From Cold War to New World Order

**Recent Titles in
Contributions in Political Science**

Germany for the Germans? The Political Effects of International Migration
Wesley D. Chapin

Out of Russian Orbit: Hungary Gravitates to the West
Andrew Felkay

Ideas of Social Order in the Ancient World
Vilho Harle

Voting Rights and Redistricting in the United States
Mark E. Rush, editor

Democratization in Late Twentieth-Century Africa: Coping with Uncertainty
Jean-Germain Gros, editor

Eisenhower's Executive Office
Alfred Dick Sander

Partisanship and the Birth of America's Second Party, 1796–1800: "Stop the Wheels of Government"
Matthew Q. Dawson

The Early Security Confederations: From the Ancient Greeks to the United Colonies of New England
Frederick K. Lister

Selected Works of Juan Donoso Cortés
Juan Donoso Cortés
Translated, edited, and introduced by Jeffrey P. Johnson

The Later Security Confederations: The American, "New" Swiss, and German Unions
Frederick K. Lister

Comparative History and Legal Theory: Carl Schmitt in the First German Democracy
Jeffrey Seitzer

The Autonomy of the Political: Carl Schmitt's and Lenin's Political Realism
Eckard Bolsinger

From Cold War to New World Order

THE FOREIGN POLICY OF GEORGE H.W. BUSH

Edited by
Meena Bose and Rosanna Perotti

Prepared under the auspices of Hofstra University
Contributions in Political Science, Number 393

GREENWOOD PRESS
Westport, Connecticut • London

Library of Congress Cataloging-in-Publication Data

From Cold War to new world order : the foreign policy of George H.W. Bush / edited by Meena Bose and Rosanna Perotti.
     p. cm.—(Contributions in political science, ISSN 0147–1066 ; no. 393)
"Prepared under the auspices of Hofstra University."
Papers from a conference held at Hofstra University, April 17–19, 1997.
Includes bibliographical references and index.
ISBN 0–313–31682–1 (alk. paper)
     1. United States—Foreign relations—1989–1993—Congresses. 2. Bush, George, 1924– —Congresses. I. Bose, Meenekshi, 1970– II. Perotti, Rosanna. III. Series.
E881.F757 2002
327.73'009'049—dc21   2001042327

British Library Cataloguing in Publication Data is available.

Copyright © 2002 by Hofstra University

All rights reserved. No portion of this book may be
reproduced, by any process or technique, without the
express written consent of the publisher.

Library of Congress Catalog Card Number: 2001042327
ISBN: 0–313–31682–1
ISSN: 0147–1066

First published in 2002

Greenwood Press, 88 Post Road West, Westport, CT 06881
An imprint of Greenwood Publishing Group, Inc.
www.greenwood.com

Printed in the United States of America

The paper used in this book complies with the
Permanent Paper Standard issued by the National
Information Standards Organization (Z39.48–1984).

10 9 8 7 6 5 4 3 2 1

Copyright Acknowledgments

The authors and publisher gratefully acknowledge perm permission to use the following:

Sections of Chapter 3 reprinted by permission of Transaction Publishers, "Saddam Surprises the United States: Learning from the Revolution of August 2," by P. Edward Haley, in *Armed Forces and Society*, Vol. 22, no. 2. Copyright © 1995–96 by Transaction Publishers; all rights reserved.

Contents

PREFACE	xiii
INTRODUCTION	xvii
Part I. International Trade	1
1. President Bush's Trade Rhetoric: Retaining the Free Trade Paradigm in an Era of Managed Trade *Delia B. Conti*	3
DISCUSSANTS:	
Stephen P. Farrar	19
Richard T. McCormack	22
John O. McGinnis	27
Olin L. Wethington	30
QUESTIONS AND ANSWERS: *Mark L. Movsesian, Moderator*	34
Part II. The Far East	41
2. Trade Policy Making in the Bush Administration: United States–Japan Trade and the GATT Uruguay Round Negotiations *Christopher C. Meyerson*	43
DISCUSSANTS:	
Carla A. Hills	63
Susumu Awanohara	66

Donald Burnham Ensenat 69
  Henrietta Holsman Fore 71
  Barbara Hackman Franklin 74
  Donald P. Gregg 78
  James R. Lilley 81

QUESTIONS AND ANSWERS: 87
  Paul F. Harper, Moderator

Part III. Personal Diplomacy: The Middle East Peace Process 89

3. It Wasn't My Fault: Or, Why Saddam Surprised the Bush Administration and Invaded Kuwait 91
   P. Edward Haley

4. The Arab-Israeli Conflict under President Bush 113
   Samuel Segev

5. The Agent-Structure Question in Theory: President Bush's Role during the Persian Gulf Crisis 137
   Steve A. Yetiv

DISCUSSANTS:
  Richard N. Haass 151
  Bobbie Greene Kilberg 156
  Joan Peters 161
  Abdel Raouf El Reedy 164
  Murray Silberman 167

PANELIST DISCUSSION: 169
  Bernard J. Firestone, Moderator

Part IV. Latin America 173

6. The Bush Administration and Panama 175
   Douglas G. Brinkley

7. The Failure of Cuba Policy 185
   Jules N. LaRocque

8. President Bush, Congress, and the War Powers: Panama and the Persian Gulf 193
   Duane Tananbaum

DISCUSSANTS:
  Edward N. Ney 220

Mark Falcoff	223
G. Philip Hughes	226
Robert Mosbacher	231
William T. Pryce	234
William H. Webster	237

PANELIST COMMENTS: 241
Robert McMillan, Moderator

9. Bush versus Castro: America's Fight
against the Banana Dictatorship, 1989–1993 243
Derrick Bradford Wetherell and Michael J. McIsaac

Part V. Somalia and Bosnia 257

10. Operation Restore Hope: Somalia and
the Frontiers of the New World Order 259
Stephen F. Burgess

11. Appointment in Sarajevo: George Bush, Yugoslavia,
and the Prospects of Federalism 275
John E. Ullmann

MODERATOR: 290
Ulric Haynes, Jr.

DISCUSSANTS:
Roy W. Gutman	291
Kenneth I. Juster	295

QUESTIONS AND ANSWERS 302

Part VI. Arms Control and Reduction 311

12. Arms Control and Military Preparedness
in the Bush Administration 313
Martin E. Goldstein

13. The Post–Cold War Peace of Europe, 1989–1992 335
Joseph P. Harahan

MODERATOR: 348
Carolyn Eisenberg

DISCUSSANTS:
Arnold Kanter 349

James M. Klurfeld	355
Kathryn R. Schultz	359

QUESTIONS AND ANSWERS — 364

Part VII. Defense Posture and Base Closings — 367

14. The Rejection of a Cabinet Nomination:
    The Senate and John Tower — 369
    James D. King and James W. Riddlesperger, Jr.

15. The Bush Administration's Defense Policy:
    Transcending the Cold War — 391
    Earl C. Ravenal

16. Defense Cuts, Base Closings, and Conversion:
    Slow Reaction and Missed Opportunities — 407
    John E. Ullmann

DISCUSSANTS:
Douglas A. Brook	420
Richard B. Cheney	423
James M. Klurfeld	428

QUESTIONS AND ANSWERS: — 431
David G. Blanchard, Moderator

Part VIII. Desert Shield and the Gulf War — 439

17. The Bush Just War Doctrine: Genesis and Application of the
    President's Moral Leadership in the Persian Gulf War — 441
    Daniel R. Heimbach

18. George Bush, Mass Nationalism, and the Gulf War — 465
    Laurence Ingram Radway

DISCUSSANTS:
Richard B. Cheney	483
Saud Nasir Al-Sabah	487
Abdel Raouf El Reedy	490
Samuel Segev	493
William H. Webster	496

PANELIST DISCUSSION: — 500
Jay R. Avella, Moderator

Part IX. Gulf War Legacies 505

19. After the War: President Bush and the Kurdish Uprising 507
    Michael M. Gunter

DISCUSSANTS:
  Peter B. Collis 521
  Edward J. Derwinski 524
  Robert W. Haley 528
  Burton J. Lee III 535
  Robert A. Newman 537
  Philip Shenon 539

QUESTIONS AND ANSWERS: 541
  Michael D'Innocenzo, Moderator

INDEX 549

ABOUT THE EDITORS AND CONTRIBUTORS 569

Preface

From April 17 to April 19, 1997, more than 200 scholars, journalists, foreign dignitaries, and alumni of the Bush administration gathered at Hofstra University to discuss the work and times of George Bush, the forty-first president of the United States. The conference, titled "George Bush: Leading in a New World," had been two years in the making. It was the university's tenth and largest presidential conference. President Bush himself attended, as well as his vice president, Dan Quayle, his wife, former First Lady Barbara Bush, former Soviet president Mikhail Gorbachev, and former Canadian Prime Minister Brian Mulroney. Members of the Bush cabinet participated, as did dozens of others who served under President Bush.

This book is one of a series of four volumes of proceedings of the conference. Each of the four volumes features the prepared papers of scholars who presented work analyzing the Bush administration. At the conference, these panel papers were then discussed by journalists who covered the Bush presidency, as well as former officials of the Bush administration. Like the conference itself, the proceedings featured fascinating exchanges between those of us who observe and analyze the presidency from the vantage point of the academic world and those who make day-to-day political decisions in our national government. As the reader will notice, sometimes the exchanges were sharp.

We have organized the proceedings thematically into four volumes. *A Noble Calling: Character and the Bush Presidency*, edited by William F. Levantrosser and Rosanna Perotti, contains papers and discussions on President Bush's upbringing, his early career, and his personal style, particularly in the handling of foreign affairs. *Honor and Loyalty: Inside the Politics of the Bush White House*, edited by Leslie D. Feldman and Rosanna Perotti, covers proceedings of panels on appointments, including the Clarence Thomas nomination, White House staffing, and relations with Congress. President Bush's campaign and rhetorical style are also discussed in this volume. *Principle over Politics? The*

Domestic Policy of the Bush Presidency, edited by Richard Himelfarb and Rosanna Perotti, details President Bush's domestic policy in areas including the economy, the budget, the disabled, civil rights, health, science, and technology. This volume also examines President Bush's emphasis on voluntarism. *From Cold War to New World Order: The Foreign Policy of George Bush*, edited by Meena Bose and Rosanna Perotti, discusses Bush administration policies in a variety of subject areas, including trade, arms control, and base closings. The geographic areas looked at in this volume span the Far East, the Middle East, Latin America, Somalia, and Bosnia.

The views from the Bush conference provided an early snapshot of how the Bush presidency stacked up four years after the president's departure from office. We have tried to edit them as little as possible for style, so that the richness of the discussion and the differing perspectives may shine through and serve as a point of departure for future studies on this important presidential administration.

Neither this volume nor the Bush conference itself would have been possible without the tireless work of many people: those in the Hofstra community, the larger academic community, and the Bush administration. At Hofstra, President James M. Shuart, Provost Herman A. Berliner, and the Hofstra Board of Trustees were most supportive of both the conference and the completion of these volumes, as was Bernard J. Firestone, Dean of the Hofstra College of Liberal Arts and Sciences. Alexej Ugrinsky, Natalie Datlof, Athelene Collins-Prince, and the able and untiring secretarial and student staff of the Hofstra Cultural Center handled all arrangements for the conference—from manuscript solicitation, to event planning, to publicity, to travel accommodations. Hofstra faculty members and deans reviewed manuscripts, provided comments, presented papers, and rallied students to attend the conference. Undergraduate Political Science student Michelle Mitchell provided expert and invaluable clerical help in the preparation of these volumes of the proceedings. In fact, cooperation from the entire Hofstra community—from student guides, to Web site coordinators, to public safety officers—was necessary to enable the hundreds of guests to assemble for this important dialogue.

The editors would like to extend a special thanks to Bill Levantrosser, a dear colleague and friend who helped to build the university's Political Science department. When Dr. Levantrosser retired from our department in 1996, we expected him to escape to some sunny climate with a stash of his beloved golf clubs and tennis racquets for much-deserved rest and relaxation. It was our immense good fortune that he instead took up the challenge of directing this very complex conference, masterminding every detail—from mobilizing students, to pitching his ideas to faculty, to arranging for a military flyover, to convincing three former heads of state that their participation would enrich the conference. Bill's vision not only brought together academics and practitioners, but it also galvanized the entire university community. Always the picture of enthusiasm, professionalism, and cheer, Bill provided us with the example of an ideal colleague. Dr. Levantrosser's fellow volume editors—Meena Bose of the United States Military Academy, and Leslie Feldman and Richard Himelfarb of

Hofstra—agree: Now that Bill has decided to really retire from Hofstra, he has left enormous shoes to fill.

Rosanna Perotti
Hofstra University
General Editor

Introduction

Hofstra's conference on the Bush presidency differed from its previous presidential conferences in the proximity of the conference date, April 1997, to the president's time in office, 1989–1993. Because the conference took place less than five years after President Bush left office, many former administration officials were able to participate, most notably, George Bush himself. Consequently, the conference served as a unique opportunity to record an early oral history of the Bush administration. While much of the archival record that scholars use awaits declassification, particularly for foreign policy, the following papers and discussions illustrate the advantages of early post-administration appraisals. Administration officials supply rich interview material in the panel discussions for researchers to evaluate, and the scholarly papers contain useful frameworks from a variety of perspectives for analyzing this material.

If one common theme can be seen in these panels on foreign policy, it is the emphasis on George Bush's personal leadership in office. Because of his extensive background in foreign policy (U.S. ambassador to the United Nations during the Nixon administration, liaison to China and director of the Central Intelligence Agency during the Ford administration), as well as his eight years as vice president, Bush already had worked with a number of the foreign leaders whom he met as president. As one former Bush administration official says, "George Bush is very much a people person and, over the 20 years before he became president of the United States, the number of relationships he developed with leaders throughout the world was extraordinary. . . . President Bush knew not just the prime ministers or the presidents, but the education ministers, the finance ministers, the defense ministers. He'd known them for 20 years." This quotation is from the panel on the Middle East, titled "Personal Diplomacy"; the comments of other Bush administration officials, on topics ranging from the Far East to Desert Shield and the Gulf War, suggest that the title would have been apt for other panels as well.

At the same time, not everyone who participated on these panels agrees that "personal diplomacy" in the Bush administration always yielded the best results. Some scholars question whether the president could have accomplished more in trade agreements with other nations, such as the Uruguay Round of GATT (General Agreement on Tariffs and Trade), while others make similar suggestions about arms control treaties. On Desert Shield and the Gulf War, disagreements surface in examining the administration's decision to begin the war in January 1991, its consultations with Congress, its decision to end the ground war after 100 hours, and its efforts to protect troops from chemical weapons as well as its awareness of such exposure. Readers will not find unanimity in these panels, among either scholars or policymakers, on evaluations of the Bush administration's leadership style and policy decisions. What does emerge are a richly detailed portrait of the administration's actions, rationale, and debates about the consequences of those decisions.

The foreign policy record of the Bush administration covers a vast range of issues, and this volume surveys the field well. The first two panels examine international trade, one generally and the other with a focus on the Far East. In so doing, they examine President Bush's rhetoric on free trade, his negotiations in the Uruguay Round of GATT, and U.S. trade with China, particularly after the Chinese government's crackdown on the Tiananmen Square demonstrations in 1989. Each panel contains extensive information about both the substance of international trade negotiations and the officials in the Bush administration, particularly the president himself, who participated in making those decisions.

The next three panels examine foreign policy in specific regions, namely, the Middle East, Latin America, and Somalia and Bosnia. The panel on the Middle East looks at both the Gulf War and the Israeli-Palestinian peace process. The panel on Latin America addresses several topics, from the invasion of Panama in 1989, to U.S. policy on Cuba, to a comparative analysis of President Bush's decision-making authority in the Panama invasion and the Gulf War. Also included in this section is a paper by two Hofstra students on the Bush administration's policies toward Cuba. The panel on Somalia and Bosnia examines the Bush administration's decision to intervene in Somalia but not Bosnia and its rationale.

The next two panels examine the Bush administration's changes in U.S. defense policy after the Cold War. The panel on arms control and reduction evaluates several treaty negotiations, including the Conventional Forces in Europe Treaty (CFE) and the Strategic Arms Reduction Treaties (START I and START II). The other panel concentrates on how U.S. base closings affected the country's defense posture and also considers the reasons behind the failed cabinet nomination of Bush's first choice for defense secretary, John Tower.

The final two panels evaluate the Bush administration's actions in the Gulf War. The first panel focuses on the president's decision to go to war, from the initiation of Desert Shield after Saddam Hussein invaded Kuwait in August 1990, to the beginning of Desert Storm in January 1991. The second panel concentrates on the aftermath of the Gulf War, looking at both the plight of Kurds in Iraq and the issue of Gulf War syndrome among veterans in the United

States and its possible causes.

While the arguments presented here certainly are not the final word on these topics, the panels raise important subjects for discussion and contain information that will influence future debates, both academic and policy-oriented. Consequently, the volume is of interest to scholars and policymakers alike.

NOTE

After the conference in April 1997, paper writers were given an opportunity to revise their analyses, based on feedback that they received at the conference. Panel discussants reviewed their remarks and also were permitted to make some changes. In all cases, the substance of the material remained as it was presented at the conference. The reader should keep in mind that the panel discussions reflect the spoken, not the written, word.

Meena Bose
United States Military Academy

Part I

International Trade

1

President Bush's Trade Rhetoric: Retaining the Free Trade Paradigm in an Era of Managed Trade

Delia B. Conti

The guiding rhetorical principle of the Bush administration's trade strategy was free trade, entailing three components: tying political security to economic strength, promoting export-led growth, and fighting for fair trade through negotiations. George Bush's trade policy was appropriate to the demands of the executive office, the tenets of free trade, and the realities of fair trade. Rhetorically, the executive must balance demands for fair trade with minimizing economic nationalism provoked by the rhetoric of reciprocity. In addition, the United States must reconcile its new role as economic leader with the nature of multilateral institutions and agreements. The arcane details of trade policy, the continuing pervasiveness of nontariff barriers, and the impending negotiation of international trade agreements combine to make presidential leadership critical. President Bush's rhetoric on trade illustrates the obstacles as well as opportunities for the executive in reconciling the ideal of free trade with increasing economic interdependence.

INTRODUCTION

In the public's perception, the enduring image of President George Bush's trade policy is unfortunately the president's collapsing into the lap of the Japanese prime minister during his January 1992 Asian tour. Yet this episode does not do justice to President Bush's trade policy. True to the executive tradition, President Bush followed a policy of free trade in principle tempered by select protectionist acts. Rhetorically, he highlighted the tenets of free trade, with fair trade not publicly broached until his Japan trip.

George Bush's tenure in office spans a volatile period in U.S. trade policy. In his vice presidential years, the trade deficit reached new highs and as a result came to new prominence on the public agenda, activating protectionist pressures.[1] In his presidential years, economic competition eclipsed military competition with the collapse of the Soviet Union and the end of the Cold War.

These circumstances have created a new political and rhetorical environment for the president. Traditionally, keeping trade off the public agenda has been to the executive's benefit, minimizing the more protectionist public's and Congress' clamor for action.[2] This is no longer possible. In the 1992 and 1996 presidential primary and general election contests, economics as epitomized by trade policy reached a new prominence. While a healthy economy has always been critical to electoral success, trade policy has not been essential in this equation. Yet the candidacies of Ross Perot and Pat Buchanan, as well as those of Bush, Dole, and Clinton, have all deemed trade—manifest in discussions of economic investment, controlling the budget deficit, labor policy, and educational reform—a vital element of the political discussion.

In this paper, I examine the trade rhetoric of the Bush administration. First, I assess the context of trade policy, including the rhetorical traditions of the executive, the rhetoric of the Reagan administration, and President Bush's continuation of this policy. Second, I assess the Bush administration's pivotal role in negotiations for the North American Free Trade Agreement (NAFTA) and the Uruguay round of GATT [General Agreement on Tariffs and Trade]. Third, I examine the elevation of trade policy in the post–Cold War era as epitomized by President Bush's Asian trip. With the return of economic nationalism and isolationism, the executive's responsibility for leadership in international affairs will keep trade on the president's agenda.

PRESIDENT BUSH'S TRADE POLICY: EXECUTIVE TRADITION AND THE PRINCIPLE OF FREE TRADE

The guiding rhetorical principle of the Bush administration's trade strategy was free trade, entailing three components: tying political security to economic strength, promoting export-led growth, and fighting for fair trade through negotiations. In advocating free trade, Bush was squarely within the tradition of the chief executive. In the 1930s, the executive branch changed from an import-based trade policy, to an export-based trade policy; from protecting American products through tariffs on imports, to promoting American products through pushing for open markets abroad. The imbalance between the United States' relatively open markets and foreign nations' closed markets did not become a problem until the strength of American manufacturing declined and the strength of foreign manufacturers increased following World War II. At this point, the executive's push for open markets and general condemnation of tariffs on U.S. imports began to be perceived by the public as an inadequate defense of American interests. As nontariff barriers grew in importance in the 1960s and the United States experienced its first negative trade deficit in 1971, the United States restricted imports. The argument was not so much for protection as for reciprocity: opening foreign markets to U.S. exports in the name of fair trade. Despite the continuing and increasing imbalance between U.S. exports and imports, presidents continued to rhetorically adhere to the principle of free trade throughout the 1970s and 1980s, managing protectionist pressures with informal restrictions via nontariff barriers and programs to assist displaced workers.

President Reagan presided over a dramatic increase in the trade deficit, correlated with an escalation of the budget deficit. Yet Reagan adhered to a strict Adam Smith free market rhetoric despite dramatic reversals on trade policy, most notably, devaluation of the dollar.[3] Despite occasional congressional outbursts calling for protectionism in the name of fair trade, especially at election time, Reagan retained executive control of trade policy with minimal congressional interference. In practice, his administration's concessions on trade policy were usually due to presidential electoral politics, for example, allowing quotas on shoes, textiles, and automobiles in politically sensitive states. Through consistent definition of free trade as fair trade, such lapses in free market economics did not interfere with his rhetorical arguments for free trade. Moreover, President Reagan's justification of fair trade was not without merit given the aggressive economic nationalism of the United States' trading partners.

Similar to Reagan, President Bush kept trade off of the public agenda, with the notable exception of the Asian trip. For the balance of his administration, trade policy consisted of minimizing protectionist pressures via fair trade measures while negotiating for free trade through international trade pacts, with GATT and NAFTA the most prominent.[4] The Bush administration extended voluntary restraint agreements on steel, autos, and machine tools. Bush limited trade speeches to affected partisan audiences and proclamations surrounding international trade summits. In President Bush's definition of the New World Order, trade—although an integral component of foreign policy—was not rhetorically potent. Free trade was an ideal to be emulated as the basis of a capitalist economy and a democratic polity, not a policy to be dramatically altered in a new era of economic interdependence and increasingly managed trade.

From the outset of his administration, President Bush reaffirmed his commitment to free trade and free markets. In his Inaugural Address, Bush proclaimed: "We know what works: Freedom works. We know what's right: Freedom is right. We know how to secure a more just and prosperous life for man on Earth: through free markets, free speech, free elections, and the exercise of free will unhampered by the state."[5]

Free trade remained an ideal, as it had been with past presidents. Yet each party's president had different rhetorical tasks. Democratic presidents had to reconcile their support for free trade with their traditional constituencies'—most notably, labor's—support for protectionism. Republican presidents had to reconcile their protectionist actions with their philosophy of limited government. The combination of the change in the nature of presidential leadership and the economic context for free trade has made both parties' presidential tasks more difficult.

According to "The Rise of the Rhetorical Presidency," the presidential office has changed for three reasons: a new, activist leadership by modern presidents, advances in communication, and the modern mass media.[6] Herein lies the paradox. Even with the dominance of the president's rhetorical powers—the foundation of the executive's constitutional power and power as party leader—modern presidents have continued to adhere to the traditional trade strategy of rhetorical neglect.[7] Historically, presidents have found it to their advantage to keep trade off the public agenda. Making trade an issue activates the inherently protectionist public, disadvantageous for the free trade-oriented executive. Yet keeping trade off the public agenda does not translate into ignoring the persuasive possibilities of television—especially the network news. Following in the tradition of the Reagan presidency, the Bush administration presented itself as fighting for fair trade abroad through appropriate venues. This included visuals of President Bush at international economic summits and using American manufacturing plants as backdrops for presidential proclamations on the strength of the economy.

The increasingly active, visible presidency coalesces with the growing presence of trade on the economic agenda. Further complicating matters, trade is an intermestic issue presenting special dilemmas in policy leadership for the president. Barilleaux writes that intermestic issues are "those matters of international relations which, by their very nature, closely involve the domestic economy of a nation. . . . In many ways, trade is the classic intermestic issue: it is about the American economy as it interacts with the rest of the world."[8] Barilleaux writes that, for the president, "the risks of leadership in intermestic affairs are greater than for other foreign-policy issues."[9] These risks are greater because the president also has to consider domestic actors in the political context, especially Congress and the pressure of public opinion. President Bush, consistent with the foreign policy emphasis of his presidency, gave preference to foreign actors in the trade equation. He extended trade benefits, such as unilateral most-favored-nation status, to reinforce political alliances.[10] However, the end of the Cold War resulted in a new political order, presenting new rhetorical opportunities as well as risks for the president. For example, political considerations eclipsed economic decisions in U.S. policy toward the East. Concurrent with the rise of Asia's trade strength was the end of the Cold War, resulting in a reversal of political and security influences: "America's stabilizing presence in the Pacific, which permitted Japan and other Asian nations to develop and prosper, no longer has its firm ideological basis: the cold war containment of the Soviet Union."[11] Economic challenges have replaced military conflict as a substantial and sustained policy problem: "The fundamental challenge facing the United States is not Soviet military might. Rather, it is the danger of economic insolvency, reflected in budget deficits, an eroding industrial base, and the growing American inability to compete with newly formidable economic rivals, especially Japan, South Korea, and Taiwan."[12]

In his 1990 State of the Union Address, President Bush acknowledged that the new political circumstances of the post–Cold War era had resulted in heightened economic competition. Placing the burden for the domestic recession on outside forces, Bush allowed that economic adjustments were necessary: "In the tough competitive markets around the world, America faces the great challenges and great opportunities. And we know that we can succeed in the global economic arena of the nineties, but to meet that challenge, we must make some fundamental changes—some crucial investment in ourselves."[13]

In advocating investment, Bush was consistent with past Republican and Democratic presidents. The distinction between the parties was in emphasis. President Bush disavowed managed trade, accepted the realities of the international marketplace, yet upheld the ideal of free trade through practicing fair trade: "I still believe that free markets work. I know that there is no such thing as pure free trade in the world today, but we believe in free trade, and obviously in fair trade as well."[14]

Yet in his personal politics emphasizing foreign policy, President Bush was careful to define trading partners as allies in the economic marketplace. Doing so disallowed a zero-sum definition of trade with clear winners and losers: "Our trade relationships are a vital factor in America's international alliances that help secure freedom and stability for so much of the world. We will apply firmness to help promote what is fair, but we will always remember that our major trading partners are not our enemies but, indeed, they are our allies."[15]

Bush recommitted the United States domestically to the ideal of the free market, in doing so nullifying the Democrats' desire for government intervention. He argued that as emerging nations chose democracy, America was obligated to continue its stellar model of economic freedom: "As the world turns to freer markets—and you're seeing this happen, some solidifying their commitment to freer markets, countries that never had the benefit of free markets—but as the world moves in this direction, this is not time to become wishy-washy about where America stands. The jury is no longer out. Markets work. Government controls do not work."[16]

Republican conservatism dictated a rhetoric of free trade in principle; allowing, yet rhetorically minimizing, fair trade in practice. However, in this post–Cold War era presidents must promote free trade, vital to international economic growth, while more aggressively protecting domestic economic interests against unfair trading practices.[17] President Bush did so through his emphasis on reciprocity, defining his administration's capitulations to managed trade as consistent with an export-led trade policy: "The goal of this administration's trade policy, simply put, is to open markets, not close them; to fight protectionism, not to give in to it. We don't want an America that is closed to the world. What we want is a world that is open to America. We're going to work to promote American exports and to see to it that in dealing with the United States other nations play by the rules."[18]

Opening markets, fighting for fair trade, propelled negotiations—multilateral and bilateral—to the forefront of administration trade policy. Throughout his presidency, Bush emphasized the importance of concluding the GATT Uruguay round: "The Uruguay round of the GATT continues to be the centerpiece of our trade strategy. While the lack of effective multilateral rules and enforcement mechanisms has forced us to resort to section 301, we look forward to the day when such actions will be unnecessary."[19]

True to the ideal of free trade, President Bush portrayed actions the United States had taken to ensure fair trade as regrettable. Strategically, these maneuvers were economically defensible. Rhetorically, this language undermined the image of a strong executive aggressively protecting U.S. domestic economic interests. Moreover, the Bush administration's pursuit of bilateral and multilateral trade agreements further promoted the perception of cooperation with trading partners openly ignoring fair trade rules. Thus, it was rhetorically advantageous for the Bush administration to pursue a largely private persuasive campaign for passage of NAFTA.

NEGOTIATING NAFTA: A PRIVATE CAMPAIGN

In promoting NAFTA and the Enterprise for the Americas Initiative (EAI), President Bush was recommitting the United States to international trade agreements in the name of free trade. The administration was pursuing a course of structural reform and regulation rather than resolving disputes on a case-by-case basis—historically disadvantageous to a free trade policy. Precisely because he was advocating free trade in an economy with a significant protectionist element, placing these pacts in a new context was critical. President Bush made adhering to the principle of free trade in a changing world order his first argument in speeches on Latin American trade policy. In June 1990 Bush announced EAI in the context of the New World Order: "Nations are turning away from the statist economic policies that stifle growth and are now looking to the power of the free market to help this hemisphere realize its untapped potential for progress. A new leadership has emerged, backed by the strength of the people's mandate, leadership that understands that the future of Latin America lies with free government and free markets."[20] Announcing the successful conclusion to NAFTA negotiations August 12, 1992, President Bush immediately placed the agreement in its historical context: "The Cold War is over. The principal challenge now facing the United States is to compete in a rapidly changing and expanding global marketplace."[21]

At home, though, President Bush stressed protecting jobs and the environment, precisely the arguments Clinton would advance in his support for the pact. Yet NAFTA was of more symbolic than economic importance to the United States: "NAFTA has become a focal point in the debate over how to maintain and improve U.S. living standards in the face of stiff foreign competition and sluggish economic growth."[22]

The argument over jobs is ultimately an argument over fairness. In essence, should the United States promote free trade despite other countries' protectionist actions, resulting in short-term disadvantages for the United States? Should American workers seem to pay the price for adhering to the principle of free trade, for the extension of economic and political prosperity as in the post–World War II period? With the passage of NAFTA, the United States would in all probability lose low-wage, low-skill jobs. Yet increased orders for machines, technology, and chemicals would add high-wage jobs to the U.S. economy. To move into these new jobs, workers would need retraining. Thus, the rhetorical dilemma for the president: the need to emphasize the positive, long-term effects of NAFTA while minimizing the short-term costs of dislocations in the workforce.

In promoting NAFTA, President Bush relied on institutional legitimacy. He relied on the powers of his office—his role as protector of the national interest in contrast to Congress' partisan instincts: "As President, only I can stand up against irrational impulses of protectionism. And as President, only I can speak for the national interests and fight for the jobs of the future."[23]

Striving for consistency in adhering to the principle of free trade, the Bush administration downplayed unilateral actions taken to punish erring trading allies and protect U.S. domestic interests. This occurred even though unilateral actions were integral to the administration's trade policy. Politically and rhetorically, such actions were defensive. The Omnibus Trade and Competitiveness Act of 1988 forced the administration to name and act upon unfair traders through the Super 301 provision. For example, on May 26, 1989, the administration named three unfair traders—Japan, India, and Brazil. President Bush stressed cooperation with allies and adherence to the principle of free trade in announcing this action: "Our goal is to open markets and to eliminate trade barriers. We oppose protectionism in any and all forms. Therefore, I urge the Governments of Japan, India, and Brazil to work with us to resolve these issues expeditiously."[24] Announcing the extension of voluntary restraint arrangements on steel July 25, 1989, Bush again stressed the ideal of free trade despite the existence of unfair trade practices:

Today I am establishing a Steel Trade Liberalization Program that will extend for 2 1/2 years the voluntary restraint arrangements (VRA's) that limit steel imports into the United States. I am taking this step to permit the negotiation of an international consensus to remove unfair trade practices and to provide more time for the industry to adjust and modernize. This Steel Trade Liberalization Program is designed to restore free-market forces to, and end government interference in, global trade in steel.[25]

If President Bush had emphasized adjustment assistance, as a Democratic president may have been more philosophically inclined to do, he would have promoted the image of a president as protector of the national interest. Bush's chosen emphasis on the ideal of free trade would have been more suitable in an atmosphere of public confidence in the growth of the domestic economy and the perception that trading partners were mending their ways. But in an atmosphere of continued foreign promises, most notably by Japan, of opening markets despite the continuation of closed markets, emphasizing commitment to the principle of free trade only perpetuated an image of the United States as trade patsy. In the era of rebuilding following World War II, trade policy was an economic tool closely aligned with political proclivities, attested to by such devices as the Marshall Plan and the dictum "trade, not aid." As foreign nations rebuilt their economies and became economic competitors with the United States, economic policies once deemed vital to U.S. political security became outmoded and indeed harmful to U.S. domestic industries. Nowhere was this more evident than in U.S. policy toward Japan.

THE INTEGRATION OF DOMESTIC AND FOREIGN POLICY: THE ASIAN TRIP AND THE 1992 ELECTION CAMPAIGN

President Bush's trip to Asia, with Japan as the centerpiece, is an exception to the administration's trade policy for with this trip, Bush prioritized domestic concerns. While President Bush retained the executive emphasis on free trade, he adjusted to domestic pressures by stressing fair trade in an export-oriented policy. The original focus of the trip was on security concerns in the post–Cold War era, to culminate in the Tokyo Declaration, affirming the importance of the U.S.–Japanese alliance. However, when former Bush attorney general Dick Thornburgh was upset by Harris Wofford in the Pennsylvania Senate race November 5, 1991, running on the slogan "It's time to take care of our own," the Bush administration rescheduled the trip from late November to January and changed the focus from security to economic concerns. With this trip, the Bush administration moved trade to the forefront of its agenda and began to integrate domestic economic politics into its former foreign policy trade emphasis.

The pressures on the executive to privilege domestic over foreign policy on intermestic issues and the tendency of the more protectionist Congress to threaten trade-restricting bills and the executive to wield such threats to pressure foreign governments were in sharp focus in the rhetorical exchanges surrounding the trip. President Bush explicitly commented on the traditional executive–congressional dance on trade policy: "I think it's ridiculous to start throwing in special legislation just before a trip to kind of look like the macho trying to dictate the foreign policy of this country. It's crazy. But they have their own constituents, and I've got mine. But it's all good-spirited, and we'll do our thing, keep it on broad international principles, and then take my case to the American people."[26]

As president, Bush remained committed to the principle of free trade while opening foreign markets on behalf of fair trade and keeping security concerns on the agenda. In his official departing statement, President Bush highlighted the role of the executive in promoting and connecting foreign economic prosperity, domestic economic success, and political security:

In this new world, old notions no longer apply. The sharp lines that once separated foreign and domestic policy have been overtaken by a new reality. If we want to put people to work here at home, we've got to expand trade and to open markets. These new economic realities have not eclipsed the security concerns that continue to demand our attention. Our Asian/Pacific friends will play a crucial role in helping us build a post–cold war world defined by prosperity and trade, not poverty and isolationism.[27]

In his less formal remarks, President Bush reiterated his new emphasis on American jobs: "But let me make very clear the focus of this trip. My highest priority is jobs, and I want us to build a foundation for sustained economic growth and an ever-increasing supply of good jobs for American workers."[28] With the 1992 presidential race looming, Bush redefined the Japan trip as essential to the recovery of the domestic economy, thereby retaining ties to export-led growth:

Here at home, all of us are concerned about our sluggish economy. One way to get this economy growing again is to open up markets abroad for American goods and services. The goods we make here in America, the services we provide, are second to none. More exports mean new jobs. Each billion dollars in new manufactured exports supports 20,000 new American jobs.[29]

President Bush was adhering to the traditional chief executive role of protecting American interests abroad through fighting for fair trade: "My message in each country I visit will be this: 'Free trade is a two-way street.'"[30] Yet with the rhetorical focus of the trip to Japan and the emphasis on domestic jobs and fair trading practices, the United States became the aggrieved actor on the defensive: "As President Bush sets off on his long trip through Asia, his exaggerated emphasis on jobs, jobs, and jobs is less than wise. He's trying to convey the useful point that foreign policy and the country's economic health are not separate subjects. But he's doing it in a way that encourages all the grievances and resentments against the Japanese on the part of American companies that have lost ground in competition with them."[31]

Compounding President Bush's difficulties in defining Japan as an ally, not an enemy, in trade, Japanese prime minister Miyazawa attempted to justify earlier remarks extending sympathy and compassion to the United States: "I believe the U.S. society is a great society, but there are homeless people; there is the problem of AIDS and so on. And for various reasons, education is not as high as in the past. And U.S. industries are not as company competitive as in the past for various reasons."[32]

Defending Americans' ability to compete accentuated these expressions of sympathy from foreign nations, reinforcing Americans' resentment toward foreign nations. Emphasizing the need to expand markets highlighted unfair trading practices. Choosing corporate executives, the first ever to accompany a U.S. president overseas, was a gesture of symbolic significance intended to showcase U.S. economic successes. Instead, it highlighted American management deficiencies.

A combination of circumstances resulted in refocusing the trip to the president's disadvantage. On January 8, the eve of his major address in Japan, Bush, weakened by the flu, vomited and collapsed into the lap of the Japanese prime minister. Immediately, the focus of the trip became the president's health. Expressions of sympathy from the Japanese only magnified their complaints about American workers, management, and the state of the U.S. economy, underscoring their attitude of economic superiority. Returning to the United States, Bush was met with the report of increased unemployment figures—7.1 percent—the highest in five years. He defined these numbers as a temporary setback, reversible given the administration's fight to open markets and thus create jobs:

> In each country on this mission we made progress on a top priority of this trip, renewing the strength of the American economy and generating world economic growth. Now, while I'm disappointed that the unemployment numbers went up in December here, our work over the last few days will help open markets for American companies and provide more jobs for our workers. Make no mistake about it, our progress this week will translate into progress on jobs and economic growth in America. The results will be clear and measurable.[33]

Yet in a *USA Today* poll, 56 percent of Americans did not believe the trip would produce more domestic jobs, and only 28 percent thought it would.[34] A *Wall Street Journal*/NBC poll found that only 19 percent of Americans blamed Japan for America's economic problems, while 53 percent blamed American management and labor.[35]

Auto executives, in statements upon returning, attempted to further resentment against the Japanese, thus undercutting the president's attempts to portray the trip as a success. The day of Bush's return, chairman of Chrysler Lee Iacocca fumed: "I for one am fed up hearing from the Japanese, and I might say some Americans too, that all our problems in this industry, all our problems, are our own damn fault. We do not have idiots running General Motors, Ford, and Chrysler, or our suppliers. And our workers are not lazy and stupid."[36]

As if to answer and thereby justify Iacocca's remarks, President Bush began a series of speeches on the strength of the American workforce. In doing so, he appropriated President Reagan's use of factories as visual backdrops of American economic strength. At the Stryker Corporation in Michigan, Bush echoed Reagan's optimistic rhetoric about the ability of the American workforce: "Don't tell me the American worker can't compete with the Japanese. You're solid proof that when the playing field is level, when you have access to the other guy's market, American workers can outthink, outperform, and outproduce anyone, anyplace in the world."[37] Bush was not merely appropriating Reagan's economic arguments but following in the tradition of the chief executive's supporting free trade. He was emphasizing his role as protector of the national interest, in contrast to a parochial Congress. At the NAFTA initialing ceremony less than one month before the election, Bush stated: "As President, only I can stand up against irrational impulses of protectionism. And as President, only I can speak for the national interests and fight for the jobs of the future."[38] The administration's export-led trade policy was rhetorically grounded in faith in the American worker and U.S. productivity, capitalizing on economic nationalism: "Americans are one of the only—if not the only—people in the world who imagine themselves to have a global mission. Successful competition from other nations threatens this sense of national uniqueness and destiny."[39]

In his 1992 acceptance speech at the Republican National Convention, Bush continued his emphasis on the domestic economy: "The defining challenge of the '90's is to win the economic competition. To win the peace, we must be a military superpower, an economic superpower, and an export superpower."[40]

With this new domestic emphasis, President Bush was not only preempting Democratic calls for investment of the "peace dividend" but also defending American interests as chief executive: "The subject of fairness in trade matters, not the esoterica of trade deficits or economic theory, is an issue with political resonance. The theme of economic nationalism—embracing education, training, technology development and getting tough on trade issues—appeals to many voters."[41]

Both Democratic and Republican presidential candidates sounded remarkably similar in calling for investment, deficit reduction, and educational restructuring. In the most critical element of trade policy, promoting international economic growth through expanding free trade in international treaties, both candidates agreed. However, the arcane details of trade agreements are no match for the persuasive potency of protectionist arguments. Therefore, although in what is most vital to American economic growth—the continued liberalization of international trade—the Bush administration was successful, this advancement of United States' interests was rhetorically invisible.

Domestically, this issue surfaced in a congressional vote over extending fast-track negotiating authority for the executive branch on trade treaties, relegating Congress to an up-or-down vote with no possibility for amendments. While opponents in Congress viewed this as an unwarranted delegation of authority, Bush argued that fast track was essential to the administration's ability to negotiate in good faith: "A vote against the extension of Fast Track authority would cut off the chance to negotiate any new agreements. Simply put, a vote against Fast Track is a vote against trade, against ourselves, against our neighbors."[42] The administration was successful. The House and Senate extended Fast Track authority in May 1991.

Yet this victory was not easily translatable into a victory for free trade and U.S. economic interests, nor was the administration's negotiation of bilateral trade agreements with Canada and Israel. Negotiations for the North American Free Trade Agreement and the extension of the GATT treaty were the focal points of the administration's trade policy, yet passage did not come during Bush's term. The logistics of trade policy are complicated and do not easily convert to rhetorical success. This problem is endemic to trade politics for any executive. Highlighting trade activates the protectionist public. The benefits of free trade are long-term and diffuse, while the immediate consequences of fair trade are readily apparent and activate the vocal few.

CONCLUSION

The Republican task is a difficult one: reconciling the ideal of free trade, reinforced by the executive preference for free trade, with the growing reality of fair trade and intervention in the economy. While the United States' domestic economy was strong, unfair trade was not problematic. Yet as the public perception of unfair trade continued with the burgeoning trade deficit and the weakening of the domestic economy, the rhetoric of free trade promoted an image of executive isolation and inaction.

George Bush's trade policy was appropriate to the demands of the executive office, the tenets of free trade, and the realities of fair trade.[43] Yet his rhetoric limited his ability to capitalize on this policy. President Bush's rhetorical strategy on trade was reactive: consisting of promoting free, but fair, trade during election years while in off years keeping trade off the public agenda. For example, when Bush allowed government and industrial cooperation within the computer industry, he downplayed intervention:

Late in 1991, when the president signed legislation providing federal assistance for development of a new supercomputer, administration officials pleaded with the media for discretion. Don't call it industrial policy, one official told a Time magazine reporter. Call it "George Bush's incredibly forward-looking applied research and development initiatives."
The irony is that at the same time Bush was trying to cloak his policies in political euphemisms, conservative opposition to the idea of industrial policy was also beginning to dissipate.[44]

The free market paradigm impinges on American economic power. While a congressional representative, the current governor of Pennsylvania, Tom Ridge, stated: "The rhetoric of free trade has been an impediment to the development of a comprehensive, responsive trade policy. It has been an encumbrance, and to those who have lost their jobs because of blind subservience to it, it has been a curse. Free trade has proven to be very expensive and continual reliance is pure folly."[45]

The free market may remain as an economic ideal. The free market paradigm, however, should not unnecessarily constrain trade policy. The president must balance demands for fair trade with minimizing economic nationalism provoked by this rhetoric. While President Bush defined free trade according to the theory of comparative advantage, in which all parties would benefit from open markets, the public viewed trade as a zero-sum game, in which there were clear winners and losers. Moreover, Bush's definition of free trade as fair trade reflected the zero-sum perception, as did his correlated trade policy of unilateral actions. Economic nationalism is also inflamed by rhetoric touting America's ability to compete while conflicting with the rhetoric of cooperation via multilateral and bilateral trade agreements. While the United States' economic leadership role is evolving, a clearer and more consistent presidential rhetoric asserting United States' goals while protecting United States' interests is vital.

The United States must reconcile its new role as economic leader with the nature of multilateral institutions and agreements. The arcane details of trade policy, the continuing pervasiveness of nontariff barriers, and the impending negotiations of international trade agreements combine to make presidential leadership critical.[46] Examining the rhetoric of President Bush, as well as the policy constraints and opportunities of trade as an intermestic issue, there are clear guidelines for presidential rhetoric on trade.

First, presidents must prioritize the domestic. If presidents are not seen as defending the United States' best interests, foreign nations trade transgressions nullify the effectiveness of trade pacts. Without a strong domestic economy, economic nationalism and isolationism will increase, as evidenced by the success of demagogic trade rhetoric in presidential primaries and in lower-level congressional rhetoric.

Second, presidents must remain consistent despite the inconsistency of trade policy. Most importantly, they must reconcile the principle of free trade with protectionist actions. This is most readily accomplished through a rhetoric stressing fair trade. In addition, presidents can address select audiences affected by trade. In doing so, they can acknowledge the existence of unfair trade, justify select protectionist actions without promoting them to prominent items on the public agenda, and convey an aura of action without publicly betraying a rhetoric of free trade.

Third, presidents must rely on institutional legitimacy through emphasizing executive wisdom, the national interest, and historical precedent. The national interest and hence the executive's prerogative remain with the economic principle of free trade. Presidents must also reconcile unilateral, bilateral, and multilateral trading pacts. The arcane nature of trade agreements and trade policy lends itself to minimizing contradictions. At the same time, this very same complexity allows simplification promoting economic nationalism.

The first three strategies—prioritizing the domestic, maintaining consistency, and emphasizing institutional legitimacy—are essential for the president to make the policy changes necessary in meeting the demands of increased economic competitiveness. In the 1990s and beyond, executive coordination of an aggressive trade offensive is necessary. It can be made acceptable only through changing the terms of debate, and this will require an active public campaign by the president. President Bush's trade policy was successful in promoting an open trading system and reducing the trade deficit. Yet his rhetoric limited his ability to capitalize on this policy. With the growing importance of economic interdependence, the breakdown of the paradigm of the Cold War, and the ensuing combination of political security and economic interdependence, the president needs to adjust the rhetorical arguments to the political realities of trade.

NOTES

1. The merchandise trade deficit rose from a negative $24.2 billion in 1980 to a negative $118.6 billion in 1988.

2. For an explanation of the "cry-and-sigh" syndrome, see Robert A. Pastor, *Congress and the Politics of U.S. Foreign Economic Policy, 1929–1976* (Berkeley: University of California Press, 1980).

3. For an analysis of President Reagan's trade rhetoric, see Delia B. Conti, "President Reagan's Trade Rhetoric: Lessons for the 1990's," *Presidential Studies Quarterly* 25, no. 1 (Winter 1995): 91–108.

4. The Bush administration negotiated six key trade accords: NAFTA, the Uruguay Round of GATT, the Enterprise for the Americas Initiative, and trade agreements with Eastern and Central Europe (the former Soviet Union), China (market access and inter-

national property), and Japan (structural and sectoral barriers).

5. George Bush, "Inaugural Address," *Weekly Compilation of Presidential Documents* (hereafter abbreviated as *WCPD*), January 20, 1989, p. 1.

6. James W. Ceaser, Glen E. Thurow, Jeffrey Tulis, and Joseph M. Bessette, "The Rise of the Rhetorical Presidency," *Presidential Studies Quarterly* (Spring 1981): 158–171.

7. For an analysis of the president's rhetorical powers, see Theodore Windt, "Presidential Rhetoric: Definition of a Discipline of Study," in Theodore Windt and Beth Ingold, *Essays in Presidential Rhetoric*, 2d ed. (Dubuque, IA: Kendall/Hunt, 1987), pp. xv–xliii.

8. Ryan J. Barilleaux, "The President, 'Intermestic' Issues, and the Risks of Policy Leadership," *Presidential Studies Quarterly* 15, no. 4 (Fall 1985): 754–755.

9. Ibid., p. 763.

10. Following the Gulf War, President Bush would cite extension of most-favored-nation status as critical to China's decision to support the United States.

11. Mortimer B. Zuckerman, "Yesterday, Today and Tomorrow," *U.S. News and World Report*, December 2, 1991, p. 86.

12. Selig S. Harrison and Clyde V. Prestowitz Jr., "Pacific Agenda: Defense or Economics," *Foreign Policy* (Summer 1990): 56.

13. George Bush, "Address before a Joint Session of the Congress on the State of the Union," *Public Papers of the Presidents* (hereafter abbreviated as *Public Papers*), January 31, 1990, p. 131.

14. George Bush, "Remarks to Members of the American Retail Federation," *WCPD*, May 17, 1989, p. 568.

15. George Bush, "Remarks at the Swearing-in Ceremony for Carla A. Hills as United States Trade Representative," *WCPD*, February 6, 1989, p. 56.

16. George Bush, "Remarks to the Chamber of Commerce in Cincinnati, Ohio," *WCPD*, January 12, 1990, p. 43.

17. See Ethan B. Kapstein, "Workers and the World Economy," *Foreign Affairs* 75, no. 4 (May/June 1996): 16–37.

18. George Bush, "Remarks to the American Farm Bureau Federation in Orlando, Florida," *WCPD*, January 8, 1990, pp. 23–24.

19. George Bush, "Statement on United States Action against Foreign Trade Barriers," *WCPD*, May 26, 1989, p. 608.

20. George Bush, "Remarks Announcing the Enterprise for the Americas Initiative," *Public Papers*, June 27, 1990, p. 874.

21. George Bush, "North American Free Trade Agreement," *U.S. Department of State Dispatch* 3, no. 33 (August 17, 1992): 641.

22. David S. Cloud, "Will NAFTA Prove a Policy Prophecy?" *Congressional Quarterly*, September 26, 1992, p. 2893.

23. George Bush, "Remarks at the Initialing Ceremony for the North American Free Trade Agreement in San Antonio, Texas," *WCPD*, October 7, 1992, p. 1877.

24. Bush, "Statement on United States Action against Foreign Trade Barriers," p. 607.

25. George Bush, "Statement on the Steel Trade Liberalization Program," *WCPD*, July 25, 1989, p. 1011.

26. George Bush, "The President's News Conference with Prime Minister Keating of Australia in Canberra," *WCPD*, January 2, 1992, p. 15.

27. George Bush, "Remarks Upon Departure for Asian/Pacific Nations," *WCPD*, December 30, 1991, p. 1.

28. Ibid.

29. Ibid.

30. Ibid.
31. "Mr. Bush in Asia," *Washington Post*, January 2, 1992, p. A22.
32. Prime Minister Miyazawa, "The President's News Conference with Prime Minister Miyazawa of Japan in Tokyo," *WCPD*, January 9, 1992, p. 65.
33. George Bush, "Remarks and an Exchange with Reporters on Arrival from Asian/Pacific Nations," *WCPD*, January 10, 1992, pp. 67–68.
34. E.J. Dionne Jr. and Howard Kurtz, "Bush's Opponents Denounce Japan Trip as Failure," *Washington Post*, January 11, 1992, p. A1.
35. John Schwartz et al., "The Push to 'Buy American,'" *Newsweek*, February 3, 1992, pp. 33–35.
36. Michael Wines, "Bush Returns, Hailing Gains in Japan Agreement," *New York Times*, January 11, 1992, p. A1.
37. George Bush, "Remarks to Stryker Corporation Employees in Kalamazoo, Michigan," *WCPD*, March 13, 1992, p. 468.
38. Bush, "Remarks at the Initialing Ceremony for the North American Free Trade Agreement in San Antonio, Texas," p. 1872.
39. Michael Prowse, "Is America in Decline?" *Harvard Business Review* (July–August 1992): 37.
40. George Bush, "Remarks Accepting the Presidential Nomination at the Republican National Convention in Houston," *Public Papers*, August 20, 1992, p. 1382.
41. Steve Lohr, "Blaming Japan Has Its Risks; So Does Bush's Visit to Tokyo," *New York Times*, January 4, 1992, sec. 4, p. 1.
42. George Bush, "Remarks at a White House Briefing for the National Leadership of the Hispanic Alliance for Free Trade," *WCPD*, March 19, 1991, p. 286.
43. During President Bush's administration, the merchandise trade deficit declined from a negative $109.6 million in 1989 to a negative $84.5 billion in 1992.
44. Kevin P. Phillips, "U.S. Industrial Policy: Inevitable and Ineffective," *Harvard Business Review* (July–August 1992): 108.
45. Thomas J. Ridge, "Should Congress Adopt the House-Passed 'Gephardt Amendment,'" *Congressional Digest* (June–July 1987): 180.
46. For a discussion of the importance of credibility in the Gore–Perot NAFTA debate, see Herbert W. Simons, "Judging a Policy Proposal by the Company It Keeps: The Gore–Perot NAFTA Debate," *Quarterly Journal of Speech* 82, no. 3 (August 1996): 274–287. For a discussion of the importance of presidential leadership in domestic congressional debate on international treaties, see C. Fred Bergsten, "Globalizing Free Trade," *Foreign Affairs* 75, no. 3 (May/June 1996): 105–120.

Discussant: Stephen P. Farrar

I'm pleased to be here today. I would like to offer some general remarks on the Bush administration trade policy, confining myself primarily to the Uruguay round issue, which I think was one of the major accomplishments of the Bush years. My colleagues may have other areas to touch on as well, and I hope we can get into even more areas in the question-and-answer time, which I personally think would be a rewarding way to spend the last few minutes of our gathering.

In my view, President Bush was remarkably consistent in his views on trade. Right from his campaign in 1988, he stressed the importance of opening markets, the importance of free and fair trade. He supported the need for negotiating authority to take on the Uruguay round, which was being discussed at the time, which is, in particular, the fast-track authority that Professor Conti referred to. He very clearly opposed the Gephardt Amendment, which was a proposal at the time to force a reduction in our bilateral trade deficit with Japan through fiat if the Japanese couldn't solve it themselves. He very clearly supported the negotiation of NAFTA—what eventually became NAFTA. He strongly favored reform of world trade in agriculture, something that I think the Uruguay round achieved remarkably well, and he also committed himself to supporting U.S. trade laws.

You may recall at the time that, because of the large trade deficit with Japan and the worldwide deficit, there was increasing pressure to use what was called Section 301 of our trade laws to take unilateral retaliation against countries that refused to open their markets to U.S. goods. In fact, in the 1988 Trade Act, Congress passed what became known as "Super 301," which, in effect, forced the president every year to point the finger at the bad guys, the countries that were keeping out U.S. goods, and if they failed to open their markets, then the president was obliged to retaliate.

I might just say a word about that before talking about the Uruguay round. In my view, President Bush's use of Super 301 was a perfect example of how he had a long-range view of where he wanted to go on trade, and incorporated domestic political pressures, stuck to the law of the land, and recognized the needs of Congress for movement in certain directions. The end result of the Super 301 decision was naming Japan as the major bad guy in the world trading system. It was very, very clear in discussions with Congress that the minimum that was acceptable in political terms was naming Japan, but at the same time, to ease the burden on Japan as a political matter, the president also named Brazil and India with serious, but less controversial, problems. The issues that we had with Japan were broken out and addressed in different ways. The big issue of agriculture, for example, access to the rice market, was put into the Uruguay round negotiations as part of our Super 301 strategy.

There were three specific sectoral issues that were identified as discrete negotiations. There was a negotiation on satellites, there was a negotiation on supercomputers, and then one on forest products. Each of those was a fairly well contained, solvable problem. Then there was a whole world of systemic macro- and other issues that was put into the structural adjustment negotiations—which Richard McCormack hopefully can tell us more about since he was one of the U.S. negotiators.

But the end was a very interesting case of melding political pressure and overall objectives to continue opening markets and I think a very good example of presidential leadership. Whether you call it rhetoric or adjusting to reality, I think President Bush maintained a sort of consistent direction all through that early test of his trade policies.

In the Omnibus Trade and Competitiveness Act of 1988, Congress provided authority for the president to enter into a huge, worldwide trade negotiation under the GATT—the General Agreement on Tariffs and Trade—and this negotiation had originally been agreed to in 1986. So it was something that was building during the Reagan administration, but the negotiating authority didn't get passed by the Congress until August 1988. So it really was the job of the Bush administration to push the negotiation to a conclusion—or to get it organized at all, for that matter. I think, to me, the signal achievement of the Bush administration—and I think both President Bush and Carla Hills as a trade negotiator deserve a lot of credit for this—is laying out the objectives and insisting that a good deal was obtained and not stopping short of a good deal. There were many opportunities to call it a day with a pretty good deal and let the other countries off without offering the access that we really needed most.

I think the best example in the negotiations is the agriculture issue, where the United States, as you may recall, had been trying to cut down its own cost of the domestic agriculture program. We had farm bills in 1985 and 1990 that pretty sharply cut the support programs. But part of the premise of our cutting our support programs was that our farmers were going to be able to export, since the U.S. farmers are among the most competitive in the world, especially in the areas of grains and dairy products. The big hooker was the European Community with its common agricultural policy, which essentially set high domestic internal prices within the European Community for its farm products. When, responding to these price incentives, European farmers grew too much or made too much butter or whatever the product, the Europeans just used subsidies to export it onto the world market and drove world prices down and made it very difficult for U.S. farmers to compete.

So that's where we were really going at in this negotiation in the Uruguay round. The round itself was scheduled to terminate December 1990. The whole negotiating strategy was built around this ministerial meeting that was supposed to occur in Brussels, and everybody was supposed to come with his or her best and final offer. It was a big jamboree, with a dozen or more major negotiations going on in a huge hall. The United States had proposed, going into the meeting, that all the countries agree to phase out agricultural restrictions over a 10-year period, and the Europeans weren't buying it. Their farm programs were still continuing to generate huge surpluses. While the cost of the U.S. support program was going down from, say, $25 billion in 1985 to roughly $10 billion in 1990, the European program, the common agricultural policy, was going in exactly the opposite direction. But the visionary leaders—and Ray McSherry, the agricultural commissioner, was one—who worked on the problem in the European Community knew that something had to change, and they were trying to get positioned where they could, in political terms, get their rhetoric in Europe to the point where they could tell their people that they had to reform their farm program. The key to their reform was getting away from price incentives and getting toward direct income payments, which they eventually did in 1990, because direct income payments really put more of the spotlight on the cost of the program and made it much harder to justify to farmers.

At this great showdown meeting, December 1990, in Brussels, the European Community essentially came with nothing to offer on agriculture—no additional movement. They were offering some progress in many other areas, in the subsidies area, nonagricultural subsidies, and in reducing tariffs on industrial products, but no movement on agriculture. To the great credit, I think, of George Bush, when Carla Hills called him up and said, "Mr. President, I'm here in Brussels and we're not where we want to be. This is supposed to be the grand finale of this negotiation"—which involved 108 countries—"but I don't think we've got enough to go on," he said, "Come on home and let's fight it another day." In the end, thanks to a showdown meeting between the United States and the Europeans at the Blair House in Washington in November 1992, where agreement was reached on cutting subsidies and converting other barriers to tariffs, agriculture was one of the huge, shining successes of the Uruguay round. I think you can see the effects today in the cost of food prices, not only in the United States but in Europe.

There were other dramatic breakthroughs in the Uruguay round. I think creation of the World Trade Organization as the successor to the GATT was particularly significant, especially because it changed the mechanism for resolving disputes and eliminated the possibility where one of the parties in the dispute could essentially hold up the agreement by vetoing the report of a dispute resolution panel. I'll stop here since my time is up, but I hope we can talk more about these issues later on.

Discussant: Richard T. McCormack

In my remarks this afternoon, I'm going to cover briefly some of the political complications in dealing with international economic policy which President Bush and his support staff faced, as seen from my perspective as Under Secretary of State for Economic Affairs.

I intend to touch upon trade policy, the Structural Impediment Initiative negotiations involving Japan, and, briefly, the G-7 Economic Summit process.

THE POLITICS OF TRADE POLICY MAKING

Having watched U.S. trade policy since my involvement in the administration of President Nixon, I find a remarkable degree of consistency in the general philosophy of the United States on trade policy. We tend to favor as open a trading system as possible, consistent with our larger strategic concerns in managing a global foreign policy, and with domestic politics.

Because of our primary strategic role in coordinating the global Cold War effort of the free world, trade policy took a distinctly second-tier supportive function during much of that period. We were anxious to see a prosperous world, integrated into an overall global economic system that would be supportive of our beliefs and values. We did not always attempt to wring the last possible concession out of our trading partners during the earlier part of that 25-year period, and by and large we succeeded in spreading prosperity around much of the globe: first in Europe, later in Asia, and finally aiming at our own hemisphere.

Because of the vast superiority of the American economy during the earlier part of that period, there were only limited constraints upon American presidents in managing trade policy. But as prosperity spread and the Cold War became history, opposition to dramatic expansions of access to the American market began to build, adding increasingly heavy political burdens in selling the policy to the American people. The recession complicated the task, as did the gradually accumulating overall current accounts deficit. This opposition crystallized during the 1992 presidential election and was one of the two issues that Ross Perot used to divide the conservative electorate in that year.

From the point of view of a U.S. president managing the domestic politics of the trade issue, there is a fundamental problem. When you negotiate a trade agreement, you are attempting to obtain lower prices for consumers and create new and better job opportunities for American workers. At the same time, you trade off access to the American market, and that means more competition for American workers domestically. Historically, this general approach is not a problem during times of prosperity. But during the inevitable downturns in the business cycle, workers naturally feel defensive about their existing jobs and less optimistic that new jobs will be created for them as individuals.

A second problem with the overall approach to trade policy has to do with the fact that the United States system is one based on transparency, laws, and rules governing our marketplace. Our strategy was to expand the geographic areas where rules and transparency existed. That was a fundamental reason why we pushed the World Trade Organization. The problem comes from the fact that, in large parts of the world, rules are less important in the marketplace, and relationships are much more important. In Japan, for example, those relationships may involve huge interlocking cartels called Keiretsu, which are both horizontally and vertically linked business combines, centered on banks but extending down to loosely tied component suppliers for manufacturers. Price is not the determinant in many buyer-seller contracts, unlike in the United States.

In attempting to expand that part of the world which is based on transparency in the marketplace, there is inevitably a lag. Many believe that competition will sooner or later push things more in the direction of conditions in the United States, but in the meantime, there is the perception of inequality of opportunity—that it is easier to sell things in the American market for foreign manufacturers than is the case with American manufacturers in large markets in Asia and elsewhere. This complicates the politics of trade policy for an American president.

Finally, there is the steady reality of the United States' current accounts deficits, now accumulating to more than a trillion dollars. Trade policy opponents attribute these to a degree of naiveté on the part of trade policy managers, who, they say, refuse to recognize the full opportunity gap that exists in our international trade policy. For a president to actually sell a trade policy in today's complicated environment is excruciatingly difficult, due in part to the enormous scope and scale of the multidisciplinary negotiations.

The Uruguay round involved agriculture, services, financial matters, textiles, and a whole host of subsidiary matters all wrapped up in a basic negotiating document that at one point was the size of the telephone directory of a large city, with print almost as small.

For a top policymaker to weigh the trade-offs in a negotiation that lasted more than six years, involving decisions of three different presidents, was not an easy task. And if this was difficult for me as Under Secretary for Economic Affairs, with responsibilities for a limited agenda, imagine how difficult it must have been for the president, who was trying at the same time to deal with the problems of the entire globe—political, military, and economic.

Never was the interrelated nature of things more stark than during the build-up to the Gulf War, when Turkey's cooperation was essential. Turkey was pressing for textile concessions, in part to compensate her for the vast losses that occurred when financial and oil ties between Iraq and Turkey had to be severed. Decisions like this do not thrill U.S. textile workers—to the degree that they are aware of them—but they do save U.S. lives in war.

And, more broadly, the fact that the Cold War was brought to a nonviolent conclusion had to do, in part, with the fact that the West held solid while the longer strategy was allowed to erode the Soviet system from within over time. Trade policy played a critical role in this, and American presidents, like President Bush, understood it, even if parts of the electorate did not always do so. But that is what presidential leadership is all about: a broader vision for our people as a whole, an ability to transcend the special interest for the sake of the general good. And that is what President Bush did in spades.

Clearly, with the end of the Cold War, other matters that occupied a secondary position require greater emphasis, and the United States cannot indefinitely run a current accounts deficit without undermining the basis of our long-term prosperity. Dealing with this problem is the task of a new president unencumbered by the Cold War, or a hot war in the Gulf. It needs to be done on a gradual basis. But it needs to be done on the basis of expanding the rule of law and a transparent market environment. It also needs to take into account the increasing use of competitive devaluations as a substitute for earlier trade regulating devices, such as tariffs and other nontariff barriers which will no longer stand muster in the WTO [World Trade Organization].

But the fact that all problems are not solved does not mean that the earlier efforts to expand trade were wrong. Rather, it means that imagination and energy need to be devoted to creating a level playing field, without which the politics of trade for any post–Cold War president can easily become unmanageable.

THE JAPAN PROBLEM AND PRESIDENT BUSH

Congress was alarmed by the growing current accounts deficit with Japan and the obvious lack of equal access to Japanese markets. By the time President Bush came into office, Congress had passed a new trade law designed to strengthen the hand of the U.S. trade negotiators in dealing with particularly intractable market access problems. It was called the Super 301 process and involved sanctions on those who had unjustifiably closed markets. It was mainly aimed at Japan.

As a substitute for deploying the full weight of this sanctions-related process, the administration launched what was called the Structure Impediment Initiative [SII] negotiation with Japan, a process which was aimed at creating a policy dialogue with Japan to deal with those things that were causing the persistent imbalance in the U.S.–Japan trade accounts. President Bush gave this negotiation direct and personal support, meeting with top Japanese leaders to encourage them to open up their markets and cooperate with the negotiation. The process was formally launched after the G-7 Economic Summit in Paris, where the final issues were hammered out in bilateral meetings on the edge of the summit.

The American participants aimed their fire at a number of Japanese business and government practices that were clearly obstructing equal access of foreigners to the Japanese market. Antitrust pressures against the Keiretsu were discussed. Closed distribution networks were assailed. Dual pricing schemes, whereby the Japanese people were forced to pay 40 percent higher prices in Japan than for the same Japanese manufactured items sold in New York were exposed. Exclusionary business practices were identified. At one point, President Bush met with former Prime Minister Takesita to give impetus to the flagging negotiation. Because it was increasingly clear in Japan that consumers were being ripped off by the system, the Japanese press became a great advocate of the American position on SII, believing that it could result in lower prices for Japanese consumers.

Unfortunately, in the middle of this negotiation, which lasted for several years, it became clear that the Japanese financial situation was growing untenable due to overheated stock markets and land prices. The entire banking system was threatened with catastrophe. Inevitably, the emphasis of the SII negotiation changed, with much greater U.S. concern that the entire Japanese financial system faced collapse. We tended, therefore, to concentrate on those aspects of the problem that would benefit both economies.

In retrospect, our concern was justified, since the financial crisis lingered and deepened, ultimately wiping out stock and land prices involving somewhere between $10 trillion and $20 trillion. The Japanese banking system still is in difficulty five years later.

THE G-7 ECONOMIC SUMMITS

President Bush played an active and central role in setting the tone and agendas for the economic summits that he led. He avoided three key mistakes that his predecessors and successors made. One of President Carter's economic summits had been poorly staffed and led to decisions that helped trigger a global economic inflation. One of President Reagan's first economic summits had led to an open rupture with President Mitterrand on basic East-West strategy, with both presidents issuing conflicting interpretations on what had been decided. This led to a permanent breech between the two leaders. One of President Clinton's summits produced a certain amount of triumphalism at the expense of his peers, which triggered bitter post-summit remarks by other heads of state, the full price of which has yet to be paid.

President Bush made none of these mistakes. Even when he had largely succeeded in carrying out his agenda at his first economic summit—namely, with a new Third World debt plan, a constructive approach to East-West strategy, and very firm ideas governing the post–Tiananmen Square China, not to mention a host of lesser matters—he refused every opportunity to engage in the public self-congratulation offered by the reporters at his post-summit press conference. He also made sure that the technical personnel were involved in a sufficiently broad consultative process so that what flowed from the preparation of summits was a reflection of his policies.

He also understood the immense value of the G-7 consultative process internationally in airing controversial and complex issues—such as the proposed Economic Bank for Reconstruction and Development that was launched for newly liberated Eastern Europe—and in dealing with other evolving technical issues in international finance and economics.

The U.S. technical support personnel for the G-7 summit, including personnel from the White House, Treasury, and State Department, regularly met with their peers from abroad throughout the year in private consultations on the whole scope of international economic issues. These consultations were among the more useful exercises in diplomacy, since they were totally confidential and usually very open exchanges of opinion. The technical support personnel, in consultation with the rest of their governments, tried to carry out the wishes of the leaders to avoid open breeches at the actual summits. This led to a process of negotiation on the press communiqués that supplemented the other private exchanges by the heads of government at the summits themselves.

Some are inclined to downgrade the importance of economic summits. But summits have the tremendous value of providing a forum for the exchange of opinion by heads of government on issues that are increasingly important for the whole globe. They also provide a useful means of educating newly elected governments and administrations about the full complexities of international finance and economics. Campaign promises sometimes are seen to be ill advised after exposure to protracted private discussions at the highest levels. Leaders also have an opportunity to interact with each other and build personal relationships that later lead to greater trust and bilateral informal consultations. During crises, such ties can be extremely important. Indeed, it was President Bush's lifetime of friendships among leaders internationally that led to the cooperation he received during the events that led up to Desert Storm. Relationships matter because they produce trust.

CONCLUSION

President Bush left an important legacy with his international economic policies. He advanced rules-based international trade politics. He managed a complicated and shifting agenda with Japan, partly through the SII process. And he used the Economic Summit process in the way it should be used: to build understanding and relationships, to provide a platform for technical personnel to do their work, to allow sound decisions to be reached on matters implicating the global economy, and to keep alive a forum that provides for collective decision-making during normal and crisis periods.

Because he was less inclined than some to take credit for his accomplishments, the American people never had a full appreciation of George Bush's accomplishments. But historians are likely to be much kinder to him than the electorate in 1992. And I suspect that is what really matters to him.

Discussant: John O. McGinnis

Professor Conti's interesting paper raises the question of presidential leadership in trade. It's a very good place to explore presidential leadership, because trade presents a dilemma for the president. Free trade is clearly in the country's interest and in his own personal political interest, but is often very difficult to sell as a policy.

Why is it in the country's interest? Well, very briefly, trade is wealth-maximizing because of comparative advantage. By allowing us to concentrate on making those goods we make most efficiently and to buy from other countries the goods they make most efficiently, free trade increases the resources of the country—that is now well understood since David Ricardo. Why is it in the president's interest? It's wealth-maximizing and increases economic growth rates, and there seems to be a lot of evidence that the president's reelection chances or that of a successor of his political party are very closely tied to the economic growth rate.

So the president is necessarily and institutionally going to be generally in favor of free trade. The difficulty is in selling it. You might ask, why is it difficult to sell when it is wealth-maximizing for people as a whole? Well, I believe Ambassador McCormack touched briefly on this, and I'll just sort of underscore it. The difficulty is that, while free trade increases the wealth of the country as a whole, there are some interest groups that lose out. So once you lower tariffs, for instance, on cars, some automobile workers lose their jobs, and stockholders in automobile companies in the United States lose some money. That is a problem because, in a democracy, concentrated interest groups have more political leverage than the diffuse populace, which is largely rationally ignorant of the advantages they're getting from trade. But the concentrated interest groups—because they have these concentrated losses from trade—pay a lot of attention and, even more importantly, pay a lot of lobbyists to look after their interests in Washington.

The other problem is the problem of nationalism. We have an ideology of nationalism for a lot of good reasons—one to do with national defense—but like any ideology it's exploited for reasons that have nothing to do with its *raison d'être*. In this case it is manipulated to support these concentrated interest groups to say we really should look at trade from the standpoint of nationalism rather than wealth creation. These are the two basic reasons that make it very hard for the president to sell a free trade policy despite the fact that it clearly is in the country's interest.

The problem for presidential leadership is how to overcome that. I think there are basically three kinds of ways the president can pursue a free trade policy, and I'll take a look at the way President Bush deployed these three different methods. The most effective way to promote trade—and the most important task of presidential leadership across the board—is mobilizing the diffuse interests in favor of a free trade policy. Generally, that is best done by connecting it to some other policy that people can understand more readily than free trade. For most of the post–World War II era, the fight against Communism has been such a policy. GATT and most of the other international economic institutions created after World War II were broadly sold as institutions that bound together the West, increasing their prosperity and their interconnectedness in the fight against the Communist foe. But President Bush presided over the end of the Cold War. Connecting free trade to the struggle against Communist became a less plausible way to mobilize these diffuse interests.

The other way, which I think Professor Conti suggests is perhaps the most important way, is what one might call the "inside game." The president just uses his political power inside the Beltway and gets various mechanisms—like the fast-track procedure—that make it easier for him to advance free trade with a minimum of public fuss in Congress. Congress might be expected to oppose such free trade–enhancing procedures because members of Congress are dependent on local interest groups, but the president counters, "Well, this is very important to me, and I'll give you something that's more important to you in return." Thus he gets this fast-track procedure. That inside game is often successful, but the problem is that the mechanisms he uses degrade over time. Over time, interest groups come to understand that the passage of the fast-track procedure is actually where they're losing out, and they become very focused on the fast-track procedure, and it becomes harder and harder to get renewal of the fast track through the quiet inside game. We're seeing that in a very acute form today as President Clinton seems to be wholly unable to get a renewal of the fast track to increase NAFTA for Chile.

The final way, I think, is to do a kind of tap dance—I don't mean to disparage it by characterizing it in that way. The president pretends to look after interest groups by promoting "fair trade," or protectionism, or getting tough with some other countries. For instance, Super 301, a trade law that permits the president to name countries that have been engaged in protectionism against the United States, is a way of conciliating these concentrated interest groups and nationalistic feelings. I think, as Stephen Farrar suggested, that President Bush used that very successfully in some ways, putting Japan and a few other nations sort of in the stocks of public opinion, but then not taking any real action against them.

Over time, however, this strategy is less effective than mobilizing diffuse interests favoring trade. The "tap dance" strategy, which necessarily tends to promise more than it can deliver, tends to degrade over time and actually can exacerbate public interest in getting tough with the Japanese. I thought one saw that in the candidacy of Pat Buchanan, who turned trade with the Japanese into an issue with which he attacked President Bush.

So the question is, in this difficult era for trying to mobilize opinion in favor of free trade policy, Were there other innovative ways the Bush administration attempted to do that? First of all you have to say that the Bush administration was never finally put to the sternest test of mobilizing opinion because, while it initialed NAFTA, and while it very skillfully conducted the Uruguay round, it never had to get these treaties through Congress. So I think the president never settled on a new paradigm to mobilize these diffuse interests in favor of free trade. I think there were two initial attempts, and I'm not sure either of them was very successful. With respect to NAFTA, there was a conscious attempt to suggest that it was in our geopolitical interest to increase the prosperity of Mexico. We might put this most bluntly: We'll either get Mexican goods or the Mexican people across our borders. I think the president tried—in a somewhat more subtle way than I'm putting it—to emphasize that geopolitical reality and mobilize opinion in that way. With respect to GATT, I think he tried to connect the Uruguay round to the New World Order that we were building post-Communism, and the interconnections that we were necessarily going to have. Will that kind of slogan be enough to mobilize these interest groups, these diffuse groups in favor of free trade? I think the jury is still out on that, and President Bush did not have the opportunity in the second term to see whether that strategy would work.

In my own view, any Republican administration in the future is going to have to face some very hard issues about how to mobilize a consensus in favor of free trade. I will thus end with just a suggestion of how one can mobilize particularly traditional Republican constituencies in favor of free trade. That is to connect it to a new regime—a new regime of limited government. One of the hard issues for the Republican Party is always the question how you're going to have institutional structures to limit the powerful state, to limit Leviathan. Free trade and global markets are the way to accomplish that for our time. They restrain government's ability to redistribute wealth and hamper enterprise. The government's tendency to confiscate wealth is the essential problem that Republicans fear about government, because since the beginning of recorded history, rulers of all kinds have used taxation and regulation to extract wealth from their citizens, thereby discouraging productive economic activity. Free trade and global markets prevent that, because they allow competition among various countries of the world for the capital and trade of companies. If a government is heavy-handed, capital goes elsewhere. To some degree, even the deregulation we're seeing going on in Washington today is a consequence of a free trade policy. We are actually mobilizing producer interest groups that now have more leverage in the political process because they can threaten to export their industries rather than submit to burdensome and unfair regulations.

I think that that is probably the secret of mobilizing these diffuse interests: to connect it up to some ideal of limited government. I think President Bush was beginning to do that at the end of his administration, and I think that will be the task for any Republican administration in the future if we're going to have a free trade policy that's going to succeed and mobilize the people against the interests that are always going to be trying to strangle free trade and global markets.

Discussant: Olin L. Wethington

It's great to be here. This subject and the Bush administration's place in history are something I care about very much. I want to address that in the area of trade, at least as I see it at this point.

But before I do that, I want to give an anecdote and convey a secret that gets passed down from administration to administration concerning the making of good trade policy. It really is, as you may know, in the quality of the options that staff like those of us up here serve up. I first heard this described in the context of the Carter administration: when the options get prepared, you make sure that, first of all, you put down a dumb option and then, second, you make sure you've got a *really* dumb option on that paper and then, third, you give another option, and I don't need to tell you which one *usually* gets chosen. Put that one in the middle!

Anyway, in thinking about this conference in terms of the trade piece of it, I was trying to sort through in my own mind, What is it, from a historic point of view, that is most significant about the Bush trade policy? Can we identify in that four-year period a common element that has permanence, that will survive beyond those four years and will continue many decades into the future and will be recognized as such by those who look back and do historic assessments? I think there is at least one very significant contribution that does relate to the framework of economic relations and the architecture of the post–Cold War global economy, and that is, the Bush administration and the president, with his very genuine commitment, made a significant contribution to structural reform conducive to American interests. I want to illustrate this by reference to four or five major areas. The kind of structural reform that I'm talking about that is conducive to American interests is market openness, the limitation of government, and I'd reflect a bit on what John McGinnis was saying earlier about the compatibility between free trade from a philosophical perspective and limited government internationally. There are a number of significant ways in which the Bush administration was catalytic in locking in, making permanent, making irreversible structural changes throughout the international economy and within the domestic economies of a number of nations that will stand to its long-term historic credit.

By way of contrast for just a second, I do not think the Bush administration will be noted for achievements in commercial diplomacy. There's been great emphasis the last four years on the ability of the president to deliver the deal, and we've seen how, at least conceived in certain ways, the process of commercial diplomacy can become tainted and lacking in integrity. I doubt also whether, in historic terms (although it was significant at the time and important to many special interests), the Bush administration will be remembered for unique contributions to individual sector deals. There were some important sector agreements that were reached. I don't think there were any, for example, that were as sweeping as the 1982 steel arrangement with Europe. But the structural element—that is, the broad, across-the-board reform that is permanent—I think will override any particular individual trade agreements that were reached. I also don't think the administration will be noted for its special protection of domestic interests in need of particular relief. There were those instances, but I don't think they, in any historic sense, will survive on a long-term basis. Nor do I think historians some years from now will note—to use a term that Professor Conti used—the rhetorical potency of the administration, in terms of free trade rhetoric. The administration saw the world as too complex for that. The central core was openness, was limiting government in foreign markets, was making that permanent. But there was a pragmatic component as well. (One could also ask how the administration would rate in terms of its sensitivity to the domestic economic origins of international competitiveness, and I think that may be a subject for another panel, and I'm not going to address that.)

But let me return to my central focus, which is the Bush administration's substantial contribution that is irreversible in terms of significant structural reform. I'd like to talk quickly about four or five areas. First, the Uruguay round. I won't go into detail on the Uruguay round because Steve has already dealt with that, but I'd like to highlight two things that in framework and architectural terms are permanent, are locked in, are irreversible, and will make a substantial difference. Number one is the Uruguay round process (which was 95 percent completed during, and in historic terms needs to be credited to, the Bush administration) brought under multilateral discipline significant new areas of economic activity that included services; intellectual property rights protection; agricultural reform, as Steve mentioned; and trade-related investment measures. In other words, it broadened substantially what was subject to the discipline of the free market internationally in ways that are irreversible. President Bush himself persisted when, at many points—as I think either Dick or Steve said—he could have quit. It would have been easy to do that; he did not.

Second, in terms of the Uruguay round framework, another essential piece of the permanent architecture that needs to be credited is the dispute settlement mechanism that is now in place in the WTO. It has substantially narrowed the scope for unilateral action by any government that is a member of the World Trade Organization. To illustrate that, one need only look at the U.S.–Japan auto dispute in 1995, which took us as close as anything that I can remember to the brink of trade war. The United States threatened massive retaliation with a very sweeping and overreaching, I think, set of demands, which, in the end, the Clinton administration surrendered on. A central factor in causing the Clinton administration to pull back at the end as the deadline for action approached and to take an agreement that was much less than what it had insisted on for many, many months was that it was not willing to have put to the World Trade Organization the issue of its unilateral retaliation against Japan for fear that it would rupture in some permanent way that organization. So we see in that instance the scope of unilateral action being very substantially narrowed by the WTO.

Let me turn next to another area, which is the Bush administration's policy toward the Western Hemisphere. Here I'm referring to three separate initiatives:

number one, the Brady Plan, which addressed the massive debt problem that existed in Latin America; number two, the Enterprise for the Americas Initiative, which I'll come back to in a minute; and number three, the NAFTA. To President Bush will go, in historic terms, the credit for having changed the face and the substance of our interaction with all other nations in this hemisphere. He launched a process of economic integration that is irreversible and that has catalyzed a profound process of economic reform, free market reform, in Latin America. I don't think we now understand even the full dimensions of what was begun by his personal leadership. One can only speculate what those might be decades hence. However, I think what was begun and for which historians will give him credit—the Brady Plan, the EAI, and the NAFTA—will someday include in this hemisphere a seamless, single capital market; I think also a de facto dollar zone and unified monetary policy, when we look out several decades; and common business regulation in many areas. The process of economic integration, although it is currently stalled—and I'm not sure when that, at least in terms of new agreements, will begin to move forward again—is irreversible. Latin America has changed dramatically from what it was 8 to 10 years ago. In that time frame, it was in turmoil: debt was massive; hyperinflation existed. In the three years before the EAI was announced, growth throughout that hemisphere was virtually zero. Governments were unstable, threatened by coups, by internal insurgency. President Bush stepped forward and took a risk and said we're going to change the face of this relationship. We're going to talk in terms of partnership, we're going to create a zone of free trade that will be a magnet for the rest of the hemisphere. Other countries must come to it. Whether they enter into an agreement or not, their policy must conform to the open market policy of the NAFTA because, without that, they will miss out on the very substantial capital flows that are required to modernize.

I see I have five minutes left. So with that, let me turn to a third area where I think the Bush administration put in place a structure conducive to American interests that will stand us in good stead in historic terms, and that is related to the breakup of the Soviet Union and the initial economic response in its immediate aftermath. There are two elements that I would mention. First, I think the administration correctly understood—even recognizing the limits of our ability to influence the policy of that new Russian regime—that Russia could not default on its massive international debt, even though there were some within Russia who were prepared to do that. Default, in a sense, was the easy thing to do. However, the United States took the leadership in the G-7, convinced the Russians that the thing to do was not to default but was to reschedule that debt, to move it out, to honor those obligations—even those entered into under the previous Soviet regime—and therefore preserve, to a great extent, its credibility in international capital markets.

The second thing that was done that is of an architectural nature was to bring, almost immediately, Russia and the other Commonwealth of Independent States countries into the international financial institutions. This provided the opening, the avenue, for affecting the domestic economic policy of Russia over the long term. Now, it may be a mistake to overemphasize the extent of the leverage that the IMF [International Monetary Fund] and the World Bank have on Russia and those other countries, but I think to some significant extent bringing them in and conditioning future economic relationships on their domestic economic reform have been central to our subsequent dealings with Russia. I think this will continue for some time. Even with all the problems that Russia faces in going forward, by linking the West to the internal reform process in a deliberate and conscious way, our interests are further down the road than they otherwise would have been.

The last thing I would mention—and maybe I've got two minutes left—is Japan. Dick McCormack touched on this, and I agree with his comments. But the point I would like to emphasize, as it relates to Japan, is that the contribution of the Bush administration is the recognition that the essence of the market access problem is not to be solved in a case-by-case, sector-by-sector battling it out over particular disputes but rather goes to the question of basic structural change and to the question of deregulation. I think the Structural Impediments Initiative that Dick talked about embodied that understanding. The Clinton administration abandoned that recognition in its early days, but I think it has come back increasingly to that view. While it's important to be responsive to individual domestic interests that are not getting a fair shake, the essence of the issue lies in broad-based structural and regulatory components of the Japanese economy.

Over time the United States has pressed the Japanese hard. We've threatened retaliation, particularly the current administration. We've begged them to stimulate their domestic economy by massive fiscal packages so that they can draw in more American products. They lowered their interest rates to virtually zero as another means of stimulating their domestic economy. The Clinton administration tried currency devalued—that is, driving the dollar to historic lows as a weapon of trade policy—and it realized that didn't work. The Japanese themselves now, I think, for their own domestic, internal reasons, have concluded that the answer long-term to opening that market up and to overcoming the kind of sluggish growth that they've experienced the last five or six years is to deregulate and to reform in a structural sense their domestic economy, which is the notion that was captured by that Structural Impediments Initiative.

I want to respond to two points very quickly that Professor Conti made that I take issue with, and one of them may be evident from what I've just said. I don't think the 1992 Japan trip was a microcosm of either U.S.–Japan policy or the general trade policy of the Bush administration. It was not guided by protectionist pressures. Rather, Bush had a genuine personal concern for the U.S. role in the world. Presidents always are going to adjust rhetoric to the particular situation. But I think President Bush was seeking a bigger change, and that goes to the structural components that he was seeking to influence.

Also in terms of rhetoric, I'd just say in concluding one sentence: I think increased interdependence in this world makes it not harder but easier for presidents to use potent free trade rhetoric in domestic politics.

Questions and Answers: Mark L. Movsesian, Moderator

Mark L. Movsesian: I think we will use that last comment of yours as the springboard for the next part of this panel. What I want to do is allow the panelists to make some comments, rebuttals, and so on, and then we'll open it up for questions from the audience. I guess we'll begin with Professor Conti. Please say whatever you wish, but I had a question for you, too, actually, and since I'm the moderator, I will take the moderator's privilege to ask it. That is, as I understand what you were saying, it is that there is an incentive, in some sense, to hide protectionism or protectionist rhetoric—that is to say, that for a president, a Republican president, for example, the idea is to speak in terms of free trade and then do all the sort of protectionist stuff, as it were, on the side, when no one is really looking. I'm curious as to why that should be, because given the nature of politics in America, wouldn't it be to the president's advantage, if one were being Machiavellian, to do just the opposite, which is to say, to talk a very tough nationalist line but then really act the free trader other times? So I leave that to you. Please feel free to come up here, if you'd like, or stay where you are.

Delia B. Conti: No, the president, throughout history, has consistently argued for free trade, and especially with the rhetorical presidency now, you have to remain consistent. You can't go to one audience and do one thing and then change it in front of another audience. So what the president will do—and Bush did this, and Reagan did this, and Clinton does this, and previous presidents did this—is that you go to an auto factory more for the setting than for what you say. So you go to select audiences to highlight trade, but otherwise you ignore it. I mean, no president has given a major speech on trade—at least recently. There has not been a major, televised speech—maybe a radio address touches it, but trade's a loser. I don't mean loser policy-wise, but rhetorically, trade for the president is still a loser. You don't touch it, OK? If you look at just the most recent general election, Dole and Clinton didn't talk about trade, in terms of trade. So no, it's not to the advantage to play up protectionist actions. It's to the advantage to hide those, to assuage the labor, and so on, and to play up the free, but fair, trade.

But what's critical, what's not being done, is now—and this would go to Mr. Wethington's point—what's critical is that, in increased interdependence, you can no longer do this. You can no longer just ignore trade. I mean, rhetorically, it's stupid now to ignore it, and there are ways you can deal with it. So I actually would agree with that, that there are—I would say because of increased interdependence, you have to have a more potent, you have to play up domestic trade rhetoric. You can no longer ignore it, but you have to do so with certain guidelines, such as play up domestic, be consistent, and so on. Does that answer your question?

Movsesian: I think so, although I'm still not entirely convinced, but I want to let other people speak also, and then we will get to questions. Mr. Farrar, if you have anything to add, please do so. I would again take the privilege to ask that you talk a little bit about the dispute settlement understanding and the Bush administration's role during the Uruguay round in regard to pushing the new dispute settlement understanding, which really has changed WTO and GATT procedures.

Stephen P. Farrar: Well, there was a big debate internally on whether to move to this whole new level of international dispute resolution—in fact, there's still a big debate today on it—because what it meant, essentially, was that the United States was giving up its ability to stop the music whenever the tune wasn't coming out to our advantage in a dispute resolution process. The decision by President Bush was to go for it, armed partly by facts that, in most cases, we're the ones who stand to gain. There are some significant issues where we have been on the weaker side, and we've, in fact, lost. We lost on a case with Venezuela and gas, was it? Our case was weak. We were discriminating against imports, and we had one policy for domestic gasoline and one for imports. We decided to bite the bullet and go for an international system. We threw our own lot in with this impartial adjudication system, where we have a say in picking who the experts are on the dispute resolution panel, but there's even a constitutional argument now that these judges or panelists are taking away rights of Americans under the Constitution because Americans are deprived of the U.S. court system to address their ills. But I think time will show—and this is the theme of Olin's remarks, of things that history will prove the Bush administration left its mark on—this WTO dispute resolution process will prove to be one of the great ones, because it has sharply taken away the unilateral action option for the United States and other countries.

Can I make a side remark that might prompt a question or two? I think there's been a little bit of confusion in some of the terminology that I've seen recently, anyway, on the difference between managed trade and fair trade. To me, managed trade is closer to industrial policy, and it's government action to build up industries, to sustain industries more directly than just using the tariff rates or other elements of the trade system. Fair trade, in the Bush administration, anyway, was usually a code word for using fair trade laws, such as Section 301 or Super 301, in a way to open markets. Section 301 ultimately provided authority to retaliate against offending countries, but really, everybody knew that the goal was to open foreign markets rather than to close our market. The WTO dispute resolution process gave him another avenue. But I think the Bush administration used that process extremely effectively, of running up to the brink of retaliation and getting market opening deals. So that almost in no cases that I can recall have the escalating threats under the U.S. trade law resulted in actually a shrinking of markets because we've created new barriers.

Movsesian: Ambassador McCormack.

Richard T. McCormack: I agree with the observations that the WTO is going to be viewed as one of President Bush's long-term accomplishments. What it has done exactly, as they say, is just reduce whole areas where nations are unilaterally in a position to determine the terms of trade, with tariffs and similar things. The challenge we have now is to make sure that nations don't turn to competitive devaluations as the weapon of choice in determining the terms of trade. We've had, in the case of the last few years, a 50 percent appreciation of the dollar versus the yen. Imagine what this does in terms of your relative ability to sell cars and all sorts of other things. It not only affects the United States and Japan directly, but it affects every single country in the world that is linked to the dollar, directly or indirectly. It affects Hong Kong, it affects Taiwan, it affects Thailand. We need somehow to figure a way of stabilizing the currency situation in such a way so that it doesn't simply overwhelm what we've already accomplished in terms of tariff eliminations. That is a challenge for the future.

Movsesian: Professor McGinnis.

John O. McGinnis: Well, I would certainly just second that point about the WTO. I think it's very important and because it is part of the new regime that I discussed. It allows the president to say that he is somewhat tied down—sort of like Ulysses and the siren, we're tied to the mast here; I can't as easily take these actions that our concentrated interest groups would like to, such as unilateral retaliation. In that sense, you can think of the new WTO regime as an emerging constitutional regime. Like all constituted regimes that succeed in getting rid of destructive passions of the polity, it's a great achievement.

Movsesian: Mr. Wethington.

Olin L. Wethington: I'll defer to the audience.

Movsesian: Yes, well, let's open for questions, then. I saw one there. Yes, ma'am?

Q: *I have a question about the contradictions in Bush's policy in terms of having free trade versus protectionism. For example, the statement by Professor McGinnis that, since the time of Jimmy Carter, everybody knows that free trade is optimal, but frankly, many trade economists today don't agree with you on that at all. Many well-known economists emphasize the economies of scale, which are in many ways very different and distinct from the Ricardian model. In that sense, the Bush administration's trade policies, as well as Reagan's and Clinton's policies, are, in fact, very consistent with trade theory, and they are doing very much the kind of things that recent trade theorists are advocating in favor of. For example, opening up markets for America's high-tech products should be a priority. I don't think that economists today are quite in agreement that free trade is always right.*

Movsesian: All right, well, I guess Professor McGinnis and then also Dr. Conti, if you want to respond.

McGinnis: Well, I certainly am aware of this new trend in the literature on trade.

I myself don't agree with it and still think that free trade is optimal. Even if there are a few areas where, if we had a perfectly knowledgeable government, we could have a sensible set of tariffs or an industrial policy—I don't think we're going to have that. Governments are going to be influenced by interest groups, and they're not going to choose the correct intervention, even if that were possible. So my view is that, at least as a practical matter, the argument that free trade is optimal is still a very strong argument, and I would say that even many of the people, like Krugman, who accept that there's theoretically some possibility of more optimal intervention agree that, in an area where government policy is going to be influenced by interest groups, you're very unlikely to get sound intervention. So while I am aware of those arguments, I reject them and still believe that a policy of free trade should be the lodestar of any administration.

Movsesian: Professor Conti, and then Mr. Farrar.

Conti: I would just take a minute and slightly build on that: that because of that, because of economic theory on free trade and Republicans versus Democrats—and I touched on this in the paper—Republican presidents and Democratic presidents have different rhetorical tasks, even though they have the same basic trade policy. Republican presidents have to go more with adhering to free trade and really play down the fair trade protectionists, but they still have that fair trade, while Democratic presidents have to do something with special interest groups—labor, especially—without playing up protectionism. So that comes into play in terms of the different rhetorical tasks for both parties' presidents.

Movsesian: Mr. Farrar.

Farrar: John's too modest to say this, I think, but during his tenure at the Justice Department, there was even a significant shift in sort of bridging the difference that we've been talking about. The Justice Department, in looking at antitrust issues, I think significantly moved to the view that there's a big world out there and broadened its interpretation of antitrust policy to sort of change the rules of the game and what competition means. I think that was at least partly an accommodation on the economies-of-scale argument that you're talking about, and I think it's been a major shift since then that's enabled several U.S. industries to compete a lot more effectively abroad.

Movsesian: Any other questions?

Q: Given that international trade issues are fairly complicated and take some attention that perhaps laypeople don't have time to give, how would a president of either party explain to the American public in a concise way the case for free trade?

Movsesian: Mr. Wethington, why don't we start with you?

Wethington: Well, the thing that comes immediately to mind, as Bush did and as Clinton did, is to say this is about your job. I'm fighting for your job. I want you to sell more overseas. It's about jobs, U.S. jobs—jobs, jobs, jobs. That's the most effective pitch, and presidents have used it. People understand it.

McCormack: But here again, there was a great complication in the 1992 race, as you undoubtedly know. Perot exploited three issues—jobs, trade deficit, budget deficit—and claimed that the administration was not concerned about these three things. He was sufficiently articulate to be able to get 20 million votes to move in his direction; it split the conservative groups down the middle, and it allowed President Clinton to win the election with 43 percent of the vote. So it is no wonder why subsequent Republican presidential candidates have been just a little cautious about how they dealt with these issues.

Conti: But it's interesting to note that, for the Clinton administration, one real turning point, in terms of that really short public campaign for NAFTA, was the Gore–Perot debate, where Gore effectively demolished Perot on *Larry King*. So that might provide some suggestions for persuasion on presidential rhetoric on trade. But you can't in a campaign say, "I'm going to educate you on the issues," because that's not what campaigns are about.

McCormack: The problem is, people don't vote because their shirt is 20 percent cheaper against or for a man, alas, but they will vote if they think that you're going to take away their textile job. I mean, it has to do with the intensity of the issue. We had beautiful editorials in the *Wall Street Journal* praising the wise policies of President Bush, but notwithstanding those excellent editorials, we got it in the ear at the precinct level in key states and lost the election.

Conti: Which is the—yeah. Primaries, protectionism comes up, and presidents aren't dealing with it right now.

Movsesian: Yes, another question.

Q: [Question inaudible]

Movsesian: Right. I'm glad you raised that because this was a major issue during the Bush administration: the periodic—I should say the annual—question whether most-favored-nation [MFN] status should be authorized for the People's Republic of China. MFN status, of course, is a nondiscrimination provision that provides that Chinese goods get in at the same basic level, essentially, as everybody else's goods. Just as historical background, China is one of the nonmarket economies that, under the law, must be approved annually for MFN status. It was a particularly acute controversy during the Bush administration because of the events at Tiananmen Square in 1989, and there were various people in Congress who were saying absolutely do not renew MFN status for China, and President Bush continued to do so. So let's start on this end, Mr. Farrar, and see if you have any comments on this, and we'll move down. The question is about trade with China.

Farrar: I say yes. Having worked some on the issue, I think that there is no alternative but to stay engaged, to keep the markets open. I think we'd do a lot better on the noneconomic issues with a country like China—on human rights, for example—if we're talking to them. I don't think the Chinese respond to the cold shoulder. I think it's interesting: this was an issue not only during the Bush administration but in the campaign, and Bush was attacked very hard by candidate Clinton on the issue. After the election, Clinton came around and essentially supported the Bush view and then supported continuing economic relations.

Conti: Well, I would just add that economics is not the primary force in trade policy; its political considerations remain. If you look at presidential rhetoric—especially Bush—Bush consistently would say, "Let's look at using trade to push for what we want in other areas." But the political priorities are more important.

McCormack: The simple truth of the matter is that we have very strong national preferences for democracy and civil rights, and we should, and we should speak about those things. When you take it the next step further and say we won't trade with anybody who doesn't maintain our standards, what that basically does is say, Boeing and the Boeing workers, you're not going to be selling your aircraft to China; Airbus is perfectly happy to come in to deal with these markets, and they will do so. So what we do is we get a nice day's newspaper article about we've taken a nice, strong stand on principle and we've cost 20,000 or 30,000 jobs. I mean, that's the basic bottom line, and that is the key problem about dealing with economic sanctions across the board. You simply cannot line up the rest of the world to support you in the absence of something truly egregious. We did succeed, for a brief period after Tiananmen Square, in having a united front on financial issues as it related to China and certain other pressures, but they were very carefully calibrated, and that's where we did have some broad support. But if you try to do that on a long-term basis with China affecting other kinds of issues, it simply isn't going to work, and it's simply going to result in further problems with our balance of payments.

McGinnis: I would reject the idea that there's any inconsistency between granting MFN policy to China and interest in human rights in China. What will ultimately bring human rights to China are increased economic wealth and prosperity. Wealth has been the root of rights, almost invariably throughout history: a rising middle class demands democracies and rights to protect their wealth. Actually, granting MFN status to China will hasten the demise, ultimately, of an authoritarian and Communist regime. So that would be the argument on which I would rely, if I were president.

Wethington: On the question of linking human rights and trade, I think the question is, Does China perceive that the Clinton administration can be bought? In other words, that it's going to go soft—I'm not talking about campaign finance, but is it going to go soft on human rights and proliferation and other issues in order to gain economic advantage? I think that's the current predicament we're in. We are currently perceived in that fashion. It seems to me that it ought to be possible to pursue a very aggressive policy on human rights and proliferation and other things that are vital to American interests and at the same time pursue an expanding economic relationship. Those two things, to me, aren't inconsistent, but I think currently they're linked in a very disadvantageous way to American interests because of the perception that we're up for sale.

Part II

The Far East

2

Trade Policy Making in the Bush Administration: United States–Japan Trade and the GATT Uruguay Round Negotiations

Christopher C. Meyerson

OPENING REMARKS

It is a great honor to participate in this conference and to have heard the presentations on the various panels up to this point in this conference. When I sent in my one-page response to the call for papers, I had no idea that I would end up on a panel with so many distinguished people. I found it quite a challenging task to prepare a paper for this conference and very much welcome comments from other members of the panel and the audience concerning my paper, which I consider to be a very tentative early appraisal of trade policy making in the Bush administration.

My paper far from covers, nor was ever designed to cover, the Bush administration's policy toward the entire Far East, and I very much look forward to hearing the other members of this panel analyze the Bush administration's policy toward the Far East.

Before presenting my paper, I would like to raise some larger questions concerning the Bush administration that have come up in the other panels that I have attended at this conference and that seem to be particularly relevant to this panel's discussion of the Bush administration's policy toward the Far East.

First is the issue of how to evaluate the Bush administration's policy toward the Far East. Roger Porter emphasized, in the Thursday night panel on "The Inner Dynamics of the White House," that the Bush administration focused more on governing than on campaigning. Is such a characterization valid for the administration's Far East policy? In other words, what were the administration's objectives, were they achieved, and were the administration's objectives at all related to the goal of winning the 1992 election?

Second, was Bush's personal network style adequate or suited for the conduct of President Bush's policy toward the Far East? Furthermore, given the pressing importance of the decline of the Soviet Union and the Gulf War, was the president able to devote adequate time to the Far East?

Third, what was the link between the president's handling of domestic issues and his policy toward the Far East?

Fourth, how was the Far East defined for the purposes of this administration? There are ambassadors to everywhere from Brunei to Korea and China on this panel. So, one of the questions to deal with today is, What is the Far East?

Fifth, to what extent was President Bush's gentlemanlike character coupled with his fierce competitiveness, which Secretary Baker commented on, reflected in his policy toward the Far East?

Sixth, were there particular phases in the Bush administration's policy toward the Far East? Were the objectives set forth in 1989 closely related to the policies that were undertaken in early 1992?

INTRODUCTION

When George Bush outlined the successes of his administration on the opening night of the August 1996 Republican National Convention, he mentioned neither United States–Japan trade relations nor the GATT Uruguay round [General Agreement on Tariffs and Trade].[1] Probably for three reasons. First, United States–Japan trade relations was one of the most difficult areas of foreign policy for the Bush administration. The administration's efforts culminated in a politically disastrous January 1992 trip to Japan. Second, while the Bush administration proclaimed the successful conclusion of the GATT Uruguay round as "its highest trade priority,"[2] the GATT Uruguay round was not concluded during the Bush administration. Third, trade policy is generally not an issue by which candidates can be singled out and win many votes in American presidential elections.

Some have asserted, sometimes without much reference to contemporaneous press accounts, that trade policy "did not receive much attention" in the 1992 presidential election.[3] In contrast, this paper argues that perhaps one of the reasons President Bush was not reelected in 1992, in the midst of a recession and rising unemployment, was that some voters lacked confidence in the Bush administration's handling of economic policy, one element of which was the administration's trade policy.

This paper begins by outlining trade policy making during the Bush administration and then briefly discusses United States–Japan trade relations during the Bush administration, focusing in particular on the Bush administration's efforts to conclude the GATT Uruguay round trade negotiations. The successful conclusion of the GATT Uruguay round was often cited as the highest priority of the Bush administration's trade policy, and this paper focuses in particular on what came to be considered the linchpin of the GATT Uruguay round negotiations—the GATT Uruguay round agricultural negotiations. This paper concludes by discussing the relationship, if any, between the Bush administration's trade policy toward Japan and the GATT Uruguay round negotiations and Bush's failure, or inability, to win reelection in November 1992.

TRADE POLICY MAKING DURING THE BUSH ADMINISTRATION

Many argue that trade was not a tremendously important issue in the 1988 presidential campaign, particularly after the August 1988 passage of the Omnibus Trade and Competitiveness Act. Of the two candidates, Democratic candidate Michael Dukakis leaned more toward trade protectionism, while George Bush adopted the more liberal, open posture that had been espoused, but not always followed, by the Reagan administration.[4]

Below the presidential election campaign level, by the late 1980s trade policy had taken center stage in American politics. Democratic congressman Richard Gephardt had developed an economic nationalism message that was strongly supported by the middle class and by blue-collar workers, particularly as the U.S. economy faltered. Gephardt called for some form of managed trade that verged on protectionism. Democrats had been trying for several years to pass some form of what eventually became the 1988 Omnibus Trade and Competitiveness Act.

During the 1988 presidential campaign, George Bush spoke of maintaining America's "commitment to free and fair trade."[5] The improvement in the trade deficit that became apparent in late 1988 helped Bush to deflect charges from Dukakis that America's trade deficit, which had risen from $19.7 billion in 1980 to a peak of $152.1 billion in 1987,[6] was the result of major flaws in the Reagan administration's policies.

The election of George Bush as president in November 1988 was seen as "a vote for continuity of policy and political direction."[7] While Bush believed most Americans were largely content with Reagan's America, Bush also recognized that he, in comparison to Reagan, had little political leverage with Congress. In contrast to the first six years of the Reagan administration, the Republican Party did not have a majority in the Senate. While George Bush had won 40 states and 53.4 percent of the popular vote, the Democrats had added four seats in the House to achieve a 259–174 majority and had retained a 55–45 majority in the Senate. This situation was to continue in the 102nd Congress, during which the Democrats enjoyed a 258–176 House majority and a 56–44 Senate majority.[8]

President Reagan had clearly been a dominant figure in Washington. Reagan had the ability at the beginning of his administration to go over Democratic congressmen's heads to their constituents through television. President Bush was somehow less of a commanding figure. Bush created more of an image of an active chief executive involved in policy formulation, in contrast to President Reagan's more passive, chairman-of-the-board style. President Bush set forth a minimalist program and made it clear that he was willing to make compromises in return for Democratic cooperation.[9]

Reacting to the escalation in the U.S. trade deficit in the late 1980s, Congress passed legislation that allowed the executive branch to take a more aggressive stance with America's trading partners and had increased congressional monitoring of trade policy making. Many felt that this had occurred because those in power in Washington had sought to distract the American public's attention from

Congress' and the Executive Branch's inability to reduce the federal deficit. It was relatively simple to blame America's ills on its trade deficit and to argue that the trade deficit resulted from other countries', particularly Japan's, unfair trade practices.

This trade strategy was popular with the general public—particularly in relation to Japan. A February 1989 *Washington Post*–ABC News poll, "conducted on the eve of President Bush's trip to Japan for the funeral of Emperor Hirohito," found that Americans held "a strong belief that the U.S. government should do more to right a perceived imbalance in the economic relationship between the countries. Two of every three respondents said the United States should restrict Japanese imports."[10] Pollsters at the end of the Bush administration obtained similar results.[11]

Trade policy in the Bush administration was dominated by the Office of U.S. Trade Representative, which negotiated trade agreements, and the Department of Commerce, which enforced trade agreements and sought to expand markets for U.S. goods. In December 1988 President Bush named Carla Hills as U.S. trade representative and Robert Mosbacher—a Texas oilman and a longtime friend of Bush's, who had been national finance chairman of Bush's 1988 campaign—as secretary of commerce. Barbara Franklin succeeded Mosbacher in February 1992. Although George Bush had promised fresh faces, many members of his cabinet had served during previous Republican administrations. Nicholas Brady stayed on as secretary of the treasury. James Baker, who had preceded Brady as secretary of the treasury during the Reagan administration, became secretary of state.

Carla Hills succeeded Clayton Yeutter as U.S. trade representative, assuming a job that had become increasingly more important and challenging as the trade deficit had risen. Hills was a Washington lawyer who had served as secretary of housing and urban development (HUD) in the Ford administration. Hills' appointment was greeted "with cautious optimism within the trade community."[12] In the words of one observer, "to be successful, Hills [would have to] satisfy both a president who want[ed] to follow a trade policy that [was] pragmatic and open, and the more militant members of Congress." In addition, the U.S. trade representative would have to "serve as 'an honest broker' among the other parties that historically have a say in setting the nation's trade policy: The Treasury, State and Commerce departments, Office of Management and Budget, labor and private industry."[13]

Clayton Yeutter, President Reagan's U.S. trade representative since 1985, became secretary of agriculture. Yeutter had an extensive background in agriculture, including ranching and government. Yeutter received support from groups representing subsidized U.S. farmers and was unanimously approved by the U.S. Senate. Yeutter hoped to use his term as secretary of agriculture to continue the American quest for agricultural trade reform in the GATT Uruguay round negotiations that he had initiated as Reagan's U.S. trade representative. Edward Madigan succeeded Yeutter in March 1991. As one reporter noted, Yeutter's appointment as secretary of agriculture "ensure[d] a historical memory in Cabinet-level discussions of the U.S. position regarding the Uruguay round and various bilateral trade issues. It also mean[t] a trade policy similar to that of the Reagan administration."[14]

Thus, at the very beginning of the Bush administration, Carla Hills and Robert Mosbacher were relative newcomers to trade policy making, while Secretary of State James Baker, Treasury Secretary Nicholas Brady, and Agriculture Secretary Clayton Yeutter had all served in the Reagan administration.

In his January 1989 Inaugural Address, President Bush stated, "We know how to secure a more just and prosperous life for man on Earth: through free markets, free speech, free elections, and the exercise of free will unhampered by the state."[15]

At the February 1989 swearing-in ceremony for U.S. Trade Representative Carla Hills, President Bush stated "that the goal of this administration's trade policy, simply put, is to open markets, not close them; to fight protectionism, not to give in to it." Bush asserted, "We will apply firmness to help promote what is fair, but we will always remember that our major trading partners are not our enemies, but indeed, they are our allies." Bush noted, "As Carla said during her own confirmation hearings, we will open foreign markets with a crowbar where necessary, but with a handshake whenever possible."[16]

During the early days of the Bush administration, George Bush's campaign rhetoric of "free and fair trade" quickly devolved into what became a rather aggressive trade policy.[17] One of the reasons for this more aggressive stance was public opinion. According to a February 1989 *Washington Post*–ABC News poll, while in reality America was still the largest economy in the world, "54 percent of those interviewed named Japan as the 'strongest economic power in the world today.' Only 29 percent named the United States." Two of every three respondents believed "Japanese companies compete successfully because 'unfair trade barriers and a cheaper labor force in Japan give Japanese companies advantages that American companies don't have.'"[18]

Such public opinion results, coupled with the poll information discussed earlier, meant that, in the words of Charles Pearson of Johns Hopkins University, there was public support for a "policy of aggressive reciprocity, attempting to beat down foreign trade barriers on a product-by-product and country-by-country basis."[19] This mood was reflected in the recommendations of the February 1989 report of the Advisory Committee on Trade Policy and Negotiations, the highest-level private sector advisory committee to the USTR [U.S. trade representative].[20]

At her Senate Finance Committee confirmation hearing, U.S. Trade Representative Carla Hills stated, "We must use the retaliatory tools that we have, not because we want to, but because they are the leverage that make credible a bilateral or a multilateral arrangement with the United States."[21] At the start of his second full week in office, Commerce Secretary Robert Mosbacher stated that "we've got to make some changes" in trade policy toward Japan. Mosbacher noted that "Japan has got to be on the top, or very close to the top, of any list" of nations engaged in unfair trade practices. "Certainly they're allies and friends, but they have been beating us 50-to-zip as far as trade goes,"[22] Mosbacher added.

The imminent threat of retaliation Ambassador Hills spoke of was used throughout the administration and led to a series of rule-oriented Section 301 cases.[23] Meanwhile, Secretary Mosbacher's desire to take a tougher stance with the Japanese concerning access to the Japanese market gradually became more popular within the White House, culminating in President Bush's January 1992 trip to Japan.

The Bush administration's trade policy was made clear in a March 1989 report to Congress that recommended "non-inflationary economic growth on the part of industrialized nations to stimulate world trade." The report from the Treasury Department and the Office of the U.S. Trade Representative said the United States and its major trading partners were committed to making the changes needed to reduce imbalances in world trade. West Germany and Japan, both countries with large trade surpluses, "need[ed] to take steps to ensure open and growing domestic markets." The United States, meanwhile, "[was] committed to substantial federal budget deficit reductions, improving its international competitiveness, and bolstering its savings rate." The United States "expect[ed] to see increases in exports exceed growth in imports, although rising payments on the national debt [would] hold back the overall reductions in the trade deficit."[24] Markets were to be forced open "through the use of multilateral negotiations as well as bilateral efforts and 'selective unilateral actions.'"[25]

While the Bush administration espoused a trade policy of liberal multilateralism, it made major exceptions to this policy in reality. America's allies noted this discrepancy, constantly complaining that the United States had an impressive number of deviations from the principle of nondiscrimination under the GATT and the pure doctrine of multilateralism. Critics pointed in particular at the 1988 Omnibus Trade Act and especially its revision of Section 301,[26] which, some said, "if it does not guarantee illiberal behavior, will certainly facilitate it."[27]

Regardless of how the Bush administration's trade policy was viewed abroad, the policy line espoused by Ambassador Hills and Secretary Mosbacher was welcomed on Capitol Hill. Congressmen from both parties believed that it was possible to reduce America's huge trade deficit by forcing Europe and Japan to open their markets further to American goods and by threatening to shut off Europe's and Japan's exports to the United States if they didn't open their markets. The 1988 Omnibus Trade Act provided the Bush administration with what some called "'process protectionism' that [could] be doled out with a heavy hand or a light touch."[28]

By July 1989 the most aggressive trade policy that America had ever taken during the postwar period began to take shape as the Bush administration designated India, Japan, and Brazil as priority foreign countries under the Super 301 process. By June 1990, however, the Bush administration had removed these designations concerning Japan and Brazil.[29]

Throughout the rest of the administration, using the new trade legislation, interest groups continued to pressure both the administration and Congress for help with coping with foreign competition. Trade, according to some, had become "a virtual obsession in Washington—particularly among Democrats, who [saw] protectionism as a sure-fire vote-getter." Lawmakers were "nearly rabid about the need to 'get tough' with Japan," and they pressured Hills to do so, using the 1988 Omnibus Trade and Competitiveness Act.[30]

While President Bush at times took strong stances against protectionism (as Ambassador Hills notes in her panel presentation), the American government had moved in the direction of what many perceived to be some form of managed trade in automobile and semiconductor agreements with the Japanese government.[31] Like other administrations before it, the Bush administration used the network of private advisory committees created by Congress[32] to receive ongoing advice from America's aggrieved industries. The Bush administration went one step further, however, with the creation of the Trade Promotion Coordinating Committee, "a council of 18 Federal Agencies that provide export assistance to U.S. businesses,"[33] chaired by U.S. commerce secretary Robert Mosbacher and created in May 1990. Bush hoped the committee would "harness all the resources of the Federal Government to serve America exporting businesses" and would "promote U.S. business in new or neglected markets through presidential trade missions, missions to be headed by the Secretary of Commerce."[34]

It was through such vehicles, however, that the Bush administration fell particularly prey to powerful American interest groups that were reluctant, and sometimes unable, to penetrate foreign markets—particularly the Japanese market—without the American government's support.

UNITED STATES–JAPAN TRADE RELATIONS DURING THE BUSH ADMINISTRATION

As the American trade deficit and the trade deficit with Japan increased dramatically in the late 1980s, United States–Japan trade friction escalated. During the Reagan administration, Japan had become the second largest economy in the world, and America's trade gap with Japan had become its largest trade deficit with any single country.

On the eve of the November 1988 election, Bush was subject to pressure from interest groups to use the recently passed Omnibus Trade and Competitiveness Act, particularly the strengthened Section 301 provisions, against Japan. On September 14, 1988, the Rice Millers' Association and the Rice Council for Market Development filed a complaint with the U.S. trade representative, charging that Japan's all-but-total ban on imported rice constituted an unfair trade practice that violated GATT rules. The petition included demands that Japan "open its domestic rice market by 2.5% of consumption per year for four years." Vice President Bush, while campaigning in California, urged U.S. Trade Representative Yeutter to take action on the petition "'so we can maintain the pressure against barriers to our exports around the world.'"[35]

However, a few days before the November 1988 election, Yeutter declined to accept the petition—"the first major trade action by the Reagan administration" since the signing of the Omnibus Trade and Competitiveness Act.[36]

Shortly after his inauguration, in February 1989, President Bush flew to Asia to attend the funeral of the emperor of Japan. Returning home from his five-day Asian trip, President Bush stated that his trip to Japan, China, and South Korea "underscored that America is and will remain a Pacific power."[37] However, many felt that East Asia remained "elusive" to the Bush administration.[38]

While President Bush selected Michael Armacost as his ambassador to Japan and was eager to fly to Emperor Hirohito's funeral in early 1989, in November 1991 Bush canceled a four-nation, Asia-Pacific visit reportedly because of "uncertainty over the congressional calendar."[39] In his January 1992 visit to Japan, Bush pressured for greater access to the Japanese market and signed the Global Partnership Plan of Action in January 1992 but became ill at a state dinner.

After his February 1989 trip to Asia, President Bush stated, "In Japan, we have our most important Asian ally and one of our largest trading partners."[40] However, by early 1992 there was concern that the United States–Japan relationship was in danger "of turning dangerously sour, given the readiness of the U.S. public to blame 'unfair' Japanese competition for all its economic problems."[41] The Reagan administration had moved toward what many have called managed trade by asking Japanese auto producers to use voluntary restraints, or self-imposed quotas, on their exports to the United States.[42] President Bush tried another tactic, bringing America's Big Three auto executives with him to Japan in January 1992 in order to "pry open Japanese markets."[43]

American frustration over a stagnating U.S. economy resulted in repeated calls for further liberalization of the Japanese market. Throughout the administration, the American auto industry, the Rice Millers' Association, and other industry groups exerted pressure on the U.S. government to force Japan to liberalize its markets. On Capitol Hill, various congressmen, most notably, Richard Gephardt, advocated confronting Japan in a wide range of legislative initiatives, some of which included erecting "reciprocal trade barriers in America" unless Japan and other countries "reduce[d] existing barriers to foreign goods in their own markets."[44]

Responding to such pressures, the Bush administration conducted a stream of sectoral negotiations with Japan. Merit Janow, deputy assistant U.S. trade representative for Japan and China during most of the Bush administration, outlines 13 new bilateral agreements that were concluded with the government of Japan between 1988 and 1992. These included "four agreements covering Japanese government procurement practices and procedures (supercomputers, satellites, construction services, and computer hardware and software); five agreements covering Japanese government telecommunications standards, regulations, and licensing procedures"; "one agreement covering technical standards (wood products); and three agreements covering market access problems."[45] As well, Janow asserts that the Bush administration worked to "bring about improvements in market access in a variety of other sectors without a formal agreement," including copyright laws, access to Japan's auto and auto parts market, and other sectoral commitments. These were included in the Action Plan signed by President Bush and Prime Minister Miyazawa when Bush visited Japan in January 1992.[46] Finally, the Structural Impediments Initiative, which began under President Bush's and Prime Minister Uno's initiative in July 1989, sought to "'identify and solve structural problems in both countries that stand as impediments to trade.'"[47]

Because a discussion of all of these initiatives is well beyond the scope of this chapter, it focuses on the Bush administration's role in the GATT Uruguay round negotiations. The roles of the United States and Japan in the GATT Uruguay round agricultural negotiations are the subject of my Columbia University political science dissertation.[48]

THE BUSH ADMINISTRATION AND THE GATT URUGUAY ROUND NEGOTIATIONS

The Bush administration identified the successful conclusion of the Uruguay round, which had begun during the Reagan administration, as its "highest trade priority."[49] In the words of one observer, "saving the GATT look[ed] like a classic Bush issue." Bush was "a liberal internationalist who [needed] an economic issue to distinguish himself from Democrats, but he [couldn't] stand domestic policy and he [didn't] want to spend money. Making the world safe for trade seem[ed] perfectly suited both to his politics and to his style of personal diplomacy."[50]

The GATT Uruguay round was initiated during the second term of the Reagan administration at Punta del Este, Uruguay, in September 1986. Although the Uruguay round was not concluded during the Bush administration, the Bush administration played a key role in the negotiations concerning the April 1989 conclusion of the GATT midterm review, the December 1990 ministerial meeting in Brussels, the preparation of the December 1991 Draft Final Act Embodying the Results of the Uruguay Round of Multilateral Trade Negotiations, and the November 1992 United States–European Community Blair House Accord. Nonetheless, the Bush administration failed to conclude the Uruguay round, and the negotiations were concluded during the Clinton administration. The Uruguay round agreement was signed in Marrakesh, Morocco, in April 1994, the agreement was ratified, and implementing legislation was passed by the U.S. Congress in late 1994.

One of the reasons the Bush administration had difficulty concluding the GATT Uruguay round was that the round included negotiations concerning areas that had not been so extensively covered in previous rounds, such as agriculture, intellectual property rights, services, and investment, as well as the GATT rules.[51]

By 1991 the GATT Uruguay round agricultural negotiations had become "the linchpin" to concluding the GATT Uruguay round. As Ambassador Hills explained to the Senate Finance Committee, "[I]f we do not deal with agriculture, then we will not get the participation of the Latin American countries or the 14 members of the Cairns group."[52]

The United States pushed for the insertion of agriculture into the GATT Uruguay round as a result of the reemergence of food grain surpluses and the loss of America's market share that had occurred in the 1980s.[53] From the beginning of the Reagan administration, the gradual, but steady, appreciation of the dollar versus other major currencies had weakened American preeminence in export markets and caused an overall contraction in global agricultural trade.[54] By the mid-1980s, U.S. agriculture was experiencing "the worst collapse in farm-asset values in a half century." As a result, the farm bill that the U.S. Congress passed in 1985 was designed "to maintain farm income, to expand U.S. agricultural exports, and to contain or reduce federal budget expenditures on farm price and income supports."[55] These policies were coupled with efforts to reduce agricultural subsidies at the Uruguay round.[56] American proposals for agricultural reform were more wide-ranging, and U.S. threats to link agricultural negotiations with the outcome of the entire round were "more serious" than ever before.[57]

During the period in which the Uruguay round was negotiated, from 1986 to 1994, although agricultural exports as a percentage of total American exports increased, the United States continued to criticize subsidized agricultural exporters, such as the EC, as unfair traders.

At the start of the Uruguay round, there were mounting fiscal difficulties resulting from the Common Agricultural Program in the European Community [EC] and from agricultural subsidies in Japan. As a result, the EC and Japan were more willing in the Uruguay round than they had been in the GATT Kennedy and Tokyo rounds to pursue comprehensive, fundamental, agricultural trade reform. Thus, such reform became a key element in the Punta del Este Declaration, with which the Uruguay round began in September 1986. The declaration stated that the Uruguay round negotiations "shall aim to achieve greater liberalization of trade in agriculture and bring all measures affecting import access and export competition under strengthened and more operationally effective GATT rules and disciplines."[58]

During the end of the Reagan administration, between early 1987 and November 1988, a split developed in negotiating positions concerning the scope and speed of agricultural reform. In July 1987 a U.S. proposal called for, in the words of President Reagan, "the elimination over a 10-year period, of all export subsidies, all barriers to each other's markets (including tariffs and quotas), and all domestic subsidies that affect trade."[59] This proposal caught Japan somewhat by surprise, particularly because of its potential impact on Japan's closed rice market, and was not exactly welcomed by Japan.[60] The EC's October 1987 proposal, on the other hand, fell "far short of President Reagan's call for the elimination of all farm aid by the year 2000"[61] and stressed the need for a more gradual reduction of protection for domestic farmers. The impasse between the United States, on the one hand, and the EC and Japan on the other, over the scope and speed of agricultural reform delayed the conclusion of the GATT Uruguay round midterm review, which was supposed to be concluded at the end of the Reagan administration in December 1998 in Montreal.

The GATT midterm review process was finally concluded in April 1989 at the beginning of the Bush administration. The United States, led by newly appointed U.S. trade representative Carla Hills, finally agreed to the compromise language that GATT director general Dunkel proposed—the long-term objective, "to provide for substantial progressive reductions in agricultural support and protection sustained over an agreed period of time, resulting in correcting and preventing restrictions and distortions in world agricultural markets."[62]

In October 1989 the United States introduced the concept of comprehensive tariffication of agriculture in a revised proposal to liberalize global farm trade that called for "the conversion of all non-tariff barriers in agriculture into tariffs and the progressive phasing down of these tariffs over a period of ten years." The intent, according to Secretary Yeutter, was "to bring these tariffs to low levels, or, if possible, to zero by the end of that ten-year period."[63] While Japan opposed this tariffication-without-exception plan until the end of the GATT Uruguay round, the European Community "proposed something less radical, talking in terms of 'degrees of reduction' of farm subsidies, and [was] less specific about what types of protection would be reduced."[64]

Partially as a result of "the lack of an agreed framework for negotiations in agriculture," the December 1990 Brussels Ministerial meeting that was supposed to conclude the Uruguay round came to a close without concluding the round.[65] Finally, on December 20, 1991, Arthur Dunkel, chairman of the Trade Negotiations Committee, presented the "Draft Final Act," which covered all issues in the Uruguay round.

Before the end of the Bush administration in January 1993, the "Draft Final Act" was discussed, and the United States and EC reached the so-called Blair House Accord in November 1992. However, the Uruguay round was concluded not during the Bush administration but during the Clinton administration. Japan announced its rice liberalization decision in December 1993. The final agreement was signed in Marrakesh, Morocco, in April 1994, and implementing legislation relating to the Uruguay round agreement was approved by the American and other governments in late 1994.

There are various reasons that the Bush administration had difficulty in concluding the Round by the time of the November 1992 election. First, various authors have questioned whether if, at the December 1988 GATT midterm review, Clayton Yeutter had taken a stance other than "the zero option" to dismantle "all trade-distorting export subsidies, price supports, tariffs, and quotas by early in the next century,"[66] the GATT Uruguay round negotiations might have been concluded earlier.[67]

Second, while the United States preached agricultural liberalization at the Uruguay round, the United States continued to wage an ongoing war to expand its share of the world agricultural market by using export subsidies. These subsidies created certain vested interests who profited from the round being prolonged, and some argue that these subsidies "provided American policymakers with an excuse for postponing reform, giving more handouts, and coddling American farmers."[68] This was particularly true for the Export Enhancement Program, which was created in 1985. "Under the program, private exporters [could] sell U.S. grain at prices below those in the U.S. to meet foreign competition, and then collect government-owned surplus grain as so-called bonuses, or subsidies."[69] Yeutter said the subsidies were "'the best way to deal with the European Community subsidies.'"[70] Such a "carrot-and-stick strategy" was designed to "make it more costly for other countries to maintain subsidies." The Export Enhancement Program was used to counter EC subsidies that had helped to turn Europe "from a net importer to an exporter of grain" but also to give U.S. negotiators leverage in the GATT Uruguay round negotiations.[71]

Congress, particularly the Senate Agriculture Committee, was repeatedly trying to place a cap on subsidies resulting from the Export Enhancement Program, although Yeutter argued that such subsidies were "'budget neutral.'"[72] By early 1992, after Edward Madigan became secretary of agriculture, American exporters themselves were openly questioning the program.[73]

Third, the Uruguay round might have been concluded earlier had negotiation strategies that reflected a greater understanding of Japan been used. The United States' declining importance in the international system affected its capacity to influence Japan and the EC concerning the conclusion of the GATT Uruguay round negotiations, and Japan's increased economic strength made it possible for Japan to assert its objectives, particularly in relation to arguing against tariffication without exception. Had different negotiating tactics been used, particularly concerning agriculture, the GATT Uruguay round might have been concluded earlier. But, as with many policy areas, actions taken during the Reagan administration determined the available options for the Bush administration. It might have been possible, for example, to pull Japan more behind the United States' stance before the GATT midterm review, rather than push Japan and the EC into the same corner against the United States, which was what resulted from the use of the so-called zero-option strategy by U.S. Trade Representative Yeutter at the December 1988 GATT midterm review at the end of the Reagan administration.

Japan had resigned itself to handling agricultural reform at the multilateral level through the GATT Uruguay round agricultural negotiations when bilateral agricultural negotiations with the United States in the late 1980s led to bilateral GATT panels that were decided against Japan, partially because of the agricultural-exporter bias of the GATT treaty.[74] The inclusion of the tariffication of agriculture in the Uruguay round forced the Japanese bureaucracy, particularly the Ministry of Agriculture, Forestry, and Fisheries, as well as the Liberal Democratic Party (LDP), to commit themselves more to agricultural policy reform than they had originally intended to do at the beginning of the Uruguay round. Of most concern to Japan in the 1991 "Draft Final Act" were the market-access provisions.[75] Finally, in late 1993 Prime Minister Hosokawa, leading a majority coalition of dissident LDP elements and former opposition parties, announced Japan's agreement to partially liberalize the Japanese rice market in order to conclude the Uruguay round.[76] The market-access rates announced by Japan were higher than the rates proposed in the "Draft Final Act."[77] However, Japan was very reluctant to bring its offer to the table. It is possible that the selection of other strategies at particular points in the negotiations might have led Japan to take a more active role in helping to conclude the Uruguay round earlier, perhaps before the November 1992 election.

TRADE POLICY MAKING IN THE BUSH ADMINISTRATION, UNITED STATES–JAPAN TRADE RELATIONS, THE GATT URUGUAY ROUND NEGOTIATIONS, AND PRESIDENT BUSH'S BID FOR REELECTION IN 1992

Trade policy making in the Bush administration occurred in the midst of heated debates between the executive and legislature concerning how best to conduct American trade policy in light of America's large trade deficit. Within the executive branch, the Commerce Department and the U.S. trade representative were the most subject to pressure from America's diverse and independent interest groups, some of which attempted to win the government to their side by using protectionist legislation, such as Section 301, to their advantage.

Reducing America's trade deficit with Japan was a major objective of the Bush administration. As Janow argues, the Bush administration's bilateral and sectoral initiatives did lead to some progress in reducing the trade deficit and can be linked, to some extent, to later decreases in the American trade deficit with Japan. Janow notes that during the Bush administration, "U.S. exports increased by 57 percent, about twice as fast as exports to Japan overall." However, as Janow notes, "how much of this growth can be attributed to bilateral agreements versus some combination of market trends and changes in government policies is difficult to ascertain" and is a debate best left to economists.[78] Bayard and Elliot's study of the effectiveness of Section 301 cases[79] shows clearly "that the Japanese have been more responsive than any other trading partner to U.S. pressure."[80] Furthermore, a survey of more than 300 American companies conducted by the American Chamber of Commerce acknowledged in June 1991 that "American companies operating in Japan sa[id] they face[d] far fewer trade restrictions than in previous years."[81]

The Bush administration, however, had difficulties selling its trade policy to the general public. While some voters were adamant about taking tough action to reduce the trade deficit, they continued to buy Japanese and other countries' products that they liked and came to have doubts about the Bush administration's overall economic policy. A recession began in July 1990, in which the GDP [gross domestic product] contracted for three consecutive quarters and in which unemployment increased from a 1989 yearly average of 5.3 percent to 7.4 percent in 1992.[82] The Bush administration's actions in relation to Japan in the midst of this recession led some American voters by early 1992 to believe that Japan was "being blamed unfairly for a trade crisis that is of the United States' own making."[83] This feeling intensified after January 1992, when the media portrayed the Big Three auto producers who had accompanied President Bush to Japan as being remarkably aware of how to pressure the U.S. government for support and noticeably unaware of some of the most obvious realities of the Japanese market. By traveling to Japan in January 1992, President Bush appeared to want "to remove trade barriers to help boost U.S. exports and create jobs at home, where a lingering recession ha[d] jeopardized his reelection prospects."[84] However, shortly after his January 1992 trip to Japan and before the beginning of the primaries, President Bush's approval rating as measured by the Gallup poll hit an all-time low.[85]

Bush was an extraordinarily popular president five months into his term—when more than 70 percent of the citizens polled viewed him favorably—and after the Gulf War.[86] However, in November 1992 Bush won only 38 percent of the popular vote, in comparison to 43 percent for Clinton and 19 percent for independent Ross Perot.[87] One reason, perhaps, among many for President Bush's failed bid for reelection was the perception of some that the administration had not been as successful as it hoped in its trade policy in the midst of rising unemployment and a domestic recession. In early 1992 the U.S. trade deficit was beginning to climb again; the highest trade priority of the administration, the successful conclusion of the GATT Uruguay round negotiations, was not likely to be achieved before the November election; the president's trip to Japan wasn't very well received. This situation largely continued through the November 1992 election, although somewhat due to certain events that were beyond the administration's control.

Much of the credit for the negotiation of the GATT Uruguay round and NAFTA [North American Free Trade Agreement] should be attributed to the Bush administration. However, significant parts of two of the "six significant trade achievements" that Ambassador Hills cites in her presentation occurred after the November 1992 election. The Blair House agreement with Europe concerning agriculture was concluded later in November 1992, and in December 1992 President Bush signed and sent to Congress the North American Free Trade Agreement. During the Clinton administration, the North American Free Trade Agreement was approved by the U.S. Congress in November 1993, and the GATT Uruguay round agreement was signed in Morocco in April 1994 and approved by the U.S. Congress in December 1994.

George Bush lost the 1992 election partially because of his perceived failure to confront domestic economic problems and arguably because of his tendency to look abroad for solutions to America's woes. There was the perception that while George Bush had played a major role in winning the Gulf War, he had neglected domestic economic policy.

President Bush clung, until the very end of his administration, to the rhetoric that "free and open trade is the key to expanding prosperity," particularly when speaking of the GATT Uruguay round negotiations.[88] But by early 1992 the perception among some was that "Bush, the avowed free trader, [had] embraced a policy of managed trade where government intervenes in markets to control results. Instead of promoting free trade by simply calling for the removal of trade barriers, as the U.S. government ha[d] done in the past, U.S. trade negotiators also pushed for higher targets on Japanese purchases of American autos and auto parts."[89]

Some American voters became disenchanted with how President Bush's free and fair trade rhetoric appeared to contradict the Bush administration's, as well as the Reagan administration's, shift toward what many perceived to be some form of "managed trade." This disenchantment increased when the combination of these policies apparently led to a recession.

The visible consequences of some of the discernible elements of the Bush administration's economic policy, such as the Bush administration's trade policy, swayed some American voters, concerned about the ongoing recession, to vote against George Bush in November 1992. As a *Los Angeles Times* journalist noted, while, during the 1988 campaign, Bush had "voiced an unquestioning American faith in American growth, by early January 1992, a persistent slump ha[d] called that vision into question." According to polls taken at the beginning of the administration, "on no issue more than prosperity did voters hold high hopes for Bush." When "asked what they expected under Bush's tenure," 74 percent of those polled in a January 1989 *New York Times*/CBS survey said "he would at least 'keep America prosperous.'" But by January 1992 "on no other issue" had "expectations seemed so much to plunge"—only one in four Americans approved of Bush's handling of the economy.[90] This perception largely continued through the November 1992 election.

President Bush's reputation within his own party was damaged by the apparent results of his economic policies. Patrick Buchanan, rallying right-wing Republicans to his side, attacked Bush's free and fair trade rhetoric and set forth an "America First" strategy, claiming in March 1992 that "'American farmers have a right to protection, just like American workers and American industries do.'" At the beginning of the presidential primary elections, President Bush tried to bury Patrick Buchanan's challenge by saying that his opponents were "peddling protectionism, a retreat from economic reality into a dangerous pre–World War II isolationism."[91] Later in the campaign, Democratic candidate Bill Clinton and Independent Ross Perot also criticized President Bush's free and fair trade rhetoric.

In the midst of this debate, a certain percentage of American voters lost faith in the Bush administration's capacity to effectively cope during the next four years with not only trade relations—particularly with Japan—but, more important, with the American economy. The unemployment rate had climbed above 7 percent, and the economy, having grown 2.5 percent in 1989 and 0.8 percent in 1990 and having contracted 1.2 percent in 1991, grew 2.9 percent in the first quarter of 1992 and 1.5 percent in the second quarter of 1992.[92]

NOTES

Most of this paper was researched and written while the author was studying as an

L.L.M. and doctoral student at Kyoto University Graduate School Faculty of Law under the auspices of a Japanese government scholarship between October 1991 and March 1997. For this reason, the version of the paper submitted to the conference in October 1996, which was used during the panel discussion, included many citations to articles in the *Japan Times*, an English-language Japanese newspaper. Many of the articles cited from the *Japan Times* were not from "the Japanese press," as Ambassador Hills stated during her presentation in the panel discussion, but rather were articles originally printed in American newspapers or articles taken from wire services, such as the Associated Press, that had been reprinted in the *Japan Times*. In revising the paper in light of the panel discussion, to the extent possible, citations to the *Japan Times* in the October 1996 version of this paper have been replaced with citations to the same articles as they were originally printed in American newspapers or have been replaced with citations to other sources that contain similar information.

I am very grateful to Ambassador Hills for her comments concerning this paper during the "Far East" panel of the Hofstra University Conference on the Presidency of George Bush, April 19, 1997.

1. "President George Bush Addresses the Convention on Family Values, Strong and Honorable United States Leadership, Foreign Policy and Former First Lady Barbara Bush," "Show: Campaign '96: The Republican National Convention," CBS News transcripts, August 12, 1996. Also, George Bush mentioned none of these issues in his speech during the Academic Convocation Ceremony of Hofstra University Conference, which was broadcast on C-SPAN, May 26, 1997.

2. *Economic Report of the President Transmitted to the Congress, February 1990* (Washington, DC: U.S. Government Printing Office, 1990), p. 256.

3. See, for example, Merit E. Janow, "Trading with an Ally: Progress and Discontent in U.S.–Japan Trade Relations," in Gerald L. Curtis, ed., *The United States, Japan, and Asia: Challenges for U.S. Policy* (New York: W.W. Norton, 1994), pp. 53–95, 73. Janow was deputy assistant trade representatives for Japan and China from February 1990 through July 1993.

4. See Hobart Rowen, "And Now, Tough Talk on Trade," *Washington Post*, February 19, 1989, sec. H, p. 1.

5. "Transcript of Bush Speech Accepting Presidential Nomination," *New York Times*, August 19, 1988, sec. A, p. 14.

6. *Economic Report of the President Transmitted to the Congress, January 1993* (Washington, DC: U.S. Government Printing Office), Table B-103, p. 466.

7. David S. Broder, "Minimalist Presidency," *Washington Post*, March 26, 1989, sec. D, p. 7.

8. Peter B. Levy, *Encyclopedia of the Reagan–Bush Years* (Westport, CT: Greenwood Press, 1996), pp. 199, 323.

9. Broder, "Minimalist Presidency."

10. Richard Morin, "Americans Rate Japan No. 1 Economic Power: Poll Finds Mixture of Respect, Wariness," *Washington Post*, February 21, 1989, sec. A, p. 19.

11. See, for example, Karl Schoenberger, "The Times Poll: Public's Views of Japan Mixed, Contradictory," *Los Angeles Times*, February 12, 1992, sec. A, p. 1.

12. "Hills' Naming as Trade Rep in U.S. Is Greeted Cautiously," *Japan Times*, December 17, 1988, p. 12.

13. Art Pine, "The Toughest Trader of Them All: In Showdowns with the Japanese and Pushy Congressmen, Carla Hills Is All Business," *Los Angeles Times Magazine*, September 3, 1989, p. 18.

14. "Hills' Naming as Trade Rep in U.S. Is Greeted Cautiously."
15. George Bush, "Inaugural Address, January 20, 1989," *Public Papers of the Presidents of the United States, George Bush, 1989, Book 1* (Washington, DC: U.S. Government Printing Office, 1990), p. 1.
16. George Bush, "Remarks at the Swearing-In Ceremony for Carla A. Hills as United States Trade Representative," February 6, 1989, *Public Papers of the Presidents of the United States, George Bush, 1989, Book I*, p. 56.
17. Rowen, "And Now, Tough Talk on Trade," sec. H, p. 1.
18. Morin, "Americans Rate Japan No. 1 Economic Power."
19. Excerpts from the American Insight Group's 1989 *Survey and Report*, No. 1, as printed in "A Tenser, Gloomier Nation: Americans Feeling Pessimistic, Protectionist," *Japan Times*, March 6, 1989, p. 19.
20. Art Pine, "U.S. Should Press Tokyo for Import Targets," *Los Angeles Times*, February 17, 1989, sec. IV, p. 1; Janow, "Trading with an Ally," pp. 56–57.
21. Senate Committee on Finance, *Hearings on the Nomination of Carla Anderson Hills to Be U.S. Trade Representative*, 101st Cong., 1st Sess., January 27, 1989, p. 16.
22. Walter S. Mossberg, "Commerce Aide Takes Hard Line on Japan Trade," *Wall Street Journal*, February 15, 1989, sec. A., p. 11.
23. Leonard J. Schoppa, "The Social Context in Coercive International Bargaining," *International Organization* 53, no. 2 (Spring 1999): 307–42, 330.
24. AP, "Bush Urges Non-Inflationary Growth: U.S. Partners' Economic Structure Could Hinder Coordination," *Japan Times*, March 3, 1989, p. 11.
25. Financial Times Service, "Seven-Point Plan," *Japan Times*, March 3, 1989, p. 11. See also Janow, "Trading with an Ally," p. 57.
26. See Raj Bhala, "Note on Super 301," in Bhala, *International Trade Law: Cases and Materials* (Charlottesville, VA: Michie Law, 1996), pp. 1123–31.
27. Peter Ludlow, director of the Brussels-based Center for European Policy Studies, speaking in April 1989 at the Japan Forum on International Relations, as quoted in *Japan Times*, April 9, 1989, p. 17. See also "EC Lists American Barriers to Trade," *Financial Times*, May 4, 1989, p. 30; "Part 3 Trading Partners' Reactions to 301," in Jagdish Bhagwati and Hugh T. Patrick, eds., *Aggressive Unilateralism: America's 301 Trade Policy and the World Trading System*, (Ann Arbor: University of Michigan Press, 1990), pp. 219–65.
28. Rowen, "And Now, Tough Talk on Trade," sec. H, p. 1.
29. See Bhala, "Note on Super 301," at 1128–30.
30. Pine, "The Toughest Trader of Them All," p. 18.
31. Leslie Helm, "Free Trade Gives Way to Intervention," *Los Angeles Times*, January 13, 1992, sec. D, p. 6.
32. For a description of the role of these committees, see House Committee on Ways and Means, *Overview and Compilation of U.S. Trade Statutes, 1995 Edition*, 104th Cong., 1st Sess., August 4, 1995, Committee Print 6, pp. 214–15.
33. George Bush, "Remarks at the Export-Generating Jobs for Americans Luncheon in Boston, Massachusetts, May 24, 1991," *Public Papers of the Presidents, George Bush, 1991, Book I* (Washington, DC: U.S. Government Printing Office, 1992), p. 560.
34. George Bush, "Remarks at the Presentation Ceremony for the 'E' Star Awards, May 23, 1990," *Public Papers of the Presidents, George Bush, 1990, Book I* (Washington, DC: U.S. Government Printing Office, 1991), p. 704.
35. Oswald Johnston, "Rice Growers Pushing for Japan to Open Its Market," *Los Angeles Times*, September 15, 1988, part IV, p. 4.

36. Clyde H. Farnsworth, "U.S. Rejects Action on Japan's Rice Imports," *New York Times*, October 29, 1991, p. 37.

37. George Bush, "Remarks upon Returning from a Trip to the Far East, February 27, 1989," *Public Papers of the Presidents, George Bush, 1989, Book I*, p. 150.

38. Editorial, "Leadership to Measure," *Financial Times*, August 10, 1989, p. 16.

39. "Statement by Press Secretary Fitzwater on the Postponement of the President's Visit to Pacific Nations, November 5, 1991," *Public Papers of the Presidents of the United States, George Bush, 1991, Book II* (Washington, DC: U.S. Government Printing Office, 1992), p. 1404.

40. Bush, "Remarks upon Returning from the Far East, February 27, 1989."

41. Editorial, "Leadership to Measure."

42. Takeshi Sato, "Big Three Leaner, Tougher, Threatening: Hurting at Home, Japanese Carmakers Brace for Tough U.S. Turf Battle," *Japan Times*, January 1, 1993, p. 9.

43. Laura D'Andrea Tyson, "Getting Japan on the U.S. Bandwagon," *Los Angeles Times*, January 5, 1992, sec. D, p. 2.

44. Richard A. Gephardt, "Perspective on U.S.–Japan Trade: Nothing Ventured, Nothing Gained," *Los Angeles Times*, January 14, 1992, sec. B, p. 7.

45. Janow, "Trading with an Ally," p. 60.

46. See ibid., pp. 65–66.

47. Ibid., p. 67.

48. Christopher C. Meyerson, "Domestic Politics and International Relations in Trade Policymaking: The United States and Japan and the GATT Uruguay round Agricultural Negotiations," summary available on Columbia International Affairs Online, http://www.ciaonet.org (cited June 8, 2002).

49. *Economic Report of the President Transmitted to the Congress, February 1990*, p. 256.

50. The Editors, "GATT and Mouse: Why the Much-Mocked Geneva Trade Talks Should Be the Centerpiece of the President's New Internationalism," *The New Republic*, December 2, 1991, p. 8.

51. Janow, "Trading with an Ally," p. 58.

52. Senate Committee on Finance, *Hearings: Extension of Fast Track Legislative Procedures*, 102nd Cong., 1st sess., March 14, 1991, p. 22. See also Keith Bradsher, "Official Tells of Progress on Trade," *New York Times*, November 25, 1991, sec. D, p. 2.

53. Theodore H. Cohn, "The Changing Role of the United States in the Global Agricultural Trade Regime," in William P. Avery, ed., *International Political Economy Yearbook*, vol. 7: *World Agriculture and the GATT* (Boulder, CO: Lynne Rienner, 1993), pp. 17–38, 36.

54. Terence P. Stewart, ed., *The GATT Uruguay Round, a Negotiating History (1986–1992)*, vol. 1: *Commentary* (Boston: Kluwer Law and Taxation, 1993), p. 172.

55. Dale E. Hathaway, *Agriculture and the GATT: Rewriting the Rules* (Washington, DC: Institute for International Economics, September 1987), p. 83.

56. U.S. Department of Agriculture (USDA), "Multilateral Trade Reform: What the GATT Negotiations Mean to U.S. Agriculture" (Washington, DC: USDA Staff Briefing, August 1990), p. 4.

57. Cohn, "The Changing Role of the United States," p. 36.

58. Punta del Este Declaration as quoted in Stewart, *The GATT Uruguay round*, p. 171.

59. Ronald Reagan, "Statement on Proposed International Agricultural Trade Reform, July 6, 1987," *Public Papers of the Presidents, Ronald Reagan, 1987, Book II*

(Washington, DC: U.S. Government Printing Office, 1989), pp. 797–98.

60. "Japan and Europeans Cautious on U.S. Plan," *New York Times*, July 7, 1987, sec. D, p. 7.

61. Julie Wolf, "EC's Agriculture Proposals on Subsidies, Tariffs Likely to Evoke U.S. Opposition," *Wall Street Journal*, October 8, 1987, p. 27.

62. "Mid-Term Meeting" [MTN.TNC/10], as reprinted in Stewart, *The GATT Uruguay round*, vol. III: *Documents*, p. 33.

63. "Press Conference with Clayton Yeutter, Secretary of Agriculture, and Carla Hills, U.S. Trade Representative re: U.S. Proposals Presented at GATT on Trade in Services and Agriculture," Federal News Service, October 24, 1989. See also Clyde H. Farnsworth, "U.S. to Offer Plan to Curb Farm Support; Other Nations Will Be Asked for Similar Cuts at Meeting in Geneva," *New York Times*, October 23, 1989, sec. D, p. 9.

64. Steven Greenhouse, "Trade Talks Stalemated after U.S.–Europe Clash," *New York Times*, May 31, 1990, sec. D., p. 2.

65. Carla Hills, "The Benefits of Open Markets and Trade, Remarks as Prepared for Delivery before Conect/International Business Centers, Boston, June 17, 1991" (Washington, DC: USTR Reading Room Speeches and Testimonies File, 1991). See also Clayton Yeutter, "Letter to the Editors: Blame Europe," *New York Times*, January 9, 1991, sec. A, p. 20.

66. Steve Drysden, *Trade Warriors: USTR and the American Crusade for Free Trade* (New York: Oxford University Press, 1995), p. 348.

67. See Gregory F. Trevorton, *Making American Foreign Policy* (Englewood Cliffs, NJ: Prentice-Hall, 1994); Drysden, *Trade Warriors*, pp. 348–50.

69. James Bovard, *The Farm Fiasco* (San Francisco: Institute for Contemporary Studies, 1989), p. 311.

69. Bruce Ingersoll, "U.S. Cancels Grain Sale Subsidy Offers following Information Leak at Hearing," *Wall Street Journal*, August 2, 1989, sec. A, p. 9.

70. AP, "Farm Export Subsidies Will Continue: Yeutter," *Japan Times*, May 25, 1989, p. 9.

71. Art Pine, "Agricultural Subsidies Would Be Jointly Cut Under U.S. Trade Plan," *Wall Street Journal*, April 7, 1987, p. 1.

72. Charles J. Abbott, "Controversy over EEP Ceiling," United Press International (UPI), September 15, 1989. See also United Press International–Kyodo, "Export Subsidy Cap Would Harm Farm Exports: Yeutter," *Japan Times*, September 17, 1989, p. 8.

73. See AP, "Cargill Rips Farm Export Subsidies," *Mainichi Daily News*, February 8, 1992, p. 6. See also "U.S. Money for Food Ads," *New York Times*, February 3, 1992, sec. D, p. 7.

74. Mitsuo Matsushita, "Constitutional Framework of the Major Trade Laws in Japan: In the Context of the Uruguay Round," in Meinhard Hilf and Ernst-Ulrich Petersmann, *National Constitutions and International Economic Law, Studies in Transnational Economic Law*, vol. 8 (Boston: Kluwer Law and Taxation, 1993), pp. 275–97, 282–86.

75. These provisions stated, "Where there are no significant imports [as in the case of Japan's rice market], minimum access opportunities shall be established. They shall represent in the first year of the implementation period [1993] not less than 3 percent of corresponding domestic consumption . . . and shall be expanded to reach 5 percent of that base figure by the end of the implementation period [1999]." ("Draft Final Act Embodying the Results of the Uruguay round of Multilateral Trade Negotiations, L. Text on Agriculture, Part B, Specific Modalities: Market Access," December 20, 1991, as printed in Stewart, *The GATT Uruguay round*, vol. 3: *Documents*, p. 633.)

76. While making concessions in other areas, Japan agreed to a special treatment clause in the Uruguay Round Agreement on Agriculture that allowed Japan to keep its rice market exempt from tariffication if it established "minimum access opportunities [that] represent[ed] four per cent of domestic consumption of the designated products in the first year of the implementation period [which would] increase annually to reach eight per cent in the sixth year [of the implementation]" ("Final Act of the Uruguay Round: Press Summary," *News of the Uruguay Round of Multilateral Trade Negotiations*, NUR 080, December 14, 1993, p. 9).

77. See note 75.

78. Janow, "Trading with an Ally," p. 68.

80. Thomas Bayard and Kimberly Ann Elliott, *Reciprocity and Retaliation in U.S. Trade Policy* (Washington, DC: Institute for International Economics, 1994).

80. Leonard J. Schoppa Jr., "Deconstructing Power: Explaining the Declining Effectiveness of U.S. Pressure on Japan," paper presented for annual meeting of the American Political Science Association, San Francisco, August/September 1996, p. 6.

81. David E. Sanger, "U.S. Companies in Japan Say Things Aren't So Bad," *New York Times*, June 12, 1991, sec. A, p. 1.

82. *The Economic Report of the President Transmitted to the Congress, January 1993*, Table B-30, p. 382.

83. Schoenberger, "The Times Poll."

84. Steve Holland, "Big Three U.S. Car Makers Urge Japan to Open Markets," *Reuter Library Report*, January 7, 1992.

85. Levy, *Encyclopedia of the Reagan–Bush Years*, pp. 417–18.

86. Richard Morin, "Poll Finds Public Is Optimistic About the Economy and Clinton," *Washington Post*, December 16 ,1992, sec. A, p. 16.

87. Levy, *Encyclopedia of the Reagan–Bush Years*, p. 136.

88. George Bush, "Remarks Following Discussion with European Community Leaders, December 18, 1992," *Public Papers of the Presidents, George Bush, 1992–93, Book II* (Washington, DC: U.S. Government Printing Office, 1993), p. 2203.

89. Leslie Helm, "Free Trade Gives Way to Intervention," *Los Angeles Times*, January 13, 1992, sec. D, p. 1.

90. Douglas Jehl, "Promises of '88 May Dog Bush in 1992 Race," *Los Angeles Times*, January 5, 1992, sec. A, pp. 1, 18.

91. George Bush, "Remarks to the Georgia Republican Party in Atlanta, Georgia, February 29, 1992," *Public Papers of the Presidents, George Bush, 1992–1993, Book I* (Washington, DC: U.S. Government Printing Office, 1993), p. 358.

92. *Economic Report of the President Transmitted to the Congress, January 1993*, Table B-2, p. 351.

Discussant: Carla A. Hills

Let me start out by saying that President Bush is remembered for six significant trade achievements: the successful conclusion of the North American Free Trade Agreement (NAFTA), which, contrary to the suggestion made earlier, was indeed signed in December 1992 by President Bush; the substantial progress made toward a successful conclusion of the Uruguay round, and, for example, without the Blair House agreement with Europe on agriculture, the round would have collapsed; the launching of the Enterprise for the Americas, with a framework agreement for open trade and investment concluded with 31 Latin American countries, which engendered a wave of goodwill toward the United States by Latin America that had not been experienced in this nation's history; the execution of formal trade agreements with the newly freed countries in Eastern and Central Europe and the republics of the former Soviet Union, bringing those closed economies into an international trading system; breakthrough agreements with China for market access and for the protection of intellectual property; and a series of well-focused agreements with Japan attacking both structural and sectoral barriers to the import of foreign goods and services. Because of this panel's focus on the Far East, I will spend my allotted less than 10 minutes in reviewing the Bush administration's trade initiatives in China and in Japan.

But I do feel first compelled to comment briefly on Mr. Meyerson's paper because, I am told, it will be part of the compiled work of this conference. I do wish so sincerely that I had the time to correct the substantial number of inaccurate statements in the conference draft of the paper, which the author bases primarily on articles from the *Japan Times*. Forty-eight of his 78 footnotes are to the Japanese press. The author claims that President Bush lost the 1992 election because of a perception of failed trade policy. A citation for this conclusion in the conference draft of the paper is a 1987 Japanese press account. He concludes at the end of his paper that the actions of the Bush administration often contradicted Bush's trade rhetoric. It is puzzling how this can be said of the president, who ended the so-called voluntary restraint arrangements made by his predecessors on steel, autos, and machine tools and twice vetoed protectionistic textile legislation. Even a cursory review of the record reveals that this president's actions matched his rhetoric more than any other president in recent history.

A profound lack of understanding of our trade laws and how they operate is apparent in the paper's accusation that the Bush administration moved in the direction of managed trade because it set up industry advisory groups. In fact, the 1974 Trade Law requires the president to establish such advisory groups. In practice, those groups included not only industry but labor, consumer, and environmental representatives who primarily supported free trade objectives.

A final comment: the conference draft of the paper incorrectly cites the emphasis upon agriculture as a reason for the failure to complete the Uruguay round agreement before President Bush left office. The fact is that we had broken the back of agriculture in 1992 with the Blair House agreement. But the suggestion that agriculture could have been shoved under the carpet to make for a speedier end to these negotiations is just plain wrong. A majority of the nations at the bargaining table refused to open their market without an address of the distortions in agricultural trade. It was extremely important to us, for 90 percent of our disputes with Europe centered on differences in agricultural policy.

Now let me turn to the Bush administration's trade policy toward Japan, which had four major aspects. First, our Structural Impediments Initiative, which we called SII. It was launched in July 1989 and sought to lower those structural barriers to trade and investment in Japan, such as the cumbersome distribution system; exclusionary business practices, including the cozy government and business relationships; and discriminatory corporate relationships in procurement, the *Keiretsu* relationship between Japanese companies. SII achieved some noteworthy objectives and successes, including a streamlined approval process for the new, large-scale retail stores, which enabled U.S. retailers to enter that market and compete head-to-head with Japanese distributors. It strengthened the enforcement of the Japanese anti-monopoly laws, accelerated customs clearance for imports, and reduced processing time for U.S. patent applications.

Second, we worked hard to negotiate strong and enforceable multilateral rules under the auspices of the Uruguay round. Now, of course, the Uruguay round was not directed at Japan in particular or even at Asia in particular, but it did cover topics and disciplines like agriculture, investment, and services, where Japanese policies and practices were extremely restrictive.

Third, we targeted specific sectors where our products were demonstrably competitive and where the Japanese barriers could be documented. These sectors included computers, paper, construction services, semiconductors, amorphous metals, telecommunications equipment, satellites, supercomputers, and wood products, just to name a few. As a result, our exports to Japan of the products covered by these agreements from 1988 through 1991 grew 54 percent, about twice as fast as our overall exports into the Japanese market.

Finally, we sought to build constituencies in Japan to support market-opening measures. That effort helped to bring about a remarkable transformation in Japanese public attitudes toward its own restrictive practices. Often, the Japanese press would support our efforts, arguing that the Japanese government should indeed open the Japanese market so as to lower consumers' costs. That's a very different reaction from that taken in the 1995 auto talks, where the Japanese press urged Prime Minister Hashimoto (then trade minister) to resist what it saw as U.S. bullying. The Japanese economy is far more open today than it was a decade ago, and I believe it will be far more open in the decade to come than it is today, but its opening, in part, is a result of the market-opening initiatives launched during President Bush's administration.

With respect to China, in 1992 we concluded agreements improving China's intellectual property laws and reducing barriers to market access. In January of 1992, the Chinese signed an agreement in which they committed to improve their intellectual property laws in copyright, patents, and trade secrets. Pursuant to that agreement, the Chinese established a bilateral copyright relationship with the United States, joined the Berne Convention, amended its patent law, and issued regulations implementing both the Berne Convention and its undertakings with us. Enforcement has lagged at the local level, but the protection of intellectual property today is far better than it was before the agreement, and the agreement provides the necessary legal framework within which to insist upon adequate enforcement.

In October 1991 we began negotiations to address China's principal market restrictions: lack of transparency; the existence of discriminatory quantitative restrictions, like import quotas and bans and unreasonable standards; and discriminatory certification standards and restrictive import licensing requirements. As a result of the agreement we concluded one year later, China committed not to enforce any trade law or regulation that had not been published; to lift 90 percent of all import licensing requirement in yearly tranches over a five-year period; to ensure that its standards and certification requirements be based upon sound science and not discriminate against U.S. products; and to reduce significantly the tariffs covering a broad range of products of concern to U.S. products.

President Bush was courageous in maintaining most-favored-nation [MFN] status with China and vetoed three times—in 1990, 1991, and 1992—bills that attached a variety of conditions on China's MFN status during the review process, believing that we were more likely to advance our objectives with China if we kept an open dialogue.

President Bush's trade policy toward Asia and throughout the world was clearly based upon the premise that open markets provide the best way to ensure growth and stability, thereby maximizing prosperity and opportunity for the American people.

Discussant: Susumu Awanohara

In Mr. Meyerson's paper, I think he is suggesting that President Bush lost the 1992 election, at least in part, because of a perceived failure in his trade policy. Mr. Meyerson says that the free trade talk, on the one hand, and some protectionist action, on the other—under duress from protectionist forces—this inconsistency was the cause of discontent among the voters and perhaps contributed to his unsuccessful election race. It's not that I've thought about such causality seriously, but reading his paper, I had a different idea, which is that perhaps he didn't cave in enough for the liking of the American public in those days. He resisted protectionist pressures too much, except at the end, symbolized by the 1992 trip to Japan, which is often described as having been disastrous for various reasons. I think maybe President Bush was too "free trade," and that was a minus for him.

I was in Washington covering the Bush administration and into the Clinton administration. I'm Japanese, but I guess you don't have to be Japanese to see which of the two trade policies was the more sensible. Listening to the Clinton trade team coming in in 1993, it sounded as though they wanted every trade deal to look like the bilateral semiconductor deal, in which the Japanese domestic market shares were predetermined so that the Japanese would guarantee to take 20 percent of imports. Of course, this didn't work. To be fair, one has to understand why the American team was so frustrated. I think the Japanese market is very difficult to crack. The Japanese, like others sometimes, negotiate perhaps in bad faith or don't deliver what they promise. There were also these structural barriers that Ms. Hills referred to, which were really becoming obvious as the impediments to trade. But the solution probably was not to predetermine market shares, as the Clinton team tried to do at the beginning and soon saw was impractical.

Coming back to Mr. Meyerson's paper, he says at one point that by July 1989—that's right after the Super 301 designations were made and just before the Structural Impediment Initiative (SII) was launched—the most nationalistic trade policy America had ever taken during the postwar period began to take shape, as the Bush administration took bilateral actions against India, Japan, and Brazil and designated them as unfair traders under the Super 301 process. Now, that may be, but I think we have to remember that Super 301 was very much a creature of the Congress and a watered-down version of the congressional initiative. It could have been worse. But it was an earlier congressional initiative that the Bush administration kind of inherited, had to deal with. I think the whole story about Super 301 is that it was applied very narrowly and softly by Ms. Hills, who in 1990 already refused to designate anybody and, after two years, dropped the law despite considerable pressure from the Congress to extend it. I will not go into the details of Super 301, for what reasons India and Brazil and Japan were hit and so on, because of time, but in 1990, as I said, Japan was not named because Japan was seen to be making progress, and India was the only one that was kept on the list because it hadn't done anything. Brazil was also taken off.

I think in 1990 the Bush administration introduced the Structural Impediments Initiative, which Ms. Hills just spoke of, partly as a sop to Congress, to appease Congress, to say that we're dealing with Japan in different ways, not just through the Super 301, but also because I think there were valid reasons why these structural barriers had to be addressed. The SII talks went on for a couple of years. It was pretty popular in the beginning but gradually lost public support—or the support of the officials who were engaged in the talks—partly because in America there was dissatisfaction that this was not actionable. As a result of the talks, if the Japanese didn't comply, you could not take action against them under the law. The Japanese were increasingly frustrated because the talks got very intrusive, because you're talking about trade practices, commercial practices, which were time-honored. Although they were not created to block imports, they were blocking imports, but from the Japanese point of view, they were not created to block imports, and there was no need for Japan to change the ways in which it did business to accommodate imports. So the SII talks didn't end very nicely, but I think these talks were nevertheless useful. After the first term of the Clinton administration, many trade officials in the administration are now looking back to the SII with a kind of nostalgia and also a design to really move back into that direction because the sector-by-sector talks are just too time-consuming and won't deal with the broad issues effectively.

I said that the Bush administration resisted protectionist pressures except at the end, with the trip in 1992 when President Bush took a whole bunch of American top executives—including the Big Three—and talked about "jobs, jobs, jobs" and wanted to open up the market. He acquiesced in the framework that was being used by the business sector, saying that the trade imbalance was being caused by Japanese protectionism and that he had to open up the Japanese market. He insisted upon a deal in the auto sector and auto parts sector, which was rather like the semiconductor agreement, although there's vagueness as to whether there was a Japanese government commitment to import as much as was indicated. But still, I think that trip was disastrous, even from the trade point of view, because after the trip, which went rather nastily for everybody, a wave of Japan-bashing resumed, and a lot of kind of America-bashing—not just by the Japanese but by a lot of Americans—about how the Detroit executives were blaming the Japanese for their own failures, and so on. I think the Bush administration may have lost control of the debate, joining this debate on the wrong side.

So that was an unfortunate ending, I think, but on the whole, coming back to the theme, I think that—and certainly in retrospect, compared to the Clinton administration—the Bush administration stood for the right principles of trade, and I think we will remember it for that.

Discussant: Donald Burnham Ensenat

Thank you for coming through the double-whammy of bad weather and an 8:30 in the morning session. I thought when I graduated from law school was the last time I'd be in a classroom at 8:30 in the morning on Saturday morning. But here I am.

When Professor Levantrosser gave us our instructions about the panel, he said we could either react to the paper, or we could ignore it and talk about what we pleased, so I'm going to choose the latter. I'm going to speak on Southeast Asia, and I'm going to make a case for the Bush presidency and its legacy in Southeast Asia. In my view, the legacy is that we got over our Vietnam hangover, and it woke up American public opinion and American business—especially small and medium American business—to what had happened out there since our 1975 pullout. After 1975, basically we tuned out and turned off Southeast Asia, expecting the dominoes to fall. Instead, what happened was that the region matured politically and boomed economically. Between 1983 and 1993 the region grew at a collective rate of 7 percent per year, making it the fastest growing place on earth. American business, on the other hand, had pulled out. Ford and Chrysler, for example, closed their operations there, leaving the market to the Japanese.

So what did the Bush administration do? Well, I submit it had a "vision thing." The political grouping of the region was the Association of Southeast Asian Nations (ASEAN), which ironically was born in 1965 out of the domino theory as an American-fostered, anti-Soviet institution. By 1989 ASEAN was 6 countries: Brunei, Indonesia, Malaysia, the Philippines, Singapore, and Thailand, with the intent of including all 10 of the Southeast Asian nations by eventually adding Vietnam, which it has, Myanmar (or former Burma), Laos, and Cambodia. The organization had institutionalized a dialogue-partner system with the United States, Japan, Canada, Australia, New Zealand, South Korea, and the European Community. It had also institutionalized something they call the "Post-Ministerial Conference," or the PMC, which was an invitation from the ASEAN foreign ministers to their dialogue partners to meet with their ASEAN counterparts at the conclusion of ASEAN'S ministerial conference, which was held each year and rotated among the ASEAN capitals. While there was a great deal of demand, as you would know, on Secretary Baker's time and physical presence in other parts of the world, he made a point of regularly accepting the invitation and attending those PMC meetings. In addition, President Bush made a visit to the region, the first since Lyndon Johnson back in the 1960s.

Also included in these dialogues and PMC meetings were private-sector participants. The American side was, and is, organized and led by the U.S. ASEAN Business Council, which has tirelessly spread the word to American business that there is "a glittering market," as the *New York Times* called it, that had developed out there and that U.S. business was missing out. From these trips and enhanced attention from the Business Council and by the administration came enhanced media attention, from which came enhanced public awareness—particularly in the business community—which generated increased interest, which brought increased trade and investment. Just as one example, American investment in the region between 1991 and 1992, which had long lagged behind the Japanese, grew 25 percent in Singapore in one year, 21 percent in Thailand, and 13 percent in Indonesia.

From ASEAN grew another grouping: Asia-Pacific Economic Cooperation (APEC). Are you following all these acronyms? First proposed by Prime Minister Hawke of Australia in 1989, which was undoubtedly as a counter to the proposal among ASEAN for its own trading block à la NAFTA (in fact, the ASEAN group was called AFTA), the grouping was to include all of the major Pacific Rim economies: the ASEAN group, its dialogue partners (which I just mentioned, except for the EC, which was its own trading bloc), and the three Chinas—the PRC [People's Republic of China], Taiwan, and Hong Kong. The Bush administration quickly endorsed this proposal and became its most ardent supporter.

In late 1990, however, Malaysian prime minister Mahathir proposed an all-Asian grouping that he called the East Asian Economic Caucus (EAEC), motivated in large part, in my view, by an erroneous news story—I'm told it was erroneous, because it made no sense for Malaysia economically to have an all-Asian grouping that didn't include the United States, because it had a booming high-tech export business to the United States and to North America—but an inaccurate story about Secretary Baker having asked about Mahathir, calling him "that funny little man in a hat" or "the man in the funny-looking hat," referring to his traditional Malay dress.

Anyway, by 1993, through American leadership and administration leadership and through the cooperation of Japan, I might add, in not giving EAEC any support or credence, APEC had taken hold and become institutionalized. It opened a secretariat in the summer of 1993 in Singapore—I remember walking through it when it was nothing but bare walls—and EAEC and any notion of an all-Asian grouping in Southeast Asia or on the Pacific Rim had become very much a subsidiary issue.

From APEC came the only other (that I know of) regular economic summit of leaders than the G-7. As with ASEAN, came enhanced media and public attention to the region, and from that enhanced trade and investment and, in particular, job-creating American exports.

Again, some other statistics: U.S. exports of manufactured goods—that is, in the United States—to the region tripled between the mid-1980s and the end of the Bush administration, accounting, at the end of the Bush administration, for approximately 2.3 million good-paying U.S. American jobs. Not bad, if you ask me, for an administration that was supposed to be "vision thing"-challenged.

Discussant: Henrietta Holsman Fore

I shall leave Ambassador Hills' remarks as the quintessential rebuttal for our panel to the paper, and I will just pick up two of the themes, the first being the United States–Japan economic rivalry and the second being the GATT Uruguay round, but as seen through the eyes of the developing countries in South and East Asia. There were really three reactions to these two events. The first was that there was a concern that the trade disputes would spill over onto their countries, and it would close off access to the U.S. markets. The second was that there would be a requirement of choosing sides, and the third, that there would be an effect on U.S. security forces in Asia. This was the time when Subic Bay (in the Philippines) was being renegotiated.

The United States–Japan trade disputes had a tough public voice in our trade negotiations, but underlying it was a diaspora of Japanese companies that were setting up corporate seedlings throughout South and East Asia. It sidestepped the trade deficit for the United States and moved it from Japan to the developing countries. Therefore, when the trade disputes began heating up, the South and East Asian countries began being worried. They were worried that they would not have access to the U.S. markets; they were worried that the Japanese companies that they were partnering with would pull back their technology and their venture capital; and they were worried that they would lose jobs, all of which were essential to the tigers and the tiger cubs emerging throughout Asia.

The idea of retaliation spilled into the question: Did you have to choose sides? There was money at stake in foreign aid budgets. At the beginning of the Bush administration, these budgets were running about even between the United States and Japan, at approximately $9 billion each. By 1992 the Japanese foreign assistance budget had become the largest foreign assistance budget in the world, and it spent more of its aid in Asia. Now, as most of you know, the foreign assistance budget for the United States has dropped to $6.6 billion; the Japanese is still around $9.5 billion, but the effect was a rivalry for infrastructure projects throughout Asia. As it heated up, it was played out at the highest levels, and there was a real issue for developing countries about choosing sides.

The third issue was that the U.S. military forces really were protecting and keeping open the trade lanes in Asia. It was essential that they stay open; it was important that there be peace and stability throughout the region.

While all of this was going on, the GATT Uruguay round came to the scene. While the developing countries looked at these specific negotiations, the Uruguay round was seen in a much larger context. The context was that of worldwide expectations that had changed significantly. The new expectations were unsubsidized market economics, and the power of the message lay in the fact that all countries in the developing world were expected now to change their economic policies. So whether the issue was trade finance, agricultural policies, intellectual property rights, or the opening of financial services or service company markets, there was a unity among the industrialized world that developing countries had to see.

The reflections that come back to me on trade are that trade is sometimes seen as a very abstract notion. It is a dialogue among nations. It is a dialogue that occurs at very high levels, it is assumed to be something that does not touch people's lives, but it is *very* immediate if you are a developing country. When Ambassador Ensenat mentioned that Secretary Baker went out to Asia, he visited Mongolia. I was one of the next high-ranking officials to come into Mongolia, and I was asked if I had brought an airplane with me. They wanted a large airplane, both for passengers as well as cargo. I indicated that I had not, but what they were saying is that the world had changed, and they wanted trade as a way to develop. Those of you who know Mongolia know that there is a narrow-gauge railroad that was built in Mongolia to deter an invasion from China. Mongolia has no major seaports, no major highways, no major rivers. Air traffic is their lifeline. For them, the notion of speaking to, and trading with, the outside world was very important. To their credit, they wanted the ideas that come with trade, and trade affects people's lives in many ways, but it brings ideas of what the outside world wants and does not want and what your country could or should become.

Ambassador Ensenat mentioned the countries of ASEAN being drivers of the economic growth in this period. They certainly were, and I also count APEC as one of the achievements of the era. But while ASEAN in Asia focused on trade, there were different winds sweeping in from Europe, and the winds from Europe were seeking capitalism and democracy. It affected U.S. policies in Asia in that there was a new urgency toward the idea of privatization of state-run companies and monopolies within Asia. There was an ineffective and inefficient allocation of resources. Private operation and/or ownership of both public services as well as many of the private services could and should be scrutinized. One phenomenon of the era was that governments had run out of money, and as a result all attention and focus went to private provision of services and the privatization of state-owned corporations. But without the winds sweeping through Europe, we would not have had the urgency in Asia.

Three successes I would count during these years were the creation and the opening of capital markets. Much of this success was a result of the international expectations that I mentioned earlier, but some of it also had to do with innovative programs. I think OPIC (Overseas Private Investment Corporation) led the way with some of their equity investment trusts.

A second area that was very important was the open markets and the open policies for the privatization of fertilizer and agricultural programs. Bangladesh is certainly one of the recipients of this change in thinking. There was a new expectation of how agricultural policy should operate in a market, and it was not just the donation of excess food from the United States.

The third area that I think was very indicative of the Bush administration was the U.S.–Asia Environmental Partnership. President Bush announced it in Singapore in 1992. It had all of the hallmarks that we have been hearing over the past few days of the Bush administration: teamwork across the agencies, in this case 28 U.S. government agencies, involvement with all the nonprofit organizations in the United States dealing with energy and environment, as well as the commitment of businesses for technologies that could be put overseas. Many U.S. companies think of environmental technologies as an afterthought, and what the Bush administration tried to do was to gather all of these forces together and use them to help clean up the air, water, and land of Asia. It is a style of this presidency that it committed to starting a dialogue and a program with 31 Asian nations. Former prime minister Brian Mulroney spoke about this aspect of President Bush as a president last night, and I think it is extremely important.

We tried to level the playing fields; it is something that Ambassador Hills struggled with time and time again. I do not think we accomplished it. But I come from the world of business, and the leveling of playing fields is next to impossible. We did, though, make a herculean effort to mix credits, to blend them, to try to address the notion of how equity loans, how development and grant finance could move projects for development and infrastructure projects forward on behalf of U.S. businesses, U.S. jobs, and the developing world.

During the Bush administration, I think we also accomplished a great deal in terms of opening up the dialogue on business being a good force, a force for change, a force for positive improvement. During these years, in the United States we woke up to the idea, finally, that trade across the Pacific had outstripped trade across the Atlantic and that we were heading into an Asia-Pacific century. It really did not quite hit our public consciousness, and it is just starting to come through now.

What lies ahead? All eyes are on China: its size, its rising nationalism, its emergence as an economic power. But I would also keep my eyes on what is going on in Europe. The euro as single currency is certainly one that will be an issue and a possibility that will be debated within Asia. If I were a student at Hofstra, I would study Asia. I would study the cultural issues, because how we deal with an individual, with a corporate responsibility, with societal responsibility is very different within the Western and the Eastern strains of thought, and how we come to terms with these will be the basis for trade, for economics, for political, for economic and social agreements in the next century.

I would also like to just mention that, from our point of view, I think, in the Bush administration, we didn't think of Asia as the "Far East," a strange and distant land. We really thought of there being no oceans, that our continents touched, and that Asia was the "Near West." It was a very important and near neighbor.

Discussant: Barbara Hackman Franklin

I'm delighted to be here and to participate in a warm discussion on a cold, rainy morning. I like the "Near West" idea very much. I think that's how we should look at Asia.

I am going to confine my brief remarks today to two areas, and they will have a commercial aspect: China is one, and Japan is the second. My brief comment about the paper will come in the context of my Japan comments.

China: President Nixon opened China in 1972; Deng Xiaoping's reforms began in 1978; the United States recognized China in 1979; and some businesses began to look toward this huge potential market. In 1983 then secretary of commerce Malcolm Baldridge, with his counterpart, established the U.S.–China Joint Commission on Commerce and Trade. The objective: to promote business between the two nations and to solve commercial problems. Business activity began to gather momentum in the 1980s but was abruptly interrupted when the Chinese government forcibly cracked down on the democracy movement at Tiananmen Square on June 3 and 4, 1989. (Jim Lilley was our ambassador at the time.) The United States, quite dismayed, placed a variety of sanctions on China. One was a ban on ministerial contact of exactly the sort required to keep the joint commission going.

However, President Bush understood the need to maintain a relationship with this emerging great power, even though we continued to be distressed by the events of June 3 and 4. So the next few years saw quiet efforts to resume a dialogue with China. By the time we reached 1992, there was the additional movement you've heard about from Ambassador Hills. There were two new market-opening agreements signed—one on intellectual property rights and the other on market access. The next logical step was to capitalize on those new agreements and expand our commercial activity.

So, after the election in 1992, President Bush asked me to undertake a mission to Beijing to reconvene with my counterpart, then [Ministry of Foreign Economics and Trade] minister Li Lanquing—he is now Vice Premier Li—the joint commission, which had been moribund since Tiananmen Square. We put this mission together in just a few weeks. We invited a small delegation of business leaders and went to Beijing in December 1992. I was the first cabinet member to visit that country officially after Tiananmen, an act that removed the ban on high-level, government-to-government contact. Before going, I met here with the Chinese ministers of aerospace and communications, strongly indicating that the growing trade deficit was going to become a political liability—and could become an issue in the upcoming most-favored-nation status trade renewal. That trade deficit stood at $18 billion in 1992, and the only way to address it was for China to buy more U.S. products. I had a list of pending U.S.

sales, at the top of which was a large Boeing aircraft purchase.

When I arrived for my first bilateral meeting with Minister Li, he informed me that we would get our Boeing contract, that it would be signed while I was in China. It was, and I witnessed the signings of some other agreements, notably involving AT&T and Northern Telecom. In total, we brought back more than $1 billion worth of new contracts for American companies. A great deal more business flowed from the trip afterward: GE engines for those new Boeing aircraft that China Southern Airlines had purchased; a large AT&T joint venture; power equipment orders; and several other things. The point is that the United States could now put the full weight of its government at the highest levels behind our businesses, and this opened the floodgates for U.S. investment. The cumulative contracted amount of investment in China today is over $28 billion, 80 percent of which occurred since 1992, making us third as an investor in China behind Hong Kong and Taiwan. Of course, each time I have returned I have been able to see the impact of that investment in the growth of China's economy.

I also addressed human rights and nuclear proliferation on that trip. Those issues are among those in the mix today in our relationship with China, together with concerns about aggression against Taiwan, the Hong Kong handover, the current fund-raising scandals, and the fears of some about the intentions of the military. These are all strands of a very complex strategic relationship the United States must have with China. It is arguably the most important bilateral relationship in the world.

President Bush understood all this and deserves credit for making the right call and sending me to China when he did. It was also courageous. If you remember, Bill Clinton had accused him of coddling dictators during the 1992 campaign. Had my mission not been undertaken when it was, it would have meant, I believe, a year's loss of commercial opportunities for our businesses. The new administration needed time to get its act together, and it would have been politically difficult for President Clinton to send a mission immediately. President Bush's action was important because our companies got a better foothold in this large, emerging market. But in addition, the presence of U.S. companies there today reinforces economic freedom and openness, brings human rights into a different perspective, and helps create conditions that I believe, over time, will lead to more political freedom in that country. President Bush deserves credit for understanding this.

Turning to Japan: As you have indicated, there was a high degree of frustration with Japan when the Bush administration came into office. We had a trade deficit of $50 billion, the yen was relatively weak against the dollar (which, of course, helped Japan's exports), and we thought Japan's markets were not truly open. The United States had employed a variety of negotiating approaches over the years trying to break down the barriers to exports. The Bush administration, as you heard from Carla, tried another, and that was the Structural Impediments Initiative (SII) to try to get at the *Keiretsu*, Japanese collusive business practices. I want to highlight another approach, which I will call "direct presidential involvement." One example is the trip the author has called "politically disastrous." I will focus on the results of that trip.

As we know, President Bush went to Japan with a group of CEOs [chief executive officers] and my predecessor, Secretary Bob Mosbacher. We also know that there was an intestinal flu going around; the president got it and got sick. That news overwhelmed everything else from the trip. However, a key result was a voluntary agreement, acknowledged by both governments in the Tokyo Declaration that was signed at the time, that Japanese companies would purchase U.S. auto parts, and that the amount would grow from $9 billion (in dollars) in Japan's fiscal 1990 to $19 billion by fiscal 1995. Japan's companies did it and, in fact, actually exceeded that target. If we relate that to jobs, every billion dollars' worth of exports translates to an estimated 19,000 jobs here in the United States. Thus, the trip yielded or protected many thousands of U.S. jobs.

Because the Big Three automakers' CEOs were on the trip, and because the trip was so politicized, the president was criticized as being a "car salesman." This is a cynical characterization and, I believe, grossly unfair. I came into office just in time to oversee the action plan that came out of the Tokyo Declaration. I can tell you that this trip captured the attention of the Japanese and made Japan more willing to negotiate the agreements that we heard about earlier. I also disagree with the author that the Japan episode had anything much to do with the 1992 election. I do not think it did.

Subsequent to the president's trip, on my watch, we did a number of things aimed at reinvigorating U.S. exports to Japan. I believe that those efforts—for example, a major conference with the U.S.–Japan Business Council to help our businesses learn how to export to Japan—all contributed to increasing U.S. export performance. What I want to emphasize in conclusion is this: it is very clear to me that the whole Bush administration, starting with the president, was four-square for free and fair trade every step of the way, from beginning to end.

I have one final concluding note, on the lighter side. I tell you this story because it's something I learned from President Bush. He was very personal in his diplomacy. Every head of state I ever met in the course of my being in office thought he was his or her best friend.

This particular anecdote is about "oatmeal diplomacy." The first time I met my then-counterpart, MITI [Ministry of International Trade and Industry] minister Kozo Watanabe, it was over breakfast in my office. He admired my bowl of oatmeal—my usual breakfast—and he said it reminded him of the kindness of the GIs when they came to Japan at the end of the war. Then he said, "There's a Japanese saying that when two people eat the same foods, they begin to think alike and they become friends forever." So, he ordered a bowl of oatmeal. We went through our issues. There was tension over semiconductors and some other things, but the oatmeal broke the tension. He ordered another bowl of oatmeal and we continued our discussion. When he left the United States, I sent him a Commerce ice bucket full of oatmeal, a Japanese flag, and an American flag, with a note suggesting that he keep eating. Every time we then met or talked and there were disagreements, it was the oatmeal that broke the tension. I do believe this helped us to make more progress than we would have otherwise.

Footnote: I had dinner with Mr. Watanabe three weeks ago in Tokyo—he's now the deputy speaker of the Diet—at his residence. I couldn't resist presenting him with a box of American oatmeal and a Japanese bowl as a symbol of our friendship and that of our countries.

Discussant: Donald P. Gregg

I want to pick up on a number of remarks made earlier, tell a couple of anecdotes that illustrate what I think the Bush presidency accomplished in trade, and then mention one completely unrelated issue.

First, on Secretary Franklin's depiction of the Tokyo meeting, we've heard a couple of people on panels who have brought with them notes that President Bush wrote them, and they've kept them as sort of precious reminders of the way he operated. I wish I had, because my favorite of all, I think, was written to Meg and me from Air Force One on the way back, in flight, from the visit to Tokyo. Prior to that, he had visited Seoul and had a very successful visit. We'd, I thought, accomplished a lot. President Bush started it out, it said, "Dear Don and Meg, thanks so much for all you did in Seoul." Then he went on and he said, "You know, apart from throwing up in the lap of the Japanese Prime Minister in front of 50 million people, the trip to Japan wasn't all bad." He then went on to allude to some of the same agreements that you mentioned. But the media were there, and that, of course, is what was remembered.

When we were in Seoul, one of our first visitors was Carla Hills, who came in as USTR. I had a meeting in the residence for her with several of the highest-ranking Korean businesspeople that I could assemble. Carla was—at that point, beef was quite high on your agenda, and we were pushing the Koreans to open their market to hotel-quality beef. One of the Koreans got up and said, "You know, Secretary Hills, if you force us to open our markets, you're going to get all the blame and you're not going to get much of the market, because the Australians and the New Zealanders are going to come in and get 80 percent of any additional percentage that we grant." So he said, "Why bother? You're going to get all the flak." Carla said, "You're right. You're absolutely right. That's our analysis. And I'm not here arguing bilateral advantage for the United States. I'm here arguing free trade, which works eventually to the benefit of all." That had a profound impact, I think, on the Koreans who heard her.

I would then pick up on Henrietta Fore's remark that trade has an impact on people's lives. A week later, six Korean college students who didn't like the fact that we were pressuring them to open their beef market came over the wall to our residence, broke into the residence, and tried to set fire to it. This caused some stress, as the Korean police seemed to be very reluctant to come into the residence and evict the students, and I think they were surprised at how easy it was to get into the residence, and they ran around and broke a lot of furniture and tried to set fire to a fireproof (fortunately) rug. But eventually they were evicted, and we went on television, and actually, it was an excellent way to start my tour as ambassador, because the Koreans were humiliated by this. We were fairly good sports about it, and it was a very good way to go. But it did cause me to give Carla a nickname, which I have told her about before: I refer to her as "the Joan of Arc of Free Trade."

But the difference between the way Carla operated and the way Mickey Kantor operated for the Clinton administration I think is very illustrative, and Mr. Awanohara got at that, in a way. When Carla appeared, she was talking about one strand of a very complex series of relationships that we had going with Korea, or Japan, or wherever else she appeared. So she was not the only spokesperson for the relationship.

Bill Clinton essentially ran against foreign policy; I think he hoped that it would stay still so that he and Mrs. Clinton could fix health care. When it didn't, he fell victim to the "nothing but" theory: that is, someone would come in and say, "Hey, we've got a problem with Japan." "What is it?" "Well, it's auto parts." So he'd say, "Okay, send Mickey Kantor." So Mickey Kantor would saddle up and gallop in and would raise the issue of auto parts. I talked to Fritz Mondale, who was out there, and he said, "This is a very difficult job. It's very heavy lifting." Mickey Kantor very frequently was perceived to be in charge of foreign policy in Asia.

This was also true in China, where I think CD-ROMs were the central issue. The dialogue with China was so nonexistent that a year ago we were reduced to really ugly muscle-flexing after the Chinese fired missiles in the Straits of Taiwan, and we had to respond by sending a couple of carrier battle groups into the straits. So there was really no broad dialogue in Asia during the first Clinton administration. I think it's going to be much better with Secretary Madeleine Albright.

I would also say that there was no micromanagement in the Bush administration, that we were all really given a lot of scope to do our jobs as we saw fit to do them. I think that the momentum that we gathered on the economic front is being carried on today. I was very distressed in the political campaign of last year to see practically no references to foreign policy whatsoever, and that seems to be a trend almost worldwide, but what you do have is economic outreach in very new and aggressive forms. The WTO [World Trade Organization] is emerging as a successor to GATT, APEC is developing, and we are reaching out to each other. I think that the true fruits of winning the Cold War lie in our ability to trade with our friends as well as our former opponents. But sooner or later, that needs political undergirding, and I hope that some of that will come in the second term of President Clinton.

Now, the thing that I want to mention that has nothing to do with trade is something that probably President Bush will never talk about, but I think it's one of the more significant things he did. I arrived in Seoul in September 1989, and one of the first things I went through was an analysis of what would happen in Korea if we had an accident with one of our nuclear weapons—and we had nuclear weapons in Korea in those days. It was a pretty horrendous scenario. There was no indication that this was going to happen; they were carefully stored, but they were old. So this led me to call in our commander there, a wonderful four-star general, and I said, "Hey, do we need these?" He said, "Well, let me check into that." So the answer came back, "Well, no, but they've always been here." So then I sort of raised the question with CINCPAC [commander in chief, Pacific Area Command]: Do we really need these? The answer, after a certain amount of harrumphing, was no, but it's sort of convenient to have them there. Then I said, "Sooner or later, these are going to become a huge issue with the North Koreans. Sooner or later, it's going to become a huge issue with the South Korean students. So if we don't need them, why don't we get them out?" So the CINCPAC and our CINC [commander in chief] said, "Well, that's okay with us, but what about the Koreans?"

So I went to the Koreans—I had an extraordinary relationship with the national security adviser to the Korean president—and after some talk, they said OK. So, in October 1990, I sent a message back to Washington saying, "I think we ought to pull our nuclear weapons out of Korea." The only response I ever got was one very short message saying, essentially, "Thank you." Sometime in the next year, there was a policy announcing that all of our tactical nuclear weapons were being removed from around the world. I've forgotten, Jim, what the formulation was on ships; I think it was usually—

James R. Lilley: No confirm, no deny.

Gregg: Yeah, still on that. But anyway, then there was sort of a back-and-forth, "Well, how can we be sure that they're really out of Korea?" President Roh of Korea made a statement saying that they were out, and then the White House said, "We have no reason to object to that statement," so that was sort of the way we did it.

I can tell you that getting them out ahead of necessity—not only there, but wherever else we had them—I think was a great step. It is not an issue with North Korea. It would have been, and we would not have taken them out under pressure. It is also a move that positions us to work, I think, much more effectively against proliferation of nuclear weapons from other countries. So this is something that President Bush did. I think it's one of his really better moves. It's something that is never talked about, but I thought this was a good place to mention it.

Discussant: James R. Lilley

My colleagues have all said it so well, so far, but I'll try to build on what they have said.

China, in some ways, is like Banquo's ghost in *Macbeth*, hovering in the background, and President Bush, being the modest man that he is, doesn't talk about it very much. I am not very modest so I will talk about it, mainly because I believe he did a very good job, and I think in some ways he got a bum rap. When protocol toasts become policy, or "coddling Communist dictators" becomes the cliché used on this brave man, it gets close to disgusting. What President Bush did was to build on the accomplishments of the Reagan administration in carrying out a consistent Asia policy that reflected our values and was characterized by consistency, balance, and toughness.

But one small anecdote: When President Bush came to power, he chose to send three people out to the three key areas of East Asia. Each man was supposed to know his area well. He sent Mike Armacost to Japan, who had spent much of his adult life on Japan; he sent Don Gregg to Korea, who knew Korea better than most people in the government; and he sent me to China, and I was born in Tsingtao. Now, in my case, it wasn't necessarily a magical mix for brilliant success, but anyway, no one could fault us on our credentials. They could fault us on our tactics, on our big mouths, or various other things, but they couldn't say that we didn't know our subject matter.

President Bush did not experiment with the Chinese relationship. After the flap in 1980, when President Reagan in the early campaign suggested that we might restore official relations with Taiwan, we got back on track with China, and that was when the dual-track policy of improving relations with both Taiwan and China succeeded. Most people are unaware that then-vice president Lee Teng-hui of Taiwan, who was part of that awful furor in June 1995, came to the United States quietly under Reagan, was treated with great dignity, went to West Point as a VIP [very important person], and then quietly left. In other words, these sensitive incidents can take place without the pyrotechnics, sulking, and petulant behavior that characterized Lee's 1995 visit to Cornell.

At that time, we established precedents for the way Asian policy should be worked. For instance, both Taiwan and China remained in the Asian Development Bank (ADB). Previously, when China wanted to join the World Bank in 1980, it said, "Boot Taiwan out," and we unfortunately cooperated. In 1985 we said no: "Taiwan is in the ADB. Let's work on nomenclature, and let's compromise and have you both in," and it was accomplished after two and a half years of tough bargaining. Both sit in the Asian Development Bank today. This was the breakthrough that took place in 1985 but may not still exist today.

At the same time, we had to bring into some balance the military capabilities of China and Taiwan. We sold Taiwan the technology to build a better fighter aircraft, its indigenous defense fighter, and we also sold F-8 avionics to Beijing. Some balance was then achieved. So, as we moved into this period, we began to make progress with both sides.

In 1984, as you also will recall, Prime Minister Thatcher signed the joint agreement on Hong Kong, which was welcomed in most circles as dealing with this necessity—the eventual turnover of Hong Kong to China—but doing it in a way that protected the equities of Hong Kong for 50 years after the turnover in 1997 in the one country/two systems arrangement. The United States quietly supported this.

In 1989 Tiananmen, of course, changed much of this for the worse. China was condemned by the world and reacted angrily. The arrival of British governor Chris Patten in Hong Kong three years later in 1992 with his idea of accelerating democracy also proved to be an added irritant for China. In contrast, Taiwan and China relations were flourishing. In the United States, trade with China also had taken off and was basically in balance. The U.S. trade deficits came later.

When I first arrived in China as a U.S. official in 1973, we were isolated in Beijing in the small U.S. Liaison Office. George Bush was our second boss. At that time there were only Pullman Chemical Fertilizer Factories, Boeing 707s sold to China, along with products from Continental Grain, Weyerhauser, and that was just about it. I returned to China last year [May 1996], spent some days in Shanghai, visited the Pudong Development Zone—I don't have to say any more about the incredible change in our relationship with China and the economic developments in China itself. The United States has a balanced China policy, Taiwan felt secure, and China knew we understood the ground rules. We formed with China various concrete programs in Afghanistan, Cambodia, and elsewhere to deal jointly with Soviet hegemonism. In 1987 China and Taiwan started to work together, and their trade went through the roof—investment grew, tourism and contacts increased, cross-strait relations bloomed. Taiwan had built up the confidence to deal with China, and China had the confidence that we understood the one-China relationship and wouldn't experiment with its sovereignty or unity. We knew what we were doing, and as a result, the two, China and Taiwan, worked together in an extraordinary development. This first happened under President Reagan, but it boomed under President Bush. U.S. problems with China on Taiwan were minimized.

What President Bush also recognized—which was true of Nixon, Carter, Ford, and Bush, and Reagan—is that in the Chinese relationship, there have to be summitry, rituals, and symbols to make it work. This is fundamental to understanding the relationship. It may be distasteful to go through suffocating banquets, hour after hour; toasts have to be made and drunk; speeches calling for "friendship forever" have to be made. This is all part of the drill. If you don't want to do this, then get out of the relationship. The administration that initially didn't get the point were the people that took over on January 20, 1993. They thought you could build a relationship with China and stick your tongue out at them at the same time. It didn't work. As Don Gregg pointed out, in March 1996 we almost went to war with China over Taiwan. Nuclear-capable missiles were fired by China into the Taiwan Strait, U.S. carrier battle groups moved in, and only after this frightening spectacle did we both pull back from the abyss. The administration had to start over—so what did they do? They invented summitry, symbols, and rituals. This started in 1996, about three and a half years late, and only having gone through some agonizing and dangerous confrontations: on trade, on human rights, on proliferation of weapons of mass destruction, on Taiwan—all three were allowed to become confrontational.

One of the ironies is that President Bush, who understood this aspect of Chinese character so well, went to China in 1989 in what was to be a triumphant visit. What distorted this was "the man who came to dinner," which almost ruined the trip. The media saw the one thing they wanted to see, a dissident leader in China who didn't get to President Bush's return banquet. It was real copy. Never mind what happened in his talks with Deng Xiaoping or various other leaders in China. The lead story was that this particular dissident couldn't get into the banquet that President Bush was giving for President Yang Shang-kun. The dissident, smelling publicity, went back and gave a press conference, and this smeared the whole trip.

The sequel to that story is this dissident and his wife had over 500 meals in my house, because he was in the embassy for 13 months after seeking refuge, and I had to negotiate his way out. He finally left in June 1990. We became, shall we say, colleagues. We ate together; we talked together. The media and our U.S. opposition were highlighting United States–China differences and used toasts like "coddling Communist dictators" to the extreme. The current administration got a taste of this when the Gore handshake with Li Peng dominated his trip. Somehow we have to work ourselves out of these negative symbols as partisan issues. They undermine U.S. interests.

In 1986–1989, the danger signals were coming from China, but we didn't notice them. The fall of Hu Yaobang on the issue of the "spiritual pollution" campaign in 1986 should have told us that something was wrong, that in China economic development was getting out of balance with political and cultural aspirations. When Charlton Heston and Arthur Miller came to China to show the Chinese *Death of a Salesman* and *The Caine Mutiny*, the Chinese got a whiff of the other world, and they wanted more. Given their dreary fare at the time, this was exciting for them. They also came in droves to see us in the United States, tens of thousands of young Chinese students. The attacks on bourgeois liberalization followed; the cultural surge was quietly suppressed by the Chinese without too much fanfare at that time. But then the inflation factor entered into the mix, and the rather moderate leader of the party at that time, Zhao Ziyang, fell largely on this issue—on inflation, which was getting out of control. He also crossed Deng on his political liberalism. Most people who study China are aware that inflation is a much bigger issue there than it is here or even in other countries. In 1949 it was part of the downfall of Chiang Kai-shek, the rival to the Communist Chinese. The Chinese of today were very conscious of this.

What happened then in 1989 was, in part, a miscalculation by both parties. In a way, we were both living in the past. The big event in Chinese eyes was Gorbachev coming to China, meeting Deng, and reestablishing party-to-party relations between the two great Communist giants. It was obvious even then that President Gorbachev wasn't going to last very long. The real story was not that these two party leaders were meeting; it was 200,000 demonstrators in Tiananmen Square. Gorbachev couldn't get into the Great Hall of the People because of the crowds. Unfortunately for the Chinese, Dan Rather, Bernie Shaw, Peter Jennings, and Tom Brokaw all were covering the summit, but the story was becoming Tiananmen Square. When I arrived, our embassy in Beijing was still entranced by the Kissingerian great geopolitical game of the triangular United States–China–USSR relationship. Gorbachev was becoming obsolete, the students instead were challenging Deng, and right at this time, the American navy was going to come to Shanghai. This was originally designed to be a triumphant naval visit to upstage Gorbachev's visit. In retrospect, it seems obtuse. Anyway, we saw to it that the U.S. navy left China very quickly, as Tiananmen was getting ready to explode.

After Tiananmen, there were those TV scenes of Chinese youth being dragged off to kangaroo courts, being humiliated before numb crowds. The impact all over the world was dreadful and compounded the negative reaction to the violent suppression at Tiananmen. President Bush had to undertake a daring act. He sent two emissaries—Brent Scowcroft and Larry Eagleburger—to China on a secret mission. One of the objectives of the mission was to let the Chinese know that Tiananmen had caused a severe reaction in the United States, and dragging those kids out and probably executing some of them were causing an even worse fallout. The relationship could not be preserved if this was kept up. The relationship should continue—and it was very important that it did—but both had to get to work on improving the relationship. It was a strategic risk. But as you know, the Bush administration was absolutely savaged for this trip. It was turned into a caricature, "coddling Communist toast," when these men were actually risking their political careers to save a relationship. The Chinese seemed aware of what Bush was trying to do.

The United States was, in fact, talking sense to the Chinese while at the same time working with our allies on a common policy toward China. It wasn't the Americans confronting the Chinese bilaterally; it was Americans working with the European Union, with Japan, with Australia, New Zealand, and Canada toward a common position. World Bank loans were halted temporarily; the Japan third-yen loan package was delayed. President Bush, who knew how to use MFN, didn't use it as a humiliating club to threaten the Chinese into a public admission that they'd made mistakes. It was used quietly and persuasively to get real concessions. In 1993 the Clinton administration demanded that the Chinese deal with the Dalai Lama, listen to *Voice of America*, let us into their prisons, and release dissidents. If not, we were going to take MFN away. The Chinese said, "Buzz off. We don't believe you're going to do it. You're bluffing." We were. In 1994 we dropped MFN–human rights linkage, but not after a great deal of poison had been spread. We had threatened that this nuclear bomb of revocation of MFN was going to be used on China. If used, it would have shattered the whole trading regime and probably broken the overall relationship between ourselves and China.

The Bush administration had used multilateral cooperation to deal with China. Added to this was the symbolism of wanting to keep the strategic relationship alive. As a result, things began to happen. President Bush could explain to the Chinese that Congress was going to try to take most favored nation away. In contrast, the administration was trying to resist this damaging move, so President Bush could veto it. But the United States needed something from the Chinese! In their own way, the Chinese responded: the 13-monthlong dissident left with his family; they pulled the guards back from the embassy; they gave amnesty to hundreds of people arrested at Tiananmen; and they lifted martial law in Tibet and Beijing. This was when the process began to move ahead and improve.

The most contentious issue was the military relationship, where we had to negotiate painstakingly with the Chinese on suspending the military relationship as part of our sanctions on China. They had $500–700 million invested in this, over $500 million for their F-8 avionics alone. The contracts were all suspended unilaterally by us.

It was a crisis in our China relationship, but personal relationships here did matter. George Bush had spotted China's paramount leader, Deng, as early as 1974, when Deng was only a vice premier, and George Bush was the head of a tiny, 26-man liaison office in Beijing. They looked each other over, and the chemistry was established, and when the crunch came, these two men could talk common sense to each other. Deng clearly wanted the American relationship to work. He would accept our unilateral military terminations. President Bush, in turn, wanted the Chinese relationship to work, so he sent Brent Scowcroft to tell Deng it was in our strategic interest to make it work. Thus, when we came to the nasty crunch on the issue of the military sales, it could be resolved because these two men knew each other, understood each other, and could speak for their respective countries. They were, of course, very different kinds of men, but there was a certain chemistry that paid off when it counted.

In late 1990 a new Bush agenda emerged. This was a three-part agenda for China: human rights, trade inequities, and proliferation of weapons of mass destruction. Bush said he was going to send Reg Bartholemew to deal with proliferation of weapons of mass destruction and Joe Massey on trade, but the first visitor would be Dick Shifter to deal with human rights. Each one came to China, and there was the first substantial discussion with China on human rights. As both Carla and Barbara have pointed out, the trade relationship began to progress. We moved ahead on intellectual property rights and market access. In addition, we signed an education agreement, a science and technology agreement, and a property agreement.

Another challenge came when George Bush decided to take on Saddam Hussein. At the time, the Chinese still had American sanctions on them. We had just terminated, on terms unfavorable to the Chinese, the military avionics deal.

When we went to the Chinese and said, "We want you to back us on Saddam Hussein; we're going to sanction him," it took the Chinese only three days to support us. We were working the problem with Ambassador Pickering at the UN [United Nations]. The Chinese then continued by supporting us on 11 UN resolutions. This involved their old Third World, revolutionary, anti-imperialist collaborator Saddam, but he was dropped, and they came with us. The only thing they could not support was the use of force resolution, but they did make it clear to me in advance by saying that on principle they couldn't support it. They did, however, abstain, and we could therefore go through with it.

The Chinese also moved away from Pol Pot and the genocidal Cambodian Khmer Rouge regime they had supported earlier. Instead, they supported the UN Security Council Perm-5 solution. The Cambodian situation is still bad, but the genocide has stopped.

Most important, too, is that the Chinese joined us on Korea. Don has already mentioned getting the nukes out of South Korea; this was followed by significant agreements between South and North Korea. During Don's tenure, there were the first inspections of North Korean nuclear installations. North Korea ratified the nuclear safeguard agreement. The first inventory of nuclear equipment was received by the International Atomic Energy Agency. This is, of course, not recognized by the administration today, but, in fact, the whole denuclearization process started then. We emphasized that the South Koreans should take the lead. The Americans were in a supporting role. This was to be solved by the Koreans themselves, and the Chinese supported this. China supported both Koreas being in the UN, and were able to swing the deal against the interests of Kim Il-Sung's stated policy of resisting a two-Koreas solution in the UN. The Chinese brought him around. The Chinese actually sent over 1 million tons of grain to North Korea last year to keep it from imploding. This dwarfed all other contributions of grain and rendered our contributions trivial.

Finally, imitation is the greatest form of flattery, and right now, Clinton is trying to look an awful lot like President Bush.

Questions and Answers:
Paul F. Harper, Moderator

Paul F. Harper: I think I will allow Mr. Meyerson, if he wishes, a minute or two.

Christopher C. Meyerson: I will be very brief, but I think at least having some questions would be—but I'll leave that to the moderator. I just want to thank Ambassador Hills for a detailed reading, and I said it was a tentative draft when I opened up, and some of the language needs to be cleaned up, sources need to be double-checked, which I mentioned to Dr. Levantrosser when I submitted the paper, and he said, "We'll leave it as is for the moment, and we'll discuss it," and I'd welcome any further advice from here on in, in revising the paper and working on my dissertation.

Harper: We'll take a question.

Q: Mr. Meyerson, Mike Smith, actually from Hofstra Law School, so I'll try and be a little bit kind. The statement that you alluded to at the beginning of your lecture, the fact that President Bush lacked a certain amount of sensitivity with regard to Far East trade issues—in light of the framework that President Bush was the liaison officer for China and also ambassador of the UN and director of the Central Intelligence Agency, do you feel the lack of sensitivity was really a substantive lack of sensitivity, in that essentially all the positions were essentially formed, or do you feel that the lack of sensitivity related to a misunderstanding of the great issues that took place during the early 1990s during the Bush administration?

Meyerson: I'm not sure whether I actually used the word "lack of sensitivity." I think I might have portrayed a little bit. I don't know if it's lack of sensitivity. I also mentioned in the beginning—and it's been emphasized throughout this conference—that the Gulf War was very pressing, as well as the decline of the Soviet Union. So I think there's a certain amount of President Bush being swept up in other events so that he couldn't devote as much time, although we have examples on this panel of the president having time to deal with the Far East. I think it's a question I really should turn to the active members of the administration to respond, perhaps, rather than I myself speak.

Harper: Anyone here care to respond?

Donald Burnham Ensenat: Yeah. We made it pretty clear there was a lot of attention to the Far East.

Harper: There was a lot of attention. The question was, Was there some lack of sensitivity there? Perhaps that's simply a misreading of what Mr. Meyerson had written.

Part III

Personal Diplomacy:
The Middle East Peace Process

3

It Wasn't My Fault: Or, Why Saddam Surprised the Bush Administration and Invaded Kuwait

P. Edward Haley

IT WASN'T MY FAULT

The defeat of Iraq in the Gulf War was a striking victory for the United States and its allies and for the Bush administration. After the Iraqi attack on Kuwait, working quickly and with tenacity and effectiveness, President Bush, Secretaries Baker and Cheney, and the national security adviser, Brent Scowcroft, not only prepared American and world opinion for war but won the consent of the Security Council of the United Nations, the governments of Saudi Arabia, France, Great Britain, and the Soviet Union, and, with considerably more difficulty, the Congress of the United States. While the awkward, but crucial, process of coalition building unfolded, the necessary American and allied forces were assembled in the Gulf, a plan prepared, and military operations set in motion that ultimately crushed Saddam Hussein's army and expelled Iraq from Kuwait.

The allied coalition's quick, decisive victory not only punctured the prestige of a brutal dictator but assured that control of the largest concentration of the world's petroleum reserves would remain in friendly hands. Not least, on the eve of the post–Cold War world phase in world affairs the United States and its allies had defeated aggression and, for a time at least, raised hopes around the world that a new, more decent world order might be established through great power cooperation in the United Nations.

If one were to judge solely by the volume of discussion, one would sense that virtually the only story worth examining is the tale of Desert Shield and Desert Storm—a truly amazing tactical and logistical feat—its preparation and realization. That feeling would grow stronger if one includes the controversy over what General Scowcroft has called the "end game," essentially what terms to impose on a defeated Iraq—over such issues as whether to have destroyed the entire Republican Guard or occupied Baghdad and hunted down Saddam and his principal supporters. Certainly, Secretary Baker keeps to this emphasis, devoting 9 of 10 chapters about the war in his memoirs to the coalition building, fighting, and its aftermath and only 1 chapter to the subject of this essay, the administration's failure to anticipate and deter Iraq's invasion in the first place.[1]

Looked at in this light, it might seem wrong-headed, ungrateful, or even spiteful to focus on what went wrong rather than right in the Gulf War. After all, who needs more naysayers these days, especially at a conference celebrating the Bush administration's accomplishments at home and abroad? However, in the post–Cold War world, with the diffusion of more and more advanced weaponry to more and more countries, diplomacy's task of understanding and helping to shape the conduct of other nations becomes ever more important. Strategically, the protection of vital interests is far more difficult if one's adversaries are allowed to use force to seize important resources and geography, particularly if those adversaries are armed with chemical, biological, or nuclear weapons. It is an accident of timing as well as testimony to Saddam's supremely bad judgment that Iraq attacked Kuwait before its programs to develop weapons of mass destruction had borne fruit. With those weapons in hand, Saddam could have forced an entirely different calculus on the Bush administration. Last, the campaign to throw Iraq out of Kuwait cost tens of billions of dollars for military operations and lost oil revenues from disruptions in production and the vastly destructive oil fires set by Saddam's agents. It would have been far safer and cheaper to have foreseen the attack and actively deterred it. For all these reasons, it is important even at this conference to focus at least a bit of our attention on a failure: the failure to stop the Gulf War before it started.

Secrecy, speed, deception, and inadequate preparation by the victim—all standard explanations—played a part in the Iraqi surprise.[2] Saddam had the surpriser's advantage of knowing when and where he would strike, and this confused U.S. and Arab attempts to interpret warning signals.[3] In addition, the United States, Kuwait, and their allies misunderstood a number of critical Iraqi concerns: the intensity of Saddam's economic motives, his assessment of the risks of war, and his beliefs that there were no alternatives to military action and that the consequences of war were acceptable and, in any case, preferable to failing to act.[4] The Bush and Reagan administrations projected their own behavior onto Saddam and predicted his action from a mistaken analogy. Projection took the form of a belief that Saddam could achieve his goals without an attack; the mistaken analogy was to a country's desire for peace after a costly war rather than to the opportunistic strike into an Iran disordered by revolution.[5]

These explanations are useful and telling. The problem, of course, is that they don't answer the question why. Why did decision makers misunderstand the intensity of Saddam's economic motives? Why did they project their views of what was rational and practical onto Saddam? Why did they misjudge Saddam's assessment of the alternatives to war?

Secretary Baker ducks these questions in his memoirs and answers instead: "It wasn't my fault." Indeed, he argues that it was everyone's fault but his own. In disregarding Iraq and minimizing the likelihood of war, he says he just acted on the prevailing judgment in the State Department, Defense Department, U.S. intelligence community, and among America's closest allies in the region, including Egypt, Israel, and Jordan.[6] Their view was confirmed by a high-ranking delegation of U.S. senators, including Bob Dole, Howard Metzenbaum, and Alan Simpson, who visited Iraq in April 1990, four months before the invasion, and told Baker on their return that "Saddam was a leader with whom the United States could work."[7] "Meanwhile," Baker emphasizes,

our new administration was grappling with one of the most revolutionary periods in world history. The demise of the Soviet empire, the dissolution of the Warsaw Pact, and the unification of Germany represented the greatest shifts in the strategic environment since the advent of the atomic bomb. The Middle East peace process and developments in Central America, as well as such unanticipated events as the June massacre of Chinese dissidents in Tiananmen Square in Beijing, also commanded large amounts of time and attention. In this environment, at that time, none of us considered policy toward Iraq to be an urgent priority. *And it was simply not prominent on my radar screen, or the president's.*[8]

Looking back, Secretary Baker is a fatalist about the war. No one expected it anywhere, at any time. No attempt to act effectively against Saddam before the invasion would have succeeded. He even suggests that President Bush might have been impeached if before the war he had said he would use force to defend Kuwait.[9] "Simply put," Baker says, "the reason why nobody believed Saddam would attack is because no realistic calculation of his interests could have foreseen a full-scale invasion of Kuwait."[10]

No one knows better than Secretary Baker the atmosphere of near-total inattention to Iraq that prevailed in Washington, Cairo, and Jerusalem. But there are serious shortcomings with Baker's analysis. His assertion that "no realistic calculation of his interests" could have foreseen the attack assumes that such a calculation had been made during the spring and summer of 1990. Instead, the administration took a quick look at Iraq during the transition in late 1988 and never looked back. The prevailing interpretations of Iraqi behavior were wrong, profoundly, tragically, dangerously, and expensively wrong. The point isn't to avoid blame for the failure, which preoccupies Baker, but to understand the mistakes in order to avoid similar kinds of errors in the future. Fatalism is useless as a basis for learning from past success and failure.

The thesis of this chapter is that Saddam surprised the United States because the Reagan and Bush administrations deceived themselves. They and their allies in the Arab world allowed the belief that Saddam could be managed and converted into a constructive international actor to blind them not only to his preparations for war against Kuwait but to the inherently aggressive and expansionist character of the Iraqi regime.

There are two periods of significance in the run-up to the invasion of Kuwait: the days and weeks just prior to the invasion and the years during and after the Iran–Iraq War, when the U.S. "tilted" toward Iraq. As "D-Day" approached, Saddam knew his preparations for war would become known. He smothered the warnings creatively by entering Arab–Arab mediation and pledging not to use force against Kuwait. A number of Arab governments recalled earlier Iraqi incursions into Kuwait territory and concluded that if military action took place, it would be strictly limited and temporary, involving the seizure of a small amount of territory along the Kuwait–Iraq border.[11] American intelligence analysts in particular found in this cover story a rationale for the Iraqi troop buildup that some of them continued to believe even after the conquest of all of Kuwait. They squared the inconsistency by arguing, implausibly given what is known of Saddam's intolerance of dissent, that "headstrong" Iraqi commanders disobeyed Saddam's orders and took the whole country.[12]

But it was earlier, during and after the Iran–Iraq War, that the basis for the surprise was laid.[13] There is little doubt that the United States provided substantial covert and overt assistance to Iraq during its war with Iran, aid that has been criticized as foolish in light of the attack on Kuwait and as criminal given Saddam's record of human rights abuses.[14] Some of the criticism ignores common sense: aiding Iraq helped contain Iran and the Iranian revolution and create the elements of a balance of power in the Gulf. Even so, some of the keenest critics, notably Congressman Tom Lantos of California, turned out to have correctly judged Saddam Hussein and earned their "I told you so" to the Bush administration after the Iraqi attack.[15] This chapter addresses not the wisdom of using Iraq to balance Iran or the dilemma of how to choose whether to isolate or engage a murderous dictator. Rather, it argues that what began as a common-sense resort to the balance of power turned into a crude psychological model for diplomacy and blinded the U.S. government to Saddam's aggressive intentions.

In the Iraqi case American decision makers believed that they could ignore the rapacity and unpredictability of Saddam's Iraq because the policy of "tilting" toward Iraq—providing military cooperation, economic assistance, and diplomatic support—gave them a way of taming Saddam and converting him to a responsible international actor. In a bureaucratic and pluralist setting motives are never simple or single. For example, intelligence agencies favored the tilt toward Iraq because it opened the way for them to recruit agents and accumulate information. The policy delighted American businesses; without it they had no legal way to beat the competition. Their representatives in Congress supported the policy because it pleased influential constituents. To some players and to many critics, the policy was nothing more than a cynical cover to greed and espionage: "Let's get ours while the getting is good." But this misrepresents the motives of those in the State Department and White House who attempted to use cooperation with Iraq to address a major security problem in the Gulf. Thus, the plan to moderate Iraqi behavior was of crucial importance because it created a common basis for action while leaving decision makers and other interested players free to pursue their own agendas at the same time.

Israeli intelligence officers deceived themselves about the meaning of the Egyptian reinforcements brought to the Suez Canal before the Yom Kippur War. Much more importantly, they deceived themselves when they assumed that Egypt and Syria would never go to war before they had significantly improved their military strength. Both examples illustrate mistakes in judgment, but to refer to them in this way dangerously minimizes the problem. The act of judging implies a decision in light of all the relevant evidence and ideas. But self-deception occurs precisely because all relevant possibilities either have not been considered or have not been considered fully. In other words, the victim cooperates with the attacker in the surprise. That is the meaning of self-deception: not just mistakes but cooperation. Surprise attack succeeds because of what amounts to collusion between attacker and victim. To avoid surprise the victim must break this web of cooperation. Here lies much of the difficulty: the attacker needs the victim's cooperation in order to achieve surprise and will marshall all possible inducements, deceptions, and threats to continue it; the victim clings to the cooperative self-deception in order to avoid facing the embarrassment, financial sacrifice, possible political loss, or greater dangers of a new course.

SURPRISE AND SELF-DECEPTION: THE IRAQI EXAMPLE

Self-deception about Saddam's intentions began as the idea that the Iraqi dictator could be tamed gradually displaced the balance-of-power approach, which had dominated American policy during the Iran–Iraq War. The new idea gained official approval in National Security Council Directive (NSD) 26, signed by President Bush on October 2, 1989. Subsequently declassified in part, NSD 26 held:

Access to Persian Gulf oil and the security of key friendly states in the area are vital to U.S. national security. The United States remains committed to defend its vital interests in the region, if necessary and appropriate through the use of military force, against the Soviet Union or any other regional power with interests inimical to our own .... Normal relations between the United States and Iraq would serve our longer-term interests and promote stability in both the Gulf and the Middle East. *The United States Government should propose economic and political incentives for Iraq to moderate its behavior and to increase our influence with Iraq* [emphasis added].... We should pursue and seek to facilitate opportunities for U.S. firms to participate in the reconstruction of the Iraqi economy, particularly in the energy area, where they do not conflict with our nonproliferation and other significant objectives. Also, as a means of developing access to and influence with the Iraqi defense establishment, the United States should consider sales of non-lethal forms of military assistance, e.g., training courses and medical exchanges, on a case by case basis.[16]

If Saddam used chemical or biological weapons or breached International Atomic Energy Agency safeguards, the directive pledged that the United States would enact "economic and political sanctions" and would seek support for them from allies and friendly nations. NSD 26 referred to human rights as an "important element" in U.S. policy; Iraq was also to be encouraged to leave Lebanon alone, settle with Iran, and join in the Middle East peace process.[17]

NSD 26 closely followed the recommendations of the Bush administration's transition team on the Middle East. The administration had to decide, the team argued, whether "to treat Iraq as a distasteful dictatorship to be shunned where possible, or to recognize Iraq's present and potential power in the region and accord it relatively high priority. We strongly urge the latter view."[18] The team took such a positive view because its members believed "the lessons of war may have changed Iraq from a radical state challenging the system to a more responsible, status-quo state working within the system and promoting stability in the region."[19] The idea, according to one of the officials who helped prepare the recommendations, was "to embrace Saddam in a cocoon of moderation."[20] The confusion in the concept underlying the opening to Saddam shows through these statements. Saddam "may have changed," but at the same time it was possible to change him by offering rewards for cooperation and good behavior.

As the assault on Kuwait came closer, Saddam began to threaten his Arab neighbors and lash out at the United States and Israel. Starting in February 1990, the most important threats included Saddam's bitter attack on the United States as the only superpower in the region and a demand for the withdrawal of American warships from the Gulf; the threat on April 1 to "burn" half of Israel with chemical weapons if Israel attacked Iraq, in retrospect probably a feint to draw attention away from the Gulf[21]; the poisonous attacks on the United States imposed by Iraq on the communiqué of the Arab League summit that met in Baghdad in May; and threats against Kuwait and the United Arab Emirates and demands for huge financial concessions in mid-July.[22] On each occasion, right up to the eve of the invasion, administration spokesmen, including the president himself, responded with assurances of their desire for good relations and support for the policy of moderating Iraqi behavior.[23] Only a burgeoning scandal involving illegal loans to Iraq from the Atlanta branch of Banca Nazionale del Lavoro interrupted Commodity Credit Corporation loan guarantees for agricultural exports. U.S. credit guarantees for commercial sales to Iraq offered by the Export-Import Bank remained in operation when Saddam struck Kuwait.[24]

Many in Congress found Saddam's threats against Israel, the United States, and friendly Arab states to be alarming and unacceptable. They wanted strong action and invited the assistant secretary of state for Near Eastern and South Asian affairs, John Kelly, to explain what the administration thought of Saddam's actions and what it proposed to do about them.[25] From Saddam's first signal of war in February until three days before the attack, Kelly simply repeated over and over the same arguments against sanctions and in favor of trying to moderate Iraq's behavior. Kelly's performance accurately reflected the attitude of the Bush administration: the surprise is complete, there is no sense of urgency or recognitions that Kuwait is about to be destroyed; and U.S. policy remained unchanged despite a profound alteration in circumstances.[26]

On April 26, 1990, after the threat to use chemical weapons against Israel and the demands for the withdrawal of American forces from the Gulf, Kelly appeared before Congressman Lee Hamilton's Subcommittee on Europe and the Middle East. "Our policy towards Iraq," he told the legislators, "has been to attempt to develop gradually a mutually beneficial relationship with Iraq in order to strengthen positive trends in Iraq's foreign and domestic policies."[27] While "serious," the recent actions by Iraq offered no grounds for imposing sanctions on Iraq and no reason for changing the concept of moderating Iraq's behavior. About sanctions, Kelly said:

> I am well aware that there is a strong sentiment on this Committee and elsewhere in the Congress for trade sanctions against Iraq. If those of us in the Administration thought legislative trade sanctions would have the effect of promoting the goals we share with this Committee and the Congress, we would not hesitate to support their imposition. We simply do not believe that to be the case. While we do not rule out appropriate responses to recent actions by the Government of Iraq, we are not prepared to see economic and trade sanctions legislatively imposed at this point. Instead, we believe Iraq has clearly received the important message of unanimous U.S. Government concern over its recent actions, and we are hopeful that the government of Iraq will move quickly to bring U.S.–Iraq relations back to a more positive level.[28]

Unless they are multilateral, Kelly asserted, sanctions will fail, and no major industrial government shows the least interest in imposing sanctions on Iraq. In addition, the Bush administration, like the Reagan administration before it, did not want to use farm exports as a weapon of foreign policy. The effect of unilateral sanctions, he repeated again and again, would be to give the business to the Europeans, Japanese, Canadians, and Australians. Moreover, sanctions would hurt the balance of payments with Iraq at a time when the United States was importing $3.7 billion in Iraqi oil. Congressman Tom Lantos objected that the picture was more complex than Kelly allowed, that Iraq faced a credit crunch and thus was vulnerable to economic pressure, and that the United States could easily obtain oil from other suppliers. Kelly turned aside the points without seriously considering them.[29]

In a sharp exchange with Lantos, Kelly was emphatic about the concept underlying U.S. policy:

> Congressman Lantos. With all due respect, Mr. Secretary, I detect an Alice in Wonderland quality about your testimony. . . . You talk about Iraq using poison gas against its own people, diplomats engaging in murder plots in the United States and the government smuggling nuclear trigger devices from here and from the U.K. and other places.
>
> We now have the big gun episode which is lied about as all other episodes are lied about and a human rights record which according to the State Department's human rights annual report is a nightmare. Then you express the hope, which boggles my mind, that somehow this will change and Iraq under Saddam Hussein will turn in the direction of being a responsible and civilized and peace loving and constructive member of the international community. . . .
>
> I believe Saddam Hussein. I don't think that he would have the slightest pangs of conscience for killing half of the people living in Israel. He would probably rejoice and have a banquet at the end of the day. There are such people, Mr. Kelly. . . . At what point will the Administration recognize . . . that conceivably sanctions are appropriate. . . . At what point can we hope that the Administration will wake up to the reality which is shouting into the ears of anybody who is prepared to listen with an open mind?[30]

In his response, Kelly shifted away from the notion of moderating Saddam's behavior, plainly becoming less and less plausible day by day, to the safer general question of how to deal with any vicious government or head of state. Coming dangerously close to patronizing Lantos, Kelly answered: "You have put your finger on a very difficult decision that successive administrations have to make in dealing with countries or leaders of countries who do atrocious things."[31] The same problem existed, Kelly said, when the Soviet Union shot down Korean Airlines flight 007. South Africa posed the same dilemma: "In other words, is there the potential of improvement in countries, regimes, and leaders who advocate atrocious and unconscionable acts. This is not a new argument."[32] Exasperated, Lantos finally asked when the administration would move to sanctions against Iraq and forced Kelly to say what he had meant all along: "We believe there is still a potentiality for positive alterations in Iraqi behavior. We do not believe that the imposition of economic sanctions now would leave that possibility open. So we are still opposed to the imposition of economic sanctions."[33]

By the end of July, while he continued to oppose economic sanctions and to refuse to admit any alternative to trying to moderate Saddam's behavior by persuasion, Kelly had to take account of the threat posed by the massing of Iraqi troops on the border with Kuwait. The formulation chosen by the administration was to say, "We have no defense treaty relationship with any Gulf country. . . . We support the security and independence of friendly states in the region."[34] Kelly said the same thing to Congress: "Historically, the U.S. has taken no position on the border disputes in the area, nor on matters pertaining to international OPEC [Organization of Petroleum Exporting Countries] deliberations, but the U.S. has taken a strong position in support of the sovereignty of all states in the area."[35] These were the words Ambassador Glaspie spoke to Saddam Hussein in Baghdad.

The weakness of the formula as an expression of deterrence is obvious. While deterrence requires ambiguity, the statement is so vague that it is meaningless as a signal and even misleading; Saddam could easily read the "take no position" phrase as a euphemism to mean the United States would look the other way when he took Kuwait.[36] In other words, the Bush administration had placed itself and its friends in Saddam's hands. The Iraqi dictator's trap was undetected and ready to spring.

Why? Why, three days from invasion with tens of thousands of Iraqi troops on the border with Kuwait, would the American government still cling to self-deception? The importance of the policy of moderating Iraqi behavior in explaining Saddam's successful achievement of surprise emerged again and with agonizing clarity in Ambassador April Glaspie's testimony after the war. Disgraced, her career in ruins, a scapegoat for the policymaker's failures, Glaspie at last was allowed to explain her actions before the war. Her attachment to persuasion and persuasion alone stands out painfully. Again and again she returns to it. To her it was the only choice and the right choice. Congressman Lantos lashed out at her as he had at John Kelly, saying, "I am appalled by the frighteningly flawed judgment you displayed even in retrospect. . . . I think you need to have a very high dose of humility in retrospect, given the pattern of appalling judgments made by you and your associates." Glaspie replied:

Mr. Lantos, . . . if we are going to talk about sanctions as a way to proceed with diplomacy, there is certainly a place for them, a place for them when you hope at least the sanctions will make the culprit change his ways.

If you do not believe that—and you clearly believe that Saddam Hussein was irredeemable; that was the point of your comments—then why put yourself in the position where you will have to leave the country, where it is clear that it will be impossible to have access to that government anymore?[37]

Glaspie pointed to what she took as success in stopping the gassing of the Kurds and obtaining compensation, after three years, for the families of the victims of the Iraqi attack on the USS *Stark*. Although his time had expired, Lantos might have pointed out that this amounted to damage control rather than the moderation of Saddam's behavior. To a gentler version of the same question from Congresswoman Jan Meyers of Kansas, Glaspie said that after the Iran–Iraq War Saddam was there, in charge of a rich, cash-poor state. If the United States had tried to isolate him, no one would have helped: "[W]e could not see any alternative, to try to work with him to work very, very cautiously—a carrot-and-stick approach, as it was characterized by the Iraqi Foreign Minister. They understood very well what we were doing."[38] She repeated the same reasoning to Congressman Eliot Engel of New York.[39]

Returning to the questioning, Congressman Hamilton summarized the signs of badly deteriorating relations between Iraq and the United States from the middle of February onward. Why wasn't there a change of policy, he asked Glaspie? Why wasn't the Congress informed of the "severity" of Saddam's actions. Why was the Congress always told by the State Department that "we had to gradually develop this mutually beneficial relationship"? Glaspie answered that the more dangerous the situation, the more important it was "to stay in there, try to maintain and improve, if possible, access to decisionmakers, and do what can be done [to ameliorate the tension]."[40] Hamilton insisted, and his probing revealed the confusion at the heart of the policy:

Mr. Hamilton. While you are telling me that our policy [from March or April 1990] was to be there, Mr. Kelly is telling me our policy toward Iraq has been to attempt to develop gradually mutually beneficial relationships.
Ambassador Glaspie. Absolutely. I couldn't have put it better. Indeed, that is just what I said. When we could, we drew out some positive trends, and we did get a few things along the way, Mr. Chairman.[41]

As the hearing closed, Hamilton asked if Glaspie would have done anything differently. Her reply is heartbreaking to read, in light of her personal disgrace and the suffering and loss caused by the war:

Ambassador Glaspie. . . . we overestimated Saddam Hussein's instinct for self-preservation, for whatever reasons. I think this was internally consistent and our mistake. You know, this is what I would change, if I could, but with the data available to me at that time I do not believe I would have come to a different conclusion no matter how hard I thought about it. . . .

Mr. Hamilton. So looking back you really see no mistakes?

Ambassador Glaspie. I think it was morally right in August 1988 to try to see if we could bring him along. We never bought the idea . . . that was promulgated in the area that this is a changed man. . . . This is not the attitude with which we began this experiment in August 1988. We hoped he might be a changed man. We hoped very much he might be a changed man, and if he wasn't, we hoped that we could change him.

Mr. Hamilton. I just want to be clear. As you look back, you see no mistakes?

Ambassador Glaspie. I can only speak to the approach that we took. If you want to go hour by hour and day by day, I am sure we made many mistakes. I am talking about . . . the approach that we took . . . the approach I think was right, and we failed. We didn't make it work.[42]

FROM BALANCE OF POWER TO "COCOON OF MODERATION": THE ORIGINS OF SURPRISE

In his study of the arming of Iraq, Kenneth Timmerman argued that the tilt toward Iraq began during the Carter administration. He pointed to news stories that described a meeting between Zbigniew Brzesinski and a senior Iraqi official in Jordan in July 1980 as the time when the Carter administration discussed "ways the United States and Iraq could coordinate their activities to oppose Iran's reckless policies."[43] Confirmation of the tilt, in Timmerman's view, came that summer with the administration's approval of the sale to Iraq of turbine engines built by General Electric to power Italian-made frigates and President Carter's public sponsorship of the sale to Iraq of five Boeing airliners.[44]

Although what actually took place in Jordan is unclear, there is little doubt that Brzensinski was interested in using Iraq against Iran. However, he apparently wanted to use Iraq against Iran not to strengthen the balance of power, much less to turn Saddam Hussein into a responsible statesman, but to prod the Iranians into releasing the hostages. After Carter lost the election to Reagan, Brzezinski noted in his memoirs, the administration continued its efforts to release the hostages because Carter's personal pride was involved and also to try to free the new administration from the burden: "During this period Christopher and Cutler continued their effort at negotiations, and I recommended that we send signals that we might be inclined to provide some military aid to the Iraqis if the Iranians were not more forthcoming."[45]

The Carter administration's concern for the balance of power in the Gulf took quite a different turn than suggested by Timmerman, one that made little room for Iraq, a Soviet ally. On January 23, 1980, President Carter spoke the words before the joint session of Congress that became known as the Carter Doctrine: "Any attempt by any outside force to gain control of the Persian Gulf region will be regarded as an assault on the vital interests of the United States of America and such an assault will be repelled by any means necessary, including military force."[46] The Carter Doctrine recognized that the events of 1979–1980 had caused what Brzezinski called a "strategic revolution" to the detriment of the global position of the United States.[47]

To meet the new threat, Carter and Brzezinski sought to call into existence a "regional security framework," which Brzezinski had been advocating since 1979. Specifically, the United States moved to "flesh out" regional security arrangements with Egypt, Saudi Arabia, Pakistan, and Turkey and to seek naval and air basing facilities in Oman, Somalia, and Kenya.[48] Like the Truman Doctrine, the Carter Doctrine warned the Soviet Union unmistakably that "the intrusion of Soviet armed forces into an area of vital importance to the United States would precipitate an engagement *with* the United States, and that the United States would then be free to choose the manner in which it would respond."[49]

The Carter administration expired before Iran found its footing and began to resist the Iraqi invaders in an effective way. At terrible human cost, the Iranians eventually pushed the invaders back and stretched out the war, thus calling into question the endurance and even survival of numerically smaller Iraq, with its majority Shiite population and rebellious Kurds. In other words, the military situation in the Gulf obliged the Reagan administration to consider far more direct and extensive assistance to Iraq than had seemed appropriate earlier.

Foreign policy making in the Reagan administration suffered from the decision to subordinate foreign to domestic policy, particularly during the first term, the president's disengaged style of governing and what followed from it—the simultaneous pursuit of conflicting policies sometimes approaching incoherence—and the refusal of cabinet officers, notably Weinberger, Shultz, and Casey but also Haig, Deaver, Baker, and Meese, to cooperate with one another in good faith.[50] Thus, U.S. support for Iraq moved fitfully, often covertly, through the Reagan administration and competed with the desire of some decision makers, particularly Casey and McFarlane, to achieve a breakthrough in U.S. relations with Iran. One of the unexpected effects of the disclosure of first the arms-for-hostages deals with Iran and then the diversion of some of the Iranian payments to the Nicaraguan contras was to scotch the idea of a rapprochement with Iran. This left Iraq as the available balance-of-power player in the Gulf when the Bush administration took office, a position heightened by the end of the Cold War.

Despite the foolishness and embarrassing inconsistencies of some of its dealings with Iran, the Reagan administration pursued a clear balance-of-power approach toward Iraq. The idea was to strengthen Iraq as a barrier against both the aggrandizement of Iran and the spread of the Iranian revolution. To lead the effort, Shultz brought Richard Murphy, then ambassador to Saudi Arabia, back to Washington as assistant secretary responsible for the region. "Our primary goal was to end the war because it was generating instability," Murphy told Kenneth Timmerman. "No matter what anybody says now, with perfect hindsight, this is what it was all about. We wanted to see an end to this unpredictable war, before it got out of hand. We wanted to contain Iran." To this end the administration fashioned an ambitious interagency approach, and Murphy began to "work the problem." The results were predictable:

One key element was a far-ranging intelligence-sharing agreement worked out by CIA [Central Intelligence Agency] Director William Casey, which included supplying the Iraqis with sensitive intelligence data on the activity of the Iranian air force gathered by U.S. AWACS [airborne warning and control system] planes based in Saudi Arabia. Other aspects of the effort were more public, such as backing Iraqi appeals at the United Nations to arrange a cease-fire in the war with Iran. The United States also encouraged Iraq's principal Western arms supplier, France, to extend new loans to Baghdad. It gave the green light to Egypt to continue its massive arms shipments to Iraq. But by far the most important part of the plan, as far as Iran–U.S. relations were concerned, was the CCC [U.S. Commodity Credit Corporation] credits. Having depleted its $35 billion reserve of foreign currency by mid-1983 and exhausted the patience of Saudi and Kuwaiti lenders, Iraq was desperately in need of cash. And the United States soon became one of its best sources of funds.[52]

The U.S. government was an important, but by no means the only, helper Iraq needed in its quest for power. During the 1980s American companies sold Iraq far smaller amounts of advanced technology than Germany, France, Switzerland, Italy, and Britain. Agricultural products accounted for the lion's share of U.S. exports.[53] The CCC and Export-Import Bank credit guarantees saved the Iraqi regime millions in interest; when war broke out, the U.S. government was left as the guarantor of about $2 billion in unpaid obligations. More importantly, U.S. suppliers often were the only source of small amounts of crucially important materials and technologies without which an entire military development would have been stalled. As Timmerman noted: "The U.S. tilt toward Iraq soon became a race to see who could sell the most and the fastest to America's newest client. Well-paid Washington lawyers and influence peddlers championed causes ranging from farm exports to high technology trade. All kinds of deals were possible now that Iraq was off the terrorism list and national security export controls no longer applied."[54]

Even at this early stage, according to Richard Murphy, decision makers looked beyond the war and sought to use the new relationship to "tame" Iraq: "Our aim was to improve relations with Iraq," Murphy said, "so the old Iraq of the 1970s didn't reemerge after the war. Beyond that, of course, Iraq was an interesting market for U.S. exporters."[55]

This was not the way Secretary George Shultz described the U.S.–Iraqi relationship in his memoirs. According to Shultz, the goal of U.S. policy was to stop the war. This meant drying up the sources of weapons to both sides.[56] It wasn't easy, Shultz admitted. There was big money to be made, and the other industrial nations had no qualms about the arms trade. At least the United States could disrupt the supply. This was the origin of what was called "Operation Staunch." The arms-for-hostages deals contradicted this policy, but so did the requisites of the balance of power:

While the United States basically adhered to the policy of not supplying arms to either side, our support for Iraq increased in rough proportion to Iran's military successes: plain and simple, the United States was engaged in a limited form of balance-of-power policy. The United States simply could not stand idle and watch the Khomeini revolution sweep forward.... In this situation a tilt toward Iraq was warranted to prevent Iranian dominance of the Persian Gulf and the countries around it.[57]

Writing his memoirs after the Iraqi attack on Kuwait, Shultz was careful to emphasize the reservations he harbored about the Iraqi regime and the measures he took to guard against an undue reliance on Saddam Hussein's trustworthiness. Shultz understandably pointed with pride to the Reagan administration's warning to Iraq not to use chemical weapons against Iran and the Kurds. Viewed from Baghdad, however, Shultz's reservations might well have taken on a superficial, for-the-record character. For example, on November 27, 1984, the same day that Shultz told Iraqi foreign minister Tariq Aziz that he was "unalterably opposed to the use of chemical weapons and ... would be watching Iraq carefully," the United States resumed diplomatic relations with Iraq after an interruption of 17 years.[58] Shultz's doubts about Saddam failed to interrupt the intelligence sharing or the CCC loan guarantees, which rose to $1 billion. When Iraq used chemical weapons against the Kurds in September 1988, Shultz warned the Iraqi government that the United States would stop developing its relations with Iraq if the use of chemical weapons continued.[59] But the Reagan administration, like its successor, opposed efforts in Congress to impose economic sanctions on Iraq and on the same grounds: unilateral sanctions would fail.

The end of the Iran–Iraq War reduced the Iranian threat to the Gulf. It was also the occasion, according to Shultz, for him to take a dim view of Saddam's Iraq. For a year or so in the mid-1980s, Shultz wrote, he thought that Iraqi regime had changed. The accomplished, articulate Iraqi ambassador in Washington, Nizar Hamdoon, had contributed ably to that impression. But a series of Iraqi actions changed his mind:

When Abu Abbas was allowed to leave Italy in October 1985 following the hijacking of the *Achille Lauro* [his plane was forced to land by American warplanes], he went to Yugoslavia and then made his way to Baghdad. This was followed by Iraq's use of chemical weapons and our increasing awareness that Saddam Hussein had not only given up his pursuit of a "military option" against Israel but was seeking to construct a regionally dominant military machine that could not be explained by his fear of Iran alone. I came to regard Iraq, once again, as one of the enemy states of the responsible world community ... it became clear to me that no further reason existed for the United States to give Iraq the benefit of the doubt for balance-of-power purposes against Iran.[60]

With these thoughts in mind, Shultz recalled, he recommended that the incoming Bush administration pursue "a new and tougher policy toward Saddam Hussein's Iraq."[61]

It is unclear how much Shultz's memory of his recommendation to get tough with Saddam was colored by the attack on Kuwait. What is certain is that while the Iran–Iraq War continued, the United States concentrated on the balance-of-power aspect of its relations with Iran. The end of the war in August 1988 created the occasion for a review of U.S. policy toward Iraq. No such review was undertaken during the six months that remained in Reagan's second term. Far from accepting Shultz's advice for "a new and tougher policy," the Bush administration chose to put at the center of its policy not the balance of power but an attempt to convert Saddam using the same generous manifestations of support for Iraq that had been the means to achieve a balance of power during the Iran–Iraq War.

AVOIDING SELF-DECEPTION AND SURPRISE

In the spring and summer of 1990, as Saddam prepared for war, it became harder and harder for American officials to find anything constructive about Iraqi behavior. Instead of reconsidering, the Bush administration defended the policy with generic arguments about the dilemmas of dealing with repulsive governments and the necessity of diplomatic representation. The arguments served their purpose by contradicting and, thereby, stalemating worried members of Congress. But they were rationalizations, not hard truths for thick-headed legislators. They became part of Saddam's deception and blinded the administration to the true meaning of developments in the Gulf.

In offering guidelines for decision makers and analysts on how to avoid surprise, one is drawn to two specific warning signals, two general propositions about statecraft, and one procedural recommendation. The specific signals concern the Iraqi regime's preparations for war and quest for the instruments of deterrence on a regional and even global scale. The general propositions concern the crucial link between force and persuasion—or strategy and diplomacy in Raymond Aaron's formulation—and the role of demandeur. The procedural insight applies to the importance of "second-guessing" policies that are obviously under stress.

Long before the invasion of Kuwait, Saddam Hussein repeatedly advertised the domineering hostility of his regime's intentions by an unrelenting search for nuclear weapons and delivery systems, by repeated use of chemical weapons, not only in the war against Iran but against the Kurds, and by a huge diversion of resources into a military buildup. Unclassified figures for 1990 show that Iraq's defense budget accounted for some 20 percent of gross domestic product and that the country possessed about 5,000 main battle tanks, 6,000 armored personnel carriers, and 3,000 artillery pieces.[62] Again, unclassified analysis warned in early 1990:

Iraq continued to expand its arms industry.... Ballistic missiles development has been relatively successful with the 900 km-range Al-Abbas and the 600-km Al-Husayn having been deployed, and five other types under development. Iraq has deployed at least six Al-Husayn launchers to an airfield close to an area commonly known as H-2 (after the pumping station) in the western Iraqi desert from where targets throughout Syria and most of Israel can be engaged. Iraq's CW [conventional weapons] capability is both well-documented and substantiated, but it is generally assessed that Iraq is unlikely to be able to produce nuclear weapons for several years. A satellite launch rocket was test-fired, but no payload was placed in orbit. Another well-publicized project was the long-range gun based on technology provided by Dr. Gerald Bull (who was responsible for the designs of the U.S. HARP guns and the South African 155 mm G-5 and G-6 guns).[63]

The point is not that these actions alone indicate a plan for war, but that together they oblige Iraq's neighbors and the great powers to reconsider their policy. With Iran spent on the sidelines, Iraq faced no strategic threat commensurate to its relentless, large-scale military buildup, especially not a threat requiring large chemical and nuclear capabilities and delivery systems.

The presentations by Assistant Secretary Kelly and Ambassador Glaspie highlighted a shortcoming in American policy throughout the critical period from 1988 to 1990. Theirs was a policy consisting of persuasion alone. It contained no element of coercion or deterrence, much less the use of force. The one-sidedness of this approach is all the harder to understand because NSD 26 explicitly refers to the use of force to defend access to Gulf oil and friendly states in the region.[64] Kelly and Glaspie defended this lapse by insisting that no one would have cooperated with the United States against Iraq before the attack on Kuwait, and that friendly Arab states in particular counseled against a threatening posture. These are valid points. But to allow them to remove force and the threat of force from American policy conveyed a profoundly misleading impression to Saddam Hussein. In effect, silence about the use of force amounted to cooperation with Saddam in the impending surprise. In other words, the policy of converting Saddam denied American decision makers and analysts the clearheadedness they needed to grasp the importance of spelling out to themselves and others when the United States would fight. There were circumstances in which the United States would fight in the Gulf and would fight alone, if necessary. There was nothing to be gained and much to be lost by remaining silent about them as the menacing evidence of Iraq's intentions accumulated.

The attempt to moderate the Iraqi regime also falsely inflated Saddam's bargaining power by putting the United States more or less perpetually in the position of the demandeur. The United States alone stood in Iraq's way. It alone possessed the power, influence, technology, wealth, and will to block or facilitate the realization of Saddam's dreams. Saddam had to turn to the United States, not the United States to Iraq. If he would not turn, he ought to have been opposed, not assisted, his enemies courted. Iran might have been off limits, but perhaps not Syria. It was Iraq that needed the most from the United States, but the United States behaved as if it held the weaker hand.

Finally, a lesson from the debacle in Iran may be helpful in understanding how to break out of the web of cooperation that leads to surprise. After the Iranian revolution and the taking of Americans as hostages, President Carter's director of the CIA, Stansfield Turner, engaged Robert Jarvis to prepare an "Iran Postmortem" that would explain the failure of the CIA to anticipate the overthrow of the shah. Two of the findings bear an eerie relevance to the Kuwaiti surprise.

The first described flaws in procedure: "No method existed to ponder alternative explanations of the data. Analysts were not forced to marshal evidence that supported alternatives; there was no peer review of any significance; there was no system for challenging the assumptions."[65] This recalls nothing so much as the leisurely State Department calendar for reviewing U.S. policy toward Iraq: Ambassador Glaspie was ordered home for a policy review five days before the invasion and was actually en route *on the day of the invasion*. She learned of the attack when she turned on the television in her hotel room in London. It is hard to imagine a more embarrassing commentary on this aspect of U.S. policy.

The second of Jervis' findings may explain why review of U.S.–Iraqi relations was delayed so long: "Circularity was the common feature of the analysis." In the Iranian case the argument was that the Shah's forces were strong enough to crush all resistance; that he wasn't using them meant that the opposition posed no threat to the regime.[66] When Kelly and Glaspie spoke of Iraq, they argued that openhanded U.S. support for Iraq's economy and generous political support would moderate Iraqi behavior. When it did not, they countered that there was no alternative to diplomacy; only multilateral economic sanctions would work, and no friendly Arab governments would back strong opposition or even criticism of Iraq. This brought the administration and the Congress full circle back to diplomacy. It was adroit and unanswerable rhetorically—critical legislators could never quite figure out how to respond—but it concealed the problem. U.S. policy now operated in profoundly changed circumstances. What had begun as an attempt to modify Iraqi behavior had become damage control, but decision makers still clung to the original concept and even confused the two, as Glaspie showed in her remarks to Congressman Hamilton. There was an alternative to diplomacy: war. The question was when it would be chosen. Because of the hypnotic, self-deceiving effect of the policy of moderating Iraqi behavior, only Saddam Hussein had the answer. He gave it on August 2, 1990.

NOTES

Sections of this chapter appeared in P. Edward Haley, "Saddam Surprises the United States: Learning from the Revolution of August 2," *Armed Forces and Society* 22, no. 2 (1995–1996): 160–85.

1. James A. Baker III, with Thomas M. DeFrank, *The Politics of Diplomacy: Revolution, War & Peace, 1989–1992* (New York: G.P. Putnam's Sons, 1995).

2. Secrecy, speed, and inadequate preparation by the victim are Clausewitz's explanations for success in achieving surprise. See Karl Clausewitz, *On War*, trans. O.J. Matthijs Jollies (New York: Modern Library, 1943), p. 145. Deception is a product of the first three and a means in its own right to achieve surprise, see Edward N. Luttwak, *Strategy: The Logic of War and Peace* (Cambridge: Harvard University Press, 1987), pp. 9–10; Richard K. Betts, *Surprise Attack: Lessons for Defense Planning* (Washington, DC: Brookings Institution, 1982), pp. 108–10.

3. Betts, *Surprise Attack*, p. 87.
4. Ibid., pp. 120–38.
5. On the Iran–Iraq War, see Shahram Chubin and Charles Tripp, *Iran and Iraq at War* (Boulder, CO: Westview Press, 1988); Ralph King, *The Iran–Iraq War: The Political Implications*, Adelphi Papers, No. 219 (London: International Institute for Strategic Studies, 1987); Efraim Karsh, *The Iran-Iraq War: A Military Analysis*, Adelphi Papers, No. 220 (London: International Institute for Strategic Studies, 1987). On the importance of projection, see April Glaspie's testimony after the Gulf War, in particular, her response to questions whether the United States had misjudged Saddam's intentions: "We clearly came to the wrong conclusion, Congressman . . . we thought that since . . . he was getting what he said he wanted or seemed to be about to get what he said he wanted, both in terms of oil prices, an Arab 'Marshall Plan' and formal cancellation of his war debts to the Arab countries, these appeared to be his short-term aims." Later, she added: "I hope I have explained to the committee very clearly why I didn't think that they were going to take all of [Kuwait], and in summary, because they were already getting what they wanted. Why do it?" April Glaspie, *U.S.–Iraqi Relations*, Hearing, House Foreign Affairs Subcommittee on Europe and the Middle East, 102nd Cong., 1st sess., March 21, 1991, pp. 33, 56.
6. Baker, *Politics*, pp. 270–71, 272, 274.
7. Ibid., p. 269.
8. Baker, *Politics*, p. 263; emphasis added.
9. Ibid., p. 273.
10. Ibid., p. 274.
11. See Judith Miller and Laurie Mylroie, *Saddam Hussein and the Crisis in the Gulf* (New York: Times Books, 1990), pp. 17–21.
12. Interview with CIA official, January 7, 1993. See also the testimony of the U.S. ambassador to Iraq, April Glaspie:

There was a mindset in the area . . . I don't think we held it, but I think the Arabs held it that if [Saddam] did anything further to bully and intimidate, perhaps as a background to the negotiations, that it would be another in a long series of incursions that Iraq had made since 1963, or even '61 since Kuwaiti independence. There had been a number of incursions, some very flagrant ones. . . . So it was true that the Arabs talked about this as a possibility, but after the 25 [of July] King Fahd and President Mubarak felt that they had a commitment that would not be broken [not to invade].

Later in her testimony Glaspie returned to the idea: "I think it is important, that since Iraq, for some years, had tried to make its point, by brief incursions, I thought that early on in this crisis a number of Arab states thought that that is what they were looking at, the beginning of another brief incursion." Glaspie, *U.S.–Iraqi Relations*, pp. 33–34, 56.

13. See Kenneth R. Timmerman, *The Death Lobby: How the West Armed Iraq* (Boston: Houghton Mifflin, 1991), especially Chapters 5, 7, 8; Alan Freidman, *Spider's Web: The Secret History of How the White House Illegally Armed Iraq* (New York: Bantam Books, 1983), especially p. 7.
14. See, in particular, the remarkable books by Kanan Makiya (pseud. Samir Al Khalil), *Republic of Fear: The Inside Story of Saddam's Iraq* (New York: Pantheon Books, 1989), and *Cruelty and Silence: War, Tyranny, Uprising, and the Arab World* (New York: Norton, 1993).
15. The group included Congressman Tom Lantos, Lee Hamilton, and Howard Berman. See especially Lantos' attack on the administration's policy and Glaspie's am-

bassadorship, Tom Lantos, *U.S.–Iraqi Relations*, pp. 14–15.
  16. NSD 26, excerpts published in Friedman, *Spider's Web*, pp. 321, 322.
  17. Ibid., p. 322.
  18. Quoted in ibid., p. 133.
  19. Ibid.
  20. Ibid., p. 134.
  21. Ambassador Glaspie confirmed that Saddam's threat against Israel had this effect:

Mr. Gilman. Ambassador Glaspie, knowing what we know today about Saddam Hussein's failure to understand ... America's determination to protect our vital interests in the Gulf, and their [sic] proclivity toward violence, is there anything we could have done in the months before August 2nd to persuade him not to attack Kuwait?
Ambassador Glaspie. In the months before August 2nd, we were afraid he was going to attack Israel, Mr. Congressman.
  He was talking, we thought in terms which suggested not simply defense, which is what he said, but also the possibility of preemption ....
  There was really nobody who had, at least that I was aware of, thought or believed that the Iraqis were thinking about Kuwait. (*U.S.–Iraqi Relations*, p. 12)

  22. See especially Saddam Hussein's address at the Arab Cooperation Council summit in Amman, February 24, 1990, in Foreign Broadcast Information Service, Daily Report, Near East, and Southeast Asia (FBIS), February 27, 1990, pp. 1–5. His speech threatening to burn half of Israel on April 1, 1990, appears in FBIS, April 3, 1990, pp. 3–36. The text of the Baghdad summit communiqué is in FBIS, May 31, 1990, pp. 1–5. In retrospect it is impossible to miss the aura of violence that Saddam had managed to create in the region. The communiqué stated that the conference had been convened at the special invitation of Saddam Hussein to consider "threats posed to pan-Arab security and the adoption of the necessary measures toward these threats" (p. 1). Of course, Saddam's Iraq posed the principal threat to the Arab states. In addition, the conference condemned "aggressive threats, campaigns, and measures" against Iraq and warned that "there are preparations to facilitate aggression against it." In this superheated atmosphere Saddam hoped it would seem plausible for the conference to extend two specific authorizations for Iraq to use force, including the use of weapons of mass destruction: "The conference affirms Iraq's right to take all the appropriate measures to safeguard and protect its national security and provide the requirements for development, including the possession of advanced means and technology and using them for legal purposes." And: "The conference affirms the right of Iraq and all the Arab states to reply to aggression by all means they deem fit to guarantee their security and sovereignty" (p. 3). For Saddam's threat against Kuwait and the United Arab Emirates, see his speech commemorating the 22nd anniversary of the July 17–30 Revolution in FBIS, July 17, 1990, p. 20.
  23. For President Bush's response to Saddam's threat to burn half of Israel with chemical weapons, see the statement given to the press in Sharon Brown Wells, ed., *American Foreign Policy: Current Documents, 1990* (Washington, DC: U.S. Government Printing Office, 1990), doc. 264, p. 438. For the official U.S. response to the threats against Kuwait and the United Arab Emirates, see the daily press briefing by the deputy spokesman for the Department of State on July 18, 1990, in ibid., doc. 271, p. 448: "We ... remain strongly committed to supporting the individual and collective self-defense of our friends in the Gulf with whom we have deep and longstanding ties." For Margaret Tutweiler's statement on July 24, 1990, see ibid., p. 450: "We do not have any defense

treaty with Kuwait, and there are no special defense or security commitments to Kuwait." She repeated the earlier wording about commitments to "friends in the Gulf" and confirmed that no "overall review of the U.S. relationship with Iraq" was under way." Ibid.

24. See Assistant Secretary Kelly's testimony on U.S. loan and credit guarantees in *U.S.–Iraqi Relations*, Hearings, House Foreign Affairs Subcommittee on Europe and the Middle East, 101st Cong., 2nd sess., April 26, 1990, pp. 27–29; *Developments in the Middle East, July 1990*, Hearings, House Foreign Affairs Subcommittee on Europe and the Middle East, 101st Cong., 2nd sess., July, 31, 1990, pp. 14–16. See also the testimony by John D. Macomber, chairman of the Export-Import Bank and other Ex/Im officials in *Iraqi and Banca Nazionale del Lavoro Participation in Export-Import Programs*, Hearing, House Committee on Banking, Finance, and Urban Affairs, 102st Cong., 1st sess., April 17, 1991, pp. 1–79 and additional materials and tables; testimony by Undersecretary of Commerce Dennis Kloske and Undersecretary of State Robert Kimmit, *United States Exports of Sensitive Technology to Iraq*, Hearings, House Committee on Foreign Affairs, 102nd Cong., 1st sess., April 8 and May 22, 1991, pp. 3–70 and 75–111, respectively.

25. This was the same John Kelly who had cooperated with Admiral John Poindexter and Lieutenant Colonel Oliver North in the arms-for-hostages sales to Iran during the Reagan administration without telling Secretary of State George Shultz. Shultz was furious and demanded that Kelly be fired. Vice President Bush intervened to protect him, as did President Reagan. Shultz was allowed officially to "admonish" Kelly, but when the administration took office, Kelly was promoted to assistant secretary. Bush had what he wanted in Kelly, someone who would follow orders and not make waves or, one must add, exercise the kind of independent and unorthodox political judgment that might have foreseen and perhaps forestalled the Iraqi attack. See George Shultz, *Turmoil and Triumph: My Years as Secretary of State* (New York: Simon and Schuster, 1993), pp. 845–54.

26. In one of the cruelest and most revealing ironies of the war, Ambassador Glaspie was on her way to Washington for a major policy review when Saddam struck:

Mr. Gilman. Ambassador Glaspie, when were you recalled to the States?
Ambassador Glaspie. I received a cable on the 28th [of July]. . . . We decided—we had decided that it would be absolutely necessary, given the extraordinary activities and remarks of Saddam Hussein over the previous months, to have a high-level policy review. . . . I certainly agreed that I should be there.

However, that was the 28th. I asked for permission to stay a couple of days longer just to be sure they [the Iraqis] went to Jidda and got the negotiations begun. As soon as it was clear that the negotiations were to begin in Jidda, as [Saddam] promised they would, I left.
Mr. Gilman. When did you leave?
Ambassador Glaspie. On the 30th.
Mr. Gilman. And the invasion began August 2?
Ambassador Glaspie. That's right. (*U.S.-Iraqi Relations*, p. 14)

27. Kelly, *U.S.–Iraqi Relations*, p. 10.
28. Ibid, p. 14.
29. Ibid., pp. 14, 15, 30–31, 36.
30. Ibid., pp. 22–23.
31. Ibid., p. 23.
32. Ibid. Kelly answered Senator Daniel Moynihan in the same way in a hearing on June 15, and he repeated the same arguments three days before the Iraqi attack. See John

M. Kelly, *United States Policy toward Iraq: Human Rights, Weapons Proliferation and International Law*, Hearing, Senate Foreign Relations Committee, 101st Cong., 2nd sess., June 15, 1990, pp. 30–31.
  33. Kelly, *U.S.-Iraqi Relations*, p. 23. See also Kelly, *Developments in the Middle East, July 1990*, pp. 14–16, 23, 36–37.
  34. Ibid., p. 14.
  35. Ibid., p. 6.
  36. Ambassador Glaspie denied this. She insisted again and again that she had told Saddam that the United States would fight and that he understood her to say that. In fact, she only believed he understood that, as persistent questioning revealed:

Mr. Hamilton. No American Ambassador is going to say to a foreign leader that we are not going to defend our vital interests. The question is what is the vital interest. There must be no doubt.
Ambassador Glaspie. We defined . . .
Mr. Hamilton. Did you define it?
Ambassador Glaspie. I said sovereignty and integrity of our friends in the Gulf. That is certainly Kuwait . . .
Mr. Hamilton. Let me quote the words of Ms. Tutweiler: We do not have any defense treaties with Kuwait and there are no special defense or security commitments to Kuwait. . . . The record shows the State Department officials are saying that there is no special defense treaty or special commitment. They are simply saying that we would be extremely concerned . . .
Ambassador Glaspie. I am sorry that they had to say it on the record, but it seems to me they were forced to do so. What else could I say?
  I am saying to you, Mr. Chairman, I spent an hour and a half with a man who railed at me. . . . He went on, and on, and on. You can't hurt us. He knew perfectly well what we were talking about. . . . And he felt secure, secure in the belief that no Arab Government would ever allow us to use their land for that purpose.
Mr. Hamilton. But you never said to him, "Mr. President, if you go across the line with your forces into Kuwait, we will fight?"
Ambassador Glaspie. Absolutely not. I did not need to say that.
  If I felt I needed to say that, I would have asked the President after the meeting for permission to say that. I had no doubt in my mind that he knew that we meant business.
  And certainly it is up to the President, not up to me to decide how to execute the policy.

U.S.–Iraqi Relations, pp. 10, 11. See also her exchange with Congressman Gilman, ibid., pp. 12–13.
  37. Ibid., pp. 14, 16.
  38. Ibid., p. 20; emphasis added.
  39. Ibid., pp. 28–29.
  40. Ibid., p. 50.
  41. Ibid., p. 53. See also p. 54: "If it was impossible at a certain period to pull out any positive threads from this relationship, then the best we could do was to be there and make sure that we did what we could to lower the tension, and hope that we would be able to influence Iran in the future along positive lines."
  42. Ibid., p. 6.
  43. Timmerman, *The Death Lobby*, p. 76. For a different view of the Bush administration's policies and their consequences, see Bruce W. Jentleson, *With Friends like These: Reagan, Bush, and Saddam, 1982–1990* (New York: W.W. Norton, 1994), especially Chapters 3 and 4.
  44. Timmerman, *The Death Lobby*, p. 78.
  45. Zbigniew Brzezinski, *Power and Principle: Memoirs of the National Security*

Advisor, 1977–1981 (New York: Farrar, Straus, Giroux, 1983), p. 506.

46. Quoted in ibid., p. 442.

47. "[T]he collapse of Iran and the Soviet move into Afghanistan preceded by the unimpeded Soviet military intrusion into Ethiopia and South Yemen, created an urgent security problem for the region as a whole, prompting by 1980 formal U.S. recognition of the security interdependence of three, instead of two, zones of central strategic importance to the United States: Western Europe, the Far East, and the Middle East." Ibid., p. 454.

48. Ibid., pp. 444, 446.

49. Ibid., 445.

50. The most revealing source about the incoherence and cabinet-level conflicts is Lou Cannon, *President Reagan: The Role of a Lifetime* (New York: Simon and Schuster, 1991), especially the sections dealing with Lebanon, Iran-contra, and Nicaragua. See also two particularly insightful reviews of George Shultz's memoirs: Jacob Heilbrun, "Curious George," *New Republic* 209, nos. 8–9 (August 23–30, 1993): 35; and Robert W. Tucker, "Shultz: Playing a Good Hand: The Secrets of Shultz's Success," *Foreign Affairs* 72, no. 4 (September/October 1993): 138–43.

51. Timmerman, *The Death Lobby*, p. 130.

52. Ibid., pp. 130–31.

53. See, for example, the tables based on figures from the Organization for Economic Cooperation and Development, the Stockholm International Peace Research Institute, the International Institute for Strategic Studies, in ibid., pp. 417–24.

54. Ibid., p. 131.

55. Ibid.

56. Shultz, *Turmoil and Triumph*, p. 236.

57. Ibid., p. 237.

58. Ibid., p. 240.

59. Ibid., p. 241.

60. Ibid., p. 243.

61. Ibid.

62. International Institute for Strategic Studies, *The Military Balance, 1992–1993* and *1990–1991* (London: International Institute for Strategic Studies, 1992), pp. 100 and 105, respectively.

63. International Institute for Strategic Studies, *The Military Balance, 1990–1991*, p. 98.

64. The policy of moderating Iraqi behavior appears to be based on an impoverished view of statecraft, one in which diplomacy (persuasion) exists.

65. Bob Woodward, *Veil: The Secret Wars of the CIA, 1981–1987* (New York: Pocket Books, 1987), pp. 107–108.

66. Ibid., p. 108.

4

The Arab–Israeli Conflict under President Bush

Samuel Segev

The Madrid Peace Conference, which opened on October 30, 1991, was one of the major foreign policy successes of the Bush administration. Nevertheless—and despite the tremendous excitement of Israelis and Arabs sitting together in the beautifully ornate Hall of Columns in Madrid's eighteenth-century Royal Palace—Israel and the Arab delegations knew quite well that the conference in itself was not a definitive act. It was only a framework for negotiating a settlement of one of the most tractable conflicts of this century.

There is a basic difference between the impressive signing ceremony of the Israeli–Egyptian peace treaty at the White House South Lawn on March 26, 1979, and the equally impressive Madrid Peace Conference. When Egypt's president Anwar Sadat and Israeli prime minister Menachem Begin put their seal on the treaty that ended the conflict between the most populous Arab country and the only Jewish state in the world, they knew that the treaty was a definitive act. Negotiated tirelessly by U.S. president Jimmy Carter, the treaty's terms were clear and not in dispute. President Sadat gave Israel total peace in return for Israel's total withdrawal from Sinai, including the dismantling of Israeli settlements that had been built over the years in the desert that separates Israel from Egypt.

This was not the case in Madrid. Despite their undeniable success, President Bush and Secretary Baker were aware of the fact that the gaps between the parties were still very wide. Hence, from the very beginning, they were prepared for many tactical shifts, angry exchanges, and frequent maneuvers. They were not deterred by this prospect. It was a part of the "game of nations."

The political ambience in 1979 was also very different from that of 1991. When the Israeli–Egyptian treaty was signed, the two superpowers were still engaged in their bitter Cold War. The collapse of the pro-Western regime in Iran and the Soviet invasion of Afghanistan demonstrated how vulnerable the American national interest in the Persian Gulf had become. Thus, the Egyptian–Israeli peace treaty was generally perceived as contributing to the security and stability of the entire region.

The Madrid Peace Conference was opened in a totally different international ambience. The end of the Cold War had left the United States as the only superpower in the world. The Iraqi defeat in the Persian Gulf War had altered the regional balance of power in Israel's favor and had reduced the threat to the oil-rich Persian Gulf states. In the aftermath of the war, the United States had found a new sense of realism in the various moderate Arab countries. Israeli restraint in the war had altered Arab perceptions and offered better opportunities for a settlement of the Arab–Israeli conflict. The moderate Arab countries, foremost among them Egypt, Saudi Arabia, and Kuwait, believed that because of the PLO's [Palestine Liberation Organization] support of Saddam Hussein, Yasser Arafat was so isolated in the Arab world that he would be forced to accept anything that he could extract from Israel.

Indeed, among the various Arab parties, the Palestinians were the most eager to settle with Israel. In the years since the Camp David accords, the increased number of Israeli settlements in the West Bank and the Gaza Strip made the situation for the Palestinians intolerable. The number of Israeli settlers in 1978 was 10,000. In 1991 it increased to 130,000. The massive Jewish immigration from the Soviet Union revived old fears that the new immigrants would be encouraged to settle in the West Bank. "Our immediate goal is to stop and freeze all Jewish settlements in the West Bank," Elias Freij, the respected and moderate Christian Arab mayor of Bethlehem and currently a member of the Palestine Authority responsible for tourism, told me. He added: "If we can stop the settlement activity and avoid its expansion, then the negotiations will be pointless. What land would we talk about, if Israel takes it all?"[1]

This Arab fear is not new. Since its inception at the beginning of the twentieth century, the Palestinian national movement consistently opposed the twin issue of Jewish immigration and settlement in Palestine. At the end of World War II, the Palestinians have even opposed the immigration of 100,000 Holocaust survivors, as recommended by the United States and other countries. The Arab opposition to this twin issue remained unchanged even after the establishment of the state of Israel. Before the gates of the Soviet Union were opened for Jewish immigration to Israel, Arab and Palestinian leaders hoped that because of their high birthrate, demography would eventually tip the balance in their favor. Now they saw this hope again shattered. When President Bush and Secretary Baker launched their peace initiative in March 1991, they came to the conclusion that, unlike previous occasions, Syria must be included this time in the American peace efforts. As a participant in the U.S.-led coalition against Saddam Hussein, Syrian president Assad won a certain degree of "acceptance" in Washington. In September 1990, after the Iraqi invasion of Kuwait but before Desert Storm, Syria made it known that it would be willing to negotiate a settlement with Israel under an appropriate international auspice. In a letter to the UN [United Nations] secretary-general, the Syrian foreign minister wrote that in Syria's view an international peace conference could be sponsored by the two superpowers only.[2]

Thus, contrary to the common view, according to which Syria changed its positions after the Persian Gulf War, the Syrian letter to the UN proves that Assad was prepared to negotiate a peaceful settlement with Israel, even before the collapse of the Soviet Union. In appreciation of this new position and especially because Assad joined the anti-Saddam coalition, President Bush met with President Assad in Geneva in late November 1990 to discuss the situation in the Middle East. Bush told Assad what he was saying in public, namely, that after the liberation of Kuwait, the United States would turn to the Arab–Israeli conflict and would try to solve the problem of the Golan Heights as well. Indeed, after Desert Storm, Secretary Baker spent many hours with Assad before he convinced him to attend the Madrid Peace Conference. Israeli diplomatic reports quoted European leaders who had met with Assad as having said, "Assad was very keen to make the point that, without him, there would be no Madrid."

Like most Israelis, however, Prime Minister Shamir was very suspicious of Syria and of President Assad. Israeli intelligence reports indicated that, despite Syria's poor economy, Assad spent the $2 billion that he received as financial aid from Saudi Arabia on buying Czech, Soviet-made T.72 tanks and North Korean "Scud" missiles. Nevertheless, Israel could not ignore the fact that the destruction of the Iraqi war machine had reduced the threat to Israel and had eliminated—temporarily, at least—the danger that Saddam Hussein would join Syria and Jordan in a new military adventure against the Jewish state. Israeli policymakers observed that while Israel should continue to be able to defeat any combination of Arab armies, the results of the Persian Gulf War could not be ignored. In private background briefings, Israeli policymakers admitted that they were aware of the new realities in the region. They also trusted the U.S. commitment to Israel's security and survival. Without spelling it out publicly, they knew that should Israel face an existential threat, the United States and other Western countries would rush to its rescue, as they did with Kuwait. Israel, however, is not Kuwait, and Israelis are too proud to depend on outside forces for their defense. Israeli military doctrine was always "self-reliance." Their conclusion was, therefore, that while Israel should definitely move toward peace with its Arab neighbors, the movement should be slow and very cautious.

The slow movement was dictated also by the nature and character of Yitzhak Shamir. The Israeli prime minister was a tough bargainer. He is less sentimental than Menachem Begin and certainly not a "visionary" or a "dreamer" like Shimon Peres. Among the Israeli leaders, the ever-cautious Yitzhak Rabin was more to his liking. Shamir's intransigence, his lack of flexibility, and, above all, his poor communications ability complicated the Israeli–American dialogue, but they were definitely not the only cause for its gradual deterioration. Shamir did not trust the Arabs, and he was also suspicious of President Bush and Secretary Baker. He knew, however, that the mood in Israel after the traumatic experience with the Iraqi "Scud" missiles was for peace. He also knew that should the opportunity for peace avail itself, the Israeli people would not let him miss this opportunity.

This, then, was the general mood in the Middle East in the aftermath of Desert Storm. However, before explaining how the road to Madrid was taken, it is important here to stress a few points concerning President Bush's Middle Eastern policy and how it was perceived by Israel and the Palestinians.

During his presidential election campaign in 1988, Bush referred to Israel as a "strategic ally, whose Western values buttressed the alliance in its vulnerable area." Indeed, nothing in Bush's career, whether as director of the Central Intelligence Agency or as ambassador to the UN, indicated any anti-Israeli bias. As vice president, both Israel and the American Jewish leadership praised his outstanding, discreet efforts to rescue Ethiopian Jews and airlift them to Israel. Uri Lubrani, the former Israeli ambassador to Ethiopia and Iran and the coordinator of both "Moses" and "Solomon" rescue operations, told American Jewish leaders in New York that, were it not for Bush's efforts with Sudanese president Jaafar Nimeiry, Ethiopian Jews would not be in Israel. Nevertheless, American Jewish leaders, most of them Democrats, described Bush in private discussions as a "cold fish" with no emotional attachment to Israel. "Bush is no Reagan," they said. Jack Stein, a former chairman of the Presidents Conference—the umbrella group of all major American Jewish organizations—and one of the very few Republican Jewish leaders, disagreed. Stein, whom Bush appointed as ambassador at the U.S. mission to the UN under Ambassador Thomas Pickering, agreed that "Bush is not emotional, he is rational," but he insisted that the president's commitment to Israel "was unshaken."[3]

American Jewish leaders were uneasy about James A. Baker III as well. Baker, the friend and ally whom Bush appointed as his secretary of state, was described as a fair and no-nonsense lawyer who, in a determined pursuit of a "deal," could become blunt and brutal.

The Israeli profile of Bush, based on his record as two-term vice president under Reagan, included the following instances when Bush held positions considered to be anti-Israeli:

- In June 1981, after Operation Opera, the destruction of the Iraqi nuclear facility near Baghdad, Bush called for punitive actions against Israel.
- Also in 1981, Bush sharply criticized Israel and AIPAC [American Israel Public Affairs Committee]—the pro-Israeli lobby on Capitol Hill—for their effort to block the sale of AWACS planes to Saudi Arabia.
- In 1982, during the war in Lebanon, Bush supported the efforts of Defense Secretary Caspar Weinberger to impose sanctions on Israel. President Reagan refused.
- In 1984, at the urging of Egypt and Saudi Arabia, Bush "tilted" toward Iraq and supported the decision to allow Egypt to sell arms to Saddam Hussein.
- In 1985–1986, Bush was very reserved about the pro-Iranian role that Israel had played in the Iran-contra affair.
- Finally, Bush disliked AIPAC and shared Baker's view that Israel had "too much influence" in Washington.

However, while Likud considered Bush as being "pro-Arab," the Labor component in the Israeli national government—and especially Rabin and Peres—did not find the president's positions different from those held by his predecessors. Rabin and Peres had no difficulty at all in working with both Bush and Baker on the basis of mutual trust.

The interesting thing about Bush and Baker was the fact that some Arab countries, especially the Palestinians, were also "not comfortable" with the new Bush administration. Like Israel, the Palestinians did not know much about the president's future approach to the Arab–Israeli conflict. They knew, of course, that Bush—as vice president—supported Secretary Shultz's decision to open a dialogue with the PLO in Tunis, and they were assured that the dialogue would continue. They were suspicious, however, of the new Middle East team that the president and the secretary of state assembled. Baker inherited from Shultz Dan Kurzer, the head of the department's "Israel Desk," who was consistent in his support for a dialogue with the PLO. Baker kept him in place. Baker added to his team two senior officials, Dennis Ross and Aaron Miller, who were not exactly "in tune" with Kurzer. Ross became the senior official who coordinated Baker's peace policy. At the same time, General Brent Scowcroft, the president's national security adviser, appointed Richard Haas as director of Near East and South Asian affairs at the White House, a position that Dennis Ross once occupied under Reagan.

In the summer of 1988, before joining the Bush administration, both Ross and Haas participated in a bipartisan study group that toured the Middle East and recommended a bipartisan policy to the new administration. The mission was organized by Martin Indyk, the director of the Washington Institute for Near East Policy, a pro-Israeli research center that within a relatively short period earned the reputation as one of the most prestigious think-tank groups in Washington. Indyk later served under President Clinton as U.S. ambassador to Israel. Both Ross and Haas were known for their preference for a low-key, step-by-step approach to the Arab–Israeli conflict, based on the principle of "land for peace" and territorial compromise. As to the Palestinians, once Shultz opened the dialogue with the PLO in Tunis, none in Baker's team challenged this new reality, and none recommended the suspension of this dialogue with Arafat. Meanwhile, pressure was building on the new Shamir government to agree to an international peace conference, with PLO participation. President Mitterrand of France, Egypt's president Mubarak, Prime Minister John Major of Great Britain, and President Gorbachev had all conveyed to Israel the same message. The Soviet foreign minister even suggested hosting in Moscow a PLO–Israeli dialogue, under the auspices of the superpowers, in return for reestablishing diplomatic relations with Israel.

Shamir rejected all these pleas. At that stage, he was interested only in the American position. On April 6, during a meeting at the White House with the newly elected President Bush, Shamir presented an outline of an Israeli peace initiative. It consisted of four elements: (1) a call on all Arab states to negotiate peace with Israel; (2) a call on the three signatories of the Camp David accords (Israel, Egypt, and the United States) to convene at the foreign minister level to review their status; (3) free elections in the West Bank and the Gaza Strip, in advance of final status negotiations between Israel and the newly elected Palestinian representatives; and (4) an international effort to help alleviate the sufferings of the Palestinian refugees.[4]

According to Shamir, the outline was well received in Washington, and he promised both Bush and Baker to submit a detailed peace plan in the near future. On Sunday, May 14, the Israeli government approved a peace plan, consisting of a preamble and 20 paragraphs and prepared in collaboration with Defense Minister Rabin. The plan, based on Camp David accords, called for an interim period of five years of Palestinian autonomy, to be followed by negotiations on the final status of the West Bank and the Gaza Strip. The plan rejected the idea of a Palestinian state and ruled out PLO participation in the peace process.

The Bush administration appeared to be satisfied that, for the time being at least, it had gotten "something" to work with. Indeed, of the entire plan, Baker took out the elections paragraph "to work with." His intention was to expand on this subject in order to make it more acceptable to the Palestinians and then present the "final product" to Shamir as though it was Israel's original idea. In this way, Shamir would find it extremely difficult to reject "his own" plan.

The PLO and Egypt rejected the Israeli plan outright. Arafat rejected it because he was excluded from the process and also because he feared the creation of an alternative leadership in the territories. Like Arafat, President Mubarak opposed the exclusion of the PLO from the process and described the Israeli plan as "not useful." Faced with the reality that Israel's peace initiative was practically deadlocked, Baker decided on a "shock therapy." Addressing the annual meeting of AIPAC in Washington on May 22, 1989, which was attended by more than 1,000 activists from across the United States, the secretary dropped a powerful "bomb." Baker opened his remarks by praising the Israeli peace initiative and describing the strength of the "strategic partnership" between Israel and the United States. Then, totally unexpected and certainly not needed at this early stage and at this very forum, Baker told AIPAC that the U.S. interpretation for Resolution 242 was "land for peace," and hence any negotiation would end in some form of Israeli territorial withdrawal. Then came his "message" to Shamir: "For Israel, now is the time to lay once and for all, the unrealistic vision of Greater Israel. Israeli interests in the West Bank and Gaza—security and otherwise—can be met by a settlement based on resolution 242.... Forswear annexation. Stop settlement activity. Allow schools to reopen. Reach out to the Palestinians as neighbors, who deserve political rights."[5]

Baker had a similar "message" to the Arabs and the Palestinians: "Speak with one voice for peace. Practice constructive diplomacy. Recognize Israel as a partner in trade and human contact. Understand that violence would not work and that no one would deliver Israel to you."[6]

Baker's remarks were received in silence and total shock. This was "AIPAC's Night." AIPAC's activists came to Washington to rub shoulders with government officials and congressmen in appreciation of their devoted support for Israel. They did not come to be "lectured" on how the United States wanted

Israel to behave. Since its establishment by Sy Kennan in the early 1950s, AIPAC hosted many of the U.S. national leaders. No one had ever dropped such a powerful "bomb" on such a devoted pro-Israel crowd. Baker's speech signaled a new modus operandi in the relations between Israel and the Bush administration. It was obvious that Bush had moved away from President Reagan's approach to build Israel's trust in U.S. mediation. Instead, Bush adopted a style of strong public discord with Israel designed to modify its policies and to force Israel into accepting policies that ran counter to positions held since the 1967 war. The response to Baker's "shock therapy" was instant. In a letter addressed to Baker and drafted that same night, senators and hundreds of representatives urged the Bush administration to endorse "strongly and publicly" Israel's peace initiative. Although it was not binding, the letter had a moral effect. It signaled to Bush and Baker that AIPAC would not be intimidated into supporting a U.S. policy that would not meet Israel's basic security needs.

In the second half of 1989, U.S. and Arab efforts were directed at convincing the PLO to allow Palestinians from the West Bank and the Gaza Strip to enter into negotiations with Israel. At the same time and as the gap between Labor and Likud widened within the national unity government, the Israeli domestic scene witnessed a unique and unprecedented diplomatic experience. Both Egypt and the United States began to treat the Israeli government as though it was "two governments." Every piece of information that was communicated to Shamir and Arens was automatically communicated to Rabin and Peres as well. Furthermore, Labor dovish elements, headed by Deputy Finance Minister Yossi Beilin, began to meet in Jerusalem with Palestinians who were identified with the PLO. Both Peres and Rabin maintained regular and intensive contacts with Egypt. One cabinet minister, Ezer Weizman, was reported to Shamir by the General Security Service (GSS) to have met in Geneva with Nabil Ramlawi, a PLO representative, and through an Israeli-Arab, Dr. Ahmed Tibi, he had also had occasional telephone conversations with Arafat himself. Shamir wanted to dismiss Weizman from his government. However, in the face of a Labor threat to dissolve the national unity government, Shamir accepted a compromise. Weizman would remain in the government, but he was excluded from the prestigious ministerial committee on security and foreign affairs. Thus, in mid-1989, Shamir knew that the Labor component of his national unity government was negotiating with the PLO, directly or indirectly.

In early September 1989 Rabin left for Washington for a meeting with Defense Secretary Dick Cheney. A few days earlier, Egyptian foreign minister Ismat Abdul Meguid met with Baker and explored with him "general ideas" about a 10-point peace plan drafted by President Mubarak. Without informing Shamir in advance, Rabin, too, met with Baker and offered a few remarks about Mubarak's 10-point plan. Rabin's meetings in Washington had a deeper meaning. Although he was associated in the preparation of the Israeli peace plan, Rabin was now ready to shift his support to the Egyptian peace initiative. He qualified Mubarak's 10-point plan as "a big step forward." Seven of Mubarak's points dealt with the procedures and with the preparations for the elections in the territories; one called on Israel to accept the principle of "land for peace"; another demanded that all settlement activity be halted; and the last point called on Israel to agree to the participation of East Jerusalem Palestinians in the proposed elections. All three last points had been rejected in the past by Shamir.[7] Upon his return to Israel, Rabin reported to the inner cabinet on his discussions in Washington. At that stage, however, Mubarak's plan was not officially presented to Israel. Therefore, Shamir saw no reason to make an immediate decision. Foreign Minister Arens was due to leave for New York on September 19 to attend the UN General Assembly, where he was expected to meet with both President Mubarak and Secretary Baker. They would certainly discuss with him the Egyptian peace initiative. A decision would be made then, upon Arens' return from New York.

The UN General Assembly in New York in September 1989 would be remembered in Israel's diplomatic history as "most bizarre." Just before Arens' arrival in New York, Peres was already there. He was meeting with the same people whom the foreign minister was due to meet and conveying to his interlocutors opposite views. As a personal snub to Arens and as a clear signal to the Israeli public that the United States favored Labor over Likud, Bush met with Peres at the Oval Office. As a counterbalance, Bush also met with Arens for a photo op in a New York hotel, just minutes before he hosted a dinner for the heads of delegations to the General Assembly. The difference in decorum was oceanwide.

The Israeli public was totally confused by the conflicting messages that Arens and Peres were conveying from the United States. Arens told his interlocutors that "Shamir wants peace," but he ruled out talking to the PLO, to Palestinians who had been deported from the West Bank and Gaza because of terrorist or subversive activity, to any Palestinian who was not a permanent resident of the territories, to Palestinians who were associated with the leaders of the Intifada, or to Palestinians from East Jerusalem. Who was left, then, as a possible interlocutor? A cartoon in the *Jerusalem Post* portrayed the "acceptable Palestinian" as an informer of the Israeli security services, armed with a gun and asking for permission to emigrate.

Peres, on the other hand, told a press briefing in Washington that he supported Mubarak's 10-point plan because it had a better chance for implementation than the original Israeli plan. Peres found Mubarak's initiative "fascinating" for what it left out. Peres explained that there was no reference to the PLO, that there was no mention of self-determination and a Palestinian state, and that there was no call for Israel to withdraw to the 1967 lines. Peres concluded his remarks by saying: "The Palestinian partner for peace who exists would not be acceptable to Shamir; the one acceptable did not exist."[8] Upon the return of Peres and Arens from the United States, the Israeli inner cabinet met on October 5 to discuss Mubarak's 10-point plan. By then, the Egyptian initiative was officially submitted to Israel. The inner cabinet was evenly divided, and Mubarak's plan was rejected. Shamir argued that to accept Egypt's plan, rather than to stick to the Israeli initiative, was tantamount to signing a "letter of capitulation."[9]

The diplomatic vacuum created by the rejection of the Egyptian plan was instantly filled by the United States. On October 6 Baker injected himself into the process. In an effort to avoid a deadlock, Baker phoned Arens and suggested what was to become known as Baker's five-point plan. It was meant to make Shamir's own plan more acceptable to the Palestinians, although it was less generous than Mubarak's plan. Peres and Rabin accepted Baker's proposal. Shamir and Arens asked for clarifications. On October 23, in an effort to avoid a misunderstanding, Arens put the requested clarifications in writing. They were all aimed at excluding the PLO from the process and denying the right of Palestinians from East Jerusalem to vote for Palestinian autonomy. Baker forwarded the requested Israeli clarifications to Egypt for comment.

In early December there was still no answer from Cairo about the requested Israeli clarifications. Israeli intelligence sources reported that, after a stormy debate in Tunis, the PLO Executive Committee rejected Baker's plan. Arafat told Mubarak that, as the "sole representative" of the Palestinian people, the PLO insisted on participating in the peace negotiations under appropriate international auspices. Baker's efforts were deadlocked too.

Developments in early 1990 changed dramatically the international climate. The brutal Communist regime in Romania collapsed, and President Ceausescu was executed by a firing squad. In the wake of perestroika and glasnost, the Eastern European nations were moving away from the Soviet Union toward political freedom and democracy. Then came the least expected of all: the gates of the Soviet Union had swung open, and thousands of Jews were allowed to emigrate to Israel. The mass immigration of Soviet Jews revived the old dispute between Israel and the United States about the settlement activity in the West Bank and the Gaza Strip. In a meeting with Arens in Washington on February 23, 1990, Baker said that the United States could not agree to settling the Soviet Jews in the territories. He wanted a public Israeli commitment to prohibit Soviet Jews from settling there. This was the first time in American–Israeli relations that a humanitarian issue was linked to a political decision. Arens explained to Baker that no Israeli prime minister—not only Shamir—would agree to such a linkage.[10]

Indeed, in the following weeks and months there was not one single subject in the American–Israeli relations more irritating than the issue of the settlements. President Carter considered the settlements to be illegal. President Reagan did not consider them illegal but saw in them an "obstacle to peace." President Bush sharpened the debate by considering East Jerusalem, too, as part of the occupied territories. Finally, after a strong lobbying effort in the United States, a compromise formula was found, according to which Israel would not "encourage" (not prohibit) Soviet Jews to settle in the West Bank and in the Gaza Strip.

The developments in the Eastern bloc had brought to the Middle East two new political realities: (1) the ex-Communist countries rushed to reestablish diplomatic relations with Israel, thus ending 35 years of Israeli isolation in Eastern Europe; and (2) radical Arab countries—foremost among them Iraq, Syria, Libya, and the PLO—had suddenly lost their Communist support and had to readjust, painfully, to the new political realities.

The most immediately affected by the new situation was the PLO. At the insistence of Egypt, Arafat dropped his condition for a personal involvement in the peace process and was now prepared to reengage in negotiations—via Egypt—about the implementation of Baker's plan. Arafat was still insisting, however, that the Palestinian delegation to the negotiations with Israel should include two deportees and at least one Palestinian from East Jerusalem. The Palestinian list would be presented to Israel and the United States by Egypt, after consultations with the PLO.

This new PLO position was discussed in Washington in late January 1990 in two secret, but separate, meetings between Baker and Rabin and the Egyptian foreign minister. The precise makeup of the list was not totally resolved. Rabin agreed, however, that Egypt would provide a list of Palestinians acceptable to Israel, without Israel's asking too many questions about the list's origin. This was a semiacceptance of the possibility that the PLO would be the discreet "kingmaker" of the Palestinian list. This was the same formula that Moshe Dayan and Menachem Begin accepted in 1979 during negotiations with Egypt about an autonomy for the Palestinians. Rabin, however, was not empowered by Prime Minister Shamir to negotiate the composition of the Palestinian delegation, nor was his formula accepted by Shamir and Arens. During a meeting in Washington on February 23, 1990, Arens submitted to Baker a counterproposal aimed to eliminate any role for the PLO in future negotiations. Without explicitly defining it so, Arens insisted that Israel should have a veto power over the composition of the Palestinian delegation. He told Baker that it was "very unlikely" that Shamir would agree to include Palestinians from East Jerusalem in the Palestinian delegation.

On March 7 Shamir convened the inner cabinet for a special meeting to discuss the issue of Palestinian representation in future peace negotiations. Labor ministers supported the formula that was discussed between Rabin and Baker. Likud ministers approved Shamir's position, as presented to Baker by Arens. In the face of such a deadlock, it became clear that the fate of the national unity government was sealed. Indeed, on March 13 Shamir opened a special government meeting by reading a short letter advising Finance Minister Shimon Peres that he was fired from the cabinet. Shamir explained that he took such a dramatic and unprecedented step because of Peres' "subversion" and his constant efforts to topple the government. Visibly shaken, his face pale, and his voice trembling, Peres hit back: "I don't recognize you as my prime minister." Immediately afterward, all Labor ministers, including Rabin, submitted their resignations to Shamir. For a while it looked as though Peres would be able to form a new, narrow-based government, without Likud participation. At the end, however, it was Shamir who was capable of forming a new government without Labor. On June 11, 1990, the new Shamir government was sworn in by the Knesset. Moroccan-born David Levy became the new foreign minister, whereas Moshe Arens succeeded Rabin at the Defense Ministry.

The immediate "victim" of the new development was a previously approved

Israeli request for $400 million in loan guarantees to help absorb Soviet Jewish immigrants. When Shamir undertook "not to encourage" the settlement of Soviet Jews in the territories, he did not mention East Jerusalem. For him, united Jerusalem was the capital of Israel. When told that thousands of Soviet Jews were settling in the new Jewish neighborhoods surrounding Jerusalem, Bush was furious. He was certain that Shamir had "lied" to him, and he sharply attacked Israel's settlement policy in the West Bank and in East Jerusalem.[11]

That was a dangerous escalation in the Bush–Shamir dispute. The very fact that the president had mentioned East Jerusalem as an "occupied territory" gave the new Israeli government the final excuse to reject Baker's plan, even at the risk of losing the $400 million in loan guarantees. Shamir argued that the president's remarks about East Jerusalem proved that he was not "objective." Tensions between Israel and the United States were never so high.

In the spring and summer of 1990, regional developments were affecting the PLO as well. The Persian Gulf crisis was already in the air, and financial arguments between Saddam Hussein and Kuwait about oil prices and production had intensified. Having lost the support of the Communist bloc and facing an Egyptian inability to affect Israeli positions, Arafat was inclined to embrace Saddam Hussein. The PLO chairman pinned his hopes on Saddam's April 1 speech, in which he revealed that Iraq possessed binary chemical weapons, which, he threatened, he would use against Israel. "By God, we will make the fire burn half of Israel, if Israel tried to do anything against Iraq," he boasted.[12]

This was not mere boasting. Israeli intelligence officials reported to Shamir's government on April 4 that Iraq had indeed become the largest producer of chemical agents in the world. Mustard gas and nerve agents were produced in three facilities in Sammara, Falluja, and Salman Pak, built with German and European technology.[13]

This belligerent Iraqi posture appealed to Arafat, and he thought it could become a viable alternative to the ineffective Egyptian and Saudi influence on the United States. The first sign of this PLO "tilt" toward Iraq came on May 30, which was the Jewish holiday of Shavuot. Jews around the world celebrated Shavuot to mark the "birth" of the Ten Commandments, which Moses received from God on Mount Sinai. Secular Israelis, however, celebrate Shavuot also as the "Harvest Holiday," packing the beaches and public parks and attending joyful folk-dance festivals. In two assaults, three hours apart, a pro-Iraqi faction of the PLO, the Palestine Liberation Front (PLF), mounted a seaborne guerrilla raid and tried to land 16 heavily armed terrorists in one of the popular beaches south of Tel Aviv. The terrorists, on two dinghy boats, were intercepted by the Israeli navy, which killed 4 and captured the remaining 12 on their vessels. It was just a miracle that no sunbathing Israelis were hurt.

In their interrogation, the terrorists admitted that they were commissioned by Abul Abbas, the man responsible in 1985 for the hijacking of the cruise ship *Achille Lauro* and for the murder of the American passenger Leon Klinghoffer. In 1987 Abul Abbas was elected by the Palestine National Council—the Palestinian parliament-in-exile—to represent his faction in the 18-member PLO

Executive Committee. His base was in Baghdad, and he received generous financial assistance from Libya and Iraq. Abul Abbas' relationship with Arafat was very close.

Israel submitted all the information relevant to the seaborne guerrilla raid to the United States and asked for an immediate suspension of the American dialogue with the PLO. American Jewish leaders and congressmen from both parties added their voices to this Israeli request. President Bush sharply condemned the raid and asked Arafat to expel Abul Abbas from the PLO's Executive Committee. As to the suspension of the dialogue with the PLO, Bush decided to buy time, hoping that the public storm would calm down. It didn't. Unwilling to antagonize his new Iraqi patrons, Arafat refused even to condemn the raid. He claimed that only the Palestinian National Council could decide on a punitive action and expel Abul Abbas from the PLO's Executive Committee.[14]

On June 8, in a desperate effort to save the "dialogue" with the PLO, Bush spoke by phone with President Mubarak and impressed upon him the seriousness of the situation. Sweden, which was instrumental in opening the U.S.–PLO dialogue in 1988, on June 9 sent a special envoy to Baghdad to convince Arafat to take action against Abul Abbas. In vain.[15]

By mid-June it was already obvious that the White House delaying tactic had not worked. On June 11 Vice President Dan Quayle and Defense Secretary Dick Cheney addressed an AIPAC conference in Washington and added their voices to those calling for the suspension of the dialogue with the PLO. What was more effective, however, was the congressional pressure. Seven senators and 36 representatives introduced resolutions calling on Bush to suspend the dialogue with the PLO. On June 20, realizing that Congress would pass the resolutions with an overwhelming majority, Bush finally suspended the dialogue with the PLO.

The suspension of the 18-month dialogue with the United States was a major setback to Arafat. After he abandoned his efforts to mediate between the United States and the PLO, Mubarak's relations with Arafat deteriorated. "We told them [the PLO], you have to find yourself a solution to your problem with the United States," President Mubarak told the editors of the Egyptian press.[16]

Iraq's invasion of Kuwait on August 2, 1990, had deepened the crisis between Egypt and the PLO and had drawn the world's attention away from the Arab–Israeli conflict. The Persian Gulf crisis caused the Intifada to gradually fade away. TV coverage of Palestinian demonstrations in the territories dropped to zero, and foreign correspondents were reassigned from Jerusalem to Saudi Arabia and Kuwait. With the lack of world interest, demonstrations in the territories also stopped. At the same time, tensions between Israel and the United States were reduced.

In December 1990, a few weeks before Desert Storm, Prime Minister Shamir came once again to Washington at the invitation of President Bush. Unlike previous encounters, the December meeting at the White House was pleasant and relaxed. Israel was not a part of the coalition that the United States had organized against Saddam Hussein. Arab leaders had made it clear that should Israel join the coalition, they would quit. They could not be perceived in the Arab world as joining hands with Israel in a war against Iraq. Bush assured Shamir that there would be no trade-off with Iraq against any aspect of the U.S. commitments to Israel. Bush, however, wanted a clear Israeli commitment not to preempt or take any retaliatory military action against Iraq without prior coordination with the United States. Shamir made this commitment. To ensure the necessary coordination, Bush instructed General Brent Scowcroft to open two secure lines of communications between Israel and the United States. One line was opened between the White House and the prime minister's office in Jerusalem and was handled by both Scowcroft and the Israeli ambassador to Washington, Zalman Shoval, and the other secure line was opened between the Pentagon and the Israeli Ministry of Defense.[17]

During that meeting, Shamir raised for the first time the possibility that Israel would request $10 billion in loan guarantees from the United States for the absorption of Soviet Jews in Israel. Bush was sympathetic but noncommittal. The president told Shamir that he would deal with this subject only after the solution of the Gulf crisis. Bush reminded Shamir, however, of his position on the settlements.[18] The most intriguing subject raised by Shamir during that meeting was Jordan. The Israeli prime minister told the president that he could understand the U.S. anger at King Hussein's support for Saddam Hussein's invasion of Kuwait. The United States, however, should understand the king's intolerable situation. Arafat's support of the Iraqi move had left Jordan with no choices. Had the king stood up to Saddam, the Palestinians in his kingdom would have rebelled against him. Therefore, it was important now to look beyond the Persian Gulf crisis. It was better to help the king to remain in the Western camp rather than push him further into Saddam Hussein's arms. Bush was impressed by Shamir's defense of Jordan, but he would not change his hostile attitude toward King Hussein.[19]

Shamir's attitude during the Persian Gulf War was, indeed, exemplary. Despite constant pressure from Arens and other ministers, the Israeli prime minister rejected any retaliation against Saddam Hussein for his launching of 39 Scud missiles into Israel. Not only did he keep his promise to Bush to show restraint, but he also made a similar promise to King Hussein himself. On January 5, 1991, just 10 days before the war started, Hussein and Shamir met secretly at the King's London residence to coordinate positions during that critical period. Both the king and Shamir knew that the war was inevitable. The king wanted to avoid a situation whereby his country would become a theater of clashes between the Israeli and Iraqi air forces. In return for Jordan's promise not to allow Iraqi planes to fly over Jordan's airspace on their way to attack Israel, Shamir promised that, in the event of a retaliation against Iraq, Israeli jets would not fly over Jordan.

At the end of the Persian Gulf War, it became evident that the tensions between Israel and the United States concerning the peace process in general and the settlements issue in particular had not disappeared but were only temporarily shelved. In its determination to initiate a peace process, the Bush administration decided to make the issue of the $10 billion in loan guarantees to help absorb

Russian immigrants in Israel its most important tool to force Shamir into moderating his positions. Indeed, the issue of the loan guarantees soon became the single most irritating problem in U.S.–Israeli relations, and it was to seriously affect the peace process.

Shortly after the war and following President Bush's launching of his peace initiative, on March 6, 1991, Ambassador Shoval explored with Secretary Baker the issue of the loan guarantees. He was asked to delay the formal request until after Labor Day in September. Secretary Baker made the same request in March 1991 during his first trip to the Middle East after the war. Baker explained to Shamir that the delay was needed in order to enable him to concentrate on the peace process. Shamir agreed to the delay. This moderate Israeli approach was adopted, despite an alarming report that the prime minister had received from the General Security Service (GSS) about a meeting that Baker had with a group of some 20 Palestinians in East Jerusalem on March 12, 1991. Baker was reported to have told the group that he wanted them to hear it from him personally. In dealing with the peace process, the United States would not yield to any "domestic pressure." The implication was obvious: Bush would not be deterred by AIPAC and by Israel's supporters on Capitol Hill. The contents of Baker's discussion with the Palestinians were leaked to Israel immediately. In order to avoid future leaks, the number of Palestinian activists who met with Baker was reduced to three only—Faisal Husseini, Hanan Ashrawi, and Zakkariya Agha (from the Gaza Strip).

In May 1991, in private discussions with key congressional leaders, Israel began to explore informally the congressional position on the loan guarantees. Because of its restraint in the Gulf crisis, Israel enjoyed at that time a period of grace in the United States. Accordingly, the congressional position was encouraging. However, as Labor Day drew closer, it became clear that the Bush administration had no intention of granting Israel the $10 billion in loan guarantees without extracting a political price from Shamir. The administration asked for a further delay of 120 days. Realizing that the approval process would take longer than 120 days, Shamir saw no reason to delay the formal Israeli request beyond Labor Day, as originally planned. Accordingly, on September 6, just a few weeks before the opening of the Madrid Peace Conference, Israeli finance minister Yitzhak Modai and Ambassador Shoval submitted to Deputy Secretary of State Larry Eagleburger the formal Israeli request for $10 billion in loan guarantees.

President Bush reacted to the Israeli request instantly. In a press conference that same day, Bush said that he would ask Congress to defer "just for 120 days" the discussion of the Israeli request. He said that the deferral was important for the peace process. He added that it was "very, very important" to do everything possible to give peace a chance.[20] Shamir was in total shock. Years later, he explained:

This was the first time in the history of Israeli–American relations that there was a political and economic blackmail. Even President Carter, whose relations with Rabin and

Begin were not always smooth, never used the U.S. economic assistance to Israel as a political stick. What President Bush was telling us was very simple: If you won't behave yourselves in the peace process, and if you won't accept the principle of "land for peace," you won't receive the loan guarantees.[21]

Congressional reaction to the president's request was ambivalent and, interestingly enough, American Jewish leadership was also divided on this issue. Not only Republican Jewish leaders, like Max Fisher and Jacob Stein, but also liberal Jewish Democrats, like Rabbi Alexander Schindler and others, did not want a confrontation with Bush on the eve of the Madrid Peace Conference. They did not consider the deferral for 120 days critical. The Israeli opposition parties also shared this view. Nevertheless, on September 12, AIPAC mounted a major lobbying effort on Capitol Hill in support of the Israeli request. More than 1,000 Jewish activists from across the United States met with their congressmen and senators and asked for their support. When told about it, Bush overreacted. In a televised news conference, the president made an emotional appeal to the American people: "A debate now on this issue could well destroy our ability to bring one or more of the parties to the peace table. . . . If necessary, I will use my veto power to keep that from happening." Bush then moved to a frontal attack on AIPAC. He said:

We are up against some very powerful political forces, very strong and effective groups that go up to the Hill. . . . We have got one lonely guy down here, doing it. . . . But I am going to fight for what I believe. It may be politically popular, but probably not. . . . The question for me is not whether it is good 1992 politics; what is important here is that we give the [peace] process a chance, and I don't care if I get [in the elections] one single vote.

That, however, was not all. In a clear distortion of history, Bush went on to say that "just months ago, American men and women in uniform risked their lives to defend Israelis in the face of Iraqi Scud missiles, and indeed Desert Storm, while winning a war against aggression, also achieved the defeat of Israel's most dangerous adversary."[22]

Bush's statement shocked Israel and the entire American Jewish community. Israelis were particularly upset by the president's remarks that "American men and women risked their lives" in their defense. Not only had Israel been excluded from the anti-Saddam coalition, but Bush had practically twisted Shamir's arm to prevent Israel from retaliating to Iraqi Scud attacks. Now Bush was telling the American people that, by sending to Israel what proved to be totally ineffective Patriot missiles, American soldiers had risked their lives in Israel's defense. When Bush made this remark, he already knew that the Patriot missiles had been ineffective. Israeli defense minister Moshe Arens had told him so back in February 1991. The angry Israeli reaction was reflected by the entire Israeli press. Editorial writers and political analysts "reminded" Bush that it was Israel that suffered human losses and material damage and that by not retaliating to the Iraqi Scud attacks, Israel had served the American national interest.

No less sharp was the American Jewish reaction. Thomas Dine, the executive director of AIPAC and former aide to Senator Frank Church (D-ID), who was the president's main target, called Bush's televised news conference "a day of shame." In an interview with Israeli radio and TV, Dine said that Bush's remarks "were an affront to the entire Jewish community, since he put a question mark on their right to lobby on behalf of subjects close to their hearts."[23]

A few days later, on September 16, Secretary Baker tried to convince Israel that there would be no further delay in approving the loan guarantees beyond January. In a joint meeting in Jerusalem with Shamir, David Levy, and Arens, Baker said: "My advice to you is to call off the dogs and strike the loan guarantees off your agenda for the next 120 days." When Shamir told Baker that, as a matter of principle, he could not accept the linkage between a humanitarian issue and the peace process, the secretary interrupted him and said: "You have no choice. If you want the loan guarantees, then you will have to accept our position on the settlements. . . . You have to stop settling in the territories. We are not going to fund settlement activity."[24]

There is no credible explanation as to why Bush and Baker would be so eager to confront Shamir on such a sensitive issue on the eve of the Madrid Peace Conference. Some Israeli observers believed that Bush apparently acted on the assumption that, when the dust settled, the divided Israeli people and the equally divided American Jewish community would accept the new reality. In the short range, Bush proved to be right and won his battle with Shamir over the issue of the loan guarantees. Neither Congress nor the American Jewish leadership was prepared for a confrontation with the administration on the eve of the Madrid Peace Conference. They all agreed to defer the consideration of the Israeli request for 120 days.

It is in this atmosphere of mutual suspicion between the United States and Israel that Secretary Baker completed his preparations for the Madrid Peace Conference. After months of tough negotiations, it was finally agreed that the Palestinian team would be part of a Jordanian–Palestinian delegation, headed by the Jordanian foreign minister. The Palestinian team would not include official PLO members, Palestinians who carried Jerusalem residence cards, Palestinians from the diaspora, or deportees who had been expelled from the territories because of their terrorist or subversive activity.

In order to "drag" Shamir to Madrid, the United States acceded to his condition that the peace conference consist of one single ceremonial opening, to be followed by separate, face-to-face negotiations between Israel and its Arab neighbors. Shamir agreed that the first round of face-to-face negotiations would be held in Madrid but would be considered as part of the "ceremonial session." The Israeli prime minister did not want American participation in the direct talks. He argued that once Israel and Egypt had signed the peace treaty between them, there was no need for "outsiders" to broker similar accords between Israel and the other Arab countries.

This argument was valid but not very convincing. Since the establishment of the state of Israel, not one single accord with any Arab government had been achieved without outside intervention. The Israeli–Arab armistice agreements in the years 1949–1950 were negotiated under the auspices of the UN. In the aftermath of the Yom Kippur War in 1973, Henry Kissinger shuttled between Jerusalem, Cairo, and Damascus to arrange for the separation of forces agreements between the three countries. Finally, had it not been for the stubbornness and patience of President Carter, there would not have been an Egyptian–Israeli peace treaty.

Shamir's real reason for refusing American participation in the face-to-face negotiations was his knowledge that the long-held U.S. positions concerning Israel's final borders were closer to the Arab position than to Israel's. Every American president from Johnson to Bush envisaged an Israeli withdrawal to the pre-1967 lines, "with minor modifications." Thus, the consistent American interpretation of UN resolution 242 was "land for peace." In the face of strong Israeli opposition, Baker agreed not to make this U.S. position public.

This U.S. promise proved to be meaningless. While the invitation to the Madrid Peace Conference did not mention the principle of "land for peace" but only stated that the negotiations would be based on resolutions 242 and 338, the private letters of assurance that Baker addressed to the various Arab parties clearly mentioned the "land for peace" principle. In his letter of assurance to the Palestinians dated October 18, 1991, Baker quoted President Bush's speech of March 6, 1991, in which he said that the negotiations would be based on resolutions 242 and 338 and on the principle of "land for peace." As to East Jerusalem, Baker's letter read: "Nothing Palestinians do in choosing their delegation members in this phase of the process will affect their claim to East Jerusalem, or be prejudicial or precedential to the outcome of the negotiations." While stating that Jerusalem must never again be divided, the United States assured the Palestinians that it did not recognize Israel's annexation of East Jerusalem or the extension of its boundaries.[25]

Baker handed the first draft of his letter to Hanan Ashrawi, the spokesperson of the Palestinian delegation, in Amman on September 20, 1991. Ashrawi told Baker that she would show the text to Arafat in a PLO meeting in Algiers on September 27. Although according to the Israeli law it was illegal for Ashrawi to meet with PLO officials, Baker did not object. He only asked her not to circulate the letter in Algiers lest it be leaked, and then "it would create problems with Israel."[26]

Even before he arrived in Madrid on Tuesday, October 29, Shamir was aware of the fact that Baker's promises about the PLO were not honored. For example, immediately after Baker sent the invitations to Madrid, the participants sent their security officials to the Spanish capital to work out the necessary security arrangements for the various delegations. Although the PLO was not officially represented in Madrid, Shamir was shocked to learn from his security official that Arafat sent to Madrid Atef Bsiso, a former aide of Salah Khalaf (Abu Iyad), the head of "Black September" who had masterminded the massacre of the 11 Israeli athletes in Munich in 1972. Bsiso also had been personally involved in several terrorist attacks against Israel. In Madrid, however, it was Bsiso who met with the FBI [Federal Bureau of Investigation] and the Spanish security authorities and made all the arrangements for the Palestinian negotiating team.[27]

As soon as he arrived in Madrid, Shamir met with President Bush and Secretary Baker. The Israeli prime minister was shocked to learn that he had been misled about the Palestinian representation. Shamir was told that while the joint Jordanian–Palestinian delegation would remain unified, it would nevertheless have two chairmen. Each of them had been allotted equal time—45 minutes—to address the conference. The meaning of this decision was clear: the "joint" delegation was a farce, and the Palestinians practically won their right to be considered as a separate entity. Another source of irritation was the unofficial PLO presence in Madrid. Dr. Haidar Abdul Shafi, a respected 72-year-old physician from the Gaza Strip who was at the time among the founders of the PLO, was the head of the Palestinian delegation to Madrid. However, Faisal Husseini, a resident of East Jerusalem and the most prominent, unofficial PLO activist in the West Bank, came to Madrid as a member of a "steering committee" composed of three Palestinians from the territories and three from Tunis whose duty was to monitor the actions of the official Palestinian team. Thus, everything that had been rejected by Shamir—Jerusalem residents, deportees, and PLO officials—had been applied in Madrid. In his memoirs, Shamir wrote: "I said [to Bush] what I had to say. The president and the secretary assured me that I need not worry; the United States was an 'honest broker.' I hadn't seen the president for a long time, but we skated over the thin ice together. He [Bush] clearly made an effort not to antagonize me, even telling me that he won't mention in his speech the words 'land for peace,' nor did he."[28]

In a recent meeting in Tel Aviv, I asked Shamir: Since you knew of the PLO's presence in Madrid, why did you continue to oppose a formal recognition of the PLO and negotiate directly with Arafat? He replied: "Of course I knew about the PLO's activities in Madrid. I had full knowledge of the contacts between the Palestinians in the territories and Yasser Arafat. I knew also about the trips of Faisal Husseini and Hanan Ashrawi to Tunis and Algiers. For me, however, Arafat symbolizes a Palestinian state, which I continue to oppose. If it was up to me, I would continue to oppose Arafat, even today."[29]

The Madrid Peace Conference was opened Wednesday, October 30, 1991, by King Juan Carlos and with the participation of Presidents Bush and Gorbachev. Although the conference was cosponsored by the United States and the Soviet Union, America alone ran the show in Madrid. Gorbachev's presence attracted little attention, his speech even less. Most of Gorbachev's speech was devoted to Soviet problems, and he said very little about the peace process in the Middle East and the Soviet role in it. This very indifferent mood was later reflected in a meeting with Shamir at the Soviet Embassy. The Israeli prime minister wrote in his memoirs: "Gorbachev didn't talk to me at all about the peace process, or the Middle East. He had other problems to worry about."[30]

President Bush's speech was balanced and well articulated. He said:

Peace will only come as a result of direct negotiations, compromises, give and take.

Peace cannot be imposed from outside, not by the United States or anyone else.... We came here to Madrid as realists. We don't expect peace to be negotiated in a day, or a week, or a month, or even a year. It will take time. Indeed, it should take time—time for parties so long at war to learn to talk to one other, to listen to one another.... What we envision is a process of direct negotiations proceeding along two tracks. One track is between Israel and the Arab states, the other between Israel and the Palestinians. Negotiations are to be conducted on the basis of resolutions 242 and 338. Soon after the bilateral talks commence, the parties will convene to organize multilateral negotiations as well.... Peace cannot depend upon promises alone. Real peace must be based upon security for all states and peoples, including Israel. For too long, the Israeli people have lived in fear, surrounded by an unaccepting Arab world. Now is the ideal moment for the Arab world to demonstrate that attitudes have changed, that the Arab world is willing to live in peace with Israel and make allowances for Israel's reasonable security needs.... Peace must be also based on fairness.... This applies above all to the Palestinians. Israel now has the opportunity to demonstrate that it is willing to enter into a new relationship with its Palestinian neighbors.... Throughout the Middle East, we seek a stable and enduring settlement. We have not defined what this means. Indeed, I have no maps showing where the final borders are to be drawn. Nevertheless, we believe that territorial compromise is essential to peace.[31]

At the end of the conference's first day, it was obvious that Israel was on the defensive. Among the Arab delegations, the Palestinians were the most forceful, and their sentiment was that of ecstasy and triumph. "Today, sitting together in the same room with Bush, Gorbachev, and Shamir, we feel as though we have placed the foundation stone for the Palestinian state," Saeb Erikat, a professor of political science at El-Naiah University in Nablus and a member of the Palestinian negotiating team, told a group of Israeli journalists in Madrid. For Erikat, bespectacled, with a bushy beard and now a member of Arafat's Palestine Authority, it was not only a question of pride but rather a feeling that the United States had finally recognized the Palestinians' right to have their own entity.

Unlike the festive opening on Wednesday, the conference's mood on Thursday, October 31, was more businesslike. With a grim face and accented English, Israeli prime minister Shamir was the first of five speakers that day. If he had any misgivings about the U.S. attitude—he had many—they were certainly not reflected in his speech. In his 45-minute address, Shamir dealt with the historic past, the situation at present, and his "vision" for the future. There was nothing unusual in his speech. While he made no rhetorical gestures, the tone of his speech was realistically consistent with a desire to negotiate. He suggested publicly what had already been secretly rejected by the United States. He invited the Arab countries to face-to-face negotiations in the Middle East, with a first round in Israel. The Arabs rejected this invitation. They wanted to remain in Madrid, although eventually they settled for Washington. However, Shamir's message was clear: Israel had come to Madrid to negotiate.[32]

After the remarks by the Jordanian foreign minister, it was the Palestinians' turn to deliver their message. The appearance of Dr. Haidar Abdul Shafi, the 72-year-old graduate of the American University of Beirut Medical School and the most prominent PLO supporter in the Gaza Strip, was the high drama of the day. The Palestinians finally found their place among the nations at a major Middle East Conference, and they made no effort to conceal their pride.

Like Shamir's, the Palestinians' message carried no surprises. Repeating all the known claims for self-determination, suspension of Jewish settlement activity, East Jerusalem, and so on, Abdul Shafi accepted publicly the two-stage approach for a solution—an interim period of five years and final status negotiations. Before the Persian Gulf War, Arafat had rejected this approach.[33]

The speech by the Syrian foreign minister was certainly the most aggressive and most abusive of the day. As expected, his political message called for total Israeli withdrawal, not only from the Golan Heights and South Lebanon but also from the West Bank, including Jerusalem, and from the Gaza Strip.

The next day, Friday, November 1, was devoted to rebuttals and closing remarks by Secretary Baker. In his remarks, Baker described what role Washington would play in the next phase of the negotiations. He said:

We have our own positions and views on the peace process and we will not forgo our right to state them. But as an honest broker ... in Middle East negotiations, we also know that our critical contribution will often be to exert quiet, behind-the-scenes influence and persuasion. ... We will do our part, but we cannot do your part as well. The United States and the Soviet Union will provide encouragement, advice, proposals, and views to help the peace process. None of this, however, will relieve you, the parties, of the obligation of making peace. If you won't do it, we certainly can't. ... [W]e cannot want peace more than you [do].[34]

With the end of the ceremonial part of the Madrid Peace Conference, the formal role of the United States and the Soviet Union also came to an end. As Baker had said in his closing remarks, the United States had some ideas of how to bridge the gaps between the parties, but it could not advance them unless both sides wanted Baker to do so. Israel, however, rejected any American involvement in the face-to-face negotiations and feared an "imposed" solution. The Arabs, in contrast, wanted the United States to continue playing an active role in the peace talks. They believed that without such an active U.S. role, there would be no progress in the peace talks.

What made this situation complicated was the fact that not only Shamir but also Yasser Arafat were suspicious of the American intentions. He feared that the United States and Israel were trying to build an "alternative leadership" in the territories and eliminate the PLO's role in the peace negotiations.

With this kind of suspicion, one could hardly expect any breakthrough in Madrid. Nevertheless, President Bush and Secretary Baker did not despair. They considered the public maximalist views of the parties only bargaining positions. They believed that once the parties moved to face-to-face negotiations, they would try to reach a fair settlement. Before coming to Madrid, Baker urged Israel and the Palestinians to exchange some confidence-building measures (CBM). He urged the Palestinians, for example, to announce the end of the Intifada in return for Israel's announcing the suspension of the settlement activity in the West Bank. This did not happen in Madrid and was unlikely to happen in the bilateral, face-to-face negotiations.

Indeed, despite its undeniable success, the Madrid Peace Conference did not achieve any breakthrough. Despite four rounds of bilateral negotiations in Washington during Shamir's term as prime minister, President Bush was unable to go beyond his initial success. By June 1992 the peace process in which Baker had invested so much energy appeared to be going nowhere. The lack of progress that characterized most of 1992 was due not only to the fact that it was an election year in both Israel and the United States but mostly to an American error in judgment as to how much pressure the Bush administration could apply on Shamir in order to force Israel to accept the new regional balance of power that emerged in the aftermath of the Persian Gulf War.

Domestic political instability in Israel and the disarray in the PLO's leadership were additional elements that brought the peace process to a standstill. In addition to the widening gap in Israel between Labor and Likud, Shamir faced a serious and genuine political crisis within his own right-wing coalition parties. Due to this crisis, in January 1992 Shamir reached an agreement with Labor to dissolve the Knesset and hold new parliamentary elections on June 23, 1992.

These sharp divisions within the Israeli political body enabled both the United States and Egypt to actively interfere in Israel's domestic affairs, trying to isolate Shamir and helping in his eventual downfall. The tool that the United States had used to achieve this goal was Israel's request for $10 billion in loan guarantees to help absorb the massive Soviet Jewish immigration. The policy target, however, was the freezing of all Israeli settlement activity in the West Bank and the Gaza Strip, including East Jerusalem. Thus, the intensity of the Shamir–Bush discord, the president's determination to achieve his policy goals and his perceived pro-Arab bias—real or imagined—were among the main reasons that brought the peace process to a standstill.

Secretary Baker himself, in a revealing private discussion with Hanan Ashrawi, the Palestinian spokeswoman in Madrid and Washington and currently a member of Arafat's Palestine Authority, seems to confirm this conclusion. Baker's meeting with Ashrawi took place shortly after President Clinton's victory, and its content was reported by Mamdouh Nofal, a former commander of the military wing of the Popular Democratic Front for the Liberation of Palestine (PDFLP), which is based in Damascus, and for some time Arafat's national security adviser. Nofal was part of the team that monitored, from Tunis, the secret negotiations in Oslo, and he had access to all documents relating to the Israeli–Palestinian negotiations. In a recent series of articles published by a London-based Arabic daily, Nofal wrote:

Arafat believed that Baker was fair with the Palestinians. Therefore, before Baker left the White House, Arafat wanted Ashrawi to hear the secretary's assessment of Clinton's future policy. Ashrawi quoted Baker as having told her that, had Bush been re-elected, he [Baker] would have pushed the peace process even more aggressively, especially after Rabin's victory over Shamir. . . . He added that "we [Bush and Baker] have paid the price for our confrontation with Shamir and for our position on the loan guarantees." As for the future, Baker told Ashrawi: "Don't expect any serious pressure on Israel from the new Clinton administration. . . . So, my advice to you—don't delay the peace process. Try to get from Israel whatever you can get."[35]

Indeed, the confrontation between Bush and Shamir was resumed immediately after the Madrid Peace Conference. It was not limited only to the issue of the loan guarantees but also included subjects related to the peace process. During a meeting at the White House on November 22, 1991, Bush, Baker, and Shamir discussed the next phase of the bilateral negotiations between Israel and its Arab neighbors. Shamir reiterated his position that the face-to-face negotiations should be held in the region, alternating between Israel and the three Arab countries—Jordan, Syria, and Lebanon. Since the Arabs had already rejected this idea, Baker said that he would explore the possibility of holding the talks in Rome or in Nicosia. Pending an agreement on the venue, Baker suggested to hold the first two rounds of the bilateral talks in Washington. Shamir again objected. The Israeli prime minister explained that his objection to Washington should not be perceived as directed against the United States. He simply feared that, instead of negotiating seriously with Israel, the Arab delegations would prefer to talk to U.S. officials, hoping that the United States would deliver Israel to them. The subject remained open for further consultations.[36]

The next day, however, while in New York, Shamir was surprised to learn that Hanan Ashrawi, the Palestinian spokesperson, told ABC in Jerusalem that the Palestinians had agreed to hold the first round of the negotiations in Washington on December 4. The Israeli prime minister was furious. In his meeting with the president and the secretary the previous day, he had not been told that the Arab parties had been already invited to Washington. Asked to comment on the ABC report, the State Department confirmed that U.S. diplomats were instructed "not to haggle" over any condition. All that U.S. diplomats had to do was just convey a message to the parties involved. That was the proposal—Washington, D.C., December 4. Let us know . . .

Angered and frustrated, Shamir decided to put an end to this modus operandi. His position was that it was not up to the United States to run the peace process. The American role should be limited to helping the parties to meet. It was up to the parties to decide what kind of American assistance they needed. However, knowing that Shamir was opposed to Washington, the Arab countries were quick to accept the American venue. Realizing that he had been outmaneuvered, Shamir decided to challenge Baker on the date of the next round of negotiations. He informed the secretary that Israel would not be able to come to Washington on December 4 "because of Hanukkah." He suggested December 9 instead. Everybody knew, of course, that Hanukkah is not a religious holiday and that even Orthodox Jews work during this period. Therefore, the administration decided to ignore Shamir's objection and went ahead with the proposed date. On December 4 the Israeli delegation did not show up in Washington. It informed the State Department that, as Shamir had proposed, the Israelis would come on

December 9. On December 9 it was the Arabs' turn to play their game. They informed the State Department that December 9 was the "anniversary of the Intifada," and they had to attend a memorial service at Washington's mosque. Some correspondents who did not know the background for this "haggling" thought that the whole episode was "childish." For the Israelis, however, it was a "message" to Baker, well conveyed.

Eventually, the bilateral negotiations opened in Washington on December 10 and lasted until December 19. To facilitate the dialogue and to build mutual trust, Baker proposed some ideas of his own. To Syria and Israel, for example, he suggested a preliminary discussion on "what if." If Israel withdrew from the Golan, what would the Syrians give Israel in return, and vice versa? If Syria gave Israel full peace, what would Israel be prepared to give in return? To Israel and Lebanon, Baker suggested that, as a confidence-building measure, the Israeli-financed South Lebanese Army should withdraw from Jezin, on the crossroad from Southern Lebanon and Beirut. Israel rejected those ideas. Israel wanted to make sure that the Arab delegations understood that these were direct, face-to-face negotiations, with no intermediaries and no cosponsors. It was up to the parties to negotiate their own agenda.

Indeed, in the next few days and weeks, American officials limited their role to administrative problems only. Despite persistent Arab requests that the United States advance proposals of its own, the United States sent the delegates back to the negotiating table.

This first round of bilateral negotiations in Washington received little attention in the American media. The front pages of the American newspapers were filled instead with stories about John Sununu's resignation as White House chief of staff and the Smith–Kennedy rape trial in Florida.

The following three rounds of negotiations in Washington did not produce any progress either. By March 1992 Israel and the Arab countries seemed resigned to the idea that no breakthrough was to be expected before the Israeli elections in June. This view was asserted following Yitzhak Rabin's victory over Shimon Peres in the primary elections within the Labor Party. The "change of guards" in Labor gave the Israelis a preferred alternative to Shamir. Unlike Peres, whom Israelis considered "manipulative" and "distrustful," Rabin, the former chief of staff and former defense minister, had always been regarded as credible, and Israelis trusted his ability to give them peace with security.

Indeed, on June 23 Yitzhak Rabin won the Israeli parliamentary elections and reduced Likud's power in the Knesset. Shortly after he was sworn in as prime minister, Rabin was invited to meet with Bush in Kennebunkport, Maine. The president granted Rabin the $10 billion in loan guarantees that he had denied to Shamir and announced the resumption of the peace negotiations between Israel and its Arab neighbors. However, due to the American presidential elections, the following five rounds of bilateral negotiations in Washington did not produce any breakthrough. The defeat of President Bush brought new players to the White House. Eventually, it was President Clinton who reaped the fruits of the secret Israeli–Palestinian negotiations in Oslo and the Israeli–Jordanian peace treaty.

NOTES

1. Discussion with author, Bethlehem, February 2, 1990.
2. Davar, Tel Aviv, September 25, 1990.
3. Discussion with author, New York, September 1990.
4. Maariv, Tel Aviv, April 14, 1989.
5. Kol Israel, Jerusalem, May 14, 1989.
6. Address by Baker, distributed by U.S. Embassy, Tel Aviv, May 25, 1989.
7. Moshe Arens, *Broken Covenant* (New York: Simon and Schuster, 1995), p. 74.
8. *New York Daily News*, October 11, 1989.
9. Maariv, Tel Aviv, October 6, 1989.
10. Arens, *Broken Covenant*, p. 117.
11. *Jerusalem Post*, international edition, week ending March 24, 1990.
12. Radio Baghdad, in Arabic, April 1, 1990.
13. Maariv, Tel Aviv, April 5, 1990.
14. Kot Israel, Radio Baghdad, Radio Cairo, May 30, 1990.
15. *Times* (London), June 13, 1990.
16. El-Masa, Cairo, July 28, 1990.
17. Discussion with Shoval, Tel Aviv, October 7,1990. Shoval was note-taker.
18. Ibid.
19. Ibid.
20. Bush press conference. Text distributed by U.S. Embassy in Tel Aviv.
21. Yediot Aharonot, Tel Aviv, January 16, 1996.
22. *New York Times*, September 13, 1991.
23. Davar, Tel Aviv, September 14, 1991.
24. Arens, *Broken Covenant*, p. 249.
25. For full text of Baker's letter, see William Quandt, *Peace Process* (Washington, DC: Brookings Institution, 1993), Appendix M.
26. Hanan Ashrawi, *This Side of Peace* (New York: Simon and Schuster, 1995), p. 100.
27. Mahmoud Nofal, El-Hayat, London, March 2, 1996.
28. Yitzhak Shamir, *Summing Up* (London: Weidenfeld and Nicholson, 1994), p. 237.
29. Author's discussion with Shamir, Tel-Aviv, June 17, 1996.
30. Shamir, *Summing Up*, p. 238.
31. *New York Times*, October 31, 1991.
32. *New York Times*, November 1, 1991.
33. Text of speech, *New York Times*, ibid.
34. *New York Times*, November 2, 1991.
35. Mahmoud Nofal, El-Hayat, London, February 28, 1996.
36. Yitzhak Shamir, briefing with Israeli correspondents, Washington, November 22, 1991.

5

The Agent-Structure Question in Theory: President Bush's Role during the Persian Gulf Crisis

Steve A. Yetiv

The 1990–1991 Gulf crisis, which was triggered by Iraq's stunning invasion of Kuwait, was far more than a political, economic, and ultimately military conflict between the U.S.-led coalition and Iraq. Behind the political machinations, the economic sanctions against Iraq, and high-tech wizardry of the air war, another story was unfolding. This was the story of individuals, acting from within their own societies and cultures, facing their own set of constraints, and attempting to shape events.

At a general level, this paper explores the role of the individual in world affairs and in the process addresses some core questions. To what extent do individuals shape their environment? How much free will do leaders have? Can specific individuals really cause great change? While the focus here is on the Gulf crisis, these questions resonate in other contexts as well. Indeed, the question of whether the environment defines the individual or vice versa is probably as old as humankind itself. It is a question that is neither time- nor culture-bound, for in every era and place the struggle to chart one's destiny against the numerous constraints and obstacles that may limit free will has been germane.

The issue of the relation between individual and environment is relevant in nearly all disciplines, from literature, where it is a classic leitmotif; to sociology, where it is central to theory; to political science, where the issue of the role and impact of particular leaders is vital. The issue crosscuts and is partly tied to three major and in some ways related theoretical literatures. The first is decision making in which competing models and explanations are given for how nations make decisions.[1] The second is the question of the three levels of analysis. Here the role of the individual is weighed against two other levels of analysis: that of the state, its government and internal processes, and that of the system of internation relations and global processes.[2] The third literature revolves around the more philosophical and abstract work on the agent-structure question.[3]

The latter question explores the nature of both agents and structures, their interrelationship, and the relative importance of the agent relative to the structure.[4] Thus, in economics we might ask to what extent the structure of the market, be it monopolistic or oligopolistic, for instance, determines the behavior of the firm, while in international relations we may examine the impact of a multipolar world structure on the state as an agent, and vice versa.

While the present work can be located and is related to parts of the literatures cited earlier, and may be read with them in mind, it restricts itself to an empirical examination of the role of the individual versus the environment. While the theoretical issues embedded in these literatures are grand, they require more anchoring in reality. Thus, if we seek to obtain a better sense of the role of the individual relative to the decision-making environment, we need more in-depth cases that assess the actions of the individuals in light of the domestic, regional, and international constraints under which they acted. Although each case will be different, an accumulation of case studies may yield some broader insights into the conditions under which individuals from a variety of backgrounds and cultures can play a central role in world affairs.[5]

ARGUMENT

This paper explores the question of the individual versus the environment in the context of one of the twentieth century's most significant events, the 1991 Persian Gulf crisis. In response to that invasion, the United States spearheaded Operation Desert Shield, which aimed to protect Saudi Arabia from further potential Iraqi aggression, and then Operation Desert Storm, which began on January 16, 1991, and forcefully evicted Iraqi forces from Kuwait. Because it occurred in the oil-rich Persian Gulf, the crisis affected states and peoples on a global level, altering their daily economic, political, and even social lives.

In particular, I examine the role of President Bush in this crisis and argue that it is a case in which the individual was crucial in defining the political environment, nature, and direction of the crisis. The United States under President Bush certainly did not take action to prevent the invasion and may have inadvertently encouraged it by courting Iraq in the 1980s and sending mixed signals about how it would respond to such aggression. However, once the crisis developed, Bush played a significant role in shaping its nature and conclusion. Both George Bush and Saddam Hussein significantly determined how the crisis unfolded through their own personal decisions. While both leaders were under a set of domestic and international constraints, they also could have made different choices at critical junctures that probably would have sent history down an alternate path.

Interestingly, prior to the Gulf crisis, Bush had a reputation in some quarters as somewhat indecisive. By reneging on his "read my lips, no new taxes" line, he reinforced this impression. The media even began to describe this propensity as reflecting a possible "wimp factor." In contrast to President Ronald Reagan, who appeared exceedingly decisive, Bush appeared much more malleable.

It is thus interesting that during the Gulf crisis, Bush played a critical, defining, and even forceful role. While we could have expected Saddam Hussein, Iraq's authoritarian leader, to play a central role in the crisis, what is more interesting is that Bush, the president of a democratic state who in theory faced greater internal pressures and constraints on decision making than Saddam Hussein, also acted in a predominant manner. While Bush, unlike Saddam, did have to consider seriously a number of constituencies in his decision making, including the public and Congress, he called many of the shots at critical junctures.

SETUP

Before discussing the empirical record, I first examine the general nature of the decision-making structure during the crisis, so as to locate where the president operated in relation to it. I then identify several questions that are important in the effort to assess the importance of the individual and explore these questions against the record. I conclude with some remarks about future research.

THE NATURE OF DECISION MAKING DURING THE GULF CRISIS

The decision-making process during the crisis involved five interrelated levels of interaction. The first level involved bilateral discussions between Bush and trusted colleagues, such as Brent Scowcroft and James Baker, with whom he had established a 35-year friendship. Other officials sometimes did not even know what was going on in these bilateral meetings because Bush, they surmised, shared certain views only with Baker.[6]

The second level consisted of Bush's exclusive group of advisers, the so-called gang of eight. This exclusive group consisted of the president plus his closest advisers—vice president Dan Quayle, White House chief of staff John Sununu, Secretary of State James Baker, Secretary of Defense Richard Cheney, Chairman of the Joint Chiefs of Staff Colin Powell, National Security Adviser Brent Scowcroft, and Robert Gates, Scowcroft's deputy, who acted as a link to the Deputies Committee. This elite group helped the president make the critical decisions of the crisis such as the timing and nature of Operations Desert Shield and Storm.

The Deputies Committee, the third layer of decision making, consisted of six individuals who represented mainly members of the gang of eight. Admiral David Jeremiah, for instance, was Colin Powell's deputy and representative. The committee was chaired by Robert Gates and also involved officials from the Security Council, chiefs of staff, Central Intelligence Agency (CIA), the core agencies of State and Defense, the attorney general, and representatives from the Treasury Department, Commerce, and, sporadically, from other departments.

The deputies, who usually met once or twice a day all week long and through secure video-conferencing, played several roles. They gathered and evaluated the mass of information on the crisis that hit them each day and in this sense were information managers. Moreover, they presented options to the gang of eight through various briefings on issues ranging from burden sharing to dealing with international terrorism. For instance, they identified what the U.S.-led coalition might do in the event that Iraq withdrew partially or fully from Kuwait, a scenario that Richard Haass and others found "quite likely." The committee established a number of tests that Iraq would have to pass, even if it withdrew partially for Kuwait, and it was prepared to release these tests publicly. The goal of the committee was to prevent Saddam from changing the political atmosphere by withdrawing partly from Kuwait, thus allowing him to remain in control of most of Kuwait.[7]

In addition, the committee executed the decisions of the gang of eight. For example, early in the crisis, the United States wanted to stop Saddam's oil flow, which meant that it had to confront Iraqi ships carrying oil. The Deputies actually sat around the room deciding how this would be done. As one member described it, "We wondered, 'Do we hit the rudder, shoot a warning shot across the bow, board the ship?'"[8]

Finally, the committee identified solutions to problems that made sense across agencies and departments. This was critical. By creating common ground for the joint goal of advancing national interests, the committee aimed to avoid the bureaucratic turf wars and miscommunication that often plagued interagency governmental relations.[9]

The fourth layer of decision making was a smaller group taken from the Deputies Committee that involved key officials from State, Defense, the CIA, and the joint chiefs, plus Richard Haass of the National Security Council (NSC), who drafted most of the papers. A separate group led by Lawrence Eagleburger of the State Department focused on the burden-sharing issue.

If the Deputies Committee dealt with day-to-day issues, the smaller group, which engaged in freewheeling discussions in the West Wing conference room of the White House, focused mainly on bigger conceptual planning questions such as: How do we take advantage of this fragile time in history to build a better world? How do we pull together elements of the Middle East peace process? After committee meetings, Haass would draw up three- to six-page summaries of the discussions, which would be sent to each member, who then took it to his boss. Revisions would then be made until a sufficient draft was produced, which might then make its way to the gang of eight and the president. Ideas would then come back down to the committee from the gang of eight for reconsideration or revision.

Finally, particular members of Congress, Congress as an institution, public opinion, interest groups, and foreign leaders affected U.S. decision making at certain junctures. However, their impact was often limited to a particular issue or time period. For instance, Egypt's Hosni Mubarak and Jordan's King Hussein did persuade Bush to allow time for an Arab solution to the crisis, but after this proved a failure, their role in affecting decisions was negligible.

JUDGING THE POWER OF THE INDIVIDUAL

Examining the importance of an individual in any given situation is complex, because innumerable variables are at play that help shape outcomes. In essence, the question revolves around how we can separate out the impact of the individual from that of other variables and from the course of history. Although such a task needs to be approached with some humility, it is useful to examine several questions in judging the significance of individuals.

Was the nature of the situation such that others would have behaved similarly? Did the individual take initiative? Did the actor overcome opposition or simply follow or build consensus? Was the individual unique in ways that contributed to decision making? I explore these questions with regard to the role of President Bush, but they can be adapted for more typical cases as well.

The Situation

The power of American presidents varies according to several general factors. First, they are more likely to exercise influence over military exigencies than over economic issues. This is because many more constituencies become involved in economic issues than in military questions. Fewer people have direct, clear interest in a major national security issues and, even if they did, would unlikely have much access to decision making on it. Second, leaders gain power in crisis situations, where time may be of the essence and where the stakes are often high.[10] Finally, presidents are more likely to have power over foreign affairs, which is the province of the president, than over domestic affairs, which are often politicized. Based on these factors, we would have expected any president to play an important role in the Gulf crisis. Indeed, it was a military crisis in a foreign land where the United States has vital interests.

Nonetheless, it is hardly axiomatic that the United States was destined to confront Iraq in the sands of the Arabian desert. History is seductive in this sense. In retrospect, events seem so logical that we sometimes assume that they had to happen that way or could not have happened in numerous other ways. But history is not so linear. Different individuals and events may send it down other pathways, pathways that remain imaginary because they never occurred but that could have been very real indeed under different circumstances that are not too difficult to fathom. As one high-level official put it, "I can easily imagine that something else would have happened under another president. Being involved in the crisis, I can say that events seem different when they are in the making than in retrospect."[11] Or in the words of another official who was close to events, "[H]ad this been four years earlier, or four years later, it may have come out quite differently."[12]

Initiative

The president definitively took the initiative during the crisis, displaying the vision that his detractors said that he lost at the domestic level. According to his closest advisers, Bush "clearly set the course for American decisionmaking"[13] and was both the "spark plug and fuel" for Deserts Shield and Storm.[14] In Secretary Baker's words, "his role was absolutely critical. He made a visceral decision to reverse the invasion and he was out in front of all his advisers."[15] He contemplated the nature of Iraq's invasion during the weekend following the invasion and then asserted his view in no uncertain terms: "This will not stand."[16] No adviser put those words in his mouth; no scriptwriter fed him those lines. Indeed, at Camp David in the immediate aftermath of the invasion, Bush and his advisers focused primarily on obtaining Saudi cooperation for U.S. entry into the kingdom. Thus, upon returning to the White House Sunday afternoon, August 5, Bush's statement to reporters struck Powell and others who heard this expression on television for the first time.[17]

From the earliest meetings with his advisers, Bush felt strongly about reversing the invasion by force if necessary, and the real question then became how it would be done. Indeed, Bush, while allowing discussion to flow without his initial interference, was determined at the second major NSC meeting on August 3, setting a serious tone against Saddam, after the first meeting on August 2 appeared too relaxed.[18] The fact that Bush was far more "forceful and convinced" than many of his advisers that the United States needed to take a strong stand decreased the range of debate on how to approach Iraq and set the parameters of the agenda on the issue.[19] While Bush initially was willing to let Arab leaders find an Arab solution to the problem, he changed course not only because Margaret Thatcher urged him to take a tougher line but, more importantly, because he thought Saddam was exploiting these efforts to consolidate his hold on Kuwait.[20]

"While the president hoped that economic sanctions would work," General Scowcroft notes, "he made up his mind fairly early on that force would be used if necessary and that planning should be based on the assumption that sanctions would fail."[21]

The controversial, romantic notion of the "New World Order" was also hatched by the president on a fishing trip with Brent Scowcroft. The president understood that failing to take a strong stand against Iraq's aggression would make a mockery of the New World Order concept and set a bad precedent for the post–Cold War world. While Bush was serious about the notion, it was subsequently distorted by the media to mean that the United States would turn over influence to the United Nations. But what the notion referred to was a world that we had sought since the League of Nations and that the end of the Cold War and the rejection of Iraqi aggression had made possible.[22]

Bush's message was repeated and clear. Saddam's brutality must be punished because no "nation should rape, pillage, and brutalize its neighbor."[23] Bush himself decided to up the ante and rhetoric against Saddam; his "spin doctors" were not pulling the strings on this one. He did not waffle or mince his words. Indeed, when aides drafted a speech for him to deliver in Rhode Island in August, he rewrote it on Air Force One for far stronger effect against Saddam.[24] This would occur repeatedly as he tried to paint Saddam into a corner.

In military matters, Bush set the general parameters of objectives but by and large let the military develop particular strategies, unlike Lyndon Johnson on

Vietnam or Jimmy Carter on Iran. However, he, along with Scowcroft, sent Powell, Cheney, and Schwarzkopf back to the drawing board after they saw the first major strategic plan for Operation Desert Storm. Bush, thus, did not hesitate to affect even the military dimension of U.S. foreign policy.

As the months wore on, Bush seemed to personalize the conflict, and Saddam returned the favor. Bush focused on Saddam the individual so much that even Colin Powell was struck by how much it affected Bush's ad hoc policy making, characterized by a lack of consultation with others and extreme vitriol against Saddam. Even Secretary Baker expressed concern to aides that the White House was speeding toward an armed confrontation with Saddam.[25]

The course was thus set—a crash course, that is. Bush drew a line in the sand and warned Saddam not to cross it. Saddam, who could care less about rules, recognized no line. Bush called for Saddam to withdraw from all of Kuwait; Saddam said he would not move an inch. Bush warned of catastrophe for Iraq if Saddam stayed in Kuwait; Saddam, using the great rhetoric of Arabic, warned that rivers of blood would flow if the United States challenged Iraq militarily. "I know I am going to lose," Saddam told French diplomats, " . . . at least I will have the death of a hero."[26] Bush asserted that the war would be quick and decisive; Saddam called for the "Mother of All Battles."

The Opposition

Assessing the opposition that an individual faces in the decision-making process is also important in the overall analysis of the role of the individual. On that score, President Bush was clearly willing, even resigned to using force against Iraq. However, the move toward war was indirectly or directly questioned, but not vigorously opposed, by important people such as Senate Armed Services Committee chairman Sam Nunn, Secretary of State James Baker, General Colin Powell, and Norman Schwarzkopf. Bush's own presiding bishop said to him that using force was immoral even after Bush gave him a report on Iraqi human rights abuses in Kuwait. Such opposition weighed heavily on the president's mind.[27]

While the president made ultimate decisions, the range of views within the gang of eight was fairly large, despite the fact that everyone knew how strongly the president felt. For his part, Schwarzkopf asserted, "If the alternative to dying is sitting out in the sun for another summer, then that's not a bad alternative." Bush's position at the same time was that waiting too long might strengthen Saddam and undermine the coalition. Baker, as well, believed that Iraq was vulnerable to sanctions, that time was "on the side of the international community," and that "patience" was in order.[28] Such differences of views were not insignificant. From his angle, Powell tried to keep options against Iraq open as long as possible, but Bush told him that the United States "couldn't wait forever," which, in Powell's words, "gives you an indication of his 'vital role.'"[29]

Unlike Powell, Bush was very skeptical about economic sanctions. He thought that running economic sanctions longer would only strengthen Saddam.

Moreover, he did not want to give Saddam the opportunity to withdraw from Kuwait with impunity, with his large army and biological, chemical, and nuclear weapons programs intact. In addition, Bush worried that if given too much time, Saddam might develop weapons of mass destruction and perfect his ability to deliver them. He was also concerned that the U.S.-led alliance against Saddam, which he helped develop and nurture, would unravel over time. Finally, time was also a factor for U.S. troops whose morale was in danger of deteriorating.

In late October 1990 Bush began to push for an offensive option against Iraq far sooner than his military officers had wanted. Schwarzkopf, for his part, argued that an effort to dislodge the Iraqi army from Kuwait would be too difficult and bloody and would require twice as much American military capability as Desert Shield forces could muster. If Bush wanted an offensive option, he would have to double U.S. firepower against Iraq. Bush, doubting that economic sanctions would affect Saddam's plans, decided in November to double the size of U.S. forces. As Secretary Baker recalls, all of Bush's advisers agreed with that decision, and all agreed that it should not be announced until after the midterm elections. The administration should have notified Congress prior to releasing this information to the press. However, as a result of a failure to follow standard consultation practices with Congress, this did not occur, thus causing a firestorm on Capitol Hill.[30]

At a broader level, Baker informed Powell, after Powell contacted him to express concern over the march to war, that the State Department was preparing a report on the advantages of waiting for economic sanctions to work. Powell, for his part, argued within the administration and with allied officials against going to war to liberate Kuwait. He viewed war as nasty business and found the discussion of a potential, U.S.-led, "surgical" strike against Iraq to be irresponsible.[31] While Bush did not view Powell as "foot-dragging" on the issue of being tough on Saddam,[32] although others did, clearly Powell preferred a go-slow approach. In the aftermath of the invasion, he tried to redirect the focus in various meetings from liberating Kuwait to defending Saudi Arabia, argued his position with influential members of the broader defense community, and was much more inclined throughout the crisis than was Bush to define U.S. objectives in a limited manner.[33]

Neither Powell nor Schwarzkopf pushed his views on the president. Both of them recognized that it was the president who was calling the shots. In Powell's words, "in our democracy, it is the President, not generals, who makes decisions about going to war. . . . If the President was right, if he decided that it must be war, then my job was to make sure we were ready to go in and win."[34] This, however, raised an interesting question: How powerful should one man be in deciding issues of peace and war in a democracy?

Opposition in Congress was strong enough that the Bush administration questioned whether it should send the "use of force" motion to Congress for a vote. Indeed, Secretary Cheney argued against the move because in his view the United States would have had to attack Iraq anyway, and it had all the authority that it already needed. Moreover, for him, a no vote from Congress, which was dominated by Democrats, would have produced an embarrassment for the administration.

General Scowcroft as well had deep reservations about taking the vote to Congress. Having spent time with the president from the first days following the invasion, he knew that Bush was determined to do what had to be done, which was to force Iraq out of Kuwait, if necessary. If Congress turned the administration down, virtually all of Bush's major advisers would have argued to launch the war anyway.

Although seeking congressional approval was not required by law, it would have increased national unity and sent Saddam, who doubted American will, a strong message. While these and other goals ultimately motivated the president to go to Congress, Bush wanted Saddam to know that his determination was unwavering in any event: "I don't think I need [a resolution from Congress]. There are different opinions on either side of this question, but Saddam Hussein should be under no question on this. I feel that I have the authority to fully implement the United Nations resolutions."[35] Later, however, Bush recalled that he also expected serious impeachment charges to be filed if he did not seek congressional and United Nations approval for launching war against Iraq.[36]

The decision to go the "last mile" in meeting with Iraq's Tariq Aziz prior to launching Desert Storm was also debated seriously. Cheney and Scowcroft were concerned that this would make the United States look weak and send Saddam the wrong message. "But," Scowcroft recalls, "the president felt that to go to war without having a direct meeting with the Iraqis would not be a good idea."[37]

At the outset, most Americans as well did not see the crisis as Bush did. In the view of one top U.S. official, "[T]he public was not united behind a strong line against Saddam at the outset; no powerful images of Iraqi brutality were coming from Kuwait because the cameras couldn't get in; and the president faced a range of opinion around him."[38] Bush had to rally the people.

The level of opposition Bush faced, however, did not manifest itself in vitriolic disagreements or in attempts to undermine his decisions. The gang of eight eventually fell in line with the move toward war, and each core agency carried out its duties. Even at lower levels of decision making, the deputies "were comfortable early on with the notion that force would have to be used if Saddam did not withdraw and believed that sanctions would not work."[39] The public slowly moved toward strong support for the war effort.

Bush's Characteristics and Background

A number of factors particular to George Bush made his role important, above and beyond what might have been expected. First, Bush's World War II experience was important. Interestingly, while Bush, the Ivy League graduate, knew war from experience, Saddam knew it only from imagination and from occasional forays into the battlefield as a self-proclaimed commander in chief. Bush had been the youngest navy pilot during World War II, an eager fighter who flew 58 missions until he was shot down.[40] By contrast, although he entered the Iraqi army at a young age and rose to the rank of colonel, Saddam knew little about military strategy. He certainly did not gain power because of his military credentials; rather, he advanced because of his political savvy, personal connections, and chance events.

Bush remembered how Adolf Hitler had tricked Britain's prime minister Neville Chamberlain in 1938 into believing that Germany's expansive claims would be limited to the Sudetenland. Hitler's ploy at Munich, which led Chamberlain on his return to England to assure the British naively of "peace in our times," was impressed on Bush's mind. He referred to it often during the Gulf crisis.

Following British foreign secretary Douglas Hurd, who compared Saddam to Hitler on the day of the invasion, Bush did the same on August 8 in revisiting the 1930s and the disastrous Western policy of appeasing Hitler. This theme would repeat itself. On October 23, for instance, he asserted that the United States was faced with "Hitler revisited, a totalitarianism and brutality that is naked and unprecedented in modern times. And it must not stand."[41]

When Bush gave the nod to double the U.S. military force in the region and to create the offensive option of Desert Storm, he reported to congressmen in November that he had been reading Martin Gilbert's lengthy history of World War II. Bush, like Maggie Thatcher, was from the old school. Aggression must never be rewarded. Thatcher lived up to that line in the Falkland Islands War, and Bush would do the same in the Gulf.

Although Bush demonized Saddam partly for American public consumption, he also believed that Saddam was treacherous, deceitful, and aggressive. Saddam, however, was no Hitler. Hitler had control over the strongest state in Europe with enormous industrial and military capability. By comparison, Iraq was much weaker. While Saddam brutalized Iraq's Kurds and Shiite populations, this was a far cry from Hitler's planned genocide, his "final solution" that murdered at least 6 million Jewish men, women, and children in the Holocaust and left as many as 4 million other political prisoners dead. While Hitler went on an ambitious, unprovoked, blatant march toward European and possibly world domination, Saddam had some reason to be disgruntled with his one primary military target, Kuwait—and could not possibly dominate the Middle East, much less the whole world.

Second, the president, unlike other U.S. presidents or even some of his key advisers, was familiar with the region. Bush's feeling that he understood foreign affairs, that he had historical experience with aggressors, and that aggression should be checked gave him the confidence and personal mandate to buck his advisers if necessary and to chart the American course through the crisis. His knowledge of the Persian Gulf was critical and evidenced itself in meetings with his advisers and in his interpretation of the level of the Iraqi threat. Dating back to his oil business and interests, his role as director of the CIA, and his lengthy stint as vice president, Bush had started developing a sense of the Middle East and its politics. As one of his close advisers put it, "[H]e was attached to and aware of Persian Gulf politics and acted on the basis of knowledge."[42]

Third, President Bush had strong, long-standing connections with leaders worldwide. To prevent China from using its UN Security Council veto to torpedo U.S.-led efforts against Iraq, Bush personally and effectively handled relations with Beijing, based on years of experience with the Chinese and with the Soviets.[43] As one high-level official put it, "President Bush was potent in part because of his foreign policy background."[44] Foreign leaders trusted and respected him, and this facilitated his effort to take a strong stand against Iraq. While the United States clearly dominated the anti-Iraq effort, allied support was important.

Fourth, Bush enjoyed good relations with his key advisers, with whom he had long-standing friendships. Unlike other presidents such as Richard Nixon, Bush trusted a range of key advisers and the bureaucracies that they represented. He did not have to worry so much about being challenged or undermined directly or indirectly by individuals or by the bureaucracies that they represented. While there were differences among the members of the gang of eight, and although there were instances of questioning who was giving the president bad advice, cooperation on the whole was strong, particularly given the high stakes. As one insider put it, "[T]he harmony, camaraderie, and rapidity of decisions was amazing and all done so well."[45] Indeed, in interviewing the principal actors and those who knew them formally and informally, I was struck not by commonplace interagency and interpersonal rivalries but by their evident absence. In confidence, I expected more backbiting.

President Bush in Retrospect

Bush played a critical role in the crisis in that he took the initiative at key points, asserted his position despite a divergence of views among his advisers, and brought to bear unique characteristics based on his background and beliefs. Although the crisis situation required strong leadership from any president, it is not at all clear that any president would have taken as strong a stand against Saddam as did Bush. Other presidents, for instance, may have let economic sanctions run far longer, thus possibly changing the outcome of the crisis.

Yet while Bush drove U.S. policy at critical junctures, he did not dictate how certain American goals should be accomplished. Military policy was largely left to the military brass, their assistants, and Secretary Cheney. As Powell notes, "Bush never told me what to do militarily."[46] Furthermore, Bush did not interfere much with the work of the deputies, although he was intensely interested in events. As one deputy committee member put it, "I have a mental image of Lyndon Johnson sitting on the floor of the Oval Office, picking targets during the Vietnam war; I also saw George Bush going over photos, but instead he was looking at post-action bomb damage assessment photos."[47]

FUTURE RESEARCH

This paper has examined several questions in the effort to assess the importance of the individual—in this case, President Bush. While the types of questions asked may vary with the case under consideration, the approach in this paper may be informative for other efforts as well.

With regard to future research on the present case, several efforts would be highly useful. First, while I have argued that President Bush played a critical role, this does not mean that other causal factors were unimportant. Further work on this question is clearly needed to offer a more detailed sketch of causality. Additional analysis on the role of bureaucracies and organizations in the decision-making process could be fruitful. This would offer not only more insight into how decisions were made but also fodder for exploring the explanatory potential of the rational actor model as opposed to contending models of decision making. In this regard, future work could explore the role of the State Department and Department of Defense and the coordination between all the major agencies and branches of government. To what extent was the decision based on organizational imperatives or bureaucratic politics? In what measure did decision making follow rational processes?

Second, the theoretical debate about the interaction and role of the agent and structure is age-old, albeit the terms that describe it have become increasingly technical and esoteric to particular disciplines. Although the complexity of the modern world seems to suggest that some of the questions generated by the agent-structure debate can be answered only on a case-by-case basis, it may be possible to identify some conditions under which the agent is likely to be more significant than the structure as a causal variable. This case study can be further explored with particular emphasis on this question.

Third, this case is fit for broader analysis with regard to the three levels of analysis touched on at the outset of this work. While this study focused much attention on the individual level and implicitly argued that the state and system levels were relatively less critical in causing outcomes, additional work on the specific role of these other levels would be useful, particularly for educational purposes. Indeed, while the three levels are taught across the country at an abstract level, more explicit case studies on the issue would be valuable as a learning tool for students.

NOTES

1. Charles F. Hermann, "Changing Course: When Governments Chose to Redirect Foreign Policy, *International Studies Quarterly* 34 (1990): 3–21. Also, on the importance of the personal characteristics of the individual leader, see Charles F. Hermann, *International Crises: Insights from Behavioral Research* (New York: Free Press, 1972); Ole R. Holsti, "Crisis Decision Making," in Philip Tetlock, Jo Husbands, Robert Jervis, P. Stern, and Charles Tilly, eds., *Behavior, Society, and Nuclear War*, vol. 1 (New York: Oxford University Press, 1989), pp. 8–84; Margaret Hermann, "Explaining Foreign Policy Behavior Using Personal Characteristics of Political Leaders, *International Studies Quarterly* 24 (1980): 7–46. On the growing literature that examines how leaders must respond to domestic and international imperatives and constraints simultaneously, see Robert Putnam, "Diplomacy and Domestic Politics: The Logic of Two-Level Games," *In-*

ternational Organization 42 (1988): 427–60; David Skidmore and Valerie Hudson, eds., *The Limits of State Autonomy: Societal Groups and Foreign Policy Formation* (Boulder, CO: Westview Press, 1993).

2. This analysis was elevated in importance in Kenneth Waltz, *Man, the State, and War* (New York: W.W. Norton, 1957). See Harold and Margaret Sprout, *Man–Milieu Relationship Hypotheses in the Context of International Politics* (Princeton, NJ: Princeton University Press, 1956).

3. For a discussion of how the agent-structure and levels of analysis problems relate, see Martin Hollis and Steve Smith, "Beware of Gurus: Structure and Action in International Relations," *Review of International Studies* 17 (1991): 393–410. See also Alexander Wendt, "Levels of Analysis vs. Agents and Structures: Part III," *Review of International Studies* 18 (1992): 181–85.

4. On the nature of the agent-structure problem, see Alexander E. Wendt, "The Agent-Structure Problem in International Relations Theory," *International Organization* 41 (Summer 1987): 335–70.

5. For one such effort, see Richard Hermann, "The Construction of Images in International Relations Theory: American, Russian, and Islamic World Views," paper presented at the 34th Annual Conference of the International Studies Association, Acapulco, Mexico, March 23–27, 1993.

6. Personal interview with General Colin Powell, Chairman, Joint Chiefs of Staff, Alexandria, VA, May 30, 1996.

7. This paragraph is based on a phone interview with Richard Haass, special assistant to the president for Near East and South Asian affairs, June 13, 1996.

8. Personal interview with David Jeremiah, vice chairman, Joint Chiefs of Staff, Washington, DC, June 26, 1996.

9. Ibid.

10. On decision making in crises, see Hermann, *International Crises*; Alexander L. George, *Presidential Decision-Making in Foreign Policy: The Effective Use of Information and Advice* (Boulder, CO: Westview Press, 1980); Richard Ned Lebow, *Between Peace and War: The Nature of International Crisis* (Baltimore: Johns Hopkins University Press, 1981).

11. Phone interview with Richard Haass.

12. Personal interview with Sandra Charles, deputy national security adviser for Near East and South Asia, Washington, DC, June 5, 1996).

13. Personal interview with Secretary of State James Baker III, Washington, DC, June 4, 1996.

14. Personal interview with General Colin Powell.

15. Personal interview with Secretary of State James Baker III.

16. Personal interview with General Colin Powell.

17. Frontline interview with General Colin Powell, broadcast January 9 and 10, 1996.

18. Personal interview with General Brent Scowcroft, national security adviser, Washington, DC, June 26, 1996.

19. Phone interview with Lawrence Eagleburger, undersecretary of state, July 23, 1996.

20. Personal interview with Sandra Charles.

21. Personal interview with General Brent Scowcroft.

22. Ibid.

23. "News Conference Remarks, November 30, 1990," *Public Papers of the Presi-*

dents: George Bush, 1990 (Washington, DC: U.S. Government Printing Office, 1991).

24. Ann Devroy, "President on Inexorable Course," *Washington Post*, February 24, 1991, p. A1.

25. Jean Edward Smith, *George Bush's War* (New York: Henry Holt, 1992), pp. 89–90.

26. Quoted in Elaine Sciolino, *The Outlaw State: Saddam Hussein's Quest for Power and the Gulf Crisis* (New York: John Wiley and Sons, 1991), p. 31.

27. George Bush, interview with Bernard Shaw, CNN, March 2, 1996.

28. James A. Baker III, secretary of state, *U.S. Policy in the Persian Gulf*, Hearing, Senate Foreign Relations Committee, 101st Cong., 2nd sess., September 5, 1990, pp. 9–11.

29. Personal interview with General Colin Powell.

30. Personal interview with Secretary of State James Baker III.

31. See Bob Woodward, *The Commanders* (New York: Simon and Schuster, 1991), pp. 220, 299–303.

32. Bush interview with David Frost, PBS, January 16, 1996.

33. Off-the-record, high-level interviews.

34. Colin Powell, *My American Journey* (New York: Random House, 1995), p. 480.

35. "Statement during White House News Conference, 9 January 1991," *Congressional Quarterly*, January 12, 1991, p. 71.

36. George Bush, interview with Bernard Shaw.

37. Personal interview with General Brent Scowcroft.

38. Personal interview with Richard Haass.

39. Ibid.

40. On Bush's life, see Fitzhugh Green, *George Bush: An Intimate Portrait* (New York: Hippocrene Books, 1989).

41. Quoted in *New York Times*, November 13, 1990.

42. Personal interview with Sandra Charles.

43. Personal interview with Secretary of State James Baker III.

44. Author's interview, off-the-record, June 17, 1996.

45. Personal interview with Sandra Charles.

46. Personal interview with General Colin Powell.

47. Personal interview with David Jeremiah.

Discussant: Richard N. Haass

I stand before you as someone who's been praised as partly responsible for some of the greatest successes of the Bush administration and tarred and feathered as responsible for some of the greatest failures. It's good to be here. My critics are half right, in any case.

We are talking this morning about the Middle East peace process and the Persian Gulf War. I would say they constitute two of the three great accomplishments on the foreign policy side of the Bush administration—the third being the peaceful end to the Cold War and the unification of Germany within NATO [North Atlantic Treaty Organization]. But I'm confident that the two things we are talking about this morning will constitute two of the cardinal accomplishments when historians get around to reviewing the record—at least when this historian gets around to reviewing the record. Let me say something about each—about the peace process and then about the Gulf crisis.

I essentially agree with what I've heard about the peace process this morning. The Madrid Conference was the foundation for a lot of the progress we have seen subsequently. It broke the taboo of face-to-face Israeli–Arab contacts and direct negotiations; it was comprehensive—it involved not simply the Palestinian track or Israel and one of the Arab states but everybody; and it enshrined the concept of step by step, or gradualism, which has been the only approach to peacemaking in the Middle East that has ever worked.

That said, Madrid revealed both what the United States could do—Madrid would never have happened without an awful lot of American involvement—but it also revealed the limits to what the United States could accomplish. By that I mean, once we got people there, what they would do was limited, which is the reality of peacemaking. The United States may be critical, but the United States is not enough.

The bulk of the impetus for peacemaking in the Middle East has to come from the parties themselves, and that was revealed during the Bush administration. It also showed, consistent with what our last speaker just said, that American presidents have to be involved at critical moments and have to be willing to take political risks. There's no safe or easy path to being an effective peacemaker, particularly when the local parties themselves are neither able nor willing to do the work. It's interesting that the two presidents who have been most successful at peacemaking—Jimmy Carter and George Bush—have largely gone unrewarded at home for it. Peacemaking is a difficult business except when the parties themselves are ready to do most of the work. That was the case, say, at Oslo, when Prime Minister Rabin and Chairman Arafat were willing to essentially do it themselves. But that is the exception. For 90 percent of the Bush administration, when you had either a Likud government or a National Unity government in Israel, peacemaking was no easy task. It is a credit to President Bush and those around him that as much was accomplished as it was.

Bobbie Kilberg will be talking later about the U.S.–Israeli relationship. I continue to think it was a bit like Wagner's music: it was not as bad as it sounded. Despite the criticism of the relationship, despite the controversy, it actually was an extraordinarily creative period for U.S.–Israeli relations. We saw things like the repeal in the UN General Assembly of the odious "Zionism is racism" resolution; we saw Israel begin to emerge from its diplomatic isolation; we saw the Madrid process, which, as I said, broke major taboos; we saw Israeli–American strategic cooperation grow; and we saw hundreds of thousands of Soviet Jews reach Israel. When some of the emotions fade, and people look back, I really do think it will be widely seen as an extraordinary period in U.S.–Israeli relations. It wasn't always good, and for some of that Israelis bear the blame; for some of it we do. If there was one thing I would do differently, I would have argued more strongly for toning down the rhetoric on our side. Our language was, at times, unfortunate, but I think the substance of the policy was quite creative and quite productive.

What about the Gulf? The Gulf War became the first crisis of the post–Cold War world, and from where we sat at the time, it had the potential to become the defining crisis. We believed that what we did and what we said would set all sorts of precedents for the way international relations were likely to unfold in the aftermath of the Cold War. So yes, the Gulf War was about oil, but it was about more than oil. It was also about the need to respond to aggression, to establish norms, and it was about the need to put together new forms of American leadership. Indeed, what I think is most important about the Gulf War, about Desert Shield and Desert Storm, is that it established a new form of American leadership.

During the Cold War, the principal form of American leadership was alliances. Well, as you know, in the Persian Gulf, we have no alliance. So when Saddam did invade Kuwait, we could not turn to some Persian Gulf security organization, there being no NATO equivalent in the Gulf. What we did was we cobbled together this unique—or, as they like to say in Washington, "very unique"—coalition of states and organizations doing different things—different divisions of labor, if you will—to meet the threat posed by Saddam. This has become the model of post–Cold War international relations. We don't depend as much on alliances; international organizations, regional bodies, the UN—all can play a role, but they can't bear the lion's share of the burden. American unilateralism offers a limited approach to the world, and what we've learned—whether it's dealing with the Saddams, dealing with the problems of the Korean Peninsula, dealing with Mexican bailouts, or now what we see in Albania (in this case, led by Italy)—is that in almost all international crises, what we are seeing is a sort of ad hoc coalition approach (or, as I like to call them, "posses") where, most often, the United States—not always, but most often—is the sheriff. We lead not simply by what we say but also by what we do. The Gulf War established this mechanism and this instrument for ordering post–Cold War international relations because, after the end of the Cold War, we had lost the structures and the mechanisms that had essentially kept the peace for nearly half a century.

The Gulf War also shows, again, like the Middle East, the importance of presidential leadership in terms of fashioning a coalition and managing public opinion. It also showed, in one area, a wise example of a lack of presidential leadership, which was in the very conscious decision not to "do a Johnson," and by that I mean not to micromanage the military. One of the things that President Bush did most was by doing less: setting the broad parameters of policy but allowing the military professionals to essentially carry it out and to implement it without someone poring over the maps and looking over their shoulders on a day-to-day, minute-to-minute basis.

Now, we've heard this morning some taste of the revisionist critique. Most of the critics say, "Yeah, you did a good job with the war, but you were pretty bad before and you were pretty bad afterward." I would simply say that the revisionists need some revising. Unlike what Professor Haley said, there was no self-deception; there was no self-delusion. None of us thought that Saddam Hussein before the war was a candidate for the Boy Scouts. What we thought was that we had had some limited cooperation with Iraq and Saddam in previous years during Iraq's war against Iran during the Reagan administration and that we thought it was worth exploring, in an extremely limited way, whether we might be able to continue or expand upon that cooperation. We didn't know if it would work; we had very few illusions. We thought we would try for two reasons. First, if it did work, it would lead to influence over the most capable country in the Persian Gulf. Iraq is the one country that has it all: population, water, oil, a very talented people. It was certainly worth exploring whether this was a country that we could potentially work with. Second, there was simply no appetite—in the region or internationally—for a policy of sanctioning or containment of Iraq. And I would just say as an aside, we've seen over the last few years what happens when the United States embarks on unilateral policies of sanctioning and containment: we tend to be the ones who get more isolated. We have seen it in the case of Cuba with Helms-Burton and in the cases of both Libya and Iran. Unilateral approaches to dealing with rogues simply do not work. So, from where we sat, it was worth exploring the potential to build ties with Iraq, especially as we didn't think we had a very good alternative.

As it turned out, the effort didn't work, and I would simply say that the fact that we tried actually made it much easier to cobble together the coalition that did succeed in winning the war. No one could argue that we had painted Saddam into a corner. You're going to hear from Ambassador El Reedy, but no one in the Arab world could say, "You forced Saddam to do this." There was an understanding, even in the Arab world, that Saddam had brought this crisis upon himself.

I am not going to stand here this morning and say everything we did was ideal, that every statement we made was pitch-perfect, that every action we took was right on the mark. It wasn't. No one bats a thousand, and we didn't either.

But by and large, I think what we tried was the right thing to try, and the fact that it didn't work doesn't mean that it was flawed in concept. It doesn't mean, to me, that simply because a policy did not succeed, there were better alternatives to put into place.

In terms of after the war, again, things did not go as well as what we wanted, but here again I think it was a good example of presidential leadership. As I noted earlier, sometimes less is more. A lot of our critics have argued that we should have "finished the job" and gone to Baghdad. I would simply say, if we had, we'd probably still be there. A lot of the same people who are criticizing us in retrospect for not having done enough would have criticized us for having done too much, for having exceeded our mandate. It's all very well to say we should have continued. Indeed, I would have argued just that if I thought we could have invaded and occupied Iraq, say, on a Tuesday; by Wednesday, we could have turned around and left; and on Thursday, we would have found Iraqis reading *The Federalist Papers* in Arabic translation. Alas, I don't think that was the most likely scenario.

History was very much on our minds—on the president's and those around him—especially the Korean War and the march of folly across the 38th parallel. What we very much wanted to avoid in the aftermath of Desert Storm was an increase in our war aims. Getting carried away in the flush of advance and victory risked snatching defeat from the jaws of victory. So yes, we put limits on what we did, but, again, it was an interesting exercise in presidential power, to limit the extent of what it was we were going to do. Again, the aftermath has clearly not gone as we would have liked, but again, that does not suggest we were necessarily wrong for what we did or didn't do.

Let me just end with one or two more comments. The first relates to the point where Professor Yetiv began, which is whether presidents matter. As he said, there is the "great man" theory of history, as opposed to the "great events" theory of history. Based on my experience of having been up close to this president for four years, the answer to the question of whether presidents matter is yes, and not only yes, but decidedly yes.

History tends to make things look a lot neater than they looked at the time. There was simply nothing inevitable about what happened with the Gulf crisis— the idea that we would say this would not stand and then actually mean it; the idea that you would have someone who would be willing to send half a million of America's young men and women across the world, thinking that the rate of casualties was likely to be far greater than it turned out to be, very uncertain about what would happen. For a president to do all this was not at all obvious at the time, and certainly it is not clear that other presidents in that position would have done it. It was a tremendous roll of the dice. A lot of the presidency at the time seemed to come down to it. For a year, the Gulf essentially defined the Bush presidency. I thought it was a remarkable act of courage to have done that. Again, it's just not clear to me that other people would have weighed the choices in the same way. Indeed, I think if some other people had been in the Oval Office at the time, we'd still be seeing if sanctions could work to get Saddam out of what little was left with Kuwait.

Similarly with the peace process. To be effective in the peace process, as I said, when the locals themselves are not willing to do the bulk of the running, means an American president has to engage. Most of all, he has to engage with his rhetoric. The words of the presidency, the bully pulpit of the presidency, are critical. That is the way we shape domestic opinion; it's often the way we shape international opinion. President Bush was essentially willing to use his words to urge countries or parties to do things and to discourage them from doing things that he and we thought were unhelpful. Needless to say, it wasn't always popular; needless to say, he probably paid a political price for it. But again, it was an effective use of presidential power.

So I end with where I began, in two areas—the Middle East and the Persian Gulf—where we saw extraordinary accomplishments. This is not to argue that everything went perfectly or to be self-serving. But in those two areas, as well as in Europe, with the peaceful end of what really was the third great struggle of this century, you have the foundation stones of an awfully impressive foreign policy record. My hunch is that, when the legacy of George Bush is finally put together, these three events—the Middle East, the Gulf, and German unification with the end of the Cold War—will stand out as probably the three principal accomplishments.

Discussant: Bobbie Greene Kilberg

I am probably the odd duck on this panel since I am a domestic policymaker and politician by trade. You might legitimately ask, What is she doing on this panel, why and how does domestic politics interrelate with foreign policy, and what was the role of that interrelationship in the White House? I should start out by saying that I headed the Office of Public Liaison and that the job of the Office of Public Liaison was twofold: number one, it was to be sure that the various groups in the American body politic had an ability to come in and express their views, particularly on domestic issues, and that those views would become part of the formulation when the president made a decision on domestic policy; and number two, once the president made a decision, it was our job to go out and to sell that decision to those interest groups as something they ought to be supporting, the theory being that if you consult them on the way in, they're more likely to support you on the way out, or at least not actively oppose you.

The foreign policy arena is obviously very different, and I think my number one point would be that George Bush, as president, never made a foreign policy decision based on domestic political concerns. Having said that, in this country there are many domestic groups who care very deeply about foreign policy issues, and it was the job of the Office of Public Liaison to keep in contact with them to be sure they knew where we were going and why, to brief them, and to try to have them feel comfortable with our decisions.

I'd like to make four general points and then one or two specific points. Number one, as I just stated, the president never made a foreign policy decision based on domestic political concerns. If you don't believe that, just look at the statistics of our election loss. In 1988 in the American Jewish community, we got between 32 and 35 percent of the overall Jewish vote and almost 50 percent of young Jewish voters under age 35. In 1992 we were down to below 20 percent, somewhere in the range of 18 to 20 percent.

Number two, George Bush's foreign policy successes, at least based on my layperson's perspective on them, were really based on personal diplomacy, and that's what the title of this panel is: "The Middle East Peace Process: Personal Diplomacy." George Bush is very much a people person, and, over the 20 years before he became president of the United States, the number of relationships he developed with leaders throughout the world was extraordinary. General Scowcroft mentioned those relationships last evening in the symposium, and Governor Sununu also tells wonderful stories about them.

When President Bush went on his first foreign trip as president to the Far East, Sununu accompanied him, and when they came back, I said to Sununu, "Well, how did it go, John?" He replied, "I'm fascinated, I'm absolutely fascinated! I never saw this side of George Bush before. We went to four or five countries. Every single place we went, the president knew all the leaders." It is important to note that President Bush knew not just the prime ministers or the presidents, but the education ministers, the finance ministers, the defense ministers. He'd known them for 20 years. He knew their spouses, he knew their kids, he knew who was going to which school, who was in trouble, and who was doing well. These were extraordinary relationships that he had carefully built and cultivated and that I think many of his foreign policy successes were based on. Richard Haass will have to confirm this, but I believe that when the president made the phone calls to foreign policy leaders immediately after Desert Shield started, he called about 120 heads of state over a period of two to three days. Individually picked up the phone and called each one. The Egyptian ambassador knows that well. There's no other president who has worked that way. You can't package that, you can't market it, you can't sell it. It was personal to George Bush, and I think it affected everything he did in foreign policy.

Number three, how did this personal approach to foreign policy relate to the Middle East? The American Jewish community has historically had a very strong relationship with American presidents, and George Bush had a strong relationship with much of the American Jewish community. He also was developing a relationship with members of the Arab American community. The Arab American community had not historically come to the White House, but he encouraged them, and we encouraged them, to do so. The American Jewish community became a conduit for messages between the White House and Israel—and I think this is what Richard indicated that I was going to talk about—and individuals within the community became the interpreters of messages and events. I can't think of American foreign policy in any other area being conducted in this manner or at least being supplemented in this manner. Arab American leaders also began to have a feel for how to do this during Desert Shield and Desert Storm, and, according to Governor Sununu, a number of Arab American leaders had discussions with leaders in Syria and Jordan during the war that were reported back to the White House.

Why did the American Jewish community become a conduit of communication back and forth between the White House and Israel? The basic bottom line—which Professor Segev referred to—was that George Bush had no rapport with Prime Minister Shamir. They didn't relate to each other, they didn't understand each other, and it was a rather difficult relationship. I will return to this fact shortly.

The fourth and last last general point I want to make is that over the long term foreign policy must have domestic support in order to succeed in the United States. The Office of Public Liaison took the generation of that domestic support very seriously. Specifically and particularly during the Gulf crisis, every briefing that we did on any subject with any group—business group, labor group, environmental group, consumer group, Jewish American group, Arab American group, African American group, Hispanic group, any group—included a briefing on Desert Storm and Desert Shield. We would line up the briefings to meet Richard Haass' schedule, and he or his deputy would address every group. We very consciously built support. That was our job in Public Liaison. The Gulf was front and center in every mailing our office sent out and every speech our staff members made.

A few specific points about President Bush and the Jewish community. George Bush's relationship with the Jewish community was complex. In front of large audiences, his personality was more reserved, certainly, than Ronald Reagan's. But in small group settings and one-on-one, he was warm, relaxed, and open. Most of the Jewish community leadership loved Ronald Reagan on Israel and felt he was devoted to its security. If you look at President Reagan's positions line by line, I don't believe they were very different from those of President Bush, yet the perception was very different, our rhetoric was different, and Ronald Reagan's personality made a big difference. George Bush also wasn't Jack Kemp. A standard joke in the Jewish community was that half its members thought Kemp was Jewish. Jack can wear a yarmulke comfortably; he can go to anybody's bar mitzvah or wedding and fit right in. George Bush, with his reserved WASP background, didn't have that advantage.

Yet, if you take a look at what George Bush did during the period of his vice presidency and presidency, it is very impressive: the rescue of Ethiopian Jews, who never would have gotten out without the firm and skillful diplomatic intervention of Vice President Bush; strong support of Soviet Jewry as vice president; the emigration of over 500,000 Soviet Jews to Israel, when he was president, with the American Jewish community actively participating in the development and implementation of this policy; lifting of travel restrictions for Syrian Jews; the rescinding of the "Zionism is racism" resolution in the UN; hate crimes legislation; a State of the Union Address in 1990 where he strongly condemned racism and anti-Semitism; the public repudiation of David Duke—Bush stood up and said, "David Duke does not represent the Republican Party, I would never vote for him for any office, and I hope the people of Louisiana will not vote for him for governor."

Having said all this, the Jewish community was still skeptical about President Bush on the Middle East and very concerned about having direct access to him on this issue. We had a number of competing power centers within the Jewish community to deal with. We had the National Jewish Coalition, which was a group of Republican Jewish leaders who believed that they should be the "gatekeepers" of who in the Jewish community could come in to see the president. We had the President's Conference of Major National Jewish Organizations, consisting of about 50 major groups, which believed that it should decide who came to see the president. We had all the individual groups—B'nai B'rith, the Anti-Defamation League, the Orthodox organizations, the American Jewish Congress, the American Jewish Committee, and so on—most of which were members of the President's Conference but also believed that each of their groups should come in separately to see President Bush.

Because of the numbers and the competition, from 1989 through 1991, we had 20 meetings between the president and the American Jewish community. That's 20 meetings in the White House around the table in the Roosevelt Room or in Room 450 of old Executive Office Building, the Roosevelt Room being a seminar kind of session. That does not count the small private meetings in the Oval Office with the president, initiated either by the president or by leaders of the American Jewish community, to talk about issues, mostly related to the Middle East. During that same time period, the Arab American community came in to see the president four times. The first was five days after the Iraqi invasion of Kuwait; the second was six weeks later; the third was during the Gulf War; and the fourth was after Madrid. They were just getting organized, and they did not have the same clout as their Jewish counterparts, but they were beginning to develop a structure and get themselves going politically. This list of meetings does not include the briefings that the Office of Public Liaison had separately with Jewish American groups and with Arab American groups without the president. Those briefings were particularly numerous with the Jewish community, totaling 22 in 1989 and over 60 during our four years in office, all aimed at listening to Jewish community concerns and discussing the president's policies on both foreign and domestic issues.

What happened when the president would sit down with the Jewish community to discuss the Middle East? It was very interesting, and it related to his relationship—or lack thereof—with Prime Minister Shamir. The president had a very difficult time getting through to Shamir, trying to understand what made him tick. There was a lack of trust there. For example, I believe there was a feeling on the president's part that Prime Minister Shamir would say one thing on settlements and then turn around and do something else the next minute and that Shamir was not being truthful with him. That was of great concern to the president, and he would use meetings in the Oval Office with American Jewish leaders to express that concern. The president would sit in his office and have a meeting with Max Fisher or George Klein or Jack Stein or Gordon Zacks, and he would talk about settlements. Like clockwork, the participants would leave the Oval Office; they'd use a West Wing phone or return to their hotels and make a call. Within 10 minutes, Shamir would know precisely what had happened in the Oval Office. The president knew that this was the routine that would be followed. He was not distressed by it; he used it. It was just the way things worked, and it was fascinating to watch. The same thing would happen in Roosevelt Room discussion meetings with a broader list of Jewish leaders.

I asked the president once whether he would spend some social time with Shamir, away from official functions in a relaxed setting. I don't know if you knew this, Richard, but we were sitting there one day, and he told me that he really enjoyed spending time with Mubarak. The president said that when Mubarak was at the White House, he asked him if he would like to go to a baseball game, and they went to the Baltimore Orioles baseball game and had a wonderful time. As you all probably know, the president played baseball at Yale, and Mubarak, if he didn't play, certainly was an active observer. So I replied, "Well, that's good, Mr. President, but I don't think Shamir is a baseball fan. Why don't you take him to Camp David just to relax?" The president looked at me in absolute astonishment and said, "What would we do at Camp David? How would we spend our time?" I think that was the crux of the problem. There was not an ability to communicate with each other.

Part of the problem with this process of communicating with Shamir through the Jewish community was that the president would say X to an American Jewish leader, but that leader perhaps would hear X plus Y and then would call Shamir, who perhaps would hear X plus Y plus Z; and, when it eventually came back from Shamir, it was W. That is of concern in running foreign policy.

John Sununu, who was our chief of staff and, as many of you know, is Lebanese American, is a very fair individual, and he didn't want anyone in the Jewish community to believe that he was hostile to the community or to Israel because of his ethnic background. So he would bend over backward to give American Jewish leaders access to the president. But when Brent Scowcroft finally said, "Enough! This process of carrying personal messages is not working," Sununu promised Scowcroft and Richard Haass and myself that he wouldn't allow it to happen any longer. However, occasionally it still occurred with close friends of the president such as Max Fisher, who would come in for a meeting with Sununu, and, before we knew it, John would be walking Max Fisher down to the Oval Office. Not knowing this, I would have gone back to my office thinking everything was fine, only to find a message from Governor Sununu's secretary saying, "You'd better come over here, Max Fisher's in the Oval Office." So I would run over to the Oval Office, and there would be Max Fisher with the president and with Governor Sununu but without Brent Scowcroft. So I would run down to the other end of the hallway and say, "Brent, Max Fisher's in the Oval Office with the president," and Scowcroft would stop whatever he was doing and would race into the Oval Office so he would know what was happening in that conversation.

Overall, I think the conduit worked from time to time, but it also caused problems. I'm not sure I would recommend it, but it occurred by necessity—the necessity of keeping those lines of communication open. The president said to me on more than one occasion that it had been so different with Rabin, and I don't think it is any surprise to anyone that, as a personal matter, George Bush much preferred Mr. Rabin because there was a genuine warmth in their relationship, which Mrs. Bush and Mrs. Rabin also shared.

Discussant: Joan Peters

I think that one of the advantages (or disadvantages, as the case may be) is that, being late in the discussant's role, I have seen a lot covered that I intended to cover.

But we're speaking of personal diplomacy, at least partly. I think we're wandering a little bit off personal diplomacy, which I'd like to do. But in the nature of personal diplomacy, it's quite interesting, I think, to look back on the Camp David accords and just before the Camp David accords, when President Sadat—the late and great President Sadat—walked over the water and went to Jerusalem to be with Prime Minister Begin. It was significant—I was at the White House at that time—that for weeks there was a bowled-over, outraged reaction within the staff of the White House; the United States had not been quite privy to the timing on this trip, so it took several weeks to formulate, with Moshe Dayan's assistance, the need for "Camp David" to bring it all together, with the United States as the leader of the group.

Personal diplomacy, no question, has colored everything that we've done with the Israel–Arab conflict since 1948, but it also is true that there has been a consistency of American policy, regardless of who was the president. I'm going to throw out a couple of posits for you because I've been thinking about them, and they may very well be wrong. But nevertheless, I'd like to throw them out.

It's not entirely clear to some of us—and we had a discussion at a foreign policy roundtable recently—that the Arab countries would have rejected Israel out of hand as a coalition partner to the Gulf War. At Desert Storm time, the Arabs were sufficiently, I believe, threatened as a group by the combined threat of the attack of Saudi Arabia and Kuwait that it was possible—among some minds, at least—that Israel could have been accepted as a partner to the coalition. How would that have affected the results of Oslo, for example? What seems clear is the fact that, at the end of the war, U.S. policy had denied Israel the right to defend itself, which had been promised to Israel; the denial of that right to retaliate against the aggression of Iraq into Israel's heartland—which was a great demoralization to Israel. However, Shamir, the prime minister, of course, later wrote that it was a necessity and that he acquiesced to the United States' demands that Israel keep its hands tied behind its back.

I was at Desert Storm; I had been in Egypt, and I was visiting there when the Desert Storm war became imminent. I went to Israel, and I shared the gas masks with people in various areas with their children. I saw that the demoralization was a different kind of attitude than I'd ever seen, and I'd been in the midst of the Yom Kippur War with the Israelis and the Egyptians at various times during that war. The demoralization and the difference came because there was no semblance of knowledge about what was in the weapons that were going to come at them, if they did come at them. Israel was isolated entirely. Israel was a client state in the eyes of the world and particularly in the Arab world.

Again, I understand the evidence to show that Israel had less than the best intelligence at times, but it's rather interesting that, until Professor Segev just mentioned it now, I've hardly ever heard Israel's prowess in taking out the Iraqi nuclear reactor described as being totally responsible for the possibility to achieve Desert Storm. Had Iraq kept the nuclear reactor, had it been intact and not been taken out in 1981, what would the world have been like? Was that an intelligence failure, or was it one of the most salient gestures that have been perpetrated in the twentieth century?

The violation by the Bush–Baker administration of its promise to accord Israel her right to retaliate was seen as a necessary violation. James Baker writes very clearly about his thoughts on why and why not the violation of the promise to Israel. Even though Prime Minister Shamir agrees in his own memoirs about this topic, one must wonder what would have happened had there been at least the capability for Israel to get the code, which would have given it permission to defend itself, even if the code was not used.

The idea of compromising Israel's security at that time is the same behavior at the present in Jerusalem. Many asked, Would the actions of Peres and Beilin, who were then the Israeli leaders at Oslo, have been the same? Would they have mentioned Jerusalem specifically? Would there have been as much acquiescence on the explicit naming of certain unmentionables as negotiable at Oslo if Israel indeed had been made to feel as if it were an equal partner and not a client state? Some students of the area have pondered that question.

James Baker was appointed secretary of state in 1989, and *Time* magazine quoted him as saying, "The trick is getting them"—meaning Israel—"where you want them: on your terms. Then you control the situation, not them. You have the options, pull the trigger or don't. It doesn't matter once you've got them where you want them. The important thing is knowing that it's in your hands, that you can do whatever you determine is in your interest to do." That was February 13 in an article by Michael Kramer in *Time* magazine. It was not the first time that such an attitude had been described by an American secretary of state, an American foreign affairs commentator, or a president. Ambassador Sam Lewis, considered a great friend to Israel, said to me during an interview sometime earlier, in the 1970s, that a particular U.S. policy decision was unfair to Israel, but that was "irrelevant, because the United States *had* to have a Middle East deal that year." In fact, from 1967 on—June 1967, when Israel won the Six-Day War and annexed "East Jerusalem"—as it's called today—the part of Jerusalem that had been off-limits for Jews—President Johnson delivered a speech on June 19. He said there must be a peaceful settlement after the Six-Day War, but he never mentioned border changes.

I have a whole list of statements by various presidents from 1967 on. All the U.S. governments for 30 years have objected to the annexation of Jerusalem on one level or another, even though it was legal. International law has said that it is legal. Annexation is on the side of international law. But in terms of personal diplomacy, it was Johnson who gave the Phantoms to Israel. It was, in the final analysis, Bush who kept the Iraqi threat against Israel from ultimately having its effect, which was, of course, as was said here earlier, to burn Israel down.

No matter how President Bush reacted, his uniqueness would have been limited in any event. Certainly, the intelligence failure of the Bush administration to anticipate Iraq's aggression was not more serious than the recognition of the extent of the ayatollah's threat in Iran against our shah. Just before the fall of the shah, I led a fact-finding mission to Iran, and we were assured by all the powers that be, in the Iranian government and in our own embassy, that the only threat to Iran was the Soviet Union. They even flew us around the perimeters of Iran and the Soviet border, replete with caviar and champagne, to show us that this was the only threat, while, on the ground, the volcano of the ayatollah was bubbling, and, just a couple of months later, would erupt.

Discussant: Abdel Raouf El Reedy

Thank you very much for being here, and for inviting me and giving me the opportunity of seeing old friends, like Richard Haass and Mr. Segev and others. I am going to speak on the Middle East peace process, because I am going to speak after this panel on Desert Storm and the Iraqi occupation and invasion of Kuwait. But before I do so, I would like to make two points that are related to what has been said today.

First point, with regard to Iraq (which I will elaborate on in the next panel), no question that we in Egypt had been deceived by Saddam Hussein. I think that Saddam Hussein had planned this aggression sometime before, and part of his planning was when he proposed to Egypt to become a member of what was called the Arab Cooperation Council. He planned to include Egypt in this council so as to neutralize Egypt when the moment came for carrying out his plan of invading and annexing Kuwait.

The other point that has been mentioned by Richard Haass and Mr. Segev is that there is no question that the environment created by the invasion of Kuwait and Desert Storm and the diplomacy that was conducted at that time made it possible for the United States—President Bush, Secretary Baker—to be able to convene the Madrid Conference. Part of this success, ironically, is due to Iraq. When Iraq made a linkage between its occupation of Kuwait and Israel's occupation of the West Bank and Gaza, that linkage created or reinforced the momentum and increased the pressure for President Bush—supported, of course, by President Mubarak—to make the commitment that as soon as Kuwait is liberated, there will be a very serious effort to solve the basic problems of the Middle East, the most important of which is, of course, the Arab–Israeli conflict.

Madrid, I think, was a success despite the problems that we have today, and they are obvious. Madrid was the first occasion when all the parties to the Middle East problem got together and negotiated around the same table, face-to-face. It allowed for the Oslo Agreement to be concluded and for the Jordan–Israeli Peace Treaty and also the negotiations with Syria, which have been actually interrupted since 1974—it was only in Madrid in 1991, 17 years after 1974, that negotiations took place between Syria and Israel—and the fact that we today have a mechanism, a structure, that could be used for negotiations. It is in place.

I also would like to agree with Mr. Segev that, without a very active American participation and role, peace negotiations—I was in Camp David for three weeks; I attended the talks. Without the role of President Carter, nothing would have happened. Also, without the active role of people like Richard Haass and, of course, Secretary Baker and others, it would not have been possible.

Now, having referred to the objective conditions that created the environment for the Madrid Conference, I would like only to add another objective factor, and that is the Soviet factor, because the Gulf crisis took place while the Soviet Union was already unraveling. The two superpowers were already working together on several fronts, including the diplomatic front in opposition to Iraq's invasion of Kuwait. The Soviet Union, being weakened, being under the pressure of the United States, turned the Soviet Union from its traditional role as a spoiler into a supporter of the peace process.

I would now wish to refer to the personal or the subjective factors that made the Madrid Conference possible. The first point I would like to make here is that which has been mentioned, and it's a theme that has been played from the very beginning of this conference on George Bush, which is the personal diplomacy of President Bush. I believe that, without the counseling and support of President Bush, Secretary Baker would not have been able to manage to have the agreement on Madrid. I would like here to refer to what I think is an important point with regard to President Bush.

President Bush was a man who knew the Middle East, and this goes back to the time when he was permanent representative of the United States to the United Nations. He attended the four-power talks that were taking place between the big powers and that were examining all aspects of the Palestine problem and of the Middle East crisis, as it was called at that time. President Bush, I know from personal experience, at that time had very strong relations with his colleagues who were versed with this problem. He knew, despite the fact that diplomatic relations were not in place between Egypt and the United States, but he had a very good relation with the permanent representatives of Egypt at that time, the late Muhammed Hasi Nisayeh and Ahmed Esmat Abdel Meguid, who is now the secretary-general of the Arab League. Of course, he became after that the head of the Central Intelligence Agency and eight years as a vice president in the Reagan administration.

I would also like to mention here the role of Secretary Baker, because I believe that President Bush was served well by the able Secretary Baker, who had the full confidence and support of President Bush. Baker was savvy in Washington politics; he did not need actually to seek the support of powerful lobbies in Washington. He employed his talents and negotiating skills, no question about that.

But also I would like, of course, naturally, to refer to the role of Egypt, President Mubarak. I think you have referred to the telephone diplomacy that was taking place. Many times I would receive a call from Richard Haass telling me that President Bush is going to telephone today President Mubarak, and President Mubarak also, from the very beginning, urged President Bush to do something about the peace process, to which, of course, President Bush responded. Even before the Gulf crisis, there were the five points of Secretary Baker, and there was one year of very active diplomacy before the Gulf crisis. But unfortunately, it did not produce anything because of the relationship that existed with Prime Minister Shamir, and Shamir did not want to cooperate with that process.

I would also like to refer to the role of Syria. One reason that the peace initiative was successful was that it had every party around the table, including Syria. Syria has its influence in the Arab world; it gained its right to be a part of the process as a result of its participation in the coalition that liberated Kuwait. Syria's participation in the Madrid Conference made it possible for Saudi Arabia and the Gulf Arab countries to come to the conference, which, in turn, brought every Arab country into the negotiation.

In conclusion, the successful construction of a peace process and putting it in place were made possible by these objective and subjective factors and the skillful diplomacy of Secretary Baker. Unfortunately, now the process is stalled, but that is another story. I hope we will have some time, either during this conference or in the future, to deal with that.

Discussant: Murray Silberman

I think another intelligence failure of the Israeli intelligence community was the failure to read that *Time* magazine interview about Baker. That perhaps may have been more significant than some of their other failures. But then again, when we talk about failures, we can talk about the failure of the CIA to anticipate the collapse of the Soviet Union—they read about it in the *Times* the way we all did—and what was going on in Iraq and also the Israeli failure to anticipate, or to understand fully, what was going on on the other side of the Suez in 1973. So maybe, since we are all really human beings and we're all fallible, the fallibility also is reflected in these intelligence communities, many of whose operatives are prisoners of their own passions and their own convictions, and they slant information to make sure that the results are in line, or the conclusions are in line, with their own thinking.

I have just a few comments. I agree with what everyone has said, that the Madrid Conference was the framework for jump-starting the peace process, and I think Iraq made an important contribution to this process—and maybe one day we should even give it credit. One day, some cartoonist might even draw a cartoon showing Saddam Hussein getting some kind of a secondary Nobel Peace Prize for that.

I'd like to dwell for a moment on this issue of vision and war aims. I'm in agreement with Professor Haley's point that there was no real understanding of what was going on in Baghdad in the years right after the Iran–Iraq War, and certainly there was no real understanding what was going on in the weeks and months just before the invasion of Kuwait. Now, I also agree with Dr. Haass that probably we couldn't have done much about it even if we had wanted to. Unilateral sanctions don't work very well for the reasons that he stated. But I think somehow we could have drawn some kind of a line—maybe not in the sand, but in the minds of the Iraqis—to understand that, "Hey, wait a second; we're not going to buy this thing," and let them start worrying what kind of reaction it will have.

But I think the more significant failure and lack of vision was when the war ended. First of all, why it ended so quickly the way it did, and I think that sudden ending of the war—which I think caught a lot of people by surprise—was a reflection of the lack of vision. Very often, the apologists in Washington said, "Well, what we were really doing is simply following the UN resolution." For the first time (or one of the few times), all of a sudden the UN was raised, or the Security Council resolution was raised. We're there simply to implement the terms of that resolution calling for the eviction of Iraq from Kuwait. But I think that didn't fly very well. I think it was somehow a weak explanation of our war aims. I don't think there was any real conception of what we should be doing in

Iraq once we had defeated the Iraqi army.

I think in terms of understanding Israeli politics and its foreign policy, many people have observed that Israel has no foreign policy. It has only domestic policy, and that domestic policy is what really drives what might be called foreign policy. For example, if one looks at the strains within the present Netanyahu coalition, or the rifts and divisions there, we understand the limits on Netanyahu's maneuverability in trying to promote or sabotage the peace process—I don't know which. But I think more attention should have been paid to that.

At one point, Professor Segev pointed out that when there was this National Unity government, in effect there were two governments, and the Arab states and the United States played on that very well, and they dealt with Shamir when they had to, but they often dealt with Rabin and Peres as really autonomous units within that government. I think we have to understand more about internal divisions within Israel in order to understand its foreign policy. That, I think, is very important. Right now, the desire on the part of many of those who want to push the peace process forward is to hope that a Labor government—not necessarily headed by Peres, perhaps by Ehud Barak—if that group came to power, perhaps the peace process would move forward. The point that I want to make is that we have to have a better understanding of internal Israeli politics because therein lie the true signs and pressures in favor of one direction or another.

Lastly, I want to touch on the settlements. I think one of the real moves forward by the Bush administration was to make the Israelis understand that settlements were not a humanitarian issue; they were not a matter of finding a place for people to live. This was an issue that was critical for the entire peace process. In his paper, Professor Segev made the point that for the Palestinians, nothing comes closer to the issue of peace or no peace, war or no war, than the settlements issue. President Bush and Secretary of State Baker really laid it on the line with the Israelis and said, "Look, this is not going to be allowed. We're not going to allow this $10 billion loan guarantee to be used for settlements." They, in effect, were telling him this is not a humanitarian issue; this goes to the heart of the peace process. Settlements will drive, or will help or hinder, the peace process.

In conclusion, I want to say this was an insightful summation and analysis of the events in the Middle East during the Bush administration.

Panelist Discussion: Bernard J. Firestone, Moderator

Bernard J. Firestone: With permission of the panelists, I do have to allow the paper presenters to respond to anything they'd like to, and I believe Professor Haley might have something to say.

P. Edward Haley: Let me repeat again that I have no desire to detract from the victory in Desert Storm, and I've certainly no wish to criticize Richard Haass personally. I use your book, Dick, for my Ph.D. students—*Conflicts Unending*—I make them all read it, so there's no personal side of this whatsoever. But to say that our policy toward Saddam before the war was just a little off is like saying it's all right to suffer Pearl Harbor because eventually we defeated Japan, and all kinds of good things came out of that defeat. After millions of casualties and dropping two atomic bombs on Japan, we had the Marshall Plan, European unification, democratization of Germany and Japan, and even the downfall of worldwide Communism. U.S. policy toward Saddam Hussein wasn't just a little off; it was way, way off, and it was pursued way too long. Assistant Secretary Murphy, for example, argued that the purpose of this policy is to wrap Saddam Hussein in a "cocoon of moderation." Ambassador Glaspie, when she was finally allowed to testify, said there was nothing wrong with the policy. We did the right thing. We thought we could change him, we hoped we could change him, and we didn't carry out the policy effectively. There's a real problem here. Saying that U.S. policy was a little off blinds us to what was wrong and to what might be done about similar problems in the future.

I'll just list a couple of effects. The Bush policy put the United States in the position of *demandeur*—of asking other countries to do our bidding when, in fact, they need our cooperation. It blinded us to the implications of a massive buildup in military strength. Unclassified figures for 1990 show Iraq's defense budget accounted for 20 percent of gross domestic product; they had 5,000 main battle tanks, 6,000 armored personnel carriers. One could go on and on. I urge us to look again at this and to apply it very carefully in the post–Cold War world.

Firestone: Dr. Haass, would you like to respond?

Richard N. Haass: I would say just two things. It's very hard to predict behavior that is 100 percent against the self-interest of the party that carries it out. So the fact that we did not accurately predict Saddam's invasion seems to me to bear out that lesson. Second, I really do think the basic idea of trying to work out a relationship with Saddam was the best of the options that we had. But this is what historians do. They fight battles long after the battles themselves are over, and I look forward to continuing it.

Firestone: Ms. Kilberg, I believe you want to say something?

Bobbie Greene Kilberg: I just want to add one last point about the carrying of messages back and forth between the Jewish community and Israel. I don't want to leave the impression that there was pandemonium out there with unauthorized messages going all over the place. It's my impression—and Richard can add to this—that, on a number of occasions, the president and Scowcroft would purposely schedule an Oval Office session with leaders of the American Jewish community to convey a message to Shamir and to be sure that the message was understood. It was the necessity of having that kind of backdoor communication that I find interesting, both from a political science and a politics viewpoint.

Firestone: Dr. Yetiv?

Steve A. Yetiv: I think the question of how the United States should have dealt with Saddam Hussein in the 1980s raises a much deeper question, and I want to focus some attention on it very briefly. The question is, How do you deal with an actor that's threatening? Sometimes accommodating a threatening actor can make that actor less threatening, and you can bring that actor back into the international arena. Sometimes if you accommodate a threatening actor, you might make that actor even more threatening. So the question is, When do you accommodate, and when do you oppose? This is a critical question, not only related to how to deal with Saddam but related to how to deal with the world writ large. I don't think we have theoretical frameworks or conceptual frameworks to deal with this question, and I hope that in the future more attention will focus on the issue of, Under what conditions do you accommodate, and under what conditions do you oppose?

Firestone: Professor Segev?

Samuel Segev: I would like to touch very briefly on a question that I did not mention in my presentation. It is in my paper, but not in the oral presentation. It is the issue of the loan guarantees. This was, undoubtedly, one of the most irritating issues in the American–Israel relationship. This was the first time that the U.S. administration used the loan guarantees as a stick to force a political solution to a purely humanitarian issue. The Israelis, at least, felt deceived by the Bush administration on this issue. I had access to information relating to a secret meeting that took place between Prime Minister Shamir and President Bush right before the Persian Gulf War. Contrary to what is generally believed, that the issue of the loan guarantees was raised after the Persian Gulf War, I can reveal here that it was raised long before. In that meeting in December 1990, when Bush asked Prime Minister Shamir not to preempt against Iraq and that, should there be a retaliation in case Saddam Hussein launched missiles on Israel, Israel should not retaliate without prior coordination with the United States, Bush got the Israeli commitment to follow the American lead on this issue. During that meeting, Shamir raised the issue of the loan guarantees, and for the first time the amount of $10 billion was mentioned. Mr. Shamir told me that he was given to understand by President Bush that, "Once we finish with this crisis with Saddam Hussein, you will raise the problem again, and I will be very supportive of the issue." Right after the Persian Gulf War, when the issue was raised, Israel was asked to defer its request for the loan guarantees until after Labor Day. Shamir agreed. But then and all of a sudden, the closer the United States came to the Madrid Peace Conference, the more the Bush administration used the loan guarantee as a stick to force Israel to take positions that it did not feel comfortable with. So I wanted to make this issue clear.

Firestone: Ms. Peters?

Joan Peters: Just a very brief comment on the settlements. The time in which the settlements that had been inaugurated after the Six-Day War by the Labor government became an "obstacle to peace" was also the time in which apartheid was allowed into the Middle East in a way that the United States never allowed it in South Africa. I think that settlements must be seen in the context that they are seen within Israel, within the Arab areas of Israel, within the Arab population of Israel. There would be no more chance of having the Arab population of Israel expelled than the man in the moon, and by the same token, I believe that, in the context of the peace process, the Arabs and the Israelis must look at the settlements that are now home to almost 150,000 Jews in the territories, in the West Bank, in Judea, Samaria—however you want to talk about it—must be seen as a community that has to live together. I think the people who live in the settlements know that better than the ones who don't.

Part IV

Latin America

6

The Bush Administration and Panama

Douglas G. Brinkley

> The lessons I absorbed from Panama confirmed all my convictions over the preceding twenty years since the days of doubt over Vietnam. Have a clear political objective and stick to it. Use all the force necessary and do not apologize for going in big if that is what it takes.
>
> Colin Powell, *My American Journey* (1995)

The first major Bush administration speech on Latin American relations was delivered on March 30, 1989, by Secretary of State James A. Baker III at the Carter Center in Atlanta. Reaganesque in rhetoric, Baker denounced the Soviet Union for using Latin America as a "dumping ground for their arms," insisting that Soviet president Mikhail Gorbachev's glasnost policy of openness did not nullify the Monroe Doctrine as hemispheric law.

But in one sense the speech represented a significant departure from the Reagan administration's foreign policies: Baker called for a "new partnership" between the United States and Latin and Central America, one that would make democracy flourish, markets open, and drug cartels vanish. With Jimmy Carter—the President who had given the canal back to the Panamanians—standing symbolically at his side, Baker made it clear that the Bush administration's approach to hemispheric affairs would be based on constant consultation, respect for the democratic process, and the ultimate goal of ousting dictators. Little did Baker realize that only five weeks later Panama would emerge as the Bush administration's first genuine foreign policy crisis—and a litmus test for the "new partnership."[1]

Throughout the hemisphere Baker's speech was hailed as a warning to Nicaragua's Marxist Sandinistas as well as to Panama's General Manuel Antonio Noriega, whose illegal dictatorial regime was about to be put on public trial via democratic elections that May. "We were confident that in open elections Noriega would lose badly," Baker later recalled.[2]

The U.S. government's obsession with purging Noriega from power arose from myriad—and complex—reasons. For starters, Noriega had been on the CIA [Central Intelligence Agency] and Defense Intelligence Agency payroll for 25 years. Then, throughout the mid-1980s he became closely associated with official Washington by joining President Reagan in support of the Nicaraguan contra army that was fighting the Sandinistas.[3]

But after Noriega shifted his allegiance to the pro-Soviet Sandinistas in 1987, U.S. officials did everything possible to punish and excoriate him. On February 4, 1988, a U.S. Justice Department anxious to flush the crooked caudillo from his palace got two federal grand juries to indict Noriega for drug trafficking and racketeering.[4] As Baker put it, Noriega was now "up to his epaulets in drug trafficking"; what's more, the sort of intelligence information he used to sell to the CIA was no longer deemed worth the risk of dealing with him. Noriega had become persona non grata to the Reagan administration.[5]

"I found Noriega an unappealing man, with his pockmarked face, beady, darting eyes, and arrogant swagger," noted Colin Powell, soon to be chairman of the Joint Chiefs of Staff (JCS). "I immediately had the crawling sense that I was in the presence of evil." Noriega had joined Libya's Muammar Qaddafi, Iraq's Saddam Hussein, and Cuba's Fidel Castro in the ranks of "dangerous thugs" whose reckless regimes were seen as threats to America's national security.[6]

It came as no surprise to Washington insiders, therefore, that shortly after George Bush was sworn in as president the ouster of Noriega became a foreign policy priority. A year earlier, when some in the Reagan administration had argued for cutting a deal with the Panamanian strongman—dropping the indictments if he agreed to go into exile—then-Vice President Bush had taken a hard line. Influenced by Los Angeles Police Chief Daryl Gates, who viewed the drug indictments as a point of law and order, Bush made a rare, fiery dissent at a White House meeting with President Reagan, arguing that offering Noriega a deal would be a catastrophic mistake. "How can we make the argument we're getting tough on drug dealers if we let this guy off?" Bush asked. Reagan shrugged off the question and offered Noriega the exile deal—which the obstinate general refused.[7]

Now, a year later, Bush was president, and a deal with Noriega was out of the question. Instead, the new administration seriously considered covert operations—including kidnapping Noriega (or "snatching" him, as Baker phrased it). "The press simply reported that Bush was going after Noriega," CIA director William Webster later complained. That just wasn't the case. He had a broader vision to protect the Panama Canal, to maintain stability in the region. In the end Bush decided that democratic elections in Panama would be the smartest way to end an illegal regime.[8]

As the May 7 elections approached, the CIA and State Department received intelligence that indicated Noriega—who wasn't himself running for office—was staging "a campaign of systematic fraud," including manipulation of voter registrations, police intimidation of opposition candidates, and ballot-stuffing on behalf of his handpicked candidates. "From all reports, Noriega has already rigged the results and will steal the election massively," Baker warned President Bush in a May 5 memorandum. The secretary of state then recommended that the United States send "a clear, decisive signal" to Noriega that it would not be "business as usual . . . once he steals the election." When it came to Panama, in other words, the Bush administration was willing to forgo the niceties of diplomatic consultations and was prepared, if necessary, for military confrontation.[9]

As Baker predicted, Noriega stole the election from opposition candidate Guillermo Endara. Worse, one of Endara's two vice presidential candidates, Guillermo (Billy) Ford, was beaten bloody on Election Day and his bodyguard murdered. Noriega had been foolish to assume that his strong-arm attempts at "retail fraud" would guarantee his flunky's victory; instead, with an international group of election observers headed by Jimmy Carter looking on, Noriega's candidate lost by a margin of 3 to 1. So Noriega officially nullified the election results. Stunned at the general's hubris, a furious Carter publicly declared in Spanish, "The government is taking the election by fraud. It's robbing the people of their legitimate rights. . . . I hope there will be a worldwide outcry against a dictator who stole this election from his own people."[10] Carter then exhorted the leaders of every country in the Organization of American States (OAS)—all of whom respected the ex-president for engineering the Panama Canal Treaties and promoting human rights—to take action against Noriega for refusing to relinquish power. "Carter's word was believed by all the OAS leaders," Baker recalled. "But we had to work hard to convince them to denounce Noriega by name."[11]

It is impossible to comprehend Noriega's refusal to relinquish control in rational terms. By thumbing his nose at the world community, he made sure that his days in power were numbered. Furious over Noriega's defiance of the ballot box, President Bush boldly declared on May 11 that "the days of the dictators are over" and announced the evacuation of American dependents in Panama not living on military bases; the recall of U.S. ambassador Arthur Davis; the reduction of the U.S. Embassy's staff by two-thirds; the dispatch of an army brigade to bolster the 12,000 U.S. Southern Command (Southcom) troops permanently stationed in Panama; and, most important, the deployment of U.S. troops to training exercises in regions outside the Canal Zone—a legal move according to a special treaty provision.

"Some of these exercises would be staged in areas the Panamanians considered their exclusive domain," Baker wrote in *The Politics of Diplomacy*. "It was psychological warfare. We wanted Noriega to believe we were coming if he didn't leave first." More to the point, the Bush administration wanted the Panamanian Defense Forces (PDF) to understand that if they were incapable of toppling Noriega themselves, the U.S. military would complete the coup, whether by covert operations or direct force.[12]

Far from overreacting to Noriega's intransigence, the Bush administration proceeded with extreme caution. Rather than order aerial bombings of Panamanian defense installments, Bush, in a policy reversal, gave diplomacy a final try, encouraging the OAS to persuade Noriega to flee into exile before it was too late. Meanwhile, Howard Air Force Base in Panama became a beehive of activity, U.S. bombers circled the skies of Panama City, and troop maneuvers out of Fort Clayton increased 10-fold. In fact, the U.S. Southern Command was conducting joint-service contingency readiness exercises designed to test U.S. forces' ability to respond swiftly and decisively to defend the Panama Canal and protect American lives and property.[13]

To make sure Noriega got the message, in July 1989 the Bush administration replaced Southcom commander General Frederick Woerner, who feared the consequences of getting too tough with Panama's strongman, with General Maxwell "Mad Max" Thurman, a dedicated hawk who reviled Panama's illegal government. "All these measures were designed to shake Noriega's confidence, to convince him and his military that U.S. patience was wearing thin," Baker said recently. Desperate for allies, Noriega sought financial assistance from Libya, moral support from the Sandinistas, and arms from Fidel Castro. To the Bush administration's national security officials, Noriega had become the Muammar Qaddafi of Latin America—"a hostile, radical militant running drugs, allied with our enemies, and in absolute control of a country where American soldiers were stationed to protect and defend the canal," as Baker put it.[14]

But rather than engage in gunboat diplomacy, Bush's people hoped that the PDF would take direct action and overthrow Noriega themselves, replacing him with the democratically elected Guillermo Endara. As Baker later admitted, "We were doing our best to foment a coup."[15]

Unfortunately, the Bush administration soon turned skittish when a disenchanted PDF military officer, Major Moises Giroldi, commander of the Panamanian 4th Infantry Company, offered to stage a coup against Noriega. Giroldi had contacted the CIA, alerting them to his eminent coup attempt, but was uncommunicative as to how the U.S. government could help out. "We were cautious not to be duped," recalled Webster.[16] "The whole affair sounded like amateur night," JCS chairman Powell concluded after reading intelligence reports about Giroldi's cockamamie hopes of ousting Noriega. Powell advised the president not to support the plan; Secretary of Defense Dick Cheney and General Thurman agreed.[17]

But on October 3 Giroldi, with the assistance of several fellow officers, went ahead and waged a coup, even getting so far as to hold Noriega captive in the Comandancia, his own headquarters. But instead of killing Noriega on the spot, a nervous Giroldi allowed the strongman to make a telephone call, which he did, shouting for military reinforcements. Within hours PDF loyalists had freed Noriega and executed nine coup plotters, including Giroldi. "The Americans had failed to accomplish their goal—elimination of me, coaxing an assassination from within," Noriega recalled about the aborted October coup, insisting that Bush was responsible for Giroldi's death.[18]

By refusing to take Giroldi seriously enough to aid his clumsy offensive strike, the Bush administration squandered a superb opportunity to wrest power from Noriega. "Instead of being so skeptical, we should have gone to Giroldi, demanded to know his plan in exchange for our help, assessed his scheme and quietly assisted in its execution," Baker confessed later.

The Bush administration, which had been showered with accolades for its diplomacy when the Berlin Wall was ripped down, was just as roundly criticized for failing to support the Panamanian coup attempt. Critics from the *Washington Post* to House Intelligence Committee Chairman Henry Hyde (R-IL) chastised the administration for its timidity and indecision. Even Senator Jesse Helms (R-NC) lambasted Bush and his men for acting like "a bunch of Keystone Kops, bumping into each other."[19]

In reality, however, the failed October coup sounded the death knell for Manuel Noriega. The Bush foreign policy team of Baker, Cheney, Powell, and NSC [National Security Council] Advisor Brent Scowcroft had learned a lesson and vowed never again to let Noriega escape the noose. "From that moment onward Noriega was finished," Scowcroft bluntly maintains. In a matter of weeks the CIA and the Pentagon had cooked up seven possible PDF coup scenarios, while General Thurman stepped up Southcom's contingency planning for a military invasion.[20]

Not surprisingly, having stared down the "gringos" and survived their coup attempt, Noriega had actually strengthened his grip on Panama and felt free to jail or torture anyone who had supported Major Giroldi. Thus reinflated with hubris, Noriega even turned down a U.S.-approved offer of political asylum in Spain, taking on the role of a modern Pancho Villa defying the Yanquis at every turn. But with polls showing 64 percent of the American public identifying drugs as the nation's number one problem, Noriega was not likely to remain a caudillo for long.[21]

Noriega's anti-Americanism came into full view on December 15 in an inflammatory speech before his puppet National Assembly, where he bragged that "we will sit along the banks of the canal to watch the dead bodies of our enemies pass by." Spurred on by the general's jingoistic posturing, the assembly declared a state of war against the United States and honored Noriega with the title "Maximum Leader."[22]

As could be expected, the day after Noriega's inflammatory anti-American diatribe the situation in Panama turned grim. All year long the PDF had been harassing U.S. soldiers in petty incidents ranging from theft to assault—occurrences that were routinely brushed aside. This time, however, with tensions running high, members of the PDF opened fire on a car carrying four U.S. military officers when it failed to stop at a roadblock outside PDF headquarters in Chorrillo. A U.S. Marine lieutenant was killed, a second soldier injured, and a third who had witnessed the incident detained and beaten. "The wanton murder of an American serviceman was a tragedy that sickened me, but I also knew that our confrontation with Noriega had reached a turning point," Baker said. "We'd just been handed the reason for doing what we should have done in October."[23]

The murder of a U.S. Marine in Panama on December 15 "caused Bush to cross his Rubicon."[24] At an emergency White House meeting on December 17, Bush polled his foreign policy advisers one by one; all agreed the United States had no choice but to invade Panama. "There will be a few dozen casualties if we go," Powell estimated. "If we don't go there will be a few dozen casualties over the next few weeks and we'll still have Noriega." Baker took the hardest line: "Let's take them up on their declaration of war. We shouldn't wait." Cheney and Scowcroft agreed that diplomacy was useless and war in order. "Let's do it," Bush resolved, calling for Operation Blue Spoon to be launched at 1:00 a.m. Wednesday, December 20. For the first time since Reagan's invasion of Grenada in 1983, the United States was going to war and in the largest deployment of troops since Vietnam.[25] Former Soviet leader Mikhail Gorbachev later cynically maintained that the entire Panamanian invasion was "to get America out of its post-Vietnam depression."[26]

The Bush team then immediately set to work, notifying congressional and OAS leaders of the imminent invasion, making certain Endara was ready to take over the Panamanian government, and ordering electronic surveillance equipment to Panama to track Noriega's whereabouts. "There was no turning back," Baker noted.[27]

A few hours before the invasion Cheney changed the invasion's code name from Blue Spoon to Operation Just Cause, a gesture designed to stress that the United States was simply enforcing the democratic will of the Panamanian people.

In the 48 hours between the emergency White House meeting and the launching of Operation Just Cause on December 20, 10,000 U.S. troops backed by gunships and fighter-bombers flew into Panama to rendezvous with the 13,000 soldiers already stationed at the American bases in the canal area. This would be the 14th U.S. military intervention since Panama had declared its independence in 1903 and the first intervention since the 1977 Carter–Torrijos treaties that had pledged the United States would never return.[28]

"[We] could scarcely even conceive of defending ourselves against an overwhelming blitzkrieg," Noriega confessed. "We had never bothered preparing for an American invasion. The idea, then and now, would be idiotic. First of all, invasion of Panama would be a violation of international laws that protected our sovereignty. How does one plan for an invasion from the United States? After all, they were already there, a permanent invasion force."

Although Noriega denied it, he had long been planning for an American invasion, and his contingency plans were executed immediately; PDF troops were deployed in roadblocks all around the capital, a civilian protest march was organized, and civil defense units called "Dignity Battalions" were activated. "But what we could not plan for was an aerial bombardment, which is exactly what happened," Noriega later lamented.

The U.S. Air Force dropped 422 bombs on Panama in 13 hours, destroying the PDF by disconnecting its principal lines of communication. A disoriented Noriega was left to dart about Panama City in a Hyundai, moving to safety from a Dairy Queen, to a schoolhouse, to a hospital. "It was like a nightmare—like falling into a swimming pool and when you try to reach for the safety of a wall or touch bottom, you suddenly realize that walls and bottom had fallen away," Noriega wrote in his memoir. "I couldn't grasp anything or stop my free fall. All

I could see was an endless limitless ocean and thousands of weapons and men hoping to find me in their sights." Eventually Noriega escaped the U.S. manhunt by seeking refuge in the residence of Monsignor Sebastian Laboa, the papal nuncio to Panama.[29]

U.S. undersecretary of state for political affairs Robert Kimmitt immediately sent a diplomatic missive to the Vatican requesting that Noriega be turned over as a fugitive from justice. But it was the Christmas season—the Vatican's busiest time of year—and the Catholic Church was uncertain what to do. On Christmas Day James Baker wrote Vatican secretary of state Agostino Cardinal Casaroli insisting that Noriega be turned over to U.S. authorities: "This is an exception to diplomatic immunity. We've indicted him as a drug dealer. He's a common criminal. We will not let him go because he's a threat to public security. He's a temporary refugee, but he's not entitled to political asylum. And you must understand that having lost American lives to restore democracy in Panama, we cannot allow Noriega to go to any other country than the United States."[30]

The Vatican was in a quandary. For the next two weeks U.S. troops circled the embassy, blaring Guns and Roses' "Eye of Destruction" and other noisy rock songs from giant speakers in a peculiar attempt to unnerve Noriega through questionable art. "It was a low moment in U.S. Army history," Scowcroft later admitted. Blasting rock music was silly, childish, reproachable, "undignified."[31] But in some strange, postmodern way it worked. CNN broadcast the United States versus Noriega showdown continuously, as Panama's "Maximum Leader" was transformed into "Hunted Fugitive," a corrupt drug dealer who had thwarted the will of the Panamanian people and was now hiding in a papal basement. Hunkered down in a dirty T-shirt, baggy Bermuda shorts, and a baseball cap pulled low over his face, forced to listen to American rock and roll, Noriega had become an international joke overnight.

The Panamanian people were demanding his head on a stick. Although the OAS had passed a resolution on December 22 urging the withdrawal of U.S. troops, a CBS News poll taken in Panama in early January found that 92 percent of Panamanian adults approved of the invasion. Before long a mob formed and approached the papal nunciature on January 3, 1990, demanding Noriega. Monsignor Laboa consulted with U.S. major general Wayne Dowling about what to do. After the meeting the monsignor found his resolve and asked Noriega to evacuate his residence; within a few hours Noriega, afraid of being lynched, walked out of the nunciature and surrendered to American forces. He was placed on a helicopter to Howard Air Force Base and delivered to the custody of the U.S. Drug Enforcement Agency.[32]

For the Bush administration, Operation Just Cause was a political as well as a military success. Although 24 U.S. servicemen and 139 PDF troops were killed, President Bush had accomplished all three of his objectives: Manuel Noriega was imprisoned in Miami, Guillermo Endara was installed as president, and the Panama Canal was secure. "The loss of innocent lives was tragic, but we had made every effort to hold down casualties on all sides," Powell stated.[33]

The arrest of Noriega also had a sobering effect on the Medellín against its own drug thugs. Although the OAS had opposed the U.S. invasion of Panama in December, in June 1991 the organization endorsed the Santiago declaration, a U.S.-drafted resolution committing the OAS to collective action wherever democracy was threatened in the region.

The American people also approved of the Bush administration's invasion of Panama, with 74 percent of those polled calling it justified. In fact, the Panamanian invasion had liberated Bush from his predecessor and allowed him to shed his image as a "wimp" once and for all. Whether bombing Panama was morally justified could be debated, but it carried no concern to Bush as he watched his overall approval rating skyrocket to 76 percent. The success also gave Bush's foreign policy team a sense of cohesion and purpose, a post–Cold War U.S. military confidence that would surface again 13 months later in the Persian Gulf War.[34]

"All this flowed from a single event: the President's determination that a naked assault on democracy wouldn't be tolerated," Baker summed up. "In dramatic fashion, the United States had demonstrated once more that it would stand up for democracy, and behind its friends in the hemisphere." The secretary's "new partnership" based on democracy building, backed by U.S military might, was off to a good start.[35]

NOTES

1. Address by James A. Baker III to the Carter Center of Emory University's Consultation on a New Hemispheric Agenda, Atlanta, GA, March 30, 1989, U.S. Department of State Press Release no. 56.

2. Author interview with James Baker III, September 1995.

3. For a discussion of Noriega's relationship with the CIA, see Manuel Noriega and Peter Eisner, *America's Prisoner: The Memoirs of Manuel Noriega* (New York: Random House, 1977), pp. 58–66. Noriega believes that the December 20, 1989, invasion of Panama would never have taken place if Reagan's CIA director William Casey had lived.

4. Ibid., pp. 195–217. Perhaps the most credible witness who claims the drug trafficking charges against Noriega were trumped up is General Fred Woerner, the southern command chief until the fall of 1989, when he was replaced by General Colin Powell. "Overall, I never saw any credible evidence of drug trafficking involving General Noriega," Woerner said. "My analysis was that the U.S. policy of isolating Panama and its military was counterproductive to U.S. interests." Yet it must be remembered that Woerner was fired for having a case of *clientitis* with Noriega.

5. James A. Baker III, *The Politics of Diplomacy* (New York: G.P. Putnam's Sons, 1995), p. 180.

6. Colin Powell, *My American Journey* (New York: Random House, 1995), pp. 412–13.

7. Baker, *The Politics of Diplomacy*, p. 179.

8. Author interview with William Webster, April 1997. Also, Baker, *The Politics of Diplomacy*, p. 181.

9. "White House Memorandum on Panamanian Elections," James A. Baker III to President George Bush, May 5, 1989.

10. Jimmy Carter quoted in L. Gruson, "Noriega Stealing Election, Carter Says,"

New York Times, p. A1. See also Rob Troester, *Jimmy Carter as Peacemaker: A Post-Presidential Biography* (Westport, CT: Greenwood Press, 1996), pp. 104–105.

11. Author interview with Robert Pastor, October 1995. For Carter's account of the May 1989 Panamanian election, see Jimmy Carter, *Talking Peace: A Vision for the Next Generation* (New York: Dutton, 1993), pp. 129–33. Also, author interview with James Baker III.

12. Baker, *The Politics of Diplomacy*, pp. 180–84.

13. For example, see copies of *The Tropic Times*, published in Quarry Heights, Republic of Panama, which detailed increased U.S. military exercises (particularly the August 18, 1989, issue).

14. Baker, *The Politics of Diplomacy*, p. 184.

15. Ibid., p. 185.

16. Author interview with William Webster.

17. Powell, *My American Journey*, p. 418.

18. Noriega and Eisner, *America's Prisoner*, pp. 165–67.

19. Baker, *The Politics of Diplomacy*, pp. 185–88.

20. Author interview with Brent Scowcroft, April 1997. Also see Michael Wines, "U.S. Plans New Effort to Oust Noriega," *New York Times*, November 11, 1989, p. A3.

21. Bruce Bagley, "U.S. Foreign Policy and the War on Drugs: Analysis of a Policy Failure," *Journal of Inter-American Studies and World Affairs* 30 (Summer/Fall 1988): 189–212.

22. Baker, *The Politics of Diplomacy*, p. 188.

23. Ibid.

24. Robert Pastor, *Whirlpool: U.S. Foreign Policy toward Latin America and the Caribbean* (Princeton, NJ: Princeton University Press, 1992), p. 92.

25. Baker, *The Politics of Diplomacy*, pp. 188–94; and Powell, *My American Journey*, pp. 419–34.

26. Author interview with Mikhail Gorbachev, April 1997.

27. Author interview with James A. Baker III.

28. For a history of U.S. intervention in Panama, see Walter LaFeber, *The Panama Canal: The Crisis in Historical Perspective* (New York: Oxford University Press, 1978).

29. Noriega and Eisner, *America's Prisoner*, pp. 10–11.

30. Baker, *The Politics of Diplomacy*, p. 192.

31. Author interview with Brent Scowcroft.

32. Ibid. See also Pastor, *Whirlpool*, p. 93.

33. Powell, *My American Journey*, p. 434. See also Stephen E. Ambrose and Douglas Brinkley, *Rise to Globalism: American Foreign Policy since 1938*, 8th ed. (New York: Viking Penguin, 1997), p. 372.

34. Pastor, *Whirlpool*, p. 93.

35. Baker, *The Politics of Diplomacy*, p. 194.

7

The Failure of Cuba Policy

Jules N. LaRocque

The policy of the Bush administration toward Cuba should be assessed on the basis of what it did not do rather than on what it did. Despite the fact that an opportunity arose to change policy toward Cuba in an important and constructive way and that that opportunity remained open at that stage of President Bush's term in office when his popularity soared due to his Gulf War success, his administration continued to pursue a Cuba policy that could be best described as one of containment of a threatening Communist empire. The analysis that follows outlines that opportunity in some detail. This paper places in sharp focus the question of whether the failure of the Bush administration to seize an opportunity to break from its pattern of vindication of past policies stemmed from lack of political courage, of confidence, of vision, or of some combination of these.

The element of vision enters into the argument that follows because of the particular circumstances that surrounded the emergence of the opportunity presented to the Bush administration to make a major shift in the policy of the United States toward Cuba. These circumstances had implications for the broader realm of policy toward, at the least, the Central American/Caribbean region and perhaps even the entire Western Hemispheric region. For example, a more visionary policy toward Cuba might have enhanced the response to, and the results of, Bush's "Enterprise for the Americas" initiative, announced in June 1990 and promoted during Bush's visits to five South American countries later that year.[1]

The opportunity in question was a set of circumstances made to order for the weaning of Cuba from its state of dependency upon the Soviet Union and its reentry into the community of nations of the Western Hemisphere. The Soviet Union, just prior to its sudden demise, was entering into its program of perestroika, to the success of which the Bush administration was avowedly committed,[2] as evidenced by its waiver of the Jackson–Vanik Amendment and by President Bush's stated desire to see that program succeed (though he had trouble enunciating the word "democratization," which could have been due to partisanship, which would, in turn, imply unfamiliarity with the word).[3]

It seemed clear that Bush's respect for democratization (as reflected by popular election of national leaders) was outcome-dependent. When the results of the voting in Nicaragua in February 1990 were hailed as "a victory for democracy," one had to wonder what the next-most-likely results would have been called. Such an outcome would, indeed, have required substantially different voting and, some might say, would have been a different election; some might have argued, for instance, that for the Sandinistas to win would have required extensive meddling with the electoral process by the government then in power.[4] But a different result need not have substantially vitiated the democratic process; they (the Sandinistas) were leading in polls until the very eve of the election.[5] A Sandinista victory might have presented a timely challenge for U.S. foreign policy. Had the Sandinistas won in what observers could have attested to have been a fair election,[6] it would have been necessary for the foreign policy of the Bush administration to take a meaningful and well-timed step away from the ideology-based Reagan policy toward Central America. That, in turn, might have hastened the day when events in the world could be looked upon as other than vindications of foreign policies of the recent past.

This criterion for evaluating the foreign policy of the Bush administration might be quite generalizable, applicable to even the broader Cold War context. However, the intended focus of the analysis that follows is the Western Hemisphere. Accordingly, events and developments that are not grounded in the hemisphere are omitted from consideration for the time being. That an electoral victory by the Sandinistas would have afforded the Bush administration an excellent opportunity to establish the credibility of its stated intent to support duly elected governments in Central America is assumed. The failure of that result to come to pass raised the price of establishment of that credibility.

So apparently determined was the Bush administration to vindicate the policy of the Reagan administration that much-needed economic assistance was withheld from the newly elected Chamorro government, presumably until the Nicaraguan army, then still under the control of the Sandinista leaders, surrendered its arms, thereby making it safe for the contras to return to their homes and take up peacetime activities. The Sandinistas were, perhaps understandably, reluctant to disarm unilaterally while the contras were still heavily armed. The crippled Nicaraguan economy worsened while the Bush administration—and the Congress—delayed assistance to Nicaragua by attaching sensitive amendments to the appropriations bill that would provide economic assistance to Nicaragua and Panama.

Meanwhile, Chamorro took a gamble in an effort to prevent the increasing economic hardships from bringing about a return to the fighting between the Sandinistas and the contras. She left the Nicaraguan forces under the command of Humberto Ortega (brother of Daniel, the defeated Sandinista presidential candidate), in order to acquire for herself a measure of control over the army. Having brought the defeated Sandinistas virtually into her government, she was able to begin the effective negotiations to reduce armaments on both sides. In sharp contrast to the Bush administration's policies toward Central America, Chamorro chose a course that she hoped would lead to a true reconciliation of the peoples of Nicaragua. On the occasion of her inauguration, she said: "Reconciliation is more beautiful than victory."[7] It was the failure of the Bush administration to inject that spirit of reconciliation into its policy toward Central America that resulted in the administration's missing an opportunity to make constructive change in its Western Hemispheric foreign policy.

During his tour of several Latin American countries in 1990, President Bush might have given the appearance (as presidents sometimes try to do when they visit regions of the Third World) of establishing a new beginning to the administration's policies toward Latin America. However, his speeches at several of his visits, proclaiming victories of democracy and "free markets," had a ring of effort at self-persuasion. They were delivered, in some instances, within earshot of some relatively serious challenges to governments that were not themselves entirely secure. The Bush administration failed, like most administrations before it (and, now, in the wake of the Helms–Burton Act, the one following it), to reconcile itself to Latin America *as it was* (is), including Nicaragua as *it* was, which is a necessary condition for moving U.S. policy toward Latin America forward to where it was in the 1930s—the Good Neighbor Policy. To accomplish this last, however, it will be necessary to welcome—indeed, encourage—Cuba, *as it is*, back into the Western Hemispheric community.

Though the permanence of the Chamorro government was far from established by mere election, economic and military assistance to Nicaragua was quite suddenly cut off by all sources other than the United States. As mentioned earlier, even humanitarian aid from the United States was held up pending satisfactory disposition of armaments by the Sandinista and contra armies. The termination of direct assistance to Nicaragua by the Soviet Union and then, immediately upon the occasion of Chamorro's inauguration, the cessation of assistance from Cuba probably marked the permanent withdrawal from Central America by nondemocratic external influences. The reversibility of those developments seemed unlikely at the time (and still seems so) and invited attention to the future of Soviet involvement in the Western Hemisphere, which is to say, the relationship between the Soviet Union and Cuba. The direction of change in that relationship was readily and easily predictable. Given the determination of the Soviet Union to put its economy on a market basis and the resistance that such reforms were facing at home, where better to make progress than in the external sector, where Cuba was a major partner of the Soviet Union? No important signs appeared suggesting that the Soviet Union *would* attempt to continue in its role of supporting the Cuban economy; indeed, the evidence much more powerfully suggested that it could not.[8]

Two kinds of economic analysis might be appropriate at this juncture. The first is an examination of the substance of the trading relationship between Cuba and the Soviet Union with an eye to determining whether the activity involved could be put on market terms without terribly dislocative repercussions. The other is an assessment of the economic cost, if any, of the failure of the United States to normalize relations with Cuba and accord that country full standing as a trading partner. The former is a relatively easy task, at least in outline form. The latter, because it would entail the use of clumsy counterfactual conditional statements, is perhaps impossible to do satisfactorily.

The annual cost to the Soviet Union for supporting Cuba has been estimated to have reached about $5 billion, though on average it was perhaps closer to $4 billion.[9] Some of the assistance was in the form of subsidies, such as paying higher-than-market prices for Cuban sugar and selling Soviet oil at lower-than-world-market prices.[10] Another important portion of it took the shape of military support. Because the adjustments facing the Soviet economy in the context of perestroika would make the continuation of these costs budgetarily prohibitive, the Soviet Union resolved to put its economic relationship with Cuba on a hard-currency market basis. In the trade in primary products between the two countries (Cuban sugar, Soviet oil), the terms of trade would change in favor of the Soviet Union.[11] However, to the extent that Cuba continued to buy manufactured commodities from the Soviet Union, the terms of trade would move back in Cuba's favor, as Soviet manufacturers would not fare well in markets in which they had to compete with manufactured goods produced in market economies, that is, goods traded for hard currencies.

It was clear that, whatever the outcome might be in terms of trade between Cuba and the Soviet Union, it was necessary that the latter shed the burden of support of an expensive client state. The move at home toward a market-based economy, an essential part of the perestroika program, required the direction of as many as possible of the Soviet Union's resources to the enhancement of supply of goods. Augmenting supplies of commodities on the newly opened markets would, other things unchanged, reduce the degree of instability in the Soviet economy. Given that a substantial portion of Soviet assistance to Cuba consisted of military support and that it might be safe to assume that there was no serious threat to the security of Cuba in light of reduced tensions between the United States and the Soviet sphere of influence, the net *economic* loss to Cuba from withdrawal of Soviet assistance would have been quite small.

Anticipating the withdrawal of Soviet aid, Premier Fidel Castro requested that Gorbachev act in Cuba's behalf in pursuit of achieving normalized relations with the United States. President Bush's reaction to the suggestion was to express surprise that Gorbachev would avail Cuba of his good offices after Castro's open criticism of the program of *perestroika*. Bush added that he would have expected the Soviet Union to react to such chastisement by joining in the effort led by the United States to remove Castro from power by means of economic sanctions or embargo. To that suggestion, Gorbachev responded that Cuba was a sovereign nation and Castro was its legitimate head of state.[12]

The foreign policy of the United States toward Cuba had been relatively stable for many years. Following the revolution that put Fidel Castro in power, each of the superpowers had made one major error. The error by the United States was the badly planned and (perhaps worse?) executed Bay of Pigs invasion. The Soviet error was the ill-advised placement of ballistic missiles in Cuba. The very serious condition created by the missile crisis made Cuba an intractable policy problem for the United States—for administrations of both parties. Democratic presidents could not appear to be amenable to improved relations with Cuba, for fear of charges of being "soft on Communism." A similar, though intraparty, problem would have arisen had a Republican president made any overtures in that direction.[13] Cuba therefore continued to be a policy problem in two ways. It maintained a highly visible Communist presence in the Western Hemisphere, demonstrating that such a presence was possible; it was, therefore an embarrassment to the United States, and it served as a conduit through which the Soviet Union could respond to efforts by the United States to assist and encourage rightist governments and parties in the region. However, the anti-Cuban rhetoric heated up during the Reagan years, and, in the context of a program of assistance to the Nicaraguan contras by the United States, a more substantive anti-Cuban policy seemed to be taking shape. This occurred even while the two superpowers, following the initiative of Gorbachev, were reaching important agreements on issues of a more global nature.

The Bush administration seemed content to continue to treat Cuba as though the contra war was still ongoing. With a diminishing number of plausible anti-Communist targets for policy, opportunities to please the ultraconservative wing of Bush's party became increasingly scarce. But such determination to vindicate past policy could, and, as suggested here, did go too far, resulting in missed opportunities to advance more important policy objectives, such as stability in the Central American and Caribbean regions and perhaps even improvement of the chances of success of perestroika. However, in order to achieve advances toward those ends, it would have been necessary that the Bush administration get into step with the rest of the world and raise the priority of reconciliation of peoples as a criterion of success in foreign policy.

Reconciliation as a basis for policy implies that there are some interests that are shared by the formulator of policy and the political entity that is the target of the policy. The shape of the policy should then become a set of actions that enhance the possibility that the objectives of both parties with respect to the shared interests are advanced. These shared interests can, and indeed usually do, include such broad objectives as security and economic development, but it is more likely that more particular objectives would motivate reconciliation as a basis for policy. The nature of involvement by the United States in Latin America in the 1980s, aside from matters pertaining to the indebtedness of the region's governments to U.S. banks, was dominated by interference in civil wars in Central American countries and efforts to control drug flows from South American countries. Military action was used (either directly or indirectly) or threatened in most cases. All of this raised the suspicion that, should there have arisen any new tensions between the United States and Cuba, the use of force by the United States might very well have occurred. In addition, it would be entirely in keeping with the practice of vindicating past policy. A substantive move of a conciliatory nature by the United States could have gone far to elevate the overall character of the Bush administration's foreign policy and the responses to it.

As mentioned earlier, the Soviet economy needed to be relieved of the burden of its long-standing policy of assistance to Cuba. It was readily apparent that, when that aid was withdrawn, the Cuban economy would have to accommodate itself to the world market system to a considerable extent. That the Cuban economy could not accomplish that accommodation without substantial transitional assistance was questionable then and the absence of much of this aid did seriously retard that transition. There is little doubt that the United States could have, by intervening to aid in the transition of the Cuban economy from dependence upon the Soviet Union to meaningful participation in the world economy, elevated the overall character of the foreign policy of the Bush administration in the Western Hemisphere. Depending upon how well the weaning was accomplished, it might have materially upgraded the administration's foreign policy in other spheres as well. The opportunity was there, and it was missed.

To be successful in reforming its economy, the Soviet Union had to be able to devote as much as possible of its productive capacity to production of goods for its own domestic use, and preferably consumption, or to exports that would earn maximal purchasing power to be applied to the same end. Making reform palatable meant demonstrating that a market economy would result in improved conditions of supply, especially in food products and in manufactured consumer goods. How far the United States was prepared to go under the Bush administration toward providing *direct* assistance to the Soviet Union was a separate issue, but a more open attitude toward Cuba would have aided the process of economic and political reform in the Soviet Union.

The argument is frequently made by members of Bush's political party that the refreshing breezes of so-called free markets, if they are allowed to blow, will sweep away the forces of oppression and bring full political and economic freedom in their wake to the previously oppressed. Yet, given the opportunity to restore normalized relations with Cuba, which would surely remove a very substantial part of the barriers to those breezes, the administration chose instead to attempt to tighten the embargo on Cuba, insisting quite contrarily to the usual rhetoric of openness and the resulting flow of political and economic benefits for the people, in order to force—or induce—Castro to do what he had not done for some 30 years in response to treatment of that kind. Either Bush's partisans and their spokespersons do not themselves believe the rhetoric they promulgate, or they believe in small-mindedly inflicting punishment on the already oppressed peoples who suffer at the hands of regimes such as that of Castro.

It has been obvious since the demise of the Soviet Union that the failure of the Bush administration to seize the opportunity to begin the process of restoring normal relations with Cuba was a serious foreign policy mistake. In the absence of a Cold War context (which did indeed complicate dealing with Cuba), the removal of the blight of a Marxist-Leninist presence in the Western Hemisphere, especially one of such small proportions as Cuba, should present no difficulty.[14] With careful diplomacy, anything offered to the Castro regime that might be called "concessionary" could be engineered in such a way that benefits conferred would, to use a phrase much-loved by Bush's economic policymakers, "trickle down" to the people through increasingly freed-up channels of transactions. What is most egregious about this foreign policy error is that it was made in a temporal context in which, within the same Central American–Caribbean area of influence, a fledgling democratically elected government in Nicaragua was extending the warm embrace of popular reconciliation to its predecessor, which was, until that time, the other Marxist-Leninist presence in the hemisphere. The overall result was a starkly contrasting set of representations of political courageousness.

It is difficult, and has always been so, to determine the economic impact of the policies of the United States toward Cuba. Attempted blockades fail notoriously unless supported by a great majority of the target country's potential trading partners. The embargo effort by the United States against Cuba has rarely, if ever, enjoyed the required support, providing a clear indication that U.S. policy toward Cuba has been out of step with that of most of the rest of the world for a long time. It is, of course, entirely appropriate to regard the *economic form* (i.e., embargo) of policy toward Cuba as mere posturing. But, of course, the Cold War context provided the country with few alternative courses of action.

That these efforts have failed has been a great frustration to some political interests in the United States. That frustration erupted into an action—called the Helms–Burton Act—by the 104th Congress, setting, in the mind of this writer, a new standard in small-mindedness as a characteristic of some foreign policies undertaken by the United States. Helms–Burton has brought forth wrath and ridicule upon the United States by many countries, including some of its closest allies, such as Canada. This current national embarrassment, the like of which should easily have been foreseen years ago, could have been prevented most easily had the Bush administration adopted the spirit of reconciliation so generously displayed by Cuba's Caribbean neighbor Nicaragua, even while the administration watched through a wide-open window.

NOTES

1. Clifford Krauss, "In South America, Bush Finds Warmth and Restiveness," *New York Times*, December 9, 1990.

2. "The Trade Decision: Bush's Remarks on Aid to Kremlin and Plans for Summit," *New York Times*, December 13, 1990.

3. The Jackson–Vanik Amendment is Section 402 of the 1974 Trade Act. Its primary purpose was to impose extra tariffs on imports to the United States from Communist countries that deny its citizens the right of free emigration. Bush announced the waiver of Jackson–Vanik to Edward Shevardnadze, Soviet foreign minister, on December 12, 1990, in order to initiate food assistance to the Soviet Union, in response to a request for same. See *New York Times*, December 13, 1990.

4. The margin of victory by Chamorro over the Sandinista Party was 14 percentage points. Mark A. Uhlig, "Turnover in Nicaragua; Nicaraguan Opposition Routs Sandinistas; U.S. Pledges Aid, Tire to Orderly Turnover," *New York Times*, February 26, 1990.

5. Polls in instances such as this are often found to be in error, due to fears on the part of voters to declare their opposition to incumbent regimes. Once convinced of the complete anonymity provided by a closely observed voting site, however, they vote their true political convictions and preferences.

6. By all responsible accounts, the election was a fair one. See, for example, Robert A. Pastor, "George Bush and Latin America: The Pragmatic Style and the Regionalist Option," in K. A. Oye, R. J. Lieber, and D. Rothchild, eds., *Eagle in a New World: American Grand Strategy in the Post–Cold War Era* (New York: HarperCollins, 1992).

7. Mark A. Uhlig, "Chamorro Takes Nicaragua Helm; Hails a New Era," *New York Times*, April 26, 1990.

8. See Susan Kaufman Purcell, "Collapsing Cuba," *Foreign Affairs* 71, no. 1 (1991–1992): 130–45.

9. Ibid., p. 13. See also Peter Shearman, *The Soviet Union and Cuba* (London: Routledge and Kegan Paul, 1987), pp. 28–29.

10. During perestroika, the reported dollar value of trade between the Soviet Union and developing countries (including Cuba) declined even as real volume increased due to price effects. See Abel Aganbegyan, *Inside Perestroika: The Future of the Soviet Economy* (New York: Harper and Row, 1989) pp. 178–80.

11. To the extent that the Soviet Union were to continue purchasing sugar from Cuba (or any other seller), it would do so at a lower price than previously; and, should the Soviet Union wish to continue exporting the oil that it had exported to Cuba, it would receive a higher price for it.

12. Mikhail Gorbachev, *Memoirs* (New York: Doubleday, 1995), pp. 512–13.

13. It might be argued that President Nixon could have enjoyed "license" to court Cuba, given that he was able to deal with the People's Republic of China, having demonstrated his anti-Communist credentials earlier and often. However, the "opening" of China had economic implications of sufficient magnitude to silence the party's far-right elements on that issue. Cuba represented no such economic potential. It is similarly likely that Nixon would not regard Cuba as being worthy of much expenditure of political capital.

14. President Clinton has been inhibited in the way that leaders of Democratic administrations always have been, but, until the unfortunate incident resulting in the shooting down of two private airplanes, he did at least refrain from tightening the embargo.

8

President Bush, Congress, and the War Powers: Panama and the Persian Gulf

Duane Tananbaum

President George Bush ordered American troops into combat in Panama in December 1989. He later sent U.S. troops to the Persian Gulf to defend Saudi Arabia and, eventually, to expel Iraqi forces from Kuwait in 1990 and 1991. In both instances the president and his advisers ignored Congress during the crucial period when decisions were made on whether the United States should intervene militarily. Congressional leaders were notified only after the decisions had already been made. The administration reported its use of American forces to Congress as required by the War Powers Resolution, but it refused to concede that it was taking such action to comply with the War Powers Resolution. In the Persian Gulf, the administration argued for months that it did not need authorization or approval from Congress to use American forces; only at the last minute did President Bush state that he would welcome a congressional resolution supporting the use of American forces in the Gulf. Bush's actions led to a major debate in Congress in January 1991 in which a reluctant Congress narrowly authorized the use of American forces in the Gulf War.

In his Inaugural Address on January 20, 1989, President George Bush called for "a new engagement ... between the Executive and the Congress." He recalled the old days of bipartisanship when "our differences ended at the water's edge" and asked for compromise, harmony, and unity between Congress and the president in foreign and domestic policy.[1]

In reality, however, the Bush administration, like the Reagan administration before it, believed that the president and his advisers should determine foreign policy with as little interference from Congress as possible.[2] This was especially true when it came to deciding when the United States would use its armed forces against other nations. President Bush, Secretary of State James Baker, and other administration officials believed, in Baker's words, that "Congress does not enjoy an equivalent right with the president for either the conduct of foreign policy or the deployment of American military forces. The Constitution is unassailable on this point: the authority to conduct foreign policy, particularly when it involves the prerogatives of the commander in chief, is preeminent in the executive."[3]

The Constitution is not nearly as clear-cut as Baker suggests. In foreign affairs, as in other areas, the framers established a system of checks and balances to prevent any one branch of the federal government from having too much power. Although Article II, Section 2 of the Constitution designates the president as commander in chief of the armed forces, Article I, Section 8 vests in Congress the power to declare war; raise, support, and regulate armies and navies; and pass all laws necessary and proper for carrying out these and all other powers that the Constitution grants to any part of the federal government. Congress and the president have fought for more than 200 years to determine how extensive each branch's powers are in this field.[4]

In 1973, in an attempt to define and limit the president's authority to commit American forces to combat without congressional concurrence, Congress enacted the War Powers Resolution. The statute reflected Congress' frustration over the war in Vietnam, especially, President Richard Nixon's decision to send American troops into Cambodia in 1970. The legislators sought to reassert their legitimate role in determining whether and when the United States would use its armed forces in hostilities short of war.[5]

The War Powers Resolution requires the president to consult with Congress "in every possible instance *before* introducing United States Armed Forces into hostilities or into situations where imminent involvement in hostilities is clearly indicated" (emphasis added). The president must send a report to Congress within 48 hours whenever he introduces U.S. forces into hostilities or situations where hostilities are likely, sends troops "equipped for combat" to a foreign nation, or substantially increases the number of U.S. forces so equipped in a foreign country. U.S. troops must be withdrawn from hostilities in foreign countries within 60 days unless Congress specifically authorizes their continued use beyond the 60-day deadline. The president can extend this deadline to 90 days by certifying that more time is needed to withdraw U.S. forces safely, but Congress is authorized to order the immediate withdrawal of U.S. military forces at any time by passing a concurrent resolution, a measure not subject to presidential veto.

The Bush administration, like most of its predecessors, considered the War Powers Resolution an unconstitutional attempt by Congress to limit by statute the president's powers under the Constitution as commander in chief of the armed forces. But the courts have never ruled directly on the War Powers Resolution, so it remains on the statute books, and the president and the executive branch are obligated to obey it.[6]

PANAMA

On May 11, 1989, in response to General Manuel Noriega's nullification of recent elections in Panama and the beatings of opposition candidates, President Bush announced that he was increasing the number of American armed forces in Panama by approximately 2,000 men. Bush reported that he had "consulted" earlier in the day with the congressional leaders of both parties and emphasized that he was taking this action "as part of his profound obligation as Commander in Chief of the Armed Forces and as President . . . to protect American life" in Panama and to safeguard American rights under the Panama Canal treaties.[7]

The administration kept a careful watch on events in Panama over the next few months. However, when elements within the Panamanian Defense Forces staged a coup and tried to oust Noriega in October 1989, the Bush administration was caught unprepared and ill informed concerned the leadership and strength of the anti-Noriega forces, and Noriega quickly restored his hold on power. As Secretary of State Baker later conceded, the administration was embarrassed that "a prime opportunity to remove Noriega had been squandered." The president and his advisers vowed not to be caught unprepared the next time an opportunity presented itself to take care of Noriega once and for all, and they secretly began increasing the number of U.S. forces stationed in Panama.[8]

The situation in Panama worsened in December 1989. On December 15, 1989, the Noriega-dominated Panamanian National Assembly declared that a state of war existed between the United States and Panama. The following day, an unarmed U.S. Marine was shot and killed by Panamanian troops, and an American navy officer was arrested and beaten by Panamanian forces while his wife was threatened. On December 17, the president met with his senior advisers and decided to take military action against Noriega's government in order to protect American lives, restore democracy in Panama, remove Noriega from power and bring him to the United States for trial on drug trafficking charges, and protect the Panama Canal. Just after midnight on December 20, Operation Just Cause began.[9]

During the months leading up to American military action against Noriega, especially during the last few days when the final decisions were being made, the Bush administration paid very little attention to Congress. Congressional input was never sought; the only time Congress was even mentioned was in compiling lists of people and organizations to be notified just before the operation began. In his speech announcing the action to the American public, the president did not even pretend that there had been any real consultations with Congress. Bush stated that he had "contacted the bipartisan leadership of Congress last night and *informed* them of this decision" (emphasis added).[10]

On December 21, 1989, in identical letters to Speaker of the House Thomas Foley (D-WA) and Senate president pro tempore Robert Byrd (D-WV), President Bush officially notified Congress of his use of U.S. military forces in Panama. The president asserted that he had acted "to protect American lives in imminent danger" and that he had acted "pursuant to my constitutional authority with respect to the conduct of foreign relations and as Commander in Chief." He was providing Congress with this information, Bush explained, "in accordance with my desire that Congress be fully informed on this matter, and consistent with the War Powers Resolution."[11]

With this letter, the Bush administration complied with the requirement in the War Powers Resolution that Congress be notified within 48 hours when U.S.

forces were used in hostilities. At the same time, however, the administration refused to invoke the War Powers Resolution formally or acknowledge its legitimacy. The president did not want to trigger the time limits imposed by the War Powers Resolution on military operations not sanctioned by Congress, and Press Secretary Marlin Fitzwater reiterated the administration's contention that the War Powers Resolution was an unconstitutional intrusion by the legislature into the president's powers in foreign affairs.[12]

Although a few legislators questioned the legitimacy of the president's actions in Panama, most senators and representatives supported Bush's decision to use U.S. military forces in Panama. Representative Don Edwards (D-CA), chair of the House Judiciary Subcommittee on Civil and Constitutional Rights, charged that the president had usurped Congress' power to declare war. Since the United States was not endangered by events in Panama, Edwards argued, Congress, not the president, had the authority and responsibility to decide whether the United States should go to war. The vast majority of legislators supported the president, however, especially when the action against Panama turned out to be so successful so quickly and with so few casualties among American forces. Bush also removed a possible point of confrontation when he announced on January 31, 1990, that American forces sent to Panama as part of Operation Just Cause would be back in the United States before the end of February. Although the president never made the connection publicly, this would be before the 60–90 day period specified in the War Powers Resolution expired.[13]

THE PERSIAN GULF—PHASE ONE

The use of American forces in Panama proved to be merely the precursor to the main event the following year—the deployment of hundreds of thousands of U.S. troops to the Persian Gulf in 1990. The debate over whether the president could dispatch such large numbers of troops to foreign soil and then order them into hostilities without congressional approval raised the controversy over the president's authority as commander in chief and Congress' power to declare war to a level not heard since the Vietnam War.

Iraqi forces invaded Kuwait on August 2, 1990, and quickly took complete control of the oil-rich sheikdom. The United Nations [UN] Security Council condemned Iraq's action and called for an immediate and unconditional withdrawal of Iraqi forces from Kuwait. A few days later, the Security Council imposed economic sanctions against Iraq in an attempt to pressure Saddam Hussein into withdrawing from Kuwait. The United States and the Soviet Union issued a joint statement deploring Iraq's action, and the Bush administration immediately began assembling an international coalition to deter any further Iraqi aggression and to restore the Kuwaiti government.[14]

On August 8, 1990, President Bush announced that he was sending American air and ground forces to Saudi Arabia to help defend that nation against a possible Iraqi attack. Bush emphasized that he was taking this action in response to a request from King Fahd of Saudi Arabia and based on the "longstanding friendship and security relationship between the United States and Saudi Arabia." He had made this decision, the president explained, only after engaging in "perhaps unparalleled international consultation and exhausting every alternative," and he had informed the congressional leaders prior to the announcement. The president was *not* implementing or carrying out a treaty commitment to Saudi Arabia, however; no formal treaty or agreement existed that called for the United States to come to the defense of Saudi Arabia.[15]

On August 9, 1990, President Bush formally notified Congress of his decision to send U.S. military forces to Saudi Arabia. Bush emphasized that he wanted to keep Congress "fully informed" and that his report was "consistent with the War Powers Resolution." The president asserted that Iraq's actions posed a direct threat to other countries in the Persian Gulf and to vital American interests in the region. Although American forces were equipped for combat, the president did not believe their involvement in hostilities was imminent. He stressed that their mission was defensive—to deter further Iraqi aggression and preserve the integrity of Saudi Arabia. The president maintained that he had acted "pursuant to my constitutional authority to conduct our foreign relations and as Commander in Chief." Bush argued that his actions were an exercise of the inherent right of "individual and collective self-defense," and he promised to cooperate with Congress in restoring peace and stability to the Persian Gulf.[16]

Once again, however, the Bush administration undercut its compliance with the War Powers Resolution at the same time that it was following the procedures set forth in that legislation. White House Press Secretary Marlin Fitzwater explained that President Bush considered the War Powers Resolution unconstitutional, so the administration was sending Congress "a notification consistent with" the resolution rather than the formal report the statute required. The administration did not want to trigger the resolution's 60–90 day limit for using military forces without congressional approval. There was also a sharp contrast between the genuine consultations President Bush was engaging in with foreign leaders such as Prime Minister Margaret Thatcher of Great Britain and President Hosni Mubarak of Egypt and the very limited notifications that the administration had given the congressional leaders. Fitzwater emphasized that the president had made 20 telephone calls to 12 different foreign leaders over the last few days. In contrast, congressional leaders were notified just hours before the deployment of American forces to Saudi Arabia began.[17]

Nonetheless, most members of Congress strongly supported President Bush's actions during the first weeks of the Persian Gulf crisis. Representative Les Aspin (D-WI), chairman of the House Armed Services Committee, declared his full support for the president's decision to send U.S. forces to Saudi Arabia, and Senator Christopher Dodd (D-CT) believed it was "the right move . . . to isolate Iraq politically and economically and put military pressure on Saddam Hussein to leave Kuwait." Warnings were sounded by Senate minority leader Robert Dole (R-KS), who wanted some of the Arab nations to play a more active role in the anti-Saddam coalition, and by Senator Alan Cranston (D-CA), who hoped the United States "won't be the Lone Ranger the way we were in Vietnam."[18]

During the first few months of the Persian Gulf crisis, President Bush went out of his way trying to keep Congress informed about his actions and objectives in the Persian Gulf. Congress was in recess when the crisis broke out, but on August 28, 1990, the president held a special briefing at the White House for all members of Congress who wished to attend. About 170 senators and representatives attended the session, which might have been prompted by the administration's realization that the cost of the American deployment in the Persian Gulf would be $2.5 billion by the end of September, more than double the earlier estimates. A reporter asked whether the president was "opening a Pandora's box" by meeting with the legislators, but Bush reiterated his commitment to work with Congress and to demonstrate American unity of purpose to the Iraqi government. He praised the congressional leaders "for the almost Vandenbergian support for the actions that we have taken." After the briefing, House Speaker Foley reported, "There's very strong support for the president's actions. He was commended by speaker after speaker. There were really no overall reservations expressed."[19]

Congress reconvened in early September, and on September 11, 1990, President Bush spoke about the Persian Gulf crisis to a Joint Session of Congress. Bush thanked the legislators for their support and emphasized how important it was for the United States to stand up to Saddam Hussein's aggression in the Persion Gulf and prevent him from gaining a stranglehold over the world's oil supply and demonstrate America's willingness to use force to defend its friends and its interests.[20]

President Bush met with the congressional leaders in mid-September to update them on the situation in the Gulf. Bush thanked the legislators for their strong support and urged Congress to approve the supplemental funds needed to pay for U.S. forces in the Gulf. The president promised "to continue to consult fully, consult regularly, with the Congress."[21]

The legislators appreciated the president's comments, but they worried that the president would not allow Congress to fulfill its constitutional role in any decision to go to war in the Persian Gulf. Senator William Cohen (R-ME), ranking Republican on the Senate Intelligence Committee, urged the president to compromise with Congress on the War Powers Resolution and to develop a national consensus before any use of American forces in the Persian Gulf. After the meeting with the president, senators wondered whether this had been "the briefing that's pointed to later as the one where they said we told the congressional leaders there's going to be shooting."[22]

In early October 1990 the House of Representatives and the Senate passed separate resolutions supporting President Bush's actions in the Persian Gulf. Both resolutions passed by overwhelming majorities, 380–29 in the House and 96–3 in the Senate. The resolutions put Congress on the record in support of the president's actions up to this point, especially his working with the UN to impose economic sanctions against Iraq. Senate majority leader George Mitchell (D-ME) cautioned, however, that this did not mean unlimited support for any actions the president might take in the future. Mitchell stressed that this was "not a blank check, . . . not an authorization for the use of force now or in the future."

Senator Edward Kennedy (D-MA), who, along with Senators Mark Hatfield (R-OR) and Bob Kerrey (D-NE), voted against the Senate bill, warned that the measure was "a Tonkin Gulf Resolution for the Persian Gulf."[23]

THE PERSIAN GULF—PHASE TWO

As the number of U.S. troops in the Persian Gulf surpassed 200,000, more legislators began to raise questions concerning the president's plans for these forces and reminding him of Congress' legitimate role in deciding when the nation should go to war. Legislators feared that a military clash in the Gulf would come after they had adjourned for the year in mid-October, and they feared that the president would use Congress' recess as an easy excuse for not consulting with the legislators before going to war against Iraq. To prevent that from happening, Congress inserted in its adjournment resolution a provision giving its leaders the authority to call Congress back into session if necessary to deal with the situation in the Gulf. Meanwhile, the Bush administration continued to demonstrate that it had a very limited view of what it considered *consultations* to be. So far, meetings and conversations with congressional leaders had been for the purpose of *informing* them of decisions already made, not to seek their input at any time in the decision-making process. This limited view of consultations become a serious problem as the Persian Gulf crisis moved into its next phase in the fall of 1990.[24]

The issue exploded when Secretary of State James Baker testified before the Senate Committee on Foreign Relations on October 17, 1990. Committee chairman Claiborne Pell (D-RI) asked Baker whether the Bush administration would promise to consult with Congress before taking any military action in the Gulf. Pell asserted that it would be in the president's best interest to have "Congress share the responsibility for taking the nation to war." After all, Pell emphasized, "shared responsibility for war is what the founding fathers intended." Pell explained that members of Congress were thinking of setting up "a bipartisan Senate-House leadership group to consult with the president prior to any decision that might be made of offensive military action." This would allow for meaningful consultations with Congress even while it was in recess.[25]

But Secretary Baker would make only the traditional executive branch pledge to consult with the congressional leaders if military action were needed. Baker noted that the president had consulted frequently with the congressional leaders concerning the military deployment in the Gulf and would continue to do so, even if Congress were in recess. Baker made it very clear, however, that such consultations would be primarily to inform legislators of decisions already made. According to Baker, the president did not need to get formal congressional approval in advance in order to use the armed forces against Iraq. Baker asserted that requiring advance congressional approval for the use of military forces or setting up a congressional committee to share in the decision for war would infringe on the president's powers as commander in chief. In addition, it would make it impossible for Bush to respond quickly to any actions Saddam Hussein might take.[26]

In response to the secretary's comments, both Republican and Democratic senators reiterated their concern that Congress be involved in a meaningful way in any decision to go to war. They believed that the Constitution required that Congress authorize the president to use the armed forces in the Persian Gulf and that congressional authorization to use the armed forces would strengthen the president's hand in dealing with Saddam Hussein. Senator Richard Lugar (R-IN) argued that rather than the Bush administration's making the decision unilaterally, "Congress ought to come back into session and authorize a declaration of war." One of the lessons of Vietnam, Lugar stressed, was that when the nation went to war, it should be with the support of the American people as expressed through their representatives in Congress. Similarly, Senator Paul Sarbanes (D-MD), in a heated exchange with Secretary Baker, emphasized, "There's a difference between consultation and authorization. It's my very strongly held view that the commitment of American forces by the president in a major assault to drive Saddam Hussein out of Kuwait would require an authorization from the Congress."[27]

On October 30, 1990, President Bush met once again with the congressional leaders to discuss the American involvement in the Persian Gulf. Legislators sought to extract from the president a promise that he would not take military action in the Gulf without congressional approval. The president promised that he would continue to consult with Congress and seek the advice and support of the lawmakers, but he refused to rule out unilateral action. Presidential spokesman Marlin Fitzwater explained that the president needed to retain his flexibility in dealing with Saddam Hussein and the situation in the Gulf.[28]

Unbeknownst to the legislators, President Bush was at that very moment deciding to send 200,000 more troops to the Persian Gulf in order to give the military forces there the ability to eject Iraqi troops from Kuwait. Secretary of State Baker later wrote that the president told him on October 24 that he was leaning toward sending more troops to the Gulf and that Bush officially approved the additional deployment on October 31. The president delayed the announcement until November 8, however, in an effort to keep the issue out of the congressional elections and to allow consultations with the other members of the international coalition.[29]

Congressional leaders were furious at the president's apparent duplicity and his failure to consult or even inform Congress before the public announcement that the additional troops were going to the Persian Gulf. In response to a reporter's question earlier in the day on November 8, Bush had emphasized the extensive consultations he had had with Congress on the Persian Gulf. The president recognized the importance of such consultations in building support in Congress for his policy, and he promised to "continue to reach out to them and keep them informed and consult." The president's actions contradicted his nice words, however. He had not mentioned anything about the coming increase in U.S. troops in the Gulf during his meeting with the legislative leaders on October 30. Moreover, this time there had not even been the customary phone calls notifying legislators of the president's decision shortly before the announcement. To make matters even worse, the president went out of his way in his announcement to list all the foreign leaders he or Secretary of State Baker had consulted before the announcement.[30]

Besides being insulted and angry at the way in which the president had kept them in the dark about the increase in U.S. forces going to the Gulf, congressional leaders were also concerned about the effects the additional troops might have on the situation there. Specifically, they feared that the large number of troops that would now be stationed in the Gulf could be used to do more than just protect Saudi Arabia. They were concerned that the president now had the capability to wage offensive operations in the Gulf without congressional concurrence, and they reiterated their previous calls for the president to seek congressional approval before using the armed forces in hostilities in the Gulf. Senate majority leader Mitchell acknowledged that the president had the authority as commander in chief to deploy American forces and respond militarily to attacks on the United States, but he reminded everyone that under the Constitution only Congress had the authority to declare war. Similarly, Representative Les Aspin, while supporting the president's decision to strengthen U.S. forces in the Gulf, recommended that any decision to go to war should be made by a formal vote of the Congress, not just informal consultations between the president and congressional leaders. Senator Sam Nunn (D-GA), the influential chairman of the Senate Armed Services Committee, emphasized that President Bush's original decision to send U.S. forces to the Gulf had enjoyed widespread support in Congress, but the recent increase in U.S. forces to provide an offensive capability had raised questions in the minds of many legislators, especially since this change had occurred without any consultation with Congress.[31]

Republicans as well as Democrats raised questions and concerns over the new situation in the Gulf and its implications. Many legislators feared that the offensive capability of U.S. forces in the Gulf meant that war was now very likely and would probably begin while Congress was in recess. Representative William Broomfield (R-MI), the senior Republican on the House Foreign Affairs Committee, advised the president to consult more widely with Congress on such a "major policy change," while Senate minority leader Dole and Senator Lugar recommended that the president call Congress back into session to explain his policy and get specific congressional approval to show that the nation was united behind the president. Dole believed that voting on a specific resolution would force most Democrats to stop criticizing the president and go on the record as supporting the commander in chief.[32]

President Bush and his advisers preferred not to contend with the uncertainties of a special session of Congress. In order to curb some of the legislators' fears, the president sent Secretary of State Baker and Secretary of Defense Dick Cheney to Capitol Hill to brief members of Congress. Administration officials also agreed to testify at hearings on the Gulf situation that would be conducted by the Armed Services and Foreign Relations Committees. In the meantime, the president met with the congressional leaders yet again and assured them that he had not changed his policy in the Gulf nor decided to take military action. The additional forces, he explained, were intended to make the threat of offensive action against Saddam Hussein more credible. The president also agreed to send Congress another letter, similar to the letter he had sent in early August, officially notifying Congress of the increase in U.S. forces stationed in the Gulf. At one point during the meeting, the president pulled a copy of the Constitution out of his pocket and assured the legislators that he understood what it said about Congress' power to declare war. He reminded them, however, that the Constitution also designated the president as commander in chief of the armed forces. The congressional leaders felt that they had made their point directly to the president, and they agreed to drop the idea of a special session of Congress, at least for the time being.[33]

As congressional committees prepared to conduct hearings on the situation in the Gulf, the Bush administration sought to strengthen its position both internationally and domestically by securing a UN Security Council resolution authorizing the use of force against Iraq. Administration officials believed that a UN resolution authorizing the use of military force would make it easier to win congressional approval for a similar measure. After considerable effort by the United States, the Security Council approved a resolution on November 29, 1990, authorizing member states "to use all necessary means ... to restore international peace and security" in the Persian Gulf unless Iraq complied with all UN resolutions by January 15, 1991. The Security Council's passage of this resolution made it more difficult for liberal Democrats, many of whom were longtime supporters of the UN and advocates of collective security, to oppose the use of military force in the Persian Gulf.[34]

The Senate Armed Services Committee opened its hearings on the situation in the Persian Gulf on November 27, 1990. According to Senator Nunn, the hearings were intended to help define America's goals and tactics in the Gulf before any military action commenced. Nunn hoped this might avert some of the division that had racked the country during the Vietnam War. Many Democrats, including Senators Carl Levin (MI), Edward Kennedy, and Robert Kerrey, complained that President Bush was rushing the country into war instead of allowing enough time for economic sanctions to work. Senator Levin also criticized the president's refusal to seek congressional approval before using military force in the Gulf. He found it "incredible that the president feels the need to obtain UN approval for a U.S. offensive but won't commit himself to seeking congressional approval."[35]

Most of the witnesses during the hearings asserted that economic sanctions, if given enough time, would force Iraq to withdraw from Kuwait. Former secretary of defense James Schlesinger asserted that the economic sanctions were working, and former chairman of the Joint Chiefs Admiral William Crowe argued that the United States should show patience and "give sanctions a fair chance before we discard them." Crowe believed that economic sanctions alone, if left in effect for 12 to 18 months, would bring Saddam Hussein "to his knees." General David Jones, another former chairman of the Joint Chiefs, believed that the Bush administration had erred in doubling the number of troops in the Gulf. He warned that the deployment of so many troops in the area "might cause us to fight—perhaps prematurely and perhaps unnecessarily." Jones would have preferred to give sanctions "a little more time to work."[36]

The Bush administration felt the need to counter the growing sense in Congress and the nation as a whole that the president was rushing toward war with Iraq. President Bush was also concerned that Saddam Hussein might be questioning America's resolve and willingness to use force given the criticism the president's policies were receiving in the congressional hearings. Consequently, on November 30, 1990, President Bush announced that he was inviting Iraqi foreign minister Tariq Aziz to Washington and would send Secretary of State James Baker to Baghdad to meet directly with Saddam Hussein to make sure that the Iraqi leader understood the consequences if he failed to withdraw from Kuwait by January 15. The congressional hearings were leaving the impression that the administration had already decided to use military force to expel Iraq from Kuwait, and the president wanted to demonstrate his willingness "to go the extra mile for peace."[37]

At the news conference where he announced this latest diplomatic initiative, the president also discussed at some length his thoughts concerning a congressional resolution. Bush declared that he would "love to see Congress pass a resolution enthusiastically endorsing what the United Nations has done." But, he explained, after extensive consultation with members of Congress from both parties, he had decided not to call a special session of Congress. There was some concern that a lame-duck session of Congress was not the appropriate body to consider such an important issue. The president reminded everyone that Congress, in its adjournment resolution, had inserted a provision allowing its own leaders to call Congress back into session but that the legislative leaders had declined to do so. Asked specifically what he thought his responsibilities were to the Congress in this situation, the president emphasized the need for "full consultation." When discussing the possibility of casualties if war should come, however, and whether such sacrifices were worth it, Bush stressed, revealingly, that "it's only the president that should be asked to make the decision." Bush clearly believed, and was stating publicly, that it was the president's responsibility and his alone to determine whether and when the nation should go to war.[38]

Bush elaborated on his concerns later in the same news conference. It was impossible to consult with 535 senators and representatives, he explained, many of whom might have different views. If Congress wanted to come back and endorse what the president and the United Nations had done, Bush would welcome their support. He feared, however, that it might deteriorate into a situation "where you have 435 voices in one House and 100 on the other saying what not to do and saying—kind of a hand-wringing operation that would send bad signals." Bush and his advisers did not believe that they needed congressional approval or authorization to use military force in the Persian Gulf, so the president would go to Congress only if he were certain that the legislators would endorse his actions by a comfortable margin.[39]

As the congressional hearings continued in early December, the gap between the Bush administration and Congress became more apparent. Secretary of Defense Dick Cheney asserted that the president had sufficient authority to take military action against Iraq without congressional approval, and Secretary of State Baker testified that it was unlikely that economic sanctions alone would force Saddam Hussein out of Kuwait. Baker angrily denied that the administration was acting recklessly or precipitously in the Gulf, and he defended what he described as the administration's unprecedented consultations with Congress. According to Baker, the president had met with legislators seven times, the secretary of defense had conferred with them 12 times, and Baker himself had met with them 11 times to discuss the situation in the Gulf.[40]

In the congressional view, however, meetings and consultations were not enough. Senator Paul Sarbanes (D-MD) told Baker that the administration's contention that the president had the power had to use military force in the Persian Gulf without congressional concurrence was "totally contrary to the Constitution." Similarly, on December 4, 1990, House Democrats adopted a policy statement declaring that the president should not initiate any offensive military action in the Persian Gulf without the formal approval of Congress unless American lives were in immediate danger. The resolution was adopted 177–37 by the House Democratic Caucus, and it was intended as a direct response to recent administration statements on the issue. The resolution put the House Democrats on record supporting the president's actions in defending Saudi Arabia and using diplomacy and economic sanctions to try to resolve the crisis, but it also served notice that the Democrats in the House disagreed with the administration over the extent of the president's power to decide unilaterally to go to war in the Persian Gulf.[41]

Not content to challenge the administration with a nonbinding policy statement, 54 Democratic members of Congress led by Representative Ron Dellums of California challenged in court the Bush administration's view of the president's power to commit the nation and its armed forces to war. The legislators sought an injunction to prevent the president from going to war without congressional approval. They argued that the Constitution clearly vested in Congress the authority to declare war and that the president should not be allowed to initiate a war to force Iraq out of Kuwait without Congress' consent.[42]

The administration's arguments in this case further exacerbated congressional concerns. Assistant Attorney General Stuart Gerson, who argued the case for the Bush administration, pointed out that presidents had frequently sent American troops into combat without a congressional declaration of war. When asked by Judge Harold Greene when Congress' power to declare war did apply, Gerson said that Congress' power to declare war was "optional"—it allowed Congress to take the initiative to start a war, but it did not limit or prevent a president from sending troops into combat. Gerson noted that the Constitution did not say when Congress had to declare war—it could be prior to or after hostilities began. If Congress disagreed with a war a president had started, Gerson asserted, the legislators' proper recourse would be to deny any funding for such a conflict. Attorneys for the legislators argued that the time for Congress to use its power to declare war "is before it begins, not while it's going on." Otherwise, it was a meaningless power if it could be circumvented or ignored by the president's sending troops into combat on his own authority.[43]

In his decision in *Dellums v. Bush*, Judge Green denied the request for a court order blocking the president from going to war without congressional approval. At the same time, however, he rejected the Bush administration's sweeping view of the executive's power to go to war unilaterally. The issue was not yet "ripe" for judicial intervention, the judge declared, because the full Congress had not determined whether it wanted the president to seek a declaration of war before sending American forces into combat in the Gulf. Since a majority of Congress would be required to declare war, the judge ruled that a majority of Congress would be required to seek a court order preventing the president from going to war. Judge Green concluded that the history of Article I, Section 8 of the Constitution made it clear that the framers had erected a system of government under which the president was not supposed to go to war without the consent of Congress.[44]

The president continued to meet frequently with legislators and emphasized his willingness and eagerness to consult with them, but he still refused to commit himself to obtaining congressional approval before taking military action in the Gulf. At a news conference on December 14, Bush was asked whether he would "ask Congress for specific authority to take offensive action." The president noted that he was talking with the congressional leaders and would welcome a resolution endorsing his actions and the UN resolution. Bush believed such a measure would send a strong signal of American determination and unity to Saddam Hussein and the rest of the world. Similarly, at a meeting with regional reporters a few days later, the president emphasized that he was "having the darnedest consultations with Congress you've ever seen," and he promised to continue meeting with legislators to discuss the issues involved. Speaking to reporters on December 22, the president reiterated that

we've had the most vigorous consultations with Congress.... We're talking to all of these Members of Congress as they come back.... We will continue to consult in every way possible. I want Congress fully on board. I'd love to see Congress say this minute that we fully endorse the United Nations resolutions and the president should fully implement them.... It would be very nice to send that solid signal out to Saddam Hussein.... But they've got to decide. The Congress is a separate body. They are entitled to do it any way they want. *But I know the powers of the Presidency, and I've had a chance to discuss that with the key members of Congress* [emphasis added].[45]

THE PERSIAN GULF—PHASE THREE

As 1990 ended and the United Nations deadline of January 15, 1991, approached, the debate over the president's authority to use American forces to drive Iraq out of Kuwait took on new urgency. On December 29, 1990, House majority leader Richard Gephardt (D-MO) reasserted the view of most Democrats that congressional approval was required before the president could wage war in the Persian Gulf and that economic sanctions should be given more time to work. But Gephardt went further and warned that if the president decided to take military action on his own authority in the Gulf, Congress would have to "reach for the only tool left to it, which is to cut off the funding for the war."[46]

President Bush still resisted the idea of asking Congress for approval or authorization to use the armed forces in the Persian Gulf. The president and his advisers believed that they did not need any such authorization from Congress, and they preferred to avoid a congressional debate where the result was uncertain. They feared that congressional rejection of a measure approving the use of force or its passage by a very narrow margin would send the wrong signal to Saddam Hussein.[47]

Faced with growing opposition in both parties to an early military strike against Iraq, President Bush announced on January 3, 1991, that he was inviting Iraqi foreign minister Tariq Aziz to meet with Secretary of State Baker in Geneva. It had not been possible to agree on dates for Aziz to come to Washington and Baker to go to Baghdad, so Bush offered this new proposal to demonstrate his willingness to go the last mile in the search for peace before the January 15 deadline. The president also hoped the Baker-Aziz meeting would delay any congressional action on the situation in the Gulf.[48]

The 102nd Congress convened on January 3, 1991, in an atmosphere of uncertainty. Members of Congress were divided over how to proceed at this point. Although there was widespread agreement that Congress should debate U.S. policy in the Gulf, the key question was when. After meeting with the president, Senate majority leader Mitchell and House Speaker Foley agreed that Congress would not formally take up the issue until after Secretary Baker's meeting with Aziz in Geneva. They feared that a divisive debate would undermine the last-ditch efforts to persuade Saddam Hussein to remove his forces from Kuwait before the January 15 deadline.[49]

Liberal Democrats, led by Senators Tom Harkin (IA) and Brock Adams (WA), immediately challenged the leadership's plan to delay the debate over the situation in the Gulf. They pointed out that debating the issue after January 15 would probably be meaningless, since the president was likely to use the armed forces soon after the UN deadline. Harkin wanted the Senate to consider a formal resolution officially stating that the president could not undertake a military offensive without congressional approval. The debate over going to war should not be limited to discussions "in coffee shops, in the workplace, and in homes," Harkin asserted. He maintained that "now is the time and here is the place to debate the constitutional prerogatives of the president of the United States."[50]

A compromise was soon worked out. Aziz agreed to meet with Baker in Geneva on January 9, and the congressional leaders then scheduled their debates and votes for the period between January 10 and January 15. That way the legislators would not be interfering with the meeting in Geneva, but they would have the opportunity to consider the situation in the Gulf before military operations began.[51]

The Bush administration now accepted the inevitability of a congressional debate and vote on whether to use American armed forces in the Persian Gulf. Baker explained that the president had been reluctant to ask for a congressional resolution because the leadership had not been able to assure him that such a measure could be passed, and asking for such a resolution and not getting it or getting a resolution passed by a narrow margin would weaken the president's hand in dealing with Saddam Hussein. However, Baker now declared that any resolution passed by Congress would be "helpful" to the administration. Senate Republican leader Dole predicted that a bill similar to the UN resolution would win a bipartisan majority and pass by a vote of approximately 60 in favor and 40 opposed, while House Speaker Foley thought the House would "narrowly" approve such a measure. The president and his advisers still believed that they did not need any sort of authorization or permission form Congress to use military force in the Gulf, but they recognized that a congressional resolution would be important politically in rallying support for any upcoming military action. Moreover, they were confident now that such a measure could be enacted by a comfortable margin.[52]

On January 8, 1991, President Bush himself formally asked Congress to pass a measure supporting the UN resolutions and the use of military force if Iraq did not withdraw from Kuwait by January 15. On the eve of Secretary Baker's meeting with Foreign Minister Aziz, the president asserted that it would "greatly enhance the chances for peace if Congress were now to go on record supporting the position adopted by the UN Security Council." Congressional action would present a united front and "help dispel any belief that may exist in the minds of Iraq's leaders that the United States lacks the necessary unity to act decisively in response to Iraq's continued aggression against Kuwait." Bush lamented that Congress had not already passed such a resolution for Baker to take with him to present to Aziz, but the president maintained that "there is still opportunity for Congress to act to strengthen the prospects for peace and safeguard this country's vital interests." Specifically, Bush requested that Congress adopt a resolution supporting "the use of all necessary means to implement UN Security Council Resolution 678." The president emphasized that he was "determined to do whatever is necessary to protect America's security," and he asked Congress to work with him and "express its support for the president at this critical time."[53]

President Bush's formal request for congressional support marked the first time since the Gulf of Tonkin Resolution in 1964 that a president had officially asked for congressional endorsement of military action. Even though it would be difficult to differ with the president at a time when hundreds of thousands of American troops were poised to go to war in the Persian Gulf, most legislators welcomed the opportunity to exercise their constitutional role in determining whether the United States should engage in hostilities.[54]

The president still did not acknowledge or concede that he needed congressional approval or authorization to go to war in the Persian Gulf. When asked by a reporter whether he needed a congressional resolution and whether he would be prevented from acting if such a resolution were defeated in Congress, Bush made it clear that he believed that he already had "the authority to fully implement the United Nations resolutions.... I still feel that I have the constitutional authority—many attorneys having so advised me." The president noted that there had been 200 or more instances in American history when U.S. armed forces had been employed, but Congress had declared war on very few occasions. Bush preferred, however, to emphasize how much he had consulted with Congress and tried to work with the legislators, Democrats and Republicans, to present a "solid front" against Iraqi aggression.[55]

Many legislators disagreed with the president's analysis of his powers and the proper role of Congress in deciding whether to engage in military hostilities in the Persian Gulf. This included many congressmen who were inclined to support the president and the use of military force in the Gulf but who did not want to see Congress taken for granted in the process. Key Democratic legislators, including Les Aspin and Dante Fascell (FL), the chairmen of the House Armed Services and Foreign Affairs Committees, and Representative Stephen Solarz (NY) now began working with congressional Republicans and the Bush administration to try to fashion a resolution that would support the president but also recognize Congress' legitimate role in declaring war or authorizing hostilities short of war under the War Powers Resolution. The administration eventually agreed to accept such a resolution on the understanding that it "would not prejudice" the executive branch's long-standing position on these issues, especially its contention that the War Powers Resolution was unconstitutional.[56]

The failure of the Baker–Aziz talks in Geneva on January 9 provided a somber backdrop as the congressional debate began on January 10, 1991. Representative Lee Hamilton (D-IN) of the House Foreign Affairs Committee spoke for many of his colleagues when he described the debate and decision as "one of the defining votes that each of us will cast in our congressional careers." The debate centered around three separate resolutions: (1) the Michel–Solarz resolution authorizing the president to use U.S. armed forces to implement UN Security Council Resolution 678 and stating explicitly that this resolution constituted the specific statutory authorization required under the War Powers Resolution; (2) the Hamilton–Gephardt resolution in the House and a similar Mitchell–Nunn proposal in the Senate recommending that diplomacy and economic sanctions be given more time; and (3) the Bennett–Durbin resolution reasserting Congress' exclusive power to declare war. Most observers expected the Michel–Solarz resolution, which had the support of the Bush administration, to prevail, especially since there was little hope that UN secretary general Javier Perez de Cuellar's last-minute trip to Baghdad would produce any significant results. Thus, Congress would have to choose between diplomacy and sanctions, which had not yet forced Iraq out of Kuwait, or authorizing the president to use military force. Most commentators predicted that, in the end, legislators would rally around the president at this time of international crisis and confrontation and give him the kind of resolution he wanted, one that would authorize him to use military force to implement the UN resolutions.[57]

The Bush administration actively lobbied for support in Congress. Bush met with about a dozen Democratic senators on January 10 to discuss specific language and strategy, and the president had approximately 100 members of Congress over to the White House for breakfast on January 11 to try to persuade them to vote for the Michel–Solarz resolution. "The last, best chance for Saddam Hussein to get the message is in your hands," the president told the legislators. Bush also spent considerable time on the telephone trying to win over legislators who were on the fence, such as Senator James Jeffords (R-VT), who favored economic sanctions but declared that he would vote for the use of force measure if pressed to do so by the Bush administration. Similarly, Senator J. Bennett Johnston (D-LA) originally supported the economic sanctions option but, after a meeting with the president, announced he would vote for the resolution authorizing the president to use military force. Johnston was persuaded that Bush was going to use military force after January 15, and Johnston believed it was important for Congress to "present a united front."[58]

Most legislators who supported the Michel–Solarz resolution argued that sanctions had not worked and that now was the time to support the president. Senator Strom Thurmond (R-SC) asserted that Congress should "demonstrate to the world and especially Saddam Hussein that we are behind our President and the United Nations." Senator John Danforth (R-MO) believed that Congress should authorize the president to use military force in order to maintain "a credible military threat," and Senator Orrin Hatch (R-UT) argued that it was "time for the Congress to join with the president and get behind him and our young men and women over there sitting in the sand and show that we're willing to back the use of force." Similarly, Representative Gary Ackerman (D-NY) maintained that "the best chance for peace that we have is for a message to be sent from here today that the American people through their Congress are behind their President and their soldiers and are willing to stand up to his [Saddam Hussein's] vicious aggression," and Representative Benjamin Gilman (R-NY) warned that the opponents of the Michel–Solarz resolution, "by creating an impression of discord within the Congress, will actually bring this nation closer to war by withholding from the president in these last few days of sensitive negotiation his most important tool: the tool of unified congressional support for military action in the event that diplomatic initiatives do not succeed."[59]

Senate majority leader Mitchell welcomed the opportunity for the Senate to exercise its "solemn constitutional responsibility to decide whether to commit the nation to war," but he urged his colleagues not to "give the president a blank check to initiate war against Iraq." All other means should be exhausted before the United States went to war, Mitchell emphasized. Speaker Foley, who did not usually participate in House debates, believed the importance of this issue required him to explain how he was going to vote and why. Foley stressed that the Michel–Solarz resolution was not simply another diplomatic tool to be added to the president's arsenal; rather, it should be seen as "a virtual declaration of war" that the president was prepared to use to its fullest extent. Foley did not believe that the time for war had come. He wanted to continue the economic sanctions instead.[60]

Senator Sam Nunn was widely regarded as one of the Senate's most knowledgeable and influential leaders on military issues. His views carried special weight and were likely to influence other legislators trying to make up their minds. Nunn conceded that there was no guarantee that sanctions alone would force Iraq out of Kuwait, but he believed there was a reasonable chance that "continued economic sanctions backed up by the threat of military force and international isolation can bring about Iraqi withdrawal from Kuwait." Nunn pointed out that there was no guarantee that a war against Iraq would be quick and easy, and he believed that "the risks associated with continued emphasis on sanctions are considerably less than the very real risk associated with war and, most importantly, the aftermath of war in a very volatile region of the world." He questioned whether "vital" American interests were really at stake and urged that every "reasonable alternative" should be exhausted before the nation sacrificed American lives in a war over Kuwait. Nunn's support for economic sanctions and his opposition to authorizing the president to use military force made it easier for some of his colleagues to take a similar position.[61]

Although the Democratic leaders in Congress all opposed the Michel–Solarz resolution authorizing the use of American armed forces unless Iraq complied with the United Nations resolutions, they made it clear that their opposition was personal, not a unified party position. House majority leader Gephardt emphasized that the Democratic leaders would not be trying to line up votes for the Hamilton–Gephardt resolution giving diplomatic efforts and economic sanctions more time before the United States resorted to war. "In this vote," Gephardt explained, "we are not Democrats. We are not Republicans. We are Americans. We expect and want all of the members to vote their conscience, what in their mind is the right thing for this country to do." Similarly, House Speaker Foley concluded his remarks with an eloquent call for unity after the vote:

But however you vote, ... let us come together after the vote with the notion that we are Americans here, not Democrats and not Republicans, all anxious to do the best for your country without recrimination as to motive, without anything but the solemn cry that on this great decision day we voted as our conscience and judgment told us we should. And then though our opinion may change over the years, we will not bear the burden of a harsh judgment on our honor and our actions at this moment.[62]

The mood in the Congress remained solemn as the historic debate drew to a close on January 12, 1991. The debate had been intense, impassioned, and emotional at times, but it had been conducted in a civil tone with a minimum of partisanship or rancor. Congressmen recognized the significance of the votes they were about to cast, as they considered whether to authorize the president to use the armed forces to drive Iraq out of Kuwait. Ninety-three senators spoke during the debate, as did 268 members of the House of Representatives. Congressmen actually listened to each other during the debate, and most legislators wrote their own speeches, often very personal statements referring back to their experiences during World War II or Vietnam. Representative David Obey (D-WI) spoke for many of his colleagues when he described the debate as "the most important of our careers."[63]

The House of Representatives began by considering the Bennett–Durbin resolution reaffirming Congress' exclusive authority under the Constitution to declare war and asserting that congressional approval was required before any offensive military actions could be initiated against Iraq. This measure passed easily by a vote of 302–131. The resolution was supported by 260 Democrats, 41 Republicans, and one Independent, while 126 Republicans and 5 Democrats opposed it. Representative Charles Bennett, one of the resolution's sponsors, emphasized to his colleagues that out of the 17,000 votes he had cast as a congressman, the only one he really regretted was his vote in favor of the Gulf of Tonkin resolution, and he urged his fellow congressmen not to make the same mistake now. Bennett typified the spirit of the debate when he stressed to his colleagues that their votes should be based on what they thought was "best for our country, not best for the Republican or the Democratic Party, not best for the president, not best for you, but what's best for our country and what's best for the world."[64]

The House next moved on to the Michel–Solarz resolution, authorizing the president to use the armed forces to remove Iraqi troops from Kuwait, and the Hamilton–Gephardt resolution, giving economic sanctions more time to work. Two-thirds of the Democrats, including all the leaders, favored the economic sanctions route, but the other one-third of the Democrats, including Representatives Aspin, Fascell, and Solarz, joined with virtually all the Republicans to defeat the Hamilton–Gephardt proposal and adopt the Michel–Solarz resolution instead. The votes on the two resolutions were identical: 250–183, with the majority consisting of 164 Republicans and 86 Democrats, while 179 Democrats, three Republicans, and one Independent made up the losing side.[65]

The situation in the Senate was much closer. The Senate first rejected the Mitchell–Nunn resolution, favoring continued diplomacy and economic sanctions, by a vote of 53–46. Ten Democrats, mostly conservatives from the South, joined with 43 Republicans to defeat the measure, which was supported by 45 Democrats but only 1 Republican, Charles Grassley of Iowa. Senators then voted 52–47 to adopt the Michel–Solarz resolution, authorizing the president to use the armed forces. This time the same 10 Democrats voted with 42 Republicans to make up the majority, while Republican Senators Grassley and Hatfield voted with the other 45 Democrats against the resolution. The 10 Democrats who voted against sanctions and for the final resolution authorizing the use of force were Senators Breaux (LA), Bryan (NV), Gore (TN), Graham (FL), Heflin (AL), Johnston (LA), Lieberman (CT), Reid (NV), Robb (VA), and Shelby (AL).[66]

Congressional approval of the "Use of Force resolution" marked a major victory for President Bush. The president had decided only late in the game to seek a congressional resolution, and had Congress refused to authorize him to use the armed forces in the Persian Gulf, it would have been a terrible defeat for the president. If the president had insisted on using American forces anyhow, it would have provoked a constitutional crisis of the first magnitude, but that possibility was rendered moot by Congress' passage of the resolution. Although the measure passed by only a narrow margin in the Senate, legislators agreed that the Congress had spoken and endorsed the president's actions, so it was now time for everyone to unite behind the president. Senator Nunn warned Saddam Hussein not to be misled by the congressional debate that represented "the voices of democracy.... If war occurs, the constitutional and policy debates will be suspended, and Congress will provide the American troops whatever they need to prevail. There will be no cutoff of funds for our troops while they engage your forces on the field of battle."[67]

President Bush had skillfully managed events to help ensure his victory in

Congress. He created conditions that strongly influenced the debate. In particular, his decision in early November 1990 to double the number of U.S. troops in the Persian Gulf had presented legislators with a fait accompli. The presence of 400,000 U.S. troops in Saudi Arabia created a momentum of its own—the troops would have to be used, rotated, or withdrawn within a few months, and any lessening of U.S. forces in the region would be seen as a retreat by the United States and a victory for Saddam Hussein. Similarly, winning UN approval for setting a deadline and using military force made it more difficult for the American Congress to refuse to give the president the same authority to drive Iraqi troops out of Kuwait. Sending Secretary of State Baker to meet with Iraqi foreign minister Aziz in Geneva was also important because it showed that Bush was still willing to give diplomacy a try right up to the last minute.[68]

President Bush welcomed passage of the resolution authorizing him to use the armed forces against Iraq. The president noted that "as a democracy, we've debated this issue openly and in good faith," and he believed that the "historic" debate showed "the best of the United States Congress at work." He emphasized that he had consulted extensively with Congress and that the legislature had now "closed ranks behind a clear signal of our determination and our resolve to implement the United Nations resolutions."[69]

Two days later, on January 14, 1991, Bush signed into law the resolution authorizing him to use the armed forces against Iraq. In doing so, however, Bush made it clear that his acceptance of this resolution "does not constitute any change in the long-standing positions of the executive branch on either the president's constitutional authority to use the Armed Forces to defend vital U.S. interests or the constitutionality of the War Powers Resolution." The president was pleased, though, that differences over these legal and constitutional issues had not prevented the president and Congress from working together in this instance against Iraqi aggression. Bush promised to continue consulting with Congress as the crisis continued.[70]

Within a few days, the United States and the international coalition went to war against Iraq. The president met at the White House with the congressional leaders on January 14 and January 15 to update them on the situation. On January 16, 1991, President Bush sent to Congress the report required under the Authorization for the Use of Force resolution stating that he had concluded that "all appropriate diplomatic and other peaceful means to obtain compliance by Iraq with UN Security Council Resolutions . . . have not been and would not be successful." That evening, the president spoke privately with congressional and world leaders to discuss events in the Persian Gulf, and then he announced to the nation that allied air attacks against Iraqi targets had begun. The president emphasized that military action had commenced "in accord with United Nations resolutions and with the consent of the United States Congress."[71]

By January 18, 1991, when the president officially informed Congress that he had ordered U.S. forces into combat operations against Iraq, Bush reverted to his earlier manner of citing his own authority as president rather than sharing responsibility and decisions with Congress. Bush made his report "consistent with the War Powers Resolution," but, rather than relying on that statute or on the just-adopted Authorization for the Use of Force resolution, the president cited only his "authority as Commander in Chief" as the basis for his actions. The only reference to the Authorization for the Use of Force resolution came when the president said, "The operations of U.S. and other coalition forces are contemplated by the resolutions of the UN Security Council, as well as H.J. Res. 77, adopted by Congress on January 12, 1991." As usual, the president promised to keep Congress informed and looked forward to "continued consultations and cooperation." Congress had spoken and authorized the president to use the armed forces, and that was exactly what the president was doing. Clearly, now that the war had begun, the commander in chief would be making all the decisions without any interference from Congress.[72]

CONCLUSIONS

The Bush administration showed during the conflict with Panama in 1989 and the period leading up to the Persian Gulf War that it preferred to work without congressional interference in foreign affairs. In the case of Panama, the only congressional involvement came when congressional leaders were informed of the invasion just before it happened. In the Persian Gulf, the president and his advisers insisted that they did not need congressional authorization or approval to use military force to expel Iraq from Kuwait. In the end, however, the administration reluctantly accepted a congressional resolution authorizing the use of American troops against Iraq. The War Powers Resolution played little role in either case, and certainly it has fallen way short of its goal of restoring to Congress its role in the process of deciding whether or when the United States goes to war or engages in hostilities.

In some ways, the system designed by the framers of the Constitution worked during the period leading up to the Persian Gulf War despite the Bush administration's reluctance to allow Congress to play its constitutional role. There was no sudden attack against American forces requiring an instantaneous response, as at Pearl Harbor in 1941. Rather, the situation evolved over a period of months, allowing adequate time for congressional participation and debate. Although the president and his advisers sought to avoid such a debate, once they realized they could not prevent it, they worked with legislators to draft a resolution authorizing the president to use the armed forces and then lobbied actively for its adoption. Even though the measure passed by only a narrow margin in the Senate, the debate itself contributed significantly to national unity. Everyone had the chance to state his or her views and opinions, and Congress and the nation rallied behind the president once the resolution was approved. Rather than getting bogged down in legal and constitutional issues, the president was now able to take a united country into war.

Events between August 1990 and January 1991 also demonstrated the president's ability to dominate in such foreign policy crises. It was President Bush who constantly defined American goals and objectives in the aftermath of Iraq's invasion of Kuwait. It was President Bush who decided in August 1990 to send 200,000 American troops to help defend Saudi Arabia. It was President Bush who decided in October and November 1990 to double the number of American forces in the Persian Gulf. It was President Bush who took the matter to the United Nations and assembled an international coalition opposing Saddam Hussein. All of these actions considerably reduced Congress' freedom and flexibility in reacting to the situation.

Although President Bush and his advisers met frequently with congressmen, they never really consulted with legislators in a meaningful way or acknowledged that they needed congressional authorization or approval to go to war in the Persian Gulf. The president, Secretary of State Baker, Secretary of Defense Cheney, and others merely informed the legislators of decisions already made, and they maintained consistently that the president had sufficient authority as commander in chief to use the armed forces to push Iraq out of Kuwait. They continued to dismiss the War Powers Resolution as unconstitutional, and they reluctantly accepted the Authorization to Use Force Resolution only when it became obvious that such a measure would pass and that it would be helpful *politically* in building national support for the conflict that was about to begin.

NOTES

1. George Bush Inaugural Address, January 20, 1989, in *Public Papers of the Presidents: George Bush, 1989*, Vol. 1 (Washington, DC: U.S. Government Printing Office, 1990), pp. 2–3.

2. See Duane Tananbaum, "Contempt for Congress: The Reagan Administration, Congress, and the War Powers Resolution," in Eric Schmertz, Natalie Datlof, and Alexej Ugrinsky, eds., *Ronald Reagan's America* (Westport, CT: Greenwood Press, 1997); testimony of State Department legal adviser Abraham Sofaer in U.S. Congress, Senate, Committee on Foreign Relations, *The War Power after 200 Years: Congress and the President at a Constitutional Impasse*, Hearings before the Special Subcommittee on War Powers, Committee on Foreign Relations, 100th Cong., 2d sess., 1988, pp. 142–59, 1046–68.

3. James A. Baker III, with Thomas DeFrank, *The Politics of Diplomacy: Revolution, War and Peace, 1989–1992* (New York: G.P. Putnam's Sons, 1995), p. 334.

4. See, for example, U.S. Congress, Senate, Committee on the Judiciary, *The Constitutional Roles of Congress and the President in Declaring and Waging War*, Hearing before the Senate Committee on the Judiciary, 102d Cong., 1st sess., 1991; Francis Wormuth and Edwin Firmage, *To Chain the Dog of War: The War Power of Congress in History and Law*, 2d ed. (Urbana: University of Illinois Press, 1989); Louis Fisher, *Presidential War Power* (Lawrence: University Press of Kansas, 1995).

5. The War Powers Resolution is P.L. 93-148 (1973).

6. The Supreme Court's decision in *Immigration and Naturalization Service v. Chadha*, 462 U.S. 919 (1983) struck down the legislative veto provision in an unrelated law and calls into question the constitutionality of a concurrent resolution ordering the president to remove U.S. troops from hostilities. But even if that provision of the War Powers Resolution were declared unconstitutional, the remainder of the statute would remain in effect because it includes a separability clause. See Section 9 of the War Powers Resolution.

7. Remarks and a Question-and-Answer Session with Reporters on the Situation in Panama, May 11, 1989, in *Public Papers: Bush, 1989*, Vol. 1, pp. 537–38.

8. Baker, *The Politics of Diplomacy*, pp. 185–87. On the confusion within the Bush administration, see also Colin Powell, with Joseph Persico, *My American Journal* (New

York: Random House, 1995), pp. 415–21; Marlin Fitzwater, *Call the Briefing* (New York: Times Books, 1995), pp. 201–11.

9. See President Bush's address to the nation announcing U.S. military action in Panama, December 20, 1989, in *Public Papers: Bush, 1989*, Vol. 2, pp. 1722–23; Baker, *The Politics of Diplomacy*, pp. 188–91.

10. President Bush's address to the nation announcing U.S. military action in Panama, December 20, 1989, in *Public Papers: Bush, 1989*, Vol. 2, p. 1723; Statement by Press Secretary Marlin Fitzwater on U.S. military action in Panama, December 20, 1989, in *Public Papers: Bush, 1989*, Vol. 2, pp. 1724–25; Baker, *The Politics of Diplomacy*, p. 189.

11. Letter to the Speaker of the House of Representatives and the president pro tempore of the Senate on U.S. military action in Panama, December 21, 1989, in *Public Papers: Bush, 1989*, Vol. 2, p. 1734.

12. Martin Tolchin, "Legislators Express Concern on the Operation's Future," *New York Times*, December 22, 1989, p. A-20. The letter to the Speaker and the president pro tempore of the Senate was dated December 21 to comply with the 48-hour deadline for reporting specified in the War Powers Resolution, but the letter was not released until December 22. See *Public Papers: Bush, 1989*, Vol. 2, p. 1734.

13. Susan Rasky, "Administration Says International Agreements Support Its Action," *New York Times*, December 21, 1989, p. A-22; Thomas Friedman, "Congress Generally Supports Attack, but Many Fear Consequences," *New York Times*, December 21, 1989, p. A-21; Tolchin, "Legislators Express Concern on the Operation's Future," *New York Times*, December 22, 1989, p. A-20; Representative Lee Hamilton, "Panama," *Foreign Affairs Newsletter* 9, no. 12 (December 1989); President Bush's address before a joint session of the Congress on the State of the Union, January 31, 1990, in *Public Papers: Bush, 1990*, Vol. 1, p. 130; Baker, *The Politics of Diplomacy*, p. 193.

14. See Baker, *The Politics of Diplomacy*, pp. 274–83; Maureen Dowd, "The Longest Week: How President Decided to Draw the Line," *New York Times*, August 9, 1990, p. A-17; Andrew Rosenthal, "Strategy: Embargo," *New York Times*, August 9, 1990, p. A-14.

15. President Bush's address to the nation announcing the deployment of U.S. armed forces to Saudi Arabia, August 8, 1990, in *Public Papers: Bush, 1990*, Vol. 2, pp. 1107–1109.

16. President Bush's letter to congressional leaders on the deployment of U.S. armed forces to Saudi Arabia and the Middle East, August 9, 1990, in *Public Papers: Bush, 1990*, Vol. 2, pp. 1116–17. The letter was dated August 9 to comply with the 48-hour deadline for reporting specified in the War Powers Resolution, but it was not released until August 10. See *Public Papers: Bush, 1990*, Vol. 2, p. 1117.

17. On Fitzwater's comments, see R. W. Apple Jr., "U.S. Set to Blockade Baghdad's Shipping," *New York Times*, August 10, 1990, pp. A-1, A-8; and Andrew Rosenthal, "Bush Sends U.S. Forces to Saudi Arabia as Kingdom Agrees to Confront Iraq," *New York Times*, August 8, 1990, pp. A-1, A-8. In her article "The Longest Week: How President Decided to Draw the Line," Maureen Dowd of the *New York Times* described the president's many contacts with foreign leaders during the first week of the crisis. Noticeably absent from her account is any mention of meetings or discussions with congressional leaders. See Maureen Dowd, "The Longest Week," p. A-17.

18. Rosenthal, "Bush Sends U.S. Forces to Saudi Arabia," pp. A-1, A-8; R. W. Apple Jr., "U.S. May Send Saudis a Force of 50,000," *New York Times*, August 9, 1990, pp. A-1, A-14.

19. Remarks and a question-and-answer session with reporters, August 27, 1990, in *Public Papers: Bush, 1990*, Vol. 2, pp. 1171–72; remarks at a White House briefing for members of Congress on the Persian Gulf crisis, August 28, 1990, in *Public Papers:*

Bush, 1990, Vol. 2, pp. 1172–74; R. W. Apple Jr., "Bush Briefs Legislators on Crisis and They Back His Gulf Strategy," *New York Times*, August 29, 1990, pp. A-1, A-14.

20. President Bush's address before a joint session of the Congress, September 11, 1990, in *Public Papers: Bush, 1990*, Vol. 2, pp. 1218–22.

21. The president's news conference, September 21, 1990, in *Public Papers: Bush, 1990*, Vol. 2, p. 1264.

22. David Hoffman, "Peace or War in Gulf?" *Washington Post*, reprinted in *Mount Vernon Daily Argus*, September 30, 1990, pp. A-1, A-9.

23. Nathaniel Nash, "Senate Gives Bush Limited Backing on Gulf Policy," *New York Times*, October 3, 1990, p. A-13.

24. Thomas Friedman, "Senators Demand Role in Approving Any Move on Iraq," *New York Times*, October 18, 1990, pp. A-1, A-12.

25. Ibid.; George Church, "Trip Wires to War," Time, October 29, 1990, pp. 48–50.

26. Friedman, "Senators Demand Role in Approving Any Move on Iraq," pp. A-1, A-12.

27. Ibid.

28. Maureen Dowd, "Congress Chiefs Urge Bush to Move Slowly over War," *New York Times*, October 31, 1990, p. A-16.

29. Baker, *The Politics of Diplomacy*, pp. 303, 329–30.

30. President Bush's remarks announcing the resignation of William Bennett . . . and a question-and-answer session with reporters, November 8, 1990, in *Public Papers: Bush, 1990*, Vol. 2, pp. 1578–79; President's news conference on the Persian Gulf crisis, November 8, 1990, in *Public Papers: Bush, 1990*, Vol. 2, pp. 1581; Baker, *The Politics of Diplomacy*, pp. 329–31, 335.

31. "Democrats, Fearing War, Warn Bush," *Washington Post* and *Baltimore Sun*, reprinted in *Mount Vernon Daily Argus*, November 12, 1990, pp. A-1, A-12; "GOP Senators Ask Bush to Spell Out Goals in Gulf," *Los Angeles Times*, reprinted in *Mount Vernon Daily Argus*, November 14, 1990, pp. A-1, A-11; Andrew Rosenthal, "Senators Asking President to Call Session over Gulf," *New York Times*, November 14, 19990, pp. A-1, A-14.

32. "Bush Faces Bipartisan Challenge," *Los Angeles Times*, reprinted in *Mount Vernon Daily Argus*, November 13, 1990, pp. A-1, A-15; "GOP Senators Ask Bush to Spell Out Goals in Gulf," pp. A-1, 11; Rosenthal, "Senators Asking President to Call Session over Gulf," pp. A-1, A-14; Baker, *The Politics of Diplomacy*, p. 337.

33. Rosenthal, "Senators Asking President to Call Session over Gulf," pp. A-1,A-14; R. W. Apple Jr., "The Barriers Facing Bush," *New York Times*, November 14, 1990, pp. A-1, A-14; Maureen Dowd, "President Seems to Blunt Calls for Gulf Session," *New York Times*, November 15, 1990, pp. A-1, A-18; President Bush's letter to congressional leaders on the deployment of additional U.S. armed forces to the Persian Gulf, November 15, 1990, in *Public Papers: Bush, 1990*, Vol. 2, pp. 1617–18. See also Baker, *The Politics of Diplomacy*, p. 338.

34. R. W. Apple Jr., "U.S. Reported Ready to Ask UN to Back a Gulf Assault," *New York Times*, November 16, 1990, p. A-12; "UN Gives Iraq Ultimatum," *Washington Post*, reprinted in *Mount Vernon Daily Argus*, November 30, 1990, pp. A-1, A-10; and Baker, *The Politics of Diplomacy*, pp. 300–328, 332, 344.

35. "Democrats Want More Time for Iraq Sanctions," *Los Angeles Times*, reprinted in *Mount Vernon Daily Argus*, November 28, 1990, pp. A-1, A-8; U.S. Congress, Senate, Armed Services Committee, *Crisis in the Persian Gulf Region: U.S. Policy Options and Implications, Hearings before the Senate Armed Services Committee*, 101st Cong., 2d sess., 1990.

36. "Democrats Want More Time for Iraq Sanctions," pp. A-1, A-8; "Even the War Experts Disagree," *Newsweek*, December 10, 1990, p. 32.

37. President's news conference, November 30, 1990, in *Public Papers: Bush, 1990*, Vol. 2, p. 1720; R. W. Apple Jr., "Bush Offers to Send Baker on a Peace Mission to Iraq, but Vows Resolve in a War," *New York Times*, December 1, 1990, pp. A-1, A-7; Baker, *The Politics of Diplomacy*, pp. 349–52.

38. The president's news conference, November 30, 1990, in *Public Papers: Bush, 1990*, Vol. 2, pp. 1721–25.

39. The president's news conference, November 30, 1990, in *Public Papers: Bush, 1990*, Vol. 2, p. 1726; Baker, *The Politics of Diplomacy*, pp. 338–39.

40. Susan Rasky, "House Democrats Caution Bush on War," *New York Times*, December 5, 1990, p. A-22.

41. R. W. Apple Jr., "The Collapse of a Coalition," *New York Times*, December 6, 1990, pp. A-1, A-17; "Excerpts from Remarks by Webster and Baker on Embargo's Drain on Iraq," *New York Times*, December 6, 1990, p. A-16; Susan Rasky, "Congress and the Gulf," *New York Times*, December 17, 1990, pp. A-1, A-13; and Baker, *The Politics of Diplomacy*, pp. 339–42.

42. Rasky, "House Democrats Caution Bush on War," p. A-22.

43. Ibid.; Editorial, "Who Can Declare War?" *New York Times*, December 15, 1990, p. A-26; *Dellums v. Bush*, 752 F. Supp. 1141 (D.D.C., 1990).

44. Neil Lewis, "Lawmakers Lose a Suit on War Powers," *New York Times*, December 14, 1990, p. A-15; *Dellums v. Bush*, 752 F. Supp. 1141 (D.D.C., 1990); Anthony Lewis, "Republic under Law," *New York Times*, January 4, 1991, p. A-27.

45. Remarks on the nomination of the secretary of labor and the Persian Gulf crisis and a question-and-answer session with reporters, December 14, 1990, in *Public Papers: Bush, 1990*, Vol. 2, pp. 1796–97; President's news conference with regional reporters, December 18, 1990, in *Public Papers: Bush, 1990*, Vol. 2, p. 1808; and remarks and a question-and-answer session with reporters at Camp David, Maryland, following discussions with Prime Minister John Major of the United Kingdom, December 22, 1990, in *Public Papers: Bush, 1990*, Vol. 2, p. 1818.

46. "Democrats Threaten Gulf Funds," *Los Angeles Times*, reprinted in *Mount Vernon Daily Argus*, December 30, 1990, p. 1.

47. Thomas Friedman, "White House Hints It May Talk If Iraq Offers a New Date," *New York Times*, January 3, 1991, p. A-1, A-8; Baker, *The Politics of Diplomacy*, pp. 333–44.

48. Andrew Rosenthal, "U.S. Offers to Fly Baker to Geneva to Talk to Iraq," *New York Times*, January 4, 1991, pp. A-1, A-8; Baker, *The Politics of Diplomacy*, p. 354.

49. Adam Clymer, "102d Congress Opens Troubled on Gulf but without a Consensus," *New York Times*, January 4, 1991, pp. A-1, A-8; "Congress to Debate Gulf Crisis," *Los Angeles Times*, reprinted in *Mount Vernon Daily Argus*, January 4, 1991, pp. A-1, A-16.

50. Clymer, "102d Congress Opens Troubled on Gulf but without a Consensus," pp. A-1, A-8; "Congress to Debate Gulf Crisis," pp. A-1, A-16.

51. Adam Clymer, "Senate Prepares for a Gulf Debate Soon after Baker Meets with Aziz," New York Times, January 5, 1991, p. A-4; Adam Clymer, "Votes Backing Use of Force Are Predicted in Congress," New York Times, January 7, 1991, p. A-11.

52. Clymer, "Votes Backing Use of Force Are Predicted in Congress," p. A-11; George Will, "Bush Cannot Legally Use Force without a Congressional OK," *Mount Vernon Daily Argus*, January 11, 1991, p. A-16; Baker, *The Politics of Diplomacy*, pp. 333–39.

53. "Bush's Letter to Congressional Leaders," *New York Times*, January 9, 1991, p. A-6; Adam Clymer, "Bush Asks Congress to Back Use of Force If Iraq Defies Deadline on Kuwait Pullout," *New York Times*, January 9, 1991, pp. A-1, A-6; "Bush Seeks OK

for War," *Los Angeles Times*, reprinted in *Mount Vernon Daily Argus*, January 9, 1991, pp. A-1, A-8.

54. Clymer, "Bush Asks Congress to Back Use of Force," pp. A-1, A-6; "Bush Seeks OK for War," *Los Angeles Times*, reprinted in *Mount Vernon Daily Argus*, January 9, 1991, pp. A-1, A-8.

55. President's news conference on the Persian Gulf crisis, January 9, 1991, in *Public Papers: Bush, 1991*, Vol. 1, p. 20. Wormuth and Firmage point out that, in most of the instances that have been cited as examples of presidents' using the armed forces without a declaration of war, they were doing so pursuant to treaty or statute or some other form of congressional authorization or approval. See Wormuth and Firmage, *To Chain the Dog of War*, pp. 135–51.

56. "Congress Appears More Likely to Back Bush," *Washington Post*, reprinted in *Mount Vernon Daily Argus*, January 10, 1991, p. A-8; Adam Clymer, "Congress Nears War Debate, as Bush Side Gains," *New York Times*, January 10, 1991, p. A-17. On Solarz, see Robin Toner, "From a Dove to a Hawk: 25-Year Trip," *New York Times*, January 14, 1991, p. A-11; Stephen Solarz, "The Stakes in the Gulf," *The New Republic*, January 7, 14, 1991.

57. "Congress Appears More Likely to Back Bush," p. A-8; Clymer, "Congress Nears War Debate, as Bush Side Gains," p. A-17; "Congress Debates Use of Force in Gulf," *Washington Post*, reprinted in *Mount Vernon Daily Argus*, January 11, 1991, pp. A-1, A-10. For the text of the various resolutions, see "Excerpts from Gulf Resolutions before Congress," *New York Times*, January 12, 1991, p. A-7. The Michel–Solarz Resolution was also known as H.J. Res. 77, 102d Cong., 1st sess., 1991, and would eventually become Public Law 102-1.

58. "Congress Debates Use of Force in Gulf," *Washington Post*, reprinted in *Mount Vernon Daily Argus*, January 11, 1991, pp. A-1, A-10; Associated Press, "Congress Appears Ready to Back Bush," *Mount Vernon Daily Argus*, January 12, 1991, pp. A-1, A-10; Adam Clymer, "Slim Senate Majority Is Expected but House Backing Appears Solid," *New York Times*, January 12, 1991, pp. A-1, A-7; Elaine Sciolino, "Senator Tries to Balance Party and Constituency," *New York Times*, Janaury 11, 1991, p. A-9; Martin Tolchin, "Southern Democrats Are Torn as Vote Nears," *New York Times*, January 12, 1991, p. A-7.

59. "War and Peace: A Sampling from the Debate on Capitol Hill," *New York Times*, January 11, 1991, p. A-8; "Day 2: Lawmakers Debate War and More Time for Sanctions," *New York Times*, January 12, 1991, p. A-6. There was a certain irony in longtime critics of the United Nations like Strom Thurmond suddenly calling on Congress to show American support for the UN.

60. "War and Peace: A Sampling from the Debate on Capitol Hill," p. A-8; "Day 3: Remarks in Congress during the Last Hours of Debate," *New York Times*, January 13, 1991, p. A-10.

61. Adam Clymer, "Slim Senate Majority Is Expected But House Backing Appears Solid," pp. A-1, A-7; "Day 2: Lawmakers Debate War and More Time for Sanctions," p. A-6. Senator Nunn would later say upon his retirement from the Senate that his vote against authorizing the use of force had been a mistake because it had been based on the erroneous assumption that the United States would suffer between 10,000 and 20,000 casualties in forcing Iraqi troops from Kuwait. See Nolan Walters, Knight-Ridder Newspapers, "Nunn Leaving Politics with Little Regret: War Vote Removed Presidential Hopes," in *Mount Vernon Daily Argus*, January 2, 1997, p. B-3.

62. Adam Clymer, "Legislators Take Sides for Combat or for Reliance on the Sanctions," *New York Times*, January 11, 1991, pp. A-1, A-9; "Day 3: Remarks in Congress During the Last Hours of Debate," p. A-10.

63. John Yang, "An Agonizing Emotional Vote in Both Houses," *Washington Post*,

reprinted in *Mount Vernon Daily Argus*, January 13, 1991, pp. A-1, A-14; David Broder, "Congress Finally Did Its Job in Somber, Civil War Debate," *Mount Vernon Daily Argus*, January 17, 1991, p. A-12.

64. Adam Clymer, "Congress Acts to Authorize War in Gulf: Margins Are 5 Votes in Senate, 67 in House," *New York Times*, January 13, 1991, pp. A-1, A-11.

65. Clymer, "Congress Acts to Authorize War in Gulf," pp. A-1, A-11.

66. Ibid.

67. Clymer, "Slim Senate Majority Is Expected but House Backing Appears Solid," pp. A-1, A-7; R. W. Apple Jr., "Bush's Limited Victory," New York Times, January 13, 1991, pp. A-1, A-11; Adam Clymer, "Congress in Step," New York Times, January 14, 1991, p. A-11.

68. Apple, "Bush's Limited Victory," pp. A-1, A-11; Anthony Lewis, "Presidential Power," *New York Times*, January 14, 1991, p. A-17; and Charles Krauthammer, "A Forceful and Shrewd George Bush," *Mount Vernon Daily Argus*, March 4, 1991, p. A-10.

69. President's News Conference, January 12, 1991, in *Public Papers: Bush, 1991*, Vol. 1, pp. 31–36.

70. Statement on signing the resolution authorizing the use of military force against Iraq, January 14, 1991, in *Public Papers: Bush, 1991*, Vol. 1, p. 40.

71. Letter to congressional leaders transmitting a report pursuant to the resolution authorizing the use of force against Iraq, January 16, 1991, in *Public Papers: Bush, 1991*, Vol. 1, p. 42; Address to the nation announcing allied military action in the Persian Gulf, January 16, 1991, in *Public Papers: Bush, 1991*, Vol. 1, pp. 42–43.

72. Letter to congressional leaders on the Persian Gulf conflict, January 18, 1991, in *Public Papers: Bush, 1991*, Vol. 1, p. 52.

Discussant: Edward N. Ney

I feel a little strange here—when I saw this lineup, I called Professor Levantrosser, and I said, "This is all about Latin America. I was in Canada. The temperature is different, lots of things were different." He said, "Oh, let's call it 'The Americas.'" So those of you who read the *New York Times* yesterday, you might have seen this wonderful article on a snake from prehistoric time, where they literally found maybe there were little feet on the side of the snake. So I feel like I'm little feet on this program.

There were three very important issues involving Canada during the Bush years that I'd like to talk about. As background for Canada, I had lunch one day with Peter Jennings, the fine ABC broadcaster, who is a good Canadian. He said, "Listen, Ney, I want to tell you one thing. When you go up to Canada, you must understand most Canadians believe that Americans take them for granted; that we're there, we're sort of your extra state, you can do whatever you want with us." Peter wasn't joking, because a lot of Canadians have that kind of view. But I must say, during the years when George Bush was president and prior to that, with President Reagan, the relationship was extraordinarily good, and there was much to do.

The most important part of the relationship between Canada and the United States centers on trade. I don't want to take away from my friend Bob Mosbacher, since he was overseeing the whole world of trade as secretary of commerce. The greatest trade relationship in the world exists between the United States and Canada. There's nothing like it. It's the biggest by far. President Reagan pushed the then-prime minister Mulroney to enact the United States–Canada Free Trade Agreement. They got it done just as President Reagan was leaving office. It started on January 1, 1989, a few days before President Bush came into office, and he had been very involved in the process. It was a tough battle in Canada, because it was done during the campaign. Mulroney was elected for his second term in November 1988, the same time that President Bush was winning his election. The biggest election issue in Canada was free trade, and the two opposition parties—the Liberal Party and the New Democratic Party (NDP)—fought hard against it. Many Canadians thought they would, as usual, "be taken by the Americans" in this deal.

Well, it turned out that Mulroney won the campaign, and boom, he put the free trade in, and it's been an enormous success. As it started off, the economy wasn't good at the time; the Canadian dollar went up to 89 cents versus the U.S. dollar—today it's 73, about where it should be. Huge numbers of Canadians drove down to Buffalo and Seattle to buy goods in the United States because they were so cheap. The United States–Canada Free Trade Agreement was obviously the basis for NAFTA [North American Free Trade Agreement], and as soon as United States–Canada free trade started, President Bush felt it was time to have Mexico come in.

Times, in the late 1980s, were not good in Mexico. There was 20–25 percent unemployment and a very tough and difficult political situation, but Bush fought for Mexico in NAFTA. It was finally signed after President Clinton came into office, but the major support for NAFTA was under the direction of President Bush, Secretary of Commerce Bob Mosbacher, Carla Hills (the U.S. Trade Representative [USTR]), and many others.

At the same time, the Canadians didn't care much for NAFTA. They'd had this terrible internal fight on the United States–Canada Free Trade pact and weren't ready to gear up again. Every single day I was in Canada—over three years—there was criticism in the media of the United States–Canada Free Trade Agreement. Politically, they were against it, and they fought it, and fortunately they didn't win anything. Its growth has been phenomenal.

Today, with NAFTA, we have $350 billion in trade between the three countries, and what we always wanted is to be right in the center of it. We have strong trade growth with Mexico, and it's continued to be great with Canada. I'm discouraged, as a lot of people are, that the current administration did not push when they could have, two or three years ago, to get a fast track set up in Congress to bring Chile and others into the NAFTA.

The second high-profile area in Canada was environment. You might think, well, Canada and the United States have the same environment. But the winds, the currents, drive pollutants more from the upper half of the United States into Canada than in reverse. We have 260 million people; Canada has 28 million people. George Bush—particularly with Bill Reilly, who was his environmental minister—did a marvelous job to get this through Congress. Senator George Mitchell, who came from Maine, knows a lot about acid rain and how it affected Maine, and he gave the pact a lot of support.

You may know that, after the morning of Friday, August 3, when the Iraq–Kuwait War started, the president did not leave the United States until after that war was over. The first trip he took outside the United States was around March 10, 1991. He came up to the Canadian capital, Ottawa, where the prime minister and President Bush, in a very moving and important ceremony, signed the United States–Canada Environmental Bill. One of the problems in the United States was that factories, U.S. industries, were going to have to spend about $30 billion to do various things to their factories to clean things up. Those were done; it's been paid. I was in Washington last week when Prime Minister Jean Chretien was making a state visit to the United States. He said, "We've never had any environmental problems since 1991."

Lastly, we've heard quite a lot here this morning about Iraq–Kuwait—in particular, Desert Storm. I received a call the morning of August 3 at 6 a.m. from Prime Minister Mulroney. He said that, as usual in a crisis, he got the "second call" from President Bush that morning—"President Bush always called Margaret Thatcher first." Mulroney promised, on the spot, that he would send some destroyers, airplanes, field hospitals—as much as they could. He later endured a bitter, tough debate in the House of Parliament—similar to what happened here in our Congress—and he won Parliament's support.

Whether it's the greatest trade relationship in the world, or critical issues in the environment, or when you get down to the real tough, final stage of going to war for some principles, I think most Americans and Canadians feel much the same about the big issues. We have an excellent relationship that has been built up over 200 years with certainly one of the most important allies that we have in the world. When tough times come, we've always been able to work together.

I'd just like to close by saying that there were an enormous number of people in the Bush administration who helped us make things happen in Ottawa. There were obviously Jim Baker, Brent Scowcroft, Bob Mosbacher, Carla Hills, and Jules Katz of the USTR, Bill Reilly and Larry Eagleberger at state, Bob "the Z Man" Zoellick, and on and on. Also, the people at the embassy and the six consulates across the country did a superb job, and I think, best of all, we had a great president, George Bush.

Discussant: Mark Falcoff

I'm going to confine my remarks to Professor LaRocque's paper, and I must say that the oral presentation was somewhat different from the paper itself, so perhaps you'll be hearing things from me that you didn't hear from Professor LaRocque but would get if you read his paper, which I understand is available.

Let me begin by making the best possible case for his argument. If we assume that the test of a successful Cuban policy for the United States is acceptance of Cuba "as it is"—and this is the term that is used in the paper—then clearly all our policies toward that island have been failed policies since the break in diplomatic relations and the imposition of the embargo in 1960, and, therefore, the Bush administration would be no exception. But that conclusion presents itself only if that is the single criterion of judgment.

Even so, it's not true, as the paper seems to suggest, that the Bush administration's refusal to recognize the Castro regime was dictated wholly by a desire to vindicate past policies. A quite different policy could conceivably have served the same purpose. For example, the day after the disappearance of the Soviet Union, President Bush could have called a press conference and simply recognized the Castro regime and lifted the embargo unilaterally in one fell swoop. He could have justified his decision with the argument that, after all, Cuba in and of itself was never a serious threat to the United States; that our legitimate concern had to do with the island's military and political alliance with the contending superpower; and that Cuba just wasn't an important enough country to merit special policies. This would have served several conceivable U.S. policies all at once: it would have removed the issue from our international plate; it would have vindicated past policies; and it would have humiliated Fidel Castro, all at the same time.

Unfortunately, as those of us who have worked in Washington know, such rapid responses to changes in the international environment are not really possible. Our system is slow and cumbersome and requires consensus building, particularly when policy structures have been in place for more than three decades. Nor is it entirely clear that reconciliation with the Castro regime—which, somewhat irritatingly, Professor LaRocque throughout his paper continually confuses with Cuba itself—is always necessarily and obviously the course of action that best serves the interests of the United States. That's a point to which I shall return.

What, then, was it that drove Bush's policy toward Cuba? Well, first of all, domestic politics. Now here, surely, I am not revealing any dark secrets. Everybody knows that the Cuban American community is very interested in our policies toward the island; it's very well politically organized; it exercises an influence disproportionate to its actual numbers thanks to its geographical concentration in states rich in electoral votes—namely, Florida and New Jersey. But that is not really saying anything very extraordinary, because the same could be said—and indeed often is said—about the American Jewish community and Israel and deserves to be noted in the cases of the Greek American community and Greece, the Irish American community and Northern Ireland, and, in recent times, the African American community with regard to South Africa and Haiti. I certainly agree that it would be nice if we could make our foreign policy in a platonic vacuum, where the only determining factor was some universally agreed-upon notion of national interest, but quite apart from the fact that no such definition exists, this really amounts to delegitimating the rights of Cuban Americans, Jews, Greek-Americans, Irish Americans, and African Americans—or any other organized group—to participate in our democratic political process.

Moreover—and this is something perhaps not often noted—in the specific case of Cuba, the success of the Cuban American community in helping to shape our policy is due largely to the fact that it is sailing with the ideological wind behind its back. Recent surveys show—and the most recent of which I cite was from the Chicago Council on Foreign Relations, carried out two years ago—that the American public is solidly behind our policy. The average American, according to this poll, places Fidel Castro on the barometer of esteem roughly halfway between Yasir Arafat and Saddam Hussein and ranks Cuba as a country well below China, Saudi Arabia, or India—it only barely edges out North Korea. By the way, when queried about the proper response to a popular uprising in Cuba, nearly half of those Americans polled—44 percent—favored military intervention there, bested only by the percentages that would favor a similar response if Russia invaded Western Europe or Iraq invaded Saudi Arabia. Now, maybe Americans are wrong, but they seem to know their own mind, and elected officials cannot be blamed for taking note of the fact.

Now, insofar as President Bush's refusal to accept Cuba "as it is" is concerned, his policy was also consistent with his administration's articulated embrace of democracy and free markets as the linchpin of its hemispheric policies. To accept Cuba without preconditions would, in effect, have sent a signal to antidemocratic forces in many countries—particularly the military—that the United States was reverting to a policy of business as usual with authoritarian regimes. Now, this point is not a trivial one because, during the Bush administration, the State Department did, in fact, confront crises of civil and military relations in Venezuela and in Haiti, the second of which triggered a serious refugee problem that, as we know, forced its successor to militarily occupy that country.

It is true that most of the Latin American governments disagreed with President Bush's Cuba policy, though far from vociferously, but at the same time, in the 1990 meeting of the Organization of American States in Santiago, Chile, for the very first time the Latin American countries discarded the Estrada Doctrine and endorsed collective intervention to restore democracy where extinguished by regimes such as the one in Haiti. So, in broad general terms, the Bush people were not that far away from the hemispheric consensus.

Now, I can quite see that Professor LaRocque is not enthusiastic about the "democracy and markets" mantra, but this was certainly not true of the Latins themselves. Both during and after the Bush administration, politicians embracing both have been elected and reelected in countries as diverse as Argentina, Brazil, Chile, Peru, Panama, Nicaragua—twice—and Mexico. Conversely, politicians who favored Latin America "as it is"—or rather, as it was around 1989—have been consistently defeated in national races.

Finally, the Bush administration's Cuba policy was held in place by the strongest force in any government, then, now, and forever: inertia. Any policy that's been in place for more than 30 years is bound to develop a wide range of diverse constituencies. This policy not only enjoys the support of the broad American public but also serves a useful foreign policy function. To the extent that, as critics often claim, it maintains the Castro regime in power, it assures the permanence of a valuable counterexample in Latin America. Let no one say that Marxism has never been given a chance to show what it can do in the region: there's the Cuban case for everyone to see.

But it is not only the United States that can derive benefit from the policy. On the Cuban side, the U.S. embargo provides Castro with an excuse for the fact that his economic system does not work and cannot work. It has also allowed him to draw on large sums on what is left of the diminishing account of Cuban nationalism at home and anti-Americanism abroad. Meanwhile, allies of the United States—like Mexico, Canada, Spain, and France—have been able to use their political and economic support for Castro to prove their independence from the United States. In the case of Canada, at this point its quarrel with the United States over Helms–Burton may be one of the very few issues that unify that country and provide a crucial element of self-definition.

I do not personally share Professor LaRocque's view that, by refusing to normalize relations with Cuba, the Bush administration, not Fidel Castro, is responsible for the calcification of the island's political and economic institutions. But if that is even true, there may be some method to its madness, for the fact is that a breakdown of Cuba's totalitarian system could indeed lead to a destabilization of the entire circum-Caribbean. At least under Castro, things in Cuba are quiet, and if there's anything Washington hates, it's disorder.

No one can predict, of course, with any certainty exactly what will happen if and when the Castro regime is overthrown, but, of course, it is possible that the island would degenerate into civil war, which, in turn, could produce a refugee crisis of massive proportions, economic dislocations, and even the accession to power of criminal elements allied to the drug lords of South America. Under such circumstances, one European critic of American policy has written, the United States and the smaller powers of the region someday may look back with nostalgia on the time when Cuba was still Castro's Cuba—Communist and safely isolated.

Discussant: G. Philip Hughes

My perspective on Bush administration Latin America policy comes from three experiences: first, working on Latin America policy for roughly the first five years of the Reagan administration as one of my portfolios as Bush's deputy foreign policy adviser when he was vice president and then later as director for Latin American affairs on the NSC [National Security Council] staff; second, from a position pretty close to the center of things as executive secretary of the National Security Council in the beginning of President Bush's administration; and then finally, observing and implementing in my area that Latin America policy of the Bush administration from one corner of the inter-American region as ambassador in the eastern Caribbean.

What for me is remarkable about the three papers presented today is the choice of topics of the authors: two papers on Panama, one specifically focused on war powers and war powers going over into the Gulf War arena, and another paper on Cuba. When I read these papers, I felt like I was on a planet different from that of the observers during the Bush administration, because from my point of view those were far from the centerpieces of Bush administration Latin America policy. So I think the most useful comment I can make today on these papers is to observe what I think Bush administration Latin America policy was really about.

What are the hallmarks of President Bush's Latin America policy? Frankly, I think the record is a mixed bag of four kinds of accomplishments or initiatives or consequences, and I'd like to touch on those briefly and then summarize at the end what I think were some of the characteristics of the policy.

The first and most salient accomplishment, I think, of Bush policy in Latin America was the clearing away and cauterizing of what I think the administration regarded as a troublesome legacy of past policies—specifically, the contra program in Central America. I believe that, right from the beginning, President Bush, Secretary Baker, perhaps Brent Scowcroft, and other advisers decided that they did not want to go down the road of the Reagan administration, spending enormous energy and political capital trying to maintain lethal aid for the contras and being embroiled in continuous wrangling with Congress over this issue. I think they reckoned that they would have bigger fish to fry eventually with Congress and didn't want to spend their capital in this way. I'm not sure how much their calculation about the emerging changes in the Soviet Union and East bloc affected the calculus in this domain, but it seems pretty clear to me that the president and his advisers reckoned that they would have to bring about peace in Central America in some other way than via the contra program and pressure on Nicaragua. That calculation, it seems to me, led to a key personnel decision—namely, the appointment of Bernie Aronson—a Democrat with great personal credibility among Capitol Hill Democrats, someone who had also worked in support of the Reagan administration's Central America policy—as the key Latin America figure in the State Department, the assistant secretary for intra-American affairs. It was basically Bernie's job to solve the Central America problem and liquidate what the Bush administration apparently regarded as the political liability of the contra program. Without going into the twists and turns of the path that led us to the Esquipulas Agreement and the first Nicaraguan elections—Bill Pryce is probably better able to do that than I am—Bernie did it, and the administration did it.

In the process, of course, the administration was aided by the collapse of the Berlin Wall and of the Warsaw Pact, the cutoff of aid from a collapsing Soviet economy to Cuba, and Cuba's distraction with its own disagreements, both with Moscow and with the Sandinistas. But still, for many, the Nicaraguan elections looked like a great gamble. If the Sandinistas had won, even if they had ceased their support for guerrilla movements in El Salvador and Guatemala, the elections could have legitimated and solidified a Marxist government in the middle of Central America—albeit one bereft of Soviet–Cuban support and no longer part of a larger global movement. As it turned out, the Bush administration won that gamble, and the festering sore of Central America policy became much less painful and costly for the administration, particularly after 1990. So I'd like to point out here that this is one dividend, it seems to me, that Latin America policy paid for the Bush administration in its other foreign policy domains. You see, if you would, by moving this very, very controversial issue off the congressional agenda, it greatly simplified the administration's dealings with Congress on the Gulf War effort. It was one more important, contentious thing that didn't have to be dealt with with Congress, or at least not nearly to the extent it was in the Reagan administration.

A second feature of Bush administration policy in Latin America, I think, was visionary initiatives that changed—or had the potential to transform—the historic relationship between the United States and its Latin American neighbors. I'll mention four. The first is the Enterprise for the Americas Initiative, announced in June 1990. I think this initiative was very largely sparked by a remarkable set of leaders who rose to power in Latin America more or less concurrently with George Bush's arrival in the presidency: Menem in Argentina; Collor, who looked so very promising and so very vibrant, in Brazil (it turned out differently, of course); Aylwin in Chile; Fujimori in Peru; Salinas in Mexico. The Enterprise for the Americas Initiative as conceived by the Bush administration had something for everybody. It was a three-part program intended to provide debt relief, via the Brady Plan and debt-for-nature swaps, for economies that were heavily debt-burdened; an investment incentive for economies that very much needed investment and infrastructure to grow, structured as an incentive program to foster market opening and liberalization of Latin economies; and the negotiation—the offer to negotiate—a hemispheric free trade area, a project that we are now actively working on, thanks to the 1994 Miami Summit of the Americas of President Clinton.

Second historic initiative: NAFTA, the North American Free Trade Agreement, which built on President Reagan's United States–Canada Free Trade Agreement, which Ambassador Ney already mentioned, gave concrete effect to President Reagan's rather vague vision of a North American accord in his 1980 campaign, capitalized on the unique personality of Carlos Salinas as president of Mexico, and changed—I hope forever—the way the United States and Mexico relate to each other.

Third initiative: the Cartagena Counter-Narcotics Summit and the regional counternarcotics strategy that combined economic incentives, the Andean Trade Preference Act, which was enacted during President Bush's presidency, intensified interdiction efforts closer to the shores of South America, a "linear," or "kingpin," strategy for targeting enforcement efforts on drug cartel leaders, and intensified efforts to combat money laundering.

Fourth initiative—here I have a little bit different twist on this from what Mark Falcoff just offered you—an effort to revitalize the OAS [Organization of American States] as a regional institution, particularly via the OAS Democracy Initiative and the 1991 Santiago Declaration that Mark alluded to, which, for the first time, made unconstitutional changes of government a matter of concern and possible response for the hemisphere's governments—in other words, that changed the Estrada Doctrine historically for the region.

A third hallmark of Bush administration Latin America policy was, of course, crisis response. Here's where Panama and Haiti and the response to the autocoups—or the attempted auto-coup in Guatemala and the actual auto-coup in Peru—fit in. There's plenty that's been written about Panama, and Bill Pryce, who served as deputy chief of mission there, is in a much better position to discuss that intervention in detail than I am. But I'd make one point about the Panama operation, and it's this—totally different from the War Powers observations that have been made: its main significance was that it put paid, once and for all, to the image of George Bush as a "wimp," an image that dogged him in his second term as vice president and during his presidential campaign. This is a second area in which Bush's Latin America policy paid dividends, it seems to me, for his Gulf War policy later on. Because there could be no doubt, I think, either in the minds of allied leaders with whom we were working in building the coalition or, frankly, in the mind of Saddam Hussein as we were trying to face him down, that George Bush was fully capable of doing what, in the end, we did.

The fourth basket of things—and this is, I think, a minor and really unintended consequence of the global foreign policy initiatives of George Bush—is that we did, I think, in the intra-American region end up shortchanging and passing over a bit some traditional friends. The crises in the northern Caribbean, in Cuba and Haiti—or the relationship with Cuba and the crisis in Haiti—and our other initiatives in the region led us to pay relatively little attention to some very tiny countries in the eastern Caribbean that had been very close and very supportive to the United States through the Reagan years and that were accustomed to enjoying a very special relationship with the United States. Our aid levels dropped, and the countries in that little corner of the world ended up feeling rather abandoned and a bit ill used. But in the overall scheme of things, this is a very, very minor consideration.

What were the characteristics of Bush administration Latin America policy? I'd point out about four or five, quickly. The first is, it seems to me, that it was a second-tier policy. One irony of Bush's political career was that people around Latin America thought mistakenly that he spoke Spanish. They clearly regarded him as someone who was *simpático*. Why? Well, perhaps it came from his 1980 primary victory in Puerto Rico; perhaps because his son Jeb was married to a Mexican woman, Colomba; perhaps because of his many friends and frequent travels around Latin America from his oil business days and from his days at the UN. President Bush was undeniably personally interested in Latin America. However, considering all the other priorities of the administration—the Gulf War, relations with Russia, relations with the allies, the Middle East peace process, China relations, Japan—clearly, Latin America was not a high priority for most of the other senior members of the administration. In fact, practically the sole exception to this was Bob Mosbacher here during his time as secretary of commerce. That, in a sense, makes the Bush administration's accomplishments in Latin America policy therefore all the more remarkable because those accomplishments had to be produced very largely on the energy of subcabinet-level officials—with occasional higher-level involvement sort of squeezed in between major world crises.

A second characteristic of Bush administration Latin America policy: it had, as has already been mentioned, two overarching unifying themes—democracy and market opening, market liberalization. However, in execution, I think, very often it was a bit fragmented. It sometimes seemed, from my vantage point, as though the Enterprise for the Americas Initiative was one thing, Central America policy was another thing, the drugs initiative was yet another thing, Haiti was still another matter. Consequently, the kind of consistency and thematic unity of policy that I think we saw more in the Reagan administration didn't quite apply here. I think particularly the Enterprise for the Americas Initiative suffered a bit (but Secretary Mosbacher can better comment on this than I can) from a tendency to sort of franchise out policy, to put USTR in charge of the trade part of the initiative, to put the Treasury Department in charge of the debt reduction part of the initiative, to have the State Department encouraging foreign contributions to the Multilateral Investment Fund. Lacking an overall coordinator, the result was that different parts of the initiative kind of never moved forward very far.

Third, I think Bush's Latin America policy fell into the trap of many other Bush policies. That is, the combination that we've heard in previous sessions of this conference of putting a premium on secrecy and announcing new policy initiatives as surprises, combined with a real phobia, a real aversion to actively promoting and selling and following up on policies—what in some of yesterday's panels were referred to as, in a derisive way, the "perpetual campaigning style" of the Clinton administration—meant that visionary initiatives like the Enterprise for the Americas Initiative often sank below the waves. Others—like the efforts to revitalize the OAS—got no notice, and the administration received scant credit for its counternarcotics efforts.

Fourth, I think the administration's policy was often, as has been mentioned, politically compromised. This is particularly true of policy toward Haiti and Cuba. What the administration could do vis-à-vis Haiti after the overthrow of Aristede was very much, I think, circumscribed by a realistic recognition of how much support there would be for an intervention in Haiti—namely, none—and how much support there would be for receiving large numbers of refugees from Haiti in the United States—namely, none. Similarly, on the embargo policy toward Cuba, its choices were politically compromised by a very important political constituency for George Bush, one that had been loyal, one that was vital, one to which Jeb Bush was personally close—the Cuban American community in Miami. It was only logical that Bush's policies in that area would respond to domestic political imperatives.

But think about what the Bush administration record on Latin America accomplished: the contra problem liquidated and Central America pacified and on a democratic road; NAFTA negotiated in a scant two and a half years; the Washington consensus of economic policies being implemented all over Latin America; and major achievements in the counternarcotics war. To have done all that in a second-tier policy area while fighting the Gulf War is a truly remarkable record.

Discussant: Robert Mosbacher

Well, it's a great pleasure to listen to many of my colleagues, and I'll comment as I go along on a few of their comments. That's one of the nice things about being in the latter part of the program.

The Bush administration developed a trade policy that, besides establishing the whole world as a market for U.S. companies and therefore building more jobs in the United States, was based on economic security, a word that was not in fashion during the Cold War years. But, as the collapse of the Soviet Union came about, George Bush understood better than most in Washington that economic security was going to be just as important as military security for the future of our country.

He also realized that opening markets around the world would be a major accomplishment and a major goal for his administration. Particularly—and perhaps demonstrably one of the greatest accomplishments of this goal—was NAFTA itself. Now, NAFTA started out dealing primarily with Mexico, because, as Ambassador Ney has told you, the United States–Canada Free Trade Agreement had been completed in 1988—went into effect January 1, 1989—and the Canadians were not too interested in getting involved in another brouhaha. That was a pretty bruising one they'd been through, and pretty bruising internally politically for them. They wanted to sit on the sidelines while Mexico and the United States duked it out on a new free trade agreement. But as the negotiations went on, and it became apparent that this was going to become a reality, then Canada, to continue to keep its own unique position with the United States, got involved, and it became really trilateral negotiating thereafter.

Another aspect of the Bush effort in Mexico was not just a normal trade agreement as we think of them traditionally but included his desire to see us work with Mexico on many levels. As you know, Mexico shares a long, long border—as does Canada—with us; it is our neighbor—was, is, and will be our neighbor forevermore—and we have had very hot and cold relations with Mexico over the years. A goal of his, typical of George Bush, was to always create a closer friendship and ties (as you heard, having a daughter-in-law from there I think was just an added incentive). But he also specifically wanted to see us work in the environmental arena with them, and he wanted to see us work in the sociopolitical area and law enforcement, and, of course, specifically drug interdiction, which was becoming more and more important, as well as the labor differential and how that could be leveled out to some degree.

I think that he felt overall—we all did—that a sound economic policy and a sound economy in Mexico would be an important step toward our own economic security. Despite the fact that there was that demagogic comment that the only thing you'd hear was the "giant sucking sound" of jobs going down there, we have found—and it has now been established, and I don't think any longer even disputed by most—that, quite to the contrary, great numbers of jobs have been created in this country, and continue to be created in this country, as our trade grows with Mexico. As you know, Mexico has been our third largest trading partner. It is getting closer to, and soon will undoubtedly replace, Japan as the second largest and will then be behind only Canada as our most important trading partner.

We will see that there's another advantage of NAFTA, and that is that these three countries—Canada, the United States, and Mexico—will become even more cohesive, and they will be able to move forward as a trading group, more effectively using the benefits of each country to compete better with Asia and with Europe and its different economies that also are affected. So these are great benefits. Of course, if it hadn't been for NAFTA and the opening up of markets in Mexico, their peso crisis that came about in the end of 1994 would have been like the one they had in 1982, which took 10 years to recover from. But because of the open trade, Mexico has largely recovered now—not totally, but has gone a long ways on the way back. Another part of this is that President Salinas used to be fond of saying, "We want our economy to grow and keep our workers busy here, because really, we want to export to you"—to the United States—"goods and services, not people." That will be coming about also as their economy grows.

Although, as in other areas, George Bush did not always articulate this totally, he realized that trade integration not only with Canada and Mexico but with all the Americas was an important next step and a building block toward worldwide free trade. So, as Philip Hughes mentioned, the Enterprise of the Americas came into being, with the goal of a free trade area for the entire spectrum of the hemisphere. At the Miami Summit attended by President Clinton, the year 2005 now is the goal for hemispheric free trade. I think there is a chance of making that come about. However, it really started and took effect because of a combination of the Brady Plan, which, as you remember, turned their debts—which were largely uncollectible anyway—into environmental and other trade benefits. Incidentally, George Bush used to say, "You know, let's call it the 'Brady Plan,' but if it works, let's change the name to the 'Bush Plan.'" It has worked, and it has been a building block, and the Latin American countries are relatively prospering. Another great fallout of the Bush NAFTA initiative is that democracy with these open markets has spread throughout the entire hemisphere, with the exception of Cuba and perhaps, to some degree, Haiti.

Incidentally, we talked about the Bush administration and the war in the Gulf: because I had made more trips to Latin America than any of the other Bush administration cabinet officers, I happened to be sitting in President Perez's, who was president of Venezuela at that time, office when he got a note. It was the evening, about 7:30, 8:30 at night, and he and I were talking about something relatively inconsequential. One of his aides—we've all seen this happen—stuck this note in front of him, and he went on talking to me. His aide then went over—you know, not knowing how far to go with the president but finally went [knocks on table]. So he said, "Oh, excuse me, I'd better read this note." It was telling him that our first air strike had just come about in Iraq, so it was interesting. Perez, who had started out in the Reagan days and the early Bush days as not very supportive, made a radio speech that very night supporting Bush and the Gulf War.

Discussant: William T. Pryce

I'd like to emphasize that although President Bush left much of the implementation of his Latin American policy to subcabinet policy officials, he gave us clear direction. For example, he let us know what he wanted in Nicaragua—a process of free elections. I'll comment a little bit on the paper on Cuba, which speaks quite a bit about Nicaragua. President Bush worked very hard and gave us clear direction as to what we should seek in Nicaragua, which was free elections, which would be respected. Throughout the hemisphere, I think the policy worked out very well—partly because the Sandinistas always thought they would win. Had they thought they wouldn't win, they would have canceled the elections, so we never let them think they would lose. The second thing we did was work very hard to get a wide network of as many people as we possibly could into Nicaragua to observe those elections. The OAS was the principal implementer of the electoral observation process. But at the end, we got the UN, the Swiss—everybody we could possibly get came in to see that the elections would be free. We—at least some of us—had a conviction that, if there were free elections, the polls indicating a Sandinista victory wouldn't make any difference; that if people really felt their vote would count, they would come out and would vote for democracy. They would vote the rascals out—the rascals in this case being a despotic regime, and that happened.

Violetta Chamorro, I think, did a great deal to bring that country healing together in a healing process. I've got to make the point that, regarding the question of our holding back aid to Nicaragua after Chamorro was elected, the fact of the matter is, in the Bush administration we worked very, very hard and successfully to get a huge aid package for Nicaragua and for Panama. When aid was held back, it had nothing to do with the political situation in terms of the contras; what it had to do with was trying to get a viable economic program in place so that the aid would be used to foster the economy.

I would also like to just mention President Bush's very deep involvement in our policy once Violetta had won. I think it's not unknown that we didn't really think that Ortega's brother should stay on as the head of the armed forces. But Mrs. Chamorro, who was elected as president, thought that that was the best thing to do, and President Bush personally said, "She's the president, she knows best, and we'll respect her wishes. We won't push all that hard to have her dismiss him." There were people, on the Hill and other places, who thought that we should push harder for Ortega's dismissal than we did. The president made the decision to do what I think was the right thing, to respect Mrs. Chamorro's wishes without question.

In Salvador—another very great success of the Bush administration—we had, when I came over to the National Security Council, a very divisive civil war going on. We have to remember that while this was a civil war, it really was a war of a terrorist insurgency against a democratically established government. You can question how good the elections were that brought the government to power. Nevertheless, there was a constitutional, democratic government in Salvador that was trying to defend itself against terrorist attacks. In the end, there was reconciliation. Some of the goals of the opposition, the FMLN [Farabundo Martí National Liberation Front], were achieved in terms of getting a broader, more democratic government. But in essence the war was finished, democracy survived, and we now have members of the violent opposition as members of Parliament—I think that's a great success.

But I want to finish on what I think was probably the single most important legacy of President Bush's vision. Believe me, it was President Bush who conceived the idea of the Enterprise of the Americas. This is how it happened. President Bush was visiting with some of the Andean presidents in Cartageña, Colombia, and they were explaining to him—and he listened—the problems that they felt they were facing in terms of development. Basically their theme was, "We really want trade, not aid." The president came back from that trip wanting to come up with a new initiative. He wanted to have it well thought out and kept secret until he announced it. He had listened, and he asked us to listen, as to what the Latins thought this policy should be. As you know, we came out with a three-pronged plan: the Enterprise for the Americas, which came out after about four months of concentrated work inside the government. It didn't leak (I could tell you the story of why it didn't leak), but we came out with a well-conceived plan, from the president's initiative, telling us what he thought ought to happen in general terms. We worked it out, and what we had was basically the concept of free trade in the hemisphere. In the speech where he announced the Enterprise for the Americas Initiative, President Bush spoke about wanting a free-trade zone from Anchorage to Tierra del Fuego. He had a vision that his administration pushed through its entire time in office and which very fortunately became a bipartisan policy being carried out today. President Clinton adopted this policy and, in the Summit of the Americas in 1995, was able to have it adopted by the entire hemisphere as a goal that we're all now working for. I can't help but plug the Council of the Americas. Chairman Mosbacher and I are trying to help on this. Through the council, our goal is to try to have free trade in the hemisphere by 2005. We're all working very hard toward that.

One of the other two facets of the Enterprise for the Americas was debt reduction through a very successful plan, the Brady Plan. President Bush had the magnanimity not to change the name to the Bush Plan when it became successful. It was always the Brady Plan, because that's the kind of person that President Bush was.

The third point was investment encouragement, and I think we've seen today the fruits of those initial moves to try to broaden markets. But I want to come back, in conclusion, to say that there were two essential objectives in the Bush administration's Latin American policy: one was open markets, free trade in the hemisphere, debt reduction; the other was promotion of democracy.

Finally, I think we have to recognize that our Cuban policy has stayed the way it is because it has had bipartisan support. All nine presidents I served as a career foreign service officer, starting with President Eisenhower, had as an objective the restoration of democracy in Cuba. You can question what's the best way to go at that. There may be different points of view, but there is no point of view that does not posit that what's necessary is a restoration of democracy. Most of the other nations—even the nations that don't agree with the embargo, and, of course, many in the United States now don't agree with the embargo— have felt that Cuba should return to the OAS only when it's a democratic nation. This should be part of a complete process. Cuba should return not as a dictatorship, which it is, but as the 35th democratic nation.

Discussant: William H. Webster

Coming at the end of a long list of distinguished members of the Bush team, I am looking for a few things to add to what you have already heard. I think it's important to realize, when we examine President Bush's decisions and policies when he became president, that he had spent eight years as vice president of the United States under President Reagan during a period of remarkable transition and turbulence in Latin America. During most of that time, I was director of the Federal Bureau of Investigation and saw, from a slightly different perspective, the two principal concerns of our government and came over to CIA [Central Intelligence Agency] two years before President Bush was elected and came into office.

The two issues that I saw that dominated the policy scene were the issues of the surrogate war and drugs. If you think back just a little bit, you'll remember that a remarkable undertaking—largely through clandestine, covert action because of the inability or unwillingness of Congress to participate in a formal action—led to meeting the Communists wherever they made incursions in areas of the world of vital interest to the United States. The principal areas that I was involved in were Angola, Afghanistan, Cambodia, and, of course, Latin America. The policy was to try to strengthen democratic insurgencies and to strengthen democratic governments against Communist efforts. In Latin America, that became known as the contra struggle, in support of a democratic insurgency in Communist-dominated Nicaragua. It was a vital part of our policy; it was carried out aggressively under the administration of Director Casey, as director of Central Intelligence. At the same time that this was going on, we were confronting the profound impact of drug production and transshipment into the United States going on primarily in Colombia and Peru, with offshoots and entanglements in Cuba and in Panama.

Against that backdrop, I would also mention that Congress was becoming disenchanted with these efforts. The amount of money involved, the apparent lack of success—three Boland Act amendments were passed, limiting access to those countries by intelligence units and enterprises. So we were shrinking down and ending the war—the hidden or secret war—against Communist efforts in Latin America.

At the same time, George Bush had served as one of the primary focal points of the drug effort, being in charge—using Admiral Dan Murphy as his surrogate—of the efforts to interdict drugs as they came into the United States and to develop intelligence throughout Latin America and on our own coastal waters that would have some impact on the effort. So he had a profound personal and political stake in the success of our effort to deal with drugs coming from Latin America.

I'll move quickly into Panama, because that's where these interests converged. Noriega had shifted his allegiance, as Mr. Brinkley pointed out, toward the Sandinistas, which put him on the wrong side of the political fence. He had been a very agile person, cooperating on both sides to his own advantage, and being slightly involved in the drug traffic as he went along. In 1988, the early part of 1988, the Department of Justice attorneys in the southern states brought in, through the grand jury, indictments against General Noriega. I disagree slightly with Mr. Brinkley's statement that the Department of Justice got him indicted. I think that he got indicted because there wasn't enough supervision over what the U.S. attorneys were doing. That's another subject of great interest for another time, and that is, to what extent should law enforcement officers get into something of profound foreign policy significance without consulting the National Security Council. But that's about what happened, and that's what we had on our hands.

That put George Bush in a position of being a primary law enforcement official, with an intelligence background, trying to shape a policy to deal with an indicted chief of state when he got there. I was present at the meeting that Mr. Brinkley referred to, one of the very few occasions when President Bush expressed a different point of view than he believed President Reagan had on the subject of what to do about Noriega in the presence of others. George Shultz was mainly one for using military force, and Cap Weinberger was mainly one for using diplomatic force when the situations arose, but in this particular case, George Shultz wanted to see if a negotiated departure of Noriega could be achieved. Interestingly enough, too, then-vice president Bush really thought I should not have been asked to attend that meeting, even though the intelligence that I was asked to bring to that meeting—which was upstairs in the residential quarters of the White House—favored the position that George Bush had. It was a very, very sharp, strong exchange of views, and in the end, President Reagan decided to see if we could work a peaceful solution to get him out of there. It didn't work.

So that's the situation President Bush inherited when he came into office. I think we slid into our policy of what to do about Noriega, and I don't believe we violated the War Powers Resolutions, if in fact the War Powers Resolutions were constitutional. Every president—every president since that law was enacted—has said, "We don't recognize it as binding on us because it is an incursion on our constitutional powers," but they've found a way to work around it. Usually, it's been a situation in which the question was, "Was this an emergency procedure?" Whenever it was an emergency procedure, there was really no question about the War Powers Resolution; no one made an issue of it. I think that that eventually happened here in Panama.

I have to say, since the Gulf War came up in discussion and will be brought up again in a few minutes in another seminar, that I worried a great deal about whether or not we weren't getting too close to the constitutional prerogative of Congress to declare war in the Gulf because, for six months, we were preparing for war. We obviously had an opportunity to consult with and obtain congressional approval, which eventually we did get.

But in Panama, we had a situation where we were gathering increasing intelligence, we were taking specific policy moves to send signals to Noriega—bringing back our ambassador, adding more troops to support the people who were there, removing civilians, sending very strong signals—yet no decision had been made, in my memory, that we were going after Noriega, the accused drug dealer.

The incident with Major Giraldo occurred while I was in Europe, and I was getting daily messages throughout the days as this occurred, even as we were about to see the breakup of the—the reunification of Germany, the end of the Berlin Wall. This was all happening at precisely the same time. Major Giraldo contacted us, told us what he wanted to do, would decline to tell us where he wanted to do it or when he wanted to do it; we had no information. He said, "We want you out of this. We do not want the United States to have been the one who did this. But we want you to know that we're going to do this." Then he made his move, where there was no ability on our part to provide any protection or support; it was an entirely independent action.

William T. Pryce: And the one thing that he asked us to do, in the end, we did. I didn't want to take the time to comment, but I was very much involved in this. I fully agree with what you were saying. One other thing was that Giraldo also had been a very close confidant of Noriega, and there was the possibility that it was a come-on, and we wanted to protect the U.S. government's integrity. But in the very end, he said he was going, and he asked us to block Noriega's troops that were on Fort Amador from coming across to his rescue. We did that, which was the only thing he asked us to do. In the end, he won. I mean, basically he had Noriega under his control.

Webster: He had him there, and then he decided that what would be really nice was if he could talk Noriega into voluntarily stepping down. Noriega made a telephone call and said, "Come after these people," and in a few hours, Giraldo was dead. It was bad judgment, but one over which the United States had no role, did not participate, and so it was not part of an ongoing process of an intent at that time to invade Panama. But there we had the situation, and when the American soldiers were killed, we were confronted with what to do now.

George Bush did have a law enforcement perspective about the drug issue. It was important to him. His feeling about Noriega was influenced by that. But I think, too, that he had a much broader vision of where we were at that moment in time, and the objectives that he put forward were very sound. Why are we going in? We're going in to protect the Panama Canal, to protect U.S. citizens who were there, to restore democracy after that abortive election that was annulled by Noriega, and to get Noriega. The press simply reported it as going there to get Noriega. In actual fact, Noriega was out of business 45 minutes after the attack, he was disoriented, he was somewhere; he was wandering around—I hesitate to say that he had just come from a dalliance that he had had out of town, but he had—and he never got back into business. Yet the papers were saying, "Where is

Noriega? You're going to fail if you don't find Noriega."

I got into a little bit of trouble because I was at American University responding to questions after a talk, and I said, "This isn't about Noriega. It's about protecting the Panama Canal, it's about protecting U.S. citizens, about restoring democracy to Panama, and, incidentally, we'd like to have Noriega back so we could try him, but we didn't wage war to get Noriega." But the press reported only the part about "This isn't about Noriega," and I got a call from the White House saying, "What was that you said?" But I explained it at the Oval Office the next morning, and what I said was exactly what the president's policy was.

I think it's remarkable, as Phil said, that so much was achieved at a time when our major focus was on the Gulf issues and the breakup of the Soviet Union, bit by bit. It was important to us that we have a measure of stability in that part of the world, and a lot of our efforts were made not to stir things up but to deal with the problems and keep them under control so that we could keep our focus on things that threatened world security. I believe that that was the view of the people who guided the president, and certainly his own intuition. I put a high stock on President Bush's intuition.

In Cuba, I suppose it was somewhat the same thing. Maintain sanctions—although sanctions have done really nothing much except reduce the country to bicycle riders. We had tried a number of things over the years and failed. Marilyn Quayle wrote a novel about Cuba; some of you may have read it. In the first chapter, Castro dies of a heart attack, and I said, "That's about the way it's going to happen." But in the meantime, we should try to encourage ways of bringing Cuba into the ranks of democratic countries so that they can enjoy the benefit of trade and enterprise.

The Latin American picture will be reviewed and rereviewed. It was an important part of the period of Bush history. His main focus and his efforts in the American public's interest were somewhere else, but I do think that it is remarkable that, throughout that period, we ended the range of insurgencies that were taking place—we allowed them to end. We didn't do it all by ourselves, but we were able to do it in a way that it did not pull from our resources the ability to achieve the major victories that occurred elsewhere in the world.

Panelist Comments: Robert McMillan, Moderator

Editor's Note: Given the time constraints and the number of participants on this panel, paper presenters were unable to respond to comments on their work. Professor LaRocque prepared a short response, which is included here at his request.

Robert McMillan: Let me just add a personal thought as someone very much involved in the Panama Canal. To hear the free trade comments that have been expressed by many people and fast-tracking Chile and recognizing that America's Hong Kong will take place in 1999 with the transfer of the Panama Canal, I'm very sensitive and very concerned about the stability of Panama beyond the year 2000. I would hope that, at some point, someone will start to beat the drum for fast-tracking Panama, because the economy of Panama is key to the stability of the future of the Panama Canal. Panama would fit well into this pattern of open free trade throughout the hemisphere.

Jules N. LaRocque: Mr. Falcoff and, to a considerably lesser extent, Mr. Hughes addressed remarks to my paper that I think deserve a response. Mr. Falcoff confined his remarks to my paper, as he said, but he did not engage the argument of the paper directly. Indeed, he talked *about* (in the sense of circumscription) my paper, perhaps in the hope that he would suffocate what he could not penetrate. Both discussants appear to view Cuba as an entity that exists only in the context of U.S. foreign policy rather than as a sovereign state that has standing in global and, especially, regional communities of nations.

Though with differing degrees of relevance to the substance of my paper, both Mr. Falcoff and Mr. Hughes suggested that I advocated foreign policy action by the Bush administration that would have constituted an excessively sharp departure from the policies of predecessor administrations. I am familiar with and fully respect the traditional arguments that politics should end at the water's edge and that, as much as is possible, foreign policy should be seamlessly continuous from administration to administration. However, the events of the period from 1989 to 1991 were such as to make these times truly extraordinary. Under such circumstances, there are good and adequate reasons for making sharp departure from the policies of the past, and this is especially the case if the circumstances at hand present an opportunity that, if not seized, is likely to prove evanescent. Events and circumstances of the mid-1990s, to which I alluded in my remarks this morning, testify to the evanescence of that opportunity that existed in 1990.

9

Bush versus Castro: America's Fight against the Banana Dictatorship, 1989–1993

Derrick Bradford Wetherell and Michael J. McIsaac

Editors' Note: The following paper was presented at a student panel during the Bush conference, "President Bush and the World." Six students presented three papers on different aspects of President Bush's foreign policy, and General Brent Scowcroft, Bush's special assistant for national security affairs, served as discussant for the panel. Because the session was not taped, it could not be included in this volume. Nevertheless, the editors decided that the quality of this paper merited its inclusion in the proceedings.

INTRODUCTION

Since that fateful New Year's Day in 1959, when Fidel Castro assumed power over the people of Cuba, a singular principle has dominated the United States' policy toward the tiny island nation, that through comprehensive economic sanctions, Castro could be forced out of power, creating an opportunity for democracy to prevail in the Republic of Cuba.

The concept of using an embargo to restrict Castro's quest for power was first put forth by the Kennedy administration after the failure of the Bay of Pigs invasion in 1961. Successive administrations continued this policy, with varying degrees of success. The initial purpose of such an embargo was to confine Castro's global sphere of influence as a Marxist ideologue. This conformed with the United States' overall foreign policy goal of containing the spread of Communism throughout the world.

The embargo proved to be a vital weapon in America's foreign policy arsenal toward combating the influence of Communism across the globe. However, with the fall of the "Iron Curtain" at the end of the 1980s, the need to continue anti-Communist policies such as the embargo came into question. President George Bush, who had inherited a world in which Communism's influence was rapidly declining, had an important decision to make: would America attempt to incorporate Cuba into the "New World Order," or would it continue with a policy of isolation toward the

Banana Republic? Bush opted for the latter, deciding that the Cold War policy pursued by previous administrations was the best way to drive Castro from power.

George Bush had an opportunity that had not presented itself since the time of President Kennedy—to implement a drastic change in the direction of the U.S. policy toward Cuba. Unfortunately, Bush did not take advantage of the situation. Instead of opening diplomatic relations between the two nations, he engaged in a series of rhetorical challenges for Castro to implement change voluntarily, while offering no incentive or rationale for him to do so. Having been familiar with Castro's unwillingness to reduce his power within Cuba in the past, it defies logic for Bush to have believed that the suffocation of the Cuban economy by a democratized entity such as the United States would make the idea of instituting democracy in Cuba appealing to the dictator.

What President Bush failed to take into account was that, in the changing geopolitical climate, certain policies whose effectiveness was never questioned during the Cold War sorely needed to be reexamined. One of these policies was the embargo against Cuba. Bush had an opportunity to explore new possibilities to improve the situation of the island nation, but instead he chose to continue with a policy whose sole purpose was to effect change by bringing the Cuban economy to its knees. Despite the best efforts of the Bush administration, Castro remains the ruler of a nation whose people's suffering increased during that time.

A BRIEF BACKGROUND OF U.S. RELATIONS WITH FIDEL CASTRO'S CUBA

Almost since the moment he took power on New Year's Day, 1959, Fidel Castro has made clear that he had no love for the United States. Within three years of taking power, Castro showed his disregard for the United States in numerous ways, including the seizure of $1.8 billion in U.S. property located on the island (*U.S. Department of State Dispatch* [*USDSD*], February 22, 1993, 103). The full U.S. trade embargo on Cuba began February 3, 1962, in response to the Communist nation's growing ties with the Soviet Union. The Kennedy administration saw Cuba as a threat to stability in the Western Hemisphere because of Castro's support for violent anti-American revolutions in the region. As part of its sanctions against the island, the administration also restricted travel between the United States and Cuba.

In 1964 the United States was able to convince members of the Organization of American States (OAS) to join the embargo in response to Cuba's various hostile actions against member states. Over the next decade, however, numerous countries reestablished trade with the island. This led the OAS to end its unified embargo in 1975 (*USDSD*, February 22, 1993, 103). In that same year, the United States allowed subsidiaries of American companies to start limited trade with Cuba. Any possibility of further reducing the embargo ended in late 1975, when Cuba sent troops to help the Soviet intervention in Angola (*USDSD*, February 22, 1993, 104).

During the Carter administration, Castro continued to aid in the spread of Communism throughout the world by sending support to various countries in Africa and Latin America (*USDSD*, February 22, 1993, 104). When Ronald Reagan took office, he vowed to stop Communist advancements in the Third World. He retightened the embargo, and he created a list of foreign firms that he claimed were Cuban fronts. American companies were forbidden to transact business with the firms on the list (De Varona, 3).

The reason Cuba was able to survive despite U.S. economic sanctions was the Soviet Union. The USSR provided billions of dollars in military assistance, economic aid, and subsidized trade, allowing Cuba to stay afloat (Kozak, 75). The Soviets realized that having a close ally near the United States could be beneficial to them. The United States, in turn, realized that the spread of Communism, which posed a threat to the democratic, capitalistic U.S. way of life, must be contained. Thus, Cuba had to be cut off as much as possible to prevent its influence from growing throughout the hemisphere. Until the Bush administration came to power, the embargo was a necessary and sound policy that prevented the United States' Communist enemies from gaining a stronger footing in the Western Hemisphere. That would change.

GEORGE BUSH: LEADING IN A NEW ERA

George Bush was born into politics and initially was hesitant to follow his father, Prescott, a senator from Connecticut, into the realm of public policy making. In fact, it was George Bush's venture into private enterprise in Texas as president of a growing oil company that first brought Fidel Castro's actions to his personal attention. In the words of Thomas G. Paterson, Bush, president of the Zapata Off-Shore Company when Castro ousted the Batista government, "contacted the State Department because he feared one of his oil drilling rigs near Cay Say Bank might be molested" during the fighting (Paterson, 141). Castro's ascension to power, not yet complete, had already threatened Bush's corporate interests.

Efforts to undermine the Castro regime in the early 1960s were part of an attempt by Bush to, in the words of Michael R. Beschloss, "please an electorate that was notably more conservative than he" during his 1964 senatorial campaign (Beschloss, 228). In his move from the moderate to the conservative Right, Bush opposed a number of liberal domestic measures, such as the Civil Rights Act, and "he wished to arm Cuban exiles to go after Fidel Castro" (Beschloss, 228). Although Bush had avoided publicly addressing such issues while becoming a wealthy Texas oil magnate, he viewed Castro as a leftist icon whom he could attack to win over conservative Texan voters.

However well this tactic may have worked politically, it did not sit well with Bush himself. "He told his Houston minister [after losing the election], 'I took some of the far-right positions to get elected. I hope I never do it again. I regret it'" (Beschloss, 229). Yet as his political power increased, Bush's hesitancy to condemn Castro's policies declined, and by the late 1980s Bush was ready to make his anti-Castro stance a campaign issue.

FIDEL CASTRO—A DANGER TO DEMOCRACY

In order to understand why the United States has had such a tense relationship with Castro's Cuba, some background must be given regarding the Cuban dictator. Whereas Bush was a democratically elected leader, Fidel Castro is an absolute dictator who must not be allowed to gain any more power than he already possesses. His devotion to Communist principles is extreme, as illustrated by his adherence to them even after the fall of the Iron Curtain. During the decades that Castro has held power, he has used his position as a tyrannical leader to suppress anything and anyone that he sees as a threat to his position. For example, in 1992 alone he had numerous human rights activists harmed to put a stop to their calls for better conditions within the country. Castro's paranoia led to his having the homes of numerous human rights leaders, including Elizardo Sanchez and Gustavo Arcos, cordoned off from the rest of the world, placing the leaders under a form of house arrest (*USDSD*, January 4, 1993, 9).

Castro has also always let it be known through his numerous efforts to undermine U.S. authority that he hates the United States. Perhaps the greatest example of his contempt for the United States was seen during the Cuban missile crisis in October 1962. As noted by Fedor Burlatsky, an adviser to Soviet leader Nikita Khrushchev, Castro sent a telegram to Khrushchev saying, "I propose the immediate launching of a nuclear strike on the United States. The Cuban people are prepared to sacrifice themselves for the cause of the destruction of imperialism and the victory of world revolution" (Burlatsky, A33).

Castro's statement illustrates how irrational he can be in his defense of Marxism. It also illustrates why the embargo will never drive him from his position. The embargo assumes that if conditions for the people in Cuba become intolerable, the logical result would be the end of Castro's power. However, Castro is an illogical person. He has made it clear that he would sooner sacrifice all of his people than bow to the United States. Therefore, it can be concluded that he would sooner allow conditions in his country to deteriorate to nothing rather than admit defeat. All Castro appears to care about is his personal power. As long as he can maintain his power, he is willing to let his people and country suffer.

BUSH'S CUBA POLICIES PRIOR TO THE COLLAPSE OF THE USSR

The first two years of the Bush administration were not marked by many significant incidents involving Cuba. However, one incident that did capture some attention dealt with the illegal drug trade. In February 1989 the U.S. Customs Service began an investigation called Operation Greyhound to look into the Cuban government's involvement in drug-smuggling operations (Isikoff, 7). Four months later, before the investigation could be completed, Castro announced that 14 senior Cuban military officials were guilty of transporting drugs into the United States. Castro's announcement followed years of denials of any knowledge of the drug trade (Kozak, 77). The Cuban dictator promptly proceeded to try to convict the officials. Four of the officers, including Cuban revolutionary hero General Arnaldo Ochoa Sanchez, were executed for the crimes (Levitsky, 46).

Why did Castro take such a public action against his men after so many years of denying the existence of a drug-smuggling operation in Cuba? One possibility is that he found out about Operation Greyhound and wanted to spare himself any embarrassment it could cause him. Castro also probably knew that he could take advantage of his new antidrug exposure by offering to help the United States in the fight against drug trafficking. The situation was a win-win one for Castro, since if the United States said yes, it might lead to an easing of the embargo. If it said no, Castro could claim that the United States was not even willing to try to give him a chance to prove that he was sincere in his anti-drug-trafficking efforts. The Bush administration did reject Castro's offer, thanks in part to the Department of State's evidence that Castro knew of the drug trade in 1985 (Kozak, 77). The administration's refusal was further vindicated when Jose Antonio Rodriguez Menier, a former major in Cuba's Interior Ministry, said Castro took a large percentage of Cuban drug profits for himself (Podesta, A17).

Another U.S. project involving Cuba was the creation of TV Martí in March 1990. Following along the lines of Radio Martí, TV Martí entailed transmitting U.S. television broadcasts into Cuba. The purpose of the project was to provide information and American entertainment to the Cuban people in the hope of reducing Castro's hold over them (Osborn, 22). The success of the project was mixed at best, owing, in part, to Cuba's efforts to jam the broadcasts. The signals could also be sent only between 3:45 and 6:45 A.M. because of international broadcasting agreements. Therefore, the ability of the Cuban people to see the programs was extremely limited. However, President Bush supported the project and pushed Congress to continue it (Ingwerson, 8).

CUBA'S POST–COLD WAR TRADE

As the Cold War ended and the Soviets scrambled to maintain their domestic economy, the powerful Communist financing machine that had assisted Castro so greatly in his attempts to maintain an iron grip over Cuba fell apart. In 1991, as perestroika and free markets prevailed over Communism in Moscow, the Soviet government began to cut off its aid to Castro, aid that, according to American estimates, totaled $6–8 billion annually (Keller, A1).

As this aid disappeared, Castro attempted to solicit foreign investors to promote the floundering Cuban economy. Although he courted significant trading partners such as Mexico and Canada, Castro maintained that his political ends would not be jeopardized by the means with which he would achieve them—even if those means, which embraced free markets and open trade, were capitalist ones. Appearing before a group of 125 foreign businessmen considering investment in Cuba, Castro made clear his unwillingness to forgo Communism when he stated, "Capital is not capitalism" (French, A8).

In his efforts to maintain the Cuban economy after the loss of Soviet aid, it appears that Castro has been minimally successful. According to the United States–Cuba Trade and Economic Council (USCTEC), a third-party, nonprofit research organization, nations other than the United States and the former Soviet Union have pledged to deliver over $5.3 billion since 1990 but have delivered only $700 million of that amount, with Mexico, Canada, and Italy having been the primary investors (U.S.–Cuba Trade and Economic Council [USCTEC], 1).

Despite these efforts at what some would liken to "market socialism," Castro's government imposed a series of rigid rationing programs to help offset the financial losses incurred since the end of Soviet aid. By 1992 the embargo had caused imports into Cuba to fall to $2.2 billion. This sum amounted to more than a 70 percent decrease from the 1989 level of $8 billion (Farah, A33). In an interview with Tomas Borge of Radio Cuba in July 1992, Castro attempted to place the entire blame for the decline in the Cuban standard of living upon the United States, stating that once the "war against Cuba" ended, "under different conditions, we could bring up in theory, and even in practice, another form of political leadership in our country" (Borge, 4).

Castro used the growth of despair and poverty in Cuba to rally the Cuban people against the 1989 amendment to the Export Administration Act sponsored by Senator Connie Mack (D-FL), as well as the Cuban Democracy Act (CDA) of 1992. The 1989 amendment forbade foreign subsidiaries of United States-based companies from trading with Cuba, while the CDA expanded the prohibition to all trading partners of the United States. Castro was able to mobilize the Cuban people against the CDA, sponsored by Representative Robert Torricelli (D-NJ), and against the American government at large. At a ceremony celebrating Cuban National Defense Day in 1992, shortly after the bill was passed, a young schoolgirl summed up popular reaction to the Cuban Democracy Act. "We are more determined now than ever that only socialism will make us free," she said. "Our loyalty is to Fidel. Down with Torricelli. Socialism or death" (Farah, A33).

The passage of both the amendment to the Export Administration Act and the CDA was not met with overwhelming approval by the entire federal government. In 1989, after passage of the Export Administration Act amendment, the State Department warned Bush of the negative ramifications of the bill, which, they stated, would "likely result in serious trade disputes with some of our allies and major trading partners" (Smith, 19). The same papers later affirm that "we [the U.S. government] are opposed to the specific provision sponsored by Senator Mack" (Smith, 19). The Bush administration itself initially opposed the Cuban Democracy Act, stating that its measures "would be difficult to enforce and would complicate trade relations with U.S. allies" (Yang, A23). However, once Democratic opponent Bill Clinton publicly endorsed the legislation, Bush quickly changed his position, realizing that he would need the support of the Cuban American community if he was to win the pivotal state of Florida in the 1992 election (Wines, A10).

As a result of the Cuban Democracy Act, companies intent on trading with the United States would face sanctions if they traded with Cuba. The act stated that "a vessel which enters a port or place in Cuba to engage in the trade of goods or services may not, within 180 days after departure from such port or place in Cuba, load or unload any freight at any place in the United States" (Cuban American National Foundation [CANF], 3). Thus, the act sought to isolate Cuba economically by punishing any nation that sought to do business with the island nation.

Another purpose of the CDA was that it would supposedly help the people of Cuba. This point is made in the "Statement of Policy," which proposes that "it should be the policy of the United States to seek a peaceful transition to democracy ... through the careful application of sanctions directed at the Castro government and support for the Cuban people" (CANF, 1). However, how the United States would hurt the Cuban government while helping the Cuban people is not clearly defined. In a Communist dictatorship such as Cuba, the state has a hand in virtually every aspect of its citizens' lives. Thus, the possibility of helping the people while hurting the government is minuscule.

The conditions for lifting the sanctions imposed by the CDA—holding free and fair elections where opposing candidates would have access to all media, creating a free market economy, and cleaning up Cuba's human rights record—while truly democratic in nature, were not practical goals that could be achieved by any means short of popular revolt. The impetus for that revolt did not exist from within Cuba itself, and all efforts by the United States to artificially implant revolutionary drive into the people of Cuba had failed. The "peaceful transition" the Cuban Democracy Act sought to achieve, as we shall see, was negated by the economic effects of that same legislation.

The end of the Cold War did not cause the United States to lessen any of the restrictions from the past three decades. The Bush administration decided not only to continue but also to strengthen the policies of its predecessors in the hope of ending Castro's regime. One reason that Bush may have decided to press on with the attack against Castro was the large anti-Castro Cuban American constituency that Bush sought to entice into supporting the Republican Party in the 1992 elections. However, passage of the Cuban Democracy Act did not assist Bush politically to the degree many in his camp had believed it would. After winning Florida overwhelmingly in 1988—by over 900,000 votes, largely due to the appeal of anti-Castro rhetoric to Cuban expatriates living in Florida—he won the state by a much lower margin in 1992 (Wines, A10). Clinton appropriated a number of Bush's anti-Cuban ideas and announced his support for the Torricelli bill prior to Bush's endorsement of it. This, along with the increasing number of Cuban exiles coming with news of Castro's nationalistic and anti-American stance, caused many Cuban Americans to view Bush as someone who had simply maintained the status quo. This discontent among the Cuban American population in Florida allowed Clinton to win seven districts in Florida during the 1992 race; in 1988, Michael Dukakis won only one (Federal Election Commission, 1).

THE HUMAN RIGHTS FACTOR

George Bush made clear that a primary reason that he was unwilling to lift the embargo was Cuba's dismal human rights record (Masland et al., 44). The human rights violations that exist on the island are numerous. For example, Castro's government is guilty of beating, harassing, and imprisoning people who speak out against the government. In certain extreme cases, the government has even incited mobs to ransack the homes of human rights activists (Gelbard 1992, 313). Citizens are not guaranteed any right to a fair trial. Rights that Americans take for granted, such as freedom of speech and assembly, are denied to Cubans. A veritable police state exists within the country, ready to stop any who oppose Castro. Citizens are not even allowed to buy food for themselves from an independent farmer under fear of punishment by the law (De Varona, 5). The United Nations Commission on Human Rights has condemned Cuba's human rights violations repeatedly, so the U.S. is not alone in its stance against Castro's despicable treatment of his people (Schifter, 43).

The Bush administration's refusal to deal with Cuba did nothing to make the human rights situation any better on the island. As conditions within the country disintegrated due to the embargo, Castro had to tighten his grip on the people in order to hold onto his power. The poor conditions gave more human rights activists within the country incentive to work for change in the government. However, since Castro would never allow anything that could jeopardize his power, he had to put a stop to the activism. He also had to take action to ensure that no other groups could rise to threaten him. Thus, the embargo gave Castro the perfect excuse to restrict human rights. As Cuban columnist Soledad Cruz noted, "U.S. aggression is the best justification for the Cuban government to reduce civil liberties and freedom of expression. If there was no blockade, there would be no government justification for not giving the opposition political space" (Scott 1993, 9).

The United States assumed a hypocritical stance by saying the embargo was due, in large part, to Castro's human rights violations. Numerous Latin American democracies with which the United States had dealings possessed human rights records that could be considered even worse than Cuba's. In Asia the Bush administration almost seemed willing to turn a blind eye on the actions of China. President Bush pushed for Congress to renew "most favored nation" status for China despite its continual refusals to allow the human rights agency Amnesty International to investigate its actions after the Tiananmen Square massacre (*America*, 527). The administration's willingness to excuse other nations for their violations sorely weakened the credibility of its stance toward Cuba.

There can be no doubt that Cuba should not be excused for its human rights violations. The problem is that the Bush administration refused to realize that instead of helping the situation, the embargo probably made it worse.

HUMAN SUFFERING AS A RESULT OF THE EMBARGO

In the months following the end of Soviet aid to Cuba, the livelihood of the people on the island rapidly deteriorated. In July 1990 the Cuban government instituted the "Special Period in Peacetime," a program that involved heavy rationing of many basic necessities (Aronson, 581). A job-swapping program was created that involved sending urban workers to farmlands for field labor. Shortages of oil caused massive cutbacks in public transportation lines (Gelbard 1992, 312) As Robert S. Gelbard, the deputy assistant director for inter-American affairs, reported before the Senate Select Committee on Intelligence on July 29, 1993: "Over the past 2 years, the Cuban economy has shrunk by over 50%. Electrical power outages have become the norm, not the exception. Across the island, major factories stand idle for want of fuel and spare parts" (Gelbard 1993, 577).

Not only was the material comfort of Cuba's population at stake, but their very lives as well. The World Federation of Public Health Associations reported at its 28th annual meeting on May 2, 1994, that "the neuropathy epidemic which appeared in late 1991 in Cuba is probably partly the result of nutritional deficiencies." The same nutritional deficiencies contributed to a rise in anemia in children and pregnant women. Severe rationing of food, which limited Cubans to six pounds of beans, one pound of rice, two eggs, a pint of oil, and fifteen kilograms of potatoes per month, resulted in the nutritional deficiencies (Chelala, 19).

A primary reason that the Cuban people were denied the necessities they needed was the embargo. The very action that the Bush administration claimed was designed to help the Cuban people was hurting them. As the embargo continued, the Cuban population became weaker and weaker as Castro tightened his grip on them. His hold on the people became stronger as he was able to claim that the United States was responsible for their suffering. When the United Nations voted to condemn the embargo in 1992, it served simply to further vindicate Castro in the eyes of his people (Kean, 19). While the embargo was supposed to primarily hurt Castro, the crafty dictator still remained dictator at the end of Bush's term. Thus, it could be said that the embargo had the reverse effect from what the Bush administration desired.

The deplorable conditions faced by the people in Cuba as a result of Bush's continuation of the embargo ultimately could not benefit anyone. The administration should have taken into account that as the people became poorer, the likelihood that they would want to leave Cuba would rise. Therefore, the possibility that the United States could have boats filled with Cuban refugees washing up on its shores increased. However, the State Department clearly stated that the United States would not allow mass migration into the country (Gelbard 1992, 315). Since Castro also maintained control of the military, the likelihood of a peasant population's being able to rise up against his was slim at best. Even if the people did rise against Castro, many people would most likely be killed in the resulting conflict. Therefore, all the United States accomplished by continuing the embargo was to make matters worse. If the embargo had ended, the increase in money and supplies could have reduced the human suffering of the people to a great extent, ensuring a higher standard of living for people in desperate need of one.

INTERNATIONAL OPPOSITION TO THE EMBARGO

While the U.S. government declared that it wanted its allies "to cooperate with the United States policy to promote a peaceful transition in Cuba," a number of multinational public and private organizations, as well as government officials speaking on behalf of their nations, overtly opposed the Cuban Democracy Act as an example of modern American imperialism (CANF, 1). "It is for the British government, not the U.S. Congress, to determine the UK's policy on trade with Cuba," according to British trade secretary Peter Lilley (Scott 1992, 1).

Canada joined 58 other members of the United Nations in voting against the Cuban Democracy Act in 1992, with only Israel and Romania siding with the United States in tightening the embargo; fearing that voting against the embargo would upset trade relations with the United States, 71 member nations abstained from the vote (AP, *Washington Post*, A14). The day after the UN [United Nations] resolution, State Department spokesman Joe Snyder defended the embargo, stating, "The U.S. embargo—and I point out it's not a blockade—is therefore a legitimate response to the unreasonable and illegal behavior of the Cuban government" (Goshko, B26). In subsequent annual votes on the embargo, the number of states in favor of opposing the embargo grew from 59 in 1992 to 117 in 1995 (Spock, 4). Several organizations, including the World Federation of Public Health Associations (WFPHA) and multiple member nations of the World Trade Organization (WTO), have condemned the Cuban Democracy Act and related legislation passed after Bush left office, including the Helms–Burton Act (Spock, 2–4).

With the European Parliament joining the growing list of international agencies condemning the Cuban Democracy Act and subsequent tightening of the embargo by President Clinton as a "'serious infringement of the GATT [General Agreement on Tariffs and Trade], World Trade organization (rules) and international law'" (Spock, 4), it has become apparent that support for the embargo has waned in recent years. While there may have been international support for the Cuban embargo in the 1960s, it has existed in a relatively nominal degree since the end of the Cold War.

CONCLUSION: BUSH FUMBLES THE BALL

The primary objective of Bush's agenda was apparently to hurt Castro rather than to ensure a decent standard of living for the Cuban people. Although Bush may never have explicitly said so, the effects of his policies speak for themselves. The more the United States tried to weaken Castro's position, the more the citizens of Cuba were made to suffer. As the quality of life declined on the island, Castro was able to use his overwhelming powers of persuasion to convince his people that he was their only hope for salvation. Having known only one leader and one form of government for their entire lives, many Cubans saw their hatred for the United States grow as their faith in their leader increased. Thus, instead of weakening Castro, U.S. policy simply served to better consolidate his position.

While tough economic sanctions may have proven to be effective in helping to bring to an end oppressive governments in other parts of the world, such as South Africa, such sanctions have proven to be ineffectual when directed toward Cuba. The difference between Cuba and South Africa is that in South Africa there is a clear difference between the white minority and the black majority. While the white minority enjoyed a relatively high standard of living and a government that catered to them, the black majority was clearly exploited and oppressed. The racial divisions made it apparent to the blacks in South Africa that they were being mistreated. Thus, economic sanctions against the white government simply served to augment the work of black antiapartheid leaders already working within South

Africa. In Cuba, where there are no noticeable race or class divisions, the Cuban people have no other group to which they can compare their situation. There is no white government they can blame their woes on besides that of the United States. Poor economic conditions are the overriding concern of the Cuban people. The people do not believe that Castro is responsible for the embargo; rather, they believe that an oppressive U.S. government is responsible for their hardships. This explains why the hard-line approach taken against a government such as South Africa's can never work with Cuba.

President Bush helped to set into motion the Cuba policy that still governs the U.S. approach today. The clearest evidence of this point can be seen in the passage of the Helms–Burton Libertad Act of 1996. The act served to tighten the already existing embargo to levels beyond those that existed during the Cold War. If Bush had taken it upon himself to change U.S. policy toward Cuba when he had the opportunity, the Clinton administration and Congress would possibly be pursuing more accommodating policies along the lines of those followed by our allies in the international community today. Instead, Helms–Burton cosponsor Jesse Helms has attempted to undermine the integrity of nations opposed to the embargo, stating that "many of the world's leading democracies continue to subsidize Castro's tyranny, perhaps hoping that if they feed the crocodile, they will be eaten last . . . it is *their* policies that have failed . . . it is *their* policies that should and, God willing, will be challenged" (Helms 1996, 2). Helms is achieving nothing but his own reelection by issuing such a statement to the global press, similar to what Bush had done years before.

Helms' conclusion that the sum of $700 million received in foreign trade by Cuba since 1990 is "subsidizing Castro's tyranny" lacks merit; no nation can convert itself from an economy that thrived on $8 billion worth of Soviet imports in 1989 to only $700 million today and be considered appropriately subsidized. The international community has continued trade with Cuba both as a means for each nation's economic success, as well as importing enough goods so that the Cubans have the ability to perhaps one day stage the revolt Bush, Helms, and other American legislators have inhibited by tightening the embargo. When Helms promised the Cuban people on the first anniversary of the Helms–Burton Act, March 12, 1997, that "at the same time that we are here building the pressure on Fidel to leave Cuba, we here in Washington are preparing to help you rebuild once Castro does leave" (Helms 1997, 2), he was perhaps overestimating the positive effects the embargo has had and will continue to have on the Cuban population. Granted, Castro has less funding to embezzle for his own interests due to the embargo; however, the Cuban people also have significantly less in relative terms than they had over 30 years ago. They have less of both the material and, it would seem, the initiative essential to installing democracy and rebuilding the nation's economy after the collapse of a despot like Castro.

Rather than engaging in ideological conflict, the United States should appeal more directly to the people of Cuba. Given that Fidel Castro is approaching the final years of his life, overtures must be made to ensure that his government will not survive past his death. By exposing the Cuban people openly to American goods, money, and ideas, the United States can help them to see that it is not the repressive nation that Castro and the embargo make it appear to be. Ending the embargo would help to ensure that when Castro is gone, a democratic, capitalistic way of life will appeal to Cuba's people. The Bush administration should have realized that the policy of isolation would serve only to increase the chance that another repressive leader would assume Castro's role after his demise.

REFERENCES

Aronson, Bernard W. "U.S. Policy toward Cuba." *U.S. Department of State Dispatch* 2 (August 5, 1991): 580–83.
Beschloss, Michael R. "George Bush, 1989–1993." In Robert A. Wilson, ed., *Character Above All*. New York: Simon and Schuster, 1995, pp. 224–45.
"Beijing's Conscience and Ours." *America*, June 27, 1992, p. 527.
Borge, Tomas. "Interview with Fidel Castro, Part 3." Gopher://lanic.utexas.edu/la/Cuba/Castro/1992/11920604/.
Burlatsky, Fedor. "Castro Wanted a Nuclear Strike." *New York Times*, October 23, 1992, p. A33.
Chelala, Cesar. "Cuba's Citizens Suffer from U.S. Blockade." *Christian Science Monitor*, June 30, 1993, p. 19.
"Cuba: Continuing Crackdown on Human Rights Activists." *U.S. Department of State Dispatch* 4 (January 4, 1993): 9.
Cuban American National Foundation (CANF). "The Cuban Democracy Act of 1992." Http://www.canfnet.org/canf-lib/torricel.txt.
De Varona, Adolfo Leyva. *Propaganda and Reality: A Look at the U.S. Embargo against Castro's Cuba*. Cuban American National Foundation, 1994 (updated 1996).
"Fact Sheet: Cuba." *U.S. Department of State Dispatch* 4 (February 22, 1993): 102–107.
Farah, Douglas. "Castro Uses Stiffer U.S. Embargo to Justify Economic Straits." *Washington Post*, December 17, 1992, p. A33.
Federal Election Commission data. Compiled by WorldMedia Inc. Http://www.worldmedia.fr/elections/electionva/1988-1992/index.html.
French, Howard. "Castro, Looking for Investors, Courts Executives from U.S." *New York Times*, June 12, 1992 p. A8.
Gelbard, Robert S. "U.S. Policy toward Cuba." *U.S. Department of State Dispatch*, 3 (April 20, 1992): 312–17.
———. "Cuba: Current Assessment and U.S. Policy." *U.S. Department of State Dispatch* 4 (August 16, 1993): 577–78.
Goshko, John M. "Bush Administration Rejects UN Call to End Cuba Embargo." *Washington Post*, November 26, 1992, p. B26.
"Health in Cuba and the U.S. Embargo." http://www.apha.org/ APHA/WFPHA/cuba.html
Helms, Jesse. "Remarks by Senator Jesse Helms, Chairman of the Senate Foreign Relations Committee, before Regent University Conference on the Cuban Liberty and Democratic Solidarity Act, Washington D.C., July 9, 1996." Courtesy of Senator Helms and the Senate Foreign Relations Committee.
———. "Message from Senator Jesse Helms to the People of Cuba on the First Anniversary of the Libertad Law, March 12, 1997." Courtesy of Senator Helms and the Senate Foreign Relations Committee.
Ingwerson, Marshall. "Testing Period Ends Today for TV Martí; Congress Awaits Report from Bush." *Christian Science Monitor*, June 25, 1990, p. 7.
Isikoff, Michael. "U.S. Probe May Have Spurred Castro to Act." *Washington Post*, July 27,

1989, p. A7.

Kean, Christopher. "UN Stance on U.S.–Cuba Relations Ill-Timed." *Christian Science Monitor*, December 8, 1992, p. 19.

Keller, Bill. "Gorbachev–Castro Face-Off: A Clash of Style and Policies." *New York Times*, April 2, 1989 p. A1.

Kozak, Michael G. "Cuba: A Threat to Peace and Security in Our Hemisphere." *Department of State Bulletin* 89 (November 1989): 75–79.

Levitsky, Melvyn. "Cuba and Narcotics Trafficking." *Department of State Bulletin* 89 (October 1989): 46–48.

Masland, Tom, Spencer Reiss, Douglas Waller, and Marcus Marry. "Running against Fidel." *U.S. News and World Report* (March 9, 1992): 44.

Osborn, Barbara. "Kate and Allie Go to Havana." *The Progressive* (June 1990): 22–23.

Paterson, Thomas G. *Contesting Castro*. New York: Oxford University Press, 1994.

Podesta, Don. "Officer Says Castro Profited from Drug Trafficking." *Washington Post*, August 26, 1989, p. A17.

Schifter, Richard. "Human Rights Situation in Cuba." *Department of State Bulletin* 89 (October 1989): 41–43.

Scott, David Clark. "Plan to Stiffen Cuba Ban Annoys U.S. Trading Allies." *Christian Science Monitor*, June 23, 1992, p. 1.

———. "Cubans Make Case for Lifting the Embargo." *Christian Science Monitor*, November 4, 1993, p. 8.

Smith, Wayne R. "Trade with Cuba: Unlearning an Old Lesson." *Christian Science Monitor*, October 20, 1989, p. 19.

Spock, Benjamin. "The Facts about the Blockade against Cuba." Http://www.igc.apc.org/cubasoli/blockade.html.

"UN Backs Cuba on U.S. Embargo." *Washington Post* (article credited to the Associated Press), November 25, 1992, p. A14.

U.S.–Cuba Trade and Economic Council. "Foreign Trade and Cuba." Http://www.cubatrade.org/foreign.html.

Wines, Michael. "Bush Plays to TV Cameras to Sell Image of Momentum." *New York Times*, October 24, 1992, p. A10.

Yang, John. "Bush Moves to Tighten Trade Embargo against Cuba." *Washington Post*, April 19, 1992, p. A23.

Part V

Somalia and Bosnia

10

Operation Restore Hope: Somalia and the Frontiers of the New World Order

Stephen F. Burgess

President Bush's decision in November 1992 to send more than 24,000 troops to Somalia in Operation Restore Hope ranks as one of the most intriguing foreign policy decisions that any president has made. While prosecuting the Gulf War will be remembered as President Bush's crowning achievement, clearly the U.S. national interest dictated that Iraq had to be driven out of Kuwait. In contrast, the Somalia mission was not in the national interest. Somalia contained no significant natural resources, and the Cold War rivalry with the Soviet Union over the Horn of Africa had ended by 1992. Operation Restore Hope was a major commitment of U.S. power, which was solely intended to put an end to a humanitarian catastrophe. As a consequence, President Bush's decision must be understood as an act of "idealism" (as opposed to "realism") and, more specifically, as the fulfillment of his commitment to a "New World Order."[1] In this paper, I analyze the events and the decision-making process, led by President Bush, that culminated in the launching of the Somalia operation. From this analysis, I draw conclusions about President Bush's foreign policy orientation and his decision-making style and make comparisons between President Bush and other twentieth-century presidents.

As the national interest was not at stake in Somalia, a number of hypotheses have been posited to explain President Bush's decision to intervene. In addition to the president's idealism and his commitment to the New World Order, there is evidence that the views of President Bush and United Nations secretary-general Boutros Boutros-Ghali converged over the need for U.S. intervention. In opposition to idealist explanations are claims that President Bush acted for political reasons. After his defeat in the November 1992 presidential elections, some observers asserted that President Bush was compelled to "do something" before he left office and that he wished to shore up his place in history. Others claimed that "CNN diplomacy," which had become so effective during the Gulf crisis, the rescue of the Iraqi Kurds, and a succession of other humanitarian disasters, influenced both the American public and President Bush to see the need for U.S. action.²

PRESIDENT BUSH'S FOREIGN POLICY AND COMMITMENT TO A NEW WORLD ORDER

George Bush came to the presidency with as much foreign policy experience as any previous president, experience that was gained during service as special representative to China, ambassador to the United Nations, and director of the CIA [Central Intelligence Agency]. Before he became vice president in 1981, his foreign policy orientation placed him on the Republican Party's "internationalist" wing (Eisenhower, Nixon, Rockefeller, and Kissinger), as opposed to the "isolationist" (Taft and Buchanan) and "anti-Communist" (Reagan, Fitzpatrick, and Helms) wings.³ However, after eight years as vice president in the Reagan administration, he campaigned for office in 1988 with a Reaganite vision of maintaining U.S. strength, while committing himself to engage Mikhail Gorbachev in winding down the Cold War.

Until the Gulf crisis, President Bush's foreign policy was largely reactive and grounded in realism. He forged a sound working relationship with Secretary-General Gorbachev and skillfully helped to manage the dismantling of the Soviet empire between November 1989 and December 1991. As a consequence of President Bush's restraint and skill, victory in the Cold War, the greatest international victory scored by the United States since 1945, did not require U.S. intervention. During 1991, as the Soviet Union disintegrated and as the elected president of Russia, Boris Yeltsin, gained ascendancy, President Bush maintained his strong links to Gorbachev and did little to encourage the independence of Soviet republics. The one exception to the president's cautious approach was his proposal of START II [Strategic Arms Limitation Talks] reductions in U.S. and Russian nuclear arsenals and the elimination of nuclear weapons in Ukraine, Belarus, and Kazakstan, once the breakup of the Soviet Union seemed inevitable after the August 1991 coup attempt. President Bush exhibited similar caution and realism in relation to China, even after the Tiananmen Square massacre of June 1989. Until Iraq's invasion of Kuwait in August 1990, President Bush maintained relations with the regime of Saddam Hussein, which had been established under the Reagan administration to balance power against Iranian expansionism.

Signs of President Bush's idealism and interventionism first emerged in December 1989 actions in the Philippines in support of the democratically-elected Aquino government and in Panama against the Noriega dictatorship.⁴ President Bush decided to launch Operation Just Cause in Panama because General Noriega had become a political liability and embarrassment to a U.S. government that had once supported him. However, President Bush also acted under the banner of democracy and used the intervention to install the more democratically inclined Endara government. This commitment to democracy represented a continuation of the policy that had begun almost accidentally during the Reagan administration with the February 1986 democratic revolutions against the Duvalier regime in Haiti and the Marcos regime in the Philippines, which the United States ended up supporting. The Panama action was soon followed by UN [United Nations]-supervised democratic elections in Nicaragua in 1990 and the resolution of the vicious civil war in El Salvador, also involving the UN. In 1990 the Organization of American States [OAS] in Santiago de Chile committed itself to the maintenance of democracy in the Western Hemisphere, which led to the imposition of OAS sanctions against Haiti after the Aristide government was overthrown in a military coup in August 1991. While events in the Western Hemisphere drew President Bush in a more interventionist and idealist direction, it was only with the Gulf crisis of 1990–1991 that he began to talk about a New World Order.

Decision-Making Style

While the Reagan administration strengthened the U.S. position in the world, the foreign policy decision-making process has been described as "anarchical."[5] President Reagan was not interested in the intricacies of the foreign policy process, and rivalries between the National Security Council, the State Department, and Defense Department persisted throughout the administration's eight years. The Iran-contra scandal was a result of the anarchy. As vice president, George Bush was forced to cope with the infighting and the uncertainty that plagued the Reagan years. When he came to office in January 1989, President Bush was determined to restore order to the decision-making process. After some initial difficulties in 1989 due to the transition process, he succeeded in forging discipline and cooperation among his advisers. First, he appointed a strong and competent foreign policy team, including Brent Scowcroft as national security adviser, James Baker as secretary of state, and Dick Cheney as secretary of defense. President Bush established a small-group decision-making style in which he played a leading role and built consensus. Rather than convene the entire National Security Council, President Bush often consulted informal groups of his top advisers, including Scowcroft, Baker, Cheney, and Joint Chiefs of Staff Chairman Colin Powell. Consequently, during the first year and a half of the Bush administration, Bush's foreign policy style could be most closely compared to that of the "consensual" style of the Johnson administration.[6]

Saddam Hussein's invasion of Kuwait emboldened President Bush, and his decision-making style became more authoritative. In both Operation Desert Shield and Operation Desert Storm, he made many command decisions on his own and stuck with them, including abruptly ending the offensive against Iraq in March 1991. As a consequence, evidence was mounting that President Bush was adopting a more "patriarchal" style somewhat reminiscent of the approach of Franklin Delano Roosevelt.[7] An indicator of President Bush's patriarchal tendencies came in his decision to launch Operation Restore Hope; when confronted with the need to act, he chose the boldest possible option and surprised his more cautious advisers.

The Gulf War and the New World Order

Iraq's invasion of Kuwait provided the Bush administration with the opportunity to lead the United Nations Security Council in mounting a collective security operation as had been envisaged in the UN Charter and as had been accomplished in the 1950 operation in the reversal of North Korea's invasion of South Korea. President Bush was able to use the UN to build the U.S.-led coalition and to maintain and ratchet up concerted pressure against Iraq. The Security Council invoked Chapter VII of the charter to impose sanctions on Iraq, then to authorize the use of force, and then to dictate postwar conditions to Iraq. Since 1987 Mikhail Gorbachev had reversed Soviet noncooperation in the Security Council, and, consequently, the Soviet Union voted with the United States instead of blocking resolutions. In the process of rallying the UN against Iraq, Secretary-General Perez De Cuellar assisted the United States, while he largely stayed behind the scenes and left negotiations with Iraq to the United States.

The Gulf crisis, the mounting of Operation Desert Shield, and the building of the coalition led President Bush to formulate his New World Order foreign policy vision. This vision was grounded in the end of the Cold War and bipolarity that had enabled the United States to lead the UN Security Council with cooperation from its former adversary. Consequently, President Bush envisaged the UN as a major vehicle for defending international law and order and democratic regimes and for mounting humanitarian operations to alleviate suffering from man-made and natural disasters. Subsequently, the Bush administration attempted to involve the UN in resolving crises in the Mideast, the former Yugoslavia, and Haiti.

President Bush also began to use U.S. forces beyond their traditional role of defending the national interest. Modest U.S. contingents were committed to help start UN operations in western Sahara and in the former Yugoslavia. Most significant was the dispatching of U.S. troops on humanitarian missions, both outside and inside the United States.[8] The first was Operation Provide Comfort to rescue and relieve Kurdish refugees in April–June 1991 in the wake of the Gulf War. The operation provided dramatic results with relatively little cost in men and matériel. Troops were also involved in flood relief for Bangladeshis and rescue of Filipinos from a volcano eruption. The U.S. military mounted Operation Provide Hope, which airlifted much needed food supplies to the newly independent Russian Federation in the volatile winter of 1992.

In January 1992 Perez de Cuellar was succeeded as secretary-general by the Egyptian diplomat Boutros Boutros-Ghali. The good relations established between Perez de Cuellar and the Bush administration carried over into the Boutros-Ghali era. A meeting of the five permanent members of the Security Council culminated in the authorization of Boutros-Ghali to provide a report on the future of United Nations peacekeeping. Subsequently, Boutros-Ghali issued *An Agenda for Peace*, in which he proposed a UN high command and a standing UN force for rapid deployment.[9] He also presented a more idealist vision of the New World Order, emphasizing collective action, poverty alleviation, and social justice. Given the idealism of the time, the Bush administration did not distance itself from these ideas, though it took no action to put them into practice.

Starting in August 1991, four months after the successful conclusion of Operation Desert Storm, the New World Order was challenged with the breakup of Yugoslavia and Serbian aggression and with a military coup in Haiti against the democratically elected Aristide government. In Croatia and Bosnia the United States and the UN failed to counteract Serbian aggression in the same way that Iraq had been thwarted in Kuwait. The Bush administration decided that the former Yugoslavia was not as important to the U.S. national interest as Kuwait and Saudi Arabia and that the costs of reversing Serbian aggression were unacceptably high. Administration officials believed that intervention in the former Yugoslavia could sink the United States and the UN into a Vietnam-style quagmire. In Haiti the United States did not intervene as it had done in Panama, because the Cedras military regime did not pose the same type of threat to U.S. interests as the Noriega regime in Panama. Instead, the United States preferred to join the OAS in applying multilateral sanctions. In 1992, the final year of President Bush's term, inaction by the United States and the UN was raising doubts about the credibility of the New World Order.

SOMALIA 1991–1992: UNITED NATIONS WEAKNESS

In January 1991 the collapse of the Siad Barre dictatorship in Somalia led to anarchy and clan warfare, which became particularly intense in the capital city, Mogadishu. From 1978–1990, the United States and Egypt had supported the Barre regime as an ally in the Cold War in the Horn of Africa. In 1990 Somalia actually sent troops to the Persian Gulf in support of Operation Desert Shield. In spite of this display of support for the United States, with the end of the Cold War and growing U.S. support for democratization, the Bush administration phased out support to the Barre dictatorship. By January 1991 Siad Barre and his regime could no longer resist rebel attacks and fled Mogadishu. The rebels installed an interim president, Ali Mahdi Mohamed, but he was unable to consolidate power in the face of clan-based "warlord" forces. The Somali state collapsed, and the country descended into anarchy. With attention centered on the Gulf, the United States, Egypt, and other countries failed to step in to mediate and impose a peace plan.[10] Throughout 1991 and 1992, the forces of the clan-based "warlords" attacked peasant farmers, stealing their food and crops. Relief supplies from international aid agencies were also stolen. Consequently, the warlords created expanding food shortages and a growing famine.

In the absence of regional peace efforts, the UN was forced to take the lead in attempting to make peace between the warring factions and to coordinate the delivery of humanitarian relief from the United States and other countries. In 1992 Mohamed Sahnoun was appointed as the special representative of the UN secretary-general and began mediation efforts. Finally, in July 1992 the UN Security Council authorized the United Nations Operation in Somalia (UNOSOM I), and 500 Pakistani troops were dispatched to stop the looting of food supplies and to halt the growing famine that threatened hundreds of thousands, if not millions, of Somalis.[11] However, UNOSOM I forces were pinned down in the Mogadishu harbor district the moment they arrived in Somalia.

A problem of UN intervention in the crisis was UN secretary-general Boutros Boutros-Ghali, who had been Egypt's foreign minister and who was perceived by the warlords as a supporter of Siad Barre. In August 1992 Boutros-Ghali unilaterally announced, without consulting the warlords, that an additional 3,000 troops were to be deployed. As a consequence, the belief arose, especially in the mind of the chief warlord, Mohamed Farah Aidid, that the UN was on the side of the ancien regime. Sahnoun's efforts failed as Boutros-Ghali undermined his credibility, as cease-fire after cease-fire was violated, and as humanitarian relief supplies were plundered or blocked.[12]

NOVEMBER 1992: PRESIDENT BUSH AND THE DECISION TO INTERVENE

On May 12, 1992, Boutros-Ghali visited the White House and alerted President Bush to the growing crisis in Somalia.[13] He informed the president that the weak Western response to the famine in Somalia was lowering U.S. prestige in the Middle East, which had been greatly boosted during the Gulf War. In the region, the perception was growing that the West was turning a "blind eye" to Somalis, because they were merely "Muslim victims." Although the Bush administration had committed more than $240 million in food aid to Somalia, starting in April 1991, the food was clearly not reaching most of the starving people.[14] In response to the secretary-general's plea, President Bush at the end of July 1992 ordered an airlift from Kenya, Operation Provide Comfort, until the roads to Somalia could be opened. In spite of the airlift, more and more Somalis were suffering from, and dying of, starvation.

By the first week of November 1992, the crisis had brought massive famine and television pictures from CNN of starving children. Bush was receiving reports that relief efforts were not succeeding and that thousands were dying each week. Deliberations began in the White House, the State Department, and the Defense Department about how to deal with the increasingly deadly situation. Private relief organizations were bombarding administration officials, including Acting Secretary of State Lawrence Eagleburger and Undersecretary of State for International Security Affairs Frank Wisner with demands that action be taken. The relief specialist, Fred Cuny, who had played a leading role in promoting the rescue of the Kurds in the spring of 1991, visited Paul Wolfowitz, the undersecretary of defense for policy planning, and lobbied for a humanitarian operation similar to Operation Provide Comfort, which had helped to save the Iraqi Kurds.[15] However, by the middle of November 1992, the Pentagon had not yet considered the option of sending ground forces to Somalia.

On November 15, 1992, the Deputies Committee met at the Pentagon and devised a plan for an expanded UN presence. Undersecretary of State Wisner proposed that the United States organize a coalition under UN command and that the United States provide logistics, but no ground forces. Accordingly, the Deputies Committee proposed to President Bush "option one-and-a-half" with an expanded UN presence with ground forces from Canada, Belgium, and other NATO [North Atlantic Treaty Organization] allies, but not from the United States. However, opponents of "option one-and-a-half" argued that Canada and Belgium would not commit troops unless the United States did. Four days later, on Thursday, November 19, 1992, Admiral David Jeremiah, vice chairman of the Joint Chiefs of Staff, argued strongly that the greatest chance of success lay in having the United States carry out the relief effort itself with a division or so of troops. For the first time, massive deployment was placed on the table as an option. However, on that day, Admiral Jeremiah did not persuade the rest of the Deputies Committee. Joint Chiefs of Staff chairman Colin Powell remained against the involvement of U.S. ground forces. However, Powell made it clear that he wanted complete command and control by the United States if ground forces were to be committed.[16]

Boutros Boutros-Ghali dispatched a letter to Security Council members urgently asking for ideas or initiatives to stem the mounting humanitarian disaster. Upon receiving the letter on Tuesday, November 24, President Bush asked the Pentagon to come up with a much bolder option. Dropping his opposition to intervention, Colin Powell requested the formulation of a plan of action based upon the principle of "decisive intervention" in which U.S. forces would intervene massively and leave quickly. A meeting of top members of the National Security Council was called at the White House on Wednesday, November 25, 1992. At the meeting, "option one-and-a-half" was discussed. However, the option was rejected, because it had been confirmed that Canada and Belgium would not commit troops unless the United States did. The chairman of the Joint Chiefs of Staff, Colin Powell, has provided the following account of the point at which President Bush made his decision:

The day before Thanksgiving, President Bush called a meeting that I attended with Cheney, Scowcroft, and a handful of others. The new CINC CENTCOM [Commander in Chief, Central Command], General Joseph Hoar, who had replaced Norm Schwarzkopf, had readied a contingency mission for Somalia, Operation Restore Hope, which I now laid out for the President. Operation Restore Hope involved putting a substantial number of U.S. troops on the ground to take charge of the place and to make sure that the food got to the starving Somalis.

"I like it," the President said after I finished. "We'll do it."

Brent Scowcroft looked uneasy. "Sure, we can get in," he said. "But how do we get out?"

"We'll do it, and try to be out by January 19," the President concluded. "I don't want to stick Clinton with an ongoing military operation."

Cheney and I eyed each other. "Mr. President," Dick said, "we can't have it both ways. We can't get there fully until mid-December. And the job won't be done by January 19."[17]

After the meeting, President Bush dispatched Lawrence Eagleburger to the

UN to meet with Boutros-Ghali and make the offer of U.S. troops. The United States would launch Operation Restore Hope on condition that the force be under U.S. command, include sizable contingents from other national armies, and be authorized under Chapter VII of the UN charter to use force when necessary. Upon receiving the offer, Secretary-General Boutros-Ghali recommended the U.S. proposal to the Security Council on Sunday, November 29, and, on Wednesday, December 2, the Security Council agreed to the terms. The Security Council approved and authorized Operation Restore Hope in the guise of the United Nations Interim Task Force (UNITAF) and invoked Chapter VII of the UN Charter to allow the force to use all necessary means to complete its mission.

Operation Restore Hope and a "Bush Doctrine"?

The United States landed marines in Mogadishu on December 9, 1992, and soon 24,000 U.S. troops came ashore. Eventually, they were joined by more than 20,000 additional troops from 20 other countries.[18] President Bush visited the troops in January 1993. Before he left office on January 20, 1993, the U.S.-led multilateral operation had succeeded in supplying humanitarian relief and curbing the famine and starvation.

On Friday, December 4, 1992, when President Bush addressed the nation and announced the commitment of U.S. troops to rescue the people of Somalia, he used idealist tones: "I want to emphasize that I understand the United States alone cannot right the world's wrongs, but we also know that some crises in the world cannot be resolved without American involvement, that American action is often necessary as a catalyst for broader involvement of the community of nations."[19]

After the speech, speculation began that a "Bush Doctrine" had been declared in which the United States would be prepared to lead humanitarian operations whenever necessary. After the speech and the deployment of U.S. troops, President Bush made a speech at West Point on January 5, 1993, in which he supported interventionism in cases where the national interest was not at stake in order to support a "democratic peace" and "less than vital interests":

But in the wake of the Cold War, in a world where we are the only superpower, it is the role of the United States to marshal its moral and material resources to promote a democratic peace. It is our responsibility, it is our opportunity to lead. There is no one else.

Similarly, we cannot always decide in advance which interests will require our using military force to protect them. The relative importance of an interest is not a guide: Military force may not be the best way of safeguarding something vital, while using force may be the best way to protect an interest that qualifies as important but less than vital.

Using military force makes sense as a policy where the stakes warrant, where and when force can be effective, where no other policies are likely to prove effective, where its application can be limited in scope and time, and where the potential benefits justify the potential costs and sacrifice.

Once we are satisfied that force makes sense, we must act with the maximum possible support. The United States can and should lead, but we will want to act in concert, where possible involving the United Nations or other international grouping. The United States can and should contribute to the common undertaking in a manner commensurate with our wealth, with our strength. But others should also contribute militarily, be it by providing combat or support forces, access to facilities or bases, or overflight rights. And similarly, others should contribute economically.[20]

The criteria for intervention were drawn from "just war theory," which had become popular during the 1980s and was used during the Gulf crisis.[21] Just war theory stipulated that force could be employed only if the problem was of crisis proportions where force would be used as a last resort, the chances of success very high, and costs very low.[22]

In conclusion, the Somali crisis brought a convergence of interests and preferences between the UN secretary-general and the United States and President Bush, which led an African observer to note: "While Boutros-Ghali was frustrated by the intransigence and unreliability of Somali warlords and faction leaders who had prevented the deployment of the initial UNOSOM I force, Bush was embarrassed by the fact that the new world order, which was identified by U.S. leadership, was now characterized by the mass starvation of Somali children."[23]

Without Boutros-Ghali's letter and the option of "decisive intervention" presented by Colin Powell, it is unlikely that Bush would have opted for massive deployment. The secretary-general's plea for action was answered in the boldest possible way by President Bush with Operation Restore Hope, a quintessential example of "decisive intervention." If President Bush's advisers harbored reservations at the meeting, he preempted them and selected the strongest possible option. He surprised many administration officials, especially top State Department staff who had proposed the far more modest proposal, "operation one-and-a-half." The president exhibited a lack of common sense in his assumption that forces could be inserted in December and withdrawn by January 19, 1993.

After the caution displayed in the Bosnia and Haiti situations and with weeks to go in the Bush administration, the decision was indeed surprising. President-elect Clinton and his advisers had little foreign policy experience and virtually no knowledge of the Somalia situation. Therefore, President Bush was, indeed, dropping a potentially dangerous foreign policy initiative into President Clinton's lap. While Clinton was consulted, he had little or no basis for vetoing or even disagreeing with President Bush's decision.

Unlike Operation Desert Storm, where the UN gave the United States a blank check and a free hand to drive Iraq out of Kuwait, the United States was called upon to work closely with UN agencies in Somalia and with the secretary-general in New York. This arrangement soon created friction between the United States and Boutros-Ghali over the goals of the mission. Specifically, Boutros-Ghali began to call for the disarming of Somali factions, which the U.S. military was most reluctant to do. However, UNITAF made little effort at disarming or demobilizing Somalia's warring factions or at "nation-building." In spite of its limited aims, Operation Restore Hope, with the idealist intervention of the

United States and forces from around the world, must be considered to be the high-water mark of the New World Order.

SOMALIA 1993: PEACE ENFORCEMENT AND NATION-BUILDING

President Bush's decision to intervene in Somalia meant that the United States maintained a major presence in Somalia when a new, inexperienced, and even more idealist administration came to office on January 20, 1993. President Clinton's foreign policy of "assertive multilateralism" built on President Bush's idealism and the New World Order. One outcome of this policy was dual leadership by the U.S. government and by the UN secretary-general. Both the Clinton administration and Boutros-Ghali pushed the mission from a humanitarian one toward peace enforcement and nation-building. "Mission creep" had begun.

UNOSOM II was created by the Security Council on March 26, 1993, with the Chapter VII mandate to enforce cease-fires and seize weapons from warring factions, as well as to protect ongoing humanitarian relief efforts. Secretary-General Boutros-Ghali was to direct UNOSOM II, with the assistance of an American special representative, a Turkish military commander, and an American second in command. UNOSOM II was to combine an aggressive peace enforcement function with peacemaking or mediation purpose, designed to bring about a cease-fire, an interim government, and the restoration of civil order throughout Somalia. The problem with UNOSOM II's peace enforcement mandate was that it threatened the power of the warlords, especially the most powerful one, General Farah Aidid. His faction's radio station in Mogadishu began broadcasting anti-UNOSOM messages, and UN forces responded by attempting to shut down the station with force. On June 5, 1993, Aidid's forces retaliated by killing 23 Pakistani UNOSOM soldiers. The UN Security Council responded by issuing a warrant for the arrest of General Aidid and by dispatching UNOSOM forces to capture him, disarm his faction, and attack Aidid's military installations in Mogadishu. U.S. forces were particularly vigorous in pursuing Aidid. Mounting violence in Mogadishu culminated on October 3, 1993, when 18 U.S. Rangers were killed and mutilated in an operation to capture Aidid. The subsequent outcry in the United States led President Clinton to announce the withdrawal of U.S. forces from UNOSOM II by March 31, 1994. The campaign of peace enforcement by UNOSOM II was abandoned in spite of Secretary-General Boutros-Ghali's pleas to continue efforts to disarm the warring factions.

SOMALIA 1994: RETREAT TO A NOT-SO-NEW WORLD ORDER

After the defeat of peace enforcement and nation-building by UNOSOM II, the mission was diminished to one of protecting humanitarian operations. The UN hoped that ongoing peacemaking efforts would bring a cease-fire among the warring factions and that peace-building efforts at the district level would provide the foundation for a new Somali state. However, General Aidid and other warlords still believed that they could seize control of Somalia through force and continued fighting each other and the UN. Finally, in November 1994 the Security Council voted to terminate UNOSOM II by March 31, 1995. Pakistani, Bangladeshi, and Egyptian forces were the last to withdraw from Somalia, as the warring clans sought to seize their military equipment. With the end of UNOSOM II, Somalia has remained racked by civil war, though the specter of famine has lurked only in the background and has not become reality again.

Ambitious U.S. plans for the UN and multilateral conflict resolution collided in 1993 with the reality of shrinking U.S. interests in the wake of the Cold War and in a unipolar world with no superpower rivalries. In addition to Somalia, the exponential growth of the UN peacekeeping budget awakened U.S. policymakers and led to a sober reassessment of the U.S.–UN relationship. Consequently, the Clinton administration in October 1993 balked at paying for a higher level of peacekeeping forces in Rwanda, the UN Assistance Mission for Rwanda (UNAMIR), which might have prevented the genocide of April–June 1994 from occurring. When the genocide began, the United States insisted on the "downsizing" of UNAMIR forces. In May 1994 the Defense Department issued a directive against U.S. involvement in peace enforcement. In sum, the Somalia debacle destroyed idealism and led to the restoration of "realism" to U.S. foreign policy. The United States distanced itself from Secretary-General Boutros-Ghali and the *Agenda for Peace*.

CONCLUSION

I have found that, in launching Operation Restore Hope, President Bush ultimately made his own decision, after reviewing the options, as he did quite often during the Gulf crisis. The decision to act came in the wake of an appeal from the UN secretary-general, Boutros Boutros-Ghali. A surprising finding (in 1997) is that the views on Somalia of President Bush and the secretary-general converged. For his part, President Bush wanted to prove that the New World Order was a reality and that humanitarian intervention was part of that order. The option presented by Colin Powell, involving the use of overwhelming force, provided President Bush with the basis for his bold decision. While the decision was bold, the humanitarian operation, backed by overwhelming force, appeared to have lower costs than intervention in Bosnia or Haiti.

Political explanations for President Bush's decision appear to be secondary in significance, though further research is needed. If not for the secretary-general's plea on November 24, 1992, the probability was high that President Bush would not have had the basis to change his position and opt for humanitarian intervention. "CNN diplomacy" and U.S. public opinion in favor of intervention provided additional pressure for action. At this time, there is little evidence that President Bush wanted to shore up his "place in history" after the 1992 elections. However, as time passes, the picture may change.

President Bush's idealism and penchant for intervention were first evident in

Operation Just Cause in Panama and became fully developed during the Gulf crisis and his conception of a New World Order. Operation Restore Hope and President Bush's speech at West Point represented the highest manifestation of his idealism. President Bush's underlying internationalism and the sudden change in international structure from bipolarity to unipolarity and U.S. hegemony help to explain the emergence and rapid development of idealism. President Bush's idealism was comparable to that of Franklin Delano Roosevelt during World War II, with the onset of bipolarity and the founding of the United Nations, and Woodrow Wilson at the end of World War I, with the abandonment of the nineteenth-century multipolar balance of power and the founding of the League of Nations.

In evaluating the decision-making style of President Bush, clearly he moved from the anarchy of the Reagan years toward consensus, and signs were evident that he was becoming increasingly decisive, if not patriarchal. If he had served a second term, President Bush's style might have become more patriarchal, once again placing him in the same category as Roosevelt and Wilson. The bureaucratic politics involved in the decision were reflective of the small-group, consensual style that Bush encouraged. As in Desert Storm, there were "realists" and "idealists" on the Restore Hope issue. In the case of Somalia, Brent Scowcroft provided one note of realism, while other realists were not on the scene to raise their objections. Surprisingly, it was Colin Powell, the realist during the Gulf crisis, who provided the "decisive intervention" option and who provided the basis for action.

The consequences of President Bush's mounting idealism and patriarchal leadership style were ultimately self-defeating. The operation was launched too late in President Bush's term. The inexperience of the Clinton team and the determination of Secretary-General Boutros-Ghali to pacify Somalia created "mission creep" and led to the overextension and eventual collapse of the mission. Both Presidents Bush and Clinton were unfortunate in having Boutros-Ghali as a partner in the Somalia operation. Starting in 1992, Boutros-Ghali and the UN were increasingly perceived by many Somalis, particularly by Mohamed Farah Aidid, as adversaries, and UNOSOM II was seen as an occupying force. With hindsight, Boutros-Ghali should have kept a low profile in Somalia, allowing his special representative, Mohamed Sahnoun, to mediate among the warlords. Instead, Boutros-Ghali undermined and removed Sahnoun and antagonized Mohamed Farah Aidid and other warlords. As a result of the Somalia debacle, the secretary-general began to forfeit the close relationship with the United States he had enjoyed in 1992 with the Bush administration.

With hindsight, President Bush and President Clinton may have been wiser to maintain Operation Restore Hope and UNITAF longer in Somalia, thereby preventing Boutros-Ghali from reappearing on the scene. President Clinton should not have agreed to UNOSOM II and its peace enforcement and nation-building terms of reference. The alternative to UNOSOM II may have been a joint Organization of African Unity and NATO forces which would have kept Boutros-Ghali out of the picture. Ultimately, President Bush's idealist decision to launch Operation Restore Hope has led to a retreat to realism, which will serve the United States and the United Nations well in the future.

NOTES

1. In an address to the nation on January 16, 1991, in which President Bush announced the beginning of hostilities with Iraq, he said, "We have before us, the opportunity to forge for ourselves and for future generations a new world order . . . where the rule of law, not the law of the jungle, governs the conduct of nations" and "in which a credible United Nations can use its peacekeeping role to fulfill the promise and the vision of the UN's founders." Peter B. Levy, *Encyclopedia of the Reagan–Bush Years* (Westport, CT: Greenwood Press, 1996), p. 255.

Also, Henry A. Kissinger, "Balance of Power Sustained," in Graham Allison and Gregory F. Treverton, eds., *Rethinking America's Security: Beyond Cold War* (New York: W. W. Norton, 1992), p. 238. In criticizing the New World Order, Kissinger calls for adherence to classical realist concepts of the national interest and the balance of power. In contrast, idealist concepts, such as the New World Order, call on states to act in concert beyond their national interests.

2. CNN diplomacy arose in the 1980s, as pictures from the sites of humanitarian disasters and wars were transmitted into the homes and offices of Americans and their leaders and resulted in mounting pressure on presidents to act.

3. The three wings of the Republican Party overlap. The "internationalist" wing tended to favor containment and the balance of power in relation to the Soviet Union, while the "anti-Communist" wing wanted to roll back Soviet influence.

4. Richard N. Haass, *Intervention: The Use of American Military Force in the Post–Cold War World* (Washington, DC: Carnegie Endowment for International Peace, 1994), pp. 30–31.

5. Cecil V. Crabb Jr. and Kevin V. Mulcahy, *Presidents and Foreign Policy Making: From FDR to Reagan* (Baton Rouge: Louisiana State University Press, 1986), pp. 323–28. According to the analysis of Crabb and Mulcahy, the "anarchical pattern" featured a president, secretary of state, and national security adviser who were "very weak" in foreign affairs. In contrast, Truman's presidency is characterized as the "classical pattern" of cooperation between the president and secretary of state; Eisenhower's as the "personalistic pattern" of dominance by the secretary of state; and Nixon's as the "palace guard pattern" of dominance by the national security adviser.

6. Ibid., p. 327. The "consensual pattern" features a "strong" president and a secretary of state and national security adviser who are both rated "average." While the decision-making style of the Bush administration was similar to that of the Johnson administration, the former was able to avoid involvement in Vietnam-like situations, particularly in Bosnia.

7. Ibid., p. 323. The "patriarchal pattern" featured a president who was "very strong" in foreign affairs and "a secretary of state who plays a largely symbolic role in foreign relations."

8. Stephen J. Cimbala, *Collective Insecurity: U.S. Defense Policy and the New World Disorder* (Westport, CT: Greenwood Press, 1995), pp. 186–87.

9. Boutros Boutros-Ghali, *An Agenda for Peace* (New York: United Nations, 1992).

10. In contrast to inaction by Egypt, the United States, and other interested parties in the Horn of Africa, action was taken to prevent another U.S. ally, Liberia, from total collapse. Nigeria and the regional ECOWAS [Economic Community of West African

States] Military Observer Group stepped in to prevent Liberia from collapse, to enforce peace, and to ensure the delivery of humanitarian assistance. See Haass, *Intervention*, pp. 63–64.

11. Samuel Makinda, *Seeking Peace from Chaos: Humanitarian Intervention in Somalia* (Boulder, CO: Lynne Rienner, 1993), p. 63.

12. Mohamed Sahnoun, *Somalia: The Missed Opportunities* (Washington, DC: U.S. Institute of Peace, 1994), p. 39. Jonathan Stevenson, "Hope Restored in Somalia," *Foreign Policy* 91 (Summer 1993): 148.

13. Fred Barnes, "Last Call," *The New Republic*, December 28, 1992, p. 11.

14. Herman J. Cohen, "Update on Operation Restore Hope," U.S. Department of State Dispatch, December 21, 1992.

15. Barnes, "Last Call," p. 12.

16. Michael R. Gordon, "Somali Aid Plan Is Called Most Ambitious Option," *New York Times*, November 28, 1992, p. A-6.

17. Colin Powell, *My American Journey* (New York: Random House, 1995), pp. 564–65.

18. Makinda, *Seeking Peace from Chaos*, p. 73. The biggest contributors were Pakistan (4,000 troops), Italy (3,800), India (3,000), and France (2,500). The African contributors were Morocco (1,250), Nigeria (550), Zimbabwe (400), Egypt (250), and Tunisia (130).

19. Barnes, "Last Call," p. 13.

20. Haass, *Intervention*, pp. 201, 203.

21. Barnes, "Last Call," p. 12.

22. Michael Walzer, *Just and Unjust Wars* (New York: Basic Books, 1977). Jean Bethke Elshtain, ed., *Just War Theory* (New York: New York University Press, 1992).

23. Makinda, *Seeking Peace from Chaos*, p. 69.

REFERENCES

Abdullahi, Mohamed Diriye. *Fiasco in Somalia: U.S.–UN Intervention*. Pretoria: Africa Institute of South Africa, 1995.

Adibe, Clement. *Managing Arms in Peace Processes: Somalia*. New York: United Nations, 1995.

Allard, C. Kenneth. *Somalia Operations: Lessons Learned*. Washington, DC: National Defense University Press, 1995.

Allison, Graham, and Gregory F. Treverton, eds. *Rethinking America's Security: Beyond Cold War to New World Order*. New York: W. W. Norton, 1992.

Barnes, Fred. "Last Call." *New Republic*, December 28, 1992.

Bartoli, Andrea, and Jeffrey Carmel, eds. *Somalia, Rwanda and Beyond: The Role of the International Media in Wars and Humanitarian Crises*. Dublin: Crosslines Global Report, 1995.

Boutros-Ghali, Boutros. *An Agenda for Peace*. New York: United Nations, 1992.

———. *The United Nations and Somalia*. New York: United Nations, Department of Public Information, 1996.

Cimbala, Stephen J. *Collective Insecurity: U.S. Defense Policy and the New World Disorder*. Westport, CT: Greenwood Press, 1995.

Cohen, Herman J. "Update on Operation Restore Hope." *U.S. Department of State Dispatch*, December 21, 1992.

Crabb, Cecil V., Jr., and Kevin V. Mulcahy. *Presidents and Foreign Policy Making:*

from FDR to Reagan. Baton Rouge: Louisiana State University Press, 1986.
Diehl, Paul F. *International Peacekeeping: With a New Epilogue on Somalia, Bosnia, and Cambodia.* Baltimore: Johns Hopkins University Press, 1994.
Elshtain, Jean Bethke, ed. *Just War Theory.* New York: New York University Press, 1992.
Gordon, Michael R. "Somali Aid Plan Is Called Most Ambitious Option." *New York Times,* November 28, 1992, p. A-6.
Haass, Richard N. *Intervention: The Use of American Military Force in the Post–Cold War World.* Washington, DC: Carnegie Endowment for International Peace, 1994.
Kissinger, Henry A. "Balance of Power Sustained." In Graham Allison and Gregory F. Treverton, eds., *Rethinking America's Security: Beyond Cold War.* New York: W. W. Norton, 1992, pp. 238–48.
Levy, Peter B. *Encyclopedia of the Reagan–Bush Years.* Westport, CT: Greenwood Press, 1996.
Lyons, Terrence. *Somalia: State Collapse, Multilateral Intervention, and Strategies for Political Reconstruction.* Washington, DC: Brookings Institution, 1995.
Makinda, Samuel. *Seeking Peace from Chaos: Humanitarian Intervention in Somalia.* Boulder, CO: Lynne Rienner, 1993.
Powell, Colin. *My American Journey.* New York: Random House, 1995.
Sahnoun, Mohamed. *Somalia: The Missed Opportunities.* Washington, DC: U.S. Institute of Peace Press, 1994.
Simons, Anna. *Networks of Dissolution: Somalia Undone.* Boulder, CO: Westview Press, 1995.
Stevenson, Jonathan. "Hope Restored in Somalia." *Foreign Policy* 91 (Summer 1993): 138–54.
———. *Losing Mogadishu: Testing U.S. Policy in Somalia.* Annapolis, MD: Naval Institute Press, 1995.
U.S. Congress, Senate, Committee on Foreign Relations. *U.S. Policy on Somalia: Hearing before the Committee on Foreign Relations, United States Senate,* 103d Congress, 1st Session, July 29. Washington, DC: U.S. Government Printing Office, 1993.
Walzer, Michael. *Just and Unjust Wars.* New York: Basic Books, 1977.

11

Appointment in Sarajevo: George Bush, Yugoslavia, and the Prospects of Federalism

John E. Ullmann

> And therefore never send to know for whom the bell tolls; It tolls for *thee*.
> John Donne, *Meditations XVII*

CHANGE AND RESPONSE

After years of steadily worsening instability, Yugoslavia finally came apart during the Bush administration and sank into a horrifying civil war. It was and is the most violent of all the changes in Europe that followed the meltdown of the Communist satellite regimes and the breakup of the Soviet Union. As such, it should have been at the center of political concern and debate, yet it became part of a failure to define a realistic post–Cold War global role for the United States and—as we will show—a failure to realize the far broader implications for human governance, *not excluding its own*.

This is certainly not to argue that the United States could have unilaterally ended the Yugoslav conflict or prevented it; its roots go too deep for that, nor is this paper intended as a comprehensive account of it. Rather, it focuses on the reaction of the Bush administration to it, which reflected a crucial failure to shed Cold War habits and other ingrained policy conflicts in the face of a vast process of change. The result was a combination of hesitation, superficial and short-sighted historical and economic analysis, letting others, notably Germany, make basic policy, and oscillations between concern and indifference. It was followed eventually by the first use of U.S. forces. They have become more directly involved since then, so that how to respond to future crises of this type, as well as what to do next in this one, are very much current issues.

Moreover, calamitous as it is in itself, the Yugoslav disaster has implications far beyond the geopolitics of its region. The most crucial is its effect on the feasibility of federalism as a political arrangement generally; by the time the Yugoslav civil war started, it had already failed in the former Soviet Union, which had broken up, and in Czechoslovakia, which was about to do so. It is now a live issue in Canada, which may split up in the not too distant future, and, a point that must now be raised with some insistence, it may become one in the United States itself. For this reason, the treatment of the Yugoslav crisis as essentially a distant diplomatic problem was as misguided as it was inadequate.

This is because the purpose of federalism is to unite areas of disparate ethnic, economic, and social characteristics for a common purpose. It becomes successful when the inevitable conflicts in such an arrangement are resolved to general satisfaction. However, recent experience in Yugoslavia and elsewhere shows that once separatism based on perceptions of injustice in any of these factors takes hold, the entire arrangement is under rising and potentially dangerous stress.

The problem has attained crucial relevance for the United States, because the demonization of the federal government became high policy during the Reagan and Bush administrations (Wills 1996; Ullmann 1990). It remains a hallmark of conservative doctrine that is by now shared by most Republicans, as shown by their Contract with America and by the 1996 party platform, as well as by conservative (or frightened) Democrats. The resultant devolution of federal responsibilities to the states and prospects of more to come are precisely the kinds of trends that were potent factors in the breakups of Yugoslavia and other federations. When the central government comes to be perceived as no longer providing a useful service, separatism begins to become attractive. Obviously, this is not a clear and present danger to the United States, but, as shown later, the similarities with the broken federations are too clear to be ignored any longer.

AULD DOCTRINES NOT FORGOT

For the four decades of the Cold War, the United States based its foreign policy on a politically bipolar view of the world, even where such judgments were questionable in themselves and were not shared by American allies. In the Yugoslav case, Marshal Tito broke with the Moscow Communists in 1948. In 1949 he received the first installment ($20 million) of what eventually became substantial Western aid to his regime (Bennett 1995, 59); the initial price was an end to Yugoslav support for the Communist side in the then-ongoing Greek civil war. Still, Tito had a hard time persuading U.S. policymakers that the split was real and that Communism was not "monolithic," as a cherished ideological notion had it.[1] Similar disbelief greeted the Sino–Soviet split some 10 years later.

Another entrenched Cold War ingredient, that of the "captive nations", was closely related to that of monolithic Communism. The Cold War began when Communist regimes were imposed on East European states that, except for Poland, had been allies of Germany; Czechoslovakia and Yugoslavia included the Nazi puppet states of Slovakia and Croatia. Soon, these "captive nations" were joined by Ukraine, the Baltic states, and just about anything else in the USSR that was not Great Russian. Regardless of their records in World War II, Congress regularly commemorated their "slavery," ignoring the overlapping of many territorial claims and sometimes creating never-before-seen entities like "Cossackia." Nevertheless, while the integrity of Yugoslavia was soon accepted and, in fact, insisted on by the United States, that did not prevent the different ethnic blocs in the United States from linking the captive nations doctrine to their own separatist inclinations, eventually coordinating their efforts with those on the scene. They played a powerful part in the U.S. domestic politics of the Yugoslav problem and its public relations aspects, where Croatian and Muslim voices were much stronger than those of Serbs (Owen 1995, 118–19).

Events in Yugoslavia were also part of the religious controversies at the beginning of the Cold War. Following World War II, there were sharp reactions in several newly Communist countries against Catholic hierarchies and the power of the church, including the still-debated behavior of Pope Pius XII toward the Nazis. In Yugoslavia the signal event was the trial and imprisonment of Archbishop Aloysije Stepinac of Zagreb, who was imprisoned for his role in Nazi Croatia (Kaplan 1993, 9–23). His treatment was part of a local settling of scores, but that was also the time when, in the name of anti-Communism, thousands of war criminals were settled in South America, Canada, and the United States, some with help from the Vatican. Thus, Ante Pavelic, the head of Nazi-Ustashe Croatia, escaped to Argentina and later Spain, and Andrija Artukovic, his notorious interior minister, was in the United States until deported in 1986 (Kaplan 1993, 12). Such ethnic and religious issues were crucial domestic factors in setting U.S. Cold War policy.[2]

The captive nations doctrine did not create, but did reinforce, a long-held American view of the meaning of "recognition." Where to others it meant little more than that a certain authority controlled a certain territory, U.S. policymakers invested it with a degree of actual approval of such authority. It had led to U.S. nonrecognition of the Soviet Union from 1918 to 1933 and later of Communist China, Castro Cuba, Vietnam, North Korea, and others. Recognition of its succession states was to play a disastrous part in the Yugoslav breakup, especially in Bosnia-Herzegovina.

The captive nations doctrine seemed to justify itself when the Soviet Union broke up in 1991 at about the same time Yugoslavia descended into war. Suddenly, the nations weren't "captive" anymore, and their independence was quickly recognized. To be sure, there were contrary views that leaving the federations in one piece would be a tidier arrangement, but in general, the Reagan and Bush administrations and their political constituencies considered the Soviet breakup as "victory" in the Cold War, so maybe it would all sort itself out in Yugoslavia as well.

While these victory claims were palpably spurious (Ullmann 1997), the breakups showed again the disastrous legacy of Wilson's Fourteen Points, which had shaped the peace at the end of World War I and led to the creation of the first Yugoslavia, the Baltic States, Czechoslovakia, and Poland. Ostensibly based on Wilson's interpretation of "self-determination," they united under one sovereignty different peoples who had never been together before. Thus, Yugoslavia included Serbia, Croatia, Slovenia, Montenegro, Macedonia, and Bosnia-

Herzegovina as well as large non-Slavic minorities; assertions of Serbian primacy and other conflicts kept the country in constant turmoil. In fact, all of the succession states had difficult minority problems and all of them, including Yugoslavia and excepting only Czechoslovakia, became right-wing dictatorships.

Eventually, ethnic and linguistic conflicts, exacerbated by German conquest and its atrocities in World War II and by perceptions of economic injustice, led to the vicious conflicts of today. Ethnic rivalry became "ethnic cleansing"; discrimination became large-scale robbery and expulsions and, at worst, genocide. It was a surprising legacy for the president of a country that then prided itself on being a melting pot and, despite grave faults, at least paid lip service to the idea of everybody living together.

GERMANY, OLD AND NEW

The central role played by Germany in the recognition of the Yugoslav succession states is obviously the result of Germany's, even before reunification, having once more become the dominant power on the Continent. While this did not faze American conservatives who had long looked on Germany as the best ally against the Soviet Union—bulwark against Bolshevism and all that (Ullmann 1990, 9–10)—it did produce a modicum of international queasiness over German reunification when East Germany collapsed in 1989. When the crowds at the openings in the Berlin Wall sang "Deutschland Über Alles," foreign listeners could hardly have been reassured by the old hymn's definition of Germany's boundaries: "Von der Maas bis an die Memel, von der Etsch bis an den Belt"—from the Meuse in Belgium to the Nemunas in Lithuania, from the Adige in Italy to the Belt in Denmark.[3]

Nowhere was this concern greater than in Serbia and Montenegro, which had lost 537,000 killed or 7.1 percent of their population in World War II; 207,000 Croats and 87,000 Muslims were also killed; in Bosnia-Herzegovina, one-eighth of the people lost their lives (Bennett 1995, 45).[4] While Serbian excesses in the civil war had created international sympathy, though little help, for their victims, their nationalists saw in the prompt German espousal of the Croatian cause a new power play, with Croatia once more a German puppet. Croatia had indeed become pro-German, but, in part, for German domestic reasons; erstwhile Croatian guest workers who had become German citizens were strong supporters of the Free German Party (FDP), whose head was Dietrich Genscher, then the German foreign minister.

The first problems came during the secession of Slovenia. As noted later, it proclaimed its independence in December 1990 for economic reasons that turned nationalistic as well but still hoped for a chance to save the federation. After brief fighting in June 1991, it was allowed to secede, apparently after promising to stay neutral in the rest of the Yugoslav war; also, the country has no border with Serbia and no comparably critical minority problems (Owen 1995, 31).

The next stage, and a very much bloodier one, was the war between Serbia and Croatia, which started in March 1991. As it escalated, it resulted in the arms embargo that was imposed by the UN [United Nations] in September 1991, with the United States in the lead (Owen 1995, 44). When Croatia and Slovenia were recognized soon afterward, the ban was lifted against Croatia, because by then Serbia and Croatia had a cease-fire in their own civil war that seemed to hold.

There were more objections to the recognition of Bosnia-Herzegovina, which had, in fact, itself opposed the recognition of Croatia and Slovenia for fear of a Serbian attack that promptly came. The extreme cruelty of the war was what prompted subsequent NATO [North Atlantic Treaty Organization] intervention, but Germany was precluded by its constitution from using its own troops. A return of Germans would, in any case, have triggered the most violent opposition in all of Eastern Europe, especially Russia (Bennett 1995, 178–79), whose support (or lack of strenuous opposition) was necessary for collective action.

Germany, however, could put pressure on the Serbs by threatening to recognize the Yugoslav succession states, and that became its main policy objective. In Britain and France and certainly in the United States, there was no support for using ground troops in Bosnia; yet, as in Balkan power games of old, there were German allegations that the British and French wanted a strong Serbia as a buffer against German geopolitical ambitions (Owen 1995, 306). In the event, the EC [European Community] recognized Croatia and Slovenia, effective January 15, 1992, and the United States soon followed. Britain had been the last EC holdout but was persuaded in return for German concessions in the Maastricht Treaty (Bennett 1995, 179). This time, however, there was no end to the conflict as there had been, at least tentatively, between Serbia and Croatia, and so the Bosnian phase spun out of control.

INTERVENTIONISM AND ISOLATIONISM: THE ARGUMENT GOES ON

We have noted that ethnic pressures influenced U.S. policy in Yugoslavia. Such pressures are often disdained by foreign policy establishments here and abroad, but, given a highly diverse U.S. population, they are inevitable in almost all foreign policy issues and in no way argue for a self-perpetuating policy group that claims a monopoly in defining the national interest without, looking at the record, the competence to back up such a claim.

Actually, the much older foreign policy conflict between interventionists and isolationists was also a potent factor, and in this case it transcended the usual liberal–conservative split. Thus, Anthony Lewis and William Safire, two columnists of the *New York Times* who differ on virtually every other issue, both advocated massive intervention against the Serbs from early on, whereas others, also of differing political orientations, argued against it.

In the conventional stereotype, interventionists are said to cast the United States as world gendarme, and the end of the Cold War during the Bush years did indeed bring proposals for continuing or widening this role. Thus, Dimitri K. Simes (1988) of the Carnegie Endowment suggested that since the Soviet Union was then preoccupied with its internal problems, the United States could intervene in many more places without concern over a Soviet response; substitute "Russian" for "Soviet," and it becomes a current policy prescription along those lines. More recently, William Kristol and Robert Kagan (1996) proposed a "neo-Reaganite" foreign policy that combines a huge military buildup with "the world-wide export of American democracy."

The contrast between this sort of thing and the isolationism of the 1990s must not, however, be overdrawn. It seldom proceeds from a prudent recognition of the limits of American power, such as came to determine the outcome of the Vietnam War (Ullmann 1988, 233ff.). Senator J. W. Fulbright put it well in 1964, when he first questioned it: "Most of what goes on in the world is either none of our business or in any case beyond our strength, our wisdom or our resources ... [we] should stop acting like a boy scout dragging reluctant old ladies across streets they don't want to cross" (Fulbright 1966, 11, 18).

Rather, today's isolationists are nothing if not traditional. While, on Yugoslavia, some still fret over what they see as the United States' once more having to help clean up a mess the Europeans had got themselves into, they are certainly not shy about viewing the United States as the "last remaining superpower." Conservative objections are not to interventions per se, but to international action, especially through the United Nations. The political record of Republicans still suggests that, ever since the League of Nations, they have had problems with U.S. membership in any international organization. The party's Grand Old "Uncle Sap" line clearly is alive and well. Yet it is a historical fact that since 1914, the United States has never won a war where it did not have powerful allies; in the Bosnian case, NATO came to fill that bill, although throughout the conflict it has often been hard to tell the difference between it and what the UN did, beyond the color of the helmets.

The collapse of Yugoslavia first took a violent turn in 1989 with the persecution and brutalization of the Albanians in Kosovo. As part of Tito's efforts to satisfy all ethnic groups, two provinces in Serbia had been given a degree of autonomy; Vojvodina in the north, next to Hungary, had a large Hungarian minority; Kosovo in the south was largely Albanian and Muslim. The violence was due to a reassertion of Serbian primacy that sought to reverse the gains the Albanians had made. It was Senator Dole who then proposed an embargo against "Yugoslavia" until there was an end to human rights violations in Kosovo, but that was not practical since sanctions would also have affected Croatia and Slovenia which opposed the action in Kosovo (Bennett 1995, 99–101, 108).

By 1992 the United Nations Protection Force (UNPROFOR), which had been deployed in Bosnia, was proving ineffectual. This led to demands for "leave, lift, and strike"; that is, let the UN leave, lift the embargo on arms sales to the Muslims, and use NATO air strikes against the Serbs. In 1993, in keeping with the familiar UN-bashing of their party, Senator Dole and then-minority leader Newt Gingrich strongly supported the plan (Owen 1995, 307); it was branded as a war strategy by the then new Clinton administration.

Actually, "leave, lift, and strike" became yet another case of the United

States' attempting to leave the messy part on the ground to others, while dealing death from the air. Eventually, of course, that did not work either, which meant that U.S. ground troops had to take a hand, unless the whole enterprise was to be abandoned. Just as happened during the Vietnam War, if there was more fighting, the Democrats would have been called the "war party"; if the United States quit, they would have been called "soft" and charged with "losing" whatever country was at issue. So the ground troops went in under NATO (meaning U.S.) command.

Objections to the widening U.S. role in Bosnia have since extended to broader issues. In an op-ed column in the *New York Times* (Dole 1994), Senator Dole complained that taking the costs of U.S. military participation out of the defense budget would "[hasten] the return of the weakened 'hollow forces' of the late 1970s." He thus dredged up the mostly spurious "gaps," "windows of vulnerability," and so on. that were used throughout the Cold War *by both parties* to justify accelerations of the arms race.

Such assertions, however, leave unanswered the questions that should have been at least partially answered during the Bush years, when the end of the Cold War was finally accepted: What else are our armed forces expected to do to justify the quarter of a trillion dollars or so a year spent on them? What wars, hot or cold, are in prospect and with whom, and, rather than working with reruns of World War II and the Cold War arms race, what kind of forces would we *really* need?

FEDERALISM IN CRISIS: THE END OF "INCLUSION"

As noted at the outset, the collapse of Yugoslavia can be seen as a crisis of federalism that goes beyond its own travail to dangers that have beset others, do so now, or are warning signs for the future. Of particular interest are some remarkable parallels with what happened at the time in the Soviet Union and Czechoslovakia and corresponding trends in Canada and the United States.

Without getting into chicken-and-egg arguments, economic troubles can quickly turn other fault lines in society into canyons. In Yugoslavia such economic issues as a general financial crisis, different levels of development, and subsidies of some parts of the federation by others came to combine with ethnic, cultural, religious, and linguistic differences to destroy the common interests that are the ultimate raison d'être of any federation.

Such conditions soon become opportunities for demagogues; two functionaries who had their start under Tito, Slobodan Milosevic in Serbia and Franjo Tudjman in Croatia, became the new nationalist leaders, followed by others like Radovan Karadjic of the Bosnian Serbs.

In the best Balkan tradition (Kaplan 1993), ancient conflicts like the final break between the Roman Catholic and Orthodox Churches in 1054, which had left most Croatians and Slovenes in the former and other Yugoslav Christians in the latter, became hideously topical. Milosevic and Tudjman were not slow in enlisting the churches of their countries in their campaigns against each other and the Muslims. The same went for the Turkish conquest of the Balkans that had begun in the fourteenth century and led to the conversion of some ethnically Serbian inhabitants of Bosnia-Herzegovina to Islam. The horrors of World War II gave further impetus to revenge. Mass murder comes more easily when opponents can be called heretics or infidels; in an interview on *60 Minutes* in July 1996, Karadjic virtually called for a new Crusade against Islam, while help from, and contact with, Muslim fundamentalist regimes, notably Iran, also became a factor in the ongoing struggles. Remaining voices of moderation soon came to be silenced.

Language conflicts are equally permanent. Slavic languages as a group resemble each other a great deal, although that has never prevented some of the world's most fervent hatreds. The ones in Yugoslavia—Slovenian, Macedonian,[5] Croatian, and Serbian—are also very similar; the last two are virtually identical but there was not even agreement on whether to call them Serbo-Croatian or Croato-Serbian. The main difference is that, for originally religious reasons, Serbian uses the Cyrillic alphabet, and Croatian the Roman one; one result of the war is an attempt to use small dialect differences to turn Serbian and Croatian into two languages. Hungarian and Albanian, also spoken, are, of course, completely different.

There also are major social and cultural differences between Slovenia, northern Croatia, and the coast, which were essentially Central European, and Montenegro, Macedonia, and the backwoods of Bosnia-Herzegovina and southern Serbia, which were among the most primitive parts of Europe. In the 70 years of Yugoslavia, they showed up painfully in its economic and social statistics.

That such factors were major ones in the breakup of the Soviet Union is too obvious to need elaboration here. It had over 100 recognized nationalities; its ruble notes came in 14 languages. Nationalism had been anathema to the Communist system, as it was in Yugoslavia, but it clearly managed to survive it. During the breakup between 1989 and 1992, ethnic Russians were worried and rightly so, as it has turned out, over the future of their people in the succession states. However, Russians also resisted the notion that their soldiers would have to break it up between second and third parties, as between Armenians and Azerbaijanis, or Georgians and Ossetians. None of these violent conflicts have as yet been permanently composed.

Czechoslovakia was another Wilsonian creation, linking two peoples that, though ethnically and linguistically almost the same, had never been under one political roof since the Middle Ages. The Czechs lived under the Austrian part of the empire, whereas the Slovaks were under Hungary, a very different arrangement. It was an uneasy combination, made worse by large non-Slavic minorities—Germans in the Czech part, Hungarians in Slovakia. The Germans were Hitler's shock troops in destroying the first republic and were expelled at the end of World War II.[6] The Slovaks established their own Nazi puppet state, much like Croatia. While these World War II memories remained very clear, postwar economic factors, as noted later, provided the impetus for nationalism and soon for separatism.

The situation in Canada is remarkably similar to that of Czechoslovakia, a point often made by English-speaking Canadians in discussions of their problems.[7] To outsiders, the primacy of French seems to be the main problem, even though, as a leading world language by any standard, it hardly seems in need of protection. Rather, the real issue is political and economic power; an earlier (and more honest) separatist slogan had been "maîtres chez nous"—masters in our house. After the narrow defeat of the referendum of 1995, there were rumblings that it had all been the fault of the "ethnics" and that the only *pure laine Québecois* were the descendants of the early French settlers. Canada's English speakers are quick to retort that the prime minister, the chief justice, the governor-general, and the chief of staff of the armed forces are all French. The main support in Quebec for continued unity comes from Montreal and its region, whereas about a third of the population, mostly in the rural French areas, demands independence regardless of the consequences. Similarly, sentiment in favor of a multiethnic community in Bosnia-Herzegovina was concentrated in its capital of Sarajevo.

Finally, similar divisions in the United States are likewise too clear to need much discussion. Racism continues to be exploited; the "cultural and religious war" proclaimed by Pat Buchanan at the 1992 convention that renominated President Bush only continued the earlier fulminations of George Wallace, Spiro Agnew, and their ilk. On the economic side, the gap between rich and poor grew ever wider in the Bush years, and, as the 1996 elections and exit polls show, the sociopolitical orientations of different parts of the country drifted farther apart. The electoral map showed an almost complete break between the Northeast, the northern Midwest, and the Pacific Coast, on the one hand, and the Southeast and mountain states, except for Florida, on the other hand.

The fact that the Republican convention of 1996 tried hard to paper over these fissures only raises the question why national unity and inclusiveness should not be secure enough without such efforts (Gleckman 1996; Herbert 1996). Whatever the variations within it, one of the two major parties is now largely controlled by those who have transferred the Cold War to the home front (Wills 1996). They, in turn, shade over into the armed paranoia at the fringe that already amounts to incipient civil war; a virtual tripling of political bombings between 1985 and 1994 makes that point rather clearly (Egan 1996).

ECONOMICS: WHO WINS AND WHO LOSES

In his *Notebooks,* Samuel Butler says that "most progress is based upon a universal innate desire of every organism to live beyond its means." Yugoslavia was no exception, but the economic situation did not deteriorate rapidly until after the 1973 oil shock; it started a European recession that has largely continued since then. One result was that the million Yugoslav (mostly Croatian) guest workers in Central and Western Europe whose remittances had been a major source of foreign exchange saw their jobs dry up, forcing half of them to return home and swell the increasing ranks of the unemployed.

One response was for both the central government and the republics to borrow massively on world markets, causing the international debt to rise from $3.5 billion in 1973 to $20.5 billion in 1982, when the debts were finally added up (Bennett 1995, 68–69). Efforts by the International Monetary Fund to provide relief were accompanied by its usual violently deflationary policy prescriptions. Such conditions inevitably produce political reactions.

The differences in Yugoslav society also extended to those between rich and poor provinces and republics. Tito's attempts to redress the balance were unsuccessful; the gap grew wider rather than narrower. In 1945 per capita income in Slovenia, the wealthiest republic, had been about three times that of Kosovo, the poorest unit, but was six times as great in the 1980s (Bennett 1995, 69); the per capita GDP [gross domestic product] of Slovenia was 3.9 times that of Kosovo in 1952 and 7.7 times as great in 1989 (Vojnic 1995, 78).

When the economic troubles hit in the 1980s, the more prosperous republics (Slovenia, followed by Croatia), became increasingly reluctant to share in national austerity. The federal government had by then become increasingly powerless because after several political purges, four republics had become supporters of Milosevic's radical pro-Serbian views; they thereby destroyed the impartiality that it had tried to maintain in Tito's times (Dimitrijevic 1995).

When Slovenia and Croatia stopped sending money to the central government, Serbia in October 1990 began levying tariffs on "imports" from Slovenia and Croatia (Bennett 1995, 122; Dimitrijevic 1995). Though it had been part of Yugoslavia from 1918 on, the economy of Slovenia had remained relatively detached from the rest of the Yugoslav market, which in 1989 accounted for only 15 percent of purchases and 21 percent of sales (Bennett 1995, 143; see also Benderly and Kraft 1994, 183–249). Still, Jože Mencinger, the first vice president of independent Slovenia and later governor of its central bank, told me in the summer of 1993 that the tariffs were the last straw.[8] All Slovenia thought it would get from the central government was having to share disproportionately in the costs of bankruptcy.

At a comparable stage in the Soviet Union, nationalism was the prime mover for the breakup, but economic issues were near the surface. For example, much of Russian industry was part of the huge military-industrial complex, whereas the manufacture of the perennially short civilian products like consumer electronics was concentrated in the Baltic republics. Nevertheless, some Russian economists at the time felt that the Russian Soviet Federated Republic, today's Russia, should secede from the other republics, several of which it had always subsidized (Kvint 1990). Such views echo Alexander Solzhenitsyn's fervent, but impractical, proposal in *Rebuilding Russia* (1991) that non-Slavic peoples should leave the Soviet Union, turning it into "Rus"—Russia, Belarus, and Ukraine. The latter two would, of course, have rejected such a proposal for their own nationalist reasons, and there would have been geographic absurdities galore.

In Czechoslovakia the two Czech provinces, Bohemia and Moravia, were likewise much more prosperous than Slovakia. To redress the balance, there was constant Slovak pressure for industrial development, which, given the republic's economy, meant Czech subsidies; in view of the Slovak role in destroying the first republic, such demands were taken seriously. Much of that investment, however, came in the form of arms factories, not only because they were the easiest for the central government to provide but because it also wanted to move them well east of its Western "hot" borders. The great Škoda arms factories in Plzeň switched over entirely to cars, machinery, and railroad equipment.

The Slovaks got a classic Faustian bargain; things were humming during the Cold War, but when it ended, the markets disappeared overnight. The Slovaks did not want any shock treatment in response and wanted to hang onto Communist-style subsidies for literally nothing. When they again put pressure on the Czechs for money and delays in reforms, they dug up their old nationalism and threatened to secede. But that became like somebody going to the boss and saying, "Give me a raise, or I quit!" and the boss replies, "Bon voyage!" As late as January 1992, a deputy minister of the economy of Slovakia told me in the presence of his Czech colleague that the country would not break up, but it did so a year later.

As to Canada, it is often noted that three provinces, Ontario, Alberta and British Columbia, subsidize the others with their federal taxes, the largest share going to Quebec, which also has by far the largest provincial debt. A Czechoslovak-style "bon voyage" has therefore become a potent view in the other provinces, which have also threatened that in the event of secession, Quebec might see its borders questioned and that it, like Slovakia, would have to have a new currency and passports. Whether all this will serve as a deterrent in the future is uncertain (Symonds 1995).

Finally, such concerns are anything but absent in the United States and promise in short order to become worse. Senator Daniel P. Moynihan (D-NY) has long tracked how federal taxes paid in the various states relate to what those states receive in federal aid and spending. New York has always paid out much more than it received; in 1988–1992 it was $65 billion, the largest amount of any state. It was $18.9 billion in 1994, again the most, or $1,040 per capita. On that basis, neighboring Connecticut ($2,128) and New Jersey ($1,816) fare even worse. In fact, the 10 states[9] that pay out more than $900 net per capita give a total of $82.9 billion; the 17 states[10] that *get* more than $900 per capita collect $71.5 billion (Moynihan, Friar, and Leonard 1995, 40, 86).

The states that lose the most are more liberal than the mostly conservative ones that collect the most but still have been the centers of opposition to social legislation. Those of the old Confederacy collect $48 billion net or an average $636 per capita; only Texas has a small ($105 per capita) surplus. The unequal treatment of the states has prompted Senator Moynihan (1995) to suggest that "sometime in the next century, we will have to reapportion the Senate."

Now New York will be especially hard hit by the cutbacks in federal welfare and Medicaid funds because these are an exceptionally large part of federal payments to New York. An editorial in *Business Week* of August 19, 1996, predicted that under the new law "a handful of states . . . will do a decent job of welfare reform [while] other states will be tempted to 'race to the bottom.'" The "leave-it-to-the-states" mentality of the Reagan–Bush years cannot fail to widen the interstate variation in business-related laws and taxes that already creates something like an internal tariff. It would surely have a more "Slovenian" effect if the worst competition were not with foreign countries rather than low cost states (Ullmann et al. 1988, 147–60).

LESSONS

As we have shown, the breakup of Yugoslavia has far wider implications, beginning with those for foreign policy in general. The often confused and contradictory response by the EC, NATO, the UN, and outside powers generally has brought predictable appeals for a more "coherent" U.S. foreign policy (for example, by Fareed Zakaria, the editor of *Foreign Affairs*). Except in vague generalities, however, such a quest is likely to be futile; the world is too irrational and complex for a "coherence" that would very likely become another ideological straitjacket, as it did in the Cold War.

The art of foreign policy is then to look at the multiplicity of conflicts and respond where possible in a sufficiently timely fashion so that the question does *not* become whether or not to send in an occupying army. The size and importance of the United States make it likely that it will be asked to take a position on most significant problems of this kind. Especially when, as in the case of Yugoslavia, the potential for further mischief is great, it is essential for the United States at least to treat the matter as "a cloud no bigger than a man's hand" rather than expect others to sort it all out. This is especially so when those others, meaning the Europeans, have a long history of ultimately involving the United States in their problems, which is exactly what happened in Yugoslavia.

It would be quite wrong, however, to think of that as something foisted on an unwilling Uncle Sam. Rather, the United States had been involved in one way or another in virtually all the current multicentric quarrels. Yugoslavia, Somalia (the "Horn of Africa"), Nigeria, Liberia, and the Middle East were all closely linked to the geopolitics of the Cold War, if not to earlier interests. While, therefore, one can understand that the Bush administration was preoccupied during crucial stages of the Yugoslav conflict with the Gulf War and such other upheavals as the breakup of the Soviet Union, a new foreign policy cannot be conducted on a "so-far-so-good" basis, losing sight of previous policies. Ignoring a problem until it gets out of hand is reducing "management by exception" to absurdity. An example was Secretary of State Baker's last-ditch visit to Yugoslavia on June 21, 1991, when he berated the leaders of Croatia and Slovenia for their separatism four days before they declared independence (Bennett 1995, 175; Owen 1995, 342).

Any response to the multicentric concerns noted is, in any case, subject to sharp limits, imposed by such factors as the ever-rising international debt of the United States and by the now-institutionalized penuriousness of its public sector. If the United States had wanted to encourage peaceful change in the changing economies or the Yugoslav succession states with a new "Marshall Plan," as was widely—and sensibly—suggested, the money for it simply would not have been there. Indeed, the United States felt obliged to ask its allies for money for the Gulf War; the $54 billion received actually produced a small and welcome profit.

Beyond the financial limits, the American public has also become (one could say "commendably") reluctant to accept casualties. Vietnam and its travail clearly remain a live memory. It is no solution, however, to sort out candidates for intervention mainly by having an "exit strategy" rather than risk quagmires. It was a point often raised in trying to decide what to do about Yugoslavia, yet its problems showed, above all, how permanent serious conflicts are. Meanwhile, a belief in military and financial minimalism, however well justified, necessarily reduces global influence—"last remaining superpower" or not.

These restrictions also reflect on the strenuous attempt by the Bush administration to "export democracy" to the changed regimes by advising them to scrap social safety nets and put faith in "markets." Markets can be sustained only if the population is not being systematically impoverished (Ullmann 1994) and the new society does not become an even worse racket than the old. After all, it was a Yugoslav, Milovan Djilas (1957), who first drew attention to the new upper crust of the Communist countries; he was imprisoned for it by his old comrade Tito, who was a rather crass denizen of one himself. The result in much of Eastern Europe has been the rise of Mafias and of "strongmen," some, like Milosevic and Tudjman, no more than "born-agains" of the old regimes (Hedges 1996), if not older ones still, as in Tudjman's shameful attempt to rehabilitate the Ustashe fascists.

As to the declining feasibility of federalism, we have dealt with only five cases in this paper, but we could easily have included others like Russia itself, Belgium, Italy, Nigeria, or Spain and the dozens of unrequited "national liberation" movements elsewhere. One useful, albeit slow, change is that the UN seems to find it easier these days to organize interventions within countries rather than using "national sovereignty" as a blanket excuse for internal barbarities. To be sure, its efforts in Rwanda, Burundi, Liberia, and Somalia did not—and probably could not—prevent slaughter and chaos as much as one would have wished. Still, matters could hardly have been worse if Bosnia had been treated as such an internal problem that deserved international concern and action, *without recognizing it as a separate country*. As we have shown, its recognition triggered the worst violence.

What is clear is that the problems of Yugoslavia were and are much too general for them to have been treated, as they largely were, as no more than faraway ancient hatreds revived that created a diplomatic problem for the United States. Rather, a fragmented population with economic and political inequities that give intergroup hatreds an opening is a far more universal danger that long ago should have been recognized as affecting the governance of the United States as well. In all the cases discussed, political factions had managed to make a central government the main enemy and, in the countries that broke up, destroy it. After the Reagan–Bush era pressure to scale back the federal role, the federal government of the United States now virtually apologizes for itself whenever it does anything other than sustain a military sector that, arguably, should instead be the focus of reassessment in the light of post–Cold War reality. A constructive rethinking of our collective needs and responsibilities is now essential to recover from this political legacy.

NOTES

1. On a somewhat farcical, though related, level, one recalls William F. Buckley Jr.'s TV interview in the late 1970s with the Archduke Otto von Habsburg on proposals for European disengagement; Buckley chided him for even talking to the Yugoslav Communists and looked censorious as only he can.

2. As part of this issue, an end to Catholic control of education and to state subsidies to the formerly established church was denounced, even though such support would have been unconstitutional in the United States.

3. The resurrection of Germany was even played for (at least German) laughs. A popular German television program I saw on May 6, 1990, showed a comedian with a broad Saxon (i.e., East German) accent as a black market operator in goods and currency who bragged about how well he was doing, because there were no longer any border controls. His straight man said: "Just think, soon there won't be any border anywhere between here and Asia!" to which the comedian replied: "Yes, but somewhere you *would* have to leave Germany, wouldn't you?" The large studio audience laughed and cheered.

4. World War II saw the murder of almost 80 percent of a prewar Jewish community of about 70,000.

5. Macedonian is spoken in another problematic Yugoslav succession state, the Former Yugoslav Republic of Macedonia (FYROM). However, in the best traditions of permanent Balkan conflict, its neighbor Bulgaria considers Macedonian as only a Bulgarian dialect, and Greece disputes the very use of "Macedonia" in the country's rather awkward name.

6. Yugoslavia also had German settlements in the northern parts of the country, but their inhabitants either left with the German army or were expelled after World War II.

7. Canadian memories of World War II are also a factor. Because of widespread French Canadian support for the Vichy regime and some local fascist movements, Canada could not have a draft, and it is estimated that some 20 percent of the population was actively opposed to the war. About 1950, I was told by a former director of the U.S. Bureau of Mines that during the war there were military contingency plans in case of serious trouble, for seizing the then strategic mica and asbestos mines of Quebec and protecting the nickel mines of Sudbury, Ontario, near the Quebec border.

8. The events in Slovenia were a reminder that the end of the Austro-Hungarian monarchy was hastened by its repeated failure—the last time in 1912—to become a true free-trade zone; instead, the Hungarian part of the empire (including Croatia) levied tariffs against the Austrian part (including Slovenia). Serbia's efforts to join this potential common market were rebuffed (Kreisky 1986, 55–56).

9. (In order) Connecticut, New Jersey, Delaware, Illinois, New Hampshire, Minnesota, Michigan, New York, Wisconsin, and Nevada.

10. (In order) New Mexico, Mississippi, Virginia, North Dakota, Alaska, West Virginia, Maryland, Alabama, Louisiana, Missouri, Montana, South Dakota, South Carolina, Maine, Georgia, Oklahoma, Arkansas, and Kentucky.

REFERENCES

Benderly, J., and E. Kraft, eds. *Independent Slovenia*. New York: St. Martin's Press, 1994.
Bennett, C. *Yugoslavia's Bloody Collapse*. New York: New York University Press, 1995.
Dimitrijevic, V. "The 1974 Constitution and Constitutional Process as a Factor in the Collapse of Yugoslavia." In P. Akhavan, ed., *Yugoslavia, the Former and Future*. Washington, DC: Brookings Institution; Geneva: UNRISD, 1995), p. 45.
Djilas, M. *The New Class*. New York: Praeger, 1957.
Dole, Bob. "Peacekeepers and Politics." *New York Times*, January 24, 1994, p. A15.
Egan, T. "Terrorism Now Going Homespun As Bombings in the U.S. Spread." *New York Times,* August 25, 1996, p. A1.
Fulbright, J. W. *The Arrogance of Power*. New York: Berkley Books, 1966.
Gleckman, H. "Dole's Reluctant Rank and File." *Business Week,* August 26, 1996, p. 25.
Hedges, C. "Isolated and Corrupt, Serbia's Economy Stagnates." *New York Times*, July 8, 1996, p. A1.
Herbert, B. "Colin's Dream." *New York Times,* August 19, 1996, p. A13.
Kaplan, R. D. *Balkan Ghosts*. New York: St. Martin's Press, 1993.
Kreisky, B. *Zwischen den Zeiten*. Munich: Siedler Verlag, 1986.
Kristol, W., and R. Kagan. "Towards a Neo-Reaganite Foreign Policy." *Foreign Affairs* (July/August 1996): 18–32.
Kvint, V. "Russia as Cinderella." *Forbes,* February 19, 1990, p. 103.
Moynihan, D. P. Letter, *New York Times* September 24, 1995.
Moynihan, D. P., M. Friar, and H. B. Leonard. *The Federal Budget and the States*. Washington DC: Office of Senator Daniel P. Moynihan; Cambridge: Taubman Center for State and Local Government, Harvard University, 1995.
Owen, D. *Balkan Odyssey*. New York: Harcourt Brace, 1995.
Simes, D. K. "If the Cold War Is Over, Then What?" *New York Times,* December 27, 1988.
Solzhenitsyn, A. I. *Rebuilding Russia*. London: Harvill, 1991.
Symonds, W. C. "The Call of the Wild in Western Canada." *Business Week,* December 18, 1995, p. 56.
Ullmann, J. E. "Lyndon Johnson and the Limits of American Resources." In B. Firestone and R. Vogt, eds., *Lyndon Johnson and the Uses of Power*. Westport, CT: Greenwood Press, 1988, pp. 233ff.
———. "Shaking Off Cold War Ideology: Cultural and Political Change in a Demilitarized Society." Briefing Paper No. 8, National Commission for Economic Conversion and Disarmament, ECD, Washington, DC, l990.
———. "The Conversion of Military Resources in the Process of Market Creation and Industrial Recovery." In M. Perczynski, J.Kregel, and E. Matzner, eds., *After the Market Shock: Central and East-European Economies in Transition*. Aldershot, England: Dartmouth, 1994, pp. 175–92.
———. "Ronald Reagan and the Illusion of Victory in the Cold War." In A. Ugrinsky, E. Schmertz, and N. Datlof, eds., *President Reagan and the World*. Westport, CT: Greenwood Press, 1997.
Ullmann, J. E., et al. *The Anatomy of Industrial Decline*. Westport, CT: Greenwood-Quorum, 1988.
Vojnic, D. "Disparity and Disintegration: The Economic Dimension of Yugoslavia's Demise." In P. Akhavan, ed., *Yugoslavia, the Former and Future*. Washington DC: Brookings Institution; Geneva: UNRISD, 1995, p. 75.
Wills, G. "Reagan Country." *New York Times Magazine*, August 11, 1996, p. 30.

Moderator: Ulric Haynes, Jr.

If you'll permit me to set the stage for this morning's discussion, let me describe ever so briefly what I see as the context in which the conflicts in Somalia and Bosnia arose.

Both conflicts typify the kind of threat to world peace that I believe is the legacy that the concluding decades of the twentieth century will leave for the twenty-first century, that is, violent conflict within nations that is often defined and legitimated by the combatants in terms of ethnicity and/or religion, and secondly, conflict that has its roots in history that is often forgotten by the adversaries and ignored by the rest of the world—conflict that defies external military solutions and that lingers even after the cessation of violence, conflict that defies the efforts of American administrations, regardless of the party in power, to—if I may use some popular expressions—"restore peace," "restore democracy," and/or "restore the rule of law and order."

The list of such latter-day conflicts is staggering and is not limited to the Third World: Northern Ireland, Spain, Nicaragua, Guatemala, Colombia, Peru, Timor, Chechnya, Azerbaijan, Afghanistan, Turkey, Iraq, Algeria, Sudan, Zaire, Kashmir, Angola, Tibet, Philippines, Lebanon, Mexico, and South Africa, and, as one of our presenters suggests, can Canada and the United States be far behind?

Discussant: Roy W. Gutman

I feel obliged, as a *Newsday* reporter here, to welcome you to *Newsday* country and to be very grateful for the turnout at this early hour on a subject that's, for most people, unsettled, unclear, if not absolutely painful to address. Just to say, to start, in listening to the papers and the presentations this morning, I thought that Professor Burgess' analysis of Somalia was quite fascinating, particularly the role of Boutros-Ghali, which really I had not ever heard singled out before in that way. I had quite a few disagreements in the analysis of Professor Ullmann, particularly on the issues of Germany and Croatia and some of the World War II history, but I did find really illuminating and insightful his whole point about the nature of federalism and the attack on federalism and how, basically, there are elements in the events in the breakup of Yugoslavia that do say a lot to us today in this country, Canada, and to other countries with a federal system.

But I want to give, as a context for discussing the policy making on Bosnia, the dramatic turn in history that occurred on George Bush's watch. We had, as was mentioned last night, the fall of the Berlin Wall, the end of the Cold War, the unification of Germany, the end of Communist rule, the breakup of the Soviet Union. These are events not just of the decade but of the century and possibly of the millennium. And George Bush and James Baker managed them, I think, with consummate skill. Brian Mulroney last night referred to "the extraordinary victory in the Cold War"—he used that phrase—and, as a reporter covering these events in the field, I can only endorse his remarks.

There was criticism of President Bush for his hesitation before and during the Gulf War, but on the whole the war was well managed. The administration certainly used the opportunities that the war opened up for peacemaking and, with courage and tenacity, pursued the peace process in the Middle East. They made a quite significant contribution, as Mr. Mulroney pointed out last night, to Israeli–Palestinian rapprochement. These achievements are beyond the dreams of most mortals, most statesmen, and they were an exhausting series of efforts. Some people sympathetic to the administration say that they entered their last year in office fatigued, exhausted, in the foreign policy sphere. In election years, no good deed goes unpunished, and so, ironically, the president found himself under attack for what was, to all accounts, a brilliant success.

One thing that struck me in the president's attitude was a kind of reticence, a reluctance to advertise his achievements but also to follow through on his achievements. He proclaimed a "New World Order," but he was reluctant to establish it. Instead, in the election year, he basically tried to avoid foreign policy issues and foreign affairs in general. This was the year, 1992, in which his reputation in foreign policy—his strongest suit—began to unravel.

I have personally had an involvement in one issue, because I was a reporter on the scene in Bosnia, and we in *Newsday* broke the story of the death camps in Bosnia and detailed the ethnic cleansing in great detail over a very long period of time. I was there writing the stories and watching the reactions. One thing I could not understand was the response of President Bush and his administration. If I got the story wrong, other reporters will prove it wrong, and then you'll know what the facts are, but the story turned out to be correct. The president, to my mind, did not address the reality that was out there. I had witnesses describing wholesale, systematic murder of citizens in detention camps that they saw firsthand. The day after my story appeared, August 2, 1992, the State Department confirmed it. Two days later, they retracted their confirmation. ITN, the British television network, got into the camp called Omarska and showed the prisoners, emaciated prisoners, looking like they feared for their lives, and with good reason. The president reacted, but he didn't demand that these camps be dismantled, that the prisoners be freed, that this whole episode somehow end quickly. He said instead that the International Red Cross should be allowed in to tend to the prisoners. Imagine the message that that statement sent to the people who were holding the prisoners, who were running the camps.

Two weeks later, in mid-August, the administration said—and I think it was Eagleburger himself—that it had no proof of systematic killing in the camps. At the State Department—and this is a unique event in modern times since the Vietnam War—officials began resigning in protest that the administration had not actually gotten out the facts but instead was putting out a version of events that was incorrect. To its credit, the U.S. government started doing its homework. It started interviewing refugees. Months later, it confirmed the stories that we did in August, but the damage had been done because the credibility of George Bush as a world leader took a nosedive.

It wasn't necessary to say what he should have done in this case, whether it's an intervention of a military sort or whether it's just simply drawing attention to the facts that were out there. But what he was doing, in fact, was to deny what was plainly visible to you in the public. If you do that, if you deny what is plainly visible, you begin to lose your charisma as a leader.

Up to that point, George Bush was almost untouchable and had a record as a gifted world leader. But beyond just simply denying what was really out there, he and his aides started misleading the public. Colin Powell wrote in his autobiography recently, "We were dealing with an ethnic tangle with roots reaching back over a thousand years." He said that at the time as well. He wrote it in the *New York Times* in a remarkable op-ed piece that was astonishing, because it's a military leader essentially laying out the outlines of policy in the public forum. It's usually left to the civilian leaders. But this is really—the British would call it "a load of codswallop," because you cannot justify mass murder of civilians—unarmed civilians—by citing some event that may have occurred six centuries earlier. That's done by the people who are organizing the camps and the repression, but that's not to say that we, the United States, an outsider, can buy such an argument. It was a rationalization, at best. I quote David Gompert, who was then on the National Security Council staff in the

White House, who commented that the administration had "wrongly portrayed the Bosnian conflict as a hopelessly complicated civil war with all parties at fault and no American interests at stake."

Now, the mistake in Yugoslavia of the administration did not occur all at once. This is a debacle that had many parents and something even of a pedigree. If you go back to June 1991, the eve of the breakup of that multinational state, James Baker went to Belgrade; he was then the secretary of state. He urged the Yugoslavs to stay together, even though by that time the breakup was really a certainty. Baker, before going out to Belgrade on that fateful trip, had had a debate, an argument, within the administration, and the person on the other side was Paul Wolfowitz, then the undersecretary of defense, as well as others. Now, Wolfowitz felt that the breakup of Yugoslavia was inevitable, and the United States basically should assist it to break up peacefully and remake it as a loose confederation. But Baker, according to accounts that I've heard, was listening to his Soviet counterpart, Eduard Shevardnadze, and Andrei Kozyrev. Shevardnadze and then Kozyrev had told him that the breakup of Yugoslavia would set a precedent for the breakup of the Soviet Union, and they wanted to avoid the breakup of the Soviet Union. Wolfowitz felt that the breakup of the Soviet Union was a very positive result, that it was to be sought in a peaceful way, and that, if Yugoslavia broke up peacefully, it would be a good example for the breakup of the Soviet Union. Obviously, the Russians were trying to avoid the breakup. Baker sided with them.

Now, whether or not Baker intended to give the signal to Slobodan Milosevic, the strongman in Serbia, Milosevic took Baker's statement to stay together as a signal to use force brutally to prevent the breakup. Worse than that, the United States essentially, after giving this advice, bowed out of policy determining the future of that part of the world. It took with it NATO, the only instrument of international security able to manage a crisis in Europe—or really, probably anywhere else—and what followed were three wars of succession. You had, first of all, Slovenia in June 1991; Croatia from June to December 1991; and Bosnia-Herzegovina from April 1992 to November 1995.

Now, I think one could argue in the administration that there was a strategic miscalculation. But they could also argue that it was made in the service of a higher goal, and the higher goal was their greatest achievement, and that was a soft and peaceful landing for the pieces of the Soviet Union. The tragedy, to my mind, is that this error was made in the service of a higher goal, but, when new facts emerged, the president didn't acknowledge them, nor the error itself, but instead distorted the facts and compounded the error.

Just to turn briefly to Somalia. The sending of American troops, as Professor Burgess makes clear, undoubtedly saved lives in Somalia. But make no mistake: it cost lives in Bosnia. Indeed, the Somalia decision can really be seen only in the light of the events in Bosnia—these things happened simultaneously—and the continuing criticism the president was receiving, especially from conservative Republicans, that he had abandoned American leadership in Bosnia. Larry Eagleburger, then the secretary of state, said, after the announcement of sending troops to Somalia, that the deployment in Somalia had no relevance for Bosnia because American resources were limited. Now, whether he intended it or not, the Serbs read this as a go-ahead signal for the conquest, and they stepped up the bombardment of Sarajevo. They totally shut down food deliveries.

In northern Bosnia, the area that I was reporting about, where these camps existed, ethnic cleansing had actually been suspended for several months, from about August until December 1992. "Ethnic cleansing" is a euphemism, as you know; it means mass killing, torture, rape, and deportation of civilians. But it had been suspended. Why? Hundreds of reporters were combing the area, and, under the spotlight, these practices stopped. There might be a lesson in that. But in any case, after the Somalia announcement, ethnic cleansing started up again there.

Now, the Somalia intervention—again, as Professor Burgess has said—was supported by Chairman Powell of the Joint Chiefs of Staff as something that was winnable, and here we come to the pithy summing up of how these two things relate. He summed up, just as the marines were landing on Mogadishu under the klieg lights of the American television networks and walking away from the heart of Europe, why Somalia and why not Bosnia. It was reported in the American press at the time: "We do deserts. We don't do mountains."

It would be wrong to fault just Colin Powell with this error of policy; clearly, when he spoke out in public or wrote in the *New York Times*, he was not doing it alone. He was doing it with, I assume, presidential approval. The fact is, we had Larry Eagleburger and Brent Scowcroft, two very distinguished men who had experience in the old Yugoslavia, Tito's Yugoslavia, and who had a kind of nostalgia for that era. I understand it, personally and perfectly, because I, too, was a reporter in the old Yugoslavia in the Tito era, and that mind-set was infectious and contagious, and most people who lived there at the time felt it. But the place had changed. The Cold War had ended. All of the previous assumptions you made about a country like that had to be reexamined. They really weren't reexamined.

To sum up, it was a series of mistakes that were made based on an old mindset and based on a refusal to reexamine the world as it had just changed, thanks very largely to the very astute leadership of Bush and Baker. They sent UN troops, peacekeeping troops, into a place where there was a raging war. They turned over control of a European problem to two European powers, Britain and France, which really didn't have the confidence of everybody else, nor really even the capabilities and the competence to lead Europe. So it's one of the tragedies of the Bush administration that their great historical achievement is not always seen—and certainly not at this phase—as the legacy it should be. Why did that happen? You know, when you ask them why the president turned away from foreign policy that year, why he ignored his best suit, people in the administration said that it was a political year, an election year. It just may be the way our democracy runs. When you have an election year, it's very hard to conduct serious foreign policy.

Discussant: Kenneth I. Juster

Two important topics—Somalia and Bosnia—have been discussed. I would like to make a few points on each in reference to the papers and the presentations made and then open up the discussion for questions and answers.

On Somalia, the overall motivation for the U.S. intervention there was really quite simple. It was as follows: when you have it in your power to prevent the deaths of several million people, you do it. The mission in Somalia arose from humanitarian concerns, and, indeed, there was always a strong commitment to limiting the mission to a humanitarian effort and not to take on the task of nation-building. The Somalia mission was not motivated by President Bush's concern about his place in history. To the contrary, any president worries that a military mission carries with it the enormous risk that U.S. soldiers will return home in body bags, so one does not undertake that sort of mission lightly or in an effort simply to enhance one's place in history.

The mission also was not, in my view, motivated by a desire to prove that the "New World Order" was a reality. Rather, there was an assessment made within the Bush administration, after seeing the devastating effects of the famine in Somalia, that the United States could lead a multilateral force to provide security to open the relief channels, feed a starving population, and help avoid a humanitarian catastrophe. That was the purpose of the mission, and I think it was accomplished.

The mission was always circumscribed from the outset; it was designed to stabilize the military situation and to avert mass starvation. The Bush administration resisted the efforts of UN secretary-general Boutros Boutros-Ghali to expand the mission and to undertake nation-building activities. Indeed, there was continual pressure from Boutros Boutros-Ghali for the United States to do more, but the Bush administration made it quite clear that it was intervening for a limited purpose, that it wanted to leave Somalia as soon as that limited purpose had been accomplished, and that it expected to turn over the mission to the United Nations within approximately three months.

It is also important to note that the Bush administration did not consult President-elect Clinton on whether to undertake the mission. Rather, President Bush made that decision as president of the United States, and the mission was sufficiently limited so that, if the incoming Clinton administration did not want to continue the mission, it could draw down the mission relatively easily early into its term of office.

Again, it should be emphasized that the undertaking in Somalia was a limited, humanitarian mission that the Bush administration felt could achieve its aims relatively easily and quickly and then could be handed over to the United Nations. Indeed, as Professor Burgess wrote in his paper, before President Bush left office on January 20, 1993, the U.S.-led multilateral operation had succeeded in supplying humanitarian relief and curbing the famine and starvation in Somalia. I think that was a correct assessment. I therefore was a bit puzzled when Professor Burgess also said that President Bush exhibited a lack of common sense in his assumption that forces could be inserted in Somalia in December 1992 and withdrawn by January 20, 1993. In effect, a drawdown really could have begun on January 20, because much of the humanitarian mission already had been completed by that time.

The problems in Somalia came, in my view, when the Clinton administration, under the auspices of the United Nations, sought to expand the Somalia mission to include nation-building. This effort was labeled by then U.S. ambassador to the United Nations Madeleine Albright as "assertive multilateralism." This "assertive multilateralism" was more than "mission creep"; it appeared to be a conscious decision to expand the mission in Somalia, and it ultimately led to violence, embarrassment, and withdrawal by the United States.

That is my brief assessment of the Somalia case. However, I would like to comment on a few other points in Professor Burgess' paper to correct the historical record.

First, it is wrong to state—and I quote here—that "President Bush's foreign policy was largely reactive" or to imply that the United States was incorrect to maintain its links with President Gorbachev as long as it did or that the United States did little to encourage the independence of the republics of the former Soviet Union. One must examine the enormous number of behind-the-scenes consultations, cables, and "quiet trips" that occurred throughout this period to appreciate how well the Bush administration actively managed the end of the Cold War, the disintegration of the Warsaw Pact, and the collapse of the former Soviet Union; how well it managed the process of the unification of Germany within NATO; and how well it managed the Gulf War without Russian or Chinese objection. All of these events did not just happen automatically; they were the result of a tremendous amount of hard work by a very committed foreign policy team that functioned extremely well together.

In terms of why the U.S. government continued to maintain strong links with President Gorbachev while he was still the leader of the Soviet Union, the answer is simple: President Gorbachev was the leader of what was still a major power, with nuclear weapons pointed at the United States. It would have been foolish not to meet with him or otherwise to snub him. At the same time, on a parallel track, the Bush administration maintained a broad range of contacts with the leaders of the republics of the Soviet Union and, again, took very careful steps to try to manage the disintegration of the Soviet Union in a way that would not lead to a backlash or incite a violent reaction from Moscow.

President Bush quite consciously did not go to Germany when the Berlin Wall collapsed so as not to throw that event back in the face of the Soviet Union. President Bush quite consciously chose not to have the United States be the first country to recognize the Baltic states because, even though the United States had supported the independence of the Baltic states throughout the Cold War, President Bush wanted to manage their independence in a way that was not going to lead to a backlash from Moscow. I would submit that, if you examine the historical record, this effort was quite successful. Indeed, if one would have predicted in 1988 all that occurred in international affairs in the years 1989 to 1992 and, with the exception of Bosnia (which I will address in a moment), that these events not only would occur but also would take place in relative peace, I think most people would have shaken their heads and said, "That just cannot happen." It was thus an extraordinary achievement to manage successfully many of the international events during this period, and that sound management occurred only through great effort.

Second, in terms of the decision-making style of the Bush administration, it is incorrect to assert that it was moving toward the end of the administration from a consensual style to a patriarchal style, in which President Bush was acting more on his own. President Bush had assembled a first-rate foreign policy team of experienced individuals—National Security Adviser Brent Scowcroft, Secretary of State Jim Baker, his deputy and successor as secretary of state Larry Eagleburger, Secretary of Defense Dick Cheney, and Chairman of the Joint Chiefs of Staff Colin Powell—all of whom had worked with each other over a number of years and respected each other. It was a team that operated extremely smoothly. There was often vigorous debate during meetings, but decisions were then made at the end of meetings, often on a consensus basis. Sure, President Bush, as the president, was the ultimate decision maker, but he acted with much advice and input from his foreign policy team and with collective agreement from the beginning of his administration to the end. Once a foreign policy decision was reached in the Bush administration, there were rarely, if ever, leaks or disagreements about implementation. Once decisions were made, they were carried out and implemented effectively.

Finally, I would like to make a point about the "New World Order" and what it was supposed to denote. It is an overused phrase; it was never, in my view, intended as a broad doctrine. It was a phrase that originated as the United States was preparing to intervene in the Persian Gulf. The New World Order was not a vision of utilizing the United Nations to resolve international crises but the notion that, with the end of the Cold War, nations could work together, often in coalitions and under the imprimatur of the United Nations, to address such crises. In other words, a UN resolution would support collective action, but the United Nations itself would not necessarily undertake military operations. Those operations would be undertaken by sovereign nations. Thus, the Bush administration did not favor granting military authority to a UN command; rather, it favored having the United Nations provide support and authority for an international coalition to act, as occurred in the Persian Gulf.

I now turn to the case of Bosnia and, again, make a few brief points before entertaining questions from the audience. I found Professor Ullmann's presentation a bit confusing at times and somewhat contradictory. Let me explain why. First, I felt that there was some inconsistency between stating, on the one hand, that what took place in terms of the disintegration of Yugoslavia was due, in large part, to historical forces and to a series of long-standing ethnic divisions and hatreds that became highly nationalistic feelings with the end of the Cold War and then asserting, on the other hand, that the disintegration was some sort of failure of U.S. foreign policy due to hesitation, half steps, and misguided historical analysis, without suggesting what one could have done to prevent what occurred.

Second, there was an implicit assumption by Professor Ullmann that the United States did not appreciate the magnitude of the problems in the former Yugoslavia and that the Bush administration neglected those problems or, as Mr. Gutman claimed, that certain members of the Bush administration were nostalgic for Tito's Yugoslavia. That is just not the case. The Bush administration was well aware of the changes going on in Yugoslavia prior to the crisis there. This can be confirmed by examining the internal memoranda and cable traffic at the time. Indeed, I recall being in Vienna, Austria, in February 1990, and there was a general discussion about how Yugoslavia might look like Lebanon very quickly. So there was not a failure of intelligence regarding Yugoslavia or a lack of attention to the situation there or a failure to reexamine the world after the end of the Cold War. Rather, there was simply no consensus among Western countries as to a good solution to the emerging problems in Yugoslavia. I have not heard any suggestions this morning as to what steps should have (and could have) been taken by the West at the time.

There was not a Western consensus as to how to prevent the accelerating and awful logic of the breakup of Yugoslavia and the resulting war. There was certainly no unity of views among the West as to what steps to take, and this obviously had tragic consequences. As Ambassador Haynes stated earlier, this was a conflict that defied external military solutions. Indeed, unless the United States and its European allies had decided at the outset to intervene with a large military force, take sides in the conflict, and impose a peace—which is what there was never an agreement on doing—it was not clear how to stop the downward spiral toward violence. That is not to excuse the tragedy of the situation, but it is to say that there had to be a game plan as to what to do before the United States and other countries could try to stop the violence.

U.S. policy at the outset was based on a judgment that a peaceful breakup of Yugoslavia would be quite difficult; that no republic should unilaterally declare independence; and that the country should remain unified until the republics could collectively decide on what would be their next phase—whether it would be, for example, a looser federation or a peaceful disintegration (as occurred in Czechoslovakia). But the United States never urged the use of force to keep Yugoslavia unified, and Secretary of State Baker's June 1991 visit to Yugoslavia was in no way a green light to Serbian leader Slobodan Milosevic to use such force. Indeed, Secretary Baker told Milosevic that, if it came to a question of using force to keep Yugoslavia unified or allowing democratic trends to lead to its disintegration, the United States would favor the path of democracy. How Milosevic may have chosen to interpret the visit is something only he can explain, and, with the warped mind of that individual, it is wrong to attribute any causality between his actions and those of the United States.

It is interesting to note that the Bush administration has generally been criticized—as Mr. Gutman indicated—for supposedly favoring the unity of Yugoslavia over its disintegration, whether peaceful or not. At the same time, Professor Ullmann implicitly criticized the Bush administration for not strengthening authority at the federal level in Yugoslavia, and thus for allowing the centrifugal forces of the republics to dominate. The fact is that the Bush administration did seek actively to assist Yugoslavia's prime minister, Ante Markovic, who had begun to implement a solid economic program for Yugoslavia before both he and his program were undermined by Milosevic and others.

It is also important to note—though the other speakers may disagree—that Yugoslavia, while a country of strategic importance during the Cold War, had lost its strategic significance with the end of the Cold War. Indeed, unlike the conflict in the Persian Gulf, neither the conflict in Bosnia nor that in Somalia involved the vital national interests of the United States. To be sure, the United States had strong humanitarian concerns relating to those conflicts and tried to develop policies to resolve the unrest in those regions, but there were limits on the extent to which the U.S. government was prepared to put American lives on the line to do so. The challenge in Bosnia was not one of isolationism versus interventionism but of how to employ limited means when vital interests were not at stake. Again, regrettably, the West was very much divided on how do to this—and, thus, immobilized.

The Bush administration felt at the time—and, in hindsight, one may disagree—that putting American troops on the ground in Yugoslavia could lead to significant casualties, which the American public, seeing no vital national interests at stake, would not support. In fact, if you look at what occurred in Somalia when 18 marines were killed, there was an outcry by the American public to get out of that country because there was no vital interest at stake.

With regard to the conflict in Yugoslavia, the United States initially relied on its European partners to take the lead. You may ask, Why did this occur? The United States had, of course, taken the lead in the transatlantic alliance throughout the Cold War. However, in organizing the Persian Gulf coalition in the aftermath of the Cold War, the United States experienced a good deal of tension with the Europeans because they very much wanted to be coleaders of that process. But the United States was putting 500,000 troops on the ground in the Persian Gulf, so the United States led the coalition, despite some European resentment. Similarly, in orchestrating the Middle East peace process, the United States also felt some European resentment because of their limited role. Again, the Europeans wanted to be coleaders in trying to stimulate the peace process.

Accordingly, when the conflict arose in Yugoslavia—in the heart of Europe, with European leaders insisting that they take the lead in this crisis, and with Luxembourg foreign minister Jacques Poos proclaiming, "The Age of Europe has dawned"—the United States had a tough time arguing against the European sentiments. The U.S. position was that we would be fully supportive of European-led initiatives in Yugoslavia and also of the Vance-Owen peace mission.

We also felt that the Europeans, being closer to the situation, might have greater leverage than we did on Yugoslavia. As we all know, however, the Europeans never were able to pull together politically to reach agreement on how to address the situation in the former Yugoslavia, and this certainly had very negative consequences. For a period of approximately one year, the Europeans tried to take the policy lead but failed in doing so.

Toward about August or September 1992, the Bush administration became more active with regard to Yugoslavia. We urged the lifting of the arms embargo, we explicitly named war criminals, and we actively discussed using airpower in the region. But the Europeans were reluctant to take any of these steps, and the United States was not prepared to act without its allies.

It is incorrect to assert that the United States denied charges of there being death camps. There was a certain amount of confusion within the intelligence community, and, at first, we were unable to confirm that there were, in fact, death camps. But there was never any effort to mislead or any active misleading of the American public about what was going on in Yugoslavia.

The next phase of the Bosnia crisis, after the European effort at leadership and after the Bush administration sought to become more assertive but was unable to reach consensus with its European allies, came with the onset of the Clinton administration. The new administration spoke of lifting the arms embargo and initiating air strikes but did neither, again because of lack of agreement with European allies. Eventually, following almost three years of problems related to the UN peacekeeping forces in Bosnia, the Dayton process led to an agreement that stopped the violence.

It is important to note that, despite the achievements of the Dayton process in halting the warfare in Yugoslavia, it does not necessarily follow that a similar peace could have been achieved four years earlier. A lot had changed during that period of time. The various parties—the Serbs, Croats, and Muslims—had been at war for four years. They were exhausted, and all had suffered greatly. Moreover, much of the "ethnic cleansing" that had motivated the fighting in Yugoslavia had occurred by the time of Dayton, especially after the Croatians evicted the Serbians from the Krajina. Indeed, the Dayton process led to complete separation among the parties. So it had achieved a tenuous peace, though not necessarily justice.

In concluding, it is important to recognize that if one undertakes an impartial intervention of a limited nature—which is really what the Western allies were seeking to do in Bosnia with the United Nations peacekeeping force—then, in some respects, the result may be further tragedy to the parties of the conflict by raising expectations that there will be a resolution of the situation but without providing sufficient means to impose such a resolution, thus leading to a sort of a slow-motion savagery on the ground. If the objective is one of "peace"—though not necessarily justice—then there may need to be a commitment to one party of the conflict—which the West was never willing to do—to intervene forcefully to resolve the situation. What has brought peace in Bosnia today is a separation of the parties but not a resolution of the conflict. It is not at all clear to me that the situation will remain stable if U.S. troops leave Bosnia next year, as announced by President Clinton.

I thus come back to the point that, despite the tragic situation in Yugoslavia, it is much easier to describe the problems there and to criticize the lack of solutions than it is to propose such solutions. Regrettably, the United States does not necessarily have policy solutions that can resolve all problems. Indeed, sometimes one is faced with selecting from among a series of less than great policy options.

Questions and Answers

Ulric Haynes Jr.: I'm sure that you all share with me the view that the presentations today have been of the highest quality and have been exemplary for their clarity. We all appreciate that on the part of all of the presenters and the panelists. Indeed, it was well worth rising from bed so early on a rainy Saturday morning.

May I have the first question or comment?

Q: Bill Brands from Texas A&M. This is a question for Mr. Juster. As the Cold War was winding down, and it was becoming apparent that there would be an opportunity or the necessity for various forms of American intervention, did anybody in the State Department or the National Security Council systematically try to devise a framework for when, and under what circumstances, the United States would intervene and when it wouldn't, or was this simply going to happen on an ad hoc basis?

Kenneth I. Juster: That is a good question. President Bush had certain guidelines as to what would make sense in terms of a military intervention. I believe if you review his speech at West Point at the end of his administration, he elaborates on those rather well. I am not sure that I can recall them all correctly, but they would include, first, defining our objective—what is the mission or the goal of the intervention? In other words, what interests are at stake for the United States, and what is the U.S. government seeking to achieve? There must be clear objectives in order to assess the scope and success of the intervention. Second, what sort of military force is required, and what will it cost? In other words, do we have the resources and the capabilities to accomplish the mission? Third, what is the exit strategy? If the United States intervenes and stabilizes the situation for 12 months, but then there is instability again once U.S. troops depart, have we truly achieved our objective or simply created, at great cost, a pause in a bad situation? Fourth, will the American people support the military intervention? Will there be support in Congress and among the public?

I believe that if you examine each of the military interventions of the Bush administration—Panama, the Persian Gulf, and Somalia—there was a clear objective and mission. It was getting Noriega out of Panama; it was ejecting Iraq from Kuwait; it was feeding the people of Somalia. There was a sense of what it would take to accomplish these objectives and that we had the capability to do so. There were consultations with Congress and with our allies to ensure that we had their support, and there was a strategy for getting out—or, in the case of Somalia, turning the mission over to the United Nations.

The assessment on Bosnia was that we just were not able to meet these guidelines. What was the mission in Bosnia? Was it to side with the Muslims and the Croats against the Serbs? Was it to separate the parties and partition the territory? If one separates the parties, how is stability achieved over time? What would it take to accomplish any of these objectives? Would the American people support the mission if there were casualties?

Reasonable people can disagree with the assessment along those lines, and I am not claiming that the Bush administration was always correct in how it answered these questions. But the administration did have a systematic set of questions that it addressed in considering any potential military intervention.

Roy W. Gutman: Just briefly, it's a good thing, if we look back at history, that Harry Truman didn't have that framework in his mind when he basically decided to return U.S. forces to Europe in the Cold War, set up NATO, committed ourselves to the defense of Germany, and so on. Because if they'd had that framework, I don't think we'd be discussing this today in the way we are.

John E. Ullmann: In response to your question, let me go back to what Mr. Gutman said about the alleged remark by Secretary Baker or General Powell or whoever it was, that "We do deserts, we don't do mountains." The Gulf War and Somalia were both in deserts, but the former was the enormously greater undertaking. So perhaps we should put it more accurately: "We do oil, but we don't do slivovitz," which, since some of you look puzzled, is the local tipple and just about the only natural resource of Bosnia-Herzegovina.

Eventually, you do have to choose whether to intervene, but I would raise a couple of points here. Number one, impartial interventions are very difficult. Ask any police department where their guys get hurt most often, and for many it is in intervening in domestic quarrels. Second, obviously—and I tried to say this a moment ago—our interests differ in different parts. I mean, we've all really said similar things about that. Also, after the terrible experience of Vietnam especially, which really tore the country apart and the aftereffects of which still linger, we don't like to see too many body bags coming home.

But there was one thing for which there really should have been opportunity, and it didn't happen. Yesterday General Scowcroft was very happy to say, "Well, we didn't come running to Russia with $50 billion." Fifty billion dollars is serious money—I agree with that—but not gigantic in a $6 trillion economy, as it then was. As Mr. Juster described it, Mr. Wolfowitz had the idea of major financial aid and other steps to ease the transition—in other words, a rerun of the Marshall Plan, which I also favored very clearly in my paper. However, given the penuriousness and the constant pressure under which our government has been put, the antitax hysteria at the federal level, and all the rest of it, we would simply not have been able to do this. What is also involved here is that, for good reason—and I would not argue otherwise—we didn't want to have American casualties. Nobody would want that, but, on the other hand, we didn't want to do it with money either. There's a limit to how much you can call the tune when you don't want to pay the piper anymore.

The Marshall Plan was an integral and essential part of our deployment at the beginning of the Cold War. We would not be able to do that now. In fact, it's interesting to read some of the rhetoric and some of the justifications for all of these things in the 1940s and 1950s. There is no political leader now who would suggest anything like it.

Haynes: Steve, did you have something?

Stephen F. Burgess: Well, since it's open season, I just want to make one comment that I think raises a question. This has to do with the transition process from one president to another and the problem, then, of initiating major foreign policy actions at the end of an administration and leaving it in the hands of an inexperienced administration. So that's a question I think really needs to be gone over in greater depth.

Haynes: Next question.

Q: *My name is George Papaioannou, and I come from the School of Business here at Hofstra. There are several conflicting views about the Bosnia crisis. One is the argument that Bosnia was allowed to declare independence prematurely, before the constitutional rights that would have safeguarded the rights of minorities were spelled out clearly and in a fashion that would protect each one of them from aggression from the other parties. The second thing is the perception, at least, about Balkan people. I happen to come from Greece, and I can understand historical causes why the West, in a way, fails to recognize the grievances and fears of the Serbians. In the process, they were demonized, and that perhaps has given purpose to the very aggressive behavior they have demonstrated.*

Dr. Ullmann said that events of 1,000 years ago look like they happened yesterday. I can attest that they are yesterday's events for many of us who come from that region. Greece, for example, had a savage civil war after World War II. I can tell you right now there are people there who would avenge past wrongdoings that they make up in their heads. Feelings are that strong. I think we see the animosity and the mistrust between Serbs and Bosnians, Serbs and Croats, Greeks and Turks, because memories die very hard. We should not judge these people; we have the historical experience and perspective of only 200 years of American history.

Haynes: Would any of our panelists care to address those comments?

Juster: Thank you for your contribution. Before I address your specific question, I would like to recall a meeting I attended in Yugoslavia in February 1990. I was with Deputy Secretary of State Lawrence Eagleburger and U.S. ambassador Warren Zimmerman at the time. Also in attendance were representatives of several dissident political parties from throughout the country, including each of the republics, and each representative made a short presentation. It was a surrealistic experience, because virtually every representative talked entirely past the others and offered a completely different version of history. So, tragically, one could begin to envision a series of trains at a distance all heading toward each other without any clear resolution of the situation.

In terms of your question as to whether the West allowed Bosnia to declare independence prematurely, I do not believe that the recognition of Bosnia precipitated the use of force by the Bosnian Serbs any more than it deterred such use of force. Once Slovenia seceded from Yugoslavia, it set in motion a series of territorial concerns and problems. The Croats followed the Slovenes, and then the Serbs wanted those Serbs outside Serbia to be part of a broader Serbia, and the Bosnian Muslims were not going to remain part of a rump Yugoslavia, dominated by the Serbs. So, tragically, events were set in motion, and I do not believe that the recognition or lack of recognition of Bosnia at that time would have changed anything.

In terms of whether the West "demonized" the Orthodox Serbs, there was plenty of demonizing going on within Yugoslavia without the West's making any contribution to it. Professor Ullmann's paper does a good job of describing, as you have yourself, a lot of the historical hatreds that existed, without any demonization by the West. One need only look at the highly nationalistic speech that Slobodan Milosevic made in Kosovo in 1989.

Finally, I would like to add one or two footnotes to the earlier discussion. First, on the issue of U.S. intervention in "deserts versus mountains," it does not relate, in my view, to oil but rather to the fact that military operations are easier to implement in a desert setting than in the mountains of Yugoslavia, where the terrain is difficult and population groups cannot be easily distinguished from each other. In other words, it was not a "clean" situation.

Second, on the point about the Marshall Plan, I agree with Professor Ullmann that the conditions that existed at the end of World War II were radically different from those that existed at the end of the Cold War—in terms of the U.S. position in the world, in terms of U.S. economic wherewithal, and in terms of domestic public opinion to support actions that the United States might take abroad. Ironically, many of the economic resources that went into the buildup in the 1980s of U.S. military power—and certainly contributed to the disintegration of the Soviet Union—also contributed to a budget deficit by the end of the decade. Moreover, public opinion in recent years has not favored spending U.S. government funds on foreign assistance. Currently, the entire foreign assistance budget is less than 1 percent of our national budget, and yet people still complain that the country is spending too much on foreign assistance. That is a major constraint for any president in conducting U.S. foreign policy.

Gutman: That raises a question: Did we go into the Gulf War not so much because of oil, but because we knew somebody else was going to pay for it? Did we not engage in Europe, in the conflict in Yugoslavia, because there was nobody who was going to pay for it? It was going to come out of operating expenses, and the military resisted for that reason. I mean, I'm just asking a question because it's kind of disturbing that the sole superpower, if this is the case, has to decide where and how it will defend security based on some kind of current calculation of defense expenditures.

Again, I come back to the point I was trying to make earlier: the lessons of the Cold War are lessons that I don't know have even been adequately discussed here in the conference and, frankly, in the country. I don't think that there's been much focus on this era that just ended, and it was really quite a successful outcome and a peaceful outcome. To my mind, one of the lessons is that we don't have to go to a hot war against a determined foe, who is well armed, in order to achieve success. What you have to do is have in mind what your aims are, and your aims—as worked out rather well in the Cold War—were democratic development, institutional development, integration in Europe; and that we would defend these values and support them in every way possible on our side of the Iron Curtain and also encourage them to develop on the other side. This is a very successful policy, and it's a policy that starts with a goal, and it works with all sorts of means brought to bear to achieve it.

What I think was missing in this period immediately after the Cold War—and especially in the case of Bosnia—were a clear set of aims and then an attempt to find means to achieve it. Instead, there was this kind of calculation of what the cost was going to be and who was going to pay for it.

Juster: I have to respond to that last comment, because I think it is a cynical view of the way foreign policy was formulated and conducted. The decision to intervene in the Persian Gulf was not an economic calculation. It was not until after the United States had put troops on the ground in Saudi Arabia that we sought financial contributions from other countries. The intervention was based on the assessment that the United States had vital national interests at stake in that area of the world, that a member country of the United Nations—Kuwait—had been wiped off the map, that Saddam Hussein possessed chemical weapons and, potentially, nuclear weapons in a tinderbox region, and that his actions could quickly destabilize the entire Middle East. These were very significant considerations, and they were the primary basis for the decision to intervene.

On Bosnia—despite the tragic situation in that country—those same vital interests were not at stake. There was a strategic interest in not letting the conflict spread to other countries in Europe, and, in that regard, U.S. policy has been successful. There has also been an interest in trying to provide humanitarian relief; the results have been mixed in that regard. But, regrettably, there are numerous conflicts throughout the world today, in places that we do not always read about in the newspapers or see on CNN but that also have tragic consequences. The United States simply has not taken on the role of international policeman to unravel these conflicts and stabilize the situation. As Mr. Gutman states, the United States has to decide on its aims and goals, on what is vital to its national interest, on what other interests it has at stake, and on what affirmative steps it is willing and able to take. Beyond that, we need to have a coherent policy that can be explained to the American public and for which support can be developed.

With regard to Bosnia, there was never any unity among the West as to what the objective should be. Moreover, I would submit that, to this day, there still is not an agreement among the West on objectives in Bosnia, which is why, when

U.S. forces depart next year according to President Clinton's timetable, there may well be a resumption of fighting by the parties to the conflict.

Burgess: I think perhaps I take the other side of the coin. When we're talking about Bosnia and the former Yugoslavia, the signs of Serb aggression began in Vukovar in 1991, and there were signs on the ground that this crisis was moving in a very nasty direction. I think a real shame of the West at the time was imposing the arms embargo on Bosnia and not being more realistic about what was going on, being more clear about it and trying, then, in more of a balance-of-power way, to aid the new government of Bosnia to resist what it was being subjected to, also to try to assist the people of Bosnia who were in these camps. I think Roy Gutman's reports were eye-opening in the summer of 1992.

Ullmann: Well, first of all, I agree that the arms embargo was not much of a help. Arms embargoes have had disastrous effects certainly, ever since the first modern one, which was during the Spanish civil war in the 1930s. Now, second, in response to my good friend George Papaioannou, one of the hardest things in all of this century, really, has been to try to assure decent treatment for people within a given sovereignty, no matter how small we make that sovereignty. One practical answer is that people just live among each other and try to live with their differences, but I can assure you from my own life experience—a dreadful one—that this is something that can truly change overnight. This is a very difficult problem, and perhaps there is no ready, universal solution to it. I've long thought that various concepts of different levels of sovereignty might do the job, but we could debate that for a long time, and we don't have time for that today.

The only thing I want to say in this connection, though, is that if there were some universal conventions—like the Universal Declaration of Human Rights—that really meant something other than rhetoric, can you imagine, if this were put to the U.S. Senate as a treaty, what the likes of Jesse Helms would say about something like that? I mean, these are people who haven't even reconciled themselves to the Civil Rights Act of 1964. Well, I think we have this kind of a problem here, and this, I think, is a bad one for us. But for others it is worse. People do remember the Serbian camps of today, certainly, and there are also Croatian camps now, but the memories of Jesenovac, the most notorious concentration camp of World War II in that region, certainly are as bright now as they ever were.

In the United States, we supposedly believe in making deals. Lots of times during the Cold War, we missed opportunities to do that. But this is not something where anybody emerges covered with glory. I would be the last one to say it's all Bush's fault, it's all the Republicans' fault, it's all America's fault, it's all Russia's fault, it's all the fault of any one entity. This has not been a particularly glorious period of history, and I don't think any of us can suggest otherwise.

Haynes: This will be the last question.

Q: *Given that our leaders have to look to the public for support of foreign policy, as a citizen, I am concerned about what I consider disproportionate power that the media have in generating foreign policy. It seems to me that when we see images of emaciated children, sometimes it gets us into a country, and when we see a soldier being dragged through the streets, sometimes it gets us out of a country. Is it a misplaced concern to feel that there's a disproportionate responsibility on the media in terms of generating foreign policy?*

Haynes: Would you like to take that one, Roy?

Gutman: I guess I have to. The talk about the "CNN effect" is a very fascinating discussion. I find it often, though, not really to the point. Our leaders make decisions based on what they think they can succeed at, what they think they can justify. I think Mr. Juster has explained that very well this morning. Then they decide on some areas where they're not going to get involved. I think the images of the people in the concentration camps in Bosnia were pretty compelling and disturbing and upsetting, and then the sight of Sarajevo being bombarded, day after day, year after year, was pretty compelling stuff. But, in fact, our leaders decided to ignore it. In the case of Somalia, they decided to pay attention. We shouldn't be blaming the media for the message. The media message gets through maybe faster and better these days; technically speaking, logistically speaking, we can do a better job in getting to the scene, and we do try to report the things that they don't want to hear in Washington, let's say. If we do that, if we remind people of the world out there that they'd like us to ignore sometimes, then that's the media doing their job. But as for whether they take it seriously, sometimes they do; often, they don't.

Juster: Until that last remark, I was going to agree with Mr. Gutman. Leaders are supposed to act responsibly. They make their decisions based on a range of factors, and they have their own intelligence-gathering capabilities. Clearly, the role of the media—the so-called CNN effect—adds another layer of complexity to decision making. It may not necessarily change what the decision maker does, but it affects the process. For example, rather than having several hours to analyze certain intelligence or cable traffic, the decision maker might have to respond to a "raw" news statement or news event almost immediately. So newsgathering operations can lessen the time for decision making, add another layer of complexity to the process, and sometimes lead to decisions made without the benefit of full analysis and reflection. But ultimately, the responsibility lies with the decision maker.

I remember when I was in Israel with Deputy Secretary of State Lawrence Eagleburger and Undersecretary of Defense Paul Wolfowitz during the Gulf War. We were negotiating with the Israelis to keep them from getting involved in the war. When the SCUD attacks occurred, we would go to a control room in the hotel that was sealed off from any chemicals that might be associated with the SCUD weapons. We had three methods of communication from that room: we had CNN on the television, we had a telephone line to the State Department operations center, and we had a telephone to the Israeli Defense Forces. Within about five minutes of the bombing attack, we invariably heard CNN reporting that the bombs had landed in a particular location and, in some instances, that there were chemicals involved. Naturally, this would create great commotion. However, about a half hour later, we would hear from the Israeli Defense Forces and from the State Department operations center that the bombs had landed in a different location and that there were no chemicals involved. So this is what happens sometimes with instantaneous, but raw, communications that have not always been fully analyzed before being aired. It does not mean that different policy decisions were made, but it does mean that we had a period of about 30 minutes when there was confusion and some activity occurring based on incorrect information. That certainly added to the complexity of the situation.

Ullmann: Well, I always wonder when people begin to blame the media for everything. But I think this is part of the political game now. If you try to suppress news in that sense, what you get instead is a self-perpetuating foreign policy establishment that claims to be the sole judge of the national interest. I made that point in a letter to *Business Week* just a few weeks ago. They didn't print the last sentence, however, in which I said that if you look at the kinds of foreign ministers we have had in this century—Berchtold of Austria, Ribbentrop, Pierre Laval, Ernest Bevin, Lord Halifax, John Foster Dulles, Dean Rusk, and so on—well, I don't find that a particularly confidence-inspiring set of résumés. So the more the newspapers and media keep tabs on what's going on, the better, as far as I'm concerned. In the battle between the document shredders and the copying machines, I stand with the latter.

Burgess: Yes, amen!

Haynes: Thank you very much, gentlemen. This has been a fascinating panel. If you'll permit me, I'd like to make one comment and step aside from my role as moderator. This has been so provocative, and I found it almost beyond my ability to control myself and not to make a comment, but I would like to leave you with one thought. Hampering the effectiveness of U.S. military intervention as a tool of American foreign policy, I think, is the pervasive notion that no American lives must be lost—the obsession with "no body bags." I mention this because I started my foreign policy career in the late 1960s as a member of the National Security Council at the height of the Vietnam War. I still find it a pervasive notion in our foreign policy that, somehow, U.S. military intervention can be clean or sanitized. It's just so unrealistic, and yet it seems to be the underpinnings of so much that we try to do to set the world aright again.

Part VI

Arms Control and Reduction

12

Arms Control and Military Preparedness in the Bush Administration

Martin E. Goldstein

The Roman god Janus is portrayed with two heads facing in opposite directions. His chief temple in Rome ran east and west, where the day begins and ends. His month, January, signifies the beginning of the new year and the end of the old.

The compelling image of Janus is relevant to any chief executive who seeks to enhance American security. Such an individual might look in two different, one might say, opposite, directions. To one side, the nation's leader spies the traditional method of securing the country's safety, namely, military preparedness. Throughout history, national leaders have accumulated weapons, military equipment, and soldiers to defend national frontiers. If military preparedness is seen as a means of enhancing security, then it stands to reason that the opposite of military preparedness, or arms control, must not serve the same purpose. Indeed, in the thinking of many laypersons, arms control is appropriate only to the imaginary world where no external threats exist. Alternatively, arms control is advocated by so-called fuzzy-headed idealists who either fail to perceive that the nation is besieged from outside or who naively believe that unilateral restraint will have such an effect on others that any existing threats will simply melt away. However, there is another view of arms control, one espoused here, that maintains that arms control, like military preparedness, is a means of strengthening national security. In this view, arms control is hardly the opposite of military preparedness; rather, arms control complements military preparedness. Like the god Janus, the leader who would increase his country's national security might look in two directions, one view leading to military preparedness and the other toward arms control.

It was the Spanish philosopher Salvador de Madariaga who perhaps best described the concept of arms control as a device for enhancing national security. De Madariaga narrated a fable that tells of a conclave of jungle animals who discuss ways of repealing the "law of the jungle." In Madariaga's fable, the lion proposes a ban on all "weapons" but claws and jaws; the eagle, all but talons and beaks; and the bear, all but embracing hugs. Translated into human terms, the approach might be termed "let's control the arms in which you are strongest." As a means of enhancing a nation's security, this approach makes eminent sense. The United States has adopted this tactic in recent years, as illustrated by successful efforts to eliminate the superheavy ICBMs [intercontinental ballistic missiles] that served as the backbone of the Soviet striking force. Even mutual cuts can serve the interest of national security. Through arms control, it is possible to reduce external threats, as the Chemical Weapons Convention holds promise of doing.

In this paper, I review the Janus-like policies of the Bush administration toward national security. In particular, I examine how this administration balanced the use of military preparedness and arms control to maximize national security.

END OF THE COLD WAR

If the international state system traversed the foothills of change during the closing years of the Reagan administration, it ascended the peaks during the Bush presidency. Due primarily to changes in the Soviet Union, the Cold War came to an end. Not only did Gorbachev renounce the long-standing Soviet commitment to global Communist revolutions, but the Soviet Union itself fragmented into 15 separate states. Furthermore, Moscow let go its grip on Eastern Europe, where one state after another replaced Communist governments with regimes that promised democracy and private enterprise. These cataclysmic changes in global politics contributed to a distinct emphasis during the Bush administration on arms control over military preparedness. I examine some of the more significant alterations in the Soviet Union before tracking President Bush's ventures into arms control and military preparedness.

Demise of the Soviet Union

Seismic alterations in the Soviet political landscape began to occur well before the splintering of the Soviet Union in late 1991. One of the most startling of these transformations was the vote taken on March 13, 1990, by the Third Soviet Congress of People's Deputies to repeal that provision in the Soviet constitution that guaranteed to the Communist Party of the Soviet Union (CPSU) a monopoly of political power.

The dramatic measure taken by the Congress reflected glasnost, or openness, proclaimed by Gorbachev at an earlier time. Indeed, in the elections of March 1989 for seats in the Congress, two-thirds of the seats were designated "free," meaning that non-Communists could run for these positions. In most cases, these candidates trounced their Communist opponents. The new legislature then witnessed something not seen in Soviet legislative behavior since the early years of the century, namely, genuine political debate and criticism of the government, including even Gorbachev himself.

In another expression of glasnost, the Supreme Soviet on June 12, 1990, approved a law establishing freedom of the press. The following month, Gorbachev ended the CPSU monopoly on radio and television broadcasting. In October the Supreme Soviet voted to guarantee religious freedom to all Soviet citizens. Restrictions on emigration were also eased.

Glasnost did not spell the arrival of democracy, but it permitted groups espousing various causes—political and otherwise—to emerge throughout the country. One cause that attracted widespread emotional support was ethnic nationalism. Several ethnic minorities demonstrated for more autonomy. In one of the Soviet Union's 15 republics after another, violent clashes erupted between ethnic minorities. By early 1991 virtually every one of these republics, including even the Russian republic, had voted to secede from the Soviet Union. The Baltic republics, which had never accepted their forced incorporation into the Soviet Union during World War II, were particularly determined to achieve independence.

On the economic front, matters were no less unsettling to the Soviet leadership. Cataracts of statistics demonstrated that the Soviet economy was plunging downward. In a desperate effort to reverse the decline, Gorbachev declared perestroika. According to this concept, the state would no longer own and manage all economic enterprise. Private enterprise was permitted. However, there was no agreement on either the scale or pace of transformation to a market economy. Obviously, such a shift would produce volcanic dislocations in Soviet economic life. Complicating the issue was the further downward slide of the Soviet economy since the proclamation of perestroika. Soviet citizens were infuriated by perestroika's failure to place more merchandise on the shelves or more food on the counters.

Deprived Soviet consumers were not the only ones incensed by the changes Gorbachev had introduced. Those who believed in Marxism-Leninism as the best guide for Soviet society accused Gorbachev of being a traitor against Communism. To halt the free fall of the Soviet Union out of the communist orbit, a number of Soviet leaders, including the head of the KGB, mounted a coup in August 1991. The plotters managed to seize Gorbachev and place him under house arrest. In Moscow Russian Republic president Boris Yeltsin courageously defied the conspirators, and consequently the coup collapsed. Communism in the Soviet Union was dead. Following a period of rivalry between Yeltsin and his former mentor Gorbachev, the latter retired from the scene. One of Yeltsin's first acts upon taking power after replacing Gorbachev was to issue a decree banning the Communist Party from Russia and seizing its assets for the state.

In December the Soviet Union splintered into 15 separate republics. Russia was by far the largest in size and population. In an effort to cement these new countries together, a Commonwealth of Independent States (CIS) was created. The CIS included 11 of the new states that arose out of the ashes of the Soviet Union; the three Baltic republics as well as Georgia elected not to join. It remains far from clear whether the CIS will survive. Power relationships among the members remain murky, including Russia's self-proclaimed prerogative to give direction to the other republics. By the time George Bush left office, the CIS had failed to provide the framework for cooperation it had promised. The CIS has also failed to resolve the ethnic conflicts plaguing the former Soviet Union, nor has it fostered significant economic cooperation among the new republics.

Europe

Ever since World War II, domination of Eastern Europe had been one of the bedrock elements of Soviet foreign policy. Aside from the desire to spread Communism, Moscow sought control of this region for defensive purposes. Eastern Europe had served as a corridor through which passed the invading armies of Napoleon, the kaiser, and Hitler. If the Soviets had one war aim in World War II, it was to block the recurrence of Western invasions by seizing control of Eastern Europe.

The incorporation of the East European nations into the Soviet orbit is a familiar tale. In 1956 in Hungary and in 1968 in Czechoslovakia, the Red Army resorted to force to maintain the obedience, if not the loyalty, of the East European satellites. In what became known as the Brezhnev Doctrine, Moscow proclaimed that no socialist state would be permitted to leave the Marxist fold. In subsequent years, Moscow actually granted a good deal of autonomy to these nations, so long as they continued to follow the basic dictates of Marxism-Leninism. Gorbachev, however, severed the cord that tied these states to the Soviet Union. Not long after coming to power, he announced that the states of Eastern Europe were free to chart their own destinies. Before long, movements for democracy and private enterprise arose throughout Eastern Europe. The year 1989 brought momentous changes. By the close of that year, democratic regimes had replaced Communist governments in Hungary, Poland, East Germany, Czechoslovakia, Bulgaria, and Romania. Soviet troops quartered in these nations remained in their barracks as these changes occurred. Soon after, Albania discarded its Communist mantle, and Yugoslavia shattered into separate warring states.

The most dramatic changes occurred in Germany. On November 9, 1989, the East German government opened the Berlin Wall. That gesture more than any other best symbolized the end of the Cold War. In another measure that marked the unraveling of the Iron Curtain, representatives of 42 industrial nations, including the United States, met in Paris in April 1990 and agreed to create a special bank to aid struggling East European economies. On September 12, 1990, representatives of East and West Germany, the Soviet Union, France, Great Britain, and the United States, meeting in Moscow, signed the Final Settlement with Respect to Germany. This document terminated occupation rights stemming from World War II and guaranteed the Oder-Neisse line as the boundary between Germany and Poland. East Germany was now completely free. In October it formally united with West Germany. The newly unified nation remained in NATO [North Atlantic Treaty Organization], but no Western troops were to be stationed in what had been East Germany. Soviet troops were permitted to remain in the East until 1994, resulting in the bizarre situation of having Soviet troops in a NATO country!

At a three-day summit meeting in Paris of the Conference on Security and Cooperation in Europe in November 1990, leaders of the 22 NATO and Warsaw Pact nations signed a Joint Declaration pledging that their nations were "no longer adversaries." The leaders also signed the Charter of Paris for a New Europe, which declared that "the era of confrontation and division of Europe has ended. We declare that henceforth our relations will be founded on respect and co-operation." In early 1991 the Warsaw Pact was dissolved as a military alliance. The Cold War was over.

Elsewhere

The Soviets displayed remarkable moderation in the developing world as well. In 1989 Moscow terminated its most costly foreign policy venture since World War II, namely, the invasion of Afghanistan, launched a decade earlier. No doubt the Soviet defeat was aided by the supply to Afghan mujahedeen of American weapons, including Stinger and Blowpipe handheld antiaircraft missiles. In Cambodia the Soviets were helpful in working with others to arrange a cease-fire among the Vietnamese-sponsored government and three internal factions opposing it. Similarly, Moscow constructively participated in the complex negotiations that yielded a cease-fire in the 15-year-old civil war in Marxist Angola. In both of these cases, the Soviet Union displayed a willingness to concur in options that might result in the withering away of Marxist regimes. Such an event transpired in Marxist Nicaragua, where democratic elections resulted in the defeat of the Sandinista government by Violeta de Chamorro in early 1990. In the Persian Gulf War of 1991, triggered by Iraq's invasion of oil-rich Kuwait, Russia placed no obstacles in the way of U.S.-led coalition forces. During the Cold War, Moscow would surely have acted strongly to block any increase in American influence in that region of the world.

U.S.–Russian Cooperation

As the epochal events just related were occurring, the leaders of the two superpowers conferred periodically to concert their policies. Bush and Gorbachev held their first meeting aboard ship off the stormy seas near Malta in December 1989. At this get-acquainted session, interrupted by occasional bouts of seasickness, Bush hinted at a willingness to extend economic assistance to the Soviet Union. Both leaders reaffirmed their determination to reach arms control agreements, and they stated their conviction that the countries of Eastern Europe should be allowed autonomy. German unification was also discussed. The Malta meeting will not be remembered for any precedent-setting agreements. Rather, it permitted the two leaders to become familiar with each other and provided an occasion to confirm the friendly convergence of the two superpowers.

In May–June of the following year, Gorbachev and Bush conducted a more substantial meeting in Washington. During a four-day summit, the two leaders signed over a dozen bilateral accords, including a framework for an agreement on reducing strategic nuclear weapons. This framework called for a ceiling of 6,000 nuclear warheads for each party. Other accords included a pledge to cease production of chemical weapons and to normalize trade.

As the decade of the 1990s unfolded, American interest in the region formerly dominated by the Soviet Union underwent a transition. No longer was blocking aggression from Moscow the principal concern (although, as we shall see, America continued to keep its powder dry). In place of this 45-year objective, the United States now elected to assist the new countries in this region to make the transition from Communism to democracy and a market economy.

A prime instrument for achieving this goal was economic aid. In November 1991 President Bush announced a $165 million program in food aid to help the former Soviet republics get through the coming winter. In January of the next year, the United States launched Operation Provide Hope, a plan to send Russia 19,200 tons of food left over from the Persian Gulf War plus excess medical supplies from Defense Department stocks. In April the Group of Seven major industrial democracies announced a $24 billion assistance program to help stabilize the fledgling market economies of the new republics. The United States was to contribute about one-quarter of this sum. The aid package included $18 billion in loans, debt deferral, and other financial assistance from international financial institutions to help the countries cover shortages in their balance of payments, plus $6 billion to stabilize the ruble. The president also announced new credits to help Russia and other republics buy U.S. agricultural products, and he called upon Congress to repeal dozens of provisions in U.S. law that limit or ban American business exchanges in the former Soviet Union.

Whether such aid and succeeding assistance will succeed in enabling the new countries to make the transition to democracy and capitalism remains an open question. Short-term economic sacrifices have strained the patience of citizens throughout the region. Some might turn to extremist demagogues who promise food and jobs immediately. Economic shortages are also exacerbating ethnic tensions, often resulting in bloody clashes. The future political and economic landscape of the former Soviet Union and Eastern Europe defies prediction. American policy, however, remains guided by the principle that the triumph of democracy and free enterprise in these lands would help shape a world in which America could flourish. Some Americans, including former president Nixon, criticized Bush for being too stingy to help consolidate and advance the fragile gains made by democracy and capitalism in Eastern Europe and the former Soviet Union. In the election year of 1992, however, the president found it difficult to win votes by giving money away.

MILITARY PREPAREDNESS

As we have observed before, governmental decisions regarding military preparedness stem, in large part, from assessments of the threat the country faces.

The monumental changes in the Soviet Union and its eventual collapse were bound to have an effect on Washington's assessment of the military threat posed by the Kremlin. At first, caution was the watchword of the incoming Bush administration in its dealings with the USSR. In February 1991 Bush issued National Security Review 3, which called for a comprehensive review of American policy toward the Soviet Union. Completed one month later, the study hailed perestroika but concluded that Moscow still aspired to be a competitive superpower (Garthoff, pp. 375–77). The cautious document resulted in no bold policy recommendations. As the decade of the 1990s began to unfold, Washington made some incremental revisions in its estimates of this military threat. Changes in procurement and planning were at first highly gradual, reflecting the caution that gripped the nation's military planners. While disappointing to those who wished to declare the Cold War at an end and to disarm precipitously, professional military planners observed that:

- the Russians continued to field strategic forces that could destroy American society;
- Russian weapons and military advisers continued to play a role in trouble spots from Cuba to Vietnam; and
- the alterations in Russian behavior were engineered by a single individual who might one day be toppled by conservatives opposed to perestroika and glasnost.

Yet, even before the Soviet Union disintegrated at the end of 1991, many agreed with Theodore Sorensen (1990):

The Soviet threat has not only been contained; it has collapsed. The Soviet empire has disintegrated. Its long-time ideology has been repudiated. Its combat forces are being unilaterally drawn down. Its military alliance is in tatters. Its attraction as a political or economic model or mentor for new and developing nations has vanished. Its ability to invade, arm, subvert, subsidize or even threaten those nations or virtually anyone else has been substantially reduced. Given the grave economic, ethnic, social and political problems that the Soviet Union faces internally, the long-term future of its present form and borders is in doubt. (p. 2)

Given these two differing views of the Soviet threat, the Bush administration started out by paring military spending only slightly. In January 1989 the Reagan administration had submitted its final military budget. It called for a rise in military spending by 2 percent above inflation. That spring, Secretary of Defense Richard Cheney reduced Reagan's request by 1 percent, from $306 billion to $296 billion. The revised budget called for a continuation of all strategic programs, including the Midgetman and MX ICBMs, B-2 Stealth bomber, and the Strategic Defense Initiative (SDI). After emerging from Congress, SDI received $3.8 billion. Each armed service lost a small number of troops. Congress reduced the ceiling on American troops in Europe by 14,500, equal to the number of persons manning the ground-launched cruise missiles (GLCMs) and Pershing

IIs that were to be withdrawn anyway. The army retained its 18 divisions, but the navy lost a carrier battle group. The air force had decided in 1988 to eliminate 2 of its 27 wings (above figures from Treverton).

As the changes in Moscow appeared less temporary, the Pentagon decided greater military cuts were in order. A study undertaken in the summer of 1990 concluded that once Russia withdrew its forces from Eastern Europe, it would take two years for it to mobilize for an invasion of Western Europe. In consequence, the United States could afford to reduce its forces-in-being and still have time to build up if an invasion seemed likely. Accordingly, the United States announced a 25 percent reduction in military forces by 1995. Since the army and air force are oriented primarily toward the defense of Europe, these services were targeted for significant reductions. The army was slated to lose 6 of its 18 divisions. The navy suffered least of all, due to its importance in dealing with Third World trouble spots. As mentioned before, however, the navy was scheduled to lose 1 of its 13 carrier battle groups.

Reflecting these planned reductions, the Pentagon requested $278.3 billion for FY [fiscal year] 1992, a figure that did not include unexpected expenses for the Persian Gulf War (*New York Times*, February 5, 1991).

By the beginning of 1992, the United States began to move away from the assumption, unquestioned for nearly half a century, that the principal security threat facing the United States emanated from Moscow. More and more military planners found themselves agreeing with the statement made in January 1992 by CIA [Central Intelligence Agency] director Robert Gates in testimony before the Senate Armed Services Committee. "The threat to the United States of deliberate attack from that quarter [Russia] has all but disappeared for the foreseeable future," Gates declared (*Washington Times*, January 23, 1992). Following the collapse of the Soviet Union as an imperial power, U.S. security concerns began a hesitating shift away from fear of expansion by Moscow. Other security problems long consigned to the background began to move toward center stage. Iraq's missile attacks on Saudi Arabia and Israel during the 1991 Persian Gulf War heightened fears of the spread of weapons of mass destruction. Suppose Iraq had affixed nuclear, chemical, or biological warheads to its SCUD missiles. More and more countries were gaining access to medium-range and short-range missiles, and this development presented another security hazard. In the next regional war, might American troops come under attack from such weapons? Terrorism, of course, represented yet another security threat.

Given the new, fluid world situation, military planners were forced to ask questions they had not posed for decades. Which countries should be placed on a U.S. "enemies list"? Who, if anyone, might entertain plans to attack the United States? How much military force did the United States require?—a perennial question that took on new urgency. A "war of scenarios" began at the Pentagon. Some planners asked such questions as, "What if" narcoterrorists sponsored a coup in Panama, or North Korea attacked its southern neighbor?

Some senior officials cited the futility of identifying potential enemies and military outbreaks as the basis for sizing U.S. military forces. Instead, they said, the United States needs certain capabilities in order to remain a superpower. According to this argument, the United States has enduring vital interests, such as the stability of Europe and northeast Asia and access to Persian Gulf oil. The United States must field the military capabilities required to protect these vital interests, whatever the source of threats.

For military planners in the Defense Department, these matters are critical, for they are charged with advising the president on the size and nature of the nation's future military forces. This recommendation is expressed in an important document known as Defense Policy Guidance. Revised every two years, the guidance statement serves as an internal planning tool for the military services on how to prepare their budgets and forces for the years ahead. To a certain extent, the Pentagon's recommendations start from a view of the world security situation.

In a preliminary effort to specify the global security situation facing the United States in the post–Cold War era, the Pentagon stated that America's political and military mission was to ensure that no rival superpower emerged in Western Europe, Asia, or the territory of the former Soviet Union (*New York Times*, March 8, 1992). In this unipolar worldview, the United States would act in a benevolent manner in order to protect the interests of the advanced industrial nations; therefore, they would have no incentive to challenge America's predominant position. Absent from this conception was the notion of collective security that had provided the underpinning for the formation of the United Nations [UN] after World War II.

Critics lambasted the Pentagon's vision of America's role in the post–Cold War world. They complained that the military's conception made the United States the world's policeman and displayed an arrogance of power. In May 1992 the Defense Department revised its Policy Guidance. The new statement dropped the idea of a one-superpower world and highlighted America's commitment to collective military action (*New York Times*, May 24, 1992). The new draft appeared to accept leadership by regional allies, such as German or Japan, when their interests were more directly involved than the United States. Still, the United States would seek to preserve a leading role in strategic deterrence and regional alliances. The document also preserved the option "to act independently, as necessary, to protect our critical interests."

The new version, intended to provide guidance for the 1994–1999 fiscal years, supported the Bush administration's call for a "base force" of 1.6 million uniformed troops. The statement also directed the military to be prepared to fight two regional wars simultaneously (a far cry from the two-and-a-half-war strategy at the Cold War's height) while maintaining a sizable military presence in Europe.

Even though the Cold War is over, and the U.S. intelligence community no longer perceives Moscow as likely to attack the United States, one determinant of the military threat facing the United States is the magnitude of Russia's military forces. Military planners cannot disregard a military force as large as Russia's. Potential upheaval could overturn those who favor democracy and a moderate foreign policy and return Russia to its long tradition of imperialism. At the beginning of 1992, Moscow fielded an impressive array of strategic weapons. This arsenal included over 2,300 missiles capable of carrying nearly 9,500 warheads plus 162 long-range bombers equipped with nearly 900 missiles and bombs. In determining U.S. force levels, American planners insisted they could not ignore the Russian arsenal.

What of the other 14 republics that constituted the former Soviet Union? Should their military forces be lumped together with those of Russia for purposes of estimating the force the United States might face? The new Commonwealth of Independent States (CIS) was supposed to coordinate the military forces of all 15 new states. However, the lance of ethnic resentment rapidly burst this bubble of military cooperation. In April 1992 Moscow established a separate military force of its own. According to the decree creating this force, the Russian military will decline from its Cold War numbers of nearly 4 million to approximately 1.5 million men in uniform. Russia also proclaimed the adoption of a defense-oriented military doctrine to replace the offensive thinking that had predominated under the Soviet Union. It is worth noting that all strategic forces stationed throughout the former Soviet Union remain under the control of the Russian military, no matter where these weapons may be located.

With the demise of the Soviet Union and the growing spirit of cooperation between Moscow and the West, many analysts have concluded that military threats from any quarter pose less of a danger to the United States than in the recent past. Nonmilitary hazards to American well-being have nudged their way to the forefront, including pollution, trade imbalances, drugs, refugees, and the degradation of America's technological leadership.

Debates in the aerial realm of philosophy tend to come to ground when the time arrives to allocate funds. This descent occurs annually when the president submits his military spending proposals to Congress. In January 1992 President Bush submitted a $272.8 billion defense budget for fiscal year 1993, $9.8 billion less than for fiscal year 1992. In several ways, the 1993 proposal signals a reduction in military preparedness. The president had already announced plans to reduce the armed forces to 1.6 million active-duty personnel by the mid-1990s (the new base force), a 25 percent cut. Two-thirds of the savings in the 1993 military budget were scheduled to come from reductions in two costly procurement programs. Orders for the B-2 Stealth bomber were lowered from 75 to 20 airplanes. Some questioned the need for any penetrating bombers in view of the Soviet Union's collapse. The Seawolf hunter-killer submarine program was terminated after construction of a single vessel. Other spending cuts came from the elimination of some strategic weapons (discussed later under "Arms Control") and the stretching out of other procurement programs. Bush also announced plans to reduce defense spending by 4 percent in each of the following five years, should he be reelected.

With defense spending on the decline, the Pentagon shifted to a new procurement strategy. In an effort to keep its technological edge in the face of shrinking budgets, the military asked contractors to design prototypes but not manufacture multiple copies. In case of war, the Pentagon would place orders for production. Some challenged this plan to put R&D [research and development] above production, questioning whether the prototypes could be rapidly translated into mass production once a crisis erupted.

Political liberals tore into Bush's military spending proposal as excessive. In the absence of a hot war or a cold war, they asked, why can't defense spending contract much further? The resulting "peace dividend" could then be used to reduce the federal deficit, repair roads and bridges, combat poverty, and the like. The age-old question of how much is enough for defense is not likely to go away anytime soon.

One of the more controversial programs that received funding for fiscal 1993 was SDI. Bush requested over $5 billion for this program. Since Reagan proposed "Star Wars" in 1983, the program has experienced several metamorphoses from protection of cities, to protection of retaliatory missiles. The collapse of the Soviet Union raised the question of whether the recession-wracked United States needed such a multibillion-dollar defensive system. In its final transformation during the Bush presidency, SDI was no longer directed against a massive missile attack but was designed to protect the country from a few "rogue missiles" that might be launched by a renegade dictator or that might be fired by accident. This new conception of SDI was given a new name, Global Protection against Limited Strikes, or GPALS. The Missile Defense Act of 1991 called for deployment by 1996 of an "ABM [antiballistic missile] Treaty-compliant" defense at a single site, with plans for expansion to additional locations should the ABM Treaty be renegotiated. President Bush remained an enthusiastic supporter of ballistic missile defense, despite critics' claims that no country is likely to attack the United States and that a nuclear adversary could circumvent GPALS by placing nuclear bombs on ships, trucks, and cruise missiles.

Finally, in a move pregnant with symbolism, U.S. and Russian warships conducted their first joint naval exercise on July 5, 1992. The exercise in the Barents Sea was named Operation Northern Handshake. The significance of this label requires no elaboration.

ARMS CONTROL

While events always manage to confound prophets, it seems safe to predict that just as Reagan will be noted for military preparedness, Bush will be identified with arms restraint.

To be sure, an inclination toward military preparedness or arms control depends, in large measure, on one's assessment of external threat. The collapse of the Soviet Union led to a reassessment of the foreign military danger facing the United States, as described earlier. The resultant downgrading of this menace paved the way for historic reductions in military preparedness and an equally historic array of arms control measures.

The Bush administration displayed characteristic caution in reevaluating the threat from Moscow. This circumspect approach was reflected in the gradual decline in U.S. military spending from the stratospheric heights of the Reagan years, as described earlier. We have also noted plans to reduce the size of the armed forces by one-quarter.

The most dramatic arms control measures of the Bush presidency concerned strategic weapons.

Strategic Weapons

When Bush entered office in 1989, experts were far from united in their views on the durability of change in the Soviet Union. Some drew plausible scenarios of a successful coup by hard-line Communists and the rebirth of Soviet imperialism. Reflecting this uncertainty, negotiations over strategic arms started out haltingly, like a train leaving the station and gingerly picking its way over switches and cross tracks. As the United States gained confidence that Gorbachev was sincere in renouncing Communist world domination and that he would not be toppled, the negotiations picked up speed. In July 1991 Moscow and Washington signed the Strategic Arms Reduction Treaty (START). Highballing along, the two powers agreed on still further strategic arms cuts in June 1992. These epochal developments merit more detailed consideration.

Not long after taking office, Bush opened strategic arms talks with Moscow. The previously noted uncertainty over the future of the Soviet Union and a long legacy of mutual distrust prevented the talks from proceeding other than at a tortuously slow pace. Meeting in Washington in June 1990, Gorbachev and Bush issued a joint statement in which they committed themselves to finalizing a strategic arms treaty in that year. They also endorsed the objectives of reducing the risk of nuclear war and ensuring strategic stability, transparency (each side's ability to monitor the other's forces), and predictability. In the interest of stability, the two leaders agreed to give priority to retaining highly survivable weapons systems.

As things turned out, the leaders missed their deadline. However, in July 1991 the United States and the Soviet Union signed the first START agreement. Reflecting the complexity of the issues and lingering mistrust, the document runs to over 500 pages. The most important features of the agreement are summarized:

- Each party will reduce its strategic nuclear arsenal to no more than 6,000 accountable warheads on 1,600 deployed delivery vehicles.
- Within these limits, no more than 4,900 warheads may be deployed on ballistic missiles, 1,540 on heavy ICBMs, and 1,100 on mobile ICBMs.
- The Soviet Union will cut its SS-18 heavy missiles and the aggregate throw weight of its strategic missiles in half by eliminating 22 SS-18 launchers every year for seven years.
- U.S. heavy bombers may carry no more than 20 long-range, air-launched cruise missiles each, and 150 of these bombers will count as carrying only 10.
- Soviet heavy bombers may carry no more than 12 air-launched cruise missiles (ALCMs) each, and 210 of these bombers will count as carrying only 8 each.

- Heavy bombers equipped with bombs and short-range attack missiles will count as carrying one warhead each.

The agreement called upon the parties to carry out these reductions in three phases over 7 years. The treaty was to remain in force for 15 years unless superseded earlier by a subsequent agreement (which occurred with the conclusion of START II). "Politically binding" agreements, not strictly part of the treaty, limited sea-launched cruise missiles with ranges over 600 kilometers to 880 for each side; the Soviets could deploy no more than 500 Backfire bombers, and these were not to be given intercontinental range.

The treaty embraces various other prohibitions, including:

- no flight testing of missiles with reentry vehicles in excess of the attributed number;
- no rapid reloading of ICBM launchers;
- no air-to-surface ballistic missiles;
- no cruise missiles on naval vessels other than ballistic missile submarines and surface ships;
- no fractional orbital ballistic missiles.

START contains verification measures that dramatically advance each side's capacity to monitor the other's performance. These measures include data exchanges; on-site inspection (OSI) to establish a base-line inventory; OSI of dismantlement and destruction; continuous OSI of critical production and support facilities; short-notice OSI of existing and former sites for systems covered by the treaty; short notice inspections, in accordance with agreed procedures, of suspect sites; a ban on encryption and other concealment devices; and cooperative measures to enhance observation by satellites.

Because of somewhat peculiar counting rules, START reduced warhead levels by about one-third, leaving the United States with about 8,500 warheads and bombs and the Soviet Union with about 6,500. The treaty promised to increase stability and predictability, decrease arms competition between the superpowers, and improve transparency. From Washington's point of view, a major attraction of the agreement was that it halved Moscow's SS-18 force and eliminated Soviet advantages in the number of ICBM warheads and throw weight.

START was signed at the very end of the era of U.S.–Soviet antagonism. Despite significant weapons cuts, the high levels of armaments the treaty allows reflected the fear that still prevailed on each side that the other might reverse course and behave aggressively. In the months after START was concluded, dramatic developments took place in the Soviet Union. These events, which we have already described, include the abortive countercoup by hard-line Communists, Yeltsin's displacement of Gorbachev, the extinction and fragmentation of the Soviet Union, and commitments by the emergent republics to implement democracy and free enterprise. (The breakup of the Soviet Union raised the troublesome question of who was responsible for implementing the START Treaty. Strategic weapons were situated in not only Russia but also the new independent states of Ukraine, Belarus, and Kazakhstan. Under a protocol signed in Lisbon in May 1992, the latter three states agreed to adhere to START and to destroy or turn over to Russia any weapons covered by the treaty.) As a consequence of the changes just mentioned, the relationship between Washington and Moscow shifted markedly from adversarial to cooperative. The new spirit of cordiality was expressed by Bush and Yeltsin—now president of the new Russian Republic—at Camp David in February 1992. The two statesmen declared, "Russia and the United States do not regard each other as potential adversaries. From now on, the relationship will be characterized by friendship and partnership founded on mutual trust and respect and a common commitment to democracy and economic freedom" (*New York Times*, February 2, 1992). In case anyone had doubted whether the Cold War were truly over, this statement drove a stake through the heart of the conflict.

The growing amity between the United States and Russia lubricated the tracks to yet further cuts in strategic weapons. In his State of the Union Address on January 28, 1992, just before his summit with Yeltsin, Bush called for strategic arms cuts that went well beyond those in the as yet unratified START Treaty. Yeltsin countered almost immediately with a speech proposing even deeper reductions. Cordial negotiations thereafter yielded yet another historic arms agreement, concluded at the June 1992 summit in Washington and designated START II. START II will:

- eliminate all 50 U.S. 10-warhead MX missiles;
- accelerate the elimination of America's 450 two-warhead Minuteman II missiles;
- download America's 500 Minuteman III missiles from three warheads each to one;
- halve the number of warheads on America's D-5 Trident SLBMs from eight warheads to four;
- eliminate all of Russia's SS-18 and SS-24 heavy ICBMs;
- impose a ceiling of 3,000–3,500 strategic warheads and bombs on each power by the year 2003; and
- eliminate all MIRVed ICBMs by 2003.

These reductions are to take place in stages, concluding in the year 2003. At this time, each country will limit itself to 1,750 SLBM warheads and may divide the other weapons among bombers, cruise missiles, and single-warhead ICBMs.

START II is remarkable in several ways. The pact reduces U.S. and Russian long-range nuclear weapons by two-thirds, a far more extensive cut than found in previous strategic arms agreements. The ceiling of 3,000–3,500 weapons is interesting in that it expresses a range rather than a precise number. This limit represents a compromise between Bush's proposal of 4,700 (made in his 1992 State of the Union Address) and Yeltsin's startling counteroffer of 2,000–2,500. In reaching the compromise position, the United States agreed to eliminate more SLBMs than it had originally wanted, while Russia agreed to scrap more ICBMs than it had first contemplated. The United States agreed to eliminate over half of its SLBM warheads. Plans to eliminate all MIRVed ICBMs are especially noteworthy. These are the most destabilizing weapons, given their accuracy, power, and large numbers. Any country considering a surprise attack would launch these first in the hope of destroying much of the opponent's retaliatory weapons, command and control system, and leadership. Resting in fixed silos, these missiles pose more inviting targets for destruction by a nuclear enemy than single-warhead missiles and thus heighten anxieties about a possible preemptive strike. In START II, the United States finally achieved one of the major objectives it had pursued throughout the nuclear era, namely, eradication of Moscow's gargantuan ICBMs. While the U.S. price for this achievement was reduction of its SLBM warheads from 3,840 to 1,750, the latter figure still represents a devastating sea force. One might wonder why Yeltsin agreed to forsake his entire MIRVed ICBM force, the backbone of Russia's nuclear arsenal. Perhaps he felt this was the price he must pay for the substantial economic aid he hoped for to rebuild the shattered Russian economy. In an interesting twist, the United States agreed to devote $400 million to help Russia dismantle its missiles and warheads in the years ahead.

The strategic arms agreements just described have generated hopes in some quarters that even deeper cuts can be made. If Russia and the United States are no longer enemies, the argument goes, why would either need 3,000–3,500 strategic nuclear warheads and bombs? Why not abolish nuclear weapons entirely?

The new international alignment has prompted military planners to address the question, How low can you go? The answer would seem to depend on the purpose one assigns to nuclear arms. If these weapons are to be used exclusively for deterrence, a few hundred might well suffice, as France and Great Britain have concluded. One would need only enough warheads to ensure destruction of some cities and important military targets. Some of these warheads could also be dedicated to the deterrence of a chemical or biological attack.

Another conceivable use for these weapons is war-fighting. A large and varied array of weapons would be required to strike not just cities and industrial sites but also a variety of military targets. These could include troop assembly points; dockyards; fleet concentrations at sea; air bases; power grids; maintenance facilities; and command, control, communications, and intelligence networks.

A third use that could be assigned to strategic weapons is insurance. This role in all probability explains why few serious military thinkers since the Baruch Plan of 1946 have recommended elimination of nuclear weapons. No one knows what might happen in the future. Might an imperialistic regime come to power in Russia or somewhere else? Could nuclear-armed China decide to flex its muscles? Might one or more radical dictators in the Third World brandish nuclear weapons? Since the future has an annoying habit of defying prediction, most military planners recommend keeping some (not necessarily 3,000–3,500) nuclear weapons on hand just in case.

Still another purpose that these weapons can serve is reassurance. America's nuclear arsenal reassures its allies that the United States is capable of defending them. Otherwise, wealthy and technologically advanced allies like Japan and Germany might decide to develop nuclear weapons of their own. America's decision to reduce its nuclear arsenal below an as yet undetermined floor might lead such allies to doubt Washington's will to come to their defense, with the consequence of more national nuclear forces around the world.

Nuclear weapons also play a symbolic role. In today's world, they are the badge of great power status, just as the great steel dreadnoughts were earlier in the century.

The uses of nuclear arms just cataloged are not mutually exclusive. The United States, it would seem, assigns all these purposes to its nuclear arsenal. If all the states that possess nuclear weapons were to negotiate verifiable reductions, then the United States could probably realize these objectives at levels in the range of 250 warheads or thereabout. Due to uncertainty about the intentions and capabilities of other states, it is doubtful the United States would ever descend much below that floor.

Before leaving the strategic area, we should mention one other development at the June 1992 summit. Bush and Yeltsin agreed to open discussions on strategic defense. No longer foes, the two nations began to seek out common ground to defend themselves against missile attacks by third parties. The most likely candidates would be rogue leaders from Third World states who sought to dissuade other powers from blocking their aggression or who wanted to engage in some form of nuclear blackmail. With the detachment of so much territory formerly belonging to the Soviet Union, Russia's radar coverage of its territory suffers from broad blind spots. At the Washington summit, the two sides agreed to make arrangements to share data on missile launches worldwide.

In 1992 the United States announced it would not resume production of the 475-kiloton W-88 warhead for its Trident II submarines. Enough warheads existed to equip two of the boats in the planned fleet of 18 Tridents. Older, less powerful W-76 warheads were to be deployed on the remaining vessels. Bush also stated the United States would not resume production of plutonium or highly enriched uranium, the key ingredients in nuclear weapons. The announcement's value was purely symbolic, however, since an abundance of these materials will be available from weapons dismantled pursuant to the START accords. It is noteworthy that Bush did not avail himself of the opportunity to propose an international treaty to halt production of fissile material.

Tactical Nuclear Weapons

Ever since World War II, arms control negotiations have been characterized by painfully slow, tortuous discussions in which every minuscule point was contested. Once Washington and Moscow moved off their collision course, however, a new process of arms control appeared, namely, unilateral reductions. Unthinkable during the Cold War, these unilateral moves bypass time-consuming haggling over minute details.

President Bush exemplified this tactic with an announcement in September

1991 that, regardless of what the Soviets do, the United States would withdraw all its foreign-based nuclear artillery shells and nuclear warheads for short-range missiles back to U.S. territory, where they would be dismantled or destroyed. The president added that the United States would also remove all tactical nuclear weapons, including nuclear cruise missiles, from its surface ships and attack submarines and that nuclear weapons associated with land-based naval aircraft would similarly be removed for destruction or storage. In effect, the president's message eliminated all U.S. tactical nuclear weapons overseas except bombs and warheads fired from land-based aircraft. The presidential initiative included other unilateral measures as well. Bush stated that all U.S. strategic bombers would be taken off day-to-day alert status, and their weapons returned to storage areas; that the United States would immediately stand down from alert all ICBMs scheduled for deactivation under START; that the United States would abandon efforts to devise mobile basing systems for ICBMs; and that the United States was canceling the nuclear short-range attack missile.

In setting forth this package of unilateral initiatives, the president explicitly invited Moscow to follow suit. However, it was equally clear that the steps announced were not contingent on Soviet reciprocity.

As it turned out, however, Moscow was more than willing to comply. Soon after Bush's announcement, Gorbachev agreed to match the U.S. nuclear withdrawals. He also called upon the United States to sign a comprehensive nuclear test ban, declare a cessation in production of fissile material, subscribe to a no-first-use policy, and remove all air-launched nuclear bombs from Europe. (In July 1992 Bush agreed to the second item, as we have mentioned.)

In October 1991 NATO defense ministers decided to reduce by 50 percent the number of U.S. and British nuclear bombs launched from aircraft. This move, combined with Bush's earlier announcement, reduced NATO's nuclear arsenal by a whopping 80 percent. NATO's decision left approximately 700 tactical nuclear bombs in Europe.

As a footnote, we might observe that after the splintering of the Soviet Union, many of the country's 17,000 tactical nuclear weapons were located outside the Russian Republic. By the summer of 1992, all of these had been transferred to Russia for storage or dismantlement.

Europe

For nearly half a century, Europe stood at the vortex of Cold War rivalry. Therefore, arms reductions in that region are of particular significance.

We have already referred to the withdrawal of nearly all tactical nuclear weapons from Europe. Such a move reflected a conviction on both sides that they were not likely to be the victims of attack (and that any plans to mount an attack of one's own had been canceled).

On the conventional front, we have noted the Pentagon's plans, finalized in the summer of 1990, to reduce the armed forces by 25 percent, primarily by disbanding a number of army and air force units designed to defend Europe. This

American reduction did not occur in a vacuum. Gorbachev had already begun to make unilateral cuts of 50,000 men and 5,000 tanks from Eastern Europe and had permitted those countries to chart their own non-Communist paths. The likelihood of a Soviet assault upon Western Europe receded rapidly during the late 1980s.

These developments were accompanied by vigorous diplomatic efforts. The Mutual Balanced Force Reductions (MBFR) talks that had been moving at a languid pace since 1973 were terminated by common consent in early 1989. In March of that year, a new series of negotiations began, known as the Conventional Forces in Europe (CFE) talks. The seven Warsaw Pact states and the 16 members of NATO participated. Progress occurred rapidly, aided by a February 1990, U.S.–Soviet understanding (not a formal treaty) limiting each superpower to 195,000 troops in Central Europe. Because of the distance from America to Europe, Washington received permission to station an additional 30,000 troops in Europe outside the central zone.

Troops, however, were not the only concern of military planners. For years NATO had been alarmed by the Warsaw Pact's menacing advantage in tanks, armored personnel carriers, artillery, and other heavy equipment useful in an invasion. These fears were laid to rest on November 19, 1990, when leaders of NATO and Warsaw Pact nations signed the CFE Treaty. This historic document limited each alliance to 20,000 battle tanks, 20,000 artillery pieces, 30,000 armored combat vehicles, 6,800 combat aircraft, and 2,000 attack helicopters. As part of these totals, each superpower was limited to 13,300 tanks, 13,700 artillery pieces, 20,000 armored combat vehicles, 5,150 combat aircraft, and 1,500 attack helicopters.

The demise of the Warsaw Pact and the disintegration of the Soviet Union played havoc with the CFE Treaty's East European force allocations. In June 1992, 29 states from NATO, the former Warsaw Pact, and the former Soviet Union, meeting in Oslo, signed a protocol that allowed Russia to keep approximately half the weapons assigned to it in the original accord. Six of the new republics were to divide the remainder.

Other developments occurred that signified the coalescence of a continent divided by nearly a half century of Cold War. Just prior to the Oslo meeting, NATO approved the use of its troops and equipment to conduct peacekeeping operations in European conflicts beyond the boundaries of member states, if requested to do so by the CSCE. This preliminary effort to transform NATO from a defensive alliance into a peacekeeping force is part of the alliance's effort to carve out a role and rationale for itself in the post–Cold War world. At the Oslo meeting, the East European states endorsed NATO's decision, and there was even talk of accepting East European countries into NATO itself!

Concern over troop levels extended beyond Russia and the United States. Accordingly, the 29 states that met in Oslo in June 1992 reconvened in Vienna the following month to conclude an understanding that limits the number of troops they may station in Europe. This nonbinding agreement applies to land and air forces in the area between the Ural Mountains and the Atlantic Ocean.

According to this understanding, the United States may station 250,000 troops in the area; Russia, 1,450,000; Ukraine, 450,000; Germany, 345,000; France, 325,000; and Great Britain, 260,000. In many cases (including the United States), these figures were higher than actual troop levels in mid-1992.

Years before this cascade of arms control agreements, President Eisenhower proposed that East and West open their military facilities to aerial surveillance, primarily to allay fears that one side was massing forces for a surprise attack. Such miscalculation could lead to unintended war. This Open Skies proposal plummeted to earth in the baleful era of Cold War hostility. In 1989 Bush resuscitated Eisenhower's proposal and offered it to Gorbachev. After the failed August 1991 coup in the Soviet Union weakened Communist hard-liners and the military, negotiations began in earnest. In May 1992 the United States, Russia, Canada, and 21 European states initialed the Open Skies Treaty. This pact opens a vast area to aerial inspection—from Vancouver to Vladivostok. It covers all 16 members of NATO and all members of the former Warsaw Pact as well as Russia, Ukraine, Belarus, and Georgia. The agreement provides for short-notice surveillance flights over military sites of signatory countries. The treaty is intended to help build confidence in the peaceful intentions of signatory states by increasing the transparency of their military forces and activities.

Other Areas of Arms Control

Since 1968 the nations of the world have been working to devise a ban on chemical weapons (CW). The 1925 Geneva Protocol bans the use of CW but not its development, production, or stockpiling. In any case, the Geneva Protocol has not served as an effective barrier to CW use, as demonstrated recently in the Iran–Iraq War and Iraqi assaults on Kurdish villages. The issue grew in urgency after the Defense Department claimed that at least 14 nations outside the former Soviet Union and NATO possessed CW and that 10 other nations were actively seeking CW (*New York Times*, March 10, 1991). The Persian Gulf War revealed that Iraq possessed substantial quantities of CW.

As part of his decided nod in the direction of arms control over military preparedness, President Bush took a special interest in limiting CW. In September 1989 he proclaimed, in a speech before the General Assembly, that the United States was prepared to reduce its CW stockpile by 80 percent, if the Soviets agreed to reduce their level to the American level. In April 1990 both countries announced agreement to lower their CW stocks to 5,000 tons each. At the Washington summit in June, Bush and Gorbachev agreed to terminate production of CW.

Meanwhile, international negotiations held under the auspices of the UN-affiliated Conference on Disarmament managed in mid-1992 to produce a draft Chemical Weapons Convention (CWC). The CWC prohibits not just the use of CW but also its development, production, stockpiling, and transfer.

Verification has long been a major bugaboo of a CW treaty. Many chemicals that go into CW have legitimate civilian uses, such as in pesticides, so the production of these substances cannot be outlawed. The only way to tell whether a chemical plant is manufacturing aphid killer or CW is to inspect the facility from within. However, unimpeded entry could easily become a form of industrial espionage. The CWC reflects a compromise on the issue. Inspectors will be given access to a facility within five days of expressing an intent to visit it. Five days, it was felt, would allow for the shrouding of sensitive materials and machinery unrelated to weapons but would not provide sufficient time to hide a weapons program. The treaty also calls for routine visits to factories known to produce dangerous chemicals.

With the end of the Cold War, the United States has begun to focus more attention than previously on another security threat, namely, the proliferation of "weapons of mass destruction" (WMD). These weapons consist of nuclear, chemical, and biological arms. Since these armaments would most likely be delivered by missiles—though artillery shells and gravity bombs could also be used—missiles are often included in discussion of WMD. We follow that practice here.

U.S. efforts to stem the spread of nuclear weapons have taken several dimensions. Washington has taken the lead in reinvigorating efforts to control the transfer of nuclear technology and equipment that could be used to manufacture nuclear weapons. With American prodding, the Nuclear Suppliers Group (NSG) renewed its formal activities in March 1991. The NSG is composed of over 20 states with the capability of producing the sophisticated items needed in a bomb-making effort. Many of these items also have legitimate uses in civilian nuclear programs and hence are referred to as "dual-use" equipment. In March 1992 the NSG agreed to an extensive list of dual-use equipment that member states will export only under stringent controls. Members of the NSG also announced they would require non-nuclear weapons states to accept International Atomic Energy Agency (IAEA) safeguards on all their nuclear activities as a precondition for any significant new supply. For certain countries of special proliferation concern, such as Libya, North Korea, and Iran, the United States has virtually banned nuclear cooperation of any kind and has urged other suppliers to do likewise. In an attempt to uncover secret nuclear weapons programs, such as that mounted by Iraq before the Persian Gulf War, the United States has supported the IAEA's proposal to conduct surprise inspections of undeclared nuclear facilities. The United States has also actively encouraged states to adhere to the Treaty on Non-Proliferation of Nuclear Weapons (NPT).

In trying to prevent the spread of nuclear weapons, the Bush administration devoted special attention to the former Soviet Union. At the beginning of 1992, the countries that once constituted the USSR possessed about 27,000 nuclear weapons, ranging from ICBMs to artillery shells. Washington shared and continues to share the concern of many other states that some of these weapons might fall into the hands of regimes that do not currently possess nuclear weapons. A related concern is that some unemployed nuclear scientists and technicians would agree to help build nuclear weapons in such states in return for lucrative salaries.

A large proportion of these weapons is scheduled for elimination under international treaties like START and the Intermediate-range Nuclear Forces (INF) Treaty. However, destroying nuclear weapons is neither simple nor inexpensive. To facilitate such dismantlement, the U.S. Congress during the Bush presidency appropriated $400 million to assist Russian efforts. The United States also offered to send experts to help with transportation and storage as well as actual destruction of the weapons. To help prevent a "brain drain" of Soviet nuclear scientists, the United States, along with Japan and the European Community, established international science and technology centers in Russia and Ukraine to provide employment for weapons specialists. In 1992 the United States said it would contribute $35 million to establish these new centers.

As mentioned before, missiles would seem to be the carrier of choice for delivering nuclear bombs. The Iran–Iraq War in the 1980s, the Falkland Islands War, and the Persian Gulf War of 1991 highlighted the dire prospects for the world of missile proliferation. Third World protagonists in all these conflicts launched missiles at their opponents. Certain countries, such as China and North Korea, are eager to earn foreign currency by exporting short-range and medium-range missiles. While the oceans insulate American territory from such attacks (for the present), there is a strong likelihood that U.S. military forces engaged in combat overseas will have to contend with missile attacks, perhaps involving chemical or nuclear warheads. American allies such as Israel and South Korea are greatly worried about missile attacks.

To help control the spread of missiles, the United States under Bush strongly pushed the Missile Technology Control Regime (MTCR), set up in 1987. The 18 countries that subscribe to the MTCR agree not to export missiles capable of carrying a payload of 500 kilograms (approximately 1,100 pounds) farther than 180 miles. Most countries where such missiles are manufactured have joined. However, the refusal of North Korea and a handful of other states to become part of MTCR as well as China's exports in seeming violation of the MTCR remain unsettling.

Finally, the issue of nuclear testing merits brief mention. It will be recalled that the Limited Test Ban Treaty of 1963 prohibits all nuclear testing except underground. Ever since, many arms control advocates have called for a comprehensive test ban for the very reason the United States long opposed it. Such a treaty would impede the development of improved warheads and bombs. In 1992 President Yeltsin announced a one-year testing moratorium and urged the United States to reciprocate. When the Bush administration demurred, Congress gave evidence it might legislate a testing halt. In large part to forestall Congress, the president announced in July 1992 certain limits on nuclear tests. Henceforward, Bush declared, the United States would conduct no more than six tests per year (not much of a reduction from recent years) for the next five years. No more than three of these annual tests would exceed 35 kilotons. Testing would be carried out only to ensure the reliability and safety of existing weapons, not to develop new ones, the president said. (President Clinton has declared a moratorium on nuclear testing.)

More so than any previous White House occupants, President Bush relied on arms control as opposed to military preparedness to enhance America's security. This stance was due primarily to changes in the Soviet Union initiated by Mikhail Gorbachev and extended by Boris Yeltsin. The splintering of the Soviet Union and Moscow's renunciation of worldwide revolution reduced America's need to maintain military forces in every corner of the globe. With the demise of the Warsaw Pact and the end of Russia's insistence on dominating Eastern Europe, Washington started to telescope its military presence in Europe. Similarly, as the threat of a Russian attack upon the United States all but disappeared, Washington found renewed hope in joint limitations of strategic arms. Since Third World disputes would no longer involve a proxy contest between the superpowers, Washington could afford to scale down military resources for deployment in developing countries.

These dramatic developments made possible a proliferation of arms control agreements under President Bush. Not only did Bush reverse his predecessor's upward leap of military spending, but he also announced a 25 percent reduction of the nation's military forces. Through unilateral, bilateral, and multilateral measures, Bush enacted deep reductions of strategic, tactical, and conventional weapons. Scarcely a single weapons system escaped the pruner's blade.

At the same time, Bush retained arms for use in those Third World regions of intrinsic importance, such as the Persian Gulf and the Caribbean. Future uncertainties also imposed a limit on the arms reductions Bush was prepared to implement. Nevertheless, Bush stands out among post–World War II presidents as the one most reliant on arms control as opposed to military preparedness. Despite the war in the Persian Gulf, it appears that President Bush ushered in a rather lengthy period that will reveal an emphasis upon arms restraint, not military preparedness, in American foreign policy.

REFERENCES

Garthoff, R. L. *The Great Transition*. Washington, DC: Brookings Institution, 1994.
Sorensen, T. C. "Rethinking National Security." *Foreign Affairs* 69 (1990): 1–14.
Treverton, G. F. "The Defense Debate." *Foreign Affairs* 69 (1989/1990): 183–96.

13

The Post–Cold War Peace of Europe, 1989–1992

Joseph P. Harahan

The Cold War, centered on Europe, ended during the years of the Bush administration. It ended suddenly, in fact, far more suddenly than anyone anticipated. That fact alone suggests that we should examine carefully those decisions taken on the cusp of a new era of European, Russian, and world history. We live in the wake of those decisions.

The Cold War in Europe entered its final days in the summer of 1989, when major political changes occurred in Poland and Hungary. Then, within a matter of months—September, October, November, and December 1989—revolutions swept across Eastern Europe as the people revolted against Communism in East Germany, Czechoslovakia, Bulgaria, and Romania. The Berlin Wall fell in November 1989. In less than a year, Germany had been unified by treaty, and the Soviet Union was carrying out its commitment to withdraw, within four years, all of its 680,000 stationed troops from the GDR [German Democratic Republic] and the other Eastern European states. Against this background of political revolution, German unification, and massive military withdrawals, the leaders of Europe, United States, Canada, and the Soviet Union met in France in November 1990 to sign the Peace of Paris. Two arms control treaties constituted the heart of that peace conference: the Conventional Armed Forces in Europe Treaty (CFE) and the 1990 Accords for the Conference on Security and Cooperation in Europe (CSCE).

Then early in 1991, in an unrelated, but coincidental, action, the United States organized and led a decisive United Nations coalition victory over Iraq in the Gulf War. Shortly thereafter, U.S. leaders declared that within three years, by 1994, the U.S. would withdraw nearly two-thirds or 160,000 American troops from Western Europe. Then, as 1991 progressed, demonstrations for national independence occurred farther and farther to the east. In April 1991 President Gorbachev, Yeltsin, and six other Soviet Republic leaders signed a new treaty of union. That measure proved insufficient to stem the tide of independence across the Eurasian continent. Communism had failed; everyone but the Soviet Union's president knew it. Following the failed coup attempt in August 1991, the parliaments of Ukraine and Belarus declared independence. At the same time, President Yeltsin and his government banned the Communist Party from Russia. Within four months, on December 25, 1991, the Soviet Union had collapsed as a nation and an empire. Subsequently in 1992, 15 new nations emerged from the former republics, a new international organization emerged—the North Atlantic Cooperation Council (NACC)—and new arms control treaties were negotiated and signed—the Open Skies Treaty, START II Treaty, and Chemical Weapons Convention. Adding to this complexity, three new nations split away from the former Yugoslavia—Slovenia, Croatia, and Bosnia-Herzegovina. By the end of the Bush administration in January 1993, a post–Cold War peace had emerged across Europe, with the important exception of the incipient civil war in the former Yugoslavia.

One way to evaluate the Bush administration's role in creating this complex European peace is to start with the previous period, the Cold War, and examine its widely held, controlling assumptions. Just what were the assumptions upon which previous administrations had based U.S. foreign policy toward Europe and the Soviet Union? Once these assumptions have been articulated, then we can ask: What role did President Bush and his senior advisers have in reconceptualizing the divided, Cold War Europe into today's Europe?

COLD WAR ASSUMPTIONS

First, the "long peace" of the Cold War had as its controlling assumption the primacy of nuclear weapons in deterring a military conquest of Western Europe. According to one of its principal historians, John Gaddis, nuclear weapons deterred those aggressor nations and leaders who sought to intimidate, or possibly invade with massed military forces, Western European nations.[1] The presence in Europe, the United States, and the Soviet Union of thousands of operationally ready nuclear forces, so the argument went, imposed great, almost overwhelming caution on the senior leaders of the United States and the Soviet Union.[2] On this issue, the Bush administration retained fidelity with America's declared military strategy of nuclear deterrence. However, President Bush and his senior advisers did engage Gorbachev, Shevardnadze, General Yazov, and the Soviet Military High Command in lengthy, detailed treaty negotiations in reducing substantially the number of strategic nuclear weapons and delivery vehicles. To a degree Bush, Baker, Scrowcroft, Cheney, and the U.S. military accepted Gorbachev's statement that strategic arms reduction treaties and agreements would permit deterrence to continue, but at a lower level.

Along this line, President Bush directed that the U.S. government would carry out the Intermediate-range Nuclear Forces (INF) Treaty with absolute fidelity. This important December 1987 bilateral treaty between the United States and the USSR stipulated the reduction of nearly 2,700 nuclear missiles and ancillary systems by May 1991. It set significant precedents. All missile reductions were conducted on schedule, and they were carried out under the direct observation of on-site inspection teams from the United States and the Soviet Union. The INF Treaty, especially in its explicit protocols and detailed procedures for inspections and eliminations, set precedents for larger and more significant strategic and conventional arms reduction treaties that were negotiated and signed during the years of the Bush administration.[3]

EASTERN AND CENTRAL EUROPE

The second Cold War assumption concerned the nations of Central and Eastern Europe. Was their status as Communist states under Soviet direction *immutable*, or were these nations subject to change through democratic and liberal pressures? Here Robert L. Hutching's recent history, *American Diplomacy and the End of the Cold War* (1997), argued cogently that the new Bush administration questioned this prevailing assumption from the beginning.[4] What did the new administration do? First, President Bush stated clearly three principles for national reform in Central and Eastern Europe: national self-determination, independence, and democracy.[5] Second, Bush, Baker, and other senior administration officials spoke directly and frequently to Gorbachev, Shevardnadze, and the other Soviet leaders on how a democratic Eastern Europe would *not* undermine legitimate Soviet security interests. The Soviet Union, by 1989, was clearly in retreat. Economically weak, militarily overextended, and politically ossified, the leaders of this decaying empire had to be reassured that the United States, Germany, and the other NATO [North Atlantic Treaty Organization] states sought no unilateral military advantage should the Central and Eastern Europe nations move toward independence.[6]

Conceptually, Bush and Gorbachev articulated their respective visions of the future of Europe in separate speeches given in Europe just 15 days apart in late May and early June 1989. Speaking in Mainz, West Germany, on May 31, 1989, President Bush began by focusing on a future Europe that would be both "whole and free." He declared,

The Cold War began with the division of Europe. It can only end when Europe is whole. Today, this very concept of a divided Europe is under siege . . . not by armies, but by the spread of ideas. A single powerful idea—democracy . . . is why the Communist world is in ferment. As president, I will continue to do all I can to open closed societies of the East. We seek self determination for all of Germany and all of Eastern Europe.[7]

Just 15 days later, General Secretary Gorbachev addressed the leaders of state at the Council of Europe in Strasbourg, France. He spoke of a "common home" for Europe, and then he laid out his vision for the future. "I know that many of you in the West," he declared, "see the presence of two social systems as a major difficulty. But the difficulty actually lies elsewhere—in the widespread conviction [that] . . . overcoming the division of Europe means overcoming socialism. But this is a policy of confrontation, if not worse. No European unity will result from such an approach."[8]

Here were the two competing visions: one stipulating a Europe "whole and free" and the other envisioning a "common home" for Europe with two, and only two, social systems. Over the next seven months, from June to December 1989, the question resolved itself. Spontaneous, popular movements (the movement of Eastern European peoples across national borders of Hungary, Austria, and East Germany) and outright political revolutions cast the people's vote for self-determination, independence, and democracy. In the summer and fall of 1989, nation after nation—from Poland, to Hungary, East Germany, Czechoslovakia, Bulgaria, and Romania—threw off their Communist governments for new independent national parliaments and governments. On this ride to revolution across the length and breadth of Eastern Europe, these were the roller-coaster months. The single overriding question became: How powerful and willing were the Soviet brakemen to stop the ride?

On October 7, 1989, Gorbachev flew to East Berlin for the GDR's celebration of its 40th anniversary. The Soviet Union's president was no mere observer; there were more than 380,000 Soviet military troops, equipped with thousands of modern conventional and nuclear weapons that were stationed in East Germany. At a critical juncture during the visit, Gorbachev observed in public that "all walls . . . will fall." This statement was widely interpreted by the restless East German people that Soviet power would not defend the Honecker East German regime.[9] Within days—less than a week after Gorbachev had departed East Berlin—thousands of East Germans took to the streets—first in Leipzig (500,000), then Dresden (100,000), and at the end of the week East Berlin (1 million). Two weeks later Honecker resigned, and then, on November 9, 1989, the East German border guards stationed at the Berlin Wall misinterpreted an order to liberalize procedures for "emigration" and for "private trips" abroad. The guards opened the gates to unrestricted, free transit. Thousands of Berliners crossed; within hours the people began tearing down the hated, symbolic wall.[10]

American leadership played a pivotal role. President Bush, Secretary Baker, General Scrowcroft, Secretary Cheney, and other senior administration officials, according to British historian Timothy Garton Ash, linked Soviet conduct in Eastern and Central Europe to continuing the U.S.–USSR relationship over arms reductions, expanding economic relations, and cooperation in scientific and technical fields.[11] Robert A. Hutchings, an NSC [National Security Council] staff member, described in his book how President Bush and Secretary Baker reassured the Soviet leaders "hundreds of times" during these critical months that the changes unfolding in Eastern Europe "did not threaten legitimate Soviet security interests."[12]

GERMAN UNIFICATION

If this statement were true, the specter of German unification did "threaten" legitimate Soviet security interests. It also called into question the third major assumption of the Cold War: that Germany would remain divided into two separate nations for the foreseeable future. Before 1989 there were good reasons for accepting this widely held assumption. Despite President Bush's statement in May 1989 that the United States sought self-determination for "all" of Germany, the idea in the summer of 1989 that the Soviet leaders would agree to a united Germany seemed almost inconceivable. The Soviet Union's national military strategy had been constructed around the concept of a divided Germany. The USSR had stationed 19 Soviet divisions, 380,000 men, and military equipment in the German Democratic Republic. Soviet war plans postulated that East German and Eastern European armies would fight within the Warsaw Pact Alliance to defend their territory and that of the Soviet Union. If the two Germanies unified, it would mean that all of these forward-deployed Soviet troops would have to be withdrawn. Soviet military strategy would have to be recast, the Warsaw Pact Alliance redefined, and all of Soviet foreign policy for the past 40 years reexamined.[13]

Yet the two Germanies were united. It took less than a year from the fall of the Berlin Wall in November 1989 to negotiate and sign the Treaty of Union uniting Germany in October 1990. This herculean act of European diplomacy was the principal work of the leaders of three nations—the Soviet Union, Germany, and the United States. Together, they forged the complex negotiations that led to the unification of Germany within the North Atlantic Treaty Alliance. This story is both exciting and well documented by the actors as well as scholars. Chancellor Kohl, Foreign Minister Genscher, President Mitterand, Prime Minister Thatcher, Secretary Baker, National Security Advisers Gates, Rice, Zeiltow, and Hutchens, U.S. Soviet ambassador Matlock, President Gorbachev, and Foreign Minister Shevardnadze have all published memoirs and analytical accounts. Scholars—Timothy Garton Ash, Horst Teltschik, Frank Elbe, Richard Kessler, and Stephen F. Szabo—in Europe and the United States have detailed and analyzed the complex, steamroller negotiations that led to unification.[14]

Events moved from possibility to reality so quickly in 1989–1990 that German unification had a strong sense of inevitability to it. For a while, the complex, multilateral diplomacy seemed to move in a straightforward direction from consensus on the process of German national unification, to consensus on retaining the Germany within the NATO alliance, to new treaties on new European security structures. But that is hindsight. During the critical, early negotiations over unification, major questions emerged concerning the future structure of European security. For European, American, and Soviet diplomats, these were days and weeks of intense bargaining and negotiations. Karl Kaiser, the diplomatic historian, characterized the months from December 1989 through November 1990 as "[t]he most intense phase of bilateral and multilateral diplomacy in European history."[15] During these months President Bush and Chancellor Kohl met 4 times, Bush and Gorbachev held and attended 3 summits, Secretary Baker and Foreign Minister Shevardnadze met 10 times, Baker and Genscher had 11 meetings, and Genscher and Shevardnadze met 8 times in May and June alone.[16] There were four major Two Plus Four meetings, several important NATO conferences, special European Community meetings, and regular sessions of the Conference on Security and Cooperation in Europe. Formal treaty negotiations on conventional and strategic weapons reductions continued major sessions in Vienna and Geneva. In addition to these face-to-face meetings, all of the key leaders and governments transmitted hundreds, if not thousands, of messages, telephone calls, and letters.

Like any complex negotiation, the process contained critical points of agreement and consensus. For Germany and the United States one critical point came in a single week at the end of November and the beginning of December 1989. Chancellor Helmut Kohl outlined his famous "Ten Points" to the West German Parliament. Essentially, Kohl's West German plan called for democratic elections to be followed by agreement on German state unity within the context of European integration and a redefined European security structure.[17] Four days later, President Bush met Gorbachev at the Malta Summit. There Bush explained the U.S. position on the Germanies: (1) self-determination should be pursued without prejudicing the outcome; (2) if German unification occurred, it should occur within the context of Germany's remaining within NATO and the European Community; (3) the process toward German unification should be "peaceful," "gradual," and "step-by-step"; and (4) the inviolability of existing borders had to be respected. Bush labeled these policies as his "four principles" on the question of German unification.[18] When presented with these two agenda-setting lists of principles, Gorbachev reacted cautiously. Aboard ship off Malta, Gorbachev asked Bush about the future status of U.S. military forces in Europe. Bush reassured him that U.S. forces would remain in Europe for the foreseeable future.

The day after the December 1989 Malta Summit, the NATO ministers endorsed President Bush's four principles for German unification. A week later, representatives to the European Community meeting in Strasbourg supported the principle of German unification, provided it occurred within the context of European integration. This was an important development because public opinion across Europe strongly supported the concept of an integrated Europe in the early 1990s. Soviet leaders sought to brake this fast-traveling roller-coaster ride to German unification. In late December 1989 Shevardnadze addressed the European Parliament and raised "seven questions" about the future of Germany, European security, and Eastern Europe.[19] As he spoke, massive, popular revolutions were succeeding in Bulgaria and turning violent in Romania. Parliamentary leaders in Latvia, Lithuania, and Estonia were preparing declarations of independence from the Soviet Union.[20] Neither Gorbachev nor Shevardnadze had a strong hand to play against a unified Western Europe. This fact became evident in late January 1990, when Shevardnadze stated that the Soviet government would support the "eventual" creation of a united, peaceful, democratic Germany. However, he insisted that German unification was *not* a matter for the Germans alone; the process had to be gradual and evolutionary.[21] This statement coincided with numerous statements and actions by the senior members of the Bush administration. They had always insisted, according to a National Security Council official, that "the German question was never about unity alone, but [instead, it was] about fitting a powerful Germany into a stable and secure European order."[22]

During February 1990 the major development that cemented Western consensus was the creation of the Two Plus Four negotiating forum introduced by the United States and West Germany. In this forum, the two German states plus the four occupation nations—the United States, Great Britain, France, and the Soviet Union—would meet in formal sessions to negotiate the external aspects of German unification. Secretary Baker personally lobbied Douglas Hurd of Great Britain, Roland Dumas of France, and Eduard Shevardnadze at the meeting of the NATO and Warsaw Pact foreign ministers in Ottawa, Canada. Following this meeting, all of the parties agreed to establish the formal Two Plus Four Meetings.[23] With this development, the German unification issue became enmeshed with the larger issue of European security and stability.

EUROPEAN SECURITY

In the spring and summer months of 1990, multilateral negotiations over German unification led to a series of consequential decisions. The "end game" took place against a background of Soviet leaders struggling to respond to popular independence movements in Estonia, Latvia, and Lithuania. In contrast, American, German, and European leaders were unified on the prospect of German unification and European integration. On the major issue of Soviet security concerns, President Bush responded with new initiatives for inclusion in the CFE Treaty, then in the final phases of negotiations. In January 1990 Bush suggested that military force ceilings for the two major "stationing force" nations, specifically, the United States and the USSR, be lowered to a ceiling of 195,000 personnel. Then in May Bush unilaterally canceled two weapons modernization programs aimed at the European theater: the follow-on missile to the Lance attack missile and the program to modernize tactical nuclear artillery ammunition.[24] That same month, May 1990, West German president Kohl declared that Germany would assume all East German obligations to the Soviet Union, compensate the Soviet Union for maintaining Soviet military forces in Germany during a three- to four-year transitional period, limit German military forces to 370,000 under the CFE Treaty IA [Issuing Authority] Agreement, renounce the production or possession of nuclear, biological, or chemical weapons on German territory, and refrain from extending any NATO structures onto the former GDR territory for three to four years.[25]

Shortly after President Bush and Chancellor Kohl's declarations to the Soviet leaders limiting U.S. and German modernization, military personnel, and weapons and amid final negotiations over the CFE Treaty, U.S. secretary of state Baker announced publicly "nine assurances" regarding the future of European security. These assurances had been agreed to by the United States, Germany, and the 14 other NATO nations. Individually and collectively, these declarations sought to address the Soviet Union's security concerns. Specifically, they:

1. agreed to limit the size of German armed forces;

2. committed to negotiate limits on short-range, tactical nuclear weapons;
3. reaffirmed Germany's non-nuclear status;
4. committed to revise NATO's strategy away from confrontation;
5. pledged not to deploy NATO forces in the former GDR;
6. agreed to a statement granting a three- to four-year transitional period for withdrawal of all Soviet forces from the GDR;
7. agreed to the renunciation of any future German territorial claims;
8. committed to a revamping of the Conference on Security and Cooperation in Europe and the Soviet Union's participation in that cross-Europe security organization; and
9. pledged German economic assistance to the Soviet Union.[26]

After this point, events accelerated. In late May 1990 Chancellor Kohl and Foreign Minister Genscher came to Washington for a series of coordination meetings with President Bush, Secretary Baker, and their aides. Ten days later, Gorbachev arrived for the Washington Summit, held at the White House and Camp David on June 1–2, 1990. It was an ambitious agenda. President Bush sought to reach agreements on German unification, CFE Treaty reductions, START Treaty reductions, and the long-term transformation of U.S.–Soviet relations. For his part, Gorbachev wanted a U.S.–Soviet trade agreement, a U.S.–Soviet agreement on Germany and European security, and a free hand to control events in the restless Baltic nations.

Over long sessions at Camp David and the White House, the two leaders agreed on a considerable number of issues. On the issue of German unification, President Bush declared at the final, public press conference that he and Gorbachev were in full agreement "that the matter of Alliance membership is, in accordance with the Helsinki Final Act, a matter for the Germans to decide." This meant, in essence, that Germany would remain within NATO. At the White House, Bush and Gorbachev signed more than a dozen agreements, including new treaty protocols on nuclear testing, agreements on bilateral chemical weapons reductions, and statements regarding conventional arms limitations and strategic nuclear weapons reductions. For the U.S. arms control agenda, this was perhaps the most significant summit of the modern era. President Bush and Gorbachev agreed that the CFE Treaty would be "the indispensable foundation for European security."[27]

COLD WAR EUROPEAN PEACE TREATIES

Bush and Gorbachev's endorsement of the CFE Treaty challenged another Cold War assumption. For more than four decades, European, American, and Soviet leaders and diplomats had assumed that there could be no all-European peace treaty following World War II. This assumption was reinforced with the creation and continuing presence of large standing armies, air forces, and navies arrayed in a quasi-permanent alliance system. Long before the Bush administration, it seemed to many that Europe's east–west divisions had solidified to the point of permanence. It seemed inconceivable that the Soviet Union would negotiate and sign a comprehensive European arms reduction treaty *and* that it would agree to a unified Germany within NATO *and* that it would agree to withdraw all of its massive, forward-deployed forces from the center of Europe. Yet, over the summer and fall months of 1990 three treaties emerged that codified many of these changes and resulted in a broad, comprehensive peace settlement for Europe. In order of their signature, these three treaties were the Treaty on the Final Settlement with Respect to Germany, September 12, 1990; the Conventional Armed Forces in Europe Treaty, November 19, 1990; and the CSCE Charter of Paris for a New Europe, November 20, 1990.

These three treaties codified into international law many of the sweeping revolutionary changes that had occurred across Europe since 1989. Under the first treaty, the Treaty on the Final Settlement with Respect to Germany, the six signatory states—Federal Republic of Germany, German Democratic Republic, French Republic, the USSR, Great Britain, and United States—accomplished two long-sought German goals. Following World War II, the four victorious powers imposed a series of agreements that extended their authority over defeated Germany and Berlin. The four victorious nations' "rights and responsibilities" delineated in these agreements were terminated. Next, the Final Settlement treaty defined for the new, unified Germany its territorial borders, confirmed its existing border with Poland, and renounced all territorial claims. Germany made an explicit pledge renouncing the manufacture, possession, or control of nuclear, biological, and chemical weapons. Germany also pledged to limit its military forces to 370,000. The Soviet Union stated it would settle the withdrawal of its military forces from the former German Democratic Republic in a separate treaty with Germany. The brief, three-page document also explicitly granted Germany the right to belong to alliances. Finally, the treaty signatories declared: "The united Germany shall have accordingly full sovereignty over its internal and external affairs." With that declaration, the longest and one of the most interesting chapters in the Cold War came to a conclusion. Three weeks later, on October 3, 1990, Germany became a unified nation.[28]

The second major treaty, the Conventional Armed Forces in Europe Treaty, encompassed 22 nations, including the 16 NATO nations and 7 former Warsaw Pact nations. Serious negotiations began in January 1989 in Vienna, Austria. Diplomats and senior military negotiators worked within the "Mandate on the Conventional Armed Forces in Europe Treaty." Developed in the final years of the Cold War, 1987–1989, this mandate had been extensively coordinated within NATO and the Warsaw Pact alliances. As treaty negotiators labored for the next 23 months, their discussions were often pierced and punctuated by outside events: political revolutions in Central and Eastern Europe, the Two Plus Four negotiations surrounding German unification, and the continuing economic and political deterioration of the Soviet Union.[29]

When the diplomatic "end game" finished in November 1990, a long-scheduled, three-day Conference on Security and Cooperation in Europe convened on November 19, 1990 in Paris, France. Leaders of 22 nations, including Bush, Kohl, Mitterrand, Thatcher, Gorbachev, and Havel, signed the CFE Treaty. At this point, the signatory states numbered 22. Later in 1992, following the collapse of the Soviet Union, eight new nations became signatory states: Russia, Belarus, Ukraine, Moldovia, Armenia, Azerbaijan, Georgia, and Kazakstan. At the time of the initial signing, many national leaders, especially among the smaller nations and the Visegrad states, stated that they regarded the CFE Treaty as the cornerstone for the future security structure of Europe, stretching from the Atlantic to the Urals.

Just what were the objectives of this new treaty? First, it established fixed levels of conventional offensive weapons for the nations of the two alliances. Five categories of offensive weapons were included: artillery, armored combat vehicles, tanks, helicopters, and combat aircraft. As one might expect in a continental-wide arms control treaty encompassing the conventional military forces of 30 nations, within each category there were many variations of equipment. For example, there were 24 types of tanks and 50 types of armored combat vehicles, including armored personnel carriers, armored infantry fighting vehicles, and heavy combat vehicles. There were 55 different types of combat aircraft. In the initial information exchange, on the day preceding the treaty signing in Paris, November 18, 1990, the 22 treaty signatory states declared 184,500 pieces of treaty-limited equipment (TLE). By category, there were 54,000 tanks, 70,000 armored combat vehicles, 43,000 artillery, 13,500 aircraft, and 3,000 helicopters. By November 1995 the total number of TLE within the area had to be below the treaty ceiling of 157,600 pieces. As envisioned in 1990, this meant that, collectively, the treaty signatory nations had undertaken obligations to reduce no fewer than 27,900 weapons. The residual figure of 157,600 weapons would be subdivided into the five categories: 40,000 battle tanks, 60,000 armored combat vehicles, 40,000 pieces of artillery, 13,600 combat aircraft, and 4,000 attack helicopters. The treaty limited each group of states, specifically NATO and the WTO [World Trade Organization], to one-half of the total in each category.

Next, the CFE Treaty divided the landmass from the Atlantic to the Urals into four large, concentric zones. Centered on Germany, the treaty limited the deployment or stationing of offensive weapons in each zone and in certain designated flank areas. The treaty also mandated that the signatory states provide extensive order of battle force data, in order to increase transparency and lower the likelihood of a surprise attack across national borders. Fourth, it mandated on-site inspections to monitor, confirm, and report on treaty compliance. Finally, it set up an all-nation consultative group in Vienna to raise and adjudicate problems with treaty implementation.

In the years after 1989–1990, the CFE Treaty became an important building block for the foundation of post–Cold War Europe. It was a major arms reduction treaty and an important conflict prevention treaty. The latter was explicit from the treaty's mandated reductions—27,900 tanks, armored personnel vehicles, artillery, fighters, and attack helicopters within 46 months. In fact, by November 1995, the 46th month after the treaty's entry into force, the reductions had exceeded 58,000 weapons. More than 2,600 on-site inspections had monitored and recorded the results of these reductions. Today, the CFE Treaty is widely viewed across Europe as a valuable, legally binding agreement for reducing military armaments and for enhancing the stability and openness of military forces across national borders.[30]

The third agreement at end of the Cold War, the CSCE Charter of Paris for a New Europe, was signed on November 20, 1990, by the leaders of 35 nations. This charter fitted squarely into the concepts and assumptions of the Helsinki Final Act of 1975. It reiterated virtually all of the declarations, principles, and ideas of the long-running Helsinki process. Since the charter was not a treaty but an accord, it did not have the same force of international law that the CFE Treaty had. It did have more signatory nations, and it did extend European consensus principles across all of Europe, Western, Central, and Eastern European nations. The security part of the charter was designated as the Vienna Document of 1990. It set up a series of confidence-building measures between the military forces of 35 signatory nations. However, in most of its essential aspects, the charter remained a consensual, declaratory document. Consequently, when violent ethnic and civil war broke out in Yugoslavia, the CSCE Charter and its organizations proved incapable of stemming the killing and massive displacement of peoples.[31]

COLLAPSE OF THE SOVIET UNION

Finally, there was one bedrock assumption during the Cold War about the future of Europe. Virtually all statesmen believed that the Soviet Union would continue into the twenty-first century as the leader of both a Marxist-Leninist state and the Soviet empire. When the Soviet Union collapsed as a nation state in the fall and winter of 1991, that bedrock assumption cracked and crumbled. With it, the last of our many long-held, fixed assumptions about Cold War Europe collapsed.[32] The Cold War was over.

EVALUATION

During the Bush administration, many long-held, controlling assumptions about Europe had been overturned. President Bush, Secretary Baker, and their senior advisers challenged many of these assumptions: first, the immutable state of Central and Eastern European governments; next, the possibility of a unified Germany; then, the existing security structure for the European continent. They, like virtually all other leaders, did not challenge the existence of the Soviet Union. It was an extraordinary period. American, German, and Soviet leaders, along with key European figures—Mitterrand, Thatcher, and Havel—became history's forcing actors. They made the European world of the 1990s.

But what of this new European world? At one point in his recent book, John Gaddis, the diplomatic historian, asked the question: "If the Soviet–American rivalry is no longer going to dominate world politics, then one can not but help wonder, what will?"[33] The answer, I believe, lies in the powerful concept of a stable, prosperous, democratic Europe that was created in 1989–1991. Most of the new assumptions about European peace, new state relations, and new security through reciprocal arms reduction treaties and alliances emerged from those years. For the first time since the mid-1920s, the same values, economic systems, and political structures are being extended across the great continent of Europe. For President Bush and his advisers, that was, and is, a lasting legacy.

NOTES

1. John Lewis Gaddis, *The United States and the End of the Cold War* (New York: Oxford, 1994), pp. 171–86. For fuller explanations see John Lewis Gaddis, *The Long Peace: Inquiries into the History of the Cold War* (New York: Oxford, 1987); Kenneth Walz, *Theory of International Politics* (Reading, MA: Addison Wesley, 1979); and Gordon A. Craig and Alexander A. George, *Force and Statecraft: Diplomatic Problems of Our Times* (New York: Oxford, 1983).

2. McGeorge Bundy, *Danger and Survival: Choices about the Bomb in the Past Fifty Years* (New York: Random House, 1988), pp. 584–86, 597. A more recent work by a member of the Bush administration is Robert M. Gates, *From the Shadows: The Ultimate Insider's Story of Five Presidents and How They Won the Cold War* (New York: Simon and Schuster, 1996).

3. For an account of the INF Treaty negotiations, see George L. Rueckert, *Global Double Zero: The INF Treaty from Its Origins to Implementation* (Westport, CT: Greenwood, 1993). For the record of how the INF Treaty was implemented, consult Joseph P. Harahan, *On-Site Inspections under the INF Treaty* (Washington, DC: U.S. Government Printing Office, 1993).

4. Robert L. Hutchings, *American Diplomacy and the End of the Cold War, an Insider's Account of U.S. Policy in Europe, 1989–1992* (Baltimore: Johns Hopkins University Press, 1997), pp. 48–89.

5. James A. Baker III, with Thomas M. DeFrank, *The Politics of Diplomacy: Revolution, War and Peace, 1989–1992* (New York: Putnam, 1995), pp. 45–46.

6. For an account of the pressures facing the Soviet leaders amid declining economic and political conditions, see Jack F. Matlock Jr., *Autopsy of an Empire* (New York: Random House, 1995), pp. 201–205. See also John B. Dunlop, *The Rise of Russia and the Fall of the Soviet Empire* (Princeton, NJ: Princeton University Press, 1993).

7. Bush speech, as cited in Hutchings, *American Diplomacy and the End of the Cold War*, p. 44.

8. *Current Digest of the Soviet Press* 56, no. 27 (1989): 6.

9. Michael J. Sadaro, *Moscow, Germany, and the West* (Ithaca, NY: Cornell University Press, 1990), pp. 376–77.

10. Timothy Garton Ash, *In Europe's Name: Germany and the Divided Continent* (New York: Random House, 1991), pp. 345–46.

11. Ibid., pp. 42–47.

12. Hutchings, *American Diplomacy and the End of the Cold War*, p. 89.

13. For American diplomacy on Germany during 1989–1990, see Philip Zelikow and Condoleezza Rice, *Germany Unified and Europe Transformed: A Study in Statecraft* (Cambridge: Harvard University Press, 1995); Stephen F. Szabo, *The Diplomacy of German Unification* (New York: St. Martin's, 1992); Michael R. Beschloss and Strobe Talbott, *At the Highest Levels: The Inside Story of the End of the Cold War* (Boston: Little, Brown, 1993); Baker, *The Politics of Diplomacy*; Hutchings, *American Diplomacy and the End of the Cold War*.

14. In addition to the authors and books cited previously, see Ash, *In Europe's Name*; Horst Teltschik, *329 Tage: Innenansichten der Eingung* [329 Days: An Insider's

View of Unification] (Berlin: Wolf Jobst Siedler Verlag, 1991); Frank Elbe and Richard Kessler, *Ein Runder Tisch mit Scharfen Ecken* [A Round Table with Sharp Edges] (Baden-Baden: Nomos Verlagsgesellschaft, 1993).

15. Karl Kaiser, "Germany's Unification," *Foreign Affairs* 70, no. 1 (1991): 179.
16. Cited in Hutchings, *American Diplomacy and the End of the Cold War*, p. 92.
17. Ash, *In Europe's Name*, pp. 346–47.
18. Baker, *The Politics of Diplomacy*, pp. 208–16; Beschloss and Talbott, *At the Highest Levels*, pp. 153–71; Hutchings, *American Diplomacy and the End of the Cold War*, pp. 99–101, 103–104.
19. *Current Digest of the Soviet Press* 51, no. 51 (1989): 9–12.
20. Matlock, *Autopsy on an Empire*, pp. 227–55.
21. *Current Digest of the Soviet Press* 51, no. 5 (1990): 23–24.
22. Hutchings, *American Diplomacy and the End of the Cold War*, p. 141.
23. Baker, *The Politics of Diplomacy*, pp. 210–16; Zelikow and Rice, *Germany Unified and Europe Transformed*, pp. 167–72, 191–97.
24. Beschloss and Talbott, *At the Highest Levels*, pp. 206–207.
25. Hutchings, *American Diplomacy and the End of the Cold War*, pp. 137–38.
26. Baker, *The Politics of Diplomacy*, pp. 250–51.
27. Hutchings, *American Diplomacy and the End of the Cold War*, pp. 131–35; Beschloss and Talbott, *At the Highest Levels*, pp. 215–28; Matlock, *Autopsy on an Empire*, pp. 367–69, 380.
28. Zelikow and Rice, *Germany Unified and Europe Transformed*, pp. 355–63; Szabo, *The Diplomacy of German Unification*.
29. Richard A. Falkenrath, *Shaping Europe's Military Order: The Origins and Consequences of the CFE Treaty* (1995).
30. Joseph P. Harahan and John C. Kuhn III, *On-Site Inspections Under the CFE Treaty* (1996).
31. Misha Glenny, *The Fall of Yugoslavia*, rev. ed. (1996).
32. Matlock, *Autopsy on an Empire*, pp. 672–47; Dunlop, *Rise of Russia*, pp. 256–84.
33. Gaddis, *The United States and the End of the Cold War*, p. 169.

Moderator: Carolyn Eisenberg

I would like to say a word or two about the nature of arms control as practiced by the United States and the Soviet Union. Many people assume that arms control is the same as disarmament—that when nations are engaged in arms control negotiations, they are engaging in the straightforward business of paring down their arsenals. While this is one possible meaning of the term, it is not the only one.

As practiced by Nixon, Ford, and Carter in the SALT (Strategic Arms Limitation Treaty) talks, arms control meant setting limits on the possible buildup of certain categories of weapons. During the Reagan years, the SALT process was scrapped, and the United States and the Soviet Union began negotiating on strategic arms reductions—START (Strategic Arms Reduction Treaty). While the two sides committed themselves to overall shrinkage of their nuclear arsenals, they left room for buildup in certain types of weapons.

Contrary to public perception, arms control has been part of the nuclear competition. Often what was going on in those very complex negotiations was the effort on the part of the participants to make deals at the negotiating table that would be of particular advantage to their side militarily. I know that can seem a paradox because, again, if people are equating arms control with disarmament, it's hard to think that the sides are jockeying for military advantage in those negotiations, but very often that's what was occurring. Arguably, that was always occurring. For policymakers who had to defend that practice and that use of arms control, the obvious reply was that we are living in a polarized world, that we still have enemies, and that it would be unrealistic in sitting down to talk about what to do about weapons not to take account of that and not, in some sense, to use those discussions as an opportunity to strengthen the military position of your own side.

It's in that context that I think that the arms control negotiations under President Bush assume particular importance and a very high level of interest, because President Bush was really the first American president since the onset of the Cold War to be in a position of supervising arms control discussions in a context where the enemy was ceasing to be the enemy and where the international polarization that had been so much a characteristic of the past four decades was really disappearing. This gave tremendous new opening to order international relationships and military relationships in a new way. So it's particularly interesting to look at how the Bush administration handled those questions and whether they began to make important changes in U.S. policy and to head the world in a different direction from where they had gone before.

Discussant: Arnold Kanter

I appreciate this opportunity to be with you today to share my impressions of the arms control process during the Bush administration. As has already been indicated by Professor Eisenberg, I do so as a kind of a participant-observer. That is, during the first two years of the Bush administration, I was very much a participant when I was on the NSC staff as senior director for defense policy and arms control. That meant that I had the distinct privilege of trying to manage the interagency process that formulated options for President Bush on the major arms control issues. Then, in 1991, shortly after START I was signed, I went over to the State Department, and at that point I became more of an observer and less of a participant as my responsibility shifted to other issues. But then, I also confess that I'm something of a fallen-away academic, as has already been indicated, as well as a continuing student of the subject. What I would like to do is draw on all three perspectives to offer a few comments organized around two topics. First, and for the most part, I want to share my impressions of arms control during the Bush administration to add to those offered by the two paper presenters; and second, I would like to derive a few lessons from that experience to help pose issues that confront arms controllers in the post–Cold War world.

Let me begin by stating two broad propositions that I think framed the approach to arms control during the Bush administration. The first proposition is that unilateral efforts to improve our defense capabilities, on the one hand, and negotiated arms control agreements, on the other, were regarded in the Bush administration as two sides of the same coin. That is, these two approaches were regarded as complementary rather than as either/or alternatives. In fact, there was a conscious and relatively systematic effort to try to negotiate provisions in arms control agreements in ways that would leverage our plans for defense modernization. We tried to take an integrated approach to defense modernization and arms control rather than either deal with them independently or deal with them as mutually exclusive alternatives.

Here I may differ a bit with Professor Goldstein's analysis, although I suspect I differ more with his shorthand than with his analysis. That is, while I do not believe it's quite accurate to say that President Bush favored arms control over military preparedness, I suspect that the difference has much more to do with what each of us means by military preparedness than with any substantive disagreement between us. In fact, I would say that to juxtapose arms control and military preparedness was, at least in the Bush administration, a false dichotomy.

The second proposition is that the arms control agreements that were negotiated during the Bush administration were obviously affected by the dramatic and almost unimaginable political changes that were taking place at the time—changes, I think, that were very ably summarized in the Harahan paper. But I think that each of these arms control agreements was affected differently by the changes that were going on. They weren't all affected in the same way.

But before I describe some of these differences, let me mention some things that these agreements had in common. The point of departure is to acknowledge that it's almost impossible to remember, let alone appreciate, the magnitude of the changes and the speed with which they occurred. As has already been pointed out, the fundamental premises that underpinned the entirety of the Cold War international system and underpinned the system for a generation—for my adult life—were overturned, all overturned, in the space of two or three years. I think, in all candor, it's fair to say that no one saw it coming. No one anticipated in advance how much and how fast and how fundamentally the world would change. But the corollary to that is that no one could bet the farm—or at least no one with responsibility could bet the farm—on how it would come out. So predicting a happy outcome on the front end of this process would not have been an act of responsibility.

Let me just be quite direct. I think that there's nothing about the end of the Cold War, the collapse of the Soviet empire in Eastern Europe, or indeed the collapse of the Soviet Union itself, that was inevitable or foreordained. I think in retrospect, it all seemed kind of easy and almost automatic. I think that is not only with benefit of hindsight but really with benefit of what happened during that period. I think that the fact that these changes happened as rapidly as they did, as peacefully as they did, and as beneficially as they did was much more the product of hard work, some genuinely courageous decisions, and, if I may appropriate a term from another era, "vision"—some vision—than it was the result of dumb luck or historical inevitability.

So, as we review the history of these arms control agreements, as Professor Goldstein has pointed out, we need to bear in mind that these arms control agreements were being negotiated with the Soviet Union that was, not the Russia that is. The Soviet Union that was in 1989 was a Soviet Union about whose motives reasonable people could have very strong disagreements. There were those who could argue with some persuasiveness (and a lot of hopefulness) that the Soviet Union was on the brink of a fundamental transformation, but there were also those who could argue with some persuasiveness (and not an abundance of paranoia) that, at least at that point, the Soviet Union might be only a case of old wine in new, more marketable bottles. At that point, no one could be sure which side would prove correct.

I would also remind you that these arms control agreements were negotiated before we or the Soviets knew that the Soviet Union was on the brink of collapse. The Soviet Union we were negotiating with, and the Soviets we were negotiating with, didn't think they were on the brink of collapse, and we didn't either.

This was a Soviet Union that not only had been our adversary for a generation but that still, in 1989, was a very serious military superpower, with 25,000 or 30,000 nuclear weapons. No matter how ideologically or economically bankrupt some people might believe the Soviet Union was in 1989, we knew that it had a history of opposing the United States and that it was a military superpower—both conventional and nuclear—and we had no reason to believe that, based on that history, this was a country or indeed a leadership that had suddenly, overnight, had a personality transplant.

Finally, it's worth emphasizing that these agreements were negotiated—not when they were signed, but they were negotiated, for the most part—during the Cold War. They weren't negotiated after the Cold War had ended. They were negotiated as the Cold War was ending, but before either side could be sure the Cold War was about to be relegated to another chapter in world history.

I could tell you a lot of war stories, but let me just tell you a brief anecdote to try to capture the sense of the time. In February 1990, after all the dramatic changes that had been going on in Eastern Europe, I attended a ministerial meeting between Secretary Baker and Foreign Minister Shevardnadze in Moscow. At this ministerial meeting, enormous progress was made in the START I negotiations. I mean, it seemed too good to be true. Sitting in a large room, I noticed that, on the Soviet side, there were no military officers; it was all foreign ministry people. I noticed it, but I confess that, at the time, I didn't do much about it or didn't make much of it beyond wringing my hands a little. After this enormously successful ministerial, we went home to Washington feeling pretty good about what we had accomplished.

When the negotiators reconvened in Geneva to translate these agreements into treaty text, however, we discovered that nothing had happened. In fact, the process in Geneva continued as though the ministerial in Moscow had never taken place, as though there had been no breakthroughs, as though nothing had been agreed. This obviously was a problem.

So, much sooner than we'd anticipated, another ministerial was held in April 1990, this time in Washington, and this time the Soviet military was part of the Soviet delegation. I remember one meeting in particular. On the Soviet side was Marshal Akhromeyev. Marshal Akhromeyev had been appointed by Gorbachev as his senior military adviser. Marshal Akhromeyev began objecting to several points we were making about provisions in the draft treaty text on START I concerning cruise missiles. He kept arguing about them, and so at one point, I asked him why he was going over all this ground again, since everything that he was raising had already been discussed and agreed in Moscow by the Soviet side. It's all agreed; the Soviet side agreed. Then he said, in very quiet, very even tones, "*I* haven't accepted them." I would remind you that this is Gorbachev's military adviser, not Brezhnev's; this is mid-1990, not mid-1970. So negotiating START I, even after these revolutionary political developments, looked a lot like a Cold War arms control negotiation.

If that's what these arms control negotiations had in common, let me briefly describe how they were affected differently by this very fluid environment. I'll confine my remarks to START I and the CFE. In my view, START was very much a product and a reflection of classic Cold War arms control. In one sense, this is obvious; I mean, the START negotiations were begun in the early 1980s, when we were still fondly referring to the Soviet Union as the "Evil Empire," and so by the time President Bush entered office, they'd been going on for several years; they had accumulated quite a heritage, shall we say, to say nothing of a lot of political history and some not inconsiderable ideological baggage. When the Bush administration took office and confronted START, it was hardly starting with a clean sheet of paper.

I think that during the Cold War, arms control succeeded to the extent that it could be carried out, if not in a political vacuum, then to the extent it could be substantially insulated from the political jockeying between the superpowers. I think that START, frankly, reflected this feature, that a lot of the progress that was made in the early days of START benefited from being insulated from the superpowers' Cold War machinations. But the flip side of that is that, as the climate between the superpowers improved, as the Cold War began winding down, START, precisely because it was insulated, didn't benefit from the improvement in relations. Instead, it sort of took on a life of its own, a rhythm of its own, and, if you will, almost an ideology of its own and continued to crank along, even though, if you looked out your window, you would see that everything else in the world had changed.

So it's a treaty in which everything imaginable is spelled out in excruciating detail. The treaty is about 500 pages long. I think its detail and its length are a reflection of a deep and abiding Cold War mistrust between the parties. If you look at what these 500 pages talk about, a lot of these 500 pages talk about verification—verifying compliance with the treaty. Now, the intrusiveness of the verification procedures, I think, speaks to a modicum of mutual understanding between the two sides; that each side would let the other engage in relatively intrusive inspection is a sign of mutual understanding. But the extensiveness of these provisions, I think, speaks to negligible mutual trust.

CFE, by contrast, was much closer to a fresh start than a continuation of the MBFR [Mutual Balanced Force Reductions] talks. While CFE, like START, was unmistakable, real, serious, mainstream, I've-seen-it-all-before arms control, it was also much more clearly part of the political competition between the United States and the Soviet Union than was START. In part, it was because CFE was a bloc-to-bloc negotiation—it was NATO on one side, Warsaw Pact on the other—rather than being a straight, bilateral superpower negotiation and, in part, because the competing proposals were aimed as much at winning the hearts and minds of the European publics as they were at enhancing stability and security in Europe. It's also in part because CFE had an overtly political, as well as security, component. Let me give you one example to illustrate this last point.

President Bush in 1989 came up with a proposal—kind of a "big idea" proposal. It was to impose a ceiling on Soviet and American troops stationed in Europe. That is, it would be a limitation on personnel rather than equipment and a limitation on the superpowers, not on the alliances. Now, from a traditional arms control perspective, it not only was a "big idea"; it was a terrible idea. It was a terrible idea because the military significance of troop limitations is, at best, problematic, and, from a verification point of view, trying to verify limits on personnel or manpower is a nightmare. So, from an arms control perspective, this is a dreadful idea, but from a political perspective, it was very important because one of President Bush's key strategic objectives was to try to lift the yoke of the Soviet military presence from the countries in Eastern Europe. By putting a ceiling, by imposing dramatic reductions on the number of Soviet troops that could be stationed in Eastern Europe, it would importantly advance that fundamental political objective. So it's important to see CFE as an instrument of not just arms control and not just security but much broader strategic objectives.

Let me briefly draw attention to three other arms control developments that Professor Goldstein mentioned in his paper and I think are worth underscoring. The first is the speed with which the START II Treaty was negotiated. While it's true that START II built on START I—you couldn't have done START II without START I—it's also true that START II went much further in reducing and restructuring forces than START I, but it did so in only a fraction of the time it took for START I. Now, my hunch is that it's because START II occurred at kind of a magic moment. It's at that moment when the Cold War had clearly ended, but while there were still two superpowers—while we still had a Russia that felt confident and secure, and was prepared to make big deals. I worry that that magical moment may have been a fleeting one and that it's now passed.

The second development is the utilization of unilateral reductions in place of negotiated agreements. Here I'm referring, obviously, to the very deep—frankly, astonishingly deep—reductions in deployed tactical nuclear weapons. I can't think of any comparable action during the first 40 or so years of the Cold War to those decisions, to those unilateral reductions, and I have to leave it to better historians than I am to think of any other earlier precedents. But I think it's worth pondering what conditions are both necessary and sufficient to permit the sides to engage in this kind of mutual but non-negotiated, nonlegally binding dramatic changes in their military force structures.

The third development is the growth of international regimes that are voluntary and norm-based rather than legally binding international agreements that enumerate the dos and the don'ts. Here I'm thinking of the Nuclear Suppliers Group and the Missile Technology Control Regime [MTCR]. These aren't agreements; they're regimes. Adherence to them is voluntary. The question is, Is this good? Is this a good way to do arms control? Or is it a case of getting in the way of more formal and more effective legal agreements?

Let me wrap up by posing three questions that I think emerge from this history as a way of helping to stimulate discussion. The first is, In the post–Cold War world, should we continue to insist on elaborate and expensive verification provisions when an impoverished Russia finds these provisions economically burdensome and politically humiliating? Do future arms control agreements still need to have all this verification stuff? Indeed, in the existing arms control agreements, do we need to continue to enforce all the very elaborate verification procedures as punctiliously as we have been doing to date? Second question: Is it necessary and desirable to continue to rely upon laboriously negotiated formal agreements, or can we rely more upon voluntary, norm-based MTCR-like regimes or simply unilateral actions that don't have benefit of international blessing at all. Last, is it possible—not just technologically, but is it possible politically, given the new world, the new relationships—to defend against theater missile attacks and perhaps even against limited missile attacks against the American and Russian homelands, without undermining either strategic stability or the strategic rationale for the ABM [Antiballistic Missile] Treaty? I think these are some of the questions that my successors face, and I'm glad it's them and not me.

Discussant: James M. Klurfeld

I'm going to try to be as brief as I possibly can, because I'm not a person who was on the inside; we have people who were on the inside and who have studied this as academics. So what I thought I'd try to do is share with you just a few observations, having listened to the presentations, and also having just returned from a trip to Germany where I spent the last couple weeks traveling and talking to people in the security areas and foreign policy. The fact is that the transformation that everybody has talked about that began in 1989 is still going on in Europe. If you look at the issues of NATO enlargement, German unification, the single monetary unit in Europe—these are all consequences, I think, of the cataclysmic events and the fundamental events that took place during the Bush administration.

Now, let me make one point. In my judgment, it's clear that the arms control achievements of the Bush administration are significant and lasting and will probably, I think, be a key part of the Bush legacy. What occurred to me as I was traveling in Europe recently, though, is that in some ways, while we have always tended to concentrate on the strategic questions and nuclear weapons because in some ways they were the most dramatic, in a way, right now, I would conclude that maybe the most significant and lasting agreement was the CFE Agreement—the Conventional Forces Agreement in Europe—because those agreements, in some ways, have fundamentally changed the security environment in Europe in a way that's never before been the case in Europe and gives Europe at least the opportunity for an era of stability and assurance about each other's motives that they've never had before. The fact is that the CFE Agreements provide Europeans with a sense of security, a transparency about what's going on, and a cushion of time if things were to go wrong that they've really never had before. It means there's a lot of time to plan for contingencies, and it also provides a basis on which to plan the future now.

Now, let me just share one observation that I've been doing a lot of writing about recently. It seems to me, in many ways, the enlargement of NATO that we are seeing happen this spring, does not—does not—seem to follow logically from all the arms control agreements and advances that were made in the Bush years. In one sense, what's very significant about all these agreements that we've been talking about is that they were done cooperatively; they were done with the Soviets' or the Russians' acquiescence. We worked with them. Arnold Kanter, General Scowcroft—they were working with the Russians. The Russians agreed to all these changes. Significantly, as it was pointed out in the papers, the Russians kept saying, "We want assurances you're not going to intrude on our basic security interests." My concern about NATO enlargement is that the Russians now are so weak, and the United States so strong, that we can do any darn thing we want to do right now, and the Russians have to accept it. But that doesn't mean it's the right thing to do, or it's going to serve our interests in the long run. It seems to me that the fact that the Russians—and I haven't talked to a single expert on Russia, whether it be here in the United States or in Europe who thinks that the Russians are really going to accept this and it's not a real problem for them. I hear that from some people in the current administration; I just don't think that it's true. They don't like it, they can't do anything about it, but it is a departure from the type of agreements that marked the Bush administration.

Also, there isn't a great—or any—military reason for enlarging NATO. This is very much a political decision; some would say it's a domestic political decision for this administration. But the point is, with the CFE Agreements, you now have the stability and transparency and the time to react in Europe that, if things were to go bad, there's plenty of time to build up your military again. So the reason for having to bring in the Czech Republic, Hungary, and Poland immediately into NATO doesn't make a lot of sense to me in that regard, either.

It also seems, if you think about this, that it is a way of drawing a new line in Europe, and I'm not sure at this stage why it makes sense to draw a new line in Europe. The issue that I came across in traveling in Europe now is not the question of what's going to happen with these three countries—it seems like it's going to happen—but now, what happens to the Baltics, what happens to Ukraine, when you're talking about Russian security interests. The Russians always referred to this as kind of their "strategic space," and that's being intruded—they see the possibility of that being intruded upon. That creates, it seems to me, a real problem.

At any rate, the important thing to understand here is that the Bush administration worked cooperatively with the Russians, and I think Bush had some vision about where he wanted to go in terms of European stability. Although let me also say that it seems to me that the underlying characteristic of the Bush administration was caution and reacting slowly to things. It always seemed to me, either from here on Long Island or if I went down to Washington to visit friends, that they were always kind of catching up with things. Events were always a little bit ahead of them. Now, you can't blame them, in some ways; these were unbelievable events. As Arnold Kanter said, no one predicted this. But where I would give the Bush administration incredibly high marks was in their ability, once having recognized something had happened—even if some of us thought they were slow to recognize it, once they did recognize it—their reactions were very solid. They were able to bring about fundamental, intelligent change in a peaceful way and that, as I said earlier, is a great legacy.

Another observation I'll give you—and I think Dr. Kanter was kind of referring to this in some ways—when you look at the pace of developments, once it was clear that things had changed in the Soviet Union, once it was clear that the Cold War was over, it reminds me of a conversation I had with Eugene Rostow, a former head of the Arms Control and Disarmament Agency. Rostow and I, we didn't agree on most things, I must say, but he always contended, "Look, arms control is not the center of policy. What you need first is an understanding, a sense of trust, a sense of mutual goals. Then arms control will fall right into place." In other words, the Canadians have a large army, but we don't need arms control agreements with the Canadians because there's obviously a sense of trust. They're not about to come across the border. So it seems to me that one of the things that happened here—and if you go back as I do (and I was covering the Carter administration), arms control was seen as an end in itself in those days. It was the way that you were going to principally move foreign policy and improve the relations between nations. I think that never really happened. Arms control fell into place after you had a sense of agreement.

I also think that maybe, when you turn to the strategic questions and you look back on them from a bit of perspective now, we ought to maybe have some appreciation for the incredible length of absurdity some of the nuclear calculations went to. You know, I remember going, in March 1977, with Secretary of State Cy Vance to Moscow. The whole purpose of that negotiation, the proposal they made then, was to try to deal with what they called land-based vulnerability. The Soviets had bigger missiles, made our missiles vulnerable. The Russians—Gromyko, basically—said, "Forget about it. Go home." Now, that remained the constant theme of American–Soviet arms negotiations right up to the START I and START II Agreements. But now, when I look back on these things, and you look at the calculations we were making, it all seems really absurd, in some ways, because the weapons, the nuclear weapons, you were dealing with are so powerful that these careful little calculations—you know, you have seven more warheads than we do—one of these things landing, of course, would have been an absolute disaster, a catastrophe. In many ways, the nuclear weapons were not—they weren't usable. They were political weapons. They gave someone the ability to say, "Hey, look, I'm strong." They certainly involved the question of deterrence, but I question now, as I look back on it, some of these excruciating calculations that we went through to see who was ahead and who was behind.

Finally, also in looking ahead—much the way Arnold Kanter looked ahead and looked at some of the problems we have—there are some other consequences I would mention that we still need to deal with that come right out of these agreements. The biggest one, I would say, is the whole question of, now that the Russians and the United States are dismantling all these nuclear weapons, what the hell are we going to do with them? Everybody has—this is called the "loose nukes" problem. You know, we have all these warheads now—I think there's something like 100 tons of plutonium floating around in Russia that's being guarded by a military that's not being paid. That's a scary problem. Then the issue becomes, how can you work with the Russians to get rid of this stuff? We have a plan for kind of putting them in canisters and burying them. The Russians say, "We spent all this money on them; we want to get some use out of them." They want to burn them in nuclear reactors. We have a whole nuclear movement in the West—not just the United States—that doesn't like nuclear reactors and thinks they're very dangerous and would oppose any type of burning, even if that turns out to be part of the solution. This is a very significant problem, and, in some ways, what concerns me the most right now is we're spending all this time debating the NATO enlargement when we should be taking a much closer look at the question of the disposal of nuclear weapons and how we should be working with the Russians in a way that the Bush administration was able to work with the Russians to solve a very difficult problem that we both face.

Discussant: Kathryn R. Schultz

Thank you for inviting me to be here. It's quite a pleasure. The papers presented by Mr. Harahan and Professor Goldstein were very interesting to read, and I will use their papers as a takeoff point for some comments.

You heard Mr. Harahan describe how the Bush administration challenged some of the underlying assumptions of the Cold War. Two of these assumptions were that nations of Eastern and Central Europe would forever remain Communist states under Soviet influence and that Germany would remain divided. In describing how the Bush administration dealt with this, Mr. Harahan stated in his paper that the leaders of this decaying empire—the Soviet Union—had to be reassured that the United States, Germany, and the other NATO states sought no unilateral military advantage should the Central and Eastern European states move toward independence. This is an important point to remember, as Mr. Klurfeld pointed out, because to some of the leaders in Russia who remember these assurances, NATO expansion is a violation of the basic understanding reached between NATO and the former Soviet Union.

The Cold War assumption with which, to use Mr. Harahan's words, the Bush administration "retained fidelity" was the primacy of nuclear weapons in deterring a military conquest of Western Europe. Not one of the leaders of the NATO states openly challenged this assumption in the 1989 to 1992 period, when it would have been relatively easy and logical to do so. This assumption about the primacy of nuclear weapons remains unchallenged in official circles to this day. For example, in the Alliance's study on NATO enlargement, it states, "The supreme guarantee of the security of the Allies is provided by the strategic nuclear forces of the Alliance." That was written less than two years ago. Instead of clinging to thousands of nuclear weapons as a hedge against a resurgent Russia, U.S. national security would be better served by reducing its reliance on nuclear weapons and by pursuing, with the other nuclear weapons states, deep cuts in nuclear arsenals with the ultimate aim of eliminating them.

While President Bush, like his European counterparts, did not confront nuclear policy or doctrine, he considerably changed U.S. nuclear posture for the better, which Professor Goldstein explains in his paper. Now, I couldn't agree more with the professor's assertion that arms control, like military preparedness, is a means of strengthening national security and that arms control complements military preparedness. On arms control in general, however, Professor Goldstein seems inclined to give more credit to President Bush than I am. In the introduction to his fine paper, the professor writes, "Cataclysmic changes in global politics contributed to a distinct emphasis during the Bush administration on arms control over military preparedness." But was it arms control *over* military preparedness or, as I would argue, military preparedness *seasoned* with arms control? For example, it should be remembered that in the START II negotiations, President Bush bargained the Russians up from 2,000 to 2,500 deployed strategic nuclear weapons, as the Russians wanted, to 3,000 to 3,500. Only now, five years later, are the United States and Russia looking again at reductions to this level.

Also, let me point out that, whenever we talk about nuclear weapons, it is *imperative* that we not fall into the trap of saying, for example, that START I would leave the United States with about 8,500 warheads and the Soviet Union with about 6,500 or that START II would reduce us to about 3,500 weapons each. We must clarify, for example, that the 3,500 warheads are strategic deployed warheads, not the total number of warheads in the arsenal. In fact, assuming that the Russians do ratify the START II treaty and that both START treaties are fully implemented, the United States and Russia will each maintain a total nuclear arsenal of about 10,000 warheads. Therefore, in terms of overall reductions, the U.S. arsenal will go from about 21,000 warheads in 1990 to about 10,000 in the year 2003. President Bush deserves kudos for this reduction, but I maintain that, given the dramatic changes in the world, we had a window of opportunity in the Bush years to eliminate even more nuclear weapons—weapons that, to this day, remain a threat not only to U.S. national security but to the fate of the world.

There were numerous other opportunities of which the Bush administration did not take advantage. There was the opportunity to follow on to the success of his initiatives on tactical nuclear weapons with a treaty eliminating all tactical nuclear weapons. After all, tactical nuclear weapons were designed and fielded by the United States to fight a war in Europe, and we have yet to see negotiations on tactical nukes. As Professor Goldstein pointed out in his paper, although President Bush officially canceled production of the W-88 nuclear warhead and terminated plans to resume production of plutonium and highly enriched uranium, he "did not avail himself of the opportunity to propose an international treaty to halt production of fissile material, as had been proposed by Yeltsin."

Also, it should be noted that the cancellation of the W-88 was a moot point, since production had actually stopped two years earlier because the Rocky Flats facility that fabricated plutonium triggers for warheads was shut down in December 1989 because of safety problems. Similarly, the termination of weapons-grade fissile materials for weapons purposes was symbolic, because the United States had not produced highly enriched uranium since 1964 and had stopped producing plutonium in 1988.

Perhaps the biggest opportunity that President Bush not only had and missed but also rejected was the opportunity to ban permanently all nuclear explosive tests. Presidents Gorbachev and Yeltsin both urged the United States to discontinue nuclear tests and to work toward a comprehensive test ban treaty. Unlike all U.S. administrations—with the exception of the Reagan administration, which preceded him—President Bush opposed any ban on nuclear testing.

Now, Professor Goldstein mentioned briefly nuclear testing in his paper, but the statements seem to date the paper. I assume the paper was written several years earlier, because it notes that Clinton had declared a moratorium on nuclear testing. As we know, President Clinton went beyond a moratorium; he was one of the driving forces behind the comprehensive test ban treaty, which was signed in September 1996. Also, President Clinton didn't technically declare a moratorium; he repeatedly extended the moratorium passed by Congress in 1992. That's the same moratorium that President Bush found "highly objectionable" because it "unwisely restricts tests necessary to maintain a safe and reliable deterrent." Nevertheless, President Bush did not veto the bill, as he had threatened.

The other point that Professor Goldstein made in his paper that I wanted to comment on, just for the record, was that he said, "Few serious military thinkers since the Baruch Plan of 1946 have recommended elimination of nuclear weapons." For the record, I'd like to remind people that many retired military leaders—including those in my organization—have called for the elimination of nuclear weapons. In December 1996 General Lee Butler, former commander of Strategic Air Command, and General Andrew Goodpaster, former commander of NATO Forces, along with 61 other retired international admirals and generals, publicly called for the nuclear weapons states to work seriously toward making the elimination of nuclear weapons a reality.

Turning our attention, for the moment, away from nuclear weapons, Professor Goldstein pointed out that significant accords were reached on conventional weapons—the CFE Treaty—and on chemical weapons—the Chemical Weapons Convention (CWC)—under President Bush. President Bush is deserving of credit for helping to make these treaties reality. As you know, the CWC will enter into force on April 29, with or without the United States. If the U.S. Senate fails to ratify the treaty in time, the Senate will not only undermine our authority on the world stage and hinder our ability to ensure that other nations do not covertly produce chemical weapons, they will do a terrible disservice to the work of George Bush and his administration.

Despite these important arms control measures, military preparedness continued to be an equally, if not more, important factor in the Bush administration than arms control. Despite President Bush's proclamation that "We won the Cold War" and General Colin Powell's claim, "I'm running out of demons, I'm running out of villains," the Bush administration did not respond to the end of the Cold War and the changed nature of the threat with corresponding reductions in military spending. Now, it's true that President Bush did cancel several weapons systems. He canceled the Short-Range Attack Missile [SRAM-II] and the follow-on tactical variant, the SRAM-T missile, as well as the small ICBM.

Reductions in military spending proposed by President Bush similarly do not show a dedication to arms control over military preparedness. We have to recognize the "Reagan phenomenon." President Reagan induced the largest peacetime buildup in military spending in military history, topping out in 1985 at $405 billion in FY [fiscal year] 1997 dollars. (All of the numbers I'm using are adjusted for inflation.) So when we speak of Bush's military spending cuts, we have to look at where spending was. In 1988, when President Bush was elected, the United States spent $365 billion on its military; by 1993, it was down to

$293 billion, which was roughly equivalent to average annual military spending during the Cold War. Even now, five years after President Bush left office and nearly eight years after the Berlin Wall fell, the United States continues to spend at roughly 85 percent of average Cold War levels. This response to the end of the Cold War is in sharp contrast to how the United States responded to the end of World War II. Again using FY 1997 dollars, within one year of the end of World War II, U.S. military spending was cut in half, from $967 billion in 1945 to $489 billion in 1946. One year later, by 1947, the United States had trimmed military spending to $123 billion. We haven't seen anything comparable in response to the end of the Cold War.

Professor Goldstein, in his paper, took it a step further. He said, "Just as Reagan will be noted for military preparedness, Bush will be identified with arms restraint." Although President Bush will definitely be associated with important arms control agreements and initiatives, I find it implausible that he'll actually be associated with arms restraint. Consider for a moment the Bush record on arms sales. Although the dramatic changes in the world provided a golden opportunity for the United States to rethink the policy of providing weapons and training to more than three-quarters of the nations of the world, the Bush administration did nothing to restrain arms sales. In fact, under President Bush, the United States became the number one weapons dealer in the world. In 1991 alone, the Bush administration authorized the sale of a staggering $63 billion worth of weapons, military construction, and training to 142 of the then-180 nations on the planet. Forty percent of this—$26.2 billion—was slated for delivery to 59 authoritarian governments.

Finally, let me close by highlighting what I think is President Bush's most important contribution in terms of arms control, which was his independent initiative of September 1991. President Bush ordered all U.S. tactical nuclear weapons, with the exception of about 1,000 air force bombs deployed in Europe, to be returned to the United States. All the army weapons were destroyed, as were many of the navy warheads. President Gorbachev ordered similar withdrawals a few days later. Why was this done? Was it because George Bush suddenly saw the value of disarmament? Was it because it suddenly dawned on the president that we didn't need to have nuclear artillery shells or Lance missiles on European soil when the only targets they could reach were now in friendly nations? Or was it to give President Gorbachev the cover to do the same? I would argue the latter. Remember that in September 1991 thousands of tactical nuclear weapons remained scattered throughout the Soviet Union. The union was still intact, but it was showing signs of splitting. The ties binding the republics to Moscow were tenuous, at best. The Armenians and Azerbaijanis were at war. Recognizing the dangerous situation in the Soviet Union, realizing that a treaty would be a laborious and time-consuming process, and with full knowledge that tactical nuclear weapons were of little, if any, military utility to the United States, President Bush took unilateral action. As was expected, Gorbachev responded in kind and returned all tactical nuclear weapons to Russia without incident. If President Gorbachev had not been given the political cover necessary to remove all tactical nuclear weapons from other republics, nuclear weapons might have played a role in the civil wars in Armenia, Azerbaijan, and Georgia. This, I believe, is President Bush's greatest achievement.

Questions and Answers

Note: Because of tape-recording problems, only the following segments of the question-and-answer period for this panel are included.

Q: I have a question for Ms. Schultz. You said in your speech that Bush made cuts in nuclear weapons but that he didn't go far enough. I was wondering if you were saying that he had an opportunity to eliminate nuclear weapons.

Kathryn R. Schultz: I don't think that he had an opportunity to eliminate nuclear weapons, nor was it appropriate or feasible to do so. But I think he had the opportunity and responsibility to get even deeper cuts, which could have enhanced U.S. national security and moved the world closer toward the goal—shared by the U.S. government—of the eventual elimination of nuclear weapons. Bargaining the Russians up, for example, from 2,000 to 2,500, 3,000 to 3,500 is a good example. Nuclear weapons are one of the greatest threats to this country, and if we can get rid of more nuclear weapons that could be used against us, we should. Although we didn't know how long Bush would be in office, we did know that the Russians/Soviets had thousands upon thousands of nuclear weapons. We had this window of opportunity that Bush should have taken as far as it could go, rather than trying to play it too safe.

Martin E. Goldstein: I would like to answer the gentleman's remarks. Basically, you and I might have some difference of opinion on the answer to the question, How low can you go? People are debating that at the present time, and it's very easy to debate. Just how many nuclear weapons do we need to defend ourselves? During the 1962 Cuban missile crisis, Secretary of Defense McNamara said that if the Soviets threatened us with only three or four nuclear weapons, we would be deterred from invading Cuba.

Ms. Schultz said the Bush administration missed many opportunities to reduce arms levels. Allow me to mention a couple of considerations. First of all, it has been pointed out that Bush is a cautious individual and that he surrounded himself with cautious people—not ideologues, not radicals, not people who said, "We're going to have arms control, no matter what." They were largely responding to what the Soviet Union was doing. Had the Soviet Union held together and bolstered its arsenal, policymakers in the Bush administration probably would have recommended we boost *our* armaments. Bush and his advisers did not know then what we know now, which is that the Soviet Union collapsed. Even today, Moscow's future course remains uncharted; Russia could reappear as a threat. So I know that you think there were opportunities missed. But remember, at the time we could not be certain how Russia would evolve.

Carolyn Eisenberg: If I could take advantage of being the moderator, I'd like to ask a question. I've been staring at Professor Goldstein's paper for an hour and half and wanting to ask it. One of the problems about reducing these complex questions to 15 minutes is that, particularly when you're in the area of arms control, much of what's important is actually in the details. Among the details that I don't think you had a chance to mention in your talk is the nature of the START II agreement itself and what's in that agreement. One of the features that Professor Goldstein mentions—and this is not a major secret—is that, as an aspect of the START II agreement, we used that agreement in order to eliminate MIRVed Soviet land-based missiles while retaining our own very substantial supply of multiple warhead ballistic missiles on ships.

When we think about the opportunities not taken, one issue has to do with how low the United States was prepared to go, but there's also another question, which is, Would the administration take this new environment as an opportunity to use arms control negotiations not to jockey for advantage but, by being equitable, to try to stop using nuclear weapons as a way of countries frightening each other and negotiating with each other? My question is, What is the explanation for an American insistence that we have a right to have a large supply of multiwarheaded ballistic missiles on ships, whereas the Soviet land-based arsenal has to be eliminated?

Goldstein: First, both sides have equal rights and equal prohibitions. It's not that the United States has a unilateral right to have submarine-based MIRV missiles, and the Russians don't; both sides have equal rights. It's not that the Russians are prohibited from having land-based MIRVed ICBMs, and the United States can have them; both sides are prohibited.

Second, let me articulate the logic for why land-based MIRVs are bad, and sea-based MIRVs are less bad. Land-based MIRV missiles are vulnerable. They can be attacked. So in times of crisis, if you think the other guy is going to attack, you have an incentive to strike those missiles and destroy them before they can hit you. Therefore, land-based MIRVs are destabilizing. The submarine-based missiles are invulnerable because you can't find them, so that even if they can threaten you, there's not much you can do about it. So even in times of crisis, you're not tempted to preempt. That's the logic for favoring sea-based missiles over fixed land-based.

I think there's another element, which is that the land-based missiles at the time were more accurate than sea-based missiles. So if a country were going to launch a surprise attack, it would use its land-based missiles to do that. Therefore, removing land-based missiles reduces the likelihood of surprise attack and affords adversaries some time to defuse the situation.

Schultz: The Trident II D-5 SLBM definitely was just as capable and accurate as any Soviet land-based ICBM. Also, under START II, there were limits placed on some submarine-based missiles that were considered a major concession by the United States—nothing comparable to the limits placed on land-based ICBMs, though. But the United States did agree for the first time to eliminate some of its weapons at sea—no more than 1,750 strategic warheads deployed on submarines—in exchange for the Soviets to agree to eliminate all MIRVed land-based ICBMs.

Part VII

Defense Posture and Base Closings

14

The Rejection of a Cabinet Nomination: The Senate and John Tower

James D. King and James W. Riddlesperger, Jr.

Presidents typically begin their administrations with a honeymoon period with Congress. This period is marked by oratory emphasizing cooperation, patience while the president prepares his legislative agenda, and Senate confirmation of the president's selections for his cabinet and other high-ranking positions. For George Bush, the honeymoon period included one remarkable setback. While most of his nominees for various executive posts were well received in the Senate, Bush's initial choice for secretary of defense, former senator and fellow Texan John G. Tower, was rebuffed after a seven-week struggle.

The Senate's rejection of John Tower as secretary of defense was remarkable for one simple reason: cabinet nominations are almost always confirmed. In 200 years of constitutional history, a president's choice for a cabinet officer has been turned down only nine times (Table 14.1). Only two twentieth-century cabinet nominations had failed to gain Senate approval prior to Tower's defeat. Confirmation by voice vote or near unanimous roll call vote has been the norm for cabinet confirmations. Presidents from Harry Truman to Ronald Reagan saw only 1 cabinet nomination in 10 experience significant opposition within the Senate.[1] Thus, the Bush administration's failure to secure Tower's confirmation is distinctive.

Why did the Senate not confirm the nomination of John Tower as secretary of defense? Were the allegations that led to the nomination's defeat unusual, or did they reflect common presidential-senatorial disagreement over cabinet appointments? We address these questions by reviewing the kinds of objections that are typically raised in Senate consideration of executive department appointments—with examples of four previous cabinet nominations that were rejected by the Senate or that encountered significant opposition—and finally examining the Tower nomination in detail within this historical context.

Table 14.1
Failed Cabinet Nominations

Year	President	Nominee	Department
1834	Andrew Jackson	Roger Taney	Treasury
1843	John Tyler	Caleb Cushing	Treasury
1844	John Tyler	David Henshaw	Navy
1844	John Tyler	James M. Porter	War
1844	John Tyler	James S. Green	Treasury
1868	Andrew Johnson	Henry Stansbery	Justice
1925	Calvin Coolidge	Charles B. Warren	Justice
1959	Dwight Eisenhower	Lewis L. Strauss	Commerce
1989	George Bush	John Tower	Defense

SENATE OBJECTIONS TO CABINET NOMINEES

As the rarity of failed nominations indicates, the Senate usually defers to the president's choices for cabinet officers. Little has changed in the nearly 50 years since Joseph Harris observed:

Well-established custom accords the President wide latitude in the choice of members of his own Cabinet, who are regarded as his chief assistants and advisors. . . . The Senate's consideration of Cabinet nominations is by no means perfunctory, but the Senate does not attempt to dictate the President's selections. Today a cabinet nomination will be rejected only if the nominee is definitely disqualified.[2]

Defining what attributes render an individual "disqualified" for a seat at the cabinet table is a problem the Senate has wrestled with on more than one occasion. As yet, no clear standard for judging nominees as qualified or not has emerged from the Senate's deliberations. Justice Potter Stewart once wrote that he couldn't define obscenity, but he knew it when it saw it.[3] Similarly, the Senate doesn't know what disqualifies someone from cabinet service until it sees the person's attributes and record.

The Senate's reasons for objecting to cabinet nominees fall into four broad categories: public policy, conflict of interest, competence, and illegal or unethical behavior.[4] The frequency of objections being raised on each basis varies widely, as does the impact of each on confirmation votes in the Senate.

Public Policy

In recent years, public policy has been foremost among Senate concerns in considering presidential nominations. This is a significant shift from the mid-twentieth century, when Harris noted that institutional norms held "that nominees should not be rejected merely because they hold views that are not agreeable to a majority of the Senate."[5] Instead, policy has moved to the forefront of many confirmation debates. Between 1945 and 1988, public policy concerns were expressed by senators in 14 percent of all cabinet nominations and 75 percent of nominations encountering significant opposition (Table 14.2).[6]

Table 14.2
Grounds for Opposing Cabinet Nominations, 1945–1988

	All Nominations	Opposed Nominations*
Policy Differences	14%	75%
Conflict of Interest	5%	25%
Competence	4%	19%
Illegal or Unethical Behavior	3%	19%
Other Reasons	4%	25%
N =	169	16

* Received less than 90% affirmative votes, rejected, or withdrawn.

Concerns over public policy focus on programs advocated by either the individual nominee or the administration. An example of the former comes from the Carter administration, when Ray Marshall's nomination as secretary of labor was viewed unfavorably by conservatives because of his support for union shops and common situs picketing.[7] Common situs picketing had been the topic of heated debate in the Congress just a year before Marshall's nomination when President Ford's labor secretary, John Dunlop, negotiated an agreement between union and management supporters on Capitol Hill. The product was legislation permitting common situs picketing while restricting wildcat strikes, a measure that Dunlop believed the president was committed to signing. Instead, Ford vetoed the bill under pressure from conservatives and building contractors. Dunlop subsequently resigned on the ground that his effectiveness had been compromised.[8] Conservatives feared the issue's revival in a Democratic administration with a labor secretary committed to the idea. With Democrats firmly in control of the Senate, Marshall's appointment was confirmed with 15 Republicans and 5 conservative Democrats dissenting.

The Reagan administration's environmental policies were questioned with the nominations of William Clark and Donald Hodel to head the Interior and Energy Departments, respectively. In these instances, senators used the nomination of a new departmental secretary to attack policies advanced on behalf of the administration by former interior secretary James Watt. Reagan's philosophy of advancing economic growth by reducing government regulations was reflected in Watt's efforts to expand natural resource development opportunities on federal lands and in coastal waters. In addition, questions of indifferent or negligent enforcement of environmental standards by the Environmental Protection Agency under Reagan were raised. These issues came to the fore during the

Senate's consideration of Clark's and Hodel's nominations but the opposition was not strong enough to block confirmation.[9]

Conflicts of Interest

The second most frequently cited reason for objecting to cabinet nominees is conflict of interest (5 percent of all nominations, 25 percent of those with significant opposition). Financial conflicts of interest are the most obvious but least troublesome to the Senate. Distress surrounding stockholdings is frequently resolved by the nominee's divesting himself or herself of shares in corporations that do business with the department or placing investments in a blind trust. For example, Presidents Eisenhower and Kennedy found their choices for secretary of defense confronting such conflict of interest allegations. Charles E. Wilson and Robert McNamara headed General Motors Corporation and Ford Motor Company, respectively, when appointed; both corporations held sizable Defense Department contracts. The apprehensions of some senators over these potential conflicts of interest were relieved when Wilson and McNamara agreed to sell their holdings. In both cases, confirmation followed shortly after the agreement was announced.[10]

Less easily dismissed by the Senate are what G. Calvin Mackenzie calls predispositional conflicts of interest.[11] These conflicts occur when the nominee has close ties to an industry or policy perspective. The essence of predispositional conflicts of interest was captured by Senator Hubert Humphrey during the hearings on the nomination of Earl Butz to be secretary of agriculture during the Nixon administration. "What I am worried about is your economic philosophy," Humphrey told Butz. "You can put all [your investments] in escrow, but I don't think you can put your philosophy in escrow."[12] Senators fear the cabinet officer will be predisposed to support a particular point of view because of his or her former affiliation. These concerns are similar to policy concerns, but the focus is on potential biases on the part of the nominee and not on explicit policy positions expressed by the nominee or policies of the administration.

Examples of nominations challenged on predispositional conflicts of interest abound, and opposition is often substantial. For example, Butz's nomination as Nixon's secretary of the agriculture was confirmed with the most dissenting votes (forty-four) of any successful nominee since World War II.[13] The effect of a predispositional conflict of interest was greatest when President Coolidge opened his second term by nominating Charles B. Warren for attorney general.[14] There was no reason to suspect that the nomination would not be confirmed. Warren was a successful businessman, respected attorney, former ambassador, and high-ranking Republican Party activist. With Republicans holding a majority of seats in the Senate and the nominee's character seemingly above reproach, confirmation appeared certain. Instead, the Senate rejected a cabinet nomination for the first time in nearly six decades.

The president and Senate leadership failed to anticipate the strength of a coalition of Democrats and Progressive Republicans. Senators allied against

Warren challenged the nomination on the ground that the attorney general-designate was closely tied to the Sugar Trust and therefore could not be relied upon to enforce federal antitrust laws.[15] According to Senator Thomas Walsh, one of Warren's leading critics: "I think that he ought not to be made Attorney General ... chiefly because for years he was a representative in his State of the Sugar Trust, one of the most offensive and most oppressive trusts with which the American people have unfortunately been familiar in the present and past generation."[16] After providing legal representation for the American Sugar Refining Company, Warren had organized and served as president of the Michigan Sugar Company, a corporation largely owned by the American Sugar Refining Company. The American Sugar Refining Company was now a target of a Justice Department antitrust investigation.

The heyday of the Progressive era had passed, but antitrust sentiment remained high. Fears that the Sherman Antitrust Act would not be vigorously applied to the sugar industry led a sufficient number of senators to oppose Warren's nomination. The roll call on the nomination ended in a tie vote. Confident of victory, the Republican leadership had not made arrangements for the vice president to preside over the debate or to otherwise be available to break a tie.[17] An angry President Coolidge again nominated Warren for attorney general, and the nomination was taken up by the Senate once more. Although better prepared to defend the president's choice, Republican leaders were unable to muster a majority of votes. The nomination failed the second time by a seven-vote margin.

After having his first choice for attorney general spurned by the Senate over predispositional conflicts of interest, President Coolidge opted for a man of substantially different experience. Nominated for attorney general was John G. Sargent, a former attorney general of Vermont. More important than Sargent's experience in the field of law was an absence of links to large corporations. The new nominee could not be painted with the brush used to discredit Warren. Sargent's appointment was quickly and unanimously confirmed.

Competence

A nominee's professional competence is also at times of concern to senators. Does this individual, either by formal training or prior experience, have sufficient knowledge of the programs entrusted to the department? Most nominees possess the training or experience to be considered specialists in the policies of their departments. Thus, objections based on the nominee's competence are infrequent, occurring in only 4 percent of all nominations and 19 percent of nominations with significant opposition.

Among the few examples of this type of objection is President Ford's selection of Carla Hills as secretary of housing and urban development [HUD]. Widely respected as an expert in anti-trust law and for her work as an assistant attorney general, Hills had no experience in housing policy. This rendered her "unqualified" in the eyes of the administration's critics and sparked charges that gender was the primary consideration in the appointment. Senator William Proxmire, chairman of the Banking, Housing, and Urban Affairs Committee, gave voice to these sentiments:

> At a time when housing starts in the country have dropped below 900,000 and when the administration has frozen virtually all assisted housing starts, this is no time for on-the-job training for a new secretary of H.U.D.
>
> We have just been through a two-year disaster period because Mr. Lynn, like Mrs. Hills, is an able and intelligent lawyer who had no background or qualifications for the job. The result: No housing.[18]

The charges of lack of competence had little effect on the outcome of the vote confirming Hills' appointment. Only five senators (including Proxmire) dissented.

Illegal and Unethical Behavior

Occurring with the same frequency as competence-based challenges but significantly more threatening to a nomination are charges of illegal or unethical behavior. In some instances, the allegations of inappropriate behavior stem from activities before the nomination is made. Construction company executive Raymond Donovan was named secretary of labor at the opening of the Reagan administration amid allegations of connections to union corruption and organized crime. Although confirmed over substantial opposition, Donovan later faced criminal indictment and was forced to resign.[19]

Others find their nominations challenged for actions in another public office. President Nixon selected Deputy Attorney General Richard Kleindienst to head the Department of Justice when John Mitchell resigned to direct the president's reelection campaign. Confirmation of the appointment was delayed five months while the Senate investigated possible links between the settlement of a Justice Department antitrust suit against the International Telephone and Telegram Corporation (ITT) and contributions by ITT to the Republican Party.[20] In the end, nearly a quarter of the Senate voted against Kleindienst's nomination. Similarly, President Reagan's nomination of longtime aide and White House counselor Edwin Meese as attorney general was stalled for more than year as the Senate and a special prosecutor investigated allegations of irregularities in his financial disclosure statements and of personal financial dealings (including personal loans and real estate transactions) with people who later received appointments within the Reagan administration. Meese was ultimately confirmed with a third of the senators dissenting, but accusations of impropriety continued to plague him throughout his tenure as attorney general.[21]

Other Senate Concerns

Senators from time to time raise other objections during deliberations on cabinet nominations. Some, such as James Abourezk's decision to oppose all Nixon administration nominations to protest presidential encroachment of congressional powers, are unrelated to the particular appointment in question.[22] Other objections expressed by senators are nomination-specific.

The most notable nomination to run afoul of the Senate on idiosyncratic grounds was President Eisenhower's selection of Lewis Strauss as secretary of commerce in 1958.[23] Strauss' career in public service dated back to relief efforts following World War I, when he was an aide to Herbert Hoover. Most recently he had been involved with atomic energy policy, serving as a member of the Atomic Energy Commission (AEC) during the Truman administration and chairing the AEC during Eisenhower's presidency. Sinclair Weeks, a member of Eisenhower's original cabinet, stepped down in 1958, and Strauss was given a recess appointment. On one hand, the president could expect the Senate to confirm Strauss' appointment as commerce secretary, as it had previous confirmed his appointments to the rank of rear admiral, as a member of the AEC, and as chairman of the AEC. On the other hand, Senate majority leader Lyndon Johnson had warned the president's aides earlier in the year that nominating Strauss for a second term as AEC chair would produce "a knockdown, drag-out fight" in the Senate.[24] Either this warning went unheeded, or Eisenhower believed that nomination to the commerce post would be unaffected by opposition to Strauss as AEC chair.

Johnson's warning proved prophetic. Opponents of the nomination charged that Strauss as AEC chairman had on more than one occasion refused to provide information requested by Congress, in particular by the Joint Atomic Energy Committee. Examples cited included details of a contract for the purchase of electrical power from the Mississippi Valley Generating Company (known as the Dixon–Yates contract) rather than from the Tennessee Valley Authority, the sharing of information on nuclear reactors aboard naval vessels with Great Britain, policy relating to procurement of uranium, and information relating to licensure of nuclear power plants. Lurking in the background was the memory of Strauss' role in the Eisenhower administration's decision in 1954 to revoke Dr. J. Robert Oppenheimer's security clearance.

Relating the story of a friendly wager between Strauss and Senator Albert Gore on whether a power plant would be constructed on schedule, Strauss' sympathetic biographer Richard Pfau writes: "Although the two men had disagreed [over AEC policies], they did so without rancor. In this case, Strauss showed he could continue to regard an opponent with respect; unfortunately, it was an exception rather than a rule for Strauss."[25] This passage captures the gist of the conflict over Strauss' nomination. Strauss and members of the Senate had not only disagreed over atomic energy policy but had done so disagreeably. This mutual contempt was reflected in the Senate hearings on his nomination as commerce secretary. Eisenhower biographers Chester Pach and Elmo Richardson note that "Strauss's combative, even truculent, manner won him no friends during his confirmation hearings."[26] In his memoirs, Strauss lists an "unfortunate trait of stubbornness in refusing to conciliate by conceding error where error had not occurred" as one factor contributing to the defeat of his nomination.[27] Yet the hearings before the Senate Interstate and Commerce Committee were marked by several instances when Strauss was forced to recant prior statements in the face of challenges by his opponents. Pfau provides an accurate summary of why the Senate rejected Strauss' nomination: "Even Strauss's supporters admitted that he had skirted the truth with his oblique explanations of his behavior. Had he been less of a perfectionist, had he been willing to admit that he, like all men, had made mistakes, he might have survived; instead, faced with a thorough review of the record of his career, he was determined to prove that he had been right about everything."[28]

Five months after the nomination was formally submitted and three months after committee hearings opened, the Senate rejected Strauss' nomination on a 49–46 vote. The roll call vote split along party lines, with 15 Democrats (mostly southerners) supporting Strauss and two Republicans opposing the nomination. The president subsequently nominated Frederick Mueller for promotion from undersecretary of commerce to secretary of commerce, an action the Senate approved without incident.[29]

The Effects of Senate Concerns

How do these types of objections affect confirmation votes in the Senate? The cases of Charles Warren, Carla Hills, Raymond Donovan, and Edwin Meese illustrate the effects of particular challenges in specific instances. They offer little in terms of generalizations. This task requires an analysis of the population of appointments to the president's cabinet.

In previous research we examined the question of how certain types of objections affect confirmation votes in the context of the political environment in which cabinet nominations since World War II were considered by the Senate.[30] Political factors included the president's popularity and the number of senators of his party. Allegations of conflict of interest, charges of illegal or unethical behavior, and whether the nominee was an expert in the prospective department's policy area were also noted. Regardless of the political environment at the time, 11 senators typically opposed a nomination when allegations of conflict of interest were present. This number more than doubled when the president's popularity was extremely low. Charges of inappropriate behavior resulted in 14 senators voting against confirmation. The nominee's status as policy expert in the field had no significant bearing on the outcome of the confirmation vote. Although no "job description" has been written detailing qualifications for being a department secretary, it is clear that many senators have a sense that conflicts of interest and illegal or unethical behavior "disqualify" an individual from service in the president's cabinet.

THE TOWER NOMINATION

The experiences of the two previous administrations suggested that one or two of George Bush's initial cabinet nominees would encounter opposition in the Senate. The Carter administration opened with the nominations of Attorney General Griffin Bell and Labor Secretary Ray Marshall being challenged. The nominations of Interior Secretary James Watt and Labor Secretary Raymond Donovan met stiff opposition at the onset of the Reagan administration. Thus, it was not a question of whether any of President Bush's nominations would stimulate a challenge but a question of which nomination or nominations would attract opposition.

Early speculation on challenges to cabinet nominations focused on Louis Sullivan, nominated for secretary of health and human services. Sullivan was president of Morehouse School of Medicine and had previously made statements expressing support for the pro-choice position on abortion. This was contrary to the pro-life positions of the president-elect and conservative Republicans. In an attempt to keep the spotlight off Sullivan and the abortion issue, his nomination was announced along with those of Manuel Lujan (interior), Samuel Skinner (transportation), William Reilly (energy), and Edwin Derwinski (veterans affairs). In addition, Sullivan publicly and privately assured members of the party's conservative wing that he supported abortion only in cases of rape, incest, or threat to the life of the mother. Either the Bush transition team's strategy was successful, or their fears were unwarranted, as Senator Jesse Helms—who argued that the nominee had changed his position on abortion to win the nomination—cast the lone vote against Sullivan's appointment.[31] Nine other Bush cabinet appointees were confirmed unanimously (see Table 14.3).

Table 14.3
Senate Action on Bush Cabinet Nominations, 1989

Department	Nominee	Vote	Date
State	James Baker III	99–0	January 25
Labor	Elizabeth Dole	99–0	January 25
Commerce	Robert Mosbacher	100–0	January 31
Transportation	Samuel Skinner	100–0	January 31
HUD	Jack Kemp	100–0	February 2
Interior	Manuel Lujan	100–0	February 2
Agriculture	Clayton Yeutter	100–0	February 8
Energy	James Watkins	99–0	March 1
HHS	Louis Sullivan	98–1	March 1
Veterans Affairs	Edwin Derwinski	94–0	March 2
Defense	John Tower	47–53	March 9
Defense	Richard Cheney	92–0	March 17

Note: Reagan appointees Nicholas Brady (treasury), Richard Thornburgh (justice), and Lauro Cavazos (education) continued in office under Bush and were not subject to Senate confirmation in 1989.

The selection of John Tower for secretary of defense was hardly a surprise. He had a long and distinguished career in the U.S. Senate, had been a political mentor and close adviser to George Bush for more than 20 years, and had openly craved the office for nearly a decade. In addition, Tower's experience on the Senate Armed Services Committee, which he chaired during his last four years on Capitol Hill, qualified him as an expert in the field of defense policy. For these reasons, Tower appeared at first blush a nearly perfect nominee for the Defense Department portfolio.

When elected to the Senate in a 1961 Texas special election, Tower was a political unknown whose victory occurred because of a combination of events. In the fall of 1960 the political science professor from Midwestern State University in Wichita Falls, Texas, had run as a Republican against incumbent Senate majority leader (and vice presidential candidate) Lyndon B. Johnson. Johnson sought both positions under a Texas law passed specifically to allow him to pursue his ambitions for national office without forfeiting his Senate seat. At the time of the election, Tower was a political novice running as the nominee of a political party that had not elected anyone to statewide office since the end of Reconstruction. Despite this handicap, Tower garnered a respectable 41 percent of the vote.[32]

When Johnson resigned his Senate seat to assume the office of vice president, the Texas special election law dictated the process for choosing Johnson's successor. Under that law, anyone can declare as a candidate for public office and appear on the ballot by paying a nominal fee. If no candidate receives a majority in the special election, the top two vote-getters, regardless of political party, compete in a runoff election. In 1961, 71 individuals ran for the office, with Tower being the only serious Republican candidate. Tower led the field in the April 4, 1961, election with 31 percent of the vote. The six serious Democratic candidates, led by the interim senator William Blakley, split the Democratic vote. Blakley was a conservative Democrat, believed by many in the party to be as conservative as Tower. As a result, many Democrats either voted for Tower, thinking him to be more vulnerable than Blakley in the future, or opted out of the election completely. In any case, Tower won a very close election by a margin of about 10,000 votes out of nearly 900,000 cast.[33]

Tower soon earned a reputation as a member of the "far right of the political spectrum" and with Senator Barry Goldwater of Arizona was a leader of Republican conservatism.[34] He became a popular speaker for conservative causes and received a perfect 100 rating on the conservative Americans for Constitutional Action (ACA) voting index for 1961–1962. Over his career, Tower never dropped below 72 and averaged 89 on the ACA index.

In many senses, Tower's election to the Senate made him the founder of the modern Republican Party in Texas. Paul C. Eggers, a longtime Republican activist and onetime Republican gubernatorial candidate, remembered that Tower "became the Apostle Paul of Republicans" in the Lone Star State.[35] One of his followers was Houston businessman George Bush. Bush was elected to the U.S. House in 1966 and made unsuccessful runs for the U.S. Senate in 1964 and

1970. Through it all, one of his most ardent supporters was Tower. Tower even took time away from the Goldwater presidential campaign in 1964 to assist Bush. While the two were never close personal friends, Tower aide Ken Towery described their relationship as "a mutual respect and a very close political bond."[36]

Tower became one of the Senate's leading experts on military and strategic defense policy, serving on the Armed Services Committee during his last 20 years on Capitol Hill. When Ronald Reagan was elected president in 1980, Tower openly coveted the office of defense secretary and was a serious candidate for appointment. Reagan ruled out Tower in part because he thought Tower's leadership in the Senate was needed.[37] Instead of becoming secretary of defense, Tower served as chair of the Armed Services Committee during Reagan's first term. His leadership and voting record during his career exhibited a strong support for the military and a consistent desire to increase military spending. This did not abate as President Reagan argued for a balanced federal budget. "I don't think we put balancing the budget as our number one priority," Tower said of this period. "We put national security as our number one priority."[38]

After leaving the Senate, Tower engaged in two notable activities. First, he was selected by President Reagan to head an investigation of the Iran-contra affair. His committee report was generally praised as balanced and appropriately critical of Reagan's lack of administrative control during the crisis.[39] Second, Tower became a consultant to many defense contractors, investigating on their behalf the political climate for defense spending in Congress. During the period between his retirement from the Senate and his nomination for secretary of defense, Tower earned $763,777 as a consultant.[40] These activities became issues during his confirmation hearings.

Bush selected Tower for secretary of defense for several reasons. First, Tower certainly qualified as an expert in the arena of defense policy. He had been a key actor in the formulation of policy concerning America's military forces from the Vietnam War to Reagan's Star Wars initiative. Second, Tower and Bush had a long history as political friends. In this way, Tower's selection was similar to those of Secretary of State James Baker, Treasury Secretary Nicholas Brady, Commerce Secretary Robert Mosbacher, HHS Secretary Louis Sullivan, and National Security Adviser Brent Scowcroft.[41] Third, the former senator was available and clearly wanted the job. Tower denied lobbying Bush for the position during the 1988 campaign but acknowledged that during the transition period he "arranged to meet with George Bush to discuss my ideas for managing the Pentagon."[42]

Tower's nomination soon encountered opposition due to several problems: questions concerning his positions on defense policy; charges of predispositional conflicts of interest; allegations of inappropriate personal behavior, including excessive drinking and indiscretions with women who were not his wife; and personal differences with members of the Senate.[43] Individually and as a group, these issues posed major obstacles to Tower's confirmation in a Democratically controlled Senate.

Critics began to investigate Tower's close associations with defense contractors soon after his nomination was announced. Senators voiced concerns that, with a record of supporting almost all defense contractor requests for funding of new weapons systems for almost a quarter of a century, Tower would be unable to act in the public interest to impose a reasonable cap on such spending in times when there was a perceived need to balance the federal budget without raising taxes. This was a particular concern as tensions with the Soviet Union began to ease. Senator Carl Levin commented:

Senator Tower, in prior years in support of increases for defense, in spite of large budget deficits, you said that we must spend whatever we need to on our defense, regardless of the domestic fiscal situation.

Today your testimony is somewhat different from that . . . I am wondering if you can explain your change in your thought processes on that. There has been a clear shift.[44]

Senator Robert Byrd used Tower's own words against him, quoting a 1988 speech at Georgetown University in which Tower said:

In its visceral reaction to budget shortfalls, Congress has required the defense budget to bear a disproportionate share of the burden. The determination of the United States in national security policy must be based unconditionally on a careful, deliberate assessment of the nature and magnitude of the threat posed by her adversaries, a task which Congress is singularly ill suited to perform.[45]

William G. Phillips, president of the National Council for Industrial Defense, remarked in his testimony before the Armed Services Committee that "John Tower has never seen a weapons system he did not like."[46]

These general policy concerns were magnified by the fact that Tower had served since his retirement from the Senate as a consultant for several major defense contractors, earning more than $.75 million during that time. His relationships had not been explicitly lobbying efforts, although at least one person testifying before the committee felt that had been a major part of his job.[47] Perhaps more importantly, some felt that the relationships gave the "appearance of using inside information for private gain."[48] Tower assured the committee that if a conflict of interest or the appearance of a conflict of interest arose, he would recuse himself from involvement in specific decision making while at defense, but some members of the committee felt that the long record of promotion of defense-related industries was a pattern that could not be broken by such an artificial distinction.

A more titillating set of charges arose during Armed Services Committee hearings on Tower's nomination. Paul Weyrich, a conservative lobbyist, suggested that Tower lacked the "moral character" necessary to be secretary of defense. There were two aspects to Weyrich's charges—that Tower had engaged in excessive drinking and in indiscreet activities with women who were not his wife.[49] Specifically, Weyrich said: "Over the course of many years, I have encountered the nominee in a condition—lack of sobriety—as well as with women to whom he was not married. . . . I encountered it frequently enough to the point where it made an impression."[50] While Weyrich made no specific charges and offered no corroborating evidence, he had raised a new set of issues that the committee felt it needed to investigate.

The two charges raised by Weyrich soon became focal points in the assessment of Tower's fitness for the defense post. Although the file produced by the FBI [Federal Bureau of Investigation] while investigating these charges remains private, some evidence was reported publicly. Perhaps the most damning charge came from Larry Combest, a Republican member of the House of Representatives and a former Tower aide, who alleged that Tower and a group of friends frequently drank an entire bottle of scotch in a single evening. Tower himself admitted that he had been a "pretty good scotch drinker" in the 1970s but denied having a drinking problem and characterized himself as "a man of some discipline."[51] Some of the nominee's supporters admitted that Tower had a drinking problem during the 1970s, but they argued that his second wife had effectively ended his heavy drinking.[52] Others, however, suggested that Tower's drinking problems had continued into more recent times. In announcing his opposition to Tower's appointment, Senator Ernest Hollings said that the record showed that Tower's abuse of alcohol was recent, credible, and overwhelming: "There are names. There are facts. There are absolute statements. The words, 'crocked,' 'bombed,' 'excessive drinking,' 'stoned,' 'comatose.' . . . There's too much of that."[53] To allay fears about his consumption of alcohol, Tower pledged to abstain from drinking if confirmed as defense secretary, but the pledge seemed to have no impact on wavering senators.[54]

Weyrich's charges that Tower had engaged in indiscreet relations with women were less well defined and drew attention to another potential problem: the way in which Tower would treat women in the workplace. Senator Sam Nunn, the chair of the Armed Services Committee, questioned Tower on this point. The nominee responded that he advocated "zero tolerance for discrimination against women, for sexual harassment of women."[55] But Nunn was unpersuaded and in his expression of opposition to Tower's nomination said that there were examples of indiscretion "which call into question his judgment and his ability to set an appropriate example for the men and women in uniform."[56]

Tower encountered some practical political problems as well. While he had one qualification that is normally thought to assure confirmation—being a long-term member of the Senate "club"—he was never able to capitalize on this advantage. Such failure might have been because Tower was "cool and aloof" from his colleagues during his time in the Senate and never a popular colleague.[57] In a Senate controlled by the opposite party and in a committee chaired by an effective leader like Sam Nunn, Tower's lack of popularity among his former colleagues was particularly a problem. Nunn and Tower were separated by character and values. Helen Dewer of the *Washington Post* described Nunn as being "as private and conventional in his lifestyle as Tower is flamboyant."[58] Moreover, Tower had developed over the years "a scrappy partisan style" that bruised a lot of sensitivities in the Senate. He was also a partisan for the Pentagon, sometimes at odds with the more skeptical Nunn.[59] The political problem was compounded, some of Nunn's critics charged, by the fact that Nunn was personally ambitious, wanting to send a message to President Bush that the Congress did not fear his leadership and to "seize the reins of defense policy."[60]

The problems associated with Tower's nomination resulted in negative votes within the Armed Services Committee and the full Senate. The vote within the committee was strictly along political party lines. On March 9, 1989, the Senate voted 53–47 to reject Tower's nomination as secretary of defense.[61] Only four senators—Democrats Howell Heflin, Christopher Dodd, and Lloyd Bentsen and Republican Nancy Kassebaum—broke party ranks in the final confirmation vote.

Why did the nomination fail? Tower offered the explanation that Senator Nunn had led a crusade against him and that Paul Weyrich had a personal vendetta against him. Nunn wanted "to cling to his apolitical image while operating in a ruthless and purely partisan manner," Tower wrote in his memoirs.[62] The confirmation debate degenerated into partisan squabbling marked by unfairness and hypocrisy, according to Tower:

Why? I can only theorize: anger and frustration at going from a twenty-point lead in the polls in July 1988 to defeat four months later in the presidential elections; fear that they were being permanently locked out of the White House; panic over the way the public lashed out at the attempt to raise congressional salaries; consternation that George Bush had grabbed the high ground on the ethics issue; paranoia about the success of negative campaigning. There is no simple, neat answer. The explanation is obviously a composite of many different factors.[63]

From Tower's perspective, Weyrich was a representative of the New Right who thought both Tower and Bush too accommodating to liberals. Not only did Weyrich oppose Tower's pro-choice position on abortion, but Tower believed he "had vowed to bring down a Bush cabinet designee." Weyrich was, Tower wrote, "the designated hit and run driver" for the New Right.[64]

Tower was also a victim of a new style of journalism currently practiced in the nation's capital. Political scientist Larry Sabato contends that there exists in Washington an atmosphere of a "feeding frenzy" akin to attacks on wounded prey in the animal world. He defines a feeding frenzy as "the press coverage attending any political event or circumstance where the critical mass of journalists leap to cover the same embarrassing or scandalous subject and pursue it intensely, often excessively, and sometimes uncontrollably."[65] Tower's case is one of many Sabato uses to illustrate journalism that emphasizes gossip over governance, titillation over scrutiny. Rather than focusing on Tower's qualifications for the post of secretary of defense, the news media focused on the charges brought by Weyrich and others, reporting the allegations without verifying their accuracy. According to Sabato,

Substance was boring; scandal was hot. . . . Alcohol use and abuse is always a legitimate concern about someone in the military chain of command; indiscreet behavior can be dangerously compromising in any top official; and womanizing is highly inappropriate for a potential Defense Department chief who serves as a role model for the men and women of the armed forces. The real threshold that much of the printed and broadcast information about John Tower failed to pass was not relevancy but the most important standard of all: proof.[66]

Political writers Rowland Evans and Robert Novak suggest that another problem for the nomination was that while President Bush showed admirable loyalty to Tower during the confirmation battle, he fared less well in the presidential effectiveness arena. Bush, Evans and Novak argue, waited too long after the election to nominate Tower and then exhibited a surprising lack of presidential influence in obtaining his confirmation: "Bush did not have a note-taker present when he made his lobbying calls. But if he twisted any arms, nobody felt the pain."[67]

Whatever the cause of the failure of the Tower nomination, it had obvious consequences for the Bush presidency. First, the delay in installing a secretary of defense resulted in a significant delay in putting in place a Defense Department management team. Many weeks passed before the various appointed positions in the department were filled. Furthermore, the rejection of the Tower nomination sent a clear message that the Democratic Congress had no fear of Bush and was an obvious early setback for the president in public relations as well. Michael Duffy and Dan Goodgame made note of this difficulty, pointing out that Bush had a very short "honeymoon" during his presidency: "Only seven weeks into his term, Bush felt obliged to call a press conference to deny that his administration suffered from 'drift' or 'malaise.'"[68] While it would be overstating the case to say that this one congressional defeat destined the Bush administration to failure, the rejection of Tower was a serious blow early in the president's term.[69]

TOWER'S DEFEAT IN PERSPECTIVE

How does the rejection of John Tower's nomination as secretary of defense compare with other troubled nominations? Were the allegations that led to the nomination's defeat unusual, or did they reflect common presidential–senatorial disagreement over cabinet appointments? Cabinet nominations are typically challenged on the grounds of public policies advocated by the administration or nominee, conflicts of interest between the nominee's finances or occupation and the responsibilities of the office, the nominee's competence in the policy area in question, and the nominee's personal behavior. The Tower nomination encountered opposition based on three of these factors.

The record budget deficits of the Reagan administration were a concern on Capitol Hill as the Bush administration opened. Since the defense buildup of the 1980s was one factor in the growth of the deficit, it is not surprising that senators would question a nominee for secretary of defense whose support for expanding the Pentagon budget was unwavering. It is unlikely, however, that Tower's career-long support of military spending alone would have killed his nomination.

Differences over environmental policy had resulted in opposition to various nominations during the Reagan years, but none of those met defeat. Few contemporary issues generate the intense debate that accompanies abortion, but the minicontroversy surrounding Sullivan's position on abortion yielded just one dissenting vote. Richard Cheney, whose congressional voting record was every bit as conservative as Tower's, was confirmed as secretary of defense after Tower's nomination was rejected. If policy differences were the only consideration, Tower would almost certainly been confirmed as secretary of defense.

An indisputable connection between Tower and other embattled nominees was the allegation of a conflict of interest. Charges of predispositional conflicts of interest doomed Charles Warren's nomination in 1925, jeopardized several others in recent years, and were a serious threat to Tower's nomination from the beginning. Anxiety over the predisposed leanings of nominees is not totally independent of policy concerns, but the assumption of many senators is that a nominee with a tight connection with an affected industry will be less open to frank discussions over the issues or will not aggressively enforce policy as secretary. Thus, Senator Kassebaum and many Democrats opposed Tower's nomination in 1989, just as Senator Walsh and others opposed Warren's nomination in 1925.

The allegations of inappropriate personal behavior that become the focus of Tower's nomination struggle were unique in the annals of cabinet confirmation battles. Previous challenges to nominations on behavioral grounds centered on charges of illegal activities (Raymond Donovan's connections to labor union corruption) or of ethical lapses (Edwin Meese's personal financial dealings). The allegations of alcohol abuse and womanizing directed against Tower were a novelty. In past eras, when public officials' private lives were truly private, Tower's alleged indiscretions would never have come to light. But in the current era of public officials' being held to high moral and ethical standards, the nominee's personal behavior is deemed an acceptable subject for consideration in confirmation deliberations.[70] The extent to which the allegations were detailed in the FBI background checks given to the president-elect is unknown, but the uniqueness of the situation makes it reasonable to speculate that Bush did not anticipate the Senate's reaction to the charges.

The Tower nomination was also like the Strauss nomination in one other respect. The opposition to both Tower and Strauss was fueled, at least in part, by personal feelings of ill will between the nominee and some senators. Both nominees had histories of conflict with members of the Senate. Neither seemed to worry about stepping on sensitive toes. That two of the three failed cabinet nominations of the twentieth century share this characteristic is unlikely a coincidence.

The Tower case was similar to the other defeated cabinet nominations in one final respect: the subsequent nominee for the position was quickly confirmed by the Senate. After the rejection of Charles Warren's nomination, President Coolidge selected a nominee without potential conflicts of interest. President Eisenhower's approach in replacing Lewis Strauss was to choose someone who had not clashed with Congress. Both nominations were quickly confirmed by the

Senate without controversy. In the wake of the rejection of Tower's nomination, President Bush looked to Capitol Hill for his secretary of defense. His choice was Representative Richard Cheney. Although not known as an expert in defense and military policy, the five-term congressman nevertheless had impressive credentials. After becoming White House chief of staff in the Ford administration at the age of 34, Cheney had risen to the post of minority whip in the House, and, most importantly, was free of any hint of scandal or conflict of interest. His nomination was confirmed unanimously one week after being announced.[71]

What lessons can a president learn from the Tower nomination? The trite answer would be to select a cabinet nominee whose policy positions match those of the Senate majority, without potential conflicts of interest, who lives a virtuous life, and who has not offended members of the Senate. This superficial answer is not too wide of the mark, however. Tower's nomination as secretary of defense probably did not fail because of any single factor but because of the combination of factors. The more vulnerabilities that a nominee has, the higher the number of dissenting votes. In one respect, this is simple addition. Senator Nunn was bothered by Tower's alleged treatment of women, Senator Hollings found the charge of alcohol abuse compelling, and Senator Kassebaum considered Tower's links with defense contractors inappropriate for a secretary of defense. The result: three votes against confirmation.

At a higher level, the combination of charges against Tower interacted to produce a doomed nomination. Interactions are well known to chemists. Glycerin, nitric acid, and sulfuric acid are relatively harmless individually but interact to produce the deadly explosive nitroglycerin. Individually, policy differences, conflicts of interest, questionable personal behavior, and a rancorous relationship with senators are unlikely to doom a cabinet nomination. The combination, however, can prove fatal. The Senate did not reject the nomination of John Tower as secretary of defense because of any one factor but because of the combination. That George Bush learned from the experience was demonstrated by his subsequent nomination of Cheney for secretary of defense. Future presidents would be well advised to heed the lesson as well.

The Senate's rejection of Tower's nomination was a harbinger of executive–legislative relations during the Bush presidency. From the outset, the Democratically controlled Congress was not receptive to George Bush's leadership. Bush's election in 1988 reflected the preferences of an electorate favoring the status quo. In this environment, Gerald Pomper noted, "issue differences were far less significant than simple approval of the past record of Ronald Reagan."[72] As a consequence, the new president had little basis for claiming a mandate from the voters. "Bush did not have a mandate" from the voters, Charles O. Jones observed; "lacking a marriage, there was no honeymoon" with Congress.[73]

Instead of the stunning first-year success of his predecessor, Bush prevailed on only 63 percent of the votes in Congress on which he took a position—the lowest first-year figure for any elected president in the post–World War II era.[74] This is often attributed to the centralization of legislative authority in the hands of Chief of Staff John Sununu and the exclusion of Frederick McClure, assistant for legislative liaison, from the White House inner circle, much of which was represented in the struggle over Tower's nomination.[75] The White House failed to recognize the dangers posed by the allegations of alcohol abuse and sexual misconduct or the need to work cooperatively with the congressional leadership. The result was a doomed nomination. It was only the first of many losing battles for the Bush White House in its relationship with Congress.

NOTES

1. James D. King and James W. Riddlesperger Jr., "Senate Confirmation of Appointments to the Cabinet and Executive Office of the Senate," *Social Science Journal* 28, no. 2 (1991): 189–202; James D. King and James W. Riddlesperger Jr., "Senate Confirmation of Cabinet Nominations: Institutional Politics and Nominee Qualifications," *Social Science Journal* 33, no. 3 (1996): 273–85.

2. Joseph P. Harris, *The Advice and Consent of the Senate: A Study of the Confirmation of Appointments by the United States Senate* (Berkeley: University of California Press, 1953), p. 379.

3. *Jacobellis v. Ohio*, 378 U.S. 184, concurring opinion.

4. The following discussion is based upon G. Calvin Mackenzie, *The Politics of Presidential Appointments* (New York: Free Press, 1981), Chapters 5–7; and King and Riddlesperger, "Senate Confirmation of Appointments to the Cabinet and Executive Office of the Senate," pp. 195–98.

5. Harris, *Advice and Consent of the Senate*, pp. 263–64.

6. The reasons for opposing particular cabinet nominations are drawn from various sources, including public record such as the *Congressional Record* and committee hearings on nominations; contemporary news reports of Senate deliberations such as those by the *New York Times* and *Congressional Quarterly*; secondary sources such as Harris, *Advice and Consent of the Senate*, and Mackenzie, *Politics of Presidential Appointments*; and histories of specific presidents and administrations. See King and Riddlesperger, "Senate Confirmation of Appointments to the Cabinet and Executive Office of the President," pp. 195–98.

7. U.S. Congress, Senate, Committee on Labor and Public Welfare, *Hearing on Dr. F. Ray Marshall to Be Secretary of Labor*, 95th Cong., 1st sess., *Congressional Record* 123 (1977): 2266–302.

8. John Robert Greene, *The Presidency of Gerald R. Ford* (Lawrence: University Press of Kansas, 1995), pp. 95–98.

9. Lou Cannon, *President Reagan: The Role of a Lifetime* (New York: Simon and Schuster, 1991), pp. 531–34; Bob Schieffer and Gary Paul Gates, *The Acting President* (New York: E.P. Dutton, 1989), pp. 151–54. U.S. Congress, Senate, Committee on Energy and Natural Resources, *Hearings on the Nomination of William P. Clark to Be Secretary of the Interior*, 98th Cong., 1st sess., *Congressional Record* 129 (1983): S16769–79, S16783–808; U.S. Congress, Senate, Committee on Energy and Natural Resources, *Hearings on the Nomination of Donald Paul Hodel to Be Secretary of Energy; and Martha O. Hesse to Be Assistant Secretary of Energy for Management and Administration*, 97th Cong., 2nd sess., *Congressional Record* 128 (1982): 29317–35.

10. During Senate hearings on his confirmation, Wilson remarked that he "thought what was good for the country was good for General Motors and vice versa." A misquote of Wilson's statement, that "what's good for General Motors is good for the country,"

has become part of political folklore. See Carl M. Brauer, *Presidential Transitions: Eisenhower through Reagan* (New York: Oxford University Press, 1986), pp. 29–30; Mackenzie, *Politics of Presidential Appointments*, p. 100.

11. Mackenzie, *Politics of Presidential Appointments*, pp. 103–105.

12. U.S. Congress, Senate, Committee on Agriculture and Forestry, *Hearings*, 92nd Cong., 1st sess., 1971, p. 57.

13. King and Riddlesperger, "Senate Confirmation of Cabinet Nominations," p. 275. Nominations to the Department of the Interior tend to generate significant opposition based on predispositional conflicts of interest more often than nominations to other departments. This is due to the tension between environmentalists and natural resources developers. Interior Secretaries Walter Hickel (Nixon), Stanley Hathaway (Ford), and James Watt (Reagan) were challenged as having pro-development leanings but were ultimately confirmed with significant numbers of dissenting votes. See King and Riddlesperger, "Senate Confirmation of Appointments to the Cabinet and Executive Office of the President," pp. 194–95.

14. Warren's nomination is discussed in detail by Harris, *Advice and Consent of the Senate*, pp. 119–24; and Richard Fenno, *The President's Cabinet* (New York: Vintage Books, 1959), pp. 54–55.

15. Warren's opponents also charged that he lacked the legal qualifications for the office. The president's supporters did little initially to refute this allegation but later presented testimonials from federal and state judges and past and present officers of the Michigan State Bar Association on Warren's qualifications. Little doubt remained concerning the nominee's competence.

16. Quoted in Harris, *Advice and Consent of the Senate*, p. 120.

17. Senator Reed switched his vote from yea to nay to enable him to move for reconsideration. Thus, the official vote count was 41–39 against the nomination.

18. Quoted in Mackenzie, *Politics of Presidential Appointments*, p. 116.

19. U.S. Congress, Senate, Committee on Labor and Human Resources, *Hearings on Raymond J. Donovan to Be Secretary of Labor*, 97th Cong., 1st sess., *Congressional Record* 127 (1981): 1439–66; Schieffer and Gates, *Acting President*, pp. 28, 150.

20. U.S. Congress, Senate, Committee on the Judiciary, *Hearings on the Nomination of Richard G. Kleindienst to Be Attorney General*, 92nd Cong., 2nd sess., *Congressional Record* 118 (1972): 19331–40, 19442–53, 19571–601, 19714–35, 19794–806, 20237–67.

21. A number of senators used the Meese nomination to extract administration support on farm credit legislation, while others used the confirmation debate as a forum for advancing general congressional interests in the context of executive–legislative relations. See Schieffer and Gates, *Acting President*, pp. 200–204; Cannon, *Role of a Lifetime*, pp. 795–802; Hedrick Smith, *The Power Game: How Washington Works* (New York: Random House, 1988), pp. 368–69.

22. "Cabinet Confirmations," *Congressional Quarterly Weekly Report*, February 3, 1973, pp. 212.

23. On the failure of the Strauss nomination, see Herbert S. Parmet, *Eisenhower and the American Crusades* (New York: Macmillan, 1972), pp. 542–44; Richard Pfau, *No Sacrifice Too Great: The Life of Lewis L. Strauss* (Charlottesville: University of Virginia Press, 1984), Chapter 13; Dwight D. Eisenhower, *Waging Peace* (Garden City, NY: Doubleday, 1965), pp. 392–96; Lewis L. Strauss, *Men and Decisions* (Garden City, NY: Doubleday, 1962), Chapter 18.

24. Parmet, *Eisenhower and the American Crusade*, p. 543.

25. Pfau, *No Sacrifice Too Great*, p. 202.

26. Chester J. Pach Jr. and Elmo Richardson, *The Presidency of Dwight D. Eisenhower*, rev. ed. (Lawrence: University Press of Kansas, 1991), p. 213.

27. Strauss, *Men and Decisions*, p. 403.

28. Pfau, *No Sacrifice Too Great*, p. 241.

29. Mueller's nomination as undersecretary of commerce was approved by the Senate just two weeks before the Strauss nomination vote.

30. King and Riddlesperger, "Senate Confirmation of Cabinet Nominations," pp. 277–81.

31. David Hoffman and Spencer Rich, "Sullivan Allays Concerns of 2 Abortion Opponents," *Washington Post*, December 22, 1988, p. A10; U.S. Senate, Committee on Finance, *Hearings on the Nomination of Louis W. Sullivan*, 101st Cong., 1st sess., 1989, p. 89; "Sullivan Confirmed As HHS Secretary," *Congressional Quarterly Almanac 1989* (Washington, DC: Congressional Quarterly, 1990), p. 175.

32. John R. Knaggs, *Two Party Texas: The John Tower Era, 1961-1984* (Austin, TX: Eakin Press, 1986), pp. 3–7.

33. Ibid., p. 15. The *New York Times* observed that "Mr. Tower and Senator Blakley are ultra conservatives of almost identical views. Thus, the only real election issue was the question of party affiliation." See Gladwin Hill, "Tower Is Elected Senator in Texas," *New York Times*, May 29, 1961, p. 1.

34. *Current Biography, 1962*, p. 426.

35. Andrew Rosenthal, "Politics, Not Affection, Is the Bond," *New York Times*, February 9, 1989, p. B10.

36. Quoted in Rosenthal, "Politics, Not Affection."

37. Senate politics played a major role in Reagan's decision against nominating Tower. If Tower left the Senate, Barry Goldwater would have become chair of the Armed Services Committee. In turn, liberal Republican Charles Mathias would assume the chairmanship of the Intelligence Committee. The former was perfectly acceptable to the new president but not the latter. See Schieffer and Gates, *Acting President*, p. 25; Alan Ehrenhalt, ed., *Politics in America: Members of Congress in Washington and at Home, 1982* (Washington, DC: Congressional Quarterly Press, 1981), p. 1147.

38. Ehrenhalt, *Politics in America*, p. 1147.

39. John G. Tower, *Consequences: A Personal and Political Memoir* (Boston: Little, Brown, 1991), pp. 286–87.

40. "Tower Nomination Spurned by Senate," *Congressional Quarterly Almanac, 1989* (Washington, DC: Congressional Quarterly, 1990), p. 404.

41. Larry Berman and Bruce W. Jentleson, "Bush and the Post–Cold War World: New Challenges for American Leadership," in Colin Campbell, S. J. Rockman, and Bert A. Rockman, eds., *The Bush Presidency: First Appraisals* (Chatham, NJ: Chatham House, 1991), p. 99; David Mervin, *George Bush and the Guardianship Presidency* (New York: St. Martin's Press, 1996), pp. 62–63.

42. Tower, *Consequences*, pp. 25–26.

43. There was also consideration of Tower's use of Senate campaign contributions. Particularly in question was an alleged illegal $1,000 corporate campaign contribution made to Tower in 1984. The charges were investigated but never became an important issue in Tower's confirmation. See David Johnston, "Finance and Behavior Questions Prolong F.B.I. Background Check," *New York Times*, February 9, 1989.

44. U.S. Congress, Senate, Committee on Armed Services, *Hearings on the Nomination of John G. Tower to Be Secretary of Defense*, 101st Cong., 1st sess., 1989, pp. 6–

7, 23, 52, 56 [hereafter referred to as *Hearings*].

45. Ibid., p. 66.

46. Ibid., p. 222.

47. Statement of William E. Jackson Jr., *Hearings*, pp. 215–16.

48. R. Jeffrey Smith, "How Valid Is Nunn's Ethical Line in the Dust?" *Washington Post*, March 3, 1989, p. A17.

49. Andrew Rosenthal, "Tower's Personal Life Is Scrutinized," *New York Times*, February 1, 1989, p. A14.

50. *Hearings*, p. 251.

51. Bob Woodward, "Nunn Shaken by Account of Ex-Tower Aide," *Washington Post*, February 28, 1989, p. A12; Tower, *Consequences*, p. 126.

52. Helen Dewar and Jim McGee, "Defense of Tower Intensifies," *Washington Post*, February 11, 1989, p. A4.

53. "Tower Nomination Spurned by Senate," *Congressional Quarterly Almanac, 1989*, p. 409.

54. Helen Dewar, "Tower's Pledge Fails to Influence Senators," *Washington Post*, February 28, 1989, p A1.

55. *Hearings*, p. 293.

56. Sam Nunn, "Sen. Nunn Replies: We Are Not Being Unfair," *Washington Post*, March 3, 1989.

57. Knaggs, *Two Party Texas*, p. 2.

58. Helen Dewar, "Nunn, a Fellow Southerner, Is Crucial to Tower's Chances," *Washington Post*, February 21, 1989, p. A1.

59. Dewar, "Nunn," p. A1.

60. "Tower Nomination Spurned by Senate," *Congressional Quarterly Almanac, 1989*, p. 405.

61. Gillian Peele erroneously reports that Bush was "forced to withdraw the Tower nomination." The nomination was rejected. Peele, "The Constrained Presidency of George Bush," *Current History* (April 1992): 153.

62. Tower, *Consequences*, p. 302.

63. Ibid., p. 323.

64. Ibid., p. 119.

65. Larry Sabato, *Feeding Frenzy: How Attack Journalism has Transformed American Politics* (New York: Free Press, 1991), p. 6.

66. Ibid., pp. 181–82.

67. Rowland Evans and Robert Novak, "The Tower Scorecard," *Washington Post*, March 15, 1989, p. A23.

68. Michael Duffy and Dan Goodgame, *Marching in Place: The Status Quo Presidency of George Bush* (New York: Simon and Schuster, 1992), pp. 56–57.

69. By some accounts, another consequence of the Tower nomination defeat was the attack on Speaker of the House Jim Wright, who resigned his office under a similar cloud to that which hovered over Tower. Wright thought that Tower's problems in confirmation were directly related to his own and that the Republicans were after him as retribution for Tower's defeat. "You mean [they want] an eye for an eye?" the speaker asked one of his Republican colleagues. "It's an even more perfect symmetry," was the reply. "They want a Texan for a Texan." It is important to note, however, that the Ethics Committee investigation that precipitated Wright's resignation began before Bush nominated Tower for secretary of defense. See Jim Wright, *Balance of Power: Presidents and Congress from the Era of McCarthy to the Age of Gringrich* (Atlanta: Turner, 1996), pp. 484–85.

70. Similar questions of personal behavior were later raised when President Bush nominated Clarence Thomas for associate justice of the U.S. Supreme Court.

71. Although he praised Cheney personally, the speed with which the Senate acted on Cheney's nomination left Tower bitter:

What standards were applied to his nomination? Rushed through the Senate to confirmation in less than a week, the FBI barely had enough time for even the most cursory of background checks. A thorough, thoughtful examination by the Senate of the nominee's views and qualifications was impossible. Sam Nunn and the rest of the Democratic majority were so eager to get out the bind they had created for themselves that all the fine sentiments about standards and process were tossed aside and forgotten. (Tower, *Consequences*, p. 364)

72. Gerald M. Pomper, "The Presidential Election," in Gerald M. Pomper, ed., *The Election of 1988: Reports and Interpretations* (Chatham, NJ: Chatham House, 1989), p. 139.

73. Charles O. Jones, *Separate but Equal Branches: Congress and the Presidency* (Chatham, NJ: Chatham House, 1995), p. 231; see also Barbara Sinclair, "Governing Unheroically (and Sometimes Unappetizingly): Bush and the 101st Congress," in Colin Campbell, S.J. Rockman, and Bert A. Rockman, eds., *The Bush Presidency: First Appraisals* (Chatham, NJ: Chatham House, 1991), pp. 156–59.

74. Lyn Ragsdale, *Vital Statistics on the Presidency: Washington to Clinton* (Washington, DC: CQ Press, 1996), pp. 383–85.

75. Mervin, *George Bush and the Guardianship Presidency*, pp. 76–77, 90–91. On Sununu's domination of the Bush White House, see: James P. Pfiffner, "The President's Chief of Staff: Lessons Learned," *Presidential Studies Quarterly* 23 (1993): 9.

15

The Bush Administration's Defense Policy: Transcending the Cold War

Earl C. Ravenal

CRITIQUES OF THE BUSH FOREIGN AND DEFENSE POLICY

The "standard" notion, looking retrospectively at the foreign and military policies pursued in the Bush administration, is that President Bush, his secretary of state James Baker, his secretary of defense Dick Cheney, and, to some extent, his chairman of the Joint Chiefs of Staff General Colin Powell, failed to "adjust" to the end of the Cold War and simply perpetuated, mindlessly, the same old Cold War defense programs and force structures. In this view, the Bush administration failed to adjust, specifically, to the demise of the Soviet Union, the vertical decline of Russian military power and international political influence, the diffuse array of lesser threats, the obsolescence of "containment," and the opportunity to distribute a "peace dividend" from the U.S. defense budget. Such critics looked, for evidence, mostly to the apparent hovering of the defense budget, in current dollars, near "Cold War levels."

Other kinds of criticism would center on the alleged mindlessness of the Bush foreign and defense policies, the lack of coherence, the absence of a unifying "theme," the eschewing of any "vision" of where the United States or the world should be going. Critics such as, for example, Fouad Ajami, reviewing James A. Baker's *The Politics of Diplomacy*,[1] would emphasize and deride the security team of 1989–1993 for its shallow manipulation, its smattering of luck masked in the pretense of skill and energy, its substitution of blunt bullying for any intellectual conceptualization of the diplomatic process—and a few other things.

But, using a rather different "model" of the security process and fixing on operational criteria for real achievement and significant action, I find that very little of the standard superficial critique is true. Yes, the Bush administration continued to insist on American primacy in international politics, and it actually broadened a kind of "containment" to extend to all regions of the world and all types of adversaries—something I have remarked elsewhere.[2] But, on the levels of both foreign policy and national strategy (and, for that matter, the further levels that constitute a model of the defense policy process: military missions, forces-weapons-operational doctrines, and budgetary resources), the Bush administration instituted real and far-reaching changes.

In order to understand policy change—even to discern policy change—you have to transcend diplomatic chit-chat and resort to a comprehensive and accurate model of the foreign policy process. The Bush administration's "New World Order" was not a mere phrase but a prescription for a definable type of international system as the object of U.S. foreign policy, with tangible requisites for national strategy and defense programs. The Bush worldview and national strategy were not beyond fault—and ultimately I identify the strains and contradictions and instabilities and thus have to define it as transient and transitional and pose an alternative national choice. But it was real and serious and different, particularly in that it pointed to, though it failed to attain, a different structure of the international system, and it stipulated—though in the long run the nation could not sustain—a national strategy and defense program appropriate to America's role in a New World Order.

In the terminology and typology of international systems that I employ— (1) the unitary imperium of a dominant state; (2) a truly systemic representation of "collective security"; (3) the bipolar confrontation of blocs; (4) a true multipolar balance of power; (5) the fragmented world that I call "general unalignment," characterized by the regionalization of power—the Bush administration seriously aimed at creating a regime of collective security. But this regime was to be a peculiarly American variant: an American-dominated and American-underpinned collective security, with the United Nations Security Council more as a cover for essentially unilateral American action or for American-led ad hoc and pragmatic coalitions (as in Desert Storm), rather than a true and autonomous source of security initiatives.[3]

In opting for this large-scale choice of collective security, the Bush administration was responding to the menu of international systems that it confronted when it came to office, and soon thereafter, in the year 1989: a choice—of the systems available, among the five differentiable "ideal types"—between collective security and general unalignment. Spokespersons of the Bush administration would have put it—and did often put it—in terms of a choice between the kind of "engagement" that was available to the United States and a retreat into "isolationism" and the accommodation of disorder in salient and not-so-salient areas of the world and the acquiescence to domineering, aggressive, and hostile nations and governments in their regions. The rhetoric may have been tendentious, but the choice of worlds was real.

Actually, the world was beginning to emerge out of a brief, though significant, structure that approximated a multipolar balance of power—a manageable, though mutually wary, consortium of great powers, dealing with each other directly in the currency of alignment and forcible opposition. The semblance of such a multipolar balance of power had been urged and partially installed through the truly radical and inventive—though widely misapprehended and misattributed—diplomacy of President Nixon and his security adviser and then-secretary of state Henry Kissinger.[4] Contrary to virtually all popular formulations, the world did not move "from bipolarity to multipolarity" in, say, 1989, with the fall of the Berlin Wall, or 1991, with the demise of the Soviet Union. It had been moved from its acknowledged structure of bipolar confrontation to a version of multipolar balance of power in about 1970 to 1973, through the deliberately structural diplomacy of Nixon and Kissinger, in such episodes as the courting of China and the partial reception of the Soviet leader Brezhnev's overtures to detente in 1972 and 1973, and the chilly treatment of the European Community exemplified in the 1972 "Year of Europe" and the threat to estrange the United States from the protection of NATO [North Atlantic Treaty Organization]. It was a further impending transformation of the international system that challenged the Bush administration, at the most "abstract" level of statecraft: the unruly and unconstructive behavior of the key multipolar balance-of-power players, the incipient rise of four or five new aspiring regional hegemons, and the loosening or fracturing of some key alliances and groupings. This fragmentation caused or allowed a plethora of diffuse and functionally different "threats" to emerge, both directly to regional order and indirectly to the sense of stability—if not really to the stability itself—of the United States. The response of the Bush administration—and it was a deliberate choice between the available large-scale structural alternatives of collective security and general unalignment—was the former, the New World Order.

The national strategy that could be virtually deduced from this choice of objective international systems would be called the "Base Force Concept." This defense policy, in its ramifications of military missions and force structures and budgets, is introduced in the next section of this paper.

THE 1992 DEFENSE PROGRAM

The real or operational point of departure for an examination of the Bush administration's political-military stance toward the world is its defense program for fiscal year [FY] 1992.[5] This defense program, developed in the mid-Bush administration, emerged in the context of Desert Storm. In a sense, the Persian Gulf War—the emphasis on the geographical region, the way America fought the war, the commitment of the portion of America's active force structure—was a representation of the shift in America's national strategy that had already been accomplished by the Bush national security organizations.

In this document, the Bush administration planned a significant reduction of general-purpose forces, measured by the decrease from 21 land divisions at the start of 1990 to 17 land divisions at the end of 1992 (and, beyond that, to 15 land divisions in 1995 if the administration were to survive into a second term). More important, in terms of the Bush administration's defense purposes, was a restructuring of the regional attributions of forces. This feature, which is not on the explicit surface, must be inferred from various indications in the secretary of defense's 1992 "posture statement." The regional attribution of forces, which incorporates the simultaneity of planned response to a number of separate geographical contingencies, is the most revealing expression of a national strategy, in the general-purpose force dimension.

In my analysis, ground forces (and, along with them, roughly proportional segments of tactical air and surface naval forces) primarily allocated to a European contingency decrease from the FY 1990 program's $11\frac{2}{3}$ divisions to the FY 1992 program's $7\frac{1}{3}$ divisions. Correspondingly, ground forces dedicated to an "other regional" (other than Europe or East Asia) contingency increase from the $5\frac{2}{3}$ divisions of FY 1990 to the $6\frac{2}{3}$ divisions of FY 1992. (Ground forces identified for East Asia decrease moderately from $3\frac{2}{3}$ to 3 divisions).

This reflects the arrival of the post–Cold War world, or the implementation of Bush's New World Order. This is more than a mere slogan. It acquired a tangible, operational concomitant in our force structure and defense budget. In effect (without quite putting it in such terms), Bush moved from Reagan's "one and one-half (ample) wars"—which followed Carter's "one and one-half (NATO-weighted) wars" and, before that, Nixon's "one and one-half wars," which radically shifted from Johnson's and Kennedy's "two and one-half wars"—to a new force-sizing concept that could be called "two times three-quarter wars," since the possible second war (such as that in the Persian Gulf) might be as large as the (now scaled-down) European War.

That was still a formidable defense establishment. The New World Order was not self-enforcing. It depended on American power. To address the possible simultaneity of conflicts, the United States had to have fairly large and redundant forces. To confront a variety of possible adversaries, it needed a range of modern, capable forces, in turn requiring advanced technology and considerable research and development. To cope with initial defense (not just counterattack) in other regions, it had to have ready either deployed or deployable units and forward logistical bases and prepositioned equipment on land and sea; and for this, it needed allies that would have to be favored in various military, diplomatic, and economic ways.

In other words, collective security does not mean net burden shifting. Rather, it creates liabilities (commitments to allies, military and economic assistance) at the same rate as assets (bases, overflight, cooperative forces, some financial contributions). In a sense, with the Bush New World Order, the United States was acquiring every nation's enemies.

True, without a permanent adversary in the form of the Soviet Union, the United States might decline some invitations to conflict. But Bush's 1992 defense program was still a prescription that was expensive and potentially escalatory. Though "beyond" the containment of a single adversary (and its proxies and sympathetic revolutionary movements), it was expressive of a globalization of containment. It universalized threats, and it hoped to collectivize the military response, always under American direction. America remained the world's policeman—perhaps even more so, since it undertook to protect against a full spectrum of challenges in any and all regions.

In order to measure how far the Bush administration traveled from the true Cold War defense program that marked its accession to the true post–Cold War military stance at which it would plan to arrive six years later (were it to remain in office), it is useful to make a direct comparison of the force structure and budgetary cost of the FY 1990 defense program with the probable force structure and budgetary cost of the projected FY 1996 defense program.[6] The "original" Bush defense program would have required, for FY 1990, $296 billion in budgetary authority; 2,121,000 military personnel; a general-purpose force structure that included 21 land divisions (18 army and 3 marine), 25 air force tactical air wing equivalents and 14 aircraft carrier battle groups with 13 navy tactical air wings; and the standard triad of strategic nuclear forces. The military personnel and the force structure would have remained constant through FY 1996, and the 1996 defense budget, in current (then-year) dollars, would have amounted to $381 billion. Over the seven years from 1990 to 1996, this program would have produced cumulative defense costs of $2.361 trillion.[7]

In contrast, a plausible projection of what the Bush defense program would have been by FY 1996, based on the administration's own anticipated budget requests and on the assumption that Congress would tend to accept the more moderate requests of that administration, is $283 billion (in current dollars); 1.7 million military personnel; and a force structure of 15 land divisions (12 army and 3 marine), 15 air force tactical air wings, and 12 aircraft carriers with 12 navy air wings, in addition to a nuclear triad reduced by a strategic arms reduction treaty. Taking the actual performance of the Bush administration, which reduced its initial anticipated requests and further acquiesced in congressional reductions in FY 1990 and FY 1991 and reflecting its requests through 1996, I calculate that those seven years of defense programs would have totaled $1.964 trillion. Thus, the Bush administration would have delivered, over seven years, savings of $397 billion, compared with projections at the time of its inauguration in 1989.

Though far from representing an extreme noninterventionist foreign policy and national strategy—which might, in theory, have produced an *additional* $300 billion of savings over those seven years—the Bush defense program delivered a substantial "peace dividend," shifted the regional emphasis of our defense from Europe to several other areas of the world, notably the Persian Gulf–Middle East–Southwest Asia, and trimmed our force structure by—across the board—about 28 percent. That is not a negligible achievement, and the point here is that it is not mindless drift but a real and deliberate shift to a post–Cold War national strategy and defense posture—the first phase of an intelligent adjustment to what were seen as the post–Cold War conditions of the international system. The Bush–Cheney–Powell Base Force Concept, the planning assumption of what I call "two times three-quarter-size wars," the inclusion of NATO-Europe in an "Atlantic Force" (along with the Persian Gulf–Middle East–Southwest Asia), and the emphasis on the Persian Gulf as the source of the principal force requisite for that Atlantic Force already, operationally, shifted the United States out of the Cold War defense policy stance. The Base Force Concept was the strategic correlative of Bush's New World Order.

One can make another kind of comment—more prescriptive and more anticipatory of the kinds of debates that would ensue in the years following the departure of the Bush administration in January 1993. The target force structure and defense budget of the Bush administration represent about the *least* that the United States could provide to sustain that administration's "regional force strategy" of two three-quarter-size wars and, in turn, Bush's foreign policy of a New World Order. It became fashionable among liberal critics and among the campaigning Clinton defense advisers to suggest that the same American global influence, projected into every significant part of the world, could be implemented with a defense structure radically smaller than that of the Bush administration. After all, the foreign policy watchwords of the Clinton administration, "Engagement and Enlargement [of Democracy],"[8] cursorily describe foreign policy objects not much different in scope (though the Bush administration eschewed, for the most part, the "enlargement" factor) from those of the Bush administration. The national strategy laid down in Secretary of Defense Les Aspin's "Bottom-Up Review"[9] posited military missions (two nearly simultaneous major regional contingencies) not much different from those envisaged in the Bush–Powell Base Force Concept and regional force strategy.

Yet, in the end, the Clinton administration sought to make only modest further reductions in the tangible Bush defense program, roughly on the order of 12 percent.[10] Such fiscally inspired cuts are not radical. So, perversely, the initially critical Clinton administration gives a backhanded validation of the Bush defense planning process, though beginning to risk a mismatch of military missions and forces.

It is fair to conclude that the liberal critics of the Bush administration's foreign policy and national strategy actually prefer those concepts but do not want to pay for them. The bottom line is that a Bush-type world order requires a Bush-sized defense budget. If critics do not want that defense budget, they have to consider adjusting American foreign policy to a different kind of world: a much more fragmented international system—which I call "general unalignment"—with a dozen and a half regional powers playing various autonomous roles and most of them not particularly subject to American dictates or desires. I might accept such a world; others would not. The point is that what is at stake here is, literally, a choice of worlds.

OPERATIONALLY DECIPHERING THE NEW WORLD ORDER

The Bush New World Order was a prescription for universal U.S. involvement to enforce order and stability in every region of the world, as a corollary of the more "structural" purpose to create and maintain a certain type of international system: what I call "collective security."

I intend collective security not as a mere schedule of individual, multilateral peacekeeping or even peacemaking expeditions, under the rubric of the United Nations [UN] Security Council, but as a *structural type* of the international system, a possible form representing the distribution of power and, particularly in the case of this kind of structure, the *regulation* of power in the world.[11]

In other words, collective security is seen as one of a number of structural possibilities of world order. It occupies a place in a typology of international systems[12]: unitary empire, collective security, bipolar confrontation, multipolar balance of power, general unalignment.

Of course, the Bush proposal was a peculiarly American version of collective security, where it could be said, cynically, that the United States would seek the rhetorical and institutional cover of the UN Security Council and assemble, typically, ad hoc coalitions of willing partners to mask essentially unilateral American exercises of force. Yet—even allowing for that interpretation—the scheme was recognizably collective security, rather than the alternative types of system, say, multipolar balance of power or the earlier, high–Cold War bipolar confrontation of alliances.

The Bush–Powell defense policy that emanated from the New World Order, that is, the Base Force Concept, was, in its time, widely tagged as a mere and mindless perpetuation of the Cold War defense policy into (in case everyone in the Bush NSC [National Security Council], State Department, and Defense Department had failed to notice) a post–Cold War era. That was a judgment manifestly unfair to the Bush administration but, more important, analytically inaccurate and methodologically obtuse.

The Bush–Powell force concept was an adaptation to not only (1) the obvious demise of a concerted Communist military threat (Soviet Union, proxy, revolutionary) but also (2) the advent of a more regionalized geopolitical situation in the world. This shift was made essentially by the Bush administration in the foreign policy form of the New World Order, which was, therefore, not an empty or meretricious phrase, and, in the Defense Department implementation, the Colin Powell (and Dick Cheney) Base Force Concept.

But Bush in his New World Order did, in effect, find a new philosophical basis for continuing into the post–Cold War period the extension of American power throughout every region of the world—that is, the U.S. *police function.* After all, what else is the overarching, semiabstract commitment to "stability" and (literally) "order" in other regions, almost for its own sake, but the enunciation of a police function? Yet this extension of American power represents more than the gratuitous and institutionally self-serving "search for enemies" (remarked by some libertarian commentators[13]), let alone the peculiarly paranoid left-wing spin that imputes some sort of "threat-filling" conspiracy to the "military-industrial complex" (i.e., the Pentagon, the military, the defense suppliers, the military research laboratories, and their hired and captive defense analysts).[14] It is simply a potentially valid alternative for the United States, at this juncture, at the level of foreign policy and national strategy, with its entailments in terms of military missions and forces/weapons/doctrines and its resource requisites in terms of dollars and personnel.

America's immediate post–Cold War stance and situation were mistaken by some ordinarily perceptive quasi theorists, such as Charles Krauthammer, who took the New World Order as affirmation and evidence of a "sole surviving superpower," enjoying and acting out its "unipolar moment" in the career of the international system. In actuality, the Bush New World Order was an important and characteristic variant of the international system of collective security and, as such, was more the progenitor of "assertive multilateralism"—asserted, at least, in the early Clinton administration by the eventual secretary of state Madeleine Albright—and of the "engagement" half of the "engagement and enlargement" formulated by President Clinton's national security adviser, W. Anthony Lake.

Thus, a fundamental question, to which we now turn, is: What are the prospects for a regime of collective security?

PROSPECTS FOR COLLECTIVE SECURITY

The validity of the Bush administration's preference for the New World Order is bound up with the prospects, both pragmatic and even theoretical, for collective security.

From a practical standpoint (and given the present and foreseeable future location of effective power in the international system), two sets of variables determine the prospects for useful and truly collective security: (1) the nature of U.S. participation (either [a] mostly disinterested and cooperative or [b] essentially self-serving and unilateral) and (2) the strength of action taken by the collective security agency or regime (either [a] "assertive," to use the catchy phrase, or [b] weak). For convenience, a matrix could be constructed to express the resulting prospects for collective security:

		STRENGTH OF ACTION	
		assertive	weak
	disinterested cooperative	ideal effective	inconsequential
U.S. PARTICIPATION	self-serving unilateral	distortive destructive	irrelevant

In other words, out of the four possibilities, there is one that it seems, by virtual intuitive certainty, that the United States will not pursue, and that is 1a and 2a—disinterested cooperation in collective action that must be waged against an important transgressor and that requires strenuous enforcement. Yet that is the sole "quadrant" that bodes well for the future of a regime of true collective security. By contrast, it is quite foreseeable that the United States will, in various circumstances, take one of the other three quadrants of action: 1b and

2a—a strong, essentially unilateral (perhaps with a veil of UN "cover") political-military response against an important adversary; 1a and 2b—implicit cooperation in a very limited and weak operation (such as traditional "peacekeeping" in a situation not involving the interests of great powers); or 1b and 2b—a perfunctory unilateral response to some unimportant slight. The three latter, likely actions and cases would have variously negative or negligible consequences for a regime of collective security. Unilateral strong action by the United States would be, at the least, distortive of any supranational regime and might bring about its destruction. Ostensibly cooperative participation in insignificant cases would facilitate UN Security Council actions, but these would be inconsequential in their implications for U.S. security and their effect on the structure of power in the international system; this is what I would call the "wastebasket" syndrome. Finally, unilateral, but unimportant, U.S. operations would be hardly relevant at all.

Thus, from a practical standpoint, the foreseeable "quality" of U.S. participation in a regime of collective security is not encouraging. Moreover, from a quasi-theoretical standpoint, none of the four possible cases carry a positive prognosis for the structural type of international system of collective security, not even the technically "ideal" combination of the strong, ostensibly disinterested support of the great powers and the attempt to apply collective power to an important member of the international system in a situation of serious transgression (case 1a and 2a). This is because of a virtual genetic defect in the nature of systems of collective security; they depend, for their very identity as well as their efficacy, on the combined array of (1) concert of the essential members of the system and (2) enforcement in demanding, difficult, important cases—that is, if necessary, against one of the essential members itself. Already we have the makings of an inescapable contradiction, perhaps even a kind of paradox (in the sense that the very elements that—together, both as necessary conditions—constitute collective security also combine to destroy collective security).

We have seen the operation of this contradiction in the crucial case of the "United Nations" intervention in Korea in 1950, which could have been initiated only through the mindless abstention through absence of the Soviet Union. This "police action"—what we would now call "peace-enforcement"—which was hailed, at the time, mistakenly and certainly prematurely, as the vindication of collective security, actually marked the fracturing of the incipient (and, in any case, already fatally flawed) regime of supranational political-military authority and the final advent of a world of bipolar confrontation (an entirely distinct structural type of international system).

The preceding exposition of the generic disabilities of regimes of collective security may seem to be a cute logical trick or, at best, an airy theoretical abstraction; but it is more real and portentous than that. One has only to consider the historical record of the architectonics of the global system builders. In the entire sweep of 350 years since the birth of the modern nation-state system in the Peace of Westphalia in 1648, there have been only three even minimally viable installations of anything asymptotically approaching the ideal type of collective security: the 1815 Congress of Vienna and ensuing Concert of Europe; the 1919 League of Nations; and the 1945 United Nations. The first (*not*, as sometimes carelessly and unsystematically characterized, a "balance of power") lasted, by operational and charitable estimate, only eight years (*not*, as often stated, until the events of 1848 or even until World War I in 1914), until it fractured on the rocks of attitude toward the New World and toward liberalism and revolution in Europe. The second was virtually stillborn at its rejection by the quintessential participant, the United States; and, after only a few years, it existed phantasmagorically and ineffectually alongside parallel diplomacy throughout the 1920s, in spite of the defection, in the 1930s, of Japan, Germany, and Italy, until World War II. The third, the United Nations, showed its true nature in the original list of permanent members of the Security Council: a cabal of the putative victors of World War II; its charter embodies a vision of the structure of true collective security, and it is, of course, still with us; but that vision was never operationalized, and even the vision faded in the events of the later 1940s.

Collective security organizations, let alone world systems, are historically rare, fragile, and short-lived. Either they do merely symbolic tasks, or they merely offer a forum and a cover for diplomatic and military actions otherwise initiated and pursued, or they operate in insignificant and dispensable cases. They do not survive their first serious test. Thus, efforts to create such regimes as types of international systems may be either heroic or cynical—and that brackets partial and oblique efforts such as the Bush New World Order—but they are "intellectually" doomed.

LESSONS OF THE PERSIAN GULF WAR

The first test of President Bush's New World Order was the American exercise of arms in the Persian Gulf in January 1991. Or was it a test? In one interpretation, what we had was merely a collection of self-seeking governments arrayed against a small regional power and a United States disdainful of allies and the real uses of an international organization but masking that disdain in the rhetoric and institutions of collective security.

Again, on one level, we saw the brilliant vindication of U.S. arms—command, planning, logistics, and weapons; but, on another level, Desert Storm enfolded all the problems that the American military will have in future regional encounters: exposure to a virulent regional power equipped with weapons of mass destruction and, undeterred, willing to use them on the battlefield against American forces.

Desert Storm was a success. But the price of success is very high and is to be measured in the perpetual cost of creating and maintaining our kind of force structure and panoply of weapons to support our kind of operational doctrines, to implement military missions that represent a national strategy of global intervention, and, in turn, to cement a foreign policy of dominance of various future coalitions to enforce universal collective security. All this cannot be done just by proclamations or even by boycotts and embargoes, unless they are enforced. Even then, the successes will be transient. The victories will come unstuck, and new challenges will arise in the regions of the world: nasty regimes, assaults on friends, manipulations and strangulations of resources. In the longer run, the price of success will be rejected by the American political-social-economic system.

Perhaps the most ironic point is that, when the fog of battle lifted, Persian Gulf oil *still* cost the United States (by my calculations) $196 to $266 a barrel in "military insurance costs" alone, not even counting the price of the oil.[15] At the height of the war, the United States had on the battlefield, around the Gulf, about 45 percent of its worldwide active force structure[16]: 10⅔ ground division equivalents (9 army and 1⅔ marine) out of 21; 18⅓ tactical air wing equivalents (9 air force, 6 navy, and 3⅓ marine[17]) out of 44; and 6 navy carrier battle groups out of 14. Although that deployment was more than the forces normally "attributable" to that region's defense, even the latter could be put as four ground divisions (three army and one marine), nine tactical air wing equivalents (four air force, three navy, and two marine), and three navy aircraft carrier battle groups. Those forces normally kept for a Persian Gulf contingency cost, in FY 1992, about $50 billion a year (now even more forces allocated to such a contingency, in the Clinton administration's force planning, and costing, in FY 1997 dollars, $82 billion a year).[18]

This interpretation of the Persian Gulf situation does not say that the United States—or more properly, its constituent individuals and groups—has no "interests" in other regions of the world, only that some interests cost more to defend than they are worth. Moreover, one larger thing is likely to happen that will make the initial taste of efficient victory turn to ashes. Such victories come unstuck in time in far-off regions (not necessarily along our own borders, of course). The only way to "nail down" a region is almost literally to nail down the lid of the coffin and sit on it forever. In general, we must provide the peacetime force structure and budget dollars, on a high, sustained level, for such probable periodic operations. (Examples are the several *re*interventions that the United States had to mount, in the years after Desert Storm, at the head of the Persian Gulf in response to repeated provocations by the government of Iraq, as well as the continuing support of the no-fly zones and the Kurdish sanctuary in the north of Iraq and the continuing economic sanctions.)

"GENERAL UNALIGNMENT": A WORLD OF REGIONAL POWERS

Of the two available structures of international system that presented themselves to the Bush administration at the demise of the Soviet Union and its external and internal empires—collective security and general unalignment—the Bush administration expressed, and attempted to implement, its preference for a world of collective security: the New World Order. It is more likely, however, that the international system will fragment, even "beyond the balance of power" that was put in place, tentatively, by President Nixon and Secretary of State

Henry Kissinger, and devolve into a world of regional powers.

Rather mistakenly, the popular conception has it that, around 1989 to 1991, the world shifted from "bipolarity" to "multipolarity." But, upon contemplation of world politics and the foreign policy of the United States over the past four decades, it emerges more clearly that a significant and substantive geopolitical revolution was accomplished by Nixon and Kissinger in the years from 1969 through 1974. Working, of course, with the grain of history, yet in a mode of real transformative statesmanship, Nixon and Kissinger moved the international system from the phase of bipolar confrontation to one of multipolar balance of power—not perfect and not classic but recognizable.[19]

Now, near the inception of the Bush administration, American foreign policy was confronted with a kind of choice of international systems as objects of our foreign policy: an attempt to create, or re-create, a version of collective security or an accommodation of the devolution of international system into a structure (or virtual nonstructure) of "general unalignment." Quite expectedly and quite rationally, in an attempt to exploit the temporary withdrawal of Russia and hasten a regime of American global dominance at a bearable cost, the Bush administration opted for an American-led and American-supported structure of collective security, which it attractively packaged and labeled as the New World Order. This attempt has not been an entire failure. Interestingly and despite its preinaugural partisan rhetoric, the Clinton administration has not only inherited but embraced the geopolitical component of the Bush New World Order; that is, it has adopted the "engagement" thesis and has added the dimension of "enlargement [of democracy and human rights]," which was deliberately missing from the Bush formula.

Yet, world politics and domestic politics have conspired to portend the failure of the Bush objective international order. A bit of what I call quasi theory is involved here. Defense policies, national strategies, and even foreign policies are not things in themselves. To understand them, you have to have a proper "model" of the foreign policy process. Foreign policies are not merely and bluntly the "resultant" of intrabureaucratic wrangling or raw, cognitive orientations of obscure origin. On the one hand, foreign policies inevitably take, as their objects, some "objective" structure of the international system. On the other hand, they have tangible requisites in terms of the national strategies necessary to implement them and, in turn, the military missions, the force structures and weapons, and, ultimately, the resources of money and troops.

Thus—in a rational relationship, from "top" to "bottom"—the New World Order would, at the top, confront the objectives of other powerful and rising nations in the world and, at the bottom, draw upon domestic resources of fiscal means and political support that might not be forthcoming.

A synoptic survey of the evolution of the international system, at this juncture, would disclose tendencies to a diffused state of general unalignment. The present putative, multipolar balance of power will further unravel to the point where the system will be marked by the rise of regional "hegemons," or at least regionally contested situations that tend to exclude or discourage extraregional intervention. A concomitant projection (contrary to prevalent expectations) would be that regional integration, even in Europe, will be truncated at levels that do not fulfill present plans. This impending situation will also bring about the irrelevance of present alliance systems, including NATO—again, despite heroic (or perhaps bureaucratically self-serving) efforts at "expansion." The entire international system will be continuously unsettled by disturbances, mostly nonstrategic, such as resource denials, restrictions of trade, environmental damage, population pressures, excessive migration, narcotics, and fanatic terrorism. Finally and most ominously, an increase of nuclear proliferation will be both a cause and a result of the tendency toward fragmentation and regionalization of power.

Yet, even though most parts of the international system may be unstable, the system as a whole may well be "meta-stable," since dangerous advantages will not thereby accrue to any of the great powers or erstwhile superpowers. Even other regional conflicts of some magnitude need not directly threaten or even indirectly implicate the United States. There are two salient exceptions to that not entirely comfortable, but minimally livable, state of affairs: (1) the long-range delivery and (2) the terroristic delivery of highly lethal munitions directly against American society; these two threats will have to be physically interdicted—not only, obviously, to ensure the security of American "core values" but to allow the United States workable freedom of action in the world.[20]

At the least, the prospect of having to sustain American domination by preparing endlessly for periodic military interventions should occasion a comprehensive revision of tactics, taking advantage of the military supertechnologies in which the United States is likely to maintain an advantage: battlefield information, precision targeting, long-range standoff strikes.[21] The irony, however, is that this kind of "new-wave" military doctrine is appropriate, not so much to the Bush New World Order, which requires definitive and lasting American control and influence in virtually every region of the world, but rather to a retrenched, "Fortress America" stance, still bristling with retaliatory power and resolve but reluctant to commit ground forces for any appreciable period of time to any region of the world and therefore devoted to the concept of (merely) punitive strikes.[22]

CONCLUSION: THE "CHOICE OF WORLDS"

The overarching significance of the Bush–Baker–Cheney–Powell foreign and military policy is that their administration faced a real and large-scale choice and made a real and large-scale response—though one that, because of some internal contradictions and several obstacles and constraints on the international plane and in the domestic political economy, remained unfinished and ultimately improbable.

At the end of a long global conflict for a brief historical moment, the Bush administration attempted to create—or re-create—a regime of collective security in world politics. Anyone would have acknowledged that the New World Order was to be an American-led effort and an American-underpinned structure, but it was a recognizable version of collective security, nonetheless, as a form of the international system. Moreover, this scheme of world order, though repudiated in title by the incoming Clinton administration, lived on in the guise of Clinton's national security adviser's "engagement" proposition and even in Clinton's (eventual) secretary of state's formula of "assertive multilateralism." Thus, the New World Order not only had tangible consequences for American national strategy and military missions (as well as force structure and defense budgets) but even constituted a coherent "theme" or, if you will, a "vision thing."

Schemes of world order, simply because they are preferred and attempted, are not self-executing, and the New World Order, representing a real structural type of international system, would impose real and severe operational costs on the United States, costs that the American political-social-economic system would probably reject. Thus, an alternative structure, which I call "general unalignment," becomes a seriously possible future—one that, with all its unnerving concomitants of disorder and loss of American control, may have to be accommodated.

In short, the Bush administration *did*, in an objective and fundamental way, transcend the Cold War. But, rather than bequeathing an effective and lasting institutional and structural resolution, it left for its successors a further set of decisions that, explicitly or implicitly, must be faced—surely, a new defense policy debate and even a "choice of worlds."

NOTES

1. "Lucky Jim," *The New Republic*, January 1, 1996.
2. Earl C. Ravenal, *Designing Defense for a New World Order: The Military Budget in 1992 and Beyond* (Washington, DC: Cato Institute, 1991).
3. Translated into the parlance of the second Clinton administration's secretary of state Madeleine Albright, this represents "assertive multilateralism," with the emphasis on the "assertive" rather than the "multilateralism."
4. This diplomatic revolution was the subject of the paper for a previous Hofstra University Presidential Conference on Richard Nixon, entitled "The Nixon Doctrine as History and Portent," November 1987, later published as Earl C. Ravenal, "The Nixon Doctrine as History and Portent," in Leon Friedman and William Levantrosser, eds., *Richard M. Nixon: Cold War Patriot and Statesman* (Westport, CT: Greenwood Press, 1992).
5. Secretary of Defense Dick Cheney, *Annual Report to the President and the Congress for Fiscal Year 1992* (Washington, DC: U.S. Government Printing Office, 1991). It is dated January 1991 but was delivered to the Senate Armed Services Committee on February 21, 1991.
6. Secretary of Defense Richard B. Cheney, "Statement before the House Armed Services Committee, in Connection with the FY 1990/FY 1991 Amended Budget for the Department of Defense," April 25, 1989, along with the news release "Amended FY 1990/FY 1991 Department of Defense Budget," April 25, 1989. Those two documents are to be read in conjunction with the outgoing Reagan administration's FY 1990 defense budget. Secretary of Defense Frank C. Carlucci, *Annual Report to the Congress, Fiscal*

Year 1990 (Washington, DC: U.S. Government Printing Office, January 17, 1989).

7. All defense budget figures used in this study are for budget authority (not outlays) for the subcategory 051 Department of Defense (not the entire category 050 National Defense, which also includes 053 Atomic Energy Defense Activities [mostly production of nuclear warheads in the Department of Energy] at $11.8 billion for 1992 and 054 Defense-Related Activities [mostly civil defense and the standby maritime fleet] at $.8 billion for 1992). The figure also excludes the added deployment and war costs for Operations Desert Shield and Desert Storm, which were represented by a supplemental appropriation request of $15 billion (net of allied pledges of $54.5 billion) for FY 1991.

In representing force structure, I do not count reserve units. In costing active combat forces, I take the cost of reserve forces as a kind of support cost and distribute it over the active units.

8. The White House (principally W. Anthony Lake, the President's national security adviser), *A National Security Strategy of Engagement and Enlargement* (Washington, DC: U.S. Government Printing Office, February 1996).

9. Les Aspin, *Report on the Bottom-Up Review* (Washington, DC: U.S. Government Printing Office, October 1993).

10. See Earl C. Ravenal, *Defending America in an Uncontrollable World: The Military Budget, 1998 to 2003* (Washington, DC: Cato Institute, 1997).

11. For a critique of collective security as a type of international system and as an object of a nation's foreign policy, see the next section of this paper; and also Earl C. Ravenal, "An Autopsy of Collective Security," *Political Science Quarterly* (Winter 1975–1976).

12. I rely here on the typology of Earl C. Ravenal presented in a number of writings, including "An Autopsy of Collective Security" and "A Rational Theory of National Action," paper presented to the Annual Meeting of the International Studies Association, San Diego, April 17, 1996. This typology is not arbitrary, and it has utility. The systemic types are identifiable and differentiable and derived from tangible and formal criteria and characteristics.

13. See Ted Galen Carpenter, *A Search for Enemies: America's Alliances after the Cold War* (Washington, DC: Cato Institute, 1992).

14. See, for example, Michael Klare, *Rogue States and Nuclear Outlaws: America's Search for a New Foreign Policy* (New York: Hill and Wang, 1996).

15. See Ravenal, "The Example of the Persian Gulf," *Designing Defense for a New World Order*, pp. 43ff.

16. Units still in the active force structure as of February 1991.

17. Actually, 1⅔ double-strength wings; marine air wings, organic to the fighting division, are virtually double-strength in terms of the number of fighter-attack aircraft.

18. The author's analysis of the FY 1997 defense budget requested authorization.

19. See Ravenal, "The Nixon Doctrine as History and Portent"; Earl C. Ravenal, *Large-Scale Foreign Policy Change: The Nixon Doctrine as History and Portent* (Berkeley: University of California, Institute of International Studies, 1989).

20. See Ravenal, *Defending America in an Uncontrollable World*.

21. Ibid.

22. Ibid.

16

Defense Cuts, Base Closings, and Conversion: Slow Reaction and Missed Opportunities

John E. Ullmann

"Is there any other point to which you would wish to draw my attention?"
"The curious incident of the dog in the night-time."
"But the dog did nothing in the night-time."
"That was the curious incident," remarked Sherlock Holmes.
Sir Arthur Conan Doyle, Silver Blaze

DECLINE AND FALL

There is general agreement that the poor state of the economy was a principal cause of the defeat of President Bush in 1992. In a real sense, his were the years of a monumental hangover, not only from the soaring debts of the Reagan years but from the Cold War itself. Central to it was the specific failure to find constructive alternatives for the growing parts of the military sector that could no longer be justified and for those who served it, no matter how hard their patrons and supporters tried.

These dislocations resulted in some of the most significant job losses in the economy, greatly affecting the already beleaguered manufacturing sector as well as a large part of the nation's technical and scientific resources. The military sector has been downsized ever since its budget reached its peak in FY [fiscal year] 1987; the process continues, in spite of huge defense expenditures that bear little relationship to changed global realities and yet are "off the table" in the ongoing budget disputes. As Senator Jim Sasser (D-TN), then chairman of the Senate Budget Committee (1994), put it, "[W]e are now in an era of military pork barrelling.... We are not responding to external threats [but] to internal threats of job losses as a result of cutting the military budget."

As Table 16.1 shows, during the Bush administration defense-related industrial jobs fell by 21.2 percent, active duty forces by 14.3 percent, and civilian employees of the Department of Defense by 10 percent, for a total of about 1 million jobs. The declines from the peak in 1987 to the estimates for FY 1997 are 44.4, 28.6, and 30 percent, respectively. However, the table also shows that at the start of the Reagan–Weinberger arms race in 1980, defense-industrial employment was about what it is now; active duty forces and civilian employees stayed about the same during the buildup.

Measured against past levels, therefore, finding jobs for those affected and helping them in the transition should not have been outlandishly difficult and, one would have thought, would have had high priority. However, ever since the subject first came up in the 1960s, few issues have generated such long, fervent, and variegated opposition by both Republican and Democratic administrations as the conversion of unneeded military assets (Raffel 1995).

Table 16.1
Defense-Related Employment, Selected years, 1987–1997

	Job Categories		
Fiscal Years	Defense Industry	Active Duty	Department of Defense Civilian
	(in millions, except percentages)		
1980	2.0	2.0	0.9
1987	3.6	2.1	1.0
1989	3.3	2.1	1.0
1993	2.6	1.8	0.9
1997 (est.)	2.0	1.5	0.7
Increase 1980–87	1.6	0.1	0.1
Percent	80.0	5.0	11.1
Decrease 1989–93	0.7	0.3	0.1
Percent	21.2	14.3	10.0
Decrease 1987–97	1.6	0.6	0.3
Percent	44.4	28.6	10.0

Source: U.S. Department of Defense, *National Defense Budget Estimates for FY 1995* (Washington, DC: Office of the Comptroller, 1994), p. 159, Table 7.7.

What made the reaction of the Bush administration different from the reaction in these earlier years was exactly that the displacement of that many relatively highly skilled as well as politically articulate people should have moved the subject of conversion to center stage rather than have it dismissed, as it largely was, as yet another liberal illusion or way to spend public money.

The decline during the Bush years thus mainly brought demands to keep going. Ever since World War II, getting defense contracts and bases for a state or congressional district had symbolized the clout of politicians. They, in turn, could count on support from the companies affected and their workers, unions, and communities. This is why many a politician who otherwise makes peaceful noises may support questionable hometown weapons or bases and why Congress often votes for weapons that not even the Pentagon wants.

For example, from the late 1980s onward, the main such problem for Long

Island was the decline of the Grumman Aircraft Corporation. Strenuous attempts were made in 1990 and 1991 to continue Grumman's production of the F-14D aircraft, which the navy wanted to cancel. The Department of Defense therefore keeps careful statistics on spending by congressional district, and its officials readily admit that they spread the work around so as to maximize the political impact of their procurement decisions.

In State of the Union messages and elsewhere, both Presidents Reagan and Bush often referred to the military sector as the "prime purpose" of the federal government. This, however, did not mean that the government felt obliged to help those displaced by the decline in the military sector, even though *it had itself created and maintained it at a very high level.*

Specifically, in a speech in Orange County, California, on June 20, 1992, Bush declared that "defense conversion puts Orange County back in the business of job creation, a skill that you mastered in the 1980s with the high-tech start-ups that made this area famous" (Berke 1992).[1] The speech was one of the rare occasions when the word "conversion" was even uttered; as noted later, it raised too many other issues that politicians like to shun.

But surely, Orange County as such had nothing to do with creating defense jobs. The federal government had done that, but there was no significant effort—nor, for that matter, is there one now—to replace those jobs through new markets in the public sector or give enough support to nonmilitary industrial research that might quickly create new products and industries.

Instead, the Bush administration opposed not only any real conversion legislation but even the extension of unemployment insurance in the then prevailing recession until forced later to accept it by a Congress controlled by the opposition. A combination of inertia, Cold War nostalgia, fear for one's livelihood, and, above all, misplaced faith in the private sector hindered virtually all attempts at positive change.

CONVERSION: WHAT GOVERNMENT RESPONSIBILITY?

The arms race of the Cold War first shifted into high gear in the Kennedy administration. Its priorities and the preemption of scientific and technical resources were soon seen as dangers to nonmilitary American industry such as the then-new area of solid-state technology (Ullmann 1970). Other clearly identifiable national needs to which the preempted skills could have been applied also fell by the wayside. A vested interest was emerging with exactly the "undue influence" against which President Eisenhower had warned in his famous 1960 speech on the rising military-industrial complex.

In the early 1960s, therefore, there were the first major proposals for feasible, yet lower, levels of military spending combined with alternative uses for the freed resources and how to plan and organize the transfers (Melman 1961; Melman et al. 1963; Ullmann 1964). In January 1963, in his maiden speech, Senator George McGovern (D-SD) made the first legislative proposal.

With some changes in emphasis, the main items in the proposed legislation have since then remained essentially the same—and so has the opposition. The most controversial part was that the government would require its contractors, facilities, and bases to have alternative-use committees of managements and employees, with community participation, to decide on future activities. Second, as needed, there would be transitional support and retraining for affected workers.

As to the objections, throughout the many years when the Cold War seemed permanent, contractors were actively discouraged by the Pentagon from thinking that there might be life after military work. When it did end, a typical first reaction was that of Murray Weidenbaum (1990), Reagan's first chairman of the Council of Economic Advisers (CEA), that the market should take care of any transition problems and that military contractors should simply merge, restructure, sell assets, and close unneeded facilities. There should be no government intervention beyond this (Ullmann 1990).

Weidenbaum's later book, *Small Wars, Big Defense* (1992), used forecasts of continuing conflict *of a similar kind* and of institutional inertia in the military sector to predict little change. In a similar vein, Gordon Adams (1989) had asserted earlier that there were so many weapons "in the pipeline" that they had to be produced, or else there would be enormous cancellation costs. Yet at the end of World War II, contracts were canceled at a few hours' notice "for the convenience of the government" without huge costs; one could but wonder why the new contracts provided otherwise. When Governor Richard F. Celeste of Ohio convened a conference of defense contractors in the state on January 24, 1990 (which I also addressed), Adams presented his predictions of little change as "good news" for his audience.

Inertia is a poor basis for planning, but it still goes on (Rauch 1996); proposals for setting the defense budget at a percentage of gross domestic product [GDP] regularly appear, even though massive changes in the composition and interpretation of GDP have made it a dubious measure of anything (Melman 1983, pp. 260–61; Alexander 1990), and defense spending must justify itself by military needs, rather than by such a simplistic "indicator." Military spending is the ultimate discretionary expenditure of any government; there is nothing that correlates with it the way indicators like consumer spending may relate to sales of a product.

Whatever responsibility the Pentagon did accept for cutbacks was centered in its Office of Economic Adjustment (OEA), but that was a poorly financed operation with limited powers and objectives. Especially in the Reagan–Bush years, it did little more than help affected communities apply for federal relief programs, rather than assist in industrial resuscitation. John E. Lynch, then its associate director, put it bluntly: "Industrial plant reuse and new product development is normally a private sector responsibility . . . in a highly decentralized investment process. . . . The conversion approach would introduce a formal "industrial policy" into the reuse of defense facilities separate from the normal plant investment process for civilian goods" (1987, p. 4). Military-industrial firms, however, are basically different from nonmilitary ones. Put more formally, what Lynch calls "private sector responsibility" are the decisions of what to make, how to make it, in what quantities, and with whose invested money. For military firms, however, there is no "highly decentralized" or "normal plant investment process." By law and regulations, the essential decisions are made by the Pentagon, with "progress payments" providing the invested money (Melman 1983, pp. 85–94; Ullmann 1985, pp. 11–20). Not getting such payments in civilian work, was, for example, cited by Grumman's top management in a panel discussion at Hofstra University on October 28, 1989, as a reason for not trying for subcontracts for Boeing's booming commercial aircraft business.

In the passage cited, Lynch also conjures up "industrial policy" as a sort of bogey; it was indeed a dreaded phrase throughout the Reagan and Bush years, much like "liberal" and "tax increase." Yet the preemption of technical industries in the huge escalation of the arms race was nothing if not "industrial policy," as complete as anything this side of the Soviet Gosplan.

In fact, in 1988 a study by the Defense Science Board (see also Ullmann 1989) proposed the extension of Pentagon control over virtually all of industry and especially of world trade. It was done in the name of "national security," which the report left conspicuously undefined, and to preserve a "defense industrial base," but designing one is impossible without defining what national security challenges are to be met. The report thus sounded like a rerun of past wars, notably the mobilization delays of World War II; it even evoked convoys laden with electronic components for which we had come to depend on imports, making their way across the Pacific to the land once known as the arsenal of democracy.

The proposal itself got nowhere, but neither did funding for the Technology Competitiveness Act of 1988 (P.L. 100-418, Subtitle B, Part I), which, in response to global trade problems, had been added to the Trade Bill of 1988. It was intended as a channel for new civilian industrial research support; instead, it is a dead letter.

By then, the chronic U.S. trade deficit had come to include even *nonmilitary* high-technology products (U.S. Congress 1986); recent contrary claims that there has always been a high-tech trade surplus take care to include its large military sector (Weidenbaum 1996). The arms race had, in fact, long served to redefine high technology in military terms (Tirman 1984).

In this connection, claims that there would be significant "spinoff" from military to commercial research and products have always been much more hype than reality; most of military technology is too different from civilian needs. Where it is not, the extreme high costs of military products require their virtual reinvention to be commercially useful, and most of such work was done in Japan, not in the United States (Ullmann 1989, pp. 16–20; 1985, pp. 22, 112–13). In the absence of specific markets, the issue of "technology transfer" is, in fact, rather moot.

CONVERSION: FROM HERE TO WHERE?

There are three problems in deciding what else military industries can do and how to get there: how the firms would have to change, retraining and reemployment of the people affected, and the alternative products and markets.

The effects of cutbacks on military suppliers vary greatly, of course, from firms selling their usual products, to those partially dependent on specialized military work, and to the large exclusive military producers. Obviously, the first category has the least difficulty; people displaced from the military sector will still eat and need other consumer products.

In the second group, while some have enough existing or readily expandable civilian business to make up for losses, many other firms are subcontractors tied to the primes in a virtual Japanese-style *keiretsu* relationship and have died when the prime contract did. The large specialized contractors in the third group have the most troubles, but that is no reason for giving up on the whole notion of conversion.

The plants themselves present the first difficulty. Today's more complex weapons are made in much smaller quantities and their manufacture has turned from the mass production lines of World War II to what a Grumman executive at the Hofstra conference cited called "handicraft methods."

Furthermore, the awesome paperwork requirements of military contracts and the related "cost-plus" habits give military work an overhead ratio of about five to one, compared with less than two to one for comparable civilian work (Ullmann 1994). There often are as many engineers as production workers in weapons production; very few nonmilitary enterprises could afford (or would need) technical talent on such a scale. For these and for other reasons noted later, conversion problems are not necessarily solvable within the existing plant or union local; this obvious fact often escalates the conflicts, or games of musical chairs, that are likely in any major changes and the political pressures to go on as before. But that should hardly be news to engineers and technical workers; for all too many of them, worry about whether a new project will materialize when the old one is finished is a fact of professional life, even without drastic product change.

There also are several levels of retraining, though there, too, opponents like to fasten on the most difficult parts. True, one would have to know the ultimate purpose of the retraining, but once that is established, it can be tailored and limited to the exact needs. To be sure, much of military work is highly specialized, but discussions with practitioners often show remarkable versatility and ideas for new products, although they tend to doubt that their existing managements could make a success of them.

Anyway, scientists and engineers are regularly exhorted "to learn all their lives" so that any conversion-related retraining would only take the place of what they would need anyway to keep up with their present fields. In the age of the Internet, computer-assisted design (CAD), and desktop publishing, potential shortages of qualified instructors and suitable teaching materials should also be manageable. One overriding topic would have to be the cost-consciousness needed in commercial products in contrast to the Pentagon's ever-open checkbook.

Proposed support while retraining and its cost itself have also run into the predictable opposition to any sort of social safety net. At the 1989 Hofstra conference mentioned, Robert E. Rauner, then the deputy director of the OEA, estimated that it would cost $200 million to "resettle" (convert) the 10,000 displaced defense workers on Long Island; he meant that $20,000 each was a lot of money, but at the time, the 40,000 U.S troops in South Korea cost $4 billion, or $100,000 each *per year*, and those in NATO even more.

Successful conversion of defense workers, moreover, would make an immediate contribution to the country's material needs and international trade, if it were, as it should be, related to a major revival of manufacturing. Oil and manufactures make up the chronic U.S. trade deficit, which has now reached a cumulative total of $1.4 trillion. This cannot go on indefinitely; it is a much greater long-term threat to the economic health of the United States than its government deficits. The decline of manufacturing, added to a long record of Pentagon toleration of waste and technical incompetence, has also already cut into the general technical literacy of the population. As a result, we have such problems as poor maintenance of technical products like commercial aircraft and a productivity crisis in construction; faster and less expensive construction would have to be a central ingredient of the alternative projects.

What would be likely candidates for such a revival? Here, over the years, a remarkably constant wish list has developed, notably involving energy and the infrastructure. In the 1980s federal support for energy conservation and new sources had been severely cut, resulting in dependence on imports of Gulf oil that had been almost eliminated by the conservation efforts of the late 1970s. The Gulf War by itself should have been a warning to the Bush administration of the renewed and growing threat to national security. Yet energy independence would be feasible through such projects as high-speed rail and local transit networks, new propulsion systems for cars, like straight electrics or hybrids, and new sources of electricity through expanded use of cogeneration and geothermal energy.

A second fruitful area is water management. Most of the major American cities need major reconstruction of their by now century-old water supply systems and other utilities. As Bob Hope said in New York in 1993 when a major water pipe burst just before the mayoral election, "New York doesn't need a mayor. It needs a plumber."

Equally urgently, as part of a global increase in climatic extremes, many vital agricultural areas have had increasingly violent alternations of droughts and floods, but instead of integrated water management, the region, by and large, is still "waitin' at the levee" for it to collapse and collects crop insurance when the next drought hits. Yet there are many ways to manage water resources better than this, even without the once-fashionable huge dams that in many areas of the globe have proved to be major ecological disasters. Water management is a task that civilizations have performed for millennia and have neglected only at their peril. A major modern effort of this sort would require huge inputs of technical equipment of a kind that the essentially technical industries of the military sector *could* provide.

Why "could" and not "can"? First, there is the long-running controversy with the alternative use committees (AUCs) for military firms and bases. Many managements simply were unequipped as well as uninterested to do any major planning for completely new product lines, let alone in joint committees with workers; rightly or not, such "codetermination" is quite alien to American practice. When a speaker at the Columbus conference asked the audience of defense contractors how many would be inclined to do such planning, nary a hand went up. Still, the only two among several workshops that attracted overflow crowds were the ones on how to become subcontractors to Honda and Siemens, both of which had large factories in the state, not that having to rely on two foreign firms reflects well on what has become of the national industrial patrimony.

In sum, there may be something to Samuel Johnson's famous dictum "Depend upon it, when a man knows he is to be hanged in a fortnight, it concentrates his mind wonderfully"; however, pressures to put a new line of work together while running an existing operation in crisis may be unavailing when the alternative is simply to shut down. Ultimately, perhaps, one cannot force people by law to be competent about planning their futures.

As defense spending declined, conversion legislation was considered in every one of the Bush years, and the AUC issue became one of the main controversies. AUCs were a central provision of the most comprehensive of the bills, that of Representative Ted Weiss (D-NY), as distinct from others, like those of Representatives Nicholas Mavroules (D-MA), Sam Gejdenson (D-CT), and Mary Rose Oakar (D-OH) (Raffel 1995).

As noted at the outset, the word "conversion" was not well regarded in polite society; it came to mean a change for keeps, whereas such other terms as "diversification" and "adjustment," preferred by the Pentagon, Gejdenson, and Oakar, implied something limited or temporary. In remarks at the Columbus conference, Oakar spoke of "diversification, with conversion somewhere down the road," as if the golden days of the Cold War would come back.

By 1992 such distinctions led to approaches such as "dual use," which is an attempt to turn out commercial products in an existing factory with existing staffing and management methods, even though those were the very factors that had made most defense facilities noncompetitive in the first place. Dual use therefore soon turned into a buzz concept made to order for the "optimists" who still were into denial that they would have to change their ways to survive. Worse still, it was a major part of the industrial advice offered to the former Communist countries; their consumer industries had for decades lived on the scraps from their military-industrial complexes and were virtually useless in their new economies.

The conversion bills, minus the joint planning provisions through AUCs, were eventually consolidated and became law; they obliged the Department of Defense to give six months' notice of major contract cancellations and sought to extend retraining, unemployment compensation, and community redevelopment; these were to be paid out of defense budget cuts. About $200 million was earmarked, but the Bush administration strenuously opposed using these funds for conversion-related activities. It wanted to use them for immediate deficit reduction, even though that would have been deflationary exactly at a time of recession.

It was not until May 1991, therefore, that the administration yielded to congressional pressure and promised to release the money to the Departments of Commerce and Labor, as provided by law. But delays continued; the Department of Commerce got its share only in January 1992. By the end of 1993, $102 million had been spent, and 38,000 workers had been served (Raffel 1995). At about $2,700 each, it thus was no more than a somewhat strengthened social safety net, without any funding for new product ideas or markets.

Is there a way out of this dead end? There is, and it is simply that *when markets are there, suppliers will follow*. In both planning and implementation, the urgent needs and initiatives previously described involve *all levels of the public sector* as well as private action. Clearly, the allergy to the former that has been central to political life for at least two decades will have to change. In fact, in a comprehensive survey of conversion projects, Jonathan Feldman (1997) has shown that market opportunities in the *nonmilitary* public sector have been most helpful to successful conversion, and, contrary to earlier fears on this subject, the firms could change internally to respond to them.

Given such opportunities, therefore, one can expect that the suppliers would include erstwhile military contractors or perhaps new users of their facilities, as well as established firms in the business; affirmative action for the former would hardly be feasible politically. Either way and depending on the size of the new markets, there would be new work to take care of many of those displaced from military work.

The ultimate problem is time. It takes at least two years (Baird 1965) to convert from one product line to another, but foresight has never been a strong suit of politicians, who look no further than the next election or, as Bush did, fail to heed ample warnings, nor of business leaders, who look to the next quarter and are given to a fault to shuffling assets rather than assuring continuity for those whose livelihood they control. We are now reminded of Richard II, one of Shakespeare's saddest heroes: "I wasted time and now doth time waste me."

BASES: DROPPING THE HOT POTATOES

In many ways, dealing with the shutdown of military bases is a more daunting problem than the conversion of industrial resources. The bases are often in remote areas, but wherever they are, the location of many, if not most, of them is the result of historical happenstance or political power plays of long ago, remote from today's cost structures and logistics. By contrast, while decisions on where to put a factory have their subjective elements, they do have to take such objective factors as labor availability, markets, energy supply, and other local costs and amenities more closely into account. Bases, therefore, are often the only employer in "company towns," as dependent as any mining or lumber community. While they often include well-equipped workshops, these may be too specialized for quick industrial conversion, especially in their remote locations.

Because of all this, political efforts to preserve bases are often even more powerful and desperate than those for defense contracts, and politicians were therefore often able to block any plans to close such facilities. There was therefore a concerted effort to take these very sensitive issues out of politics. On November 5, 1990, President Bush signed Public Law 101-510 (Title XXIX), which established the bipartisan Defense Base Closure and Realignment Commission. It required the secretary of defense to provide it with a list of proposed changes by March 15, 1993, which, in turn, were to be based on a "force-structure plan" to be submitted to Congress. Most important, Congress could disapprove the recommendations only in toto, not pick and choose among them.

In its report (1993), the commission noted that the secretary of defense had recommended 165 installations, to which the commission added a further 73, to be closed or used to consolidate the work of others to be closed. The final recommendation to the president was for 130 bases to be closed and 45 more to be realigned.

An immediate and very serious issue was that many of the bases turned out to have been environmental abominations with difficult, if not impossible, cleanup requirements. The Rocky Mountain Arsenal near Denver, closed in the 1970s, was the first notorious case; local, state, and federal environmental laws and, in some cases, building codes had been simply ignored. The Presidio in San Francisco, otherwise one of the most splendid parcels of potential urban real estate anywhere, not only had its share of toxic waste, but its water supply did not have enough pressure to fight fires. Congressional hearings have shown how widespread and serious such problems are (U.S. Senate 1993), but from the start, Congress has failed to provide enough cleanup funds.

There have been conversions of bases to industrial parks, a logical step, and now there is interest in turning more air bases into civilian airports. However, location is again a problem. For instance, Stewart Air Force Base near West Point and the onetime navy air base in Calverton, Long Island, have been suggested, but they are over 75 miles from New York and would, at the least, require high-speed rail access; there is only a freight line ending in New Jersey that could serve Stewart, and only the most decrepit line of the Long Island Railroad passes near Calverton.

Finally, some military bases have been turned into prisons or boot camps. These may be the only "housing booms" right now, but such a new "Gulag Archipelago" reflects social desperation instead of constructive development.

The process has now gone on long enough to make some judgments. Michael Closson and his associates (1996) of the Center for Economic Conversion in California note that the practical difficulties are such that even most of the bases named for closure in 1988 are far from fully converted. Luck was the prime factor in some cases; there is more to base conversion than real estate development, but sometimes success came through just happening to find a customer. The military still controls most of the conversion process, and its priorities and timetables often make it difficult for communities and others to make effective plans. Amendments to the original law in 1994 have tried to reduce what was becoming a mountain of red tape. Sometimes, however, strong community opposition to such proposals as low-cost housing on a closed base has been enough to cause long delays.

The main policy contribution to the base issue during the Bush years is the bipartisan commission; it has enabled politicians to set aside the patriotic or military fig leaves that kept unneeded facilities, even though it does not free the resources needed for success; that, of course, is what defines the only real bottom line and also, unfortunately, the inadequacy of the response.

UNFINISHED BUSINESS

In a real sense, how to reduce oversized military establishments and how to use the freed resources are key to a decent life for humanity everywhere. It goes beyond finding new jobs for displaced workers and released military personnel and new uses for the facilities. It must serve as a means of meeting the needs of society, many of which are unmet to an ever more dangerous extent. Encompassing as they do foreign and domestic policy, science, technology, and business, the issues discussed in this paper are indeed multifaceted, but they are not a single inextricable mess either; they can be addressed in steps, base by base, project by project. However, like those before or after it, the Bush administration was unwilling to shake loose enough resources from the military sector to create and sustain the alternatives. Its ideological rigidity caused it to object to virtually any action, insisting that nothing should be done and nothing would work. Yet here was a multiplicity of potential projects in the public and private sectors that, by diverting funds, would have contributed greatly to the devolution of federal control of resources that was otherwise proclaimed as a major ideological plank of the Bush administration.

Some of the nation's economic problems were easing somewhat as it ended, as well as since then, but a disaster does not have to be complete in order to qualify as one. A government has an *ongoing* obligation to ease the travail of its citizens rather than wait or hope, like Dickens' Mr. Micawber, for something good to turn up or for matters to right themselves—meaning all too often a conviction that people will continue to put up with the physical and socioeconomic deterioration of their societies. The worst lesson to be drawn from the Bush experience would be that it is not necessary to address these problems and that an ever escalating arms race (which is once again in clear prospect) will not make them infinitely worse. Most of the political pathologies of this century promised that while the current miseries were real, they would lead to future happiness. When a colleague once gave Sigmund Freud the Communist version of this gambit, Freud reported, "I told him I believed the first part." So did the voters in 1992.

NOTE

1. What also "made [Orange County] famous" at the time was the bankruptcy of its government as a result of speculation in derivatives.

REFERENCES

Adams, G. "Defense Cuts: Little Gain, Modest Pain" (op-ed). *New York Times*, December 5, 1989.
Alexander, D. "How Big Is the Military Economy? GNP vs. Resource Use." Briefing Paper 5, National Commission for Economic Conversion and Disarmament (ECD), Washington, DC, 1990.
Baird, J. E. "A Network Model of the Conversion Process." In J. E. Ullmann, ed., *Conversion Prospects of the Defense Electronics Industry*. Hempstead, NY: Hofstra Yearbooks of Business, 1965, pp. 429–70.
Berke, R. L. "Bush Pushes Himself as Good for the Economy." *New York Times*, June 20, 1992.
Closson, M., et al. "Military Base Conversion." *Positive Alternatives* (Fall 1996).
Defense Base Closure and Realignment Commission. *1993 Report to the President*, Arlington, VA, 1993.
Feldman, J. M. "Diversification after the Cold War: Results of the National Defense Economy Survey." Working Paper 112, Project for Regional and Industrial Economics, Rutgers University, New Brunswick, NJ, 1997.
Lynch, J. E. *Economic Adjustment and Conversion of Defense Industries*. Boulder, CO: Westview, 1987.
Melman, S. *The Peace Race*. New York: Ballantine Books, 1961.
———. *Profits without Production*. New York: Knopf, 1983.
Melman, S., et al. *A Strategy for American Security*. New York: Lee Services, 1963.
Raffel, J. "Economic Conversion Legislation: Past Approaches and the Search for a New Framework." In L. J. Dumas, ed., *The Socio-Economics of Conversion from War to Peace*. Armonk, NY: M. E. Sharpe, 1995, pp. 195–232.
Rauch, J. "Tooth Fairy Defense Budgets." *New York Times*, September 25, 1996.
Sasser, J. *Congressional Record*, March 23, 1994.
Tirman, J. *The Militarization of High Technology*. Cambridge, MA: Ballinger, 1984.
Ullmann, J. E. "Problems of Occupational Conversion." In U.S. Senate, Subcommittee on Employment and Manpower, *Convertibility of Defense Resources to Civilian Needs: A Search for New Employment Potentials*, 88th Cong., 2d sess. Washington, DC: U.S. Government Printing Office, 1964, pp. 675–92.
———. "Conversion and the Import Problem: A Confluence of Opportunities." *IEEE Spectrum* (April 1970): 55.
———. *The Prospects of American Industrial Recovery*. Westport, CT: Quorum Books, 1985.
———. "Economic Conversion: Indispensable for America's Economic Recovery." Briefing Paper 3, National Commission for Economic Conversion and Disarmament (ECD), Washington, DC, 1989.
———. "Let Government Help Defense Industry to Switch." Letter, *Newsday*, April 11, 1990.
———. "Conversion: The Prospects for Long Island." *Hofstra University Business Review* (April 1994).
U.S. Congress, Joint Economic Committee. *The U.S. Trade Position in High Technology*. Washington, DC: U.S. Government Printing Office, 1986.

U.S. Department of Defense, Defense Science Board. *The Defense Industrial and Technology Base*. Washington, DC: Office of the Undersecretary of Defense for Acquisition, 1988.

U.S. Senate, Committee on the Environment and Public Works. *Environmental Issues and Military Base Closings*, Hearings, 103rd Cong., 1st sess., May 27 and December 7. Washington, DC: U.S. Government Printing Office, 1993.

Weidenbaum, M. "Defense Firms Should Fight, Not Switch." Viewpoints, *Newsday*, March 26, 1990.

———. *Small Wars, Big Defense*. New York: Oxford University Press, 1992.

———. "Neoisolationism and Global Realities." Policy Study 130, Center for the Study of American Business, St. Louis, MO, 1996.

Discussant: Douglas A. Brook

George Bush occupied a substantial portion of 13 years of my life, and I'm very happy to have the chance to give him at least one more day. Let me begin by making a couple of observations, in my role as a discussant, about the papers that have been presented here.

Regarding Dr. Ullmann's disappointment with our disinclination to fund and manage aggressive conversion programs, one of the most fascinating things for a financial manager in the Department of Defense is to see how many good ideas people have about how the defense budget can be spent to achieve nondefense objectives. I would suggest to you that the list includes the manufacturing base and social disintegration. Remember for a moment that the budget savings that we were supposed to achieve through base closure disappeared from our resource base almost as fast as the bases were coming down. The revenues that we were supposed to get from base closing—primarily from the sale of prime properties—did not materialize because alternative public uses were found for many of them. So there was no property sale to generate revenue for us. Base closure costs money. There are environmental costs, there are costs to moving people, there are costs to closing down. It takes money to save money, and I would suggest that, faced with declining resources and the requirement to keep our army trained and ready at every point during the transition, it cannot be so surprising that we didn't entertain thoughts of a new mission—an essentially nondefense one at that.

Now, that's not to say that we weren't conscious of what was going on in the communities and with our people. The Army Career Alumni Program, for instance, was dedicated to assisting the transition of people who were leaving the service and moving to civilian life. Similarly, our commanders were active participants in community efforts to ease the economic impacts of base closure. As last week's *National Journal* reports, there is plenty of evidence that many of these communities have done quite well in devising and implementing survival strategies.

On the subject of the Tower nomination, Dr. King suggests that the subsequent nominations are important, that after a failed presidential nomination, presidents and Congress look for a new candidate whose personal and professional qualities at least avoid the problems that the failed nominee had. We will never know, of course, what kind of secretary the late Senator Tower would have made. But the qualities that President Bush eventually found in Secretary Cheney were exactly what was needed to lead DOD and engender the public and congressional confidence that was needed in our day-to-day management of the Defense Department, especially in times of stress like Desert Shield and Desert Storm.

The Senate may have been right or wrong with regard to Senator Tower. I think many of the reasons that were discussed today are probably quite valid as explanations for why the Senate did what it did. But President Bush certainly got it right with Dick Cheney, and I think that went a long way toward minimizing any long-term negative results in terms of our relationships with the Congress.

A protracted confirmation fight in a new administration also has organizational consequences. Institutions like the Department of Defense do not function well without leaders. The Tower fight not only delayed the appointment of a secretary; it delayed even further the appointment of his management team. Secretary Cheney was confirmed in March 1989; Sean O'Keefe was confirmed as comptroller in May 1989; my colleagues and I in the army were among the last to be appointed because there was a further delay in the appointment of the secretary of the army. I didn't take office until March 1990, 15 months after President Bush's inauguration. For this reason if no other, I think Professor Ravenal's paper is correct in the assertion that, even though George Bush took office in January 1989, the 1992 budget was the real point of departure for the Bush defense program.

Having said that, let me make a few observations about that budget and the environment in which we made it. First, it's important to understand that at any one time, not one budget but three budgets are being worked in the Department of Defense: first, there's the current-year budget, running from October 1 to September 30, that we're executing; the second is next year's budget request, which we're justifying, either at OMB [Office of Management and Budget] or on Capitol Hill; and the third is the following-year budget that is under development in the department. This is the federal budget cycle: formulation, justification, and execution. That means that the fiscal 1992 budget was under development in the summer and fall of 1990, while we were executing the 1990 budget and defending the 1991 budget proposal.

Consider for a moment what was going on while we were developing the 1992 budget. We were solidly on a budget reduction track, as Professor Ravenal describes. We had long-term plans calling for substantial reductions in our forces. Our budgets were coming down. We were implementing the defense management review and looking for cost-saving ways to change the way DOD did business. The army budget was planned to go from nearly $80 billion in 1990 to the low $60s in 1993. Then, in August 1990, along came Desert Shield. Suddenly, our attention was yanked away from formulating the 1992 budget and into the current-year budget—the one that usually gets the least attention from senior managers. The simple question was, How do we pay for the deployments that we're about to make?

Everybody looks at war from one's own perspective, I suppose. If you're on the front lines, it means one thing; if you're a logician, it means something else. If you're a financial manager, the rule is: Don't go to war in the fiscal fourth quarter. You can't afford it. If you are in the first or second quarter, you can revise your spending plans and pull money forward. But in the fourth quarter, you have spent at least three-quarters of your annual appropriation, probably more. We simply didn't have the funds to finance Desert Shield.

Fortunately, someone discovered the Civil War-era Feed and Forage Act, which allowed us to continue operations without jeopardizing the mission due to lack of funds. We spent the largest amounts of Feed and Forage money in history—about $19 billion in 1990. This had to be repaid, through appropriated funds, supplemental appropriations, and the Defense Cooperation Account, which was funded by our allies. The point is that we were preparing for war in 1990, spending in the current year as though we had the money but knowing we didn't have it yet, while we continued the separate track of fiscal 1992 budget reductions. This means that we were literally ramping up and ramping down simultaneously.

I would spend the morning of every day in the Army Operations Center listening to overnight reports about Desert Shield (and eventually Desert Storm) and dealing with resource issues to make sure that the funds were available to support the operation. Later in the morning, I would go on to my office and work the rest of the day on a downsized budget. This is troublesome fiscal schizophrenia. You begin to wonder which of those is reality. We had to segment two separate and conflicting financial missions, and we met them both—on the one hand, through Feed and Forage supplemental appropriations and the Defense Cooperation Account and, on the other hand, in force reductions, base closures, and management reform.

Now, I don't think that any of us at the time really thought much about how strange this situation was or that we might be making some sort of financial management history. But I've had some time to think about this, and I think we made the Comptroller's Hall of Fame. There are some serious issues here for future administrations. In determining policies and strategies for resourcing national defense, is it really possible or desirable to fund at reduced levels over a long period and plan to fund occasional surge requirements on an exception basis? In recent years, surge requirements have proven to be more than occasional. I would suggest, therefore, that there are some important issues involved here. Some important lessons in defense financial management can be learned from our experiences.

Discussant: Richard B. Cheney

It's always fun to go back and reflect a little bit on history, and I thought Doug did an excellent job on the financial aspects of some of the problems we had to deal with in the Bush Defense Department. Let me do a couple of things. I thought I might say just a word to Dr. Ullmann—we have slightly different views about the role of government and the private sector—and then I thought what I'd do is take a couple of minutes and talk sort of from the policy perspective about some of the strategic kinds of decisions and force structure issues that were so ably addressed in Dr. Ravenal's paper.

With respect to this whole notion of defense conversion, we went through the process of downsizing the U.S. military and cutting back. I think we closed some 800 bases and installations. I know that on my watch we laid off 400,000 people out of the Department of Defense, military and civilian, and obviously a lot more than that when you added up the private sector employment that was affected by it. We shut down dozens—literally dozens—of production lines and terminated various and sundry weapons systems. We were well aware of the economic consequences of doing that, and of the political consequences of it. I think one of the things George Bush deserves credit for is that he never blinked once. He knew that when it came time, for example, to cut back on the defense budget, we were going to have an impact, for example, on his political standing in California. California was going to get hit because there were a lot of bases there. But there was never a time, when I'd go over and brief him and tell him what we were about to do, that he ever said, "Dick, don't do that; politically we can't take the heat." As a matter of fact, in the first round of base closings, two of the bases that figured prominently on the list included the base right near Kennebunkport, Maine, that he used to fly into with Air Force One whenever he wanted a vacation to go up home, and the other was a naval air station in [Beeville], Texas, where he used to go turkey hunting every year. When those came up on the list as no longer necessary, I must say I swallowed hard, but I left them on the list, and we went forward, and he never said a word about it to me. He just rerouted his aircraft, and we went forward with our business.

But the notion of using public funds for defense conversion, I think, is a fundamentally bad idea. I'm now the chairman and CEO [chief executive officer] of a company, Halliburton. We're in the oil and gas business, engineering and construction; Brown & Root Engineering is one of our companies. We would benefit significantly if the government wants to spend money on public works programs. We're not a major defense contractor—only about 10 percent of our revenue comes from the government, from government services—but I've got to tell you, if you are going to pay companies like mine, even though you no longer need what we produce as a result of cutbacks in the defense budget, you're not only wasting public funds that ought to be devoted, perhaps, to maintaining the readiness of the force or investing in new military capabilities down the road, you're also creating an environment in which I won't do what I need to do as the chairman and CEO of that company when a certain line of business dries up, in terms of restructuring, reengineering, getting more competitive, remaining lean and mean. The competitive pressures that drive the private sector to do the right thing are enormously important, and I always looked upon defense conversion as funneling money in to maintain inefficient operations to produce goods the Department of Defense no longer needed or wanted. So I think it's a serious mistake for us to go down that road.

Let me say a word about how we tried to adjust to the Cold War. When we took over in the spring of 1989, there was still a Cold War—at least that certainly was our perception. You may remember we were in the midst of intensive negotiations on conventional force reductions in Europe. That was one of the first arms control matters we had to deal with as we tried to negotiate new force levels between the Warsaw Pact and NATO [North Atlantic Treaty Organization]. The strategy that we were tied into that we'd inherited from our predecessors in the spring of 1989 was the old Cold War scenario. It was driven by the following set of assumptions: first, that if a war began in Europe, we would have perhaps only two weeks' warning time; second, that depending upon how much mobilization time there was, we would face as many as 100 Soviet-led Warsaw Pact divisions; third, that the conflict would begin on the inner German border—that is, between East and West Germany; fourth, that as the Soviets had that kind of massive power—over 100 divisions, mind you, and the entire U.S. Army at that point had 18 divisions—we would probably ultimately have to use nuclear weapons in order to halt that Soviet assault; and that any major conflict in Europe ultimately was likely to go global and involve our forces on a worldwide basis.

That was the set of assumptions we had when I took over in the spring of 1989, which had been there for a long time. What that led to, in turn, were certain decisions from our standpoint about what kind of forces we needed: that we had to have, for example, under our commitment to NATO, a commitment to have 10 divisions in Europe within 10 days of a decision to mobilize. No way you could move 10 divisions in 10 days, so we had to keep 4⅔ divisions deployed forward at all times. That dictated, in effect, the size of our forces in Europe, that we had to maintain the sea-lanes open in the North Atlantic to be able to resupply our forces in Europe in the event of an all-out global conflict with the Soviets, and so on. So the force structure we had, the scenarios we dealt with, all were built around that notion of all-out global conflict with the Soviets that would begin, perhaps, with as little as two weeks' notice.

Then in the fall of 1989, of course, the world changed dramatically. All of a sudden, the Warsaw Pact started to come apart. Eventually, the Berlin Wall came down in November 1989, and that led to a decision internally that was signed up to by myself and our civilian leadership, as well as the Joint Chiefs, that it was time, obviously, given what we could see—the winding down of the

Cold War—for us to adjust and to adapt to that, and that if we didn't come up with our own plan generated internally, in terms of what we thought was appropriate in this new environment, then some kind of change would be imposed on us, but it would be imposed from external sources. It probably wouldn't have any kind of coherence to it, and it would simply be a reaction to the demise of the Soviet Union. Therefore, we thought it was incumbent upon us to come forward with a new strategy, a new force structure, a new budget in order to reflect the radical changes that were under way at that point in the Soviet Union.

This, in turn, led to the development of what we called our regional strategy. It's part of the Defense Planning Guidance Process. The Defense Planning Guidance is a document that's put together, signed out by the secretary of defense. The basic work that goes into it is done by the undersecretary for policy and his staff on the civilian side, and the Joint Staff under the chairman of the JCS (Joint Chiefs of staff). This Defense Planning Guidance becomes the basic document, then, that the services have to build their long-range budgets toward. In effect, what we did to replace that old strategy, based on the notion of global conflict, was a new one that said: Look, with the end of the Soviet empire and the demise of the Warsaw Pact, the demise of the Soviet Union, we are not likely in the future to face a global threat without having significant warning time to get ready for it. That is to say, we've moved to the assumption that we would not have all-out global conflict in a matter of weeks but rather that it would be a matter of years before that kind of threat arose and that, given that time frame, we would have time to regenerate sufficient forces to fight a global war. So we could downsize the force below what we'd maintained it at before.

A second major consideration was the belief that there were certain key regions of the world that we cared about very much that were strategically vital to the United States. We didn't care about all regions, or there were a lot of regions out there where significant military requirements for the United States weren't likely to occur—Latin America being one; very important to us, but no significant military threat—but that we needed to size our forces and build forces based on this notion that we needed to be able to deny an adversary the ability to dominate a region of the world that was strategic from our standpoint: Europe, probably the eastern Pacific, and certainly the Middle East and the Gulf region.

All of this thinking, then, was being done in late 1989 and the first half of 1990, and we'd scheduled a date when the president was going to make a major speech laying out this new regional approach with respect to our strategic considerations. That was going to be followed up by a briefing to the press, to the White House press corps, by myself and General Scowcroft. Then, following that, there was going to be a series of briefings and publicity for this new strategic perception over the course of the next several months. Unfortunately, the day that we scheduled all of this kick-off for was August 2, 1990—same day Saddam Hussein invaded Kuwait. So on that day, we had a quick meeting early in the morning in the Cabinet Room to first begin to discuss how we were going to respond to the Iraqi invasion of Kuwait, which had occurred the night before, and then the president went off to Aspen, Colorado, and he gave the speech, but

Brent and I couldn't go because we had to stay home, given the developing crisis, and there was never any follow-up in terms of our going out and explaining and trying to educate and articulate this new approach—primarily because we were too busy doing it instead of talking about it. We had a classic example of the kind of situation we thought we might face, where we had a regional threat, a region vital to the United States, and the prospect that somebody hostile to the United States—namely, Saddam Hussein—was trying to dominate that region.

As we went into Desert Shield and Desert Storm, then, we had all the problems that Doug mentioned: on the one hand, we were on this glide path down, looking at what we required long-term with respect to our forces; on the other hand, we were engaged in the largest deployment of forces overseas in 25 years—half a million men and women halfway around the world, to the Gulf, to participate in Desert Storm. It was a bit of a paradox to try to wrestle with both of those issues and both of those concerns, but I think we got it done.

I can't say we did it perfectly—I'm sure there were some slips along the way. But even as we were going through Desert Shield and the buildup in the fall of 1990, you may remember there were the big debate with respect to budget policy here at home and the major negotiations under way between the administration and the Congress over what was going to happen on budget and tax policy. That's when the president made his famous, or infamous, decision that he would, in fact, raise taxes and I think got himself into great trouble given his earlier, and I thought very wise, policy of "Read my lips: No new taxes." That decision was made in October 1990 at the same time that we were getting ready to deploy the second wave of forces to the Gulf, and it also, obviously, then led us to come up with a new number for the defense budget. But that new number for the defense budget was based on that prior work we'd been doing earlier, in terms of developing the base force, a 25 percent cut in force structure—all of those decisions that flowed out of that basic assumption that we no longer had to deal with global conflict, but we had to be prepared to pursue this regional strategy that I mentioned previously.

In the end, I think that it's important as well to recognize—although we sometimes were criticized then for not reacting aggressively enough to the end of the Cold War—if you look at the record of the Bush administration, it's amazing how much we did get done, even as we were undertaking a major military operation simultaneously in the Gulf. We haven't said anything at all today about the radical reduction in our nuclear force posture that occurred throughout this period of time, too. In August 1991, just a few months after the Gulf conflict ended, of course you had the coup attempt in Moscow—the Old Guard rose up and attempted to overthrow Gorbachev—and then President Yeltsin as the president of Russia as the Soviet Union came apart in September 1991. President Bush put forward what I think was the most far-reaching proposal for the reduction of nuclear weapons in history—ultimately, it became START II. We proposed eliminating land-based multiple warhead systems; we brought home most of our tactical nukes from Europe; we took all of our tactical nukes off our ships at sea; we stood down the bomber force for the first time since 1957—we didn't have bombers fueled, loaded with nuclear weapons, parked at the end of the runway ready to go to war at a moment's notice anymore. Radical, radical change in our nuclear force posture. That was a direct result of wanting to take advantage of the demise of the Soviet Union and get them to sign up to START II, which they did. Unfortunately, they haven't ratified it yet, and that's still a very important piece of business.

As I look back on it, I feel pretty good about the record that we established during that period of time. I do think there were major, major activities under way in the Defense Department. We did have a very full platter with the end of the Cold War, coupled with our operations in Panama, coupled with the operation in the desert. So I will be happy to defend the record; I think it's a good one. I'm not certain we've done justice to Dr. Ravenal, who's tried to put it all into some broad, comprehensive, analytical scheme, which we appreciate, and it wasn't quite that orderly as we went through the process, I can assure you. There were days when we were making it up as we went along, but thanks to the likes of Doug Brook and Sean O'Keefe and a great many others who were part of the effort, I think it came out pretty well.

Discussant: James M. Klurfeld

This reminds me of a time I was once at the Naval War College, and we were participating in some war games. Once they gave us the problem, they sat us around a table, and then they went around the table asking people what they would do about the problem. They asked me first, and I looked at them in absolute horror, and I said, "Hey, wait a second: I'm an editorial writer. Let everybody else go first, and then I'll second-guess them." So I appreciate being in this position.

Let me just share some observations with you from all the very interesting presentations we've heard. First of all, I think, overall, from someone from the outside watching this, my sense is that, despite Dr. Ravenal's wonderful attempt to give the Bush administration a grand vision, my sense was that this was essentially a cautious, reactive administration that dealt with problems as they came to them. But I would also say that when they dealt with those problems—especially in the foreign policy field—they dealt with them very, very well.

I also think there were some underlying principles that the members of the administration brought to dealing with these problems, and I think the principles had to do with the sense that, even though the Cold War was ending, and this great conflict that had lasted all these years was now over, in the new world, the United States needed to be active. The Bush administration clearly rejected the notion of the United States retreating to its borders in a sense of a new isolationism. I think some of that came—any number of members of the administration were people who had worked with Henry Kissinger previously, and I think, in a sense, if they didn't have Kissinger's grand vision about how to do things, they did believe that American interests were what was needed to dictate American policy—not a sense of doing good, not a sense of morality, but basically, you had to act on where American interests were.

I also think that there was a very steady sense of how to use American power in this administration. Now, this comes from an editorial page editor who has supported a string of Democratic candidates for president, but I have to admit that I think, when it comes to the use of power, the Republicans have demonstrated a much surer footing than the Democrats have, and this has been over a period of 20 years.

I think the other thing you have to recognize, while you say this was a reactive administration, my gosh, they were reacting to cataclysmic events taking place at the speed of light. The whole world changed, and I think when you listen to people like Dick Cheney and Brent Scowcroft and others at this conference talk about how they were dealing with that change, it is really fascinating and a very special opportunity, because there were other administrations that went through years and years and didn't have to face that type of problem.

Now, in terms of the question of the administration's approach, while they were slow to react, I would say that the advances in arms control—and that was the subject of the panel I was on previous to this—were fundamentally important. Dick Cheney talked about the fundamental, important changes in nuclear weapons, and they were just that. I would also make the point I made this morning very quickly, that I think the CFE Treaty—the Conventional Forces in Europe Treaty—is also of fundamental, lasting importance and has changed the face of Europe in a way that no one could have possibly imagined before.

I now look back on the Gulf War and say this was maybe sui generis, and the problems presented in Bosnia represent a more typical type of problem that we are now facing in this post–Cold War period. It might be interesting to hear, as we ask questions, what Secretary Cheney and some of the others feel about, if there had been a second administration, how the administration would have handled Bosnia, whether they could have continued to resist not doing anything.

Finally, on the question of the political aspects of dealing with the defense budget, I think you have to give this administration very high marks. I mean, the fact is that you always have to deal with these political questions. One of the things I learned as a young reporter in Washington, when I started to cover the defense budget, my first inclination was to sit down and say, "Okay, let's see: What are the threats, and then what are we spending?" One of our veteran reporters stopped me and said, "Wait a second, Jim, that's not how you study the defense budget. It's all politics. It's all about pork." That is certainly, to a large extent, true. When you go through the defense budget and try to ask, "Why do we have this program? Why do we have that program?" it's because this is a powerful congressman, and this is a powerful senator, and they didn't want to give up those programs. So the ability of this administration to form the base closing agreement, I think, was very significant in the way they packaged it and gave it to Congress on an up-or-down vote. It was still very tough politically to do, but they were able to do it, and it was an interesting and significant precedent. And you hear many times now in Washington, when the Congress has to do something tough politically, and it seems unable to do it, a lot of people refer to, "Let's do a base closing-type of package approach."

Finally, just very quickly, let me say something about the conversion argument. You know, Long Island, where we're situated right now, certainly felt the effects of the defense downsizing. The fact is—and once again, this comes from someone who's basically supported Democrats over the years—I think the market's ability to respond and be flexible is very impressive. Here we are on Long Island; we have unemployment less than 4 percent. Granted, a lot of the jobs we now have aren't as good as the defense jobs we had, but if you've spent your career watching government as I have, you develop a certain degree of skepticism about the ability of government to do things and not simply try to perpetuate itself. So I'm skeptical, at best, about whether an industrial type of policy would have done anything other than to provide bureaucratic jobs.

And I'll just say quickly—and we can get into it in the question-and-answer session—as a member of the press, I will not take either the credit or the blame for the John Tower situation. I'll leave that to Sam Nunn.

Questions and Answers: David G. Blanchard, Moderator

David G. Blanchard: I think we do have some time for maybe four or five questions.

John E. Ullmann: May I make a response?

Blanchard: Yes, sir, Dr. Ullmann.

Ullmann: First, I do not advocate now, nor have I ever done so, that the Pentagon should run any alternative activities. I am not even sure if it can be trusted to clean up the environmental horrors on various bases that it is now giving up, horrors that should never have been permitted to be there in the first place. Why, for example, did the Presidio that Secretary Cheney mentioned have a water system that didn't have enough pressure to put fires out?

I was putting forth two general ideas: We need energy independence—our import dependence is a threat to our security—and we ought to take care of our water supply and the rest of our infrastructure. Four years ago, just before the mayoral election, a big water pipe broke in Manhattan. Bob Hope was a few blocks away at Madison Square Garden, and he said, "New York doesn't need a mayor; it needs a plumber." It's that kind of thing that's been going on now, and if that isn't a threat to national security, I don't know what is. I don't want the Pentagon to run it; we need people, public or private, who would run these things properly and more efficiently. But note I said "public" too. I don't know any private enterprise that would want to invest in flood control for Fargo, North Dakota, but that's the sort of thing that we now need.

Blanchard: Dr. Ravenal, you have a point, too?

Earl C. Ravenal: I think that, embedded in this discussion, which is so various—we have everything from, in a sense, a biography of failed defense secretary John Tower and so forth, and base closing issues, and some comments on weapons systems and things—there are some very fundamental methodological problems here, and that's what I would like to underline without trying to seem overly academic. But that's where the action is. The question that's very much disputed here under the surface of the papers is what makes a difference, a big difference, between one kind of defense policy and another kind of defense policy. I'll try to keep it short, but this is what we have to keep our eye on: what makes the big differences.

Now, there was a suggestion in Professor King's paper about John Tower, that he never met a weapons system that he didn't like, and somehow this is supposed to be a disqualification for an objective view of defense policy. This comment—although it's an interesting one; it's a witty comment—reflects part of the false fixation of the Congress particularly. The Congress is fixated on big-ticket weapons systems, and, if I can shift to Professor Ullmann's point, it's fixated on such issues as base closings. I will submit that this is an instinct for the capillaries and not the jugular, as Kissinger once said. Base closings, with all due respect to the immensity of the research that is reflected in a paper such as this, don't mean a thing. A couple of billion dollars here, a couple of billion dollars there, as somebody said, pretty soon it adds up to real money. It doesn't add up to real money. The money is in the force structures. To keep one average army division in the active force structure for one year, including all the overheads that all of our newly modernized forces would certainly have to incur—all the support costs and overhead—cost $7.1 billion a year. One division—you see? To keep an aircraft carrier battle group in the force structure for one year costs $4.1 billion, and it takes three of them on rotation just to keep one in a forward position, where it can make a difference in some kind of a regional confrontation in terms of the projection of American force. The money is in the force structures, and the force structures are derived in a way that is much more rational than people would even begin to believe—much more deductive and rational, from the kinds of military missions that the people who plan these things decide have to be confronted in the world, have to be addressed. So we get to a question of the military missions for which forces must be designed and created and maintained, and that is where the action ultimately is.

The Bush administration settled on two major regional contingencies (although it did not use that term), and that is still the planning factor that is being used in the Clinton administration. Those military missions create a need, an objective need for certain active forces in the force structure, endowed with certain kinds of weaponry that are deemed to have the characteristics to prevail in the battlefields that result from the selection of those particular regional missions. That's really what I want to suggest. I think there is a tremendous methodological divide here, and I think that in order to understand—*appreciate*, let's put it that way—the defense policy of any given administration, whether one agrees with it substantively or not (a very different story), one has to keep in mind the kinds of threats, the kinds of military missions, and the design of the force structure that that administration had to deal with.

Blanchard: Let's see if we can get the audience in here. First question.

Q: Yes. *As head of a large organization, can you comment at all on President Bush's style of delegating decisions and following up, or could you shed any new light on his decision to stick with the UN [United Nations] mandate and pull out of Iraq, basically, without going to the capital?*

Cheney: You talking to me?

Q: *Please.*

Cheney: I'm just checking! I've worked in three administrations. I was a junior staffer in the Nixon administration, I worked for President Ford, and I worked for President Bush. In terms of the way he managed the Defense Department, the relationship with the Defense Department, the national security apparatus, I thought President Bush was superb. I don't mean to blow smoke—obviously, I'm a fan of his, and I enjoyed working for him—but he was very good about giving us an objective—for example, liberate Kuwait—and saying, "You guys go figure out how to do it." We then had to come up in the Defense Department with what forces we wanted to use, what the strategy was going to be, how we would deploy the force, and he was very good at then giving us the support we needed. We never got second-guessed in terms of—oh, for example, the way the Johnson administration second-guessed the military and the Defense Department during the Vietnam War. He was very good at maintaining the integrity of the chain of command.

One of the problems you have in Washington, every time you deploy the forces, everybody and his brother want to tell you how to do it. That includes an awful lot of senior military personnel in the Department of Defense who are experts, who've got a lot to say, but they're not in the chain of command. The chiefs are not in the chain of command when you deploy the force. It runs from the president to the secretary of defense to the CINC [commander in chief] out in the field—the commander who's running the region—and, if you want, you can loop it through the chairman of the Joint Chiefs, which we did. But basically, the commandant of the Marine Corps or the chief of Naval Operations is not in the chain of command for using the force. So there's this natural tendency for everybody to sort of want to get into the operation, commit forces, decide how they're going to be used, and so forth. The key to protecting that and keeping the State Department out of the business of selecting, for example, bombing targets is to have a president who believes in the chain of command and who'll back you up all the way, and George Bush was superb in that regard. He was very good.

In terms of supporting the UN resolution, this age-old debate—I suppose it will go on for a long time—we stopped when we stopped because we'd done what we said we were going to do. Our objective was to liberate Kuwait and destroy Saddam's offensive capability. We'd done that. The morning the president made the decision, everybody—military and civilian alike—agreed that we'd achieved our objectives. If we were to go beyond that, if we'd gone to Baghdad to get Saddam Hussein—which is what you'd have had to do: you'd have to go in and occupy all of Iraq to track him down—we would have been all alone, the coalition would have come apart; none of our Arab allies were prepared to support that kind of operation. While it's messy to have it the way it is today, I think it would have been messier if we had converted from a collective security arrangement that we led, where we were reversing somebody else's aggression, into a situation where the United States moves in as an occupying colonial power and starts taking down governments. I think we would have been in much worse shape than we are today.

Blanchard: Since we started a little late, I'm going to go over a little bit, but I'm going to hold it to you five people who are standing in line.

Q: Secretary Cheney, just another question about how to think about the future, both for yourself and for President Bush. As Dr. Ravenal laid out, the main changes, it appears, in the defense structure were reductions of the military—25 percent of the force structure being the main definition of the base force, and changes in percentages of the defense budget—but also acknowledgment of the idea that the defense forces that we had were based on a conflict starting in Europe. A lot of what we built and a lot of the assumptions about the navy's mission, a lot of the assumptions about the army's mission, and so on, were all based on that European contingency. Changing to a regional contingency didn't necessarily mean the same forces would be appropriate. To the degree that— I'm sort of curious as to what sense you and the president thought about the future in terms of what different forces, or what differently structured forces, we might need—not just a smaller number of tanks, a smaller number of aircraft carriers—

Cheney: But different kinds.

Q: But what different sort of structure would we need?

Cheney: Well, we had an example of how you can get in trouble in the Gulf War in terms of operating with forces that were designed for the Cold War in Europe. All of our heavy divisions that we'd planned to use in Europe in a scenario against the Soviets, we assumed rail transport. We've got a lot of railroads in the United States, a lot of railroads in Europe, and we could deploy and debark in the ports in Western Europe and put everybody on railroad cars and move them to the front. There aren't any railroads in Saudi Arabia. What we discovered when we started moving the Seventh Corps from Germany down to Saudi Arabia was that we didn't have enough heavy-equipment trucks in our divisions to move those tanks and Bradleys around.

The way we solved the problem—again, this was our good luck—the Cold War had ended. It turned out that the German military had inherited from the old GDR [German Democratic Republic] one hell of a lot of great big trucks for moving tanks around. So it was those East German trucks that were originally part of the Warsaw Pact force that we were going to have to fight in Europe that we sent to the desert, courtesy of the demise of the Warsaw Pact, to move those tanks out into the desert so we could get organized and move Seventh Corps, as we did in that operation. It was a classic example of how those forces were not configured for that kind of regional contingency that you're talking about.

I think you've got to give the military credit, the Defense Department; there is a lot of work under way in terms of new capabilities. A lot of the technologies we used in Desert Storm were old technologies. Those cruise missiles dated back to the 1970s. The first time we used them in combat was 1991. That really was old technology, all the "gee-whiz" stuff. We used a lot of laser-guided bombs at the end of the war in Vietnam that later played such a prominent role in the desert. There's a lot of work now going on to develop that next generation of stuff.

What I worry about more than anything else is that we aren't spending enough today. If I could reorient the budget, I'd close more bases and take the money and spend it in those new technologies, because those are the capabilities we're going to have 10, 15, 20 years from now, and we're not making enough investment there. Our procurement budget last year was the lowest since 1950. We've got to replace that stuff, we've got to buy new capabilities, especially the kind of sensors and improved intelligence capabilities that let us go and look at a battlefield, know where everything is, and be able to target it.

Q: *I guess this is for anybody. What are the odds of a Cheney–Kemp ticket?*

Cheney: Of a Cheney–Kemp ticket? Jack, I assume, is going to be number two.

Blanchard: Next question.

Q: *Hi, I'm a cadet here at Hofstra University, in Army ROTC [Reserve Officers' Training Corps], and I was wondering about, because of the cut in defense spending, how are we supposed to, at the lowest level—as in Army ROTC—train our cadets to become soldiers to be equivalent to our international counterparts enough that we're actually able to be deployed and know what we're supposed to do and actually be able to fight a war if we ever had one?*

Cheney: Well, your training funds have been cut back now?

Q: *Yes, they have. What we usually do is called Advance Camp over the summer, and there usually used to be one in Fort Bragg, and there's one in Fort Lewis. Because of the cut in spending, we're no longer going to Fort Bragg. They cut back a bunch of schools, like airborne air assault schools. Now we go only to Fort Lewis. The camp has actually been shortened. There's a lot less— we learn a lot less. We're cut back on branch orientation; we learn a lot less in-the-field work. This is our major officer training before we actually get commissioned. Something like that, how are we supposed to actually be trained enough that we're able to be an officer in the United States Army?*

Cheney: Well, that's unfortunate if it's happening, because—we've got the "hockey stick model," I guess: the notion that, yes, the budget's going down again this year for the 12th year in a row, or whatever it might be, but next year it's going to be different. Next year we're going to start back up, because everybody who looks at it knows that you can't stay on that downward slope forever. There are inflation and increased costs of doing business. There's some floor below which you cannot cut the defense budget without doing serious damage to the force.

Unfortunately, every year that goes by, the uptick in the hockey stick gets pushed one more year farther down the road. We're at the point now, especially given the additional peacekeeping missions we've taken and so forth, that we are soaking up all of our dollars—I can't say all, but I think a very significant portion—in terms of maintaining the readiness of the current force and carrying out these peacekeeping missions—deployments to Bosnia, deployments to Haiti and Somalia, and so forth. Gradually, over time, you start to cut back not only into your R&D [research and development] and your procurement, but you begin to affect training as well, too.

Our theory always was, in the Bush years, that we wanted the best force we could possibly have; that we would cut the size force to whatever level we had to cut it to, but when we got to that level, we wanted to make certain we had enough adequate training, equipment, and so forth for the force. When we begin to cut back on some of the things you're talking about, what happens is you begin to lose people. If you don't allow a pilot enough flying hours a month, he'll quit and go to work for United. Then, all of a sudden, what you've got is difficulty maintaining the quality of the force. We saw that back in the late 1970s; it's devastating when it happens, and we need to guard against it now.

Blanchard: Final question.

Q: This is to Mr. Cheney. I'm a graduate student in political science at Long Island University, and my question is, since the collapse of the Soviet Union, we've seen a very large arms buildup by China. I'm just curious if this could threaten our interests in the future, and are we ready? Did we cut back too much in some of our spending?

Cheney: Well, China obviously bears watching. If I look at the next century, I think if you were to try to put together a list of nations that could potentially become strategic adversaries of the United States—could mount a strategic threat to us the way the Soviets did for the last 50 years—China clearly has to be on the list. I think it's very important that we avoid that. I don't think we're there today, I don't think we ought to look at China as an adversary today. I think it would be very important for us not to fall into that trap of sort of automatically assuming they're the bad guys, and we've got to contain them, and so forth.

The Chinese seem to be absolutely determined, relative to where they were 20 or 30 years ago, to try to be part of the global economy, part of the world system. We don't obviously approve of their human rights record and so forth, but there's been some phenomenal change in China. They've opened themselves up in fairly significant ways, and we need to work on that. If we look at their military capability today, very large army; very, very limited capacity to project power beyond their borders. They've got a few strategic missiles. They obviously have the technology and the know-how to build more if they decided they wanted to do that, but they don't really have a blue-water navy; their air force is very limited. I think they'd have difficulty if they tried to take Taiwan by force.

I'd say it's a very hard thing to do, when you think about how you project significant military power beyond your own borders. Internally, inside, obviously, they're the dominant force, but I'm not worried today about a military threat from China. I would be concerned 15 or 20 years from now if we don't manage that relationship properly and find a way to sort of bring them into the society of nations and avoid a situation in which they become the kind of adversary the Soviets were.

Blanchard: One more comment from Dr. Ullmann.

Ullmann: First of all, I very much agree with Secretary Cheney on this part of his interpretation. I will put it perhaps a little more concretely. To the extent that China is now financing its development out of its participation in the global economy, that participation depends enormously and centrally on what the United States does. You might say, in a way, that we have a hold over each other that we never had in the case of the Soviet Union. After the Cold War began, the Soviet Union moved essentially from a devastated country that didn't have anything much to export to a country whose products were boycotted by the United States. So to the extent that trade has any positive effects, and I am well aware of some negative ones, I think this is something that is likely to reduce the dangers.

Part VIII

Desert Shield and the Gulf War

17

The Bush Just War Doctrine: Genesis and Application of the President's Moral Leadership in the Persian Gulf War

Daniel R. Heimbach

> I read every word of "The Bush Just War Doctrine" . . .; and it accurately states my feelings . . . . Many thanks for setting the record straight. I was very glad that you made those references to Bishop Browning. He and those other ministers did all they could to counter our use of force. I never quite understood how they seemed so indifferent to what Saddam had done to Kuwait.
>
> George Bush[1]

The explicit appeal made by President George Bush to just war principles during his leadership of the Persian Gulf War surprised some and heartened many. For both those who agreed with and those who criticized his use of this historic framework of moral analysis, the fact that the U.S. president presumed the continued relevance of this historic framework in defending a moral warrant for his actions was a matter of intense interest both practical and academic. Yet, although just war commentary in connection with U.S. military involvement in the Persian Gulf War caught national attention during the period of hostility itself,[2] very little has been published since the heat of the actual events.[3] This paper for the first time reviews the inner workings by which President Bush came to apply the principles of just war doctrine. It then goes on to evaluate the application of just war principles in the Persian Gulf War and to respond to major critics of the president's moral leadership of coalition forces seeking the liberation of Kuwait from Iraqi occupation.

GENESIS OF THE BUSH JUST WAR DOCTRINE

While no one doubts that George Bush employed just war reasoning in his leadership of coalition forces opposing Saddam Hussein, the sources of his recourse to the tradition are not well understood. While some facets have been available to scholarly research, others have not been known except to the immediate participants. Needless to say, the way by which George Bush came to justify engaging Saddam Hussein in just war terms cannot be fully understood until all facets have been adequately explained. The genesis of President Bush's recourse to just war tradition arose from three sources: established structures, including international law and military doctrine; the president's personal intuition; and an internal staff memorandum I first initiated and then wrote once the president's need for specific clarification was confirmed by the White House chief of staff John Sununu.

As to the first source, James Turner Johnson has nicely documented the way important elements of just war moral doctrine have been incorporated into international law and have been used to shape military doctrine of the U.S. armed services.[4] The notion of international law is built on the idea that moral principles exist that transcend the particular interests of individual nations and ought to limit their conduct in war. For example, the *jus in bello* principles of discrimination involving noncombatant immunity, the avoidance of evil means (including fair treatment of prisoners and rejection of certain warfare methods) as well as requirements related to proportionality are featured in the body of law that was worked out in a series of international conventions, beginning with the Geneva Convention of 1964 and concluding most recently with the Geneva Protocol of 1977. Though *jus ad bellum* principles have not been treated with the same intensity, explicit *ad bellum* restraints are worked into Articles 2 and 51 of the United Nations Charter.[5]

Johnson also shows how military doctrine as it is currently defined in conduct regulations, standing orders, strategic policies, and service manuals is another locus in which various just war principles have been included in established structures that necessarily affect leadership decisions involving the U.S. armed services.[6] While military service manuals do not treat *jus ad bellum* issues since these are properly left to civilian political authority, they do cover moral limits to the use of force in combat. Thus, as tensions mounted in the Persian Gulf, George Bush from his experience in international affairs and his reliance upon the training and experience of military advisers clearly knew that his options and methods were shaped by the contours of international law and military war doctrine. Accordingly, his actions were already guided by major principles of the just war tradition even before he made conscious appeal to just war thinking by way of explicit terminology.

The second source from which President Bush's recourse to just war tradition arose was his personal intuition. This source was significant, even though he never was formally schooled in just war as such and did not assume the presidency with command of the traditional vocabulary by which principles of the just war are commonly recognized. Nevertheless, despite this lack of formal schooling, the categories of moral analysis by which George Bush responded to tensions in the Persian Gulf displayed a decidedly just war cast because just war assumptions had been thoroughly absorbed by informal means over a lifetime oriented by Western history and driven by strong commitment to received traditions of public service.

How strongly the president's moral intuition was shaped by just war tradition was evident from the beginning even before he was intentionally conscious of employing just war terminology. In a letter to the president after a private meeting in the Oval Office on December 20, 1990, Edmond Browning, presiding bishop of the Episcopal Church, recalls how Bush handed him a copy of an Amnesty International report on atrocities perpetrated by Iraq in occupied Kuwait and said, "[M]orally, are we to do nothing?"[7] At this meeting, Bush had expressed deep moral outrage concerning the injustice of the invasion, the violence against basic human rights, and the mounting numbers of innocent civilian deaths. Although he was aware of the economic, political, and military stakes involved, Bush here revealed how intensely he was focused on the moral stakes raised by the situation.

Later, recalling his December meeting with the bishop to members of the Republican National Committee, Bush relayed how he had told Browning, I want you to read the Amnesty International Report on the abuses of these Kuwaiti families. And then you tell me whether it's right or wrong to use force to stop the cruelty—literally the rape, the pillage, and the plunder of Kuwait— that's going on now."[8] The question expressed the president's conviction concerning the relevance of a just cause in deciding when or whether it would be necessary to go to war. Going on, Bush also had expressed to Browning his concern regarding the relative costs involved in making such a decision. On this, Bush suggested that just as the allies of World War II learned (in their case, too late) that it would have cost many fewer lives to stop Hitler if they had acted in 1939, when he invaded Poland, so stopping Saddam in Kuwait was likely to be much less costly than continued delay—another classic just war calculation.[9] Beyond these remarks, the indirect influence of just war reasoning was evident in other statements. For example, there was Bush's application of last resort in the letter of ultimatum he sent to Saddam Hussein on January 9, 1991,[10] and one can see his understanding of the need to ensure approval by competent governing authority reflected in the January 11, 1991, statement issued with his signing of the House Joint Resolution granting congressional approval for the use of military force against Iraq.[11]

The third source of President Bush's recourse to just war tradition—the single source directly responsible for his conscious application of historic terminology—was an internal White House staff memorandum I initiated and wrote immediately following his December 20, 1990, meeting with Bishop Browning.[12] As tensions in the Persian Gulf mounted following Iraq's August 2, 1990, invasion and occupation of Kuwait, President Bush started taking steps in line with just war thinking as the tradition had taken shape in his own intuition and become embedded in international law and military doctrine. But the moral warrant for his actions, while present, was not clear. Certainly, it was not apparent to those who needed convincing at the time. Thus, while many statements issued by the president and other members of his administration gave multiple "reasons" for U.S. involvement in efforts to expel Iraq from Kuwait,[13] criticism stirred by a network of left-leaning church leaders was raising doubts in the public mind about the morality of presidential leadership in opposing the Iraqi occupation of Kuwait.[14]

Indeed, so much uncertainty about a moral warrant for the president's course was stirred by the end of 1990 that despite constant attempts to explain stakes at risk in the Persian Gulf, the message carried by the media in early January 1991 was that Bush still had not given the American people a "reason" for sending troops to the region. Watching this evolve, I knew the media were not actually irrational as some members of the White House staff thought at the time. Rather, it was a call for President Bush to answer the question of moral justification. That was the need of the hour, and I knew I had something to offer.

Although my assignment on the president's staff had to do with domestic policy and not defense or foreign policy, as a former military officer and a veteran of the Vietnam War, I was familiar with military doctrine and training. But, in addition to military training and experience, I also had a doctoral degree in ethics that included a specialty focus on the morality of war. The practical challenge confronting me at that point was how someone at a midlevel staff position in domestic policy could get a policy memorandum to the president on a moral framework for decisions in matters of war. That opportunity came after a conversation with Leigh Ann Metzger, deputy assistant to the president for public liaison.

Leigh Ann had coordinated Bishop Browning's meeting with Bush and well knew the weight of the bishop's campaign challenging the morality of the president's leadership in the Gulf.[15] Talking in her office just after the Browning visit, I made two observations and a suggestion. First, I believed the media were not irrational, despite numerous press releases and statements, when they said the president had not yet given a "reason" for sending troops to the Gulf. Rather, they were asking the president to deliver a convincing moral warrant for his actions. Second, Bishop Browning, while ostensibly applying just war principles, was, in fact, mixing appeal to just war tradition with what amounted to pacifism.[16] Following these observations and in view of the opposition being stirred by Browning and others, my suggestion was that someone write a memorandum to the president summarizing just war principles and recommending he make explicit use of just war reasoning to guide and justify his decisions in the Gulf. I added that I was prepared to write such a memorandum if the need could be approved through necessary channels.

Leigh Ann favored the idea and soon secured its approval from the White House chief of staff, John Sununu, who, in turn, assured the memorandum would go to the president without delay. The result was a cover memorandum from me, sent to the president on January 15, 1991, through Sununu, on the subject "Just War and Bishop Browning."[17] Attached to this cover was a two-page outline of just war principles listing eight *ad bellum* principles and four *in bello* principles, along with a short descriptive summary of each.[18] Without the introduction and descriptive summaries, the specific just war principles recommended to President Bush were:

FOR BECOMING ENGAGED IN A JUST WAR
Just cause
Competent authority
Comparative justice
Right intention
Last resort

Probability of success
Proportionality of projected results
Right spirit

FOR CONDUCTING A JUST WAR
Proportionality in the use of force
Discrimination
Avoidance of evil means
Good faith

Bush made his decision to order the use of military force the day he received my memorandum, and the liberation of Kuwait began the day after on January 16, 1991.[19] This is *not* at all to say my memorandum on just war itself "caused" the president to make his decision. Clearly, by that time, he had already made up his mind. But, the memorandum *was* responsible for quickly bringing focus to the president's understanding of the moral framework from which he was already operating, it *was* responsible for the way he articulated his moral reasoning in explicit just war terms from that point forward, and it *was* responsible for perceptibly shaping the moral boundaries of presidential decisions through Operation Desert Storm.

APPLICATION OF THE BUSH JUST WAR DOCTRINE

The effect of my memorandum to the president recommending conscious, explicit application of just war principles was immediate and dramatic.[20] President Bush not only showed appreciation for review provided but also approved the recommendation and ordered the Office of Presidential Communications to use my outline of just war principles to compose an address in which he would explain to the nation and the world the moral framework for his leadership of forces opposing Iraqi aggression in the Persian Gulf. This crucial job was assigned to speechwriter Curt Smith, who was assisted by Carolyn Cawley; and the annual convention of the National Religious Broadcasters scheduled for the Washington Sheraton Hotel on January 28, 1991—only a week and a half away—was selected as the forum for its delivery.

I contacted Curt at once to see if he could use any help. This turned out to be a good thing, because Curt first reacted by confessing lack of familiarity with just war tradition. In fact, he had not even known it existed. After explaining this was a long tradition and the core ethic of Western civilization on the morality of war, we got down to work. Curt used my outline of just war principles to compose the text, while I reviewed it for accuracy. Of course, the text was not final until the president looked it over and concluded it met his expectations.[21]

This was the president's first national address that focused clearly on the question of moral justification, and it showed without doubt—whether one agreed with him or not—that George Bush was conscious about operating within a clear moral framework, was respectful of established moral limitations, was motivated by moral intentions, and was prepared to defend his actions on moral grounds against any who wished to question the moral legitimacy of his judgment. It was also the first time a president of the United States had ever applied principles of just war reasoning in such a deliberate, explicit, and public fashion in order to explain and justify decisions of war.

The result was dramatic. Public commentary about the morality of U.S. involvement in the Gulf suddenly shifted from ambiguity and suspicion to the surprising relevance of the president's reliance on just war thinking and the propriety of applying specific just war principles in confronting the aggression of Saddam Hussein. Major stories appeared in the media for several weeks,[22] pundits focused their attention on discussing the revival and relevance of just war reasoning,[23] and the moral criticism voiced by mainline church leaders and the protest vigils that had started meeting at the gates of the White House dissipated quickly—all because the president of the United States had identified a clear moral framework for his decisions.

Certainly, when George Bush adopted the explicit language of just war reasoning, it made a rhetorical difference. But was it *merely* rhetoric? Was his embrace of the just war tradition *no more than* marketing? Was it, after all, *simply* a device for shaping public perception while lacking genuine moral conviction and substance? The answer to these questions is a definite no! As far as President Bush was concerned, it was not mere rhetoric, and it was not simply a device for shaping public perception. It did affect public perception, but it was also thoroughly genuine. The proof of authenticity comes first from the nature of its origin, that is, it was not produced by a search for a strategy to generate desired political effects. Second, its authenticity is confirmed by the level of consistency by which the president's leadership actions in the Gulf actually matched the moral framework he espoused. The first has been covered. We turn now to the second and see how the president's actions did conform and conform very well to the principles included in his just war doctrine.

Was It Right to Engage Saddam Hussein?[24]

Just Cause. By just war reasoning, going to war must have adequate moral warrant, consideration of which starts with addressing the most basic of all moral questions relating to war. Is there a just cause? By his own analysis George Bush did not doubt that just cause existed for opposing the aggression of Saddam Hussein against Kuwait. When reviewing the warrant for military action, he said:

The first principle of a just war is that it seek a just cause. Our cause could not be more noble. We seek Iraq's withdrawal from Kuwait—complete, immediate and without condition; the restoration of Kuwait's legitimate government and the security and stability of the Gulf. We will see that Kuwait once again is free, that the nightmare of Iraq's occupation has ended, and that naked aggression will not be rewarded.[25]

Later, when the president gave Congress four basic objectives he said justified his decision to order the use of military force against Iraq, each manifested some aspect of just cause. These were:

1. the immediate, complete, and unconditional Iraqi withdrawal from Kuwait;
2. the restoration of the legitimate government of Kuwait;
3. the protection of U.S. citizens abroad; and
4. the security and stability of a region vital to U.S. national security.[26]

But behind these objectives, the president was convinced the primary reason for using military force against Saddam Hussein—primary because he returned to it repeatedly as forces of opposition were building in the Persian Gulf region—was the need to make sure there would be no reward for such a blatant act of tyrannical, brutal, and unprovoked aggression.

Iraq's August 2, 1990, invasion of Kuwait was such a flagrant act of aggression against a legitimate government and showed such disdain for principles of international order, it is hard to imagine a more clear case of just cause warranting the use of military force. Nevertheless, there were voices that questioned the justice of U.S. involvement, much less the leadership of George Bush, in efforts to reverse the situation. These voices came from different sources but seemed either to misappropriate the just cause principle in order to cloak a more fundamental commitment to pacifism or to misidentify the aggressor in the moral equation.

Borrowing capital from the more widely accepted just war tradition in order to support a pacifist rejection of any recourse to war at all is consistent neither with just war nor with pacifism. Nevertheless, this was the line taken in public statements issued by the delegates of the Middle East Peace Pilgrimage, as well as in arguments published by Edmond Browning of the Episcopal Church.[27] On this, James Turner Johnson has explained that "pacifist arguments must be assessed on their own terms, not confused with just war reasoning."[28] The idea that war can be justified under specific, even if regrettable, circumstances is so fundamentally contrary to the core notion of pacifism, one simply cannot with consistency replace one with the other. The notions of justice involved are not the same, and integrity—especially in the suasion of public opinion by moral argument—requires honest appeal by honest means.

Objection to the justice of President Bush's evaluation of force as an option by which to expel the forces of Iraq from Kuwait also came from those who determined to misidentify the aggressor in the Gulf. Ignoring Saddam Hussein's unprovoked attack on Kuwait and turning a deaf ear to UN [United Nations] resolutions denouncing Iraq's initiation of an unjust conflict, United Methodist bishop Melvin Talbert called President Bush the "real aggressor" in the Gulf and called others to speak out against "U.S. aggression in the region."[29] Bishop Browning of the Episcopal Church accused the president in much the same way,[30] as did the "Peace Pilgrimage" delegates on their return from the Middle East.[31] This criticism was so patently contrary to observable facts that it took little to refute it, and thus it was never persuasive to any except those already predisposed to entertain the validity of such outlandish claims. That the argument was made at all revealed more about the disposition of those who made them than it did to clarify the situation for others. Action to free Kuwait from the nightmare of tyrannical occupation obviously did not constitute an attack on parties otherwise at peace, and it did not involve any action to acquire territory or realign established borders.

Competent Authority. The moral warrant for President Bush's decision to use military force also recognized the importance of authorization by competent authority. In fact, when President Bush finally did order the use of military force to expel Iraqi forces from Kuwait, it was endorsed by an extraordinary unanimity secured at every conceivable level. After initially insisting the U.S. Constitution allowed him as president to order forces into combat independently of whether Congress had acted to issue a declaration of war, Bush worked hard to secure congressional approval.[32] He also secured international approval by building a multinational coalition dedicated to the principle of self-defense[33] and by obtaining UN authorization to use "all necessary means" to remove Iraqi forces from Kuwait.[34] When it came to using military force against Saddam Hussein, there is no question the president's decision was made by and with competent authority.

Comparative Justice. President Bush's decision to use force not only required a just cause but also demanded a moral assessment weighing the possible merits of competing claims. By just war reasoning, the morality of going to war cannot be limited to discovering some matter of injustice without reference to degree or to distribution justice in the overall context. The degree injustice discovered may be small, and the interest of justice overall may be divided, with some level of justice or injustice on opposing sides. Thus, the Bush doctrine also required conviction that more legitimate, more significant issues of justice were at stake on the side of restoring a free and independent Kuwait than might possibly maintain Iraqi claims on the territory of its neighbor. While Saddam Hussein sought to justify his claim by denying the legitimacy of internationally recognized borders and by asserting a need for Islamic nations to stand up to the forces of "atheism, treachery, [and] hypocrisy,"[35] it was not considered valid by either the United States or the United Nations. Nor was it persuasive even to most of the Islamic world.

Right Intention. Right intention was the fourth principle affecting President Bush's decision to resort to force. It was not enough that justice called for vindication. The intention had to be right, and by historic just war reasoning this has meant the restoration of peace and stability, including recognition of established territorial rights. Negatively, this meant rejecting any lust for power or revenge either by the president himself or by the United States as a nation.

Some, indeed, doubted the nature and authenticity of the president's intentions in the Gulf, and they maligned his leadership by accusing Bush of harboring ulterior motives. Indeed, during the time coalition forces were building following the Iraqi invasion of Kuwait, U.S. involvement was frequently castigated as an economic attack of the rich on the poor, of developed nations on undeveloped, or of the greedy on the needy.[36] This sort of accusation continued even after the war, with the *Christian Century* claiming Americans had been led to war by "the twin gods of financial power and military security,"[37] and Lewis Lapham, editor of *Harper's*, saying, "The line Mr. Bush so boldly drew in so empty a desert was the line between profit and loss."[38] These charges made out

Saddam Hussein as a hero and George Bush a villain. But the criticism was never rooted in fact, first, because the president consistently stressed it was the intention of the United States to restore peace to Kuwait and stability to the Middle East, second, because it completely ignored the raw aggression of Iraq against its neighbor, and, third, because Bush followed through and, true to his word, seized no territory but simply restored the legitimate government of Kuwait.

Not only did these accusations misrepresent the president's motives, but they also misconstrued the just war principle of right intention—the moral norm by which his motives were purportedly evaluated. Just war principles limiting decisions about going to war are never more than rules of permission. Even if all conditions are met, they do not on their own establish a mandate to fight. They only justify the moral legitimacy of going to war—should that decision be made. At the threshold of decision in any actual case, an assessment of moral warrant (i.e., permission) must be coupled with extramoral stakes that can be and usually are political, economic, or military in nature.

In the Gulf War, Bush's decision to engage Saddam Hussein did involve political (regional balance of power), economic (access to oil), and military (security interests) factors. But none of these extramoral stakes served to constitute the *moral* warrant motivating the president's decision. Rather, the logic of their relevance *followed* the moral warrant that made his decision permissible and offered only practical and strategic motives for a decision the morality of which was already well established. Thus, a realistic assessment of political, economic, and military factors important to the national interests of the United States did not compromise the morality of the president's decision. The charges raised by his critics were simply wrong.

Last Resort. Perhaps the most debated component of the just war framework employed by President Bush was the idea that military force must be a last resort. Resorting to war cannot be right until all reasonable nonmilitary alternatives have been tried unsuccessfully or rejected. The debate over last resort did not arise from its meaning, which is rather unambiguous. Rather, it arose over different interpretations as to application. Senator Nunn of Georgia, serving as chairman of the Senate Armed Services Committee, while favoring the use of military force as a last resort, led an effort in Congress to delay military action against Iraq, arguing that economic sanctions might be successful if given more time. While Congress was debating the president's request for a resolution authorizing the use of force against Iraq, Nunn explained: "Many of us strongly believe a war to liberate Kuwait should be the last resort, and that sanctions and diplomacy combined with a threat, a continuing threat of force, should be given more time."[39]

For his part, President Bush was no less focused on establishing last resort in order to justify the use of military force. He differed with Senator Nunn on a matter of application that depended on contrary interpretations of what was reasonable or likely to transpire under alternative courses of action. In seeking congressional approval, Bush argued forcefully that all reasonable means short of military force had been attempted in order to obtain compliance by Iraq, but always to no avail. Indeed, he had come to believe more time would only worsen the situation by diminishing opportunities for success. A reasonable, even generous amount of time had been granted already, and Saddam Hussein would use further delay only to his advantage.

In justifying his request for authorization to use force as indeed a matter of reasonable last resort, Bush said:

For over five and half [sic] months, the international community has sought with unprecedented unity to reverse Iraq's brutal and unprovoked aggression against Kuwait....

The nearly seven week "pause of goodwill" established in UN Security Council Resolution 678 has now passed. Iraq has taken no steps whatever to fulfill these requirements. Iraq has forcefully stated that it considers the Security Council's resolutions invalid and has no intention of complying with them at any time. Iraqi forces remain in occupation of Kuwait and have been substantially reinforced in recent weeks rather than withdrawn. Iraq has strongly and repeatedly reiterated its annexation of Kuwait and stated its determination that Kuwait will remain permanently a part of Iraq....

In short, the Government of Iraq remains completely intransigent in rejecting the UN Security Council's demands—despite the exhaustive use by the United States and the United Nations of all appropriate diplomatic, political, and economic measures to persuade or compel Iraq to comply.[40]

There can be no doubt that last resort was a major principle shaping the timing of the president's decision to employ military force in the Persian Gulf.

Probability of Success. George Bush's just war reasoning also required evaluating the probability of success. This involved judging the hope of achieving just objectives because it can never be right to risk life, property, and national treasure for objectives that are clearly beyond reach. Thus, however just a cause may be, diminishing prospects for success will undermine moral justification for using force. By just war reasoning, putting others in harm's way for a futile cause is never justified.

Logically, the probability of success weighs against an open-ended interpretation of last resort. In fact, appealing to an indefinite view of last resort was just the course taken by Senator Nunn and others who urged delay so as to give sanctions and diplomacy "more time." Since time is a perpetual commodity, calls for "more time" can amount to denial of the actual relevance of last resort. Thus, a reasonable interpretation of last resort must be balanced against the probability of success, and that is the strategy Bush used in making his case to Congress.

According to the president, last resort had been reached because of limits arising from his evaluation of the probability of success. In his judgment, economic sanctions alone were "highly unlikely to compel Saddam to retreat from Kuwait" even if continued for another 12 months.[41] Delay, he argued, would only erode the ability of coalition forces to achieve their objectives by enhancing Iraq's ability to find and exploit factions in the coalition united against them, increasing opportunities for Iraq to coerce other nations in the area, and degrading the readiness of coalition forces. In particular, he stressed, the longer the sanctions continue, the more likely it is that leaks in the sanctions enforcement system will develop.... [I]f the coalition fails now to carry through on the UN Security Council's demands for immediate Iraqi withdrawal from Kuwait, there will be strong pressures and temptations on various countries to ease their enforcement of sanctions and to compromise on demands that Iraq meet existing objectives fully and unconditionally.[42]

Proportionality of Projected Results. According to just war reasoning, resort to the use of force cannot be justified unless one can reasonably expect the good achieved by war to be greater than losses caused by the destruction of war. Bush's decision to use military force in the Gulf had to satisfy this assessment as well. But, while his assessment was proven sound in retrospect, it was not so readily discerned by everyone at the time. Predictions of doom, mass destruction, worldwide instability, and nuclear warfare proliferated and were especially prevalent among the delegates who had gone on the Peace Pilgrimage to the Middle East. When they returned from their trip, these peace pilgrims argued the likelihood of mass destruction so catastrophic any recourse to war had to be impossibly immoral.

It is entirely possible that war in the Middle East will destroy everything....

War will not liberate Kuwait, it will destroy it. War will not save us from [the forces of] mass destruction, it will unleash them. War will not establish regional stability, it will inflame the entire Middle East....

War will not stop aggression, it will instead rapidly accelerate the cycle of violence and revenge, which will not be limited to the Middle East.[43]

Although Bush based his decision on the best intelligence, best character analysis, and best technical information anyone had available at the time, it could not have been more than a best guess. However, his assessment of expected results was realistic, even if it could not be made with complete certainty. As it turned out, Bush was right, and his critics were wrong.

Right Spirit. The last just war principle pertaining to the president's decision to employ military force against Saddam Hussein was right spirit. By historic just war reasoning, right spirit is distinguished from right intention as a matter of attitude as opposed to reason and of emotion as opposed to mind. Whatever else, a leader ought not to choose war except with an attitude of regret and should consider his decision suspect if he becomes aware his decision is either driven by anger or entertained with zeal.

George Bush, to his credit, never addressed the prospect of war in the Gulf with anything but regret should it ever be necessary. He always signaled a sincere preference for a peaceful solution if Iraq could be removed from Kuwait by any means short of force. This spirit was evident regularly in what the president said throughout the period of Desert Shield, but it was perhaps nowhere better evident than in the letter of ultimatum George Bush addressed to Saddam Hussein on January 5 and attempted to deliver on January 9, 1991. While Bush was absolutely clear nothing would be accepted short of full compliance with all relevant UN resolutions, he also displayed the unique spirit in which he approached the prospect of war. "I write this letter," he said, "not to threaten, but to inform. I do so with no sense of satisfaction, for the people of the United States have no quarrel with the people of Iraq."[44]

Was Force against Iraq Used within Moral Limits?

The framework of just war reasoning employed by President Bush in expelling Saddam Hussein from Kuwait not only addressed the morality of justifying his decision to use military force but also included principles limiting the use of force once that decision was made.[45] Like those relevant to his decision to go to war, the authenticity of these principles restraining the use of force in war must also be judged by how well they match the course of his leadership during the Persian Gulf War.

Proportionality in the Use of Force. Just war reasoning requires that attention be given to proportionality in the means employed while engaged in war, not only in assessing whether it is right to go to war in the first place. Once military forces are in combat, it is important that deadly force be used only to the degree needed to achieve established objectives, and no more. In a just war framework, injustice does not warrant "total" war. That is, it does not warrant a "no holds barred" use of force. Rather, a leader's response to unjust aggression must be restrained and kept only to that needed to reverse the unjust situation.

The relevance of this notion during Operation Desert Storm was evident in several ways. A swift flanking maneuver that took Iraqi forces by surprise limited the casualties on both sides as compared to the number they would have sustained in a frontal attack on Kuwait City. Technically advanced "smart bombs" limited unnecessary collateral damage. Leaflets were dropped on Iraqi troops for days before coalition forces attacked in order to maximize understanding of opportunities for surrender. The Republican Guard was allowed to escape just before being surrounded, and coalition forces did not "continue to Baghdad" as many observers desired and expected, because President Bush, at that time, determined all established objectives were accomplished, and these did not include annihilation of opposing forces, replacement of the Iraqi government, or border realignment.

The only real question regarding possible violation of the proportional use of force by coalition forces arose when the Cable News Network (CNN) broadcast pictures showing what remained of Iraqi forces fleeing Kuwait City with the spoils of occupation. Bombs dropped at the head of the convoy stopped the retreating troops in their tracks, and U.S. planes then continued to destroy much that came behind. It should be noted the attack took place at night over a short period of time and under circumstances that made it difficult to distinguish between forces in retreat and a feint by forces trying to reposition. But whether that distinction was clear or not, the proportional use of force in combat does not restrict using the level of force needed to ensure established goals are accomplished effectively. While the loss of life on the road north was regrettable, Iraqi forces had been given ample time to withdraw without risk of casualty, and their determination to leave with plunder minimized the moral status of their departure. These were not forces in honorable retreat. They were more nearly brigands fleeing the scene of a crime.

Discrimination. The president's just war reasoning on the use of force also included a principle of discrimination. This meant it was important to maintain and respect a distinction between combatants and noncombatants. Historically understood, the principle of discrimination does not rule out the possibility noncombatants may sometimes lose their lives or suffer loss as a result of military action. But it does restrict direct attacks on nonmilitary targets and any intentional threat upon civilian life and property. In other words, the principle of discrimination in combat repudiates indiscriminate slaughter.

Application of the discrimination principle during Desert Storm was especially evident in the targeting guidelines followed by planners of the bombing missions. Special care was taken to avoid damaging religious sites and locations of special historic value. Furthermore, civilian residential areas along with hospitals and schools were spared intentional damage. Indeed, the coalition bombing limitations were so well defined, the Iraqis located some of their antiaircraft batteries on the roofs of schools and hospitals knowing they would be safe from attack. Even though coalition fliers were vulnerable where batteries so located remained, they were not destroyed out of respect for the principle of discrimination.

The most noteworthy challenge to coalition observance of noncombatant immunity came when Saddam Hussein accused U.S. bombers of intentionally attacking civilians who were killed when a bomb shelter was destroyed in Baghdad. Although he did not himself respect the discrimination principle, the Iraqi leader knew how damaging such a charge could be to moral support sustaining American leadership of the forces aligned against him. Of course, the loss of civilian life in this case was never intentional, and it certainly was regretted. According to intelligence at the time, the site destroyed included a military command center. Whether it actually did or not has never been fully determined. But, however that may be, the charge by Saddam Hussein did not hold because there never was any intention to target civilian lives.

Avoidance of Evil Means. The avoidance of evil means was a third moral principle limiting the use of force during Operation Desert Storm. While an important part of the president's moral framework, it certainly was not new and with the other principles of moral engagement in combat had long been a part of U.S. military doctrine and international law. Traditionally interpreted, the avoidance of evil means includes the rejection of actions such as executing prisoners, taking hostages, terrorizing the civilian population by rape, pillage, or plunder, and desecrating places of worship.

Little needs to be said about its relevance for coalition forces in the Gulf War because respect for the principle was thoroughly obvious. What was interesting about the relevance of this principle were the rumors circulated among Iraqi troops to discourage them from surrendering. Most of these were claims immediately contrary to the avoidance of evil means principle. But perhaps charges of torture and execution seemed credible to Iraqi front-line troops because means of this sort were part of their own repertoire. Hostage taking, rape, pillage, and plunder were also evident on the Iraqi side of the equation.

Good Faith. The last principle restraining the use of force in combat was good faith. By this principle, enemies are not denigrated either as "infidels" or as subhumans unworthy of common decency. Nor are they intentionally humiliated or punished. Rather, they are treated with human dignity, civility, and even honor within reason. This is required for its own sake but also because it is required for consistency with a genuine intention to resume peaceful and friendly relations with former enemies once hostilities have ceased.

The good faith principle was particularly evident in the way coalition forces treated prisoners of war (POWs). Surrendering troops were treated with decency, fairness, and even generosity—generosity that is compared to conditions in which they had been living before coalition forces came through. One of the most memorable images to come out of the Gulf War had to be the large number of surrendering Iraqis who seemed actually eager to be taken under U.S. supervision. Indeed, so many surrendering Iraqis were accommodated that in some cases the good faith obligation to provide adequate care for POWs actually preempted chances for a more rapid advance into enemy territory.

In this review we have tried to demonstrate that President Bush did not use just war terminology merely for effect or merely for the purpose of enlarging public support. While it did affect public thinking by building confidence in the morality of his leadership, it did so legitimately because it was entirely authentic. Genuinely held moral convictions shaped his decisions through one of the major international security crises of the twentieth century, and their authenticity was demonstrated by their consistent application throughout the crisis provoked by Iraq's invasion and attempted annexation of Kuwait. The president's leadership actions in the Persian Gulf did conform very well to the principles set forth in his just war doctrine.

Throughout the history of the United States, the moral leadership of a president in time of war has rarely been so evident, and *never* has a U.S. president applied the principles of just war reasoning with such clear intention as was demonstrated by President George Bush in the Persian Gulf War.

NOTES

1. George Bush, "Letter to Daniel Heimbach" (from Kennebunkport, ME, to Wake Forest, NC, May 27, 1997).

2. See, for example, Kenneth T. Walsh, "Bush's 'Just War' Doctrine," *U.S. News & World Report*, February 4, 1991, pp. 52–53; Richard John Neuhaus, "Just War and This War," *Wall Street Journal*, January 29, 1991, op-ed; Jeffery L. Sheler, Joannie M. Schrof, and Dorian Friedman, "Holy War Doctrines," *U.S. News & World Report*, February 11, 1991, pp. 55–56; Richard N. Ostling, "A Just Conflict, or Just a Conflict? George Bush Invokes a Long-Standing Christian Doctrine to Defend His Military Action against Saddam," *Time*, February 11, 1991, pp. 42, 51; Kenneth L. Woodward, "Ancient Theory and Modern War," *Newsweek*, February 11, 1991, p. 47.

3. The major publications in this category are James Turner Johnson and George Weigel, *Just War and the Gulf War* (Washington, DC: Ethics and Public Policy Center, 1991); Micah L. Sifry and Christopher Cerf, eds., *The Gulf War Reader: History, Documents, Opinions* (New York: Random House, 1991); Thomas C. Fox, *Iraq: Military Victory, Moral Defeat* (Kansas City: Sheed and Ward, 1991); Brien Hallett, ed., *Engulfed in*

War: Just War and the Persian Gulf (Honolulu, HI: Matsunaga Institute for Peace, 1991); Jean Bethke Elshtain and Stanley Hauerwas, *But Was It Just? Reflections on the Morality of the Persian Gulf War* (New York: Doubleday, 1992); Alan Geyer and Barbara G. Green, *Lines in the Sand: Justice and the Gulf War* (Louisville, KY: Westminster/John Knox Press, 1992); and Kenneth L. Vaux, *Ethics and the Gulf War: Religion, Rhetoric, and Righteousness* (Boulder, CO: Westview Press, 1992). The first two feature reprints of various documents released or written to explain or shape events as they transpired, while the first and the third through the seventh involve personal reflections based on limited information available to outside observers immediately following conclusion of the war.

4. Johnson and Weigel, *Just War and the Gulf War*, pp. 12–20.
5. See ibid., pp. 15–16, for a more complete description.
6. In particular, see Turner's reproduction of U.S. Air Force instructions on the conduct of armed conflict. Ibid., pp. 16–17.
7. Edmond L. Browning, "Letter to President Bush" (Washington, DC: White House, Executive Office of the President, January 7, 1991, received January 14, 1991, unpublished). A copy of this letter is included in the appendix.
8. George Bush, "Excerpt from Remarks to Republican National Committee" (Washington, DC: White House, Office of Cabinet Memorandum, January 25, 1991, unpublished), p. 1. For news coverage of this event, see Ann Devoy, "Describing Moral Debate: Bush Spellbinds Audience," *Washington Post*, January 26, 1991, pp. A1, A18.
9. Bush, "Remarks to Republican National Committee," p. 1.
10. George Bush, "Letter to Iraqi President Saddam Hussein," reproduced in *Dispatch* (Washington, DC: U.S. Department of State, Bureau of Public Affairs, January 14, 1991). Reprinted in Sifry and Cerf, eds., *Gulf War Reader*, pp. 178–79. The original letter was dated January 5, 1991. Delivery of the letter was attempted by Secretary Baker but was refused by Iraqi foreign minister Tariq Aziz during their meeting in Geneva, Switzerland, on January 9, 1991.
11. George Bush, "Statement on Signing H.J. Res. 77 (1991)" (Washington, DC: White House, Office of Cabinet Affairs Memorandum, January 11, 1991, unpublished).
12. Daniel R. Heimbach, "Just War and Bishop Browning" (Washington, DC: White House, memorandum for the president, January 15, 1991, unpublished); Daniel R. Heimbach, "Just War in the Persian Gulf" (Washington, DC: White House, attachment to memorandum for the president, January 15, 1991, unpublished). Copies of these documents are included in the appendix.
13. For example, see "Gulf Policy Themes" (Washington, DC: U.S. Department of State, Bureau of Public Affairs, Office of Public Communications, January 1991, unpublished); George Bush, "Excerpts from President Bush's Press Conference" (Washington, DC: White House, Office of Public Affairs, December 3, 1990, unpublished); Colin L. Powell, "Statement of General Colin L. Powell, USA, Chairman of the Joint Chiefs of Staff before the Senate Committee on Armed Services on Operation Desert Shield" (Washington, DC: Senate Armed Services Release, December 3, 1990, unpublished); Richard Cheney, "Excerpts from Secretary Cheney's Statement to the Senate Armed Services Committee" (Washington, DC: White House, Office of Public Affairs, December 4, 1990, unpublished); James A. Baker, "Statement by the Honorable James A. Baker III, Secretary of State, before the Senate Foreign Relations Committee" (Washington, DC: U.S. Department of State Release, December 5, 1990, unpublished).
14. This was best (though not uniquely) embodied in a press statement released by an 18-member party of mainline church leaders. See Delegation to the Middle East, "War Is Not the Answer: A Message to the American People" (December 21, 1990, unpublished). This delegation came to be known as the church leaders' "Peace Pilgrimage," and its members as the "Peace Pilgrims." Their statement to the press was later published in *Sojourners* (February-March 1991): 5. Other examples of this effort can be found in

Edmund L. Browning, "The Church and War," *Washington Post*, January (day unknown), 1991, op-ed; and Lynda Richardson, "Catholic Bishops Caution Bush on 'Just War,'" *Washington Post*, November 16, 1990.

15. Browning was a leading member of the "Peace Pilgrimage" of mainline Protestant denominational heads to the Middle East in December 1990, was a signer of the statement critical of U.S. involvement issued by the delegation on its return on December 14, 1990, and had been selected by the group to personally convey their criticism to the Oval Office using his leverage as head of the denomination of which the president was a member. In addition to these actions, Bishop Browning followed his private conversation with the president with a letter (Browning, "Letter to President Bush") and an op-ed in the *Washington Post* (Browning, "The Church and War"), both of which argued that war with Iraq would be morally wrong under all conceivable circumstances.

16. My criticism of Bishop Browning's pacifist use of just war reasoning was made earlier and independently, but it was, in fact, exactly the same point later leveled by James Turner Johnson. In criticizing pacifistic misuse of just war principles, Johnson says that:

frequently the two issues [i.e., just war claims and pacifism] are mixed, with just war reasoning used to support a pacifist rejection of the use of force as an instrument of national policy .... Yet historically just war tradition rests on a different presumption, a fundamental rejection of injustice .... pacifist arguments must be assessed on their own terms, not confused with just war reasoning. (Johnson and Weigel, *Just War and the Gulf War*, p. 6)

17. Heimbach, "Just War and Bishop Browning." A complete copy of this memorandum (cover with all attachments) is provided in the appendix.

18. Heimbach, "Just War in the Persian Gulf." The list of principles compiled for this submission to President Bush represented a more complete range of just war principles than can be found in any other published source. Readers will note that, while just war reasoning is an ancient tradition, there is no one source that authoritatively defines all accepted principles important to the tradition. Thus, the particular compilation sent to President Bush was unique, even though each principle listed had been articulated in one form or another by earlier proponents of the just war tradition.

19. George Bush, "The Liberation of Kuwait Has Begun" (Washington, DC: White House, Office of the Press Secretary Press Release, January 16, 1991, unpublished). Also reprinted in Sifry and Cerf, eds., *Gulf War Reader*, pp. 311–14.

20. The conclusion of this memorandum read: "Because the American people deeply desire to do the right thing and are seeking moral as well as political leadership in the Gulf, I recommend that you consider using the principles of just war as you seek to persuade others of the moral necessity of your actions" (Heimbach, "Just War and Bishop Browning," p. 2).

21. George Bush, "Remarks by the President in Address to the National Religious Broadcasters Convention" (Washington, DC: White House, Office of the Press Secretary Press Release, January 28, 1991, unpublished).

22. For example: Tom Roberts and Gary O'Guinn, "Persian Gulf Makes 'Just War' Debate No Longer Academic," *Washington Post*, February 2, 1991, p. G1; "Philosophers Agree on Criteria for Justifiable War," *Washington Post*, February 2, 1991, p. G1; Walsh, "Bush's 'Just War' Doctrine"; Sheler, Schrof and Friedman, "Holy War Doctrines"; Ostling, "A Just Conflict?"; Woodward, "Ancient Theory and Modern War."

23. For example, Neuhaus, "Just War and This War"; Cal Thomas, "Moral Purpose: Vision of a Just Cause," *Washington Times*, February 4, 1991, pp. D1, D4. Furthermore, a roundtable on the president's use of just war principles was organized by the Ethics and Public Policy Center and held on February 12, 1991. Actually, the article by Neuhaus in

the *Wall Street Journal*, while appearing just after the president's speech, had been written before it was reported in the news. Of course, Neuhaus responded favorably when he learned of it and told me so in a personal letter, dated February 4, 1991, commending the president's use of just war reasoning to frame the moral argument for his actions in the Persian Gulf.

24. The analysis provided by James Turner Johnson (in *Just War and the Gulf War*) matches five of the eight *ad bellum* principles listed in the Bush just war doctrine, these being just cause, competent authority, last resort, probability of success, and proportionality of projected results. Johnson does not distinguish between right intention and right spirit (although these do, in fact, address different matters), and he distinguishes the aim of achieving peace as a separate principle from right intention, even though historically the intention to pursue peace has constituted the meaning of right intention. Lastly, Johnson fails to address the question of comparative justice. This historic just war principle included in the moral framework employed by President Bush was first discussed by Saint Augustine in the fourth century and then was elaborated more completely by Francesco Vittoria in the sixteenth century.

25. Bush, "Address to the National Religious Broadcasters Convention," p. 2.

26. George Bush, "Text of Letter and Report from the President to the Speaker of the House of Representatives and the President Pro Tempore of the Senate Pursuant to Section 2(B) of Public Law 102-1" (Washington, DC: White House, Office of the Press Secretary Press Release, January 16, 1991, unpublished), p. 1.

27. Delegation to the Middle East, "War Is Not the Answer"; Browning, "The Church and War."

28. Johnson and Weigel, *Just War and the Gulf War*, p. 6.

29. Melvin Talbert, quoted in a Religious News Service wire story, December 7, 1990.

30. Browning, "Letter to President Bush."

31. Delegation to the Middle East, "War Is Not the Answer."

32. "Authorization for Use of Military Force against Iraq," *House Joint Resolution 77* (January 12, 1991) and *Public Law 102-1*. Also reprinted in Sifry and Cerf, *Gulf War Reader*, pp. 287–89.

33. This was the manner in which Bush on January 28, 1991, explained his effort to the National Religious Broadcasters (Bush, "Address to the National Religious Broadcasters Convention").

34. "UN Resolution 678" (New York: UN Security Council, November 29, 1990).

35. Saddam Hussein, "The Mother of All Battles" (Speech of January 20, 1991), reprinted in Sifry and Cerf, *Gulf War Reader*, pp. 315–16.

36. For a published example of this accusation, see Fox, *Iraq: Military Victory, Moral Defeat*.

37. "Another Failure in a Bankrupt Foreign Policy," *Christian Century*, April 17, 1991, p. 419.

38. Lewis H. Lapham, "Onward Christian Soldiers," in Sifry and Cerf, *Gulf War Reader*, p. 458.

39. *Congressional Record—Senate*, January 11, 1991, p. S-190.

40. Bush, "Report Pursuant to Public Law 102-1," p. 1.

41. Ibid., p. 3.

42. Ibid., p. 4.

43. Delegation to the Middle East, "War Is Not the Answer." A similar case was made in Browning's op-ed, "The Church and War."

44. Bush, "Letter to Saddam Hussein."

45. James Turner Johnson, in *Just War and the Gulf War*, identifies only two such principles. These he identifies as proportionality of means and discrimination, which cor-

respond to the first two *in bello* principles listed in the Bush just war doctrine. He does not identify or discuss the *in bello* principles of avoidance of evil means and good faith.

APPENDIX: White House Memorandum to the President Outlining Principles of Just War (with Attachments), January 15, 1991

January 15, 1991

MEMORANDUM FOR THE PRESIDENT

THROUGH: GOVERNOR SUNUNU
FROM: DANIEL R. HEIMBACH
Deputy Executive Secretary
Domestic Policy Council

SUBJECT: Just war and Bishop Browning

Leigh Ann Metzger has suggested to me that you may be interested in a brief summation of just war principles. (See the list of principles attached.) It is my understanding that this may be useful in light of Bishop Browning's recent visit and letter (also attached) in which he takes the position that moral considerations preclude the United States from becoming involved in military action in the Persian Gulf.

I believe you have a strong moral case for the measured steps you have taken leading the world coalition in opposing the aggression of Saddam Hussein. Indeed, you can respond to Bishop Browning, and to the American people, by urging that the circumstances now existing in the Gulf, together with the actions you have pursued, present a *classic situation in which an engagement of war is morally just*.

Bishop Browning's primary effort has been to press you on whether you have exhausted all solutions short of war. Since his reasons for questioning last resort are the alleged alternatives of negotiation and waiting indefinitely for the effects of an economic embargo, the morality of your actions can be established by explaining why these are false alternatives. Bishop Browning also challenges you by discussing the cost of engaging in a shooting war. Taken alone, this is a pacifist consideration. Consistent pacifism denies there is ever a sufficient moral reason to justify the cost of war. Just war, however, considers the cost but requires that the good expected by resorting to war be greater than the costs you are able to foresee. In responding to the Bishop, you may wish to recognize both the tragedy and the cost of war but emphasize the greater good we intend to achieve (regional stability, restoration of just order, restoration of legitimate authority, restoration of human rights, moral precedent for post–Cold War world order).

As you are well aware, the views expressed by Bishop Browning represent a number of mainline church leaders and not a few Democrats in Congress. These, some more explicitly than others, would like to claim the moral legitimacy of just war to challenge your leadership. Because the American people deeply desire to do the right thing and are seeking moral as well as political leadership in the Gulf, I recommend that you consider using the principles of just war as you seek to persuade others of the moral necessity of your actions.

There is a wealth of material available on the history and theory of just war. Furthermore, some articles are being written on the Persian Gulf situation based on an evaluation of just war principles. If you would like more information on just war, these materials can be made available.

Attachments

JUST WAR IN THE PERSIAN GULF

"Just war" is a set of ethical principles regarding the morality of war. Other models on the morality of war are pacifism, and crusade. The principles of just war originated with classical Greek and Roman philosophers like Plato and Cicero. Later they were taken up and expounded by Christian theologians such as Ambrose, Augustine, and Aquinas. Although pacifism and crusade have been influential, the just war approach has always been the primary model used by Western Civilization.

While pacifism denies there is ever any moral justification for theuse of deadly force, the crusade approach treats war as an unconditional effort of good against evil. By contrast to both, just war recognizes that the use of deadly force is sometimes a tragic but moral necessity that cannot be avoided because evil is ever present in the fallen human nature, and rulers have a moral responsibility to vincidate justice and oppose tyrannical aggression. The theory treats war as a secular affair conducted by the legitimate civil authority but subject to certain moral limitations. A "just war" is a limited, morally necessary, short-term response to a specific violation of peace and order.

What Are the Principles for Becoming Engaged in a Just War?

Just Cause. The cause of initiating war must be just. Just causes may include reasons such as: the vindication of justice, the restoration of a just international order that has been violated, the protection of innocent human life, or the restoration of basic human rights.

Competent Authority. War cannot be initiated justly except by those who hold the requisite authority for engaging the government and the nation in such activity and who bear responsibility for the public order. It should not be initiated by those who do not (or do not yet) have full authority to do so.

Comparative justice. War cannot be initiated justly unless the moral merit on our side clearly out weighs [*sic*] the moral merit on the other. The values at stake must override all presumptions against war. No state has absolute justice on its side, and a sober judgment must be made between relative claims: is the justice of our cause greater than theirs?

Right intention. The intention of going to war must be morally right. War can be initiated justly only as a means to obtain genuine peace and reconciliation. In this case, genuine peace includes the pursuit of a just and humane order and is not restricted to the mere absence of hostility. Desires merely to punish or humiliate are not generally thought to be adequate intentions.

Last resort. All non-violent alternatives must be exhausted before resorting to war.

Probability of success. No war is justified if achievement of a successful end is clearly futile. An irrational resort to military force is not justified no matter how just the cause.

Proportionality of projected results. The good expected by resorting to war must be greater than the summation of costs (estimated in the loss of human life and property) that may be foreseen as the result of a war.

Right spirit. War should not be engaged except with an attitude of regret that a just settlement can be achieved no other way. War is regarded as a tragic necessity.

What Are the Principles for Conducting a Just War?

Proportionality in the use of force. The response to unjust aggression should not exceed the nature of that aggression. No action should be taken that generates more harm than good. Deadly force should be used only in the proportion needed to achieve a just objective and no more.

Discrimination. A distinction must be maintained between combatants and non-combatants. Although non-combatants may lose their lives, or suffer, as a result of military action, there must be no direct intention to take the lives of innocent civilians by attacking non-military targets. Nothing can justify indiscriminate slaughter.

Avoidance of evil means. There can be no use of evil means (even for a just cause). Evil means may include such actions as: execution of prisoners, the taking of hostages, pillaging, the threatening and violation of civilians, and the desecration of holy places.

Good faith. As much as possible, the enemy must be treated in good faith in order to keep open the possibility of reconciliation once hostilities have ceased. Even enemies should be treated with human dignity.

1/15/91

January 7, 1991

The President
The White House
Washington, DC 20500

Dear Mr. President:

When I visited you on December 20, you handed me a copy of the Amnesty International report on Iraq/Occupied Kuwait and asked me to read it. I have done so, and now respectfully ask that you consider my response.

Like Mrs. Bush, I was unable to finish the report. The brutal Iraqi invasion of the sovereign nation of Kuwait and the human rights violations reported so graphically demand condemnation. You asked, when you handed me the report, "morally, are we to do nothing?"

Morally, we must respond to such an outrage, both as a member nation of the community of nations and as individuals who seek to respect and uphold the human rights of others. Furthermore, you and I, as Christians, have an obligation to respond on the basis of our baptismal vows, in which we promised to "strive for justice and peace among all people, and respect the dignity of every human being."

Morally, we must respond. The question, of course, is how. Do we continue to apply the sanctions adopted by the United Nations or do we go to war to force the issue?

You have said that you are prepared to go to war. You do more: you threaten to invade Iraq and destroy Saddam Hussein, his regime and his army. Your military leaders have described some of the likely consequences of the war you envision, which minimally would issue in thousands of innocent civilian deaths beyond the carnage among the armies. The damage could easily be many times greater, including lasting enmity between Arab peoples and our own country.

Mr. President, I do not believe war is the answer. I do not believe it is God's will that such devastation be unleashed as a just response to Iraq's invasion and violation of Kuwait. War for me can never be a moral option unless all attempts at a solution short of war are exhausted.

Mr. President, I do not know a single person who believes you have exhausted options short of war. If the Soviet Union could be contained for forty years without a shooting war, surely a united international community could find ways to contain and punish Saddam Hussein without the additional tragedy of war. In a word, to resort to full scale war now would be immoral, in the judgement of the majority Christian tradition which we both share.

Furthermore, even if all options short of war should be attempted and prove ineffective, the likely consequences of war must not be out of proportion to the injustice it seeks to prevent or correct. As justifiable as international action against Saddam Hussein may be—and I believe condemnation and sanctions are justified—would not the inevitable deaths in war of women, children and other innocents make the tragedy immeasurably worse?

One further observation about the Amnesty report. While I share your outrage over the atrocities reported from Kuwait, such atrocities should not be used as the necessary or sufficient basis for our actions against Iraq when we have not acted in similar fashion towards other nations commiting [sic] abuses of human rights. How, for example, have you responded to repeated Amnesty International reports of atrocities committed by the El Salvador armed forces? Have you sanctioned the government of El Salvador for its repeated unwillingness or inability to bring to justice those in its own ranks accused of outrageous human rights abuses?

I have been told that Amnesty International has also issued highly critical reports of our current allies Saudi Arabia and Syria. Where do we draw the line?

I appreciate more deeply than I can sya, Mr. President, your willingness to have me meet with you and Secretary Baker in the Oval Office and your gracious and attentive listening. As I said then, I believe you have thepower, the ability and the opportunity to lead the international community into a new world order (of which you yourself have spoken), a new order that can address and adjudicate conflicts, including human rights violations, without immediate recourse to violence. I pray that God grants you the wisdom and courage to seize the moment.

Faithfully and respectfully yours,

Edmond L. Browning
Presiding Bishop

cc: Secretary James Baker

BIBLIOGRAPHY

Adams, Lawrence E., and Fredrick P. Jones. "Are These Angels Really Heralds of Peace?" Washington, DC: Institute for Religion and Democracy, January 1991, draft article.

Baker, James A. III. "Statement by the Honorable James A. Baker III, Secretary of State, before the Senate Foreign Relations Committee." Washington, DC: U.S. Department of State Release, December 5, 1990, unpublished.

Browning, Edmond L. "Letter to President Bush." Personal letter from the Presiding Bishop of the Episcopal Church. White House, Executive Office of the President, January 7, 1991 (received January 14, 1991), unpublished.

———. "The Church and War." *Washington Post*, January 1991, op-ed.

Bush, George. "Video Address to the Community of Nations United against Iraqi Aggression." Washington, DC: White House Office of Cabinet Affairs Memorandum, January 7, 1991, unpublished.

———. "Statement on Signing H.J. Res. 77 (1991)." Washington, DC: White House, Office of Cabinet Affairs Memorandum, January 11, 1991, unpublished.

———. "Letter to Iraqi President Saddam Hussein." *U.S. Department of State Dispatch*. Washington, DC: U.S. Department of State, Bureau of Public Affairs, January 14, 1991.

———. "Text of Letter and Report from the President to the Speaker of the House of Representative and the President Pro Tempore of the Senate pursuant to Section 2(B) of Public Law 102-1." Washington, DC: White House, Office of the Press Secretary Press Release, January 16, 1991, unpublished.

———. "Excerpt from Remarks to Republication National Committee." Washington, DC: White House, Office of Cabinet Affairs Memorandum, January 25, 1991, unpublished.

———. "Remarks by the President in Address to the National Religious Broadcasters Convention." Washington, DC: White House, Office of the Press Secretary Press Release, January 28, 1991, unpublished.

———. "Address by the President on the State of the Union." Washington, DC: White House, Office of the Press Secretary Press Release, January 29, 1991, unpublished.

———. "Economic Report of the President." Washington, DC: White House, Office of Cabinet Affairs Memorandum, January 31, 1991, unpublished.

———. "The Persian Gulf War: Excerpts from President Bush's News Conference." *Washington Post*, February 6, 1991, p. A21.

Cheney, Richard. "Statement by the Honorable Dick Cheney, Secretary of Defense, concerning Operation Desert Shield before the Committee on Armed Services, U.S. Senate," Washington, DC: Senate Armed Services Release, December 3, 1990, unpublished.

———. "Excerpts from Secretary Cheney's Statement to the Senate Armed Services Committee." Washington, DC: White House, Office of Public Affairs, December 4, 1990.

"Chronology: The Gulf Crisis: UN Security Council Actions." Washington, DC: U.S. Department of State, Bureau of Public Affairs, Office of Public Communications, January 1991, unpublished.

"Crisis in the Gulf: Background Information." Washington, DC: U.S. Department of State, Bureau of Public Affairs, Office of Public Communications, January 1991, unpublished.

Devoy, Ann. "Describing Moral Debate, Bush Spellbinds Audience." *Washington Post*, January 26, 1991, pp. A1, A18.

Elshtain, Jean Bethke, and Stanley Hauerwas. *But Was It Just? Reflections on the Morality of the Persian Gulf War*. New York: Doubleday, 1992.

"Gulf Policy Themes." Washington, DC: U.S. Department of State, Bureau of Public Affairs, Office of Public Communications, January 1991, unpublished.

Heimbach, Daniel R. "Just War and Bishop Browning." Washington, DC: White House, Memorandum for the President, January 15, 1991, unpublished.

———. "Just War in the Persian Gulf." Washington, DC: White House, Attachment to Memorandum for the President, January 15, 1991, unpublished.

———. "Presidential Precepts: A Moral Code for Conflict." *U.S. News & World Report*, February 4, 1991, p. 52.

———. "DOKTRINA <<SPRAVEDLIVOY VOYNI>> DZh. BUShA" ["The 'Just War' Doctrine of Geo. Bush."] *Kentavr* 1 (March–April 1992): 63–70.

Johnson, James Turner, and George Weigel. *Just War and the Gulf War*. Washington, DC: Ethics and Public Policy Center, 1991.

Langley, Norma, and Leon Freilich. "What Really Happened between the President and America's Leading Preacher in the Countdown to War." *Star*, February 5, 1991.

Neuhaus, Richard John. "Just War and This War." *Wall Street Journal*, January 29, 1991, op-ed.

Ostling, Richard N. "A Just Conflict, or Just a Conflict?: George Bush Invokes a Long-Standing Christian Doctrine to Defend His Military Action against Saddam." *Time*, February 11, 1991, pp. 42, 51.

Pearce, Kimber Charles. "George Bush's 'Just War' Rhetoric: Paradigm." *Journal of Communication and Religion* 16, no. 2 (September 1993): 139–52.

Powell, Colin L. "Statement of General Colin L. Powell, USA, Chairman of the Joint Chiefs of Staff, before the Senate Committee on Armed Services on Operation Desert Shield." Washington, DC: Senate Armed Services Release, December 3, 1990, unpublished.

Resolution 660. New York: UN Security Council, August 2, 1990. [Condemns the invasion of Kuwait by Iraq and demands unconditional surrender.]

Resolution 661. New York: UN Security Council, August 6, 1990. [Imposes economic sanctions against Iraq.]

Resolution 662. New York: UN Security Council, August 9, 1990. [Declares Iraq's annexation of Kuwait null and void.]

Resolution 678. New York: UN Security Council, November 29, 1990. [Authorizes member states cooperating with the government of Kuwait to use "all necessary means" to uphold earlier UN resolutions, while giving Iraq "one final opportunity" to abide by the resolutions by January 15, 1991.]

Robertson, Pat. "Pat Robertson's Perspective: A Special Report to Members of the 700

Club." Virginia Beach: 70 Club, January–February 1991.

Sheler, Jeffrey L., Joannie M. Schrof, and Dorian Friedman. "Holy War Doctrines." *U.S. News & World Report*, February 11, 1991, pp. 55–56.

Sifry, Micah L., and Christopher Cerf, eds. *The Gulf War Reader*. New York: Random House, 1991.

Smith, Jean Edward. *George Bush's War*. New York: Holt, 1992.

Staff of *U.S. News & World Report*. *Triumph without Victory: The Unreported History of the Persian Gulf War*. Westminster, MD: Time Books, 1992.

"To the Protestants of the United States of America." Statement of Czech and Slovak Religious and Civic Leaders. New York: Research Center for Religion and Human Rights in Closed Societies, January 14, 1991, unpublished fax.

Walsh, Kenneth T. "Bush's 'Just War' Doctrine." *U.S. News & World Report*, February 4, 1991, pp. 52–53.

"War Is Not the Answer: A Message to the American People." Statement of the Church Leaders "Peace Pilgrimage" Delegation to the Middle East. *Sojourners* (February–March 1991): 5.

Woodward, Kenneth L. "Ancient Theory and Modern War." *Newsweek*, February 11, 1991, p. 47.

18

George Bush, Mass Nationalism, and the Gulf War

Laurence Ingram Radway

This paper is part of a longer study of the influence of mass opinion in American foreign policy since the 1930s. During that period mainstream Americans often exhibited a self-regarding or parochial nationalism in their approach to foreign countries, and political leaders were usually rewarded if they shared or catered to this disposition. George Bush is the last of 10 presidents whose foreign policy decisions I examine in light of this thesis.

Bush entered the White House quite sensitive to public opinion. Transplanted from North to South, he twice won races for the U.S. House of Representatives, but his wins were sandwiched between two losses, one in a 1964 Senate race against Ralph Yarborough, the other in a 1970 Senate race against Lloyd Bentsen. Thereafter he held at least four major public positions: U.S. ambassador to the United Nations [UN], de facto ambassador to China, director of the CIA [Central Intelligence Agency], and chairman of the Republican National Committee. In light of the argument that follows, this last deserves special attention. To my knowledge no other modern president had held this partisan job, and none has held it since. Moreover, Bush held it when the Watergate scandal was rising to a boil, a time calling for exceptional sensitivity to public opinion. The record also suggests that he may have been particularly sensitive to the conservative wing of the Republican Party. It was alleged that he modified what had earlier been a somewhat more liberal position on abortion. During his 1964 Senate race he questioned the Civil Rights Act and suggested that the United States resign from the UN if it seated Communist China. As director of the CIA he catered to hawkish critics by appointing "Team B"—something like a visiting committee—to reassess his own agency's estimate of the military balance between the United States and the Soviet Union. Heavily weighted with hard-liners, Team B concluded that the military balance between the United States and the USSR had tilted dangerously toward Moscow. At a later point Bush resigned from the Council on Foreign Relations and the Trilateral Commission, two prestigious organizations criticized by militant conservatives for excessive internationalism. By 1980 he bore at least a passing resemblance to a trio of earlier American presidents identified by historians as northern men with southern principles.[1] Nonetheless, he lost a race for his party's 1980 presidential nomination to Ronald Reagan, who was considered to stand farther to the right.

During his tenure as Reagan's vice president, Bush kept a relatively low profile on sensitive foreign policy issues. But in one speech he described as "brutal murder" Soviet conduct in shooting down a civilian airliner. Some State Department officials were described as "appalled" by the language and convinced that it was motivated by "domestic political considerations."[2] Later the Soviet ambassador in Washington described him as "politically ambitious." He was certainly careful. When questions were raised about his role in the Iran–contra affair, he answered that he had been "out of the loop." At the same time he kept an eye on public opinion, on the White House's elaborate systems for gauging opinion, and on the sophisticated staffers who worked those systems.

During his 1988 presidential campaign Bush was aided by Robert Teeter, a major opinion analyst. Half a year before Election Day Teeter assembled a focus group in Paramus, New Jersey. It consisted of 30 Democrats who had voted for Reagan in the past but were now considering a return to the Democratic fold. They were told that Massachusetts governor Dukakis, Bush's opponent, had granted a furlough to a convicted black criminal, that Dukakis was also a card-carrying member of the American Civil Liberties Union, and that while governor he had vetoed a law that would have required the Pledge of Allegiance to be recited in public schools. Half of the members of the focus group then changed their minds about voting for Dukakis, and Bush's team now knew it had hot-button issues in hand.[3] Flags were featured at Bush's televised campaign events. As Election Day drew close, a growing proportion of the electorate perceived him as the tougher candidate.

Though Teeter continued to interpret polling data as an analyst for a research firm with Republican clients, some time was to pass before he followed Bush to the White House. But Bush also obtained opinion data and advice from the Wirthlin Group, from John Sununu, former governor of New Hampshire and now chief of staff in the White House, and from Secretary of State James Baker, who appeared to some onlookers to view world events through the prism of American politics. The relevance of the information and advice thus obtained is suggested in the following account of Bush's dealings with Central America and Iraq.

THE NORIEGA AFFAIR

One of the first moves made by the Bush administration was to disengage from Reagan's unpopular and unsuccessful campaign to topple a Marxist regime in Nicaragua. On their list of "most important problems," Americans now put drug trafficking and drug addiction much higher than the contras. Opinion polls disclosed concern that the United States was not doing enough to deal with the matter. Panama had become a major center of the drug traffic. General Manuel Noriega was its increasingly dictatorial and corrupt leader. In 1989, only a few months after Bush took office, Noriega declared himself the victor of an election the outcome of which was hotly disputed by his opponents. Seeking to avert another Noriega regime, the Bush administration broke diplomatic relations with Panama. In October it also gave covert support to an attempted anti-Noriega coup, but the uprising ended in failure, complete with televised scenes of the dictator's henchmen wielding metal pipes to club unarmed opponents. Senator Jesse Helms characterized Bush and his advisers as "Keystone Kops." Representative David McCurdy used the word "wimp." But shortly before Christmas 1989 the alleged wimp ordered more than 20,000 troops to invade Panama. Noriega was captured and flown to the United States to stand trial for violating American antidrug laws.

What did opinion have to do with all this? One year before the matter came to a head, a polling organization had asked whether people favored the idea of kidnapping major drug traffickers and bringing them to the United States to stand trial. It found general support for this hypothetical scenario.[4] More to the point, polls taken *after* U.S. troops reached Panama disclosed that most Americans would not consider the intervention a success unless Noriega was apprehended. When he was carried off to the United States, most Americans were convinced that their president had acted neither lightly nor illegally. Americans found Noriega a readily detestable adversary, probably the best in sight given Khomeini's death and Quaddafi's quiescence. During the episode Bush also improved his standing by going to the public. Earlier he had held few press conferences of any kind. Now he held three within three weeks, each devoted primarily to Panama. Television also helped by showing scenes of grateful Panamanians bestowing flowers and kisses on their gallant liberators. The episode dominated the media. Three out of every five people questioned claimed to follow it "very closely." For every American who chose the momentous changes under way in Warsaw Pact countries as "most important," three chose the invasion of Panama. The press identified the episode as the most powerful to date in defining the Bush presidency.

Within a week of Noriega's capture polls also reported that Bush's overall job rating was higher than that of any prior president at an equivalent time. Approval of his conduct of foreign affairs—a more specific matter—exceeded that of any president since Kennedy.[5] When poll respondents were asked what they thought Bush had done best in his first year, of the 30 optional answers offered them, the invasion of Panama was mentioned three times as often as any other. The president had not only seen to it that justice was done but had made the additional point that the United States remained a force to be reckoned with. In observing that the episode had alleviated public doubts about the president, the *New York Times* account also noted that "Mr. Bush's political advisers are delighted." Given his ambition and the difficulties he had experienced in his rise to prominence, it must have been an exhilarating and memorable experience. Together with the president's other memories, hopes, and fears, Panama must be kept in mind in attempting to fathom his subsequent conduct of American foreign policy in a vastly more important crisis that soon erupted in the Persian Gulf.

IRAQ INVADES KUWAIT

Iraq's invasion of Kuwait triggered the largest deployment of American military force since the Vietnam War, and the brief battle that ensued generated an outburst of American nationalism so fervent as to make the crisis an ideal case study of the influence of mass opinion on Bush's foreign policy. The moral is best told at the start because the story is complicated. Though Bush had a consuming interest in public opinion, it was not contemporaneous pressure from fellow Americans that drove his policy; there was no prewar consensus on Main Street. It was a mixture of inner conviction about aggression, stability, and oil and political calculation about the future of George Bush. Policy was grounded in opinion in the sense that it was driven by memory of how people had thought in the past and by anticipation in the form of hopes and/or fears about what they might think in the future. The latter process has often been downplayed by social scientists because it is hard to document and impossible to quantify. But those who have labored in the pit of politics know it well.

In retrospect it also appears that Bush had at least two serious problems in dealing with the Gulf crisis. One was that he was more interested in foreign policy than in domestic policy, while the public's priorities were the reverse. The other—less important but not insignificant because it eventually took much of the glow off the trophy—was that he let Saddam Hussein survive. He did so in an understandable desire to minimize (1) casualties, (2) complications with third countries, and (3) the responsibilities of an occupation power in Iraq. But he did so also at the cost of letting down a public that he had aroused. For these reasons Bush ultimately became something of a victim of opinion, though less of a victim than Truman by 1952 or Carter by 1980.

Next, some key facts. In August 1990, following disputes about oil prices and access to oil fields, Saddam Hussein, ruler of Iraq, ordered an invasion of Kuwait and declared that small country an Iraqi province. This posed a threat to Saudi Arabia and other lands in a region with a significant portion of the world's estimated oil reserves. The United States and the UN Security Council condemned the invasion and joined in imposing economic sanctions on Iraq. A sizable contingent of American forces was sent to defend Saudia Arabia, next in line for a potential attack. Saddam Hussein responded by proposing to withdraw in exchange for (1) the removal of economic sanctions, (2) guaranteed access to the Persian Gulf, and (3) sole control of a major Iraqi oil field that dipped into Kuwait. But no such agreement was reached.

The dispute dragged on into November, at which time Bush announced that American forces in the Gulf region would be augmented enough to provide an adequate offensive option. Later in November the UN Security Council authorized member countries to take "all necessary action" to liberate Kuwait if Iraq failed to withdraw by January 15, 1991. This was followed by (1) unsuccessful diplomatic negotiations, (2) Congress' decision to authorize the president to use force if the Security Council's deadline was not met, and (3) the start of American air and missile attacks on January 16, 1991. One week later American and allied ground forces entered the fray. A few days thereafter Iraqi forces surrendered. The victorious forces, largely but not wholly American in composition and leadership, left soon after. But Saddam Hussein remained in power.

OPINION

To most Americans the crisis appeared to have come out of the blue. Many weren't sure where Kuwait was, whether it had been attacked by Iraq or Iran, or where those countries were. Like their leaders, the American people were also divided about what to do. Most wanted some retaliatory move. More than two-third supported the initial deployment of U.S. troops described by Congress as a deterrent force. The Democratic opposition also supported the deployment. Few accepted the argument that no American interest was at stake. Even fewer urged serious consideration of Iraq's claims. A seasoned observer concluded that the force deployment had more support than that given to any similar precombat troop movement since World War II.[6] Polls taken in October revealed that a small plurality of the public felt that U.S. action to date was "not tough enough." During the midterm elections held on November 7, exit polls were taken of the somewhat upscale subset of the public that chooses to turn out for such elections. These disclosed majority support for Bush's decision to increase U.S. force levels in the Gulf.

Combat was another matter. Between November 14 and 18, three surveys were made of carefully chosen samples of the electorate—subsets more representative than those that had chosen to vote in the midterm elections. The surveys revealed more support for a defensive strategy than for an offensive strategy. Neither then nor at any other time prior to the actual start of hostilities was there a clear national consensus that the issue at stake was "worth going to war over" or, to put it another way, that, given the stakes, war was a reasonable and doable option. Many feared that Bush "will have failed if Kuwait is not liberated" and that it would be humiliating if the United States had to accept a compromise settlement.[7] But on the question of *how* Kuwait was to be liberated, polls continued to reveal a fairly even split between those ready to fight and those who wanted to give sanctions more time to work.[8] They also disclosed a "swing" group composed of people who changed position depending on how questions were worded. A certain fatalism or weary resignation also hung in the air. Many who opposed war also doubted that the dispute would ever be settled by negotiations. Expecting hostilities, they were nevertheless reluctant to accept them. Similar ambivalence appeared in Congress. As two respected Washington sources put it at the time, Desert Shield enjoyed a reasonable amount of support in November and December, but no such consensus existed for Desert Storm.[9]

FINER TUNING

The foregoing portrays opinion before war started on January 16. But given the extraordinary behavior of the American people after January 16, it is necessary to pry open the box of aggregate views to find clues to what happened later.

Support for intervention came disproportionately from middle- and lower-middle-income families, less highly educated workers, young males, and southern whites. In late September, for example, white males with no more than a high school education were readier than any other subset of the population to initiate attacks on Iraq. They were less ready than any other subset to support such goals as achieving a lasting peace in the Middle East or opposing aggression per se. As time passed, the size of the attentive audience also grew, and as it grew, this downscale component of the interventionist coalition became larger and more vocal. Between the start of the crisis and the start of battle, the greatest increase in support for war came from Americans whose college education had ended short of a degree, that is, from what two sociologists called middle America.[10]

Opponents of war also varied widely in background, interests, and motives. Skeptics included not just members of Congress and the State Department—even Secretary Baker was said to be dubious at earlier stages of the crisis—but an impressively large number of Pentagon leaders who reflected views long held by the "Never Again Club," an informal group wary of entrapment in difficult and unpopular wars. Born of Korea and coming of age in Vietnam, the club had reached maturity during Reagan's presidency when a risk-aversive defense secretary, Caspar Weinberger, debated openly with a more aggressive secretary of state, George Schultz.

Weinberger's precedent emboldened other high-ranking national security officials to speak up. By January 1, 1991, resort to force in lieu of diplomacy and economic sanctions had already been criticized by five former secretaries of defense, two former chairmen of the Joint Chiefs of Staff, two former army chiefs of staff, President Carter's national security adviser, and, from what one gathers, the then-current chairman of the Joint Chiefs of Staff, the already designated commander of the Gulf operation, and a large majority of European and American experts on Arab affairs.[11]

In the larger public, opponents of war were more often black than white, more often women than men, more often holders of postgraduate degrees than college dropouts or people who admitted to "high school only," more often from the Boston-Washington corridor than from Dixieland, more often Dukakis voters than Bush voters, more often Catholic, Jewish, or high-church Episcopalians than Christian evangelists or fundamentalists. Catholic bishops supported a peaceful solution. The National Council of Churches of Christ called for withdrawal of troops. So did Pat Buchanan and supporters of his "America First" movement.

BUSH'S FRAME OF MIND

The questions are how Bush reacted and why he reacted as he did. The president clearly felt deeply because of his office and his long-standing interest in foreign affairs. The matter before him also involved oil, and he had been in the oil business in Texas, where oil was important. But even he may not have been fully aware of why he acted as he did. With the acknowledgment that the following does not pretend to be a full account of his mind-set and that it includes a hefty dollop of conjecture, I will make a stab at trying to fathom the influence of public opinion on what went on in his mind.

A good place to start is with memory, especially memory of Panama, but not only of Panama. Grenada and the Falkland Islands were probably in the back of his mind as well. As vice president he had been in a position to observe how Reagan's decision to invade Grenada had diverted attention from a failed policy in Lebanon. The case for the relevance of the Falkland Islands precedent takes more arguing but is far from groundless. Bush had also been vice president when Britain's military action in the Falkland Islands had restored the standing of Britain's prime minister Margaret Thatcher and her beleaguered Conservative Party. The *New York Times* carried that story under the headline "Mrs. Thatcher's Heady Moment: Jubilant Britons Acclaim their Prime Minister."[12] Almost immediately after Iraq attacked Kuwait David Shribman mentioned it in the *Wall Street Journal*. Thatcher, he reminded readers, had "consolidated her position atop the greasy pole of British politics and had won for herself a reputation as a tough prime minister willing to use force to protect British interests." In the next general election her party had won hundreds of seats that had been expected to go to the Labor opposition. The conflict was extremely good to the leaders in power.[13]

Concern about the future pointed the same way as memory of the past. Bush had two reasons to worry about the near-term economic future. One was the condition of the national economy; the other was growing partisan conflict over the federal budget and tax policy. The economic outlook was bad. Housing starts and sales were down. Prices, unemployment, and the trade deficit were up. Several major corporations had lost money in the first part of the year. The savings and loan industry was in shambles, the Department of Housing and Urban Development wracked by scandal. For Bush, this posed an issue of agenda control, one that surfaced in August, grew in September, and assumed ominous proportions in October. At its height 70 percent of the American people—more than at any time in the previous 20 years—felt that their country was pretty seriously off on the wrong track. A still more pressing difficulty for the White House was a budget deficit already big and predicted to grow. Throughout August the press ran unsettling stories that left readers worried about how Bush was dealing with the problem. The following material has been condensed from the *Washington Post* and *New York Times* on the dates cited. Quotation marks have been omitted, but most words appear in the original account and convey the essence of the published material. The October 1 story had been preceded by 10 days of hard bargaining between Bush and a bipartisan group of congressional leaders.

October 1. Congress Critical of Budget Agreement. Shouts of Revolt.
October 2. Hostility between Congressional Republicans.
October 3. Pivotal Moment for Bush. From Long Honeymoon to Bad Times.
October 5. Stunning Defeat. House of Representatives Rejects Bipartisan Budget Plan.
October 6. George Bush Suffers Humiliation. Setback May Be Watershed.

October 7. President Vetoes Stopgap that Would Allow Government to Proceed with Temporary Funds for Essential Services. Shutdown of Government Begins.
October 8. House OK's New Budget Plan to Avert Government Shutdown.
October 9. Plurality Disapproves of Bush's Handling of Budget Issue. It Has Ruptured the Republican Party and Damaged the Bush Presidency.
October 11. Bush Shifts Stand on Tax Rise Again. Endangers His Image.
October 12. Tug of War Goes On. Absence of Guiding Principle.
October 13. Big Jump in Producer Prices.
October 14. Drop in Bush's Standing[14]
October 22. Dispute over Surtax on Millionaires. White House Exits from Talks.
October 25. Deal on Finances. Will Raise Taxes $140 Billion over Five Years. Sharply Higher Taxes on Wealthy.
October 26. Three-Month Budget Struggle Ends.
October 28. Politics of Confusion.
October 29. Advantage Democrats.

It must have been galling to a former chairman of the Republican National Committee to discover that well-known fellow partisans were urging Republican candidates to keep their distance from him before the November elections. One was Ed Rollins, cochair of the Republican Campaign Committee. Another was Kevin Phillips, whose analysis of the 1968 presidential campaigns had almost biblical prestige in the Nixon White House and who now described fellow partisans as alarmed that Bush "has reason to fear 1992."[15] A third was Patrick Buchanan, already gearing up to contest the 1992 Republican presidential nomination. A fourth was Richard Viguerie, a major Republican fund-raiser. "Conservative Republicans," he stated flatly, "have no business in the Bush White House." Night after night the president was also exposed to negative television commentary. Words like "wimp," "flip-flop," and "moral indecision" were used often enough to make it conceivable that he would labor under the handicap of a prospect analogous to one that had contributed to Carter's demise: a reputation for inconsistency and appeasement in a foreign crisis that left the initiative to the adversary and was a daily reminder of the limits of American power.[16]

Although I can find no conclusive evidence on the point, I think the odds are good that this had some effect on Bush's position. Analysts the world over have long contended that leaders may be tempted to use force to divert attention from domestic difficulties. Presidents don't like to admit this, which is one reason that few smoking guns can be found. Nor does it always work. But for present purposes the important point is that one seldom gets to be a modern American president without ambition, enough ambition to be highly sensitive to one's standing. Consider Truman, Kennedy, Johnson, Nixon, even Ford, certainly Carter, and Reagan. No shrinking violets here. Truman intervened in Korea when his approval rating fell to 36 percent. Nixon put U.S. nuclear forces on alert when the Watergate crisis was coming to a head. Ford distanced himself from détente when his reelection appeared uncertain. He also directed a rescue operation to recover the *Mayaguez*. Carter activated the plan for a hostage rescue mission when his popularity was plummeting. Bush was neither less nor more ambitious than these predecessors.

More controversial is the contention that Bush's views were influenced by knowledge that his predecessor's administration had tilted toward Iraq in an effort to counter Iran's ambitions. To that end it had shared intelligence data, facilitated the transfer of technology and arms to Iraq's armed forces, and more generally depicted Saddam Hussein as a haven of sanity in a sea raging with Muslim fundamentalists. The Bush administration had adopted much the same policy—often working through intermediaries—to help Saddam Hussein pursue military programs, including nuclear, chemical, and biological weapons programs.[17] Less than a month before Kuwait was attacked, the president had also written to Saddam Hussein, stating, "My administration continues to desire better relations with Iraq." One must choose words carefully here, but uneasiness about this record may have contributed to a presidential conclusion that further forbearance toward Saddam Hussein could be politically dangerous for a president already struggling with economic problems at home.

INITIAL POLICY DECISIONS

Informed observers felt from the start that this would be a high-stakes game. An August 7 headline read "Iraq Crisis Presents Bush Crucial Opportunity to Define His Presidency, Determine His Future." The reporter predicted "decisions that will color the rest of his term and help determine whether he will win another one." Liberals and conservatives agreed on the point. A leading Democratic pollster said, "He'll either look strong or he will begin the slide down the slippery slope of public opinion." The president of the Heritage Foundation, a Washington think tank that often reflected Republican views, said that "he's got to show" that he knows "how to use America's influence and power."[18]

Bush's immediate reaction was to state publicly that Iraq's invasion constituted "naked aggression" and to consider economic sanctions or military action to protect Saudi Arabia if Iraqi troops advanced farther. On August 3 he told senior staff aides, "We are not going to plan how to live with this." He also asked Defense Secretary Cheney to brief him on military options.[19] On August 4 he announced publicly that the invasion "will not stand." This implied a determination not only to protect Saudi Arabia but to free Kuwait. Four days later, having received permission from King Saud of Saudi Arabia, he announced that American forces would be sent there. He described their mission as "wholly defensive ... they will not initiate hostilities." But as if he had read the previous day's *Wall Street Journal*, he displayed little interest in a negotiated settlement. An unidentified senior official later dismissed Iraq's negotiating proposals as "not serious." Throughout the months that followed, the administration also resisted Soviet, French, Jordanian, and other efforts to resolve the dispute by diplomatic means.

It is nevertheless hard to pinpoint when Bush decided on offensive war because there appears to be no evidence on this in the available written record. My guess is that it was his intention right from the start but that time was needed to cope with logistical problems and to win international support. As early as August 6, General Scowcroft, who was not only Bush's national security adviser but his constant companion from the start of the invasion, had put the question hypothetically: Can the United States go to war for carefully defined national interests?[20] After meeting the president at Camp David a few days later, Lieutenant General Thomas Kelly concluded that war was already the president's leading option. As director of operations for the Joint Chiefs of Staff [JSC], Kelly was familiar with "Instant Thunder," a now nearly completed contingency plan for intensive air attack. Later he told a research group that there had never been doubt in his mind that the country was going to war. David Gergen, who had worked with Bush for some years, identifies an early August briefing in which JSC chairman Colin Powell, himself reluctant to embrace the war option, told senators that the United States would rely primarily on airpower in any battle.

The real question was not *why* war but *when* and *what kind*.[21] Saudi Arabia's ambassador was told that imposition of an embargo precluded a military offensive "for the time being."[22] A week later Bush stated publicly, "I don't . . . rule out the use of force," whereupon the Dow Jones stock market index dropped 77 points. On August 27 the press revealed that a pollster had raised the question of whether the public could stand a stalemate like the one in Korea in 1952, or whether pressure would build for a quick and decisive solution, as in Grenada and Panama. A few days later the press reported that an unidentified senior official had stated that a major air attack was planned "if, as expected, the economic embargo and UN initiatives fail within the next four to ten weeks." Presumably, that would be a long enough time to persuade potential critics the world over that enough consideration had been given to testing the efficacy of measures short of war. Another observer later sharpened the point. "It was evident from very early on" that some officials believed it would come to war and saw sanctions and diplomacy "as the necessary precursors of war." That would be "a box to check."[23]

Though the military still needed more time to complete its buildup, by September Bush himself was perceived to be "spoiling for a fight."[24] Secretary of Defense Cheney described his boss as belonging "to what I call the don't screw around school of military strategy." In mid-September the direction of the wind was also indicated by the so-called Duggan incident. General Michael Duggan, recently appointed air force chief of staff, was an ardent exponent of strategic bombing. In Saudi Arabia he talked publicly about offensive air war against Iraq. In so doing he not only threatened the fragile international coalition that the administration was building—another matter that took time—but threatened to spill the beans back home. Cheney promptly fired him.

At this stage Bush's 1988 presidential campaign pollster conducted a survey that included the following tortuous question: "Suppose at some point, due to a potential loss of support of allies or Congress, or for whatever reason, it seemed to the President that any further waiting would begin to jeopardize our chances of winning. In that case would you want or not want the President to start war against Iraq as soon as he thought the opportunity for success was possibly about to slip away?"[25] The fact that this issue was raised in this way at this time and by this man, together with the fact that Gallup had earlier posed a roughly similar question about combat, indicates that Bush was thinking and talking about offensive moves. Before September ended, his national security assistant had already told reporters quietly that the time for military action was shortening.

With the domestic fiscal crisis coming to a head, this was a hard time for the president. A press story described him as "increasingly testy and frustrated." He worried that his international coalition might fall apart. Ambivalence surfaced not only among Saudi Arabian notables but in other Arab states, France, Germany, China, Japan, and a now-collapsing Soviet Union. Those close to the president found him obsessed. In a worst-case scenario the crisis could drag on, with idle and unhappy troops sequestered in a strange and not highly hospitable land and with an increasingly frustrated domestic audience soon to vote in midterm elections. When JCS chairman Colin Powell told Cheney it would be a mistake to move from sanctions to attack, Cheney replied, "I don't think the president will buy it."[26] Powell dutifully relayed this to another high-level skeptic, General Norman Schwarzkopf, telling him bluntly, "My President wants to get on with this thing."[27] On October 6 the Pentagon received an unpublicized official notice that the president wanted an offensive military option. The next day the press reported that the administration would think it "a nightmare scenario" if Saddam agreed to withdraw and if Saudi Arabia then asked the United States to reciprocate.[28] A little more than two weeks later Defense Secretary Cheney told the press to expect notice of an offensive military option.

PARTISAN IMPLICATIONS

Questions were now raised about the president's motives. A week after Cheney's statement to the press a reporter probed further by asking the president whether his recently disclosed policy had domestic political implications. "The question," the reporter wrote, "struck a nerve." Any such suggestion, Bush had retorted, was "the ultimate of cynicism and indecency. I'm offended that anyone would ever suggest that. I don't think that any decent, honorable person would."[29] When stories began to appear that imminent increases in U.S. force levels in the Gulf might permit offensive operations, a reputable columnist nevertheless wrote that Bush has "suddenly found an issue on the campaign trail." Earlier he had been criticized by Republican candidates who sought to put space between themselves and their president. Now such candidates were fewer. The problem of agenda control also became a bit more manageable. Eyes were no longer focused solely on a sluggish economy and tax increases. In October, when the fiscal crisis was at its height, Bush still managed to address Persian Gulf problems in a briefing for congressional leaders, 2 briefings for the media, 5 speeches, and 10 news conferences.[30]

Analysts also speculated that electoral calculations were contributing to White House decisions. Only five days after Iraq invaded Kuwait, a reporter wrote that Bush now had a "crucial opportunity to ... determine his future."[31] Two days later another reporter observed a consensus in the press corps that Bush's pledge to liberate Kuwait, if kept, "could virtually assure reelection."[32]

Peter Hart, who polled for Democratic candidates, had predicted that the dispatch of troops to Saudi Arabia would provide a cover for Republican difficulties like the savings-and-loan scandal and the federal budget crisis. After Bush had reluctantly agreed to raise taxes, Republican analyst Kevin Phillips observed on National Public Radio that no one should be surprised if Bush now sought to take military action to divert attention from his fiscal defeat. Other presidents, he noted, had acted forcefully abroad for partisan advantage.[33] Roger Ailes, a Bush media consultant, was blunt. "If Saddam Hussein leaves Kuwait head first or feet first, George Bush wins." It was also alleged that John Sununu, Bush's chief of staff, had told the press that "a short successful war would be pure political gold."[34] Vice President Quayle and Defense Secretary Cheney were said to share this calculation.[35]

Critics of the administration had to be careful. More of them surfaced after Bush announced plans for a major increase in U.S. force levels in the Gulf. Eighty congressional Democrats disagreed openly with the decision, in part on the merits and in part because Congress had not been consulted. Republicans countered that Democrats might face attacks questioning their patriotism if they protested. Adopting the constitutional definition of treason, they warned against "giving aid and comfort" to Iraq. The president made the point more delicately by showing congressional critics an Iraqi newspaper story about their opposition to his policies. Stephen Solarz, a Democratic member of the House of Representatives, warned his colleagues that angry voters might "keep us out of the White House forever." In early January 1991, with war increasingly likely, an article in the *New Republic* described Democrats as killing themselves by being "weak and indecisive" when Americans wanted a credible and assertive commander in chief. Anticipatory reactions galore.

SALES JOB: ROLES FOR POLLS

While activists engaged in calculation and maneuver, the public remained undecided. As noted earlier, it was still far from ecstatic about an "offensive capability" and a trifle less enthusiastic than it had been two months earlier about how its leader was handling the crisis. At the same time there was no torrent of demand to "bring the boys home." A sizable number of leaders and followers wanted to give sanctions more time to work. Perhaps the best way to put it is that the public, like Congress, was still up for grabs. To grab it, the president had to know its mind about such matters as the rationale for military action and the sequence in which moves should be made. Like his immediate predecessors, he tried to fathom the public mind by consulting polling organizations, in this case Market Strategies and the Wirthlin Group. Throughout the crisis the latter tracked opinion daily on behalf of Citizens for a Free Kuwait, an organization created soon after Iraq's invasion. Headed by Republican activist Robert Gray, it was, in effect, an ally of the administration. Another source of advice was the Washington public relations firm of Hill and Knowlton, another ally, one of whose functions was to convene focus groups to test the efficacy of war-related themes.

These organizations helped Bush select means to accomplish the ends on which he had set his heart. Many arguments were available for the proposition that Iraq had to be dislodged, for example, that aggression must not go unpublished, that lasting peace must be brought to the region, that Saudi Arabia must be protected, that the legitimate rulers of Kuwait must be restored, that oil must remain available at reasonable prices, that Iraq's monstrous ruler must be removed, and that Iraq must be kept from acquiring a nuclear capability. The question of the hour was which arguments were most compelling. The answer provided by the polls was that they are listed here in order of increasing importance to the American people.

From the start, efforts were made to demonize Iraq's ruler by comparing him to Hitler. (Four months before the invasion, Abe Rosenthal had done so in the *New York Times*.) In using focus groups, analysts discovered that this argument was more effective than any based on the need to liberate Kuwait. The oil argument was also somewhat less persuasive than those that follow it on the preceding list. Bush's opinion analysts told him he needed a more "emotion-grabbing" theme. He took their advice. On a preelection swing through New Hampshire in November he stated flatly, "It's not oil." Polls suggested that Iraq's nuclear ambitions might be a highly effective issue. The White House and the media responded quickly.[36] On November 20 a *New York Times* story speculated that references to Iraq's nuclear ambition "may be a way to sustain public support." Bush spent the next two days in Saudi Arabia. A major—possibly *the* major—item on the agenda was a televised Thanksgiving address by the commander in chief to American troops. His entourage included a bipartisan congressional delegation plus General Norman Schwarzkopf, commander designate of allied forces. Bush penciled into his speech a statement that Saddam Hussein's progress toward his goal of a nuclear weapons arsenal lent great importance to the mission of the allied troops.[37]

Another attractive theme was that the United States was not acting alone. America was out front, but other countries were following by condemning the invasion, imposing economic sanctions, and contributing troops, equipment, or money. Both Congress and the public welcomed such burden sharing, and Bush played a key role in encouraging it, often by giving something significant in return. Egypt sent troops in return for relief from its debts to the United States. China was promised continuing normalization of political and economic relationships in return for refraining from casting a veto on a key measure before the UN Security Council. Late in November the council set a January 15 deadline for Iraq to withdraw and authorized member states to take "all necessary steps" in the event the deadline was not met. Only Yemen and Cuba, neither with a right to veto, voted no.

Congress was the remaining problem. Polls had made it clear that the public wanted Congress to approve any decision that might require Americans to risk their lives. Convinced that prior approval by the UN would influence Congress favorably, Bush had arranged to schedule the UN vote first. Following that vote he made another gesture to satisfy the public's desire, again attested by polls, to go the last mile diplomatically. To open what was ostensibly a direct negotiating channel with Iraq, he proposed that Secretary of State Baker go to Baghdad and that Foreign Minister Tariq come to Washington. This was welcomed not only by Congress but by the UN and the American public. But nothing came of it. William Quandt, a respected Middle East specialist at the Brookings Institution, concluded that it "wasn't meant to work." David Gergen, a former member of Regan's White House staff, described it as "a sop to doves, proof that we did all we could."[38]

In the end Congress authorized Bush to act in accordance with the UN resolution. It did so after serious and sometimes eloquent debate held shortly before the January 15 deadline. The House voted approval 250 to 18. A majority of Americans concluded that their leader had "done all he should." He, in turn, was quick to assure them, "This will not be a protracted, drawn-out war.... We will not permit our troops to have their hands tied behind their backs." Behind this language was a public whose opinion counted.

EFFECT OF WAR ON PUBLIC OPINION

The Gulf War increased the size of the audience for foreign affairs by temporarily mobilizing mainstream America. This had happened before, but seldom, if ever, had mass communication played so important a role in the process. Before the shooting started, the crisis had generated the most intensive television news coverage logged up to that time, far more, for example, than was being given to the unification of Germany, a process taking place concurrently. After the shooting started, the percentage of poll respondents who said they were following the situation "very closely" nearly doubled within two weeks. Bush's January address was heard by an estimated 78 percent of American households, then the largest television audience in American history. For weeks thereafter the story dominated the print media, network news programs, local TV stations, and radio talk shows. Bush played a major role in sustaining such media interest. During the month before the attack he met almost daily with the press.

Not all were persuaded by the avalanche of public support that followed. Many blacks living in urban poverty and elderly whites living in rural poverty remained aloof, wired out of the communications network. Women were less supportive than men. Some of the most highly educated Americans remained skeptical or resistant.[39] But the combined total of outright opponents and nonsupporters was insignificant compared to the number of middle-class Americans who had earlier displayed some signs of militancy and were now mobilized by reports from the field. Gallup interviews conducted in the third week of January revealed that 45 percent of poll respondents favored the use of tactical nuclear weapons if this might save American lives. Respondents with no more than a high school education were half again more disposed to support such use than college graduates. Few of these now-mobilized hawks read prestigious publications. Many read tabloids and/or listened to talk shows, sometimes turning to the latter for ideological guidance and reassurance. The progress of the war increased their confidence in cause, country, and leaders. Retired military officers were invited to share their expertise and devotion by commenting sagely on the evolving drama and on the skill and virtue of its American actors. Polls disclosed a leap in the percentage of people who felt that the situation had been worth a war and that the country was now on the right track. Despite objective evidence that the economy was in recession, confidence in the economy also grew. As qualified opinion analysts could have predicted, Bush's popularity rose. What they did not and probably could not foresee was that his approval rating would soar to 89 percent.

An immediate and important consequence was a yearning to demonstrate communal solidarity. Bumper stickers revealed a strain of boosterism verging on sycophancy. Patriots flew flags, gave blood, attended rallies, demonized the enemy, and rejoined in the efficacy of their country's weapons. In CBS' widely viewed *60 Minutes* program, Andy Rooney paid tribute to "the best war in history." Successive issues of *Life* magazine displayed a smiling youngster clutching a small American flag, a solitary marine walking across the sand, and a victorious General Schwarzkopf surrounded by grinning soldiers.[40] But the most distinctive symbols of support were yellow ribbons. Television commentators in Buffalo wore them to show that they cared, that they had a stake, and that they wanted a role in the epic unfolding before their eyes. Near the border between Maine and New Hampshire yellow ribbons were tied around trees, doorknobs, mailboxes, and television—not so often in better residential neighborhoods as along back roads where weathered frame houses sheltered working people who cut their own wood, owned snowmobiles, hunted deer, and drove pickup trucks equipped with citizen band radios or gun racks or both.

Happy hour continued after fighting ended. Bush gave a televised address to a joint session of Congress. Democrats arrived with flag pins on their lapels, Republicans with flags to wave at cameras. Some wore pins captioned, "I voted with the President." The scene was reminiscent of the day Congress gave thunderous ovations to General Macarthur upon his return from Korea. In an atmosphere charged with patriotism, Bush's message was, "Tonight we lead the world." America had determined the strategy and outcome of a great campaign, and fully 80 percent of its citizens felt good about it. The chant of the house was "USA! USA! USA!" Returning troops marched the streets of Washington and New York in elaborately staged parades. As late as midsummer 1991 a reporter described the president as striding the scene like a tested commander in chief with an extraordinary approval rating.

As noted later, this outburst of national pride proved temporary. It also had a flip side: indifference and intolerance—indifference to the plight of Iraqi civilians, intolerance toward anyone viewed as an actual or potential critic of the war. To many Americans, the human cost to the Iraqi people counted for little. A careful analyst of opinion described his countrymen as "remarkably insensitive" to the fact that over half a million Iraqis had been killed or wounded in six weeks and that many more had been driven from their homes.[41] There was a marked tendency to understate such facts or to shrug them off as what should be expected in wartime or what was richly deserved. Remorse was in short supply. Most Americans thought that the United States should not pay any part of the cost of repairing or replacing what had been destroyed. Most also felt that their allies were not picking up their fair share of the bill. Little interest was taken in postwar aid to needy countries like Egypt that had helped in the fight. For most Americans the question was not what the war had meant to "them"—whether allies or enemies. It was what the war had meant to "us."

A related question was what home-front critics of the war were doing to "us." Protest was much less common or vehement than it had been in the Vietnam War. Still, supporters had little patience with critics. With less-educated white males leading the way, almost one out of every four poll respondents favored a total ban on all antiwar demonstrations. Skeptics were denounced on talk radio programs, sometimes by hosts, more often by callers. An Italian member of Seton Hall's basketball team was abused by fans because he refused to wear an American flag pin on his shirt. Peter Jennings, the ABC news anchor, was called a "jerk" for reporting that an Iraqi civilian bunker had been bombed. War reporters in the field were viewed suspiciously. Military authorities tightened restrictions on where, when, and how members of the press could travel, whom they could question, and about what. Some private citizens wanted still stricter surveillance. At least one poll found a majority in favor of outright censorship.

Given this climate of opinion, few were prepared to find fault with the administration. After Iraq surrendered, a question arose about whether its government was complying with a UN mandate to end its nuclear weapons program. Bush threatened to send U.S. aircraft to the scene to check. Hardly a peep came from Democratic Party leaders. A columnist observed that "yellow ribbons are still on doorways around the country." A prominent Democrat noted, "Every time something like this happens, you can almost see the voters running for shelter to the Republicans and George Bush." The consensus was that the country had won a great victory in a righteous cause.

Yet as early as March 1991 a report by the Americans Talk Security polling project had warned that all this "might be temporary." Domestic issues soon began to regain attention. Only five days after the cease-fire the Labor Department announced that unemployment had increased more in the previous month than in any other month in the previous five years. Savings and loan bank failures made news. By summer, crime, drugs, and jobs were again on center stage. Only 2 percent of the public still identified foreign policy issues as "most important." Eighty percent agreed that "we should not think so much in international terms." There was a sharp rise in discontent with "the way things are going in the United States," with a corresponding decline in belief that the country had "won a great victory" and was "moving in the right direction." Large majorities felt that Bush was devoting too much time to foreign policy and too little to the economy. His approval rating dropped. By November, in what may have been an ironic reference to an earlier celebratory parade, a headline announced, "Dark Skies for Bush: Rain on His Parade Buoys Democrats." Behind such ominous signals was a datum from polls taken back in March, when the national mood was still euphoric: people with working-class backgrounds and relatively limited education, though strongly in favor of Desert Storm, were also "decidedly insular."[42]

As 1992 began, at least a plurality of Americans was unaware or unenthusiastic about the conception of a "New World Order." They also opposed the idea of giving the UN priority over American laws, placing U.S. forces under foreign commanders, and engaging in protected combat likely to entail heavy U.S. casualties. Though they supported the armed forces and defense spending, they were suspicious of economic aid and free trade agreements and in many cases favored imposing restrictions on commerce with economic rivals like Japan. While the better educated tended to view globalization as an opportunity, many of the less educated saw it as a threat.

How did this play out in the 1992 election? The preceding views were closer to those held by Pat Buchanan and Ross Perot than to those held by Bush and Clinton.[43] But of the latter, Clinton conformed more closely to dominant opinion in the sense that foreign policy got little attention in his campaign. The message in his headquarters read unequivocally, "It's the economy, stupid." Or, as his equally succinct campaign ad put it, "Saddam Hussein still has his job. Do you?" Both were appeals to opinion that President Bush was unable to match.

NOTES

1. Millard Fillmore, Franklin Pierce, and James Buchanan are the presidents placed in that category

2. Raymond L. Garthoff, *The Great Transition: American–Soviet Relations and the End of the Cold War* (Washington, DC: Brookings Institution, 1994), p. 128. It should be added that Garthoff had long been critical of Washington hard-liners.

3. Haynes Johnson, *Sleepwalking through History: America in the Reagan Years* (New York: W. W. Norton, 1991), pp. 396–97.

4. Market Opinion Research, *Americans Talk Security*, National Survey #11, November 1988.

5. *New York Times*, January 19, 1990.

6. David Gergen, "America's Missed Opportunities," *Foreign Affairs* 71, no. 1 (1991/1992).

7. John T. Rourke, *Presidential Wars and American Democracy* (Knoxville, TN: Shooting Star Press, 1994), p. 32.

8. For this and the following summary of opinions, see the invaluable data in John E. Mueller, *Policy and Opinion in the Gulf War* (Chicago: University of Chicago Press, 1994).

9. *Congressional Quarterly Weekly Report*, November 17, 1990; *National Journal*, December 15, 1990.

10. Howard Schuman and Cheryl Rieger, "Historical Analogies, Generational Effects, and Attitudes toward War," *American Sociological Review* 57 (1992): 315–26.

11. Those with doubts included Robert McNamara, James Schlesinger, Harold Brown, Frank Carlucci, Caspar Weinberger, Admiral William Crowe, General David Jones, General Edward Meyer, General Carl Vuono, General Colin Powell, and General Norman Schwarkopf. Other skeptics were William Odom, former head of the National Security agency, a highly secret communications agency, and Zbigniew Brzezinski, Carter's national security adviser. Henry Kissinger opposed ground combat but favored air attacks. A contemporary *New York Times* op-ed piece by Leslie Gelb, himself a former senior Pentagon official, stated that sanctions were preferred by eight of the nine recent defense secretaries and by such militant commentators as Paul Nitze, Pat Buchanan,

Rowland Evans, Robert Novak, and Edward Luttwak.

12. "Mrs. Thatcher's Heady Moment: Jubilant Britons Acclaim their Prime Minister," *New York Times*, June 16, 1982.

13. Jean Smith, *George Bush's War* (New York: Henry Holt, 1992), p. 66.

14. During the economic crisis it dropped 20 points.

15. *New York Times*, October 10, 1990.

16. Robert W. Tucker and David C. Hendrickson, *The Imperial Temptation: The New World Order and America's Purpose* (New York: Council on Foreign Relations Press, 1992), pp. 129–31.

17. *Los Angeles Times*, February 23, 1992; *New York Times*, May 18 and July 19, 1992. Columnist William Safire and Representative Henry Gonzales also publicized such activity.

18. David B. Shribman, "Iraq Crisis Presents Bush Crucial Opportunity to Define His Presidency, Determine His Future," *Wall Street Journal*, August 7, 1990.

19. Alex R. Hybel, *Power over Rationality: The Bush Administration and the Gulf Crisis* (Albany: State University of New York Press, 1993).

20. *New York Times*, August 7, 1990.

21. *Newsday*, August 31, 1990.

22. Dilip Hiro, *Desert Shield to Desert Storm: The Second Gulf War* (New York: Routledge, 1992), p. 78.

23. Elizabeth Drew, "Letter from Washington," *New Yorker*, February 4, 1991, p. 82.

24. Ibid., p. 82. See also Michael R. Gordon and General Bernard E. Trainor, *The General's War: The Inside Story of the Conflict in the Gulf* (Boston: Little, Brown, 1995), pp. 47–49.

25. *Americans Talk Security*, Survey #14, September 20–26, 1991.

26. Bob Woodward, *The Commanders* (New York: Pocket Books, 1992).

27. H. Norman Schwarzkopf, *It Doesn't Take a Hero* (New York: Bantam Books, 1992), p. 433.

28. *New York Times*, October 7, 1990.

29. *Hartford Courant*, November 1, 1990, as cited in Rourke, *Presidential Wars*, p. 32.

30. Paul Brace and Barbara Hinckley, *Follow the Leader: Opinion Polls and the Modern Presidents* (New York: Basic Books, 1993).

31. Shribman, "Iraq Crisis Presents Bush Crucial Opportunity," p. A16.

32. *Los Angeles Times*, August 9, 1990.

33. National Public Radio, November 1, 1990.

34. *New Republic*, January 7 and 14, 1991; Drew, "Letter from Washington," p. 82.

35. Smith, *George Bush's War*, p. 175.

36. Mueller, *Policy and Opinion*, p. 118.

37. Hiro, *Desert Shield to Desert Storm*, p. 250; *Bulletin of Atomic Scientists* (March 1991).

38. Drew, "Letter from Washington," p. 82.

39. Schuman and Rieger, "Historical Analogies."

40. John R. Macarthur, *Second Front: Censorship and Propaganda in the Gulf War* (New York: Hill and Wang, 1992).

41. Mueller, *Policy and Opinion*.

42. *Americans Talk Security*, Survey #15.

43. Mueller, *Policy and Opinion*.

Discussant: Richard B. Cheney

Thank all of you for being here today to listen to us tell old war stories and pontificate about the past. I heard Dr. Radway begin to discuss *Roe v. Wade*; for a minute there, I thought I was on the wrong panel. But I am delighted to be here to talk about what obviously was a significant event from the standpoint of the Bush administration.

I thought what I'd do is say a few words at the outset about the president as the manager of the Gulf crisis and the different skills and capabilities that he brought to the job. Then I'll say a few words toward the end about his mind-set—some of the things that were mentioned in both the first and second papers—with respect to public opinion as well.

Let me say at the outset that, if I had to design a president to manage a crisis like the Gulf crisis, you'd be hard put to define someone better suited for that role than George Bush. I worked for three presidents: I was a junior staffer in the West Wing in the Nixon administration, President Ford's chief of staff, and George Bush's secretary of defense. I watched Ronald Reagan from the perspective of the Congress. I've got respect and admiration for all of them in one way or another. But again, as I come back to the Gulf crisis itself, and I think about George Bush's role as a World War II combat pilot in the Pacific, as a congressman, as ambassador to the United Nations, as ambassador to China, as director of the CIA, as vice president for eight years—when you look at those experiences, those are exactly the kinds of experiences you'd want to design into somebody that you were going to trust with the fate of the nation, if you will, when faced with the kind of crisis we were faced with in the Gulf.

I would highlight, in terms of his contribution, obviously, his diplomatic skills. Assembling the coalition was really a remarkable performance, and it was a very personal kind of performance. Jim Baker did great work, as did many others involved in the effort, but I always remember the first weekend of the crisis, the president sent me to Saudi Arabia to obtain Saudi permission to deploy forces to the kingdom. When I called him to tell him that King Fahd had signed off on that and got his approval to go ahead and deploy the force, he said, "I want you to stop in Egypt on the way back and meet with President Mubarak," which I was happy to do, and he'd already called President Mubarak before I'd arrived. We were able to work out some very important understandings and arrangements at that point; got on the airplane, headed back for Washington. The president called me on the plane and said, "Stop in Morocco. I want you to see King Hassan." Again, he'd been on the phone, working the phones, and lined up Moroccan support. As we worked putting the coalition together, it was very much the personal stature, if you will, of George Bush and his ability to call in chits and work on relationships that he'd spent a lifetime building.

The role at the United Nations was crucial. There wasn't anybody in the administration who knew more about the UN than the former ambassador to the United Nations. One of the reasons I think that relationship worked so well was that he had enormous respect for the institution. He was frankly willing to go a lot further in order to build support within the United Nations than some of us in the cabinet who, frankly, wouldn't have devoted as much time to it. But he obviously was right. He had that correct.

The Chinese role and the Soviet role, obviously, were very significant, both of them with permanent seats on the UN Security Council. Either one of them could have blocked, at any time, all of the activities and initiatives that we undertook at the UN. Obviously, both of them also had the capacity to resupply Iraq. They didn't do that. A lot of that, again, was directly a result of George Bush's diplomacy.

In his role as commander in chief, I thought his performance was as good as we've ever had, in terms of how he managed that process. He had a great love and knowledge of the military; he will tell you to this day that the best days he spent as president were the days he spent with U.S. forces in various places around the world. There was never a time when I went to the White House as secretary of defense and asked for something that we needed for military reasons, even though it oftentimes entailed considerable political costs, that he didn't sign off on it. Every single time I made those requests, he was immediate and quick in his support. I would cite such things, for example, as calling up the reserves. It's a very difficult thing to do, to issue orders to call a quarter of a million people away from their private daily lives, bring them to active duty, and send a large number of them halfway around the world to participate in a tough military operation. He never hesitated a moment. Contrast that, for example, with the way Lyndon Johnson refused to call the reserves in connection with the war in Southeast Asia.

When it was time for us to function from a military perspective, he gave us a very clear-cut objective in terms of what we were supposed to do—liberate Kuwait, restore the rightful government of Kuwait—an objective that could be achieved by the application of military force. He gave us the overall strategic direction, signed up to the basic war plans themselves, but he made a very clear delegation of authority. Having established the objective, then he went to the military and the professionals in the Department of Defense to put together the war plan in terms of how we would actually use the force, and that's exactly what we did.

He was very good at preserving the integrity of the chain of command, which is something that I placed great importance by. What happens when you deploy the force—and this is true in virtually any of our crises—everybody in Washington becomes an armchair general. Everybody wants to tell you how to use the force. In the Pentagon itself, of course, there are large numbers of people who truly are expert in the application of military force, who know and understand the operational art very effectively—including, for example, the members of the Joint Chiefs of Staff. But the Joint Chiefs are not in the chain of command. The commandant of the Marine Corps, the chief of naval operations, the army chief of staff—they are not in the chain of command, since we put Goldwater-Nichols in force, in terms of using the force. The chain of command runs from the president, to the secretary of defense, down to the commander in the field, the CINC [commander in chief]—in this case, General Schwarzkopf; and, at the discretion of the secretary, if you want, you go through the chairman of the Joint Chiefs, General Powell, which, of course, we did. But that is the chain of command, and it's very important to keep it short, to have accountability, and to have everybody else in town keep their fingers out of the pie, so to speak. The president did that very ably. We had ample historical precedent when we had people who should not be making essentially military decisions trying to make those decisions. That did not happen in connection with the Gulf War.

I think in terms of talking about his state of mind as we walked through the crisis—and you can look back on it now, cite some of the various statements and so forth that were made at the time—I would say, from my perspective as secretary of defense, there was never any doubt in my mind after that first weekend. When we made the decision to deploy forces to Saudi Arabia, and when King Fahd agreed and joined in that effort, the president came down from Camp David, got off the helicopter on the South Lawn of the White House, and announced, "This aggression will not stand." From that point on, there was never any doubt in my mind about what the outcome was going to be. I think it was true—certainly was true throughout—that the president always hoped there would be a peaceful resolution to the conflict, but there were two other factors that were absolutely essential, and first of all, that was that he was absolutely unwilling to compromise on principle. Total and complete withdrawal meant total and complete withdrawal. He was not willing to accept leaving the Iraqis with a piece of Kuwait. Second, there was never any doubt in my mind, from the very early stages of the crisis, that if it came to it, that if there was no other possibility, if diplomacy failed, if negotiations didn't work, no question but that we were going to use military force to liberate Kuwait.

I would argue that the president had pretty well embarked upon that course of action, certainly as early as the end of August, when we began to talk privately within the administration about offensive operations. In the early weeks of the crisis, of course, we were focused more on a defensive deployment than offensive deployment, until we were able to get forces in sufficient numbers over there. But there was never any hesitation on my part, in terms of the understanding I had of what the president wanted, that he wanted me, as secretary of defense, to develop military options; that those had to be realistic military options—this wasn't a sham. We were sending real forces, and they were to be prepared to go to war if necessary, because if, in fact, Saddam refused to comply with the resolutions on any other basis, then, in fact, we were going to use the force to get him out of Kuwait.

Let me, in closing, say just a couple of things with respect to this question of public opinion. It would be a mistake to look at the decisions that the president made with respect to whether or not we were going to pursue this course of action, setting the objective, ultimately going to war, as being driven by public opinion. It's just wrong. It doesn't work that way. Didn't work that way in this case. It wasn't a matter of holding focus groups or taking polls trying to find out whether or not we ought to go to war. But at the same time, you're very sensitive to the question of public opinion. You need to be—it's a democracy; you govern by consent. You obviously are going to be much more successful if you take that into account in your planning, and if you do what you can do to try to build public support for your policy and to bring people along. So the president was always very much aware of the need to try to build public support for our position. But I would put forth the proposition that I believe, without doubt, that we would have gone forward with a military operation to liberate Kuwait if all we had was the request of the government of Kuwait for assistance and the approval of the Saudis to operate from bases in Saudi Arabia. The coalition was great; it was tremendous having them on board, but we could have gone forward from a military standpoint if we'd had to on our own.

I think also I'd put forward the proposition that if the Congress had not approved the use of force, the president might well—probably would have; I would have argued, and I'm sure he would have, too—have used forced anyway. We wanted the Congress on board if we could get it on board, but the principles that were involved here and the question of responding to naked aggression and of restoring the rightful government of Kuwait were sufficiently great that the president would have risked all, including his standing with the American people and with the Congress, and gone forward even if Congress had not granted its approval with respect to the vote in the Congress.

It's not a matter of polling to see if the public will support your policy in this situation; it's a matter of leadership. It's a matter of doing what's right, convincing the American people you know what's right, telling them why you're doing what you're doing. Frankly, as was true in this case, I think if you exert that kind of leadership—as I think President Bush did—the American people will follow. Of course, in the end, all of those critics who went to Capitol Hill and testified in opposition to what we were doing and all of the talking heads on television who gave us all that great advice that turned out to be wrong—in the final analysis, when the troops came home from what was one of the most successful military operations in history, everybody was on board. It's hard today to find anybody who, in fact, disagreed with that basic policy or who, having disagreed with it, is willing to admit it.

Discussant: Saud Nasir Al-Sabah

First of all, let me express my deep gratitude to Hofstra University for convening this conference to honor a man who we all share the belief is one of the greatest presidents the United States has seen in its history.

We are here to honor a president who not just changed the course of history in our troubled world but brought stability and the respect of the rule of law around the world. We are here to honor, as you've heard from academicians and from politicians, the role the president played during those crucial years from 1988 to 1992 and, during the most challenging period, during the invasion of Kuwait. It's extremely easy to hear the views of academics, and we have heard very important and very fruitful papers this morning on this view. But let me give you my view here from experience and from practice rather than from an academic point of view.

First of all, let me say that, had it not been for President Bush and the United States of America and the coalition forces, I would not have been among you today speaking to you as a member of the cabinet of government of the sovereign, independent Kuwait. Going back to 1990, August 2, is a nightmare to every Kuwaiti and to every peace-loving individual around the world: where a country, a member of the United Nations, was invaded in an attempt to annihilate a whole nation—to throw the people out of the country, to annex the country—by a dictator, as was termed by President Bush, "Hitler relived." This kind of aggression cannot and will not stand in our days where law and order should prevail, through the United Nations and through peace-loving nations. The United States and the Security Council of the United Nations immediately took action by Resolution 660 at that time and followed it by many, many various resolutions calling upon the Iraqi invaders—Saddam Hussein, mainly—to withdraw from Kuwait and restore the legitimate government of Kuwait. But, of course, we were dealing with a dictator who had ambitions over the whole region, to divide the whole region among the dictatorships in that part of the world.

Many resolutions passed, but I think, as has been mentioned by my good friend, secretary of defense then, Dick Cheney, the issue was survival: whether the world was to go to war in order to free a sovereign nation, a member of the United Nations, that has been invaded by a dictator who has ambitions in the region. There was the issue of whether the war was just, whether the war was moral. There is no moral war in this world. No war is moral. But there is moral self-defense, according to Article 51 of the Charter of the United Nations. What we practiced in 1990–1991 was the moral right of self-defense. What Saddam committed was an immoral war against Kuwait, invading a neighboring sovereign country. Had that been left untouched, unnoticed, we would have seen another war, another Hitler in the region. By the way, the hobby of Saddam Hussein at that time was watching documentaries of Hitler during World War II, and that was one of his most beloved habits.

We all wanted a peaceful solution to the problem. We did not want to see bloodshed, especially from our allies, for the purpose of the liberation of Kuwait. We went through many, many, many avenues politically to resolve this problem. Secretary Baker and all the Bush administration were active in trying to find a peaceful resolution, but not a solution that would leave one inch of Kuwait in the hands of Saddam. There was unconditional withdrawal from all Kuwait, and that was the position by the Security Council collectively, by the world community collectively. A New World Order was to be set by President Bush and by the United States.

Resolution 678 was passed, which gave the members of the United Nations the authority to use all means to eject Saddam Hussein out of Kuwait. That was passed in November 1990 and gave him until January 15, 1991. That was painful for us all in Kuwait, where a country was pillaged; people were tortured, thrown out of their homes; women were raped. These days were the most difficult times that we had to go through, but we knew that the whole world community was behind us, and the greatest nation on this earth was behind us.

The day of the air strikes on January 16, 1991, everyone was holding his breath because we had heard many, many calls before about using economic sanctions; that the coalition forces would be defeated by the 1-million-man Iraqi army. But there was no consensus, as far as I'm concerned, with the U.S. administration at that time that the Iraqi army would be in a position to fight the greatest nations on the earth. People talked about maintaining the economic sanctions. Let me tell you quite frankly right now: had we listened to those pundits who came before the Senate and the House committees advocating the issue of maintaining sanctions, we would have still been today under Saddam Hussein's occupation.

It's been seven years now since Saddam was defeated and ejected from Kuwait. There are still economic sanctions on Iraq and Saddam Hussein is still in power in Iraq. That is something that we all have to think about. The issue of humanitarian reasons, the "just war" doctrine, the morality of war—we all agree with it. I don't believe anyone disagrees with this. We are a peace-loving nation; we respect all the norms of international law and the Charter of the United Nations. We respect the integrity of every sovereign nation on the face of this earth. But we cannot accept dictators. The cry in this world now is freedom and democracy and human rights. These are the three important issues that every peace-loving nation in the world is calling for. There'll be no place for dictators among us.

Let me just give you one or two examples that I've had with the man called George Bush. He called me into the Oval Office on August 8, 1990, and we talked openly about what was going on inside Kuwait. I knew he did not need the information from me; he had ample information from all the intelligence and all the surveillance he had. I went on talking about the violation of human rights inside Kuwait, the pillaging, torture, rape, and killings—and then I just did not mention the word "rape." He looked at me—and I think Brent Scowcroft and Richard Haass and others were in the White House at that time with me—and he said, "Mr. Ambassador, are there any rapes?" I said, "Mr. President, I did not want to use that word in view of respect of this office here, the Oval Office. But yes, there are," and I could see tears in the man's eyes. He took off his glasses and wiped his tears. I knew from August 8, 1990, that I was dealing with a man—not just a politician, but a man who had respect for human rights and was touched by human affections.

The issue of public opinion was very important, as Secretary Cheney said, because we all live in a democracy in this country. You need the people, you need the Hill and the Congress with you. It's very important also to bring home to U.S. public opinion the legitimacy of the involvement and the just cause for self-defense.

I would not dwell on that much longer, but the issue, I think, that has always been in the minds of people about the cease-fire: did President Bush make a mistake in accepting the cease-fire and thereby Resolution 687? Let me answer you very bluntly and very clearly as the victim of this war: the president did not make a mistake, and the answer is no. The mandate of Resolution 687 was very clear: to eject the Iraqi forces out of Kuwait—not to invade Iraq or occupy Iraq. Had the coalition forces proceeded even north (which was very easily accessible to the military), they could have been in Baghdad in 48 hours. Well, that wasn't the mandate of the Security Council resolutions. The coalition would have broken apart, and you would have been, up to today, an occupying power in Baghdad. That would have been a political mess for everyone, I think. The war was clean, with a minimum loss of life, and the victory was achieved by virtue of the wisdom, the leadership of a great president of this country, and this country itself.

Discussant: Abdel Raouf El Reedy

It's a hard act to follow after Secretary Cheney and Sheikh Saud, my friend. We were both ambassadors at that time, in that very difficult time. There is a film called *Back to the Future*. I think what we are having today is "Looking Forward to the Past," and it is a very interesting exercise.

I would like to give an Arab perspective to the Gulf War and to Iraq's invasion of Kuwait. There have been rare occasions in modern history where an Arab army fought another Arab army, but the Gulf War was the first instance when Arab armies joined non-Arab armies in fighting against an Arab army. That was made possible only as a result of the blatant aggression by Saddam Hussein against Kuwait, where an Arab country invaded, occupied, and annexed another Arab country.

Saddam's aggression was not a reaction or an event among a chain of events as he tried to make it appear; it was premeditated and planned a long time in advance. In his planning for the takeover of Kuwait, Saddam tried to create, immediately after the end of the Iran–Iraq War, an Arab coalition that would encompass Egypt, with its predominant role in the Arab world, as well as Jordan, Yemen, and Iraq. That was the ill-fated Arab Cooperation Council (ACC). Egypt joined the council in good faith.

Saddam's eye was particularly on Egypt for its central position in the Arab world and its international standing. During the preparatory work for the constitution of the ACC, Iraq tried to include in the agreement establishing the organization provisions that would have given it the character of a military alliance or a joint defense pact. But Egypt refused to be dragged into a military alliance with the unpredictable Saddam and insisted that the ACC had no military component. Iraq's attempts to change the character of the ACC continued, however, till shortly before the invasion, but they were rebuffed by Egypt.

Saddam's plan was to create conditions where Kuwait would find itself without effective support in the Arab world when the hour would come to carry out his planned takeover of Kuwait. His first disappointment was when Egypt, a fellow member of the Arab Cooperation Council, did not act according to his design and turned instead to lead the Arab Coalition against the invasion and later to join the U.S.-led coalition that managed to liberate Kuwait. Saddam tried hard to lure Egypt so that it would not take the principled stand it actually took in opposition to his annexation of Kuwait.

The news of the invasion caught the Arab world—as everybody else—by complete surprise. Just a few days before, Saddam had assured President Mubarak that he would not invade Kuwait. It just happened that on August 2, the day of invasion, the Arab foreign ministers, as well as the secretary-general of the Arab League, were in Cairo, by pure coincidence, to attend a meeting of the Islamic Conference. After consultation between the Egyptian, Saudi, and Kuwaiti ministers, Egypt arranged for an emergency meeting of the Arab foreign ministers. I attended that conference. Iraq was represented by its minister of planning.

There was an attempt to neutralize the conference and to prevent it from making a decision. The Jordanian foreign minister, who had just flown from Amman, pleaded with the ministers not to make a decision, with the argument that such a decision would complicate the situation. His point was that consultations were under way between the heads of states, who were Arab heads of states, who were going to meet in a mini-Arab summit to find an Arab solution. President Mubarak accepted that the Arab ministers would postpone making a decision for a short interval, to give time to King Hussein to convince Saddam to commit himself to the withdrawal from Kuwait and to restore the legitimate government of Kuwait. When the meeting was resumed 36 hours later, there was no commitment by Iraq to withdraw or to restore the legitimate government of Kuwait. On the contrary, at the meeting of the Arab ministers, the Iraqi minister only reaffirmed Iraq's policy of threats and intimidation to the Gulf Arab countries.

The scene of that meeting can never be erased from my memory. The Iraqi minister was speaking in no apologetic terms. He was speaking of the invasion bombastically, as if it would usher the Arab world into a greater era, where Arab oil wealth would be shared by all Arabs according to everybody's needs. But he was the only one who displayed such jubilation. Most of those in the room were in a state of disbelief and shock. He went on with his attempt to prevent the conference from making a decision, on the pretext that it should continue to search for an Arab solution. But the Egyptian foreign minister challenged that attempt and insisted on making a decision calling for Iraq to withdraw and for the legitimate Kuwaiti government to be restored. Egypt felt that it would be a disaster for the Arab world and the Arab system if the Arab ministers failed to make a decision on such a grave matter: a blatant aggression by a member against another member state.

Egypt succeeded, after so much haggling by the Iraqi minister and his few supporters, to push for a decision by the council. The decision called for Iraq's withdrawal and the restoration of the legitimate government. That decision was the precursor for the more significant decision made by the Arab heads of state a few days later, on August 9. President Mubarak called for that Arab summit that was attended by the Arab heads of states.

I will not go on about this summit because I have just been told that there's only two minutes, and I have to make the rest of my speech. But I would like, just before leaving the rostrum, to say that, realizing that his stand in the Arab world was rapidly eroding and the Arab mass did not rise against the Arab governments that joined the coalition, Saddam decided to play the Israeli card, trying to inflame Arab public opinion against the United States, a friend of Israel. At one point, he even declared that Iraq would withdraw from Kuwait if Israel withdrew from the West Bank and Gaza. During the war itself, he launched the SCUD missiles against Israel. All these were ploys designed to change the character of the conflict into a war with Israel.

Now that I have one minute, I'm going to speak about the personal role of President Bush. I would like to say a few words about the personal diplomacy of President Bush, a theme that has come to dominate the conference from its very beginning. The personal role of the president of the United States played significantly in the making and maintaining of the coalition. How and why, of course, the personal chemistry had something to do with it, but more important, it was a sense of confidence and trust President Bush was able to convey to the leaders of the coalition. The confidence and trust emerged out of mutual respect and consultations. Nobody felt that he was taken for granted. Our opinions were constantly sought. We felt that, indeed, we were partners.

President Bush's basic character was the main factor in all of this. His caring, personable, humane, and reaching out for others came to build these bonds of trust and friendship with the other leaders of the coalition. President Bush also gave the example for the other high officials in his administration to follow and to emulate. The president himself invited the coalition's ambassadors in Washington to meet with him at the White House. Our channels of communication were open to the top echelon of his administration. At no given moment have I ever encountered any difficulty in reaching his top aides. We all felt that we were part of the team. Such is a prerequisite for winning this war, and thank God we have won it.

Discussant: Samuel Segev

I have a problem with our chairman: he forces me to include all the clever things that I have to tell you in 10 minutes. My problem is that I start speaking to the point after 12. Being a real Middle Easterner, we are accustomed to bargaining. I will bargain for another three minutes; altogether, it will be—what? About 20 minutes?

Everyone is talking about Desert Shield and Desert Storm and its success, but I think that we cannot proceed on this subject without saying two sentences about what preceded Desert Storm. I think we must here acknowledge that we came to Desert Storm after a failure of the Bush administration's understanding of the Iraqi policy. My good friend Ambassador El Reedy already mentioned a policy of deceit, and it's true that Saddam Hussein conducted a policy of deceit that was totally ignored in the United States in the years preceding the Persian Gulf War.

To what extent the policy of deceit was well planned and premeditated, I can tell you here that in late 1989, when in Israel there was still a National Unity government, Saddam Hussein tried to arrange a meeting between him and the late prime minister of Israel, Yitzhak Rabin, who was at that time defense minister, and the meeting was to take place here, in the United States. There were preparatory meetings in preparing for such an encounter between Saddam Hussein and Rabin in Philadelphia. So everyone fell into the trap of the tilt toward Iraq.

Having said that, I think that in the West and in the United States, there was not enough appreciation for the tremendous success of President Bush in assembling such a coalition with 10 Arab countries and, as it was already mentioned, joining in a war against an Arab country. There has never been a precedent; I'm not sure there will be such a precedent in future, but this is an unprecedented success that we must attest to.

Because of this success, the exclusion of Israel—and I'm saying it as an Israeli—I think it was 100 percent justified, because it was enough for the Arab world to swallow a situation where Arab countries were fighting against an Arab country. To have Israel in the coalition, it was too much to swallow. I was not surprised when, in a meeting between Prime Minister Shamir and President Bush in December 1990—just before the war started—Shamir agreed not to preempt and to coordinate possible retaliation against Iraq with the United States. What is more surprising, Shamir spoke to President Bush about the need to keep Jordan in the Western camp and not to overreact to King Hussein's support of the invasion of Kuwait. Well, at that time, I don't think that the president was in a situation to follow this advice.

Now, I have a few remarks about the preparations for the war and its aftermath. The overcautiousness of President Bush, the concern about the loss of human lives, led to a situation where the preparations for the war dragged on too long. It reminded me of a similar situation in 1956 in the Suez War, when Israel, Great Britain, and France joined in a war against Egypt. The cautiousness of France and Great Britain at that time led to a situation that, when they intervened in Suez after six days, Israel was already on the banks of the Suez Canal, and the war was practically over. Israel achieved its goals; the allies—the French and the British—did not, because they waited too long.

This could be also a result of lack of adequate intelligence. I think we all remember the first two or three days of the war, when the first reports said that everything was done; the military machine of Iraq was annihilated; the Republican forces decimated. I still remember the reports on CNN and so on. Whether it was intentionally misleading or not, I cannot say, but the fact was that in Israel we knew that the reports were not correct. In the first three days, not all of the targets were hit. Many of the things that were said to be destroyed during the war were destroyed only after the cease-fire.

Now, a few things about the coalition. A coalition, no doubt, has many advantages, but it has also disadvantages. Because of the large coalition, the United States was forced to limit itself to a very narrow mandate: the liberation of Kuwait. After the liberation of Kuwait, if the war continued, it was beyond the UN mandate. If there was not a coalition—this is a very hypothetical situation— there could have been—I'm not saying that I'm certain, but there could have been—a situation where the U.S. forces would have gone and probably removed Saddam Hussein from Baghdad. The capacity of the United States to do it was not in doubt. There was no doubt that there was overwhelming military superiority over the Iraqi army, but the limitations were political.

Now, finally, I will try to say a few words about the aftermath of the war. I said it already before, in a previous panel; I want to repeat it here. If there was no Desert Storm, there would be no Middle East peace process. Just as I said that there was a failure of the Bush administration in understanding the deceptions of Saddam Hussein before he invaded Kuwait, I must here also say that the Madrid Peace Conference was undoubtedly the biggest foreign policy achievement of the Bush administration.

Now, during the war, when things were clear, and it was obvious that the war was won—and there was no doubt about it even before the first shot was fired that the war was won—there were many talks about the Israeli restraint. I was in Israel when the SCUDs landed in Israel. I must tell you that it is a very scary experience, because you don't know when and where and how the SCUD will land. I saw two of the SCUDs that did not explode. It's really scary to see one big missile, the size of this hall, lying on the ground, and to see what could have happened if it exploded. Now, people say about the Patriot and the Israeli restraint and so on—I told you that already Shamir committed himself not to react and not to preempt, and I think that he took the right decision. But the weapons used to defend against the SCUD missiles were not very effective, and I think it is not a secret anymore that the Patriots did not fulfill their job, from day one.

Why did Israel remain quiet? Because of two reasons: one, the question of morale. Israel could not have come and justified its restraint if it had admitted that the Patriots did not do the job. So the question of morale was very important, and Israel remained quiet. What is more important, I think Israel remained quiet about the ineffectiveness of the Patriots because it did not want to encourage Saddam Hussein to launch more SCUDs. If Israel had said that the SCUDs were ineffective, it would have been an invitation to Saddam Hussein to launch more SCUDs. So Israel accepted the fact, kept its restraint, and only after the war were the results of the Patriots communicated to the United States.

I already mentioned that without the Persian Gulf War, there would be no peace process. I sincerely believe that the Persian Gulf War did the job. If it were not for the Persian Gulf War, if the military balance that even before the war was already in favor of Israel, if this balance was not altered even further in favor of Israel after the destruction of the Iraqi military machine, I don't think that Israel would have felt secure enough to enter a peace process where it gets only verbal commitments in return for tangible land and surrendering of territory.

The second thing was that the PLO [Palestine Liberation Organization] was weakened to a degree that Arafat was forced to accept anything that he was offered after the Persian Gulf War, because of his support of Saddam Hussein. Many things that the United States proposed and Arafat rejected before the war, he accepted after the war. That's how the road to Madrid was opened. We continued to Oslo; we continued with the peace process with Jordan. We have now many difficulties, but I have no illusions about it. What was started in Madrid is irreversible, and the course is very clear, and it will continue. There will be ups and downs, there will be suspensions of negotiations, there will be crises and accusations and counteraccusations, but the process is clear. Eventually, the next conference here will be devoted to the successful peace process in the Middle East.

Discussant: William H. Webster

If any of you are tempted to subscribe to Thomas Carlyle's theory that history is largely a composition of great moments and great people, I submit that the story of Desert Storm reflects the great coincidence of the presence of George Bush as president of the United States at a point in our history when great decisions needed to be made and were made. I don't want to overstate that, but I feel it deeply. It came at the time of the fruit of his preparation for this important event in our world, which could have gone in an entirely different direction and led to an entirely different set of circumstances. Dick Cheney has outlined the president's background; he was enormously prepared and ready for something that we were not fully anticipating.

I want to start with what we knew at the time and what was available to the president at the time that this event happened. A long, seven-year war had ended between Iraq and Iran. Both countries were economically and militarily exhausted. It was the opinion of the intelligence community—and I include the entire intelligence community, not just the Central Intelligence Agency—that Saddam Hussein needed a time for rest and reconstruction but that he intended to be the bully in the neighborhood when he was next able to do so. The October estimate in 1990 did not fully contemplate his interest in aggrandizement in Kuwait, and we have to accept that as a judgment based on common sense, when common sense was not the hallmark of Saddam Hussein. But we did begin to report the military buildup in Iraq on the south, the assembly of his Republican Guard, and this was all correctly and promptly reported. What was absent was a clear foreign policy at this point as to what we would do in a situation in an area where we had no historic record of participation, where I think only in Dubai—was it Dubai we had troops, Dick?

Richard B. Cheney: Bahrain.

Webster: Yeah, Bahrain. We were denied a presence in every other part of the Gulf area. When it happened, Ambassador Gillespie had given an ambiguous message to Saddam Hussein, which reflects that we did not have a clear policy at that point. We were focused elsewhere, and I think we have to accept that. Some people in the State Department were talking about a filling station in the desert. What can we do about that? George Bush never viewed it that way.

When the invasion occurred—and incidentally, the intelligence community had reported to the Deputies Committee that we anticipated an invasion within 24 hours; it came 12 hours later—everything changed, and I think it changed because of the team that George Bush had assembled around him to give him the kind of advice that this particularly important event demanded. He was also fortified by support from Mrs. Thatcher, who was in our country with the president, participating in an event at the Aspen Institute. He came back, as Dick Cheney has said, saying that this will not stand. There was never any question about it. The question was only, How do we make it happen?

The first thing we had to confront was 180,000 troops marshaled along the Saudi Arabian border. What did this mean? Kuwait was already occupied. Was this a threat? Was this mere saber-rattling? What kind of concession did he need? The Saudis were already prepared to write checks, which was the Middle East method in those days of dealing with this kind of dispute among Arabs. We all concluded that it meant invasion.

The president asked Dick Cheney to go there. He's described his trip in a very modest way, but I think that his ability to deal with a very fractious royal family at that point made all the difference. King Fahd's great respect for George Bush, I think, played another role in this, the confidence that they would have in our promise of support. Prince Bandar raised the question: "You send a couple of battalions or air flights over, and then you fly away." The confidence that they needed that we were bringing support, and more support would be there as required, was crucial in that decision. Many members of the royal family wanted to proceed in the traditional way and not let us come. Dick Cheney delivered—in his quiet, thoughtful, firm way—the message: "Do you want us to defend you, or do you want us to liberate you?" When you think about it, those were the options at that time. The answer from the king was, "Come and defend us." From that point, a great alliance began to grow. It was a historic coalition. As has been pointed out to you by Ambassador El Reedy, this was the first time that Arabs had joined with non-Arab forces in preparing to deal with a military situation in their area.

The buildup took a good many months, partly because General Colin Powell, the president, and Dick Cheney believed that if we did anything, we were going to do it with overwhelming force. There should be no doubt about the outcome.

On the other hand, we were confronted with a range of side issues. I call them side issues because they were not common to ordinary, conventional military confrontations. Saddam Hussein was fighting the war of the past; he thought we were coming in from the sea. He built obstacles for our helicopters; he dug trenches and filled them with oil; he loaded cargo ships and sent them down toward Gebayel—a very serious risk: if the cargo ships had gotten through to the desalinization plants at Gebayel, they could have done enormous damage to the oil production capability of Saudi Arabia. We were worried about chemical warfare [CW], and that's a story for another time. Saddam had the equipment, and, unlike other countries in the world, he had used it. He had used it against the Kurds and had used it successfully against Iran. So our troops had to be prepared for that eventuality, and we had to assess his capability to put any of that CW on board a missile, a SCUD missile—the elongated SCUD missiles that he used against Riyadh and against Israel. We judged that he had it. There was considerable doubt in the military that he did; when the war was over, and he had to account for what he had, and he had acknowledged that he had some 30 or 40 of these missiles, I got a very nice handwritten note from Colin Powell saying,

"You guys had it right." But there was a lot of uncertainty about these side issues.

He threatened to send terrorists around the world—and he did. One of the great stories not yet told is about the teams of two that he sent to different parts of the world and how, through good intelligence, we identified their modus operandi, knew who they were, where they were going, and had the full cooperation of the nations of the world that George Bush had put together to make sure that nothing happened. They were either arrested, moved on, interrogated, or flushed out, but not one team successfully delivered.

Then, as you've already heard from Professor Segev, there were the attacks on Israel. Yes, the Patriots were not as effective as we'd like them to be, but they did add to morale. They did go up, and they did shoot down the SCUDs. The unfortunate part about the elongated SCUDs were that the Patriots went for the heat part of the missile, and that still left the warhead to drop somewhere, some unintended target—usually in an apartment area in Tel Aviv. But they did succeed in helping the leadership of Israel avoid being pressured into getting into the conflict in retaliation in accordance with their standard rule that no attack on Israel will go unretaliated. That was an important part of maintaining the coalition.

While we were getting ready for the war, while we were preparing the air and the ground forces, an enormous debate was taking place in Congress. Hugely respected senators, such as Sam Nunn, believed that sanctions ought to be given more of a chance. I had already testified earlier that we believed that the sanction initiative had been successful in one respect: it had isolated Saddam Hussein from further strengthening his resources from others who might provide him with additional armaments and were willing to do so—weapons and other things of that kind. What we did not say is that it would cause him to modify his behavior and leave Kuwait. That was the subject of the debate.

Finally, Les Aspin, who was chairman of the Armed Services Committee of the House, asked specifically for the intelligence perspective. Would it cause Saddam Hussein to leave? It was our judgment—and I reported it—that we did not believe it would cause him to leave, first, because an extended period of grace would not weaken his troops; that only the air force would be affected by a delay of sanctions. As it turned out, he flew his air force off at the first break of war, and they were not heard or seen from again. They were in Iran and in Jordan.

I mention these things because the president was constantly challenged by these distractions. He met on a regular basis with his military team. He finally made the signal. He overcame the objections; he got his war resolution passed—and I think it was necessary, even though he may have exercised his prerogative anyway. I think it was necessary because the length of elapsed time brought into play the constitutional authority of Congress to declare war, and it seemed to me that he needed to have that resolution behind him, and I'm glad he got it. Whether or not he would have gone without it, I'm glad he got it.

The hundred-hour war—that will be debated: did we stop too soon? You know the limitations on the United Nations resolution, on the War Powers Resolution. I suppose in some way, if you had your druthers, we maybe would have carried the fight on a few more hours. We knew the Republican Guard was leaving. Many got out and are still around to cause trouble for the future. But war is not entirely neat. It was a remarkable victory and a remarkable achievement, with minimal casualties to our coalition forces.

We then were confronted with the aftermath and the problems that we had dealing with respect for existing boundaries and how we reacted to the internal affairs of nations that engaged in human rights abuses, and Saddam Hussein was right at the top of the list. When the Kurds broke loose and the Shiites in the south rebelled, the Baathist Party—the people we most counted on to take Saddam out—being a minority party in power, viewed this as a greater threat and elected to suppress the Kurds and the Shiites. This left us looking as if we'd waited too long to help the Kurds, and I suppose we can take some criticism for that.

But George Bush was looking for a New World Order—one we have not yet achieved, one in which there is great opportunity to see the nations of the world join up to insist upon leaders of the world acting in a civilized and law-abiding manner, not only with their neighbors but with their own citizens. In the absence of a crisis, nations tend to fall back on old tribal hatreds and cultures, such as we have seen in Bosnia. But I think that there were some slight movements forward in the efforts to solve the problems in the Middle East. The participation of Syria, for example, showed some small sign of hope. They're an indispensable party to the solution, and we hope they'll stay engaged.

As I look back on those two years—the preparation and execution—I think we see in it a model of what a principled man, with principled colleagues, who has built a reputation throughout the world with other leaders can do to take on a tyrant and deal with him with minimum loss of life to those who are supporting the project. What remains to be done is to see to it that you and I can somehow advance this hope of a New World Order in which these things happen rarely, if at all.

Panelist Discussion:
Jay R. Avella, Moderator

Jay R. Avella: Before we open it up to questions from the floor, is there any— Your Excellency?

Saud Nasir Al-Sabah: If you would just forgive me for coming back again, because what Professor Samuel Segev said, I think I need to make some comments, if you'll allow me to do that. I think for the sake of our distinguished guests here, ladies and gentlemen, I think some might have come out with the impression that what Saddam Hussein did that led to the peace process was somehow tantamount, implicitly giving Saddam Hussein some credit here. And Saddam Hussein doesn't deserve one iota of credit in this whole damn process! Because I knew President Bush, from 1988 and even before that, was so interested in getting the Arab–Israeli conflict resolved by any kind of means. But to say because of the Gulf War, because of the liberation of Kuwait, that the peace process started. I remember having a discussion with the president and with Secretary Baker on this, and the president made a commitment to the General Assembly of the United Nations, when he was accused that the United States did not lift a finger to resolve the Arab–Israeli conflict at the same time they're sending half a million U.S. troops to Kuwait—that was a double standard, which it was called at that time. He made a commitment before the whole world at the General Assembly (and also Secretary Baker later on), that once this whole conflict is resolved, we will look into the Arab–Israeli conflict.

But I just don't want our distinguished guests to leave this room here saying, "Well, because of Saddam Hussein, we have a peace process." That's wrong. That's not right. I do not agree with this, because by saying this, we're giving him some credit for it. The reason is that, when he lost all reasons for invading Kuwait—when he said it was to overthrow the government, that he came in to support the revolution in Kuwait, and then talked about historic rights—and then when he lost all excuses for being in Kuwait, he connected the issue of Israel withdrawing from the West Bank and the occupied territories in lieu of his withdrawing from Kuwait. This is just a game that Saddam Hussein was playing into the hands of the masses in the Palestinian community and the occupied territories. That's one. I just don't want you to leave this room with this kind of impression, and I hope Samuel will forgive me for saying it.

Number two: Israel took so much pounding, and it was a nightmare for us. It was a nightmare also for, I remember, Secretary Eagleburger, when he was sent by the president to Israel to convince them not to get into the war. Because we knew, had Israel got into the war, then the coalition would have broken up— especially the Arab side of the coalition—and I believe credit should be given to

Israel not to get into the war for the sake of keeping the coalition intact and to achieve the goal for which the coalition was formed by President Bush and by the mandate of the Security Council. That's number two.

The destruction of the Iraqi forces—I'm not a military analyst here. I can't tell between M1-A2 tanks or M1-A1 tanks here. I could tell between the F-15 and F-16, maybe. But to say that the Patriots had no effect, again, I think is an underestimate of the capability of what the United States was able to provide to protect Israel, Saudi Arabia, and many countries in the region against those stupid SCUD missiles. I think everyone did what they could do to protect Israel and Saudi Arabia from the SCUD missiles. They were called "SCUD Busters" at that time; they had been developed for that reason. Secretary Cheney knows about this far more than I do. But I think we did, and everyone did, what they could to do it.

The Iraqi forces were not totally destroyed for many, many reasons. Let the cat out of the bag here. We're talking here, I think, very frankly. The Republican Guards that were allowed to escape, they could have been destroyed with four or five further air strikes. There was no reason it could not have been. But I think we had to maintain the balance of power in the region. We had Iran on one side and Iraq on the other side with the balance of power in the region. Had the United States and the coalition forces proceeded to destroy all of Iraq's military capability, we would have—and this might be hypothetical here—Iran could have moved into Iraq, and we'd have been facing Iran right down the throat in Kuwait again. So we tried to maintain the balance of power in the region; we, and I think our allies and the coalition forces, decided to keep some part of Iraq's military capability intact in order for them to remain as a balance of power in the region facing Iran, for the sake of maintaining peace for the future. I just wanted to touch on these points, I think. I didn't want to leave them. Thank you.

Avella: I know Dr. Heimbach has some comments, but I think Professor Segev would like to respond to the minister.

Samuel Segev: I thank the minister for the clarifications. I also did not want you to leave this room with the impression that because of Saddam Hussein—and I'm insisting on the words "because of Saddam Hussein"—there was a peace process. But I do repeat my statement before that, had it not been for the victory in Desert Storm, there would not have been a peace process. Notwithstanding the commitments that President Bush had made publicly before the war, during the war, and immediately after the war, but if there was not an overwhelming victory, and if there was not an alteration of the regional balance of power, Israel would not have felt secure enough to engage in a meaningful way in the Madrid Peace Conference and to agree to the things that have developed since then.

Just to give you another example—another fact, probably, that was not published, and I'm contributing to the audience—when I mentioned that Shamir, in his meeting with President Bush in December 1990, before the war, committed himself not to preempt and to coordinate possible retaliation with the United States, I also said that he spoke about the importance of Jordan—to keep

Jordan in the coalition. Now, maybe you will be interested to know that, on January 5, 1991, just 10 days before the war started, Shamir and King Hussein met secretly in London.

It was already clear that the war was inevitable, and the king was concerned that his country would be torn between the Iraqis and the Israelis. He wanted to make sure that Israel would spare his country the horrors of the war. He said something that only strengthened what both Ambassador El Reedy and I have told you before about the deception tactics of Saddam Hussein. He told Shamir that he felt a little bit used by Saddam Hussein because he told him that he had no intention to invade Kuwait, that all his concentration of troops was meant only to bring about a raise in the prices of oil. So he used him as a channel and King Hussein, of course, as a responsible leader, that the world is concerned about an impending war, was quick to relate this information to the others. But belatedly, he felt that he was used by Saddam Hussein. At that meeting on January 5, 1991, he gave Shamir a pledge not to allow Iraqi troops to enter his country or Iraqi planes to use his airspace for attacks against Israel, if Israel would give a similar commitment to him that we would not use the Jordanian airspace to attack Iraq.

So you will understand that the restraint of Israel during the Persian Gulf War was not only directed to the danger of launching of SCUDs but had also shown some sensitivity to the regional balance of power, to the regional importance of the countries in the region, to the role that Jordan can play after the war in the peace process, and so on. So it took the hits of the SCUDs, it did not react, only looking far beyond the immediate war that, as I said before, there was no doubt that the war was going to be won. There was no doubt about it. That's the importance of what had happened after the war. Thank you.

Avella: Secretary Cheney?

Richard B. Cheney: Just one brief comment in terms of Israeli restraint. I think it was absolutely the right decision. It made sense for Israel, it made sense for the United States, it made sense for the coalition. But I must say, those of us who were dealing with Israel at the time, in the early days of the air war, when the SCUDs first began to fly, were not of the opinion that this was a precut deal. In fact, there was a major effort by the Shamir government to get an arrangement with the United States. We were specifically asked to seek permission for the Israeli Defense Forces to fly through Saudi airspace in order to be able to strike Iraq, or if not Saudi airspace, then Jordanian airspace, a request for us to deconflict—that is, to give the Israelis the code so we wouldn't have conflict between their air force and our air force. In the end, of course, they decided not to proceed, but it was a touch-and-go proposition in the early days of the air war whether or not they would pursue that course, because they tried very hard to persuade us to let them, in fact, attack Iraq.

Avella: Dr. Heimbach?

Daniel R. Heimbach: Just two very brief comments—first in relation to

Secretary Cheney's comment about the president's decision to use force not being driven by public opinion. I want to build on that and say there also had been charges, or speculations, that his use of "just war" terminology and "just war" moral framework was only for rhetorical purposes and for the purpose of enlisting public support. I also want to underscore that was not true and for two good reasons: one, his decision to use and to adopt "just war" terminology (which was, of course, in conformity with the actions he had already taken up to that point) did not arise out of some search for a strategy to spin public opinion. It was also confirmed, of course, by the way he followed up on his principles throughout the rest of the operation.

The second point has to do with whether George Bush stopped at the right time and place, and did he make a mistake. Minister Al-Sabah has said absolutely no and has mentioned a number of practical concerns that serve to justify making the decision to stop when he did. But Professor Segev has suggested perhaps it was a failure not to continue the war until Saddam was removed. That's an important division of opinion, and it's been reflected by many others. I want to point out here only that if the president had allowed the operation to go further and had not decided to end it when he did, not only were there practical matters at stake—such as going beyond the UN mandate, the coalition breaking up, the United States being an occupying power, or disturbing the balance of power in the region—continuing also would have gone beyond the just war moral framework he was using. It would not have been consistent with the just cause that warranted going to war initially, and that was to deny Saddam Hussein the fruits of tyrannical aggression. This was accomplished once his forces had been pushed across the border. But also, it would have been entirely inconsistent with a just war moral framework to pursue anything that looked like punishment or conquering or humiliating. So for moral reasons as well as practical reasons, it was the right time to make the decision.

Part IX

Gulf War Legacies

19

After the War: President Bush and the Kurdish Uprising

Michael M. Gunter

BACKGROUND

The Kurds in Iraq[1] have been in an almost constant state of revolt ever since Britain artificially created that state out of the former Ottoman vilayets (provinces) of Mosul, Baghdad, and Basra following World War I. There are three major reasons for this situation. First, the Kurds in Iraq long constituted a greater proportion of the population than they did in any other country they inhabited.[2] Accordingly, despite their smaller absolute numbers, they represented a larger critical mass in Iraq than elsewhere, a situation that enabled them to play a more important role there than they did in Turkey and Iran. Second, as an artificial, new state, Iraq had less legitimacy as a political entity than Turkey and Iran, two states that had existed in one form or another for many centuries despite their large Kurdish minorities. Thus, discontent and rebellion came easier for the Iraqi Kurds. Indeed, since the creation of Iraq, it had been understood that they were to negotiate their future position, a right that the Kurds in other states did not have. Third, Iraq was further divided by a Sunni–Shiite Muslim division not present in Turkey or Iran. This predicament further called into question its future.[3]

For its part, the Iraqi government has always feared the possibility of Kurdish separatism. Kurdish secession would not only deplete the Iraqi population; it would also set a precedent that the Shiites, some 55 percent of the population, might follow and thus threaten the very future of the Iraqi state. What is more, approximately two-thirds of the oil production and reserves, as well as much of the fertile land, were located in the Kurdish area. This being the case, the government felt that Kurdish secession would strike at the economic heart of the state. Thus were sown the seeds of a seemingly irreconcilable struggle between Iraq and its Kurdish minority.

Number 12 of U.S. president Woodrow Wilson's Fourteen Points had declared that the non-Turkish minorities of the Ottoman empire should be granted the right of "autonomous development." In addition, the Treaty of Sevres (1920) had provided for "local autonomy for the predominantly Kurdish areas" (Article 62) and in Article 64 even looked forward to the possibility that "the Kurdish peoples" might be granted "independence from Turkey."

The definitive Treaty of Lausanne (1923), however, which made no mention of the Kurds, overruled both of these documents. What is more, the British, who held Iraq as a mandate from the League of Nations, already had decided to attach the largely Kurdish vilayet of Mosul to Iraq because of its vast oil resources.[4] It was thought that this was the only way Iraq could be made viable.

Nevertheless, both the British and the Iraqi government issued a number of statements that theoretically recognized and guaranteed Kurdish rights. On December 24, 1922, for example, an Anglo–Iraqi Joint Declaration to the Council of the League of Nations clearly recognized the right of the Iraqi Kurds to some type of autonomy.

His Britannic Majesty's Government and the Government of Iraq recognize the right of the Kurds who live within the frontiers of Iraq to establish a Government within those frontiers. Our two Governments hope that the various Kurdish groups will reach some mutual agreement as quickly as possible as to the form they wish this Government to take and as to the boundaries within which they wish to extend its authority. These groups will send responsible delegates to negotiate their future economic and political relations with His Majesty's Government and the Iraqi Government.[5]

Interestingly, it was not until 1926 that the Council of the League of Nations formally recognized the incorporation of Mosul into Iraq; before then Turkey had continued to claim the area.[6] At that time, however, the International Commission of Inquiry established by the council required that "the desire of the Kurds that the administrators, magistrates and teachers in their country be drawn from their own ranks, and adopt Kurdish as the official language in all their activities, will be taken into account."[7] Although Baghdad issued a so-called Local Languages Law, these pledges to the Kurds were not included in the Anglo–Iraqi Treaty of 1930, which granted Iraq its independence in 1932.

On the other hand, Stephen H. Longrigg, an authority on Iraqi history, has argued that "in adopting a hesitant attitude to Kurdish claims, the Iraq Government was not always unreasonable. These claims were at times frankly separatist.... The fear existed, in addition, that privileges granted to the Kurds would be demanded immediately by the Shi'is of the Euphrates."[8] Longrigg therefore concluded that, as a result, "the Kurds ... represented a profoundly unsatisfactory and even a menacing element in the national life [of Iraq]."[9]

From the very beginning, important Kurdish elements opposed the cavalier manner in which they were treated. It also should be noted, however, that other Kurdish groups supported the British and, later, Baghdad. The *jash* [little donkeys]—a derogatory term for the Kurdish militia who supported Baghdad—continued to do so into the 1990s.

As the British prepared to accept the league's mandate for Iraq, they invited a local Kurdish leader, Shaikh Mahmud Barzinji of Sulaymaniya, to act as their governor there in 1919. Despite his inability to overcome the divisions among the Kurds, Shaikh Mahmud almost immediately proclaimed himself "king of

Kurdistan," revolted against British rule, and began secret dealings with the Turks. In a precursor to subsequent defeats at the hands of the Iraqi government in Baghdad, the British Royal Air Force (RAF) successfully bombed the shaikh's forces, putting down several of his uprisings during the 1920s.

Meanwhile, the only serious opposition to the British institution of the Hashemite monarchy in Iraq occurred in the Kurdish regions. Most of the negative votes came from Kirkuk, while Sulaymaniya did not even participate in the referendum that approved it. Indeed, Shaikh Mahmud styled himself "king of Kurdistan" in part to show his opposition to Faisal's becoming king of Iraq. It would be a mistake, however, to see the activities of the shaikh as exercises of Kurdish nationalism. At the height of his appeal, he never exceeded the primordial bounds of tribalism.

Genuine Kurdish nationalist feeling did manifest itself in September 1930, however, when strikes and demonstrations broke out in Sulaymaniya. For perhaps the first time it appeared that the Kurdish leadership was moving from the countryside with its religious and tribal leadership to the cities and their emerging middle classes.

If so, the change was only partial. With the final defeat of Shaikh Mahmud in the spring of 1931,[10] Mulla Mustafa Barzani (1903–1979) began to emerge as the leader almost synonymous with the Kurdish national movement in Iraq. Despite his long and eventful career, however, Barzani remained ultimately a traditional, tribal leader. Indeed, primordial tribal loyalties still plague the Kurdish movement at the dawn of the twenty-first century. Barzani himself was finally defeated in 1975, when Iran and the United States suddenly dropped their support, and the Kurdish national movement lay crushed until the Iran–Iraq War (1980–1988) offered new, but in the end false, opportunities.

THE 1991 GULF WAR

Following the Iran–Iraq War—with its legacy of chemical warfare and refugees—the Kurds were left exhausted and demoralized. Saddam's invasion of Kuwait in August 1990 and the international alliance it provoked, however, once again created new possibilities for the Kurds, since they were obviously potential allies against the Baghdad regime. Amid much speculation, Jalal Talabani—the leader of the Patriotic Union of Kurdistan (PUK), one of the two main Iraqi Kurdish parties—journeyed to Washington. He warned, however: "We have been deceived many times by foreigners. We are determined not to make the same mistakes again."[11] For its part, the United States appeared wary of alienating its important Turkish and new Syrian ally, as well as Iran, by supporting the Kurds.

Asked whether the Kurds would join the allies if war broke out, Talabani replied, "We would not." He even threatened that "if the Turkish Army invades Iraq's Kurdistan, we would stand against it."[12] The Kurdish leader softened his position, however, by noting that "we have fought Saddam since he assumed power and will continue to fight him until he is toppled," adding that "if the Arab forces liberate Kuwait, we would urge the Kurdish troops to join them."

He maintained, though, that "our fighting would be Kurdish, independent, and separate ... not ... as part of foreign armies invading or fighting Iraq."

Despite the golden opportunity the events presented, Talabani continued to maintain a sober attitude: "We don't want to be like the Palestinians and ask for the impossible. If there were a democratic government in Iraq, we would be happy to be Iraqis."[13] Hussein Guzelaydin, a Kurdish refugee who had settled in Canada, also reflected this apparent caution when he stated: "We want United States help against Iraq, but we also need guarantees that 1975 won't happen all over again."[14] For his part, Izzat Ibrahim, the deputy chairman of the Baathist's ruling Revolutionary Command Council (RCC), warned the Kurds: "If you have forgotten Halabja, I would like to remind you that we are ready to repeat the operation."[15] Ibrahim's reference was to Baghdad's notorious chemical attack that had killed some 5,000 Kurdish civilians in March 1988.

Once the war began in January 1991, however, Talabani declared that "the Kurds are really happy because they believe that this war will put an end to Saddam Hussein's dictatorship."[16] This belief, the fear that they would be left out of the postwar settlement, and the call from U.S. president George Bush for the Iraqis to overthrow Saddam after he was defeated in late February help to explain why the Kurds rebelled when their earlier statements implied they would not.

FALSE VICTORY

After the rebellion failed, Talabani claimed that "the leadership of the Kurds has never called for an uprising."[17] Instead, he maintained that following "the appeal of the Americans, spontaneous and unorganized demonstrations erupted everywhere. The Peshmerga [Kurdish guerrillas] fighters were outside the towns, and only later did we decide to support the demonstrators."

Although there is probably some truth to Talabani's assertion, it ignores the fact that the Kurdish leadership also had made preparations. One report, for example, indicated "that 2,500 Kurdish guerrillas who had escaped to Syria have infiltrated back into northeastern Iraq,"[18] while another declared that "several thousand Kurdish *peshmerga* [guerrillas] ... are poised to take control of the biggest population centres of northern Iraq in the event of Saddam Hussein's government collapsing in the face of the allied offensive."[19]

Most of the major cities in Iraqi Kurdistan fell with astounding alacrity to the rebels in early and mid-March: Arbil, Sulaymaniya, Jalula, Dohuk, Zakho, and Kirkuk, among others. Dr. Kamal al-Karkuki, a well-placed Kurdish official, claimed that most of the members of two Iraqi army corps had joined the rebels,[20] while Talabani added that "in the province of Sulaymaniya alone, 43,000 had deserted, and in ... Karkuk, 29,000."[21] It should be noted, however, that these deserters were the *jash* or pro-Baghdad Kurdish militia, not Iraqi regulars.

Massoud Barzani—the son of Mulla Mustafa and the current leader of the other main Iraqi Kurdish party, the Kurdistan Democratic Party (KDP)—declared: "I feel that the result of seventy years of struggle ... is at hand now. It is the greatest honor for me. It is what I wanted all my life."[22] One Kurdish radio broadcast exulted: "Our dear listeners, the crucial battle has been decided . . . in the most splendid victory in the contemporary history of the Kurds."[23] Meanwhile Hoshyar Zevari, a spokesman for the KDP, asserted: "This is the nearest we've ever come to achieving our objectives."[24]

In Beirut, both the PUK and KDP belonged to the recently established Free Iraqi Council or Joint Action Committee of 17, disparate Iraqi opposition groups chaired by Saad Salih Jabr. By the middle of March this group announced plans to establish a provisional government to replace Saddam. Speaking from the offices of the PUK in Damascus, Talabani reiterated that he wanted Iraq to maintain its territorial integrity[25] and claimed that the rebels had liberated "virtually all" of the Kurdish areas of Iraq. He then predicted that the Kurds and Shiite fighters in the south along with the opposition groups would topple Saddam. If the Iraqi leader resorted to chemical weapons, Talabani threatened, "we will blow up the dams and Baghdad will be submerged in water."

On March 26 Talabani left Syria and crossed into northern Iraq in a triumphal motorcade. He entered Zakho to a tumultuous welcome to tell more than 10,000 cheering Kurds: "This is the first time ever that the whole of Iraqi Kurdistan has been liberated."[26] Before captured heavy Iraqi arms, antiaircraft guns, and recoilless rifles on display in the main square, Talabani then vowed that "we will continue the struggle until we defeat the regime of oppression in Baghdad and liberate the whole of Iraq." He also announced that he would confer with other opposition leaders, some of whom had just arrived with him from Syria, about the formation of an interim government in the Kurdish region.

TALKS WITH THE TURKS

On March 8, 1991, Turkey broke its long-standing policy against negotiating with any Kurdish groups when Ambassador Tugay Ozceri, undersecretary of the foreign ministry, met in Ankara with Jalal Talabani and Mohsin Dizai, an envoy of Barzani. A second meeting between Ozceri and Dizai occurred on March 22. Talabani declared "that a new page had been turned in relations between Turkey and the Kurds of Iraq."[27]

For the first meeting, the two Kurds arrived together in Istanbul on a flight from Damascus and were immediately flown to Ankara's military airport by personnel of the National Intelligence Organization (MIT). After it was over, Talabani said that for the Iraqi Kurds, "the most significant result . . . was Turkey's lifting its objection to the establishment of direct relations between the Kurdish front in Iraq and the United States."[28] He also repeated that the Kurds did not want to establish an independent state in northern Iraq and that he had calmed Turkey's apprehensions in this regard. Talabani then elaborated on the following points:

Turkey has for years been putting forth effective and significant obstacles to the struggle we have been waging in northern Iraq. We wanted to explain our goals and eliminate Turkey's opposition. . . . We were received with understanding. . . . I believe that we were able to convince them that we do not pose a threat to Turkey.... Our goal is to establish a federation of Arabs, Turkomans, and Kurds.[29]

The talks created a furor in Turkey.[30] To some, Turkish president Turgut Ozal was simply being realistic in seeking to build reasonable relations with those who looked likely to establish an autonomous Kurdish region on his state's border. To others, however, he in effect was lending support to circles threatening Turkish territorial integrity. If the Turkish president could countenance some sort of federal solution for the Kurds in Iraq, might he not also be contemplating one for the Kurds in Turkey? Former president Kenan Evren and the current chief of general staff Dogan Gures both spoke of the possible dangers of the Ozal overture.[31] The military commanders added that "we believe that there will be subsequent demands and we think that this is harmful to our national integrity."

DEFEAT

Defeat proved as swift as victory. Indeed, in retrospect, the victory had been false because the territorial gains made by the Kurds had little strategic importance and could not be held once Saddam subdued the Shiites in the south and turned his modern army north. In reporting the Iraqi recapture of Arbil, which for two weeks had served as Barzani's headquarters and been considered the capital of "liberated Kurdistan," the Kurds admitted that they had been "outclassed by the Iraqi Army's tanks, heavy artillery, and helicopters."[32]

Barzani charged that by permitting Saddam to use helicopters, the United States had given him the "green light ... to continue massacring Iraqi civilians."[33] Mahmud Uthman, a leader of the Socialist Party of Kurdistan in Iraq (SPKI), declared: "They are bombing us, and using napalm, and civilian casualties are heavy."[34] He added that the Kurds were equipped with "many light weapons taken from the enemy" but lacked more sophisticated weapons such as antiaircraft missiles. Talabani declared that "the rebels were left in the lurch at the decisive moment, when ... Saddam was permitted to use any kind of planes, helicopter, heavy artillery, gasoline and napalm-phosphorous bombs."[35] Even when the Kurds were able to capture heavy weapons such as tanks and armored personnel carriers, it was reported that "they don't know how to use them."[36]

THE U.S. ROLE

With hindsight, only the United States could have helped the Kurds to avert defeat by (1) continuing its war against Saddam longer so that more of his army would have been destroyed, thus depriving him of the capacity to crush the Kurds; (2) preventing Saddam from using fixed-winged airplanes and helicopters, which were so effective against the Kurds and were supposedly denied Baghdad by the terms of the cease-fire; and (3) giving actual military support to the Kurds. For a variety of reasons none of these options were taken.

The United States originally had justified its decision to halt the war when it did on the grounds that the goal of ejecting Iraq from Kuwait had been achieved, and virtually all the Iraqi armor appeared to be trapped. There was no United Nations [UN] mandate to go any further. In addition, the United States did not want to appear to be slaughtering an already beaten enemy.

A month after the cease-fire, however, the United States admitted that "the number of Iraqi tanks and armored vehicles that survived the war is much greater than American military authorities initially reported," adding that "many of the weapons have been used by the Government of President Saddam Hussein to quell resistance by Iraqi insurgents."[37] These new estimates "raise questions about the wisdom of the Bush Administration's decision to halt the ground war ... when the White House did."

The allied commander, U.S. general Norman Schwarzkopf, agreed, claiming that, had the war continued just another day, "we could have inflicted terrible damage on them."[38] Ending it earlier "did leave some escape routes open for them to get back out." Talabani concurred: "If President Bush had only continued the fighting two more days, Saddam's armed forces would have completely broken down."[39]

As Saddam began to put the Kurdish rebellion down, both Talabani and Barzani appealed to Bush for help by reminding him: "You personally called upon the Iraqi people to rise up against Saddam Hussein's brutal dictatorship."[40] In addition, Talabani pointed out that "with the approval of the allies a transmitter, 'Voice of Free Iraq,' was set up, which also called for an uprising."[41] (The Kurdish leader was referring to secret orders Bush had given the CIA [Central Intelligence Agency] in January to aid rebels in Iraq with a clandestine, antigovernment radio station.[42])

For a number of reasons, however, the United States chose not to intervene in the internal Iraqi strife. Doing so could lead, it was feared, to an unwanted, protracted American occupation that would be politically unpopular in the United States and to an unstable government in Iraq or even "Lebanization" of the country and destabilization of the Middle East. What is more, the United States also concluded that Saddam could win. To support the Kurds against him might require an unwanted, perpetual U.S. commitment. Also, Kurdish success in Iraq might provoke Kurdish uprisings in Turkey, Syria, or Iran, states whose cooperation the United States needed. A U.S. Senate foreign relations staff report written by Peter Galbraith and issued a month after Saddam had put down the rebellion confirmed that the United States "continued to see the opposition in caricature" and feared that the Kurds would seek a separate state and that the Shiites wanted an Iranian-style Islamic republic.[43] Another reason was that the United States had fought Iraq to vindicate the principle of Kuwait's territorial integrity without which instability and chaos would reign. To support uprisings that threatened Iraq's territorial integrity would make the United States look hypocritical.

Given these factors, it might be concluded that the United States implicitly had returned to its pre-August 1990 policy of seeing Saddam as a source of stability in the volatile region. As National Security Directive (NSD) 26, signed by President Bush on October 12, 1989, had put it: "Normal relations between the United States and Iraq ... would serve our longer-term interests and promote stability in both the Gulf and the Middle East."[44] On the Kurdish issue this meant and indeed was emphasized that "in no way should we associate ourselves with the 60-year-old Kurdish rebellion in Iraq or oppose Iraq's legitimate attempts to suppress it."[45] What is more likely, however, is that the United States was simply reacting on an ad hoc basis to circumstances but certainly did not want Saddam to remain in power. The problem was how to remove him without exceeding what were felt to be the legitimate bounds of intervention.

REFUGEES

The failed rebellion quickly led to a human tragedy of unbelievable proportions. Reports spoke of "hundreds of thousands of Kurds fearing government reprisals . . . fleeing by any means possible into the mountains along the Iranian and Turkish borders, turning roadways into ribbons of humanity."[46] By early May Ahmad Hoseyni, the director general in charge of foreign nationals and immigrants in Iran, announced that "the number of the Iraqi refugees arriving in Iran has surpassed 1.117 million."[47] In late April Hayri Kozakcioglu, the regional governor in the southeast of Turkey, reported "that there are currently around 468,000 northern Iraqis in Turkey's border region with Iraq."[48] These new arrivals joined the 30,000 Iraqi Kurdish refugees remaining in Turkey from the 1988 exodus that had followed the end of the Iran–Iraq War. That earlier event now seemed to pale into insignificance in comparison.

These new refugees threatened to overwhelm their hosts. Indeed, there were some in Turkey who thought the problem was in part Saddam's revenge for that state's having supported the allies in the Gulf War: "This is the sneakiest form of aggression and Saddam should not be allowed to get away with it."[49]

In response, Turkish president Ozal called on all countries to join together as they had in that war, adding that "otherwise, a new dispute will be created in the Middle East" and that "a problem threatening peace and stability will be created."[50] Elaborating, he argued that "even the most perfect organization cannot cope with such an influx within such a short period. . . . It is impossible for any country to solve a problem of such proportions by itself."

What could be done? With the understanding that the settlement of the refugees on or near the Turkish border could be only a temporary expedient, the following possibilities existed. First, everything should be done to pressure Baghdad to allow the refugees to return home under guarantees for their safety. As the regional governor, Hayri Kozakcioglu, maintained: "The solution to this problem is to be able to send them back to their own homes. All countries of the world should unite and put pressure on the Iraqi Government for the safe return of these people to their own homes."[51] Certainly, Iraq did not want to face a new allied intervention. What is more, Turkey and its UN allies could use the economic carrot, since Turkey currently was the only state that could provide an outlet for Iraqi oil.

Massive Western aid was a second possibility. The lack of such a response in 1988, however, did not bode well for this idea. Indeed, at that time Turkey not only had to assume most of the refugee burden itself but also was subjected to sanctimonious Western criticism for not doing enough. In faulting the initial Western response this time, one Turkish journalist argued that "the amount of the aid these countries have provided to the refugees to date does not even equal that which the people of Turkey's Hakkari province have provided."[52]

Nevertheless, this time, unlike in 1988, the West was more involved in the situation, since it had just fought the war and then encouraged the uprising that had led to the problem. In addition, Turkey's decision to keep most of the refugees on the border, instead of allowing them into the country, may actually have helped them by forcing the West and the UN to become more involved.

Would the West have responded as readily to the problem if only Iran had been involved as a host state? Referring to the meager aid his country had received up to that point, Iranian president Ali Akbar Hashemi-Rafsanjani declared: "Shame on you. The costs are astronomical, and what you gave is equal to what a single Iranian village has donated. All your mouth-filling titles of human rights, International Red Cross, are lies, all lies."[53] Dr. David M. Reed, a volunteer with the private relief organization Americares, "praised Iran's effort to assist the Kurds, but said that it had been overwhelmed by the exodus of refugees."[54] After Iran finally appealed for international assistance, the European Community responded, while the United States continued to concentrate on the problem in Turkey.

SAFE HAVENS

Initially proposed by Turkish president Ozal and then picked up and advocated by British prime minister John Major, the concept of "enclaves," later changed to "safe havens,"[55] in northern Iraq, where the refugees would be protected from being attacked by Saddam's forces, eventually caused the United States and the United Nations partially to reverse their position on interference in postwar, domestic Iraqi strife.

The U.S. action produced a variety of political and legal problems. Politically it might have (1) enmeshed the United States in an interminable conflict between Baghdad and the Kurds; (2) resulted in an embryonic Kurdish state that would act as an unwanted model for the Turkish Kurds; (3) served as a base for the Kurdish Workers Party (PKK) guerrillas of Turkey to stage raids on Turkey; and (4) become a second Gaza Strip or home to generations of permanent refugees, stateless, embittered, and therefore disruptive.

Legally, it was doubtful that the UN Security Council would approve such a restriction on Iraqi territorial integrity because of the precedents it might set for the Soviet Union and the Baltic states (which at that time were still not independent) as well as China and Tibet. The United States, in effect, accomplished the functional equivalent, however, by warning Iraq not to use either fixed-wing airplanes or helicopters north of the 36th parallel or to interfere with relief work anywhere in Iraq. By the middle of May, more than 250,000 Kurds had moved into the safe havens, leaving some 180,000 in Turkey; 8,000 United States, British, and French troops occupied the zone, while thousands more were "just over the horizon" in Turkey and the eastern Mediterranean if needed. Kurds who had escaped into Iran, however, returned much more slowly.

Iraqi foreign minister Ahmad Husayn Khudayyir declared that the U.S. action "constitutes a flagrant interference in the internal affairs of Iraq, an independent country and member of the United Nations,"[56] while *Al-Thawrah*, the mouthpiece of the Baathist Party, denounced the move as a "precedent the likes of which never existed in the history of relations among countries."[57] Nevertheless, Iraq was in no position to offer overt opposition.

Although many observers might have had legalistic qualms, most still would have agreed that the egregious situation justified some such extraordinary action. As President Bush said: "We simply could not allow 500,000 to a million people to die up there in the mountains."[58] What is more, as the victor in the Gulf War, the United States might be deemed to have had residual rights of conquest to take such action. In addition, some argued that the 1948 Convention on the Prevention and Punishment of the Crime of Genocide provided a legal basis. Massoud Barzani was already on record as having described the concept of safe havens as "a great humanitarian gesture and a big step forward."[59]

A possible way out of the legal problem was offered by seeing the U.S. action as a logical extension of UN Security Council Resolution 688 of April 5, 1991,[60] which condemned "the repression of the Iraqi civilian population . . . in Kurdish populated areas, the consequences of which threaten international peace and security in the region" and demanded "that Iraq . . . immediately end this repression." It was the first time in its 46-year history that the world body had so explicitly addressed the Kurdish question in Iraq. This resolution was then followed by an agreement signed by the United Nations and Iraq on April 18 to permit the international organization to assume refugee assistance operations in Iraq.[61]

CONCLUSION

By the middle of July 1991, however, the entire question had become moot because the allied forces had been withdrawn. Indeed, by the fall of 1991, as Baghdad consolidated its position by withdrawing its troops southward, the Kurds had reoccupied most of the cities in northern Iraq. Behind the protection of the allied no-fly zone of Operation Provide Comfort, the Kurds then held elections in May 1992, created a regional government in July, and declared themselves a federal state of Iraq in October 1992.

Fearing the breakup of Iraq, however, no one recognized this de facto Kurdish government and state. Increasing political and economic problems then led to a civil war between Talabani and Barzani in 1994 and 1995. Although a cease-fire seemed to have taken hold by the beginning of 1996, the fate of the Kurds remained uncertain.

NOTES

1. The Kurdish question in Iraq up to the 1970s and the fall of Mulla Mustafa Barzani in 1975 have been well covered. See Edmund Ghareeb, *The Kurdish Question in Iraq* (Syracuse, NY: Syracuse University Press, 1981); Edgar O'Ballance, *The Kurdish*

Revolt, 1961–1970 (Hamden, CT: Archon Books, 1973); Sa'ad Jawad, *Iraq and the Kurdish Question, 1958–1970* (London: Ithaca Press, 1981); Ismet Sheriff Vanly, "Kurdistan in Iraq," in Gerard Chaliand, ed., *People without a Country: The Kurds and Kurdistan* (London: Zed Press, 1980), pp. 153–210. For more recent events, see Michael M. Gunter, *The Kurds of Iraq: Tragedy and Hope* (New York: St. Martin's Press, 1992); Human Rights Watch/Middle East, *Iraq's Crime of Genocide: The Anfal Campaign against the Kurds* (New York: Human Rights Watch/Middle East, 1995).

A number of useful studies of the Kurds in general also exist. In particular, see Thomas Bois and Vladimir Minorsky, "Kurds, Kurdistan," *the Encyclopedia of Islam*, new ed., vol. 5, 1981, pp. 438–86; Martin van Bruinessen, *Agha, Shaikh and State: The Social and Political Structures of Kurdistan* (London: Zed Books, 1992); David McDowall, *A Modern History of the Kurds* (London: I. B. Taurus, 1996); Nader Entessar, *Kurdish Ethnonationalism* (Boulder, CO: Lynne Rienner, 1992); Mehrdad Izady, *The Kurds: A Concise Handbook* (Washington, DC: Crane Russak, 1992).

2. No reliable estimates of the Kurdish population exist because most Kurds tend to exaggerate their numbers, while the states in which they live undercount them for political reasons. In addition, a significant number of Kurds have partially or fully assimilated into the larger Arab, Turkish, or Iranian populations surrounding them. Furthermore, debate continues whether such groups as the Lurs, Bakhtiyaris, Qashqais, Afshars, or Mamesanis are Kurds or not. Thus, there is not even complete agreement on who is a Kurd. Nevertheless, a reasonable estimate is that there may be as many as 10 to 12 million Kurds in Turkey (18 to 21 percent of the population), 6 million in Iran (11 percent), 3.5 to 4 million in Iraq (20 to 23 percent), and 800,000 in Syria (7 percent). In 1974, before Barzani's final defeat and the subsequent population depletions through fighting, executions, and exile, the Kurds in Iraq probably represented as high as 26 percent of the total population.

3. All of this, of course, is not to deny that there were three great Kurdish revolts in modern Turkey, as well as the increasingly virulent guerrilla insurgency there of the Kurdish Workers Party (PKK) since 1984. For analyses, see Michael M. Gunter, *The Kurdish Problem in Turkey: A Political Dilemma* (Boulder, CO: Westview Press, 1990); Ismet G. Imset, *The PKK: A Report on Separatist Violence in Turkey (1973–1992)* (Ankara: Turkish Daily News, 1992). In addition, the only Kurdish state to be established in the twentieth century was the short-lived Mahabad Republic in Iran following World War II. See William Eagleton Jr., *The Kurdish Republic of 1946* (London: Oxford University Press, 1963); and Archie Roosevelt Jr., "The Kurdish Republic of Mahabad," *Middle East Journal* 1 (July 1947): 247–69.

4. On this point, see C. J. Edmonds, *Kurds, Turks and Arabs: Politics, Travel and Research in North-Eastern Iraq* (London: Oxford University Press, 1957), p. 398.

5. Cited in Vanly, "Kurdistan in Iraq," p. 161.

6. Peter J. Beck, "A Tedious and Perilous Controversy: Britain and the Settlement of the Mosul Dispute, 1918–1926," *Middle Eastern Studies* 17 (April 1981): 256–76. See also Edmonds, *Kurds, Turks and Arabs*, for an earlier analysis.

7. Cited in Vanly, "Kurdistan in Iraq," p. 162. See also Amir Hassanpour, *Nationalism and Language in Kurdistan, 1918–1985* (San Francisco: Mellen Research University Press, 1992), pp. 101–25.

8. Stephen H. Longrigg, *Iraq, 1900 to 1950: A Political, Social, and Economic History* (London: Oxford University Press, 1953), p. 196.

9. Ibid., p. 328.

10. During the pro-Axis coup of Rashid Ali al-Gaylani in 1941, the shaikh once again escaped from house arrest and called for a Kurdish attack on the Arabs. Nothing came of this appeal, and Mahmud finally died on October 9, 1956.

11. Cited in Suzanne Goldenberg, "Kurds Would Not Fight Iraq," *The Guardian*,

November 27, 1990.

12. This and the following citations were taken from Najm Abdal al-Karim, "Talabani Tells Al-Majallah: We Would Fight Alongside Arab Forces to Liberate Kuwait!" *Al-Majallah*, December 19–24, 1990; as cited in *Foreign Broadcast Information Service—Near East and South Asia*, January 4, 1991, p. 39, hereafter cited as *FBIS-NES*.

13. Cited in Elaine Sciolino, "Kurds: Stateless People with a 70-Year Grudge," *New York Times*, March 27, 1991, p. A6.

14. Cited in Olivia Ward, "Silent Nightmare of Kurds May Return to Haunt Saddam's Chemical Warriors," *Toronto Star*, September 2, 1990.

15. Cited in Jonathan C. Randal, "Kurdish Rebels Weigh Attack," *International Herald Tribune*, January 25, 1991.

16. Cited in "Kurdish Leader Predicts Saddam's Collapse," *Vienna Die Presse*, January 23, 1991, p. 6, as cited in *FBIS-NES*, January 24, 1991, p. 28.

17. This and the following citation were taken from Lucian O. Meysels, "Interview with Jalal Talabani ... ," April 11, 1991, pp. 28–29, as cited in *FBIS-NES*, April 16, 1991, p. 25.

18. William Safire, "Remember the Kurds," *New York Times*, January 28, 1991, p. A23.

19. Harvey Morris, "Kurds Set to Strike If Saddam's Rule Ends," *The Independent*, January 29, 1991.

20. "Behind the News," Damascus Syrian Arab Television Network in Arabic, 1918 GMT, March 24, 1991, as cited in *FBIS-NES*, March 26, 1991, p. 26.

21. Cited in "Kurdish Leader Jalal Talabani Interviewed," *London Keyhan*, March 7, 1991, p. 12, as cited in *FBIS-NES*, March 20, 1991, p. 63. These troops were the *josh*, not Iraqi regulars.

22. Cited in Jonathan C. Randal, "Kurdish Commander Invites Saddam Foes to Meeting in Iraq," *Washington Post*, March 27, 1991, p. A25.

23. (Clandestine) Voice of the People of Kurdistan in Arabic, 1745 GMT, March 20, 1991, as cited in *FBIS-NES*, March 21, 1991, p. 15.

24. Cited in Lisa Beyer, "Getting Their Way," *Time*, April 1, 1991, p. 34.

25. The following data were taken from Judith Miller, "Iraqi Dissidents Preparing for Rule If Hussein Topples," *New York Times*, March 22, 1991, p. A8.

26. This and the following citation were taken from Alex Efty, "Rebels Hold North Iraq: Army Forces Claim South," *Tennessean*, March 27, 1991, p. A-6.

27. "Kurdish Leader on Significance of Talks in Ankara," Ankara Anatolia in English, 1515 GMT, March 14, 1991, as cited in *FBIS-NES*, March 15, 1991, p. 39.

28. Ibid.

29. "Kurdish Leader Wants 'Democratic Regime,'" Ankara Anatolia in Turkish, 1415 GMT, March 31, 1991, as cited in *Foreign Broadcast Information Service—West Europe*, April 1, 1991, p. 33, hereafter cited as *FBIS-WEU*.

30. The following analysis is largely based on "Talabani Affair Overshadows Soviet Tour on Eve of U.S. Talks," *Briefing* (Turkey), March 18, 1991, pp. 3–7; and "Free Debate in Ankara But Death and Injury Elsewhere," *Briefing*, March 25, 1991, pp. 5–6.

31. This and the following citation were taken from Tayfun Talipoglu, "Ozal Reassures Commanders against Kurdish State," *Millivet*, March 26, 1991, p. 19, as cited in *FBIS-WEU*, April 1, 1991, p. 27.

32. "Rebels Admit Government Has Upper Hand in Irbil," (Clandestine) Voice of Rebellious Iraq in Arabic, 0615 GMT, April 3, 1991, as cited in *FBIS-NES*, April 3, 1991, p. 14.

33. "Kurdish Leader on United States 'Green Light' to Saddam," Paris AFP in English, 1645 GMT, March 28, 1991, as cited in *FBIS-NES*, March 29, 1991, p. 12.

34. This and the following citation were taken from "Kurds Appeal for Help: Face

Saddam Counterattack," Paris AFP in English, 1545 GMT, March 28, 1991, as cited in *FBIS-NES*, March 29, 1991, p. 12.

35. Lucian O. Meysels, "A Shame for the Entire World," *Vienna Wochenpresse*, April 11, 1991, pp. 28–29, as cited in *FBIS-NES*, Apr. 16, 1991, p. 25.

36. Michael Wines, "Iraqi Revolts Ebb as Kurdish Rebels Flee to Borders," *New York Times*, April 3, 1991, p. A6.

37. This and the following citations were taken from Michael R. Gordon (with Eric Schmitt), "Much More Armor Than United States Believed Fled Back to Iraq," *New York Times*, March 25, 1991, p. A1.

38. This and the following citation were taken from Patrick E. Tyler, "Schwarzkopf Says Truce Enabled Iraqis to Escape," *New York Times*, March 27, 1991, p. A7.

39. "Saddam Will Not Survive," *Der Spiegel*, March 25, 1991, pp. 214–17, as cited in *FBIS-NES*, March 26, 1991, p. 28.

40. Cited in "United States Turns Down Plea to Intervene as Kirkuk Falls," *International Herald Tribune*, March 30, 1991.

41. Meysels, "A Shame for the Entire World."

42. Jim Drinkard, "Bush Reportedly Gave Secret Orders to Aid Rebels in Iraq," *Cookeville Herald-Citizen*, April 3, 1991, p. 1; and Clifford Krauss, "Baker Aide Talks with Iraqi Dissidents in United States," *New York Times*, April 4, 1991, p. A6.

43. See U.S. Congress, Senate, Committee on Foreign Relations, *Civil War in Iraq: A Staff Report to the Committee on Foreign Relations, United States Senate*, by Peter W. Galbraith, 102d Cong., 1st sess., May 1991.

44. Cited in Bruce W. Jentleson, *With Friends like These: Reagan, Bush, and Saddam, 1982–1990* (New York: W. W. Norton, 1994), p. 94.

45. U.S. Department of State, "Guidelines for U.S.–Iraq," n.d., but apparently written during the Bush transition period to the presidency, as cited in ibid., p. 104.

46. "Kurds Head for Mountains under Withering Iraqi Fire," *Tennessean*, April 2, 1991, p. 4-A.

47. "Only Unused United States Refugee Aid Said Acceptable," Tehran IRNA in English, 1000 GMT, May 2, 1991, as cited in *FBIS-NES*, May 2, 1991, p. 27.

48. "State of Emergency Governor Discusses Refugees," Ankara Domestic Service in Turkish, 2000 GMT, April 22, 1991, as cited in *FBIS-WEU*, April 23, 1991, p. 56.

49. Turhan Dede, "The Iraqi Refugee Catastrophe," *Turkish Times*, April 15, 1991, p. 11.

50. This and the following citation were taken from "Ozal Proposes Kurdish Camps in North Iraq," Ankara TRT Television Network in Turkish, 1700 GMT, April 16, 1991, as cited in *FBIS-WEU*, April 17, 1991, p. 29.

51. "Governor Estimates 400,000 Iraqi Refugees," Ankara Anatolia in English, 1600 GMT, April 11, 1991, as cited in *FBIS-WEU*, April 12, 1991, p. 37.

52. Arslan Bulut, "Cyprus and Beyond," *Tercuman*, April 16, 1991, p. 6, as cited in *FBIS-WEU*, April 23, 1991, p. 57.

53. Cited in "Iran Leader Blames United States and Iraq for Deaths, Disaster and Refugees," *New York Times*, April 13, 1991, p. 4.

54. Michael Wines, "United States May Send More to Kurds in Iran," *New York Times*, April 30, 1991, p. A5.

55. The connotation given by the term "safe havens" implied more of a humanitarian purpose and less of a restriction of Iraqi territorial integrity than that of "enclaves."

56. "Foreign Minister Denounces West's Move on Kurds," Baghdad INA in Arabic, 1716 GMT, May 1, 1991, as cited in *FBIS-NES*, May 2, 1991, p. 8.

57. "Paper Calls United States Presence 'Illegitimate,'" Baghdad INA in Arabic, 0650 GMT, April 29, 1991, as cited in *FBIS-NES*, April 29, 1991, p. 17.

58. Cited in George J. Church, "Mission of Mercy," *Time*, April 29, 1991, p. 41.

Bush's explanation ignored, however, the situation of the Kurdish refugees in Iran, as well as the pressure put on him by his Turkish ally to return them home.

59. Youssef M. Ibrahim, "Iraq Rejects European Plan for Kurdish Haven in North," *New York Times*, April 10, 1991, p. A6.

60. For the text of this resolution, see "UN Security Council Resolution 688 on Repression of Iraqi Civilians," *U.S. Department of State Dispatch*, April 8, 1991, pp. 233–34.

61. See Princeton N. Lyman, "Update on Iraqi Refugees and Displaced Persons," *U.S. Department of State Dispatch*, May 27, 1991, p. 379.

Discussant: Peter B. Collis

Given the participants on the left side of the table, I guess I feel a little bit—I don't see a target up here, but there may be one there. This is reminiscent of when I had to go on *Nightline* to defend our medical deployment to the Gulf War. The other hazard we have today, of course—and I never would have done this if President Bush were still in office—and that is, you don't go up against the First Lady, who is also presenting at this time.

Now, in response to Dr. Gunter's comments about the Kurds, I'm a physician and was involved with the medical deployment and medical policy in the Pentagon. So I was not involved with the political policy, but I can comment on the medical response of Provide Comfort, our humanitarian response in northern Iraq following the Gulf War. For those of us who had worked with the president and Secretary Cheney, it was very clear to us from the start that the Pentagon was going to be involved in providing medical support, logistic support—basically providing the food, keeping the camps clean, immunizations, and so on, to the Kurds in northern Iraq. There was talk about the United Nations, Health and Human Services, the refugee organizations, but it was clear that we were there; the military knows how to do a lot of things very well, and one of those is they know how to camp for long periods of time and keep order and also maintain the health of a civilian population.

So, we knew because of President Bush's attitude, very simply, as Secretary Baker said, he did what was right. When he saw the plight of the Kurds, he just knew that the right response from a humanitarian country like the United States was to provide support. We had prepared for that knowing that was going to be his decision, and I think it was a correct one.

Now, what I want to do is to provide a framework for the other discussants to talk a little bit about what has emerged as still a syndrome of unknown cause or causes—this is Gulf War illness, often referred to as Persian Gulf illness (PGI). I would like to take you back to August 1990, when this war broke out unexpectedly. I was given a responsibility by the secretary of defense to do whatever we could to provide maximum protection for our troops, from both the biologic and the chemical threats that we feared we may face. It was a very clear mandate: He said, "You've got all the money, you've got all the access, and you've got all DoD [Department of Defense] resources available." Unfortunately, as we had to explain to him, the bacteria to grow vaccines don't care about the money and the resources; they'll only grow so fast. The priority was there, but we did not have enough time to do everything.

What bothered us the most all that time—I can tell you it woke me up at two and three and four o'clock in the morning very consistently—was the question, Are we doing everything we can to, number one, identify what those potential biologic and chemical threats are; and then, number two, are we providing our troops with the maximum amount of protection and the maximum amount of potential treatment?

We had first to try to identify the threat, which was not easy. We made some judgment calls given a large amount of data that was provided to us by the intelligence community, and we determined that there were two likely biologic agents, and we also determined that there were two likely chemical agents—one mustard and the other organophosphate chemicals such as sarin.

We then had to turn to, What do we have to protect the troops? Now, they all have what we call "mopp gear," which is basically the chemical/biologic protective gear that they can wear. Of course, it requires a warning, and it works very well. It's a little difficult to function in that gear, although they did learn how to do that in the Gulf War, which is again a tribute to the military leadership and the type of troops that we had over there. But were there other things? Were there medical preventive measures? There was something for chemical agents that was recommended: pyridostigmine, which was a pill that was provided to the troops and to be carried by them and to be used only (and this was previous doctrine as well and part of their training) when their commanding officers gave the order to use it, because it does have some side effects. Not permanent side effects, we didn't believe at the time from our studies. The other medical protection was vaccinations for biologic agents. There were some vaccines available, and we produced as much as we could and distributed those to the troops.

With one of the agents, anthrax, the type of exposure would have never been encountered in the world before. It normally is an agent that is contracted by contact through the skin and in a biologic warfare environment would come through the lungs, so we didn't know for sure whether the vaccine would prevent disease from that type of exposure. There is no animal model to test it, and we certainly would not test it on human beings. We also provided them with an antibiotic, ciprofloxacin, that they also carried with them with the understanding that it would provide them with antibiotic protection potentially long enough to obtain more extensive treatments.

Those were real threats. Remember what Speaker Foley said yesterday, and that was, going into this war, we didn't have any idea how many casualties we were going to face, and we feared the worst. The two biggest fears, clearly, were the chemical and the biologic, and that often gets lost in a lot of the retrospective talk now because we did, fortunately, have very few casualties. But that was the biggest fear, and that's what kept us busy around the clock. As a physician, I kept asking myself, am I doing everything I can to protect those troops from the two biggest unknown and most catastrophic threats our troops faced? Fortunately, they were not used, and you could have a whole conference to speculate on why they were not used. I think the policy of President Bush and Secretary Cheney had a lot to do with that in terms of real and implied threats if they were used, and the bombing war for 30 days prevented a lot of this material from being shipped to the front lines where it could be used.

Certainly, we looked into everything we could with the research community on all the agents we provided to these troops, not knowing that there would be any permanent side effects. I wonder always today, when I read the papers, was there something in a combination of those agents for bio and chem protection that could cause side effects? Could be. It could explain the Persian Gulf illness. Obviously, we still haven't been able to figure out if that's true or not, so if I can't figure it out retrospectively, I certainly couldn't figure it out prospectively.

Do I think there's something there? Absolutely. There's something with PGI—I mean, I'm an emergency physician, so if I see that patient in my emergency department, I don't send him away saying there's nothing wrong with him. The diagnosis is you've got to admit him, and let's look at him further and evaluate it. Whether it's a combination, and even if it includes a large amount of stress, it still has to be identified because we'll face it again, and a lot of this hopefully can be prevented or recognized and treated early. So I just wanted to give some background on working in 1990 for the Bush administration, and hopefully we'll have a good discussion.

Discussant: Edward J. Derwinski

This is an interesting panel. Theoretically, we have one target, and I'm reluctant, Professor, to rebut your paper, but I can't resist it. I should explain that I have my academic degree, theoretically, in history from Loyola University of Chicago, but I really am a graduate of the school of hard knocks of politics. There's nothing better than to be able to rebut someone who's already made his point and shouldn't be given the microphone back again. But let me pick up this point of what we did or didn't do with the Kurds and state it as simply as I can.

The Kurds are unfortunate victims of geography. They are scattered among four countries, all with a history of autocratic rule, all of them previously under the Ottoman empire, which wasn't a model of democracy. Then the Kurds themselves, as the professor indicated, tended to spend more time fighting each other than they have outside forces. The battles between their clans and tribes are legendary.

Remember, the Bush administration went in with a Democratic Congress waiting to pounce on us the moment casualties started to mount. You already had what I would politely refer to as the far-left flank of the Democratic Party saying this is an unholy effort because you're just doing this to save the national oil companies and the sheiks in the Persian Gulf and the royal family of Saudi Arabia. Then you had others saying that this will be another Vietnam. They were all ready—all ready to pounce on us. If you understand that background, then you understand the political restraint.

Also understand that you had a commander in chief, notwithstanding his military service in World War II, who was a civilian; the secretary of defense is a civilian; our military takes orders from civilian authorities, and our military—Colin Powell, especially—was not the kind of a swashbuckling type you see in the movies. We would never need John Wayne to play Colin Powell. They weren't looking for a prolonged, costly war—costly in terms of casualties. So when that war ended, it was a practical political decision based on the fact that we'd achieved the one goal: the only stated reason for our first going into Saudi Arabia was to expel the Iraqis from Kuwait—to liberate, if you would use a better term, Kuwait. It was never our intention to wipe Iraq off the map. It wasn't our intention to parcel out Iraq to its neighboring states. Certainly, it was not our intention to see that Iraq was so weak that it would be in a very poor position vis-à-vis its neighbor Iran. All those practical factors of geopolitics were involved.

If we had continued—and Professor, know that General Schwarzkopf said, "Give me a couple more days"—those couple of days, we could have taken some bad losses. One of our units could have raced out ahead of its artillery and air cover and been ambushed by the Iraqi presidential guard. We'd have lost 500–

600 men in one swoop. Then what would the pundits have said? They would have said plenty. So what we did, we ended that war when it was clear that they had to sign the agreement. We did not enter the war to liberate either the Shiites in southern Iraq or the Kurds in the north.

Now, I also know—and Professor, I agree with you completely—that the start of the false hopes for the Kurds go way back to World War I and Woodrow Wilson's Fourteeen Points. But history has proven that Woodrow Wilson's Fourteen Points, while a beautiful, flowery, poetic expression of foreign policy, was eminently impractical and as much as anything else contributed to the problems that eventually produced World War II.

I also have to throw this in, only as an extra dig: you quoted Galbraith, who was a Democratic staffer at the time on the Senate Foreign Affairs Committee. He is now, I think, just leaving his position as our ambassador to Yugoslavia—or Croatia, specifically—and he's done, as much as any other man, damage in keeping the tensions and problems and controversies alive in that part of the world. Yugoslavia, as such, was one of the innocent, but misdirected, creations of President Wilson's Fourteen Points. It really wasn't freedom for all the pieces of Yugoslavia; it was really punishment of the Austro-Hungarian empire. All of these countries were lumped into one new entity to punish the Austrians and punish the Hungarians and indirectly punish the Turks and Germans, but under the noble cloth of Wilson's Fourteen Points.

The other point I'd like to, if I may, point out is that when the war ended, President Bush's public popularity—one poll hit 90 percent. It faded rapidly after that because foreign affairs euphoria comes and goes very quickly, and by the time of the 1992 election, the president didn't benefit from any of the leadership or patience he showed in that period. That's unfortunate, but, by the way, that's not particularly surprising. But in that situation, if you remember, you had all the ingredients for disaster as well as tremendous success. It could have led to thousands of casualties.

Now, let me switch off—I beg your pardon, again, Professor, but you made a wonderful target, and I think you're a great man to follow on any panel.

Michael M. Gunter: I intend to come back, though.

Derwinski: OK. Now, one thing we did at the time in the VA [Veterans Administration] was, the moment it was determined that hundreds of thousands of men would be committed to the war area, we immediately were called upon, by law, to coordinate with the medicine elements in the Department of Defense. Under the law, the VA is the basic backup for medical facilities, hospital treatment, needed for veterans who are injured in the war. So we were told, first, give us a count of the empty, but serviceable, beds you have in the VA.

Now, I had been secretary for about two years, a year and a half by then. I had a feeling our count was not completely accurate; it might have been some exaggeration. So I had to call in my top docs and the top bureaucrats and say, "OK, we're not playing games with each other anymore in our little bureaucratic world. We have to tell the DOD exactly how many empty but serviceable beds we have." You know, overnight, 10,000 beds disappeared from the VA system. The reason is, you had a budgetary procedure at the time that each hospital was allocated its budget based on the number of serviceable beds that it maintained. So honest accounting wiped out almost 10 percent of the VA's serviceable beds. We still had 30,000 empty, serviceable beds that were available to the military if they had to use us.

The other thing we did was to set up, immediately at the end of the war when the first reports came in of possible exposure to chemical elements, four VA centers—one in each of our four regions—as a center for analyzing any and all complaints that came in from the troops that could have been exposed to anything of damaging nature. What we did was set up a system whereby any VA hospital would take a veteran if the veteran said, "I was in Kuwait" or "I was in Saudi Arabia or Iraq, and I've got such-and-such a symptom." They were given a physical; their records immediately went to one of the four centers for analysis. The immediate presumption was made that, if they served in those combat areas, their ailment, even before it was diagnosed, was connected to their service. That's been expanded since then. The Clinton administration has added two or three hospitals for specific, very specific research. The basic system is the one we established in the Bush administration in the fall of 1991.

Now, I give you one statistic. This is from the latest report from Dr. [Kaiser], who's the chief medical officer of the current VA. According to his figures—and I'm quoting him specifically—there were 697,000 men and women in the general combat area during the Gulf War. There have been 300,000 additional troops go through the area, serve in the area, since that time. Now, that does not take into account the navy sailing up and down the Persian Gulf. It takes into account air force, marines, army, the units on the ground in those areas. To this date, the VA has received 65,000 registered requests for medical care or medical analysis based on possible exposure. That's less than 10 percent of the people—well, if you actually carry it out to those who've been there since then, if there's residual problems, almost about 6½ percent. To this date, they have not determined a specific cause of any pattern of ailment. In fact, most of the ailments have been effectively diagnosed, either in the military or in the VA, and there's treatment proceeding based on the presumptions involved in the analysis. There are very few unknown or mysterious cases which are being faced.

I should add one technical qualification: you are not a veteran until you leave the active military. So those men and women who served in the area, who are still continuing their careers in our all-volunteer military, get their medical care and attention to these problems from military medicine. If you have left the service, have your discharge, you then are a veteran by definition. Therefore, you become at that point a patient of the VA, and that's the one connection. We do not serve any active-duty personnel.

Late in the 1992 campaign, a month or two before the election, an issue was raised by some of the veteran groups: What are you in the VA doing for the boys and girls who served in the Persian Gulf? Well, the answer was, we were doing very little because most of them were still on active duty, and they were being served by the army, by the navy, by the air force medical personnel. Meantime, our researchers and their researchers were coordinated. The moment they left the service, and there were any medical questions in their discharge, they were directed to go to the VA, and we were receiving them, and we were starting the process. But all of that was well done and stayed in place.

Last but not least—I'm running out of time—we have an emergency network that we set up in Martinsburg, West Virginia, and it's there to work directly with military medical people on any complication that might arise in which the VA would have to absorb military casualties. This is one of the positive benefits from that. Once we knew we had to work with them, we set it up on a permanent basis, and that's still functioning.

Discussant: Robert W. Haley

Our research group published three papers in the January 15 issue of the *Journal of the American Medical Association*, in which we presented evidence that the so-called Gulf War syndrome or Persian Gulf illness, or at least some component of that, appears to be a real illness related to brain damage or neurological damage that's subtle, very difficult to diagnose; and that it probably is due to combinations of neurotoxic chemicals to which the veterans were exposed in the war.

Now, that's all on record, and you can read the articles. There's been a lot of press coverage of it, which you can go follow, so I'm not really going to focus on that. First, I want to follow Dr. Collis' comments on decisions made to protect our troops from chemical weapons. Our epidemiologic research suggests that we may have had casualties from the chemical combinations, part of which we designed. But let me emphasize, I think, as I've reconstructed and thoroughly reviewed all of the scientific literature that was available as of the end of 1990, I'm firmly convinced that what was done was nothing short of a brilliant effort to protect our troops. On the other hand, I think since then we've learned biochemical and pharmacologic lessons from almost unrelated research that has shown that there were probably flaws, but they were flaws that we could not have foreseen.

Let me just reiterate some of the things that Dr. Collis mentioned. When our troops were preparing to go over—once we got the word it looked likely that we were going to have to go over—there were three major potentially life-threatening health threats that our troops would face.

One was insects. In deployments of Allied troops during World War II to this very same area, there were large numbers of casualties from sandfly fever and other vector-borne or mosquito- or sandfly-borne illnesses that had to be prevented to keep our troops in fighting shape for the Gulf War. So there was a great deal of work put into deployment of pesticides around the camps to hold down the sandflies, use of personal protection with insect repellents containing DEET [diethyl-m-toluamide]. Some of the troops—and it's important to emphasize without the military command's approval, in fact, against orders—were wearing flea collars on their boot tops, around their wrists, and some around their necks, to prevent the bugs from crawling down into their clothes. But that was because the troops had been fairly warned accurately warned, that insects represented a very real threat to their health and fighting shape in the war.

There was a clear chemical weapon threat. Sarin and mustard agents were the most likely, but I understand that we were also concerned about soman. Now, soman is a chemical agent that's much more deadly than the others because it becomes permanent within 5 to 10 minutes after exposure. With all of the other chemical nerve agents, you have an hour or two to get off the field, get the postexposure treatment, and perhaps survive. But with soman, you have five minutes, and you can't get off the field in time to be treated successfully.

So there was an elaborate effort to give the troops an injector gun with at least a little postexposure treatment, but it was felt that that would not work for soman. If soman had been used, we would have had mass deaths on the battlefield. However, on the basis of very good chemistry, biochemistry, and pharmacologic studies that had been going on with military support for 20 years, the military command made the decision for the first time to use pyridostigmine bromide (PB) tablets as a pre-exposure antidote for soman exposure. If a person is already taking pyridostigmine and the chemical is already on board, the PB binds to the active site on the cholinesterase enzymes that are attacked by the chemical nerve agent and consequently the nerve agent can't get onto the active site to attack the enzyme. So you have time to rush off the battlefield, get the injection of the postexposure antidote, and reverse the pyridostigmine, and it doubles the survival rate of the postexposure treatment. Thus, it was a good idea, and it was not known to have serious side effects. The PB drug is given to patients with myasthenia gravis and has been for decades—very safely, we thought.

Third was the threat of biological warfare, particularly anthrax and some others, and we provided our troops with ciprofloxacin, as Dr. Collis mentioned. It was a great idea and, as far as we know, had no side effects.

As I mentioned, this was based on the best available science. I've reviewed all of that science that was known up until then, and I have no quarrel with those decisions. It was under a very tight time schedule to figure out what to do, to get it in the field so it could be delivered, and I think it was brilliant and masterful, and I would not have disagreed with any of it, and there were no experts who were disagreeing at the time. Many very eminent pharmacologists had performed all that research, and I'm sure were probably polled, and I think there was wide agreement.

Three false assumptions, however, underlay all of this, that are still mistakenly held by most of the people who are discussing this subject now. The first one is that the pre-exposure treatment with pyridostigmine bromide tablets is clearly safe. It was thought so at the time, but that is falling by the wayside. Second, that low-level exposure—exposure to low-level chemical nerve agents, not enough to make you sick on the battlefield—cannot produce long-term effects. The third assumption is that these various organophosphate chemicals—that's the generic name for this class of chemicals, which includes the nerve agents; pyridostigmine also is part of this similar type of chemicals, and pesticides—the assumption that all of these compounds act only individually and have no combined synergistic effect. Again, let me emphasize, at the time in 1990, when the war occurred, all of those assumptions were considered correct, and so I think the doctrine was rational.

However, now let me talk about what's happened since. Well, as you all know, as early as February—between the air war and the ground war—some troops were beginning to report illnesses that since have remained with them and have been incapacitating and that physicians in private practice—both at the VA, as well as out in private practice and the military—have been unable to diagnose and unable to cope with and unable to treat because we've not known what they were. For example, wives will tell you—and I've had many wives of veterans tell me—this is not the same hearty fellow who went over there. He was different when he came back, and he can't cope anymore, and he's not crazy.

Military physicians, private physicians—all of us—examined these people, and you ask them, "What's wrong with you?" and they say, "Well, my brain just isn't working the way it used to. My body doesn't work the way it used to." You say, "Well, what is it?" "I can't describe it. I can't think right, I can't remember right." You say, "Where does it hurt?" "Well, my joints." But you do an examination, and it's all normal; you do lab tests, and they're all normal; and you do brain MRIs, and they're all normal. So we say there's no illness, and so we then write in the chart, "Everything's taken care of," and so we then have statistics that everything's fine, and we've taken care of these fellows. Yet, they're still in sad shape and unable to function.

Now, soon after the war, many people in the service—particularly in the Naval Epidemiology Unit in San Diego—did quite a heroic bit of work and believed that there might be something to this and did some initial investigations and came up with some leading ideas. However, at that point, something happened. You see, there's a usual one-two-three-step method for how to work up an epidemic, which this would fit if it were true. You first establish a case definition. You examine a number of people who have this thing, and then you say, "What characteristics do all these people have in common?" You write down a case definition—usually it's one long sentence. Then you apply this case definition to a group of people who are potentially at risk and separate them into the cases (meeting the case definition) and the controls (not meeting it), and then you say, "What were the cases expressed that the controls were not?" and that's how you solve the problem. That tells you, one, is it really a disease and, two, what's it due to.

Unfortunately, for some reason—I don't know the reason; it probably was just the confusing nature of this condition, and this is the most confusing condition that we've probably seen in this half a century, at least—no one followed through the three steps and completed an epidemic investigation. So the epidemiologic work was never done. So we relied then only on clinical—individual doctors looking at individual patients and saying, "Well, I can't find anything, so therefore there must not be anything to it," but that is not valid. That cannot tell you that there's not a disease here. If the clinical approach found a disease, that would be fine, but that approach is not capable of saying there's no disease here. That can be done only with comparing cases and controls, and that was not done.

Well, the doctrine and the theory unravel at this point. Now, let me explain this. First of all, there are two diseases here, and not one, that we think are at play. Every doctor knew that, when you're exposed to an organophosphate chemical like a sarin nerve agent or a pesticide (or pyridostigmine, although it's not very bad, obviously), when you're exposed to these, two things can happen to you. One is, you can die immediately or have a very serious, what we call "immediate syndrome," immediate illness. Paralysis, maybe death on the battlefield or in the field where you're spraying pesticides and make a mistake—that's called the immediate syndrome. If you get so overcome that you collapse, and you stop breathing for a little bit, you can have brain damage, and in the Iran–Iraq War, some of the Iranians who were gassed ended up with severe neurological problems because they almost died, and they lost oxygen to their brains for a while. That didn't happen in the Gulf War, and so everyone has been saying, "Well, we couldn't have brain damage from chemical weapons because nobody came near death. No people were overcome on the battlefield."

The problem is, that's only half the story. There's another syndrome, and it's called the "delayed neurotoxicity syndrome." It's unrelated to the first syndrome. It involves paralysis of different enzymes in the body, cholinesterase in the first syndrome and what's called neuropathy target esterase in the second. The point is, there are two different toxicity syndromes. The first is immediate, but the second one is more insidious. You can be exposed to one of these organophosphates; it attaches to your neuropathy-target esterase anywhere in your brain and nervous system; it doesn't cause you to be sick immediately—you feel no pain at all; and two weeks, three weeks, even six months later, you can gradually start having difficulty thinking, difficulty concentrating. In fact, your memory's still intact; it's the switching stations down deep in your brain that are affected. That progresses, can involve the spinal cord and the peripheral nerves in any combination, depending on chronicity (how long the exposure lasts), the dose, and the different combinations of chemicals that you were exposed to.

Well, let me tell you, whereas the immediate syndrome is known to every doctor who ever went to medical school, the delayed neuropathy, delayed chronic syndrome, is known to almost no physician in the world except toxicologists. I can tell you because I've taken polls of many doctors—some of the most erudite chiefs of medicine in various places—and they've never heard of it, because it's a very rare syndrome seen only by toxicologists.

All right, now, here's where the theory unravels. In 1990, the December issue of *Journal of Applied Toxicology*, Dr. Cary Pope from Northeastern Louisiana University in Monroe published an obscure paper in which he showed that a chemical like pyridostigmine protects you from brain damage if you give it before the exposure to an organophosphate chemical—it protects you from the effects. He showed that if you give it *after* the exposure, however, it not only does not protect you—and it has nothing to do with the immediate syndrome; it doesn't protect you from the immediate syndrome—what it does, however, is it makes you more likely to get the chronic brain damage syndrome. So it not only does not prevent you from getting the acute syndrome, it promotes the chronic syndrome. So it appears that down the drain goes the first assumption—that is, that the pretreatment pyridostigmine would be safe. Yes, it's safe if you give it before, but if you continue giving it after—so says Pope's paper—it may promote the long-term syndrome. In fact, that's been now duplicated in at least 15 additional studies.

Second, Dr. Husain of India—no kin to Saddam—published papers in 1993 and 1995 in which he showed, if you give sarin every day for 10 days at a very low dose—a dose too low to produce immediate symptoms—you can get the long-term syndrome. So all the statements you've been hearing over the last three years that low-dose chemical nerve agents do not cause chronic brain damage are false. That is well shown in Husain's studies, but no one will quote them out loud. But they've been in the literature since 1993 and 1995, duplicated in two different species.

Third, in 1996 and 1997, our group, in collaboration with researchers at Kansas State University (Dr. Fred Oehme), Duke Medical Center (Dr. M. Abou-Donia—you know him because he was the first author on those papers), and the EPA [Environmental Protection Agency], who did the neuropathology of these studies, we showed that if you give pyridostigmine, DEET in insect repellents, or various pesticides in the same class of agents, if you give them individually in low doses to hens (which is the preferred model for this), they do not produce a problem. But if you give them in any two-way combination, they'll produce mild brain and nerve damage. If you give them in a three-way combination, they produce severe nerve and brain damage. That indicates that these chemicals— including pyridostigmine bromide—act synergistically to produce the long-term syndrome, even in doses that do not produce the immediate syndrome. So combinations act synergistically.

Finally, our epidemiologic studies in a Seabees unit. We studied a group of Seabees—this is what we published January 15, 1997, in the *Journal of the American Medical Association*—and showed that, in fact, there are three syndromes—three groups of these unusual, vague symptoms—that are identifiable. That is, there's one group that has impaired cognition and related symptoms; a second group that has severe mental confusion and ataxia (difficulty with their balance); and a third group that has joint and muscle pains and weakness. Each of these three groups appears to have brain damage as the cause of the symptoms. We brought a sample of them, a small group of these fellows with the symptoms, and a group of people without the symptoms, looked at them with very sensitive neuropsychological tests that can differentiate brain damage from psychological problems—stress and so forth—and with neurophysiological studies that can measure how fast nerves are conducting their impulses, looking for delays in conduction that would indicate a brain or nerve abnormality, looking at spinal cord conduction, brain stem conduction, and so forth.

We found, in fact, the ones with the syndromes do not have unusual psychological problems; their psychological profiles are normal or no different from general medical patients in a medical clinic. But what they have are indicators of mild brain and nerve dysfunction compared to the controls.

Finally, epidemiologic analysis shows that those different syndromes are related to different combinations of exposure to these chemicals. Those with our syndrome were the ones who wore flea collars containing pesticides, for example. Syndrome 2, the most severe one, these fellows are the very ones who were complaining that they were at a site where the chemical weapon alarms went off. They had symptoms; subsequently, they felt they had been exposed to chemical nerve agents. Also, they are the ones who had extraordinary side effects from the PB tablets. In our third syndrome were the fellows who used the government-issued insect repellent with highly concentrated DEET in ethanol, and also had extraordinary side effects from the PB tablets, indicating the possibility of chemical interactions.

So, in conclusion, what we think has happened is, despite the best-laid plans of our military under a very difficult circumstance, being guided by the best science available, we think that the chemical weapons somehow liberated into the environment (and I'm not qualified to talk about that aspect) and interacted with the PB tablets they were taking and the pesticides to which they were exposed in the flea collars and/or in the spraying around the camps. These chemicals produced mild, very difficult-to-diagnose brain-stem, lower-brain problems that are almost impossible to make a diagnosis in an individual case. We think our findings are supported by the large VA study by Dr. Han Kang, in which he compared the computer records of all 697,000 deployed with approximately 700,000 nondeployed era veterans, and found that there's about a 10 percent excess mortality since the war in the deployed veterans which is all concentrated in automobile accidents. There's been about a 50 percent increase in automobile accident-related deaths in Gulf War-deployed veterans compared to nondeployed veterans, and we think what we're seeing there are the effects of inability to drive a car safely in people with this subtle neurological damage.

Anecdotally, I've had a number of veterans tell me that their wives have stopped them from driving. One veteran is a 27-year-old prewar motorcycle racer. When he came back, he tried to go around the track and kept running into the wall, couldn't make the turns. Another fellow, the night he came back, they went out to eat on the rural route, and when they came home, he took out a half mile of mailboxes and hasn't driven since.

The contention that the Gulf War syndrome is due to stress is absolutely without support. The studies that have alleged that they are stress-related do not show it, and I recently published a paper to point that out. When you really look at the evidence, it does not hold up. So this is not post-traumatic stress disorder as we saw in Vietnam.

Finally, I believe now, on the basis of this, that there may be somewhere between 10,000 and—nobody knows the upper limit. The reason we don't know the upper limit is because one of the other findings we showed is that having one of these syndromes is age-related. The older the veterans were when they served in the war, the more likely they were to have this, one of these syndromes. There are several possible explanations for that. One possible explanation is what's called "brain reserve capacity." As we get older, we lose neurons. Every day you lose neurons, and your brain becomes less able to function, as those of us who are 50 or older know. It's well known that certain diseases that affect your brain create more severe symptoms, more manifestations, in people with less brain reserve capacity, and that makes plain why the age relationship with our syndrome, too.

Also what happens, what we see, is certain diseases like postinfluenzal

Parkinson's disease—Parkinson's following the 1919 influenza epidemic. The symptoms of Parkinson's come on years later after your brain starts losing capacity. So we're afraid it's possible that we're seeing maybe 10,000 veterans right now complaining of this and that, but as these veterans age, as the 25-year-olds get to be 50, it may unmask symptoms that were created by brain injuries to lower parts of their brains from these chemical exposures.

Now, let me say this: I am a great supporter and a great admirer of our military and what was done in Desert Storm. It was brilliant from all respects. It was a great show. We need to work together—the academic community, the military, the VA—to figure out what's gone on here because it's going to happen again. I think some of this happened in Vietnam. Some of what we call post-traumatic stress disorder may have been subtle brain damage from the contaminants—from the organophosphate contaminants—of the various herbicides that were used. That's a possibility. I don't know that for sure. But we're going to see this again, and before we put our troops in harm's way again in a very chemical environment, we need to understand this. We need a really crash effort—this is like inventing an atomic bomb from Einstein's equation. It's an extremely complex thing to figure out, and there's a pitifully small amount of support for people who would like to research this.

Discussant: Burton J. Lee III

Well, this will be short because Dr. Haley said everything that I was going to say. I couldn't agree with him more. I have been belaboring this from an unfortunate vantage point in that I haven't been in a place where I could do this research or have the leverage I had in the White House, but I am absolutely sure that what he is saying is the truth.

Let me bring out just a few points before I sit down. When you do clinical medicine—and I'm a clinician—the first thing that you always know is there's tremendous variability in your patient population. What you can do to 1, to 100 people, with impunity can kill the 101st, and you have to be aware of that. He gave those three assumptions that had been made, which I carefully wrote down. I won't repeat them. They all bear on the point that I was going to make. When are these drugs safe? In what sequence are they safe? Are they safe after the fact, before the fact, during the fact? Are they safe in combination? In cancer chemotherapy, people are always saying, "Well, your dose is too low, you're not achieving anything." That's nonsense. You can have profound biologic effects with minimal doses. Frequently, you get your best results with very moderate doses. The points that he made are excellent. I know these people are sick. I have seen some of them—not as many as he has—and I also feel that, when you know more, that we're going to be able to find the Vietnam people who had the same chemical exposure with the same type of thing.

One of the best articles that I've read about the Gulf War syndrome was in *The Economist*—not in any medical magazine. Most of our doctor friends have been running large comparative studies, not examining the patients, and concluding that there is no Gulf War syndrome of any consequence. We even have an article—a couple of articles—of this type in the *New England Journal of Medicine*. Now, in *The Economist* they pointed out a very interesting thing to me which I hadn't read before. The British had a small amount of what we're experiencing, but the French had none, and the Kuwaitis and Saudis report none. What are the differences? They point out that the French, the Kuwaitis, and the Saudis did not receive the various vaccines that we gave; they were not exposed to any of the low-level organophosphate pesticides; and, as far as the French are concerned, they weren't in the area of—I can't pronounce the name of it—where the sarin dump was blown up. So I wonder myself, Dr. Haley and Dr. Collis, not only the chemicals, not only the cholinesterase inhibitors, but I wonder—I have a sneaking feeling that these immunizations don't do a few people a lot of good. It certainly happens in civilian life when you immunize large numbers of people. No American company, for instance, wants to put out a vaccine because of the known certain number of bad responders that you're going to have and the lawsuits that will follow.

There were two other things that are not proven. One is infection with organisms that we don't know about. During our whole careers, all the doctors on this panel have been told that duodenal ulcers were due to stress, and we found out only four or five years ago it's due to a bacterium that's sitting in your stomach—absolutely a revolutionary finding for somebody like me, who considered myself to be an expert on duodenal ulcers. The last thing that I wonder about is—and I believe Secretary Derwinski has seen it—did you see the oil wells blown up there and what the guys were working with? It was so extraordinary to watch the environmental destruction and the oil and petroleum products in the air. I couldn't imagine people living with that very long and not getting sick.

Anyway, I'm learning more than anyone else is here.

Discussant: Robert A. Newman

Our subcommittee, which is chaired, as mentioned, by Congressman Christopher Shays of Connecticut, has oversight jurisdiction of five cabinet departments of government, including the Department of Veterans Affairs. Among issues we have dealt with is the so-called Gulf War syndrome. Why are tens of thousands of veterans sick, so sick? Why has the VA failed to properly diagnose, treat, and compensate these veterans? What role have the DOD and the CIA played in these mysterious illnesses? Is there a cover-up? If so, why?

We've investigated this matter for two years, held 10 hearings. We've talked to hundreds of veterans—Gulf veterans, sick veterans. We've heard from over 70 expert witnesses. Here are highlights of what we have come to believe about this subject.

For five years—from 1991, when the war ended, until 1996—the DOD had insisted that no U.S. troops were exposed to chemical warfare agents. They insisted in the face of valid detections of such agents during the war by trained military specialists, UN inspectors, and Czech experts. Soldiers reported thousands of chemical alarm warnings, and many of the troops have developed flu-like symptoms, rashes, joint pain, headaches, memory loss, and other maladies within hours, or days, or perhaps years. DOD disregarded all these indications.

For five years, the VA—assuming the DOD knew what it was talking about when it said no chemical exposures—disregarded veterans' health complaints as malingering, "all in the head," stress-related, somatoform disorder, or post-traumatic stress disorder. Although the VA has maintained in hearings they always had an open mind about the possibility of chemical exposures in their diagnosis and treatment of sick veterans, there's no evidence that they tested for it until 1996. They didn't put it in the VA Health Registry until the fall of 1995.

The stone wall began to crumble last June. In what was described as a watershed event, the Pentagon admitted that 400 troops were "presumed exposed"—their words—to chemical fallout when army engineers detonated Iraqi munitions bunkers at Khamisiyah. The numbers were revised to 20,000 in October. A few weeks ago, the DOD and the CIA suggested that southerly winds may also have carried chemical fallout from Khamisiyah over hundreds of thousands of troops stationed in Kuwait, Saudi Arabia, and southern Iraq. The CIA previously said the winds were northerly. Information about Khamisiyah chemical weapons, we believe, has been in DOD files before, during, and after the war. The CIA has recently admitted this information has been in their own files since 1984. The CIA said they warned DOD about the threat before the demolitions. The DOD said they had no such warning.

Now, where does this leave the sick veteran? Not only was he perhaps exposed by these Khamisiyah events, he was also possibly exposed—he or she—to a variety of other chemicals and hazards, as has been mentioned here: pesticides at levels not permitted in this country, insect repellents, smoke from burning oil wells, leaded fuel, side effects from the experimental drug, the pyridostigmine bromide antinerve gas pills (experimental except for civilian myasthenia gravis patients). Now, these troops were forced to take these pills. This was a war like no other, a war against the health of the veterans.

The veteran faces another problem: 80 percent of the Pentagon's chemical logs from the war are missing, lost, or destroyed, and this is under investigation by the inspector general of the DOD. Most CIA logs indicating chemical threats are still buried in classified files. Antinerve gas pill information sheets for informed consent by the troops were never given to the troops. Now, all these are part of the veterans' complete medical record. To make matters worse, the veterans' personal medical records have also either been lost or destroyed or inadequately kept. In the absence of such full documentation needed to prove a service connection, how do sick veterans get proper treatment and compensation?

Personally, after investigating this whole situation full-time for a year, I am convinced Gulf War veterans are fighting another war against a cover-up or incompetence or both by the DOD, the CIA, and the VA. Now, there are some indications that DOD and the VA may be willing to accept the fact that these troops were perhaps poisoned by chemical toxins. However, they are still relying heavily on stress as a diagnosis in most cases. They are supported in this by the Presidential Advisory Committee and the Institute of Medicine. Medical experts—including doctors who have treated sick veterans—and a number of scientific studies on returning veterans indicate that many sick veterans have nerve damage from exposure to neurotoxins, and some medical experts believe that stress alone does not cause peripheral nerve damage. Stress has caused health problems to some veterans of all wars, including the Gulf War, but something far more serious has happened to these Gulf veterans.

As a result of these Khamisiyah events, subcommittee chairman Shays called on the VA seven months ago to immediately reevaluate their medical protocols, including diagnosis, treatment, and compensation of sick Gulf veterans. The VA is promising still more research, and they're still reviewing the situation.

In answer to the question of why government would stonewall on the issue of chemical exposures, *U.S. News & World Report*, November 25, 1996, stated:

If exposure to chemicals is ever tied to widespread illnesses among veterans, the government may face other dilemmas. A link could open the door to thousands of disability claims, plus legislation mandating greatly expanded health coverage for veterans. The repercussions could reach into future battlefields as well. An official determination that chemicals have seriously harmed U.S. soldiers would be an admission of vulnerability.... The next time the alarms start going off, the all-clear signal may not be so quick to follow.

Discussant: Philip Shenon

My journalism career—at least as it regards the Gulf War—has really come full circle. In the fall of 1990, I was one of the youngest members of the Washington bureau, so therefore I was seen as cannon fodder and was sent off to Baghdad for several weeks at a time when Americans were being held hostage there. At that point, they weren't holding American journalists as hostages, though we had some suspicions that might happen. Eventually we were all thrown out, and I finished up in Saudi Arabia, where I covered the air war, and then I joined with the United States Seventh Corps, with the ground troops, as they went into southern Iraq and then into Kuwait during the four days of the ground war.

And certainly, when I came home a few weeks later from the Gulf, the legacy of that war was one that was entirely positive. Here we had routed a rogue nation, American servicemen and women were returning home to be hailed as heroes, and certainly they deserved all the praise that was heaped upon them. As soon as I got home, I was sent again, almost immediately, overseas, and I finished up in Asia for four years. And in truth, I can't say I thought a whole heck of a lot about the Gulf War past that point, except to hear from a very great distance across the Pacific Ocean that some Gulf War veterans were saying that they were falling ill, and that they believed that their illnesses were somehow related to what had happened to them during the war. I had no reason to believe that was true, and I certainly noted from afar that the United States government was issuing blanket denials that there had been any exposure—that any American service members had been exposed to any of the Iraqi chemical and biological agents that we knew they had stored prior to the war. I knew while I was in the war that the chemical alarms had sounded, but they had always been described to us as false alarms, and again, I had no reason to doubt that at the time.

Early last year, I returned to the United States and was reassigned to the Washington bureau and was given the Pentagon beat. And I had always thought I would get around at some point to doing a story about this thing called Gulf War Syndrome, and the servicemen and women who were saying they were falling ill. But in all honesty, it wasn't a priority until June 20 of last year.

It was a remarkable day. I remember sitting in my office in the Washington bureau and receiving an urgent call from the Pentagon that all the journalists covering the beat should gather immediately at the Pentagon in the press room because there would be an important announcement. This was a Friday afternoon, very late in the day. And let me tell you, as a long-time Washington correspondent, whenever there's a news conference late on a Friday afternoon, you know there is very bad news to come. And sure enough, that's what the case was. We were called together, and the Pentagon spokespeople went up to the podium to announce very sheepishly that, after years of denial, they would finally acknowledge that some small number of American troops—and the figures we were given at that point were three to four hundred—may have been exposed, were potentially exposed to chemical weapons when they blew up an Iraqi ammunition dump a few days after the war. This is the depot near the southern Iraqi village of Khamisiyah. You may have read a lot about Khamisiyah in the last year, or certainly seen that name.

And so began a journalistic odyssey for many reporters—myself included—and over the last year, we've found really a tremendous amount of evidence to suggest that the Pentagon, the Central Intelligence Agency, and other government agencies have been deceitful in dealing with the men and women of the military about what went on during the war. At this point, we still really have no proof, I would argue, that American soldiers were made sick from exposure to chemical or biological weapons. Dr. Haley's work is enormously respected, but I think he would acknowledge that there are other prominent scientists who really aren't sure what is going on here, or what is making these men and women sick.

But we do have proof, at this point, in abundance that the government had detailed evidence before, during, and after the war to suggest that chemical weapons had been released in the vicinity of American troops, and that there was some reason to be concerned for their health. They had this information knowingly at a time when they were issuing statement after statement after statement assuring Gulf War veterans that they had no reason to be fearful for their health. Just in the last few days, we've learned that the CIA had detailed evidence as early as 1986—strong evidence as early as 1986, and this is five years before the war—that chemical weapons were stored at this place called Khamisiyah, but apparently this information was never passed along to the Pentagon and to a good number of American military commanders before they blew up this thing.

Gulf War veterans really have reason to be very proud of their service in that war, and certainly the legacy of the war is one of tremendous American military accomplishment. But I would argue that the legacy really has been tarnished over the last four years, five years, by the unwillingness of many in the government to tell the truth about what really happened on the battlefield.

Questions and Answers: Michael D'Innocenzo, Moderator

Michael D'Innocenzo: If you'll be good enough to step to the microphone here so you can be heard, and please be good enough to keep your questions or comments as brief as possible.

Q: *As a citizen who feels that he likes to get what he's paying for with his taxes, I have just adjusted to the fact that the CIA let Aldridge Ames float around for seven years without realizing that he was living over his head and that everybody was out of the loop, that the people high up didn't know that foreigners were contributing to the government. But is there any logical accounting for the fact that the CIA knew that there were poison gases in Khamisiyah and did not advise the DOD at the time of the war? Is there a logical explanation for that?*

Robert A. Newman: Who are you asking this? Me?

Q: *Yes, or anybody on the panel.*

Newman: Well, they claim—CIA claims, and Phil Shenon can correct me if I'm wrong—that there was a confusion of names—names such as An Nasariyah, Khamisiyah, and they had one incident in which UN inspectors were going to Khamisiyah to inspect this—I don't recall the year—but their plane landed 25 miles away in a similar-sounding name of a town, and they were baffled. They looked around, and they didn't see these bunkers. But they say that they didn't make a connection between Khamisiyah and some other towns nearby, so they disregarded it. Their coordinates should have told them that they were one and the same. Now, that's what I heard from CIA's Robert Walpole, and maybe Phil can explain it.

Philip Shenon: To be clear, I don't think anybody can see any reason at all why the CIA wouldn't have happily shared this information with the Pentagon. This may be incompetence during the war, intelligence failures, or whatever. I think the question is, why has it taken them five years to find this information, especially when they claim they've been actively investigating this case now for a year and a half? All of these documents suddenly appeared just in the last several weeks.

Q: *Is there going to be a follow-through on this to some conclusion to justify this lack of cooperation between departmental agencies, or is it just going to disappear?*

Shenon: Well, Bob's on the case.

Newman: Well, we don't happen to have jurisdiction over DOD and CIA, only the VA. However, the full committee we serve on, we can easily bring in the full committee on this hunt. Right now, the full committee, headed by Congressman Burton, has its hands full on other matters.

D'Innocenzo: Thanks. Next question, please.

Q: *I'm Arnold Abrams of* Newsday. *This is for Dr. Collis. A good deal of the testimony here today makes it very clear that, professionally, there is no blame being laid on you for your work while you were in the government service. I'd like to know what your personal feelings are on hearing what has been disclosed today.*

Peter B. Collis: My personal feelings go way beyond today, because I've been following this. I think the likelihood is that the same things that you worry about as a physician are to prevent problems. Our first rule of medicine is *primum non nocere*, which is "first, do no harm." So I constantly ask myself and our colleagues, who I still stay in touch with, is there something that we could have predicted or known? And I do think, number one, that there is something—I don't know what it is, what combination it is. Certainly, I think those of us in medicine are like everyone else in life: the longer we practice, and the more we know, the more we know we don't know. I make the diagnosis all the time in the emergency department, "I don't really know what's wrong with you, but I do know we need to look at it further." I think that's what this is.

I'll comment a little bit on the intelligence community from a physician's point of view. We are not looked upon as strategically important and necessarily important to the intelligence community because they don't consider us part of the fighting force, if you will. But I'll offer you some observations as a civilian about the intelligence community that I think may explain some of the recent problems. I don't think it's incompetence. My experience trying to find answers from the intelligence community about the potential agents, I got a lot of data but very little information. My analysis of part of that problem is that you have too many intelligence agencies producing competitive data. They get to be hesitant about stepping out and making a recommendation because if one of them makes a recommendation, the other one's going to say, "You silly fool, that's not correct." So they're competing intelligence agencies afraid to make a mistake. I think Congress has looked at that; the Department of Defense has also looked at it. I think as the reorganization of government continues to look at that, the intelligence community will be slimmed down.

There's certainly no reason for the Department of Defense to have covered this up intentionally. I can tell you also from our point of view as physicians, when we looked at the detection equipment that was available to the U.S. forces, it was not under the medical group development, nor was it under what I considered highly scientific groups of people. In other words, to me it wasn't state of the art in terms of what we were doing for diagnosis in medicine. It was run by engineers, and it's a separate section. I was distressed by that. We did have to go out and buy vehicles from Germany and other places, because our detection equipment was not as good as it could be. Again, we still don't have perfect equipment, and that's one of the problems. There are a lot of false alarms. One guy told me for the biologic, if a camel goes by and has a bowel movement, it'll set off a biologic alarm because of the biologic aspect of the feces. So we didn't have the state of the art, and is there state of the art that can really work? So that is one of the problems. There were a lot of alarms going off, and you tend to ignore them because so many of them are false alarms. I think in retrospect, with some of this equipment, when they've gone back and looked at it, it's very possible they were real alarms.

Q: What do you answer when you say to yourself, "Should I have known?"?

Collis: I've looked at it, and I couldn't. There's no way I could have predicted, because there still is no answer, even retrospectively.

D'Innocenzo: Thanks, Dr. Collis.

Q: I think a lot of what we've heard is not a surprise to some of us who served a long time ago in World War II, when we coined the word "snafu"—situation normal all fouled up. That happens in the military. What really shook me up today—and I'm directing this to Dr. Haley—if I understood you correctly, the real villain in this may very well not be the fact that there was some gas let loose, but our good faith and, from what Dr. Collis says, good science efforts at the time to prevent illness. Am I correct in that?

Robert W. Haley: Our best guess is it was a combination of those, but had any one of them been absent, probably there would not have been as much illness. So it may well be that's true. However, I think we really need to keep in mind that, had we not been so prepared, had we not been taking PB tablets, had Saddam Hussein felt that we were unprepared for a soman attack, we might have gotten a soman attack and lost 20,000 troops on the battlefield with horrible deaths. So second-guessing this, at this point, is really—

Q: Oh, no, I'm not trying to blame anybody—I understand that.

Haley: Yeah, I just wanted to make that comment.

Q: But I think what you pointed out about the French and the Kuwaitis, who presumably were exposed to the same things, not having this symptom, it's kind of chilling to think that our own efforts to protect ourselves are the things that hurt us.

Haley: Right. What I think it may be telling us is that our doctrine that we have a defense against chemical weapons at this point may be, appears to be, false. It's ironic that, at the same time we're learning that that's false, our Senate is going to not ratify the Chemical Weapons Convention. We're going to make a statement that we're not opposing chemical weapons in the world. So this situation is full of ironies.

Collis: Also, remember the numbers. The British sent—when you talk to the Brits a lot of times, you'd think they won the Gulf War. They sent 50,000 troops; we sent half a million. I sent more medical troops than the Brits sent totally, and the French were below that. So clearly the numbers are lower. I wouldn't—and not to make digs on French science, but French medical science, in terms of how carefully they're going to look, is not comparable. So I would be a little hesitant about comparing those two populations unless they're both studied by Dr. Haley at the same institution.

Q: *I have two questions. They're both to Dr. Haley. First, the Iraqi soldiers—has there been any research done to see if they have the same side effects as the U.S. soldiers, or has there been any consultation with the government of Iraq? Second, I heard and I read about depleted uranium that was used in the Abrams tanks. Could that have also been something that soldiers, that's why they have the Gulf War syndrome?*

Haley: First of all, with the Iraqi soldiers, I would echo Dr. Collis' point. We're not sure—in fact, we're probably pretty sure—that the Iraqi troops, if they were having problems, would not be able to come forward and say it. I suspect the same might be true of the French. I'm not sure how open the French society is to have their soldiers step forward with complaints as our very free society is. So I would agree with Dr. Collis. I wouldn't interpret that until there were very firm studies.

There was a very interesting incident that we've referred to in some of our writings. We received an abstract from an Iraqi physician, otolaryngologist, who delivered a paper at an Iraqi medical convention. It was a convention on the health effects of the American embargo, so it was OK in Iraq, I guess, to present at this conference. This otolaryngologist presented an epidemic of unusual ear, nose, and throat illness that was characterized by scotomas—that means spots before your eyes, balance disturbances, strange seizurelike activity (in other words, a strange neurological condition)—that began several months after the war, primarily in southern Iraq. The number of cases presenting to his office increased, increased, and a year or so after the war, he said, "And it's now down to only about 20 a week." He didn't say how many there were, but he's now down to only 20 a week. So we wondered if that might be the acute phase of people who were exposed to some unusual combination of chemicals, or some infectious agent, or something in Iraq. But, of course, there's no answer to that.

Now, as for depleted uranium, I think just the physics behind that suggest that's not a risk. Also, in our study, we measured that and found that it was not associated with any of our syndromes. So empirically, it appears not to be a risk. Specifically, depleted uranium rods that are inserted into the projectiles, tank projectiles, are depleted uranium so they no longer give off gamma rays, which are the ionizing radiation that's associated with most health effects. They still emit small amounts of alpha particles, but those don't go but a few inches before they decay and are lost. So I think the best medical suggestion is that, if one were wounded with a fragment from a depleted uranium shell, you might have long-term health effects because the alpha particles are right in you—are being emitted right in you. Actually, there's a registry where all the known wounded soldiers who might have been wounded with depleted uranium munitions have been enrolled into a surveillance project, and they're being watched to be sure whether there are health effects.

D'Innocenzo: Thanks. We'll take the last two questioners, and in order to stay on schedule for those of you who want to go to the upcoming events, I'm also going to give Professor Gunter a chance for a brief response, and any of the other panelists who want to get a last word in.

Q: Kathryn Schultz with the Center for Defense Information in Washington. I'm particularly interested in the panel's assessment—and particularly Dr. Collis'—about the Pentagon's efforts to fight the next war. As you know, in the Defense Counterproliferation Initiative, where we're planning to defend, deter, and prevent attack from nuclear, biological, and chemical weapons, there's this part called "passive defense": you know, build better gas masks and BW [biological warfare] suits, and also do vaccines. What is your assessment of those efforts?

Collis: Well, first, I was part of an administration that's no longer in power, and hopefully I'll get a chance to go back there at some point in the near future. I think there's room for improvement. We do fight for dollars—for vaccines or any treatments—against dollars for helicopters, tanks, ships, and so it's a tough battle. Also, the funding is going dangerously low in the Pentagon. But a battle is still being fought, and they're still looking at it, and hopefully, at least in the area of vaccines, they're going to do something fairly quickly, or within the near future. But I can't give you details of what's going on with the present administration.

Shenon: As you pointed out, the General Accounting Office has looked at this question in recent years and has found that, actually, the Defense Department may be less ready to fight a chemical war than it was during the Gulf War. As Dr. Collis was saying, the funding for that has been cut dramatically, which is intriguing in light of things like the subway attack in Tokyo. This is a danger we face every day now.

D'Innocenzo: The *Defense Monitor* is widely read on campus, and you render a service by your perspectives.

Kathryn Schultz: Thank you. We may be doing a television show on this topic.

Q: Hello. I have three quick questions, the first one for Dr. Collis, the second two for Dr. Haley. I wanted to know, I know, right before a war, you don't have time—you want to be sure you win the battle and that everyone can win the battle the best they can. But before the Persian Gulf War, and we knew that it was going to be Iraq, did they do any kind of in-depth blood profiling that would somehow try to get a profile on blood toxicity so maybe after the war, they could *do some kind of very subtle, best-available-technology studies to see any kind of a difference that would show up?*

Collis: The answer to that is no, we didn't. We did some routine—actually, there was an initiative to try to do some of the early DNA testing for identification. As you may be aware, that has run into some ethical complaints, and we need more protection of that data if you're going to start doing DNA tests, and that's primarily to identify personnel. I'll just give you a brief example why it's useful. Unfortunately, with the new weapon systems (especially some of our friendly fire), there were some cases where there were very badly damaged parts, and we couldn't put those patients back together for shipping them home adequately without DNA studies. The Bosnia deployment, they have been very careful, and they have spent a lot of your hard-earned tax dollars to try to do a number of blood studies, psychological profiles—a number of things—to see, if this happens in Bosnia, if we will have a better way of tracking it down. So we have learned our lesson in that regard.

Q: I just wanted to clarify from Dr. Haley, with these neurophysiological signals conduction profiles that you say is something that you could really spot there's something physical going on, does that show something for all the variations in Persian Gulf War syndrome, or not?

Haley: What we did in our initial studies—our studies were privately funded by the Perot Foundation, and we had a very limited amount of money. What we did is the initial, what we call a "quick-and-dirty" study to see, is this a go, or is it not? Is there enough evidence to say there's really an illness here or not? That's all we did. We've recently proposed to the Defense Department what we call the "Manhattan Project for the Gulf War Syndrome." What we need is a concerted effort that follows along half a dozen tracks simultaneously to look at the various types of neurological, neurophysiological parameters that would ultimately, within two or three years, lead to insights that would give us a diagnostic set of tests and a treatment for these disabilities. But that really is as complicated as developing an atomic bomb from Einstein's equations. We're that far away from really being able to test accurately for this and to do treatment—which should be, by the way, the main focus of all of the effort. Cover-ups and all that notwithstanding, everybody ought to be focused on figuring out how to diagnose this problem and treat it, and that is not going on. We're so focused on cover-ups that we're not working on treatment, and that's really the issue. We're nowhere on that subject yet.

D'Innocenzo: I hope that you or others who might want to ask questions of the panel can do it afterwards, if they can stay, or walk with them. I promised Professor Gunter an opportunity for a very brief rebuttal, and then we'll see if any of the other panelists want to comment quickly.

Michael M. Gunter: Okay, thank you. Getting back quickly to the Kurds, who, after all, were the victim of documented 5,000 deaths at Halabja at the hands of

Saddam's chemical warfare in March 1988. I agree, and I made this clear in my paper, that the Kurds are a victim of geography, which has placed them as a minority in four Middle Eastern states: Turkey, Iraq, Iran, and Syria. However, there is one suggestion I would make where American policy could have been more wise toward the Kurds, and that is what I call the double-economic blockade—the double-economic blockade the Kurds have suffered from. Namely, once the Kurds had set up this de facto state in northern Iraq after the Gulf War, Saddam economically blockaded them, as could be expected. But two, the United Nations, with U.S. support, also economically blockaded the Kurds because the Kurds were legally still part of Iraq, and all of Iraq was under UN economic boycott. I think this was not—and it continues to be unwise policy because, far from rewarding Kurdish democratic behavior—after all, the Kurds had this democratic election in May 1992—we seem to be punishing them. Even not knowing what we're doing with one hand, because with the right hand we're economically blockading the Kurds as part of Iraq, and with the other hand, we're giving them a little help. We could really apply the blockade just to Saddam and not to the Kurds, and I think that would have been wiser policy.

Index

Abbas, Abul, 123–24
Abdel Meguid, Ahmed Esmat, 165
ABM Treaty, 323
Abourzek, James, 375
Accords for the Conference on Security
  and Cooperation in Europe
  (CSCE), 335
Ackerman, Gary, 209
Adams, Brock, 206
Adams, Gordon, 410
Advisory Committee on Trade Policy
  and Negotiations, 47
Afghanistan, 317
Aidid, Mohamed Farah, 264, 268, 269,
  270
Ajami, Fouad, 391
Albania, 280, 316
Albright, Madeleine, 79, 296, 398
Alternative use committee, 414
American Israel Public Affairs
  Committee (AIPAC), 116, 118–19,
  126, 127, 128
Americans Talk Security, 480
Amnesty International, 443
Andean Trade Preference Act, 228
Anglo-Iraqi Treaty, 508
Angola, 317
Arab Americans, 157, 159
Arab Cooperation Council, 108 n.22,
  490
Arab-Israeli conflict, 113–36, 151–52,
  155, 161, 162–63, 164–66, 168,
  291, 494, 495, 500, 501–2. *See also*
  Middle East
Arab states: and Arab-Israeli conflict,
  131, 132, 134, 151; and Persian
  Gulf War, 105, 124–25, 140, 142,
  161–62, 490–92, 493. *See also
  specific countries and leaders*
Arafat, Yasir, 114, 117, 118, 121, 122,
  123, 124, 129, 130, 132, 151, 495.
  See also Palestine Liberation
  Organization
Arens, Moshe, 119, 120, 121, 122, 125,
  127, 128
Aristide, Jean Bertrand, 263
Armacost, Michael, 50, 81
Army Career Alumni Program, 420
Aronson, Bernie, 226–27
Ashrawi, Hanan, 129, 130, 133–34
Asia, 6, 36, 43, 72–73, 87–88, 395. *See
  also* China
Asia Development Bank, 81
Asia-Pacific Economic Cooperation
  (APEC), 70
Aspin, Les, 197, 201, 208, 211, 498
Assad, Hafez al-, 114, 115
Association of Southeast Asian Nations
  (ASEAN), 69, 72
Atlantic Force, 395
AT&T, 75
Austria, 338
Awanohara, Susumu, 66–68, 79
Aziz, Tariq, 145, 203, 206, 207, 208,
  212, 478

Baathist Party, 499
Baker, James A., III: as advisor, 261, 297; appointment of, 46, 47; and Arab-Israeli conflict, 113, 114, 115, 118, 119, 121, 122, 123, 126, 128, 129, 133–34; and Asia, 72; and Assad, 115; and Association of Southeast Asian Nations, 69; and Aziz, 206, 207, 208, 212, 478; on Bush, 141–42; and Cold War, 291, 345; and Congress, 193–94, 199–200, 201, 204; and defense policy, 391, 403; and Eastern Europe, 337, 338; and European security, 341–42; and General Security Service, 126; and Hussein's motivation, 92–93; and Iraq sanctions, 204; and Israel, 113, 114, 115, 117, 118, 119, 121, 126, 128, 129, 134, 162; and Jewish community, 116; and Kuwait, 93; and Latin America, 175; and Madrid Peace Conference, 113, 114, 129, 130, 132, 164, 165; and Mahathir, 70; and Milosevic, 293, 298–99; and Noriega, 177, 178–79, 180, 181, 182, 195; and Palestinians, 126; and Panama, 175, 176, 177, 178–79, 180, 181, 182, 195; and Persian Gulf War, 91, 139, 141–42, 143, 144, 162, 164, 199–200, 201, 204; *The Politics of Diplomacy,* 391; and presidency, 193–94; and Serbia, 293; and Soviet Union, 293; and Strategic Arms Reduction Treaty, 351; and Yugoslavia, 293, 298–99
Baltic states, 296–97, 315, 340, 341, 342
Bandar, Prince, 497
Bangladesh, 72
Barak, Ehud, 168
Barre, Siad, 263, 264
Bartholemew, Reg, 85
Barzani, Massoud, 510–11, 511, 512, 513, 516
Barzani, Mulla Mustafa, 509
Barzinji, Shaikh Mahmud, 508–9
Bayard, Thomas, 55
Begin, Menachem, 113, 115, 122, 161
Beilin, Yossi, 119, 162
Belarus, 326, 336
Belgium, 265

Bell, Griffin, 377
Bennett, Charles, 208, 210–11
Bennett-Durbin resolution, 208, 210
Berlin Wall, 335, 338
Beschloss, Michael R., 245
Big Three automakers, 50
Black September, 129
Blair House Accord, 53, 56, 63, 64
Blakely, William, 378
Boeing Corporation, 75, 100
Boland Act, 237
Bosnia, 429; and ethnic cleansing, 294; and ethnicity, 290; failure in, 263, 292–93, 297–98; and media, 292, 307; mission in, 302–3; and United Nations, 300; and United States, 306; and West, 304–5, 306–7
Bosnia-Herzogovina, 278, 279, 283, 293, 336
Bosnian Serbs, 281
Boutros-Ghali, Boutros, 262–63, 264, 265, 266, 267, 268, 269, 270, 291, 295
Brady, Nicholas, 46, 47
Brady Plan, 32, 227, 232, 235
Brazil, 9, 19, 48
Brezhnev Doctrine, 316
Brinkley, Douglas G., 175–82, 238
Brook, Douglas A., 420–22, 423, 426
Broomfield, William, 201
Browning, Edmond, 443, 444, 447, 456 nn.15, 16, 458, 460–62
Brzesinski, Zbigniew, 100, 101
Bsiso, Atef, 129–30
Buchanan, Patrick, 4, 28, 57, 283, 470, 481
Bulgaria, 316, 335, 338, 340
Burgess, Stephen F., 259–71, 291, 295–96, 304
Bush, George:
—Congress and: Democratic, 45, 524; difficulties with, 385–86; and Israel, 126, 127, 128; and Latin America, 226, 227; and Panama, 194–96; and Persian Gulf War, 144–45, 196, 197, 198, 199–213, 214, 238–39, 443, 446–47, 448, 449, 450, 468, 486; and Structural Impediments Initiative, 67; and Super 301, 66; and Tower, 369, 376–86, 388 n.43; and trade, 9, 13, 28, 55; and Use of Force resolution,

Index 551

211, 212, 213, 214; and War Powers Resolution, 193, 194–96, 197, 198, 200, 201, 202, 207–8, 213, 238–39
—domestic policy/relations: and abortion, 377; and advisors, 147, 261, 297, 364; and African American community, 224; and agriculture, 19, 20–21, 49, 50, 52, 53–54, 64; and Arab community, 157, 159; and Big Three automakers, 50, 56, 67; and budget deficit, 471; and budget (military), 319, 322, 323, 361, 395, 401, 407–8, 421–22, 423, 429, 436; and Civil Rights Act, 245, 465; and Cuban American community, 223–24, 230, 248, 249; and defense conversion, 414–15, 417; and defense cuts, 407–8; and Democratic party, 7, 13, 45, 145, 204, 208, 466, 524; and Department of Defense, 433, 484–85; and deregulation, 33; and economy, 4, 6–7, 10–11, 12–13, 44, 45, 55–56, 57, 283, 305, 306, 448–49, 471–72, 479, 480; and election of 1988, 49, 66, 156, 249, 466; and election of 1992, 4, 44, 56, 57, 63, 76, 134, 156, 249, 291, 318, 472, 481; and energy, 73, 413; and environment, 8, 73, 221, 416; and federalism, 276; and impeachment, 145; and industry advisory groups, 63–64; and interest groups, 49, 156, 157–58, 159, 223–24, 230, 248, 249; and Irish community, 224; and Jewish community, 156, 157, 158–59, 160, 224; and jobs, 8, 9, 10–12, 70, 76, 231–32, 407–8, 409, 423; and media, 6, 63, 64, 179, 240, 259, 264, 269, 444, 477; and military, 342, 349, 452–53, 484; and military bases, 416, 417, 423, 429; and military budget, 319, 322, 323, 361, 395, 401, 407–8, 421–22, 423, 429, 436; and military defense cuts, 407–8; and military/defense policy, 143, 147, 153, 177, 195, 302, 391–404, 407–17, 424–27, 428–29, 432; and military force structure, 393–96, 425; and military jobs, 407–8, 409, 414–15, 417, 423; and military policing function, 397; and military preparedness, 318–34, 349, 359–60, 361, 362; and Office of Public Liaison, 156; and peace dividend, 395; and politics, 471, 472, 475–76, 484; and Republican party, 260, 443, 472, 475; and Tower, 369, 376–86, 388 n.43; and War Powers Resolution, 193–214; and Watergate, 465; and White House staff, 443, 444
—and foreign relations, 393; and Arab-Israeli conflict, 113–36, 151–52, 155, 291; and arms control, 79–80, 260, 317, 318, 323–34, 336–37, 348, 349, 350–51, 352–53, 359–60, 361, 362–63, 364–66, 424, 426–27, 429; and Assad, 115; and Baltic states, 296–97; and Base Force Concept, 395–97; and Bosnia, 292–93, 302–3, 304–5; and Brady Plan, 32, 232, 235; and Caribbean, 228–29; and Cartagena Counter-Narcotics Summit, 228; and Castro, 244, 245; and Central America, 186, 187; and Central Europe, 337; and chemical weapons, 331; and Chemical Weapons Convention, 361; and China, 147, 327, 484; and Cold War, 23–24, 28, 151, 186, 262, 275, 291, 314, 335, 336, 345, 391, 395, 404, 424; and collective security, 396–97, 398–401, 402; and commercial diplomacy, 30; and Communism, 185, 189, 237, 397; and Conference on Security and Cooperation in Europe, 343, 344; and conservatism, 465; and containment, 391–92; and Contras, 226, 227, 234, 237; and Conventional Forces in Europe Treaty, 341, 342, 355, 361, 429; and democracy, 186, 224, 229, 236, 260–61; and drugs, 229, 231, 237, 238, 239, 246, 466; and Eastern Europe, 337, 338, 353; and Economic Bank for Reconstruction and Development, 25; and Egypt, 116; and El Salvador, 234–35; and Enterprise for the Americas

Initiative, 8, 32, 63, 185, 227, 229, 232, 235; and Ethiopian Jews, 158; and ethnic cleansing, 292, 300; and Europe, 337, 355; and European security, 341, 342; and Fahd, 497; and Falkland Islands War, 471; and foreign aid, 234, 318; and Germany, 151, 275, 296, 339, 340, 342; and Global Partnership Plan of Action, 50; and Gorbachev, 260, 296, 317; and Grenada, 471; and Guatemala, 228; and Haiti, 228, 229, 230, 232, 263; and humanitarianism, 262, 264, 266, 269, 295, 296, 306, 516, 521; and human rights, 85, 95, 443, 453, 454, 488–89; and Hussein, 85–86, 93, 96, 108 n.23, 143, 145–46, 198, 199, 202, 203, 205, 206, 207, 260, 443, 468, 469, 473; and idealism, 259, 263, 266, 269–70; and international disputes, 21, 35; and international economy, 22; and internationalism, 260, 270, 466; and international law, 442; and international system, 392, 393, 396–97; and Iraq, 91–106, 97, 98, 99, 153, 154, 167–68, 169, 197, 473; and Iraqi-Egyptian arms deal, 116; and Iraq sanctions, 143, 144, 147, 154–55, 198, 202, 450–51, 468, 473; and isolationism, 392, 428; and Israel, 113–36, 151–52, 157, 159–60, 163, 168, 291, 493; and Israeli settlements, 123, 125, 128, 159, 168; and just war doctrine, 441–54, 458–60, 503; and Korea, 78–80, 81; and Korean War, 154; and Kurds, 510, 512–14; and Kuwait, 443, 446–47, 448; and Latin America, 175, 224, 225, 226–30, 234–35, 237–40; and Madrid Peace Conference, 130–31, 132, 151, 164, 165; and Malta Summit, 317, 340; and Middle East policy, 91–106, 113–36, 146, 151–55, 161–63, 164–66, 291; and morality, 442–43, 444, 445–46, 448, 449; and Mubarak, 197; and multilateralism, 398; and NATO, 151; and New World Order, 6–7, 29, 142, 259, 261, 263, 267, 269, 270, 271 n.1, 291, 295, 297, 391–92, 393, 394, 397–98, 401, 402, 403–4, 488, 499; and Nicaragua, 186, 187, 226, 227, 234, 237, 261, 466; and Noriega, 176, 238, 239, 240, 466–67; and North American Free Trade Agreement, 5, 8–10, 12, 13, 19, 28–29, 32, 56, 63, 220–21, 228, 231; and Organization of American States, 228, 230; and Palestinians, 291; and Panama, 175–82, 194–96, 213, 228, 238–40, 260, 263, 270, 302, 466–67, 471; and Peres, 120; and perestroika, 189; and Perez, 233; and personal relationships, xvii, 26, 43, 76, 78, 85, 147, 156–57, 159–60, 161, 165, 492, 497; and Peru, 228; and Philippines, 260; and post-Cold War world, 142; and realism, 259, 260, 271; and Saudi Arabia, 196–97, 201, 474, 475; and secrecy, 229–30; and Serbia, 263; and Shamir, 157, 159–60, 165, 168, 170; and Somalia, 259–60, 264–71, 293–94, 295–96, 302; and Southeast Asia, 69–70; and Soviet Jews, 158; and Soviet Union/Russia, 32, 63, 185, 190, 223, 260, 277, 296, 297, 303, 317, 318, 319, 320, 356, 364–66, 391, 484; and Strategic Defense Initiative, 323; and Syrian Jews, 158; and Team B, 465; and Thatcher, 142, 146, 197; and Third World, 25, 327, 328; and Turkey, 23; and unilateralism, 35, 36; and United Nations, 142, 158, 165, 214, 262–63, 271 n.1, 297, 392, 397, 448, 468, 499; and United States-Asia Environmental Partnership, 73; and War Powers Resolution, 499; and Yeltsin, 328; and Yugoslavia, 263, 293, 298–300
—and foreign relations/trade, xviii, 3–15, 19–21, 22–26, 27–29, 30–33, 34–40, 43–57, 63–65, 66–68, 69–70, 71–73, 74–77, 78–80, 81–86, 87–88, 190; and Andean Trade Preference Act, 228; and Asia, 43, 81, 87–88; and Blair House Accord, 56, 63, 64; and Canada,

Index 553

220, 221–22, 231, 232; and China, xviii, 25, 38, 39, 63, 65, 74–75, 79, 81–83, 85, 250, 260; and Cuba, 185–86, 187, 188, 189, 190, 191, 223–25, 228, 230, 232, 236, 240, 243–54; and exports, 4, 53–54; and fast track, 13, 19, 28; free, xviii, 4, 8, 31, 35, 56–57, 65, 66, 76, 78, 190, 224, 229, 235; and GATT (Uruguay Round), xviii, 5, 7, 13, 19, 20, 21, 28–29, 31, 44, 51–55, 56, 63, 64; and Gephardt Amendment, 19; and G-7 Economic Summit, 25–26, 32; and intellectual property rights, 65, 74, 85; and Japan, 9, 10–12, 19, 22, 24–25, 26, 28, 31, 33, 36, 44, 46, 49–51, 54, 55, 57, 64, 67, 75–76, 81, 232; and Japan trip, 48, 50, 56, 66, 67; and Latin America, 32, 63; managed, 7, 35, 49, 56–57; and Mexico, 221, 231–32; and most favored nation status, 38, 65, 84–85, 250; and oil, 97, 477; and Omnibus Trade and Competitiveness Act, 9, 45; and protectionism, 3, 4, 5, 7, 8, 13, 33, 47, 49, 55, 66, 67; and rhetoric, 3, 4, 6–8, 9, 10, 11, 12–13, 14, 31, 33, 34–35, 63; and Structural Impediments Initiative, 24, 25, 33, 51, 64, 67, 75; and Super 301, 28, 35, 48, 55, 66–67; and World Trade Organization, 21, 23, 31, 35, 36
—and Persian Gulf War, xviii, 91, 291; and allied coalition, 143, 144, 147, 196, 221, 475, 477, 483, 484, 492, 494, 497; and Arab states, 493; and Canada, 221; and casualties, 524–25; and collective security, 400–401; and decision-making, 261, 270; and defense policy, 393; and deployment, 434–35; and economy, 305, 306, 448–49, 471–72, 479; and election of 1992, 472; end of, 433, 498–99, 512–14; frame of mind during, 470–73, 485; and human life, 494; and interest groups, 157–58, 159; and Israel, 493; and just war doctrine, 441–54; and leadership, 137–48, 153, 213–14, 483, 486; and Madrid Peace Conference, 164; management of, 296; and marketing, 476, 477; and media, 477; and New World Order, 262, 488, 499; objectives of, 302; and personal diplomacy, 157; and politics, 471, 472, 475–76; and postwar policy, 167–68; and public opinion, 468, 469–70, 471–72, 474–75, 476–77, 478–80, 485–86, 489, 503; reasons for, 306, 477, 484, 485, 513; and strategy, 497; success in, 153–54; and War Powers Resolution, 196–213, 238–39
—personal characteristics: background/career, 145, 146, 165, 260, 465, 466, 483, 484; character, 44, 138, 145, 182, 442–43, 488–89, 492; decision-making, 261, 270, 297; leadership, xvii, 137–48, 153, 213–14, 234, 261, 432–33, 434–37, 441–54, 483, 486
—presidency: and Carter, 143, 163, 175; and Clinton, 75, 396, 398, 402, 404; and Johnson, 142, 147, 261, 271 n.6; and Reagan, 6, 12, 45, 54, 119, 121, 138, 186, 238, 261, 270, 323, 334, 409, 471; and Roosevelt, 261, 270; and Wilson, 270
—and public opinion: and Bosnia, 292; and drugs, 466; and economy, 55–56, 479, 480; and election of 1988, 466; and jobs, 12; and Noriega, 467; and Panama, 182; and Persian Gulf War, 228, 444, 446, 468, 469–70, 471–72, 474–75, 476–77, 478–80, 485–86, 489, 503; and Somalia, 259, 269; and trade, 14, 55–56
—rhetoric: and Arab-Israeli conflict, 155; and defense policy, 392; and just war doctrine, 446, 454, 503; and Persian Gulf War, 142, 143, 146, 446, 454; and trade, 3, 4, 6–8, 9, 10, 11, 12–13, 14, 31, 33, 34–35, 63
—speeches: and defense conversion, 409; Inaugural Address, 5, 193; and just war doctrine, 445–46; and Persian Gulf War, 142, 203, 271 n.1, 445–46, 477, 479; Republican National Convention, 44; and

Somalia, 266–67, 270, 271 n.1;
State of the Union (1990), 6, 158;
State of the Union (1992), 326; and
trade, 5, 12; at West Point, 266–67,
270
Bush, Jeb, 230
Butler, Lee, 361
Butz, Earl, 372
Byrd, Robert, 195, 380

Cambodia, 86, 317
Camp David accords, 117, 161, 164
Canada, 220, 225, 231, 232, 252, 265, 276, 283, 285, 288 n.7, 331
Canada Free Trade Agreement, 220, 221
Carlos, Juan, 130
Cartagena Counter-Narcotics Summit, 228
Carter, Jimmy: and Arab-Israeli conflict, 129; and cabinet nominations, 371, 376, 377; and Camp David accords, 161, 164; and Cuba, 244; and economy, 25; and Iran, 100, 143, 163; and Iraq, 100–101; and Israeli-Egyptian Treaty, 113; and Middle East policy, 151; and military force structure, 394; and Noriega, 177; and trade, 30; and war, 472
Carter Doctrine, 100–101
Casey, William, 102, 237
Castro, Fidel, 176, 188, 190–91, 224, 244, 245, 246–47, 250, 251, 252, 253
Catholic Church, 470
Cawley, Carolyn, 445
Ceausescu, Nicolae, 121
Celeste, Richard F., 410
Central Europe, 63, 337–38
Central Intelligence Agency, 146, 176, 178, 320, 496–99, 513, 537, 538, 540, 541
Chamberlain, Neville, 146
Chamorro, Violeta Barrios de, 186–87, 234, 317
Charter of Paris for a New Europe, 317, 343, 345
Chemical Weapons Convention (CWC), 331–32, 336, 361
Cheney, Richard: as advisor, 261, 297; and Arab-Israeli conflict, 119, 124; and arms control, 429; and Base Force Concept, 395; and Congress, 144–45, 201, 203–4; and defense policy, 395, 403, 423–27; and Eastern Europe, 336, 338; and Halliburton, 423; and military budget, 319; and Panama, 178, 179, 180; and Persian Gulf War, 144–45, 147, 201, 203–4, 420, 426, 434–35, 473, 474, 475, 483–86, 497, 502; and public opinion, 485–86, 503; record of, 420, 421; and Saudi Arabia, 497; and Tower, 384, 385, 390 n.71
China, 25, 73, 147; and Cambodia, 86; and culture, 83; and economy, 83, 436; and human rights, 39, 75, 250; and Korea, 86; and missiles, 333; and most favored nation status, 38, 65, 84–85, 250; and nuclear weapons, 327; and Persian Gulf War, 477, 484; threat of, 436; and Tiananmen Square demonstrations, xviii, 74, 82, 84–85, 260; and trade, xviii, 25, 38, 39, 63, 65, 74–75, 79, 81–83, 250, 260; and United States, 436–37. *See also* Asia
Christopher, Warren, 100
Church, Frank, 128
Citizens for a Free Kuwait, 476
Civil Rights Act, 245, 307, 465
Clark, William, 371, 372
Clinton, William J.: and Arab-Israeli conflict, 134–35; and Bosnia, 300; and budget, 396; and China, 39, 75, 79, 81, 83, 84; and Cuba, 248, 252; and defense policy, 404, 432; and economy, 4, 25; and election of 1992, 38, 57, 481; and fast track, 28; and GATT (Uruguay Round), 51; and Japan, 31, 33, 66; and Miami Summit of the Americas, 227, 232, 235; and military, 396, 398, 402; and North American Free Trade Agreement, 221; and nuclear testing, 361; and Somalia, 267, 268, 270, 295, 296; and Structural Impediments Initiative, 67; and trade, 31, 66, 79
Cohen, William, 198
Cold War, 391, 424; and arms control, 352; and Cuba, 249; and defense

Index   555

policy, 404; end of, 6, 314, 335, 350, 425; and Israeli-Egyptian Treaty, 113; lessons of, 305–6; and Madrid Peace Conference, 113; and military budget, 362; peace following, 336–46; and trade, 23–24; and United States, 22–24; and Yugoslavia, 299
Collis, Peter, 521–23, 528, 542–43, 545, 546
Combest, Larry, 381
Commerce Department, 55
Common Agricultural Program, 52
Commonwealth of Independent States, 315–16, 322. *See also* Soviet Union
Communism, 185, 324; and Arab-Israeli conflict, 123; and Bush, 189, 397; and Castro, 246; and Catholicism, 277; and Cuba, 243, 249; and Eastern Europe, 335; and Latin America, 237; replacement of, 314; and Russia, 314, 336; and Slovakia, 285; and trade, 28; and Trade Act (1974), 191 n.3; and Yugoslavia, 276
Comprehensive Test Ban Treaty, 361
Concert of Europe, 400
Conference on Security and Cooperation in Europe (CSCE), 343
Congress, 45, 302; and agriculture, 52, 54; and Arab-Israeli conflict, 124, 126; and cabinet nominees, 370–76; and captive nations, 276–77; and Chemical Weapons Convention, 361; and Communism, 276–77; and Cuba, 253; and defense conversion, 414; Democratic, 379–80, 383, 385, 524; and economy, 46; and environment, 416; and Europe, 48; and fast track, 13, 19, 28; and funding, 204, 205; and Iran-Iraq War, 94; and Iraq, 96–100, 103, 104, 202, 204, 209, 210, 211; and Israel, 126, 127, 128; and Japan, 24, 48, 50; and Latin America, 226, 227; and military, 302, 395, 416, 429, 432; and nuclear weapons, 333; and Omnibus Trade and Competitiveness Act, 20; and Panama, 194–96, 213; and Persian Gulf War, 140, 144–45, 196, 197, 198, 199–213, 214, 443, 446–47, 448, 449, 450, 468, 469, 470, 477, 478, 479, 486, 498; and president, 369; and Reagan, 45, 193; and Structural Impediments Initiative, 67; and Super 301, 19, 24, 66; and Tower, 369, 376–86; and trade, 5, 9, 10, 13, 28, 45, 48, 49, 50, 55; and Trade Act (1988), 19; and Use of Force resolution, 211, 212; and War Powers Resolution, 193, 194–96, 197, 198, 200, 201, 203, 204, 207–8, 210, 213, 238–39. *See also specific legislation and legislators*
Congress of Vienna, 400
Constitution of the United States, 35; and War Powers Resolution, 193–94, 196, 197, 198, 200, 201, 204, 205, 208, 212, 213, 238
Conti, Delia B., 3–15, 27, 28, 31, 33, 34–35, 37, 39
Contract with America, 276
Conventional Forces in Europe (CFE) Treaty, 330, 335, 341, 342, 343–45, 352, 353, 355, 356, 361, 429
Convention on the Prevention and Punishment of the Crime of Genocide, 516
Coolidge, Calvin, 372–73, 384, 387 n.15
Courts, 204, 205
Cranston, Alan, 197
Croatia, 263, 277, 278–79, 280, 281, 284, 286, 291, 293, 300, 305, 336. *See also* Yugoslavia
Crowe, William, 202
Cuba, 153, 185–91, 236; and Bush, 185–86, 187, 188, 189, 190, 191, 223–25, 228, 230, 232, 236, 240, 243–54; and Communism, 243, 249; and democracy, 249; and economy, 187, 188, 190, 225, 244, 245, 247, 248, 249, 250–51, 253; and human rights, 246, 249–50; and military, 188; and Nicaragua, 187; and nuclear weapons, 364; and Organization of American States, 244; and Soviet Union, 185, 187, 188, 189, 223, 227, 244, 245, 247, 250; and trade, 247–48
Cuban Democracy Act, 248–49, 251

Cuellar, Perez de, 208, 262
Cuny, Fred, 264
Czechoslovakia, 282, 284–85, 298, 316, 335, 338
Czech Republic, 356

Danforth, John, 209
Davis, Arthur, 177
Dayan, Moshe, 122, 161
Dayton process, 300
Defense Base Closure and Realignment Commission, 416
Defense Cooperation Account, 422
Defense Intelligence Agency, 176
Defense Planning Guidance Process, 425
Defense Policy Guidance, 321
Defense Science Board, 411
Dellums, Ron, 204
Dellums v. Bush, 205
Democratic party: and Bush, 7, 13, 45, 145, 204, 208, 466, 524; and cabinet nominations, 371, 372; and economy, 13; and Israel, 127; and Persian Gulf War, 145, 201, 204, 205, 206, 208, 210, 211, 480; and protectionism, 49; and Tower, 379–80, 383; and trade, 7, 37, 45, 49, 51
Deng Xiaoping, 84, 85
Department of Commerce, 46
Department of Defense: and bases, 416, 420; and budget, 421–22; Bush's management of, 433; and cabinet nominations, 383; and chemical weapons, 331, 545; and deployment, 433; and Europe, 329; and illness, 537, 538, 539–40, 542; and leadership, 421; and military industry, 410, 411, 413, 414–15; and peace enforcement, 269; and Persian Gulf War, 148, 470, 474, 481 n.11, 484–85; and post-Cold War situation, 320, 321; and research, 434–35; and Veterans Administration, 525
Department of Justice, 37, 176, 238
Deputies Committee, 139–40
Derwinski, Edward J., 524–27
Desert Shield. *See* Persian Gulf War
Desert Storm. *See* Persian Gulf War
Developing world. *See* Third World
Dine, Thomas, 128

Dizai, Mohsin, 511
Dodd, Christopher, 197
Dole, Robert, 4, 93, 197, 280, 281
Donovan, Raymond, 374, 376, 377, 384
Dowling, Wayne, 181
Duggan, Michael, 474
Dukakis, Mike, 45, 466
Duke, David, 158
Dumas, Roland, 341
Dunkel, Arthur, 53
Dunlop, John, 371

Eagleburger, Lawrence, 84, 126, 140, 264, 265–66, 292, 293–94, 297, 304, 307, 500
East Asia, 394
East Asian Economic Caucus (EAEC), 70
Eastern Europe, 63, 121, 276, 314, 316, 330, 334, 335, 337–38, 353
East Germany, 335, 338, 434. *See also* Germany
East Jerusalem, 120, 121, 122, 130, 133, 162. *See also* Jerusalem
Economic Bank for Reconstruction and Development, 25
Edwards, Don, 196
Eggers, Paul C., 378
Egypt, 101, 102; and Arab-Israeli conflict, 117, 118, 119–20, 121, 122, 133; and Iraq, 164; and Israeli-Egyptian Treaty, 113; and Persian Gulf War, 477, 480, 483; and United States, 165
Eisenberg, Carolyn, 348, 349, 365
Eisenhower, Dwight D., 331, 372, 375–76, 384
Election, of 1988: and Arab-Israeli conflict, 134; and Cuba, 249; and interest groups, 156; and public opinion, 466; and trade, 45, 49
Election, of 1992: and economy, 4, 57; and foreign affairs, 481; and foreign aid, 318; and interest groups, 156; and Japan trip, 76; and New World Order, 291; and Perot, 22; and Persian Gulf War, 472; and trade, 38, 44, 56, 57, 63, 66
Elliot, Kimberly Ann, 55
El Reedy, Abdel Raouf, 153, 164–66, 490–92, 497

El Salvador, 234–35, 261
Endara, Guillermo, 177, 178, 180, 181
Engel, Eliot, 99
Ensenat, Donald Burnham, 69–70, 72, 87
Enterprise for the Americas Initiative (EAI), 8, 32, 63, 185, 227, 229, 232
Environmental Protection Agency, 371
Episcopal Church, 443, 447
Erikat, Saeb, 131
Esquipulas Agreement, 227
Estrada Doctrine, 228
Ethiopian Jews, 116, 158
Europe, 73; and arms reduction, 329–31; and Blair House Accord, 56; and Bush, 337; and Cold War, 335; and Cold War peace treaties, 343–45; and Congress, 48; and Conventional Forces in Europe Treaty, 355; and German unification, 340, 341; and Gorbachev, 337; and international system, 403; and Middle East peace, 299; and military, 343–45; and Open Skies Treaty, 331; and Persian Gulf War, 299; and security, 341–43; and United States force structure, 394; and Yugoslavia, 299–300
European Community: and agricultural subsidies, 54; and agriculture, 20, 21; and GATT (Uruguay Round), 52, 53, 54, 63; and German unification, 340; and Kurds, 515
European Parliament, 252
Evans, Rowland, 383
Evren, Kenan, 512
Export Administration Act, 248
Export Enhancement Program, 54
Export-Import Bank, 102

Fahd ibn Abdul Aziz, 196, 483, 497
Falcoff, Mark, 223–25, 240
Falkland Islands War, 333, 471
Farrar, Stephen P., 19–21, 28, 31, 35, 38–39
Fascell, Dante, 208, 211
Feed and Forage Act, 422
Feldman, Jonathan, 415
Final Settlement with Respect to Germany, 316, 343
Firmage, Edwin, 218 n.55

Fischer, Max, 127, 159, 160
Fitzwater, Marlin, 196, 197, 200
Foley, Thomas, 195, 198, 206, 207
Ford, Gerald R., 371, 373–74, 387 n.13, 472
Ford, Guillermo, 177
Fore, Henrietta Holsman, 71–73, 78
Fort Clayton, 178
France, 102, 117, 279, 294, 316, 331, 341, 544
Franklin, Barbara Hackman, 46, 74–77, 78, 85
Freij, Elias, 114
Fulbright, J. W., 280

Gaddis, John, 336, 345
Galbraith, Peter, 513
Gates, Daryl, 176
Gates, Robert, 139, 320
GATT (Uruguay Round), xviii, 5, 19, 20, 21, 23, 28–29, 31, 44, 46, 51–55, 63, 64
Gaza Strip, 114, 118, 119, 121, 125, 130, 132, 133, 164
Gejdenson, Sam, 414
Gelbard, Robert S., 250
General Electric, 75, 100
Geneva Convention, 442
Geneva Protocol, 331, 442
Genscher, Dietrich, 278, 342
Gephardt, Richard, 45, 50, 205, 208, 210
Gephardt Amendment, 19
Gergen, David, 478
Germany: and Berlin Wall, 335; and Conventional Forces in Europe Treaty, 331; and economy, 48; and military, 343; and nuclear weapons, 328; and Persian Gulf War, 434; and Soviet Union, 316; and unification, 296, 338–41, 342, 343; and Yugoslavia, 275, 278–79, 291. *See also* East Germany
Gerson, Stuart, 204
Gilbert, Martin, 146
Gilman, Benjamin, 209
Gingrich, Newt, 280
Giroldi, Moises, 178, 179
Glaspie, April, 98, 99–100, 105, 106, 107 n.12, 108 n.21, 109 n.26, 110 n.36, 496
Global Partnership Plan of Action, 50

Goldstein, Martin E., 313–34, 349, 350, 353, 359, 360, 361, 362, 364, 365
Goldwater, Barry, 378
Gompert, David, 292–93
Goodpaster, Andrew, 361
Gorbachev, Mikhail: and Arab-Israeli conflict, 117; and arms control, 317, 318, 362–63; and Bush, 260, 296, 317; and chemical weapons, 331; and China, 84; and Communism, 314; and Conference on Security and Cooperation in Europe, 343; and Conventional Forces in Europe Treaty, 342; and coup, 315; and Cuba, 188; and Eastern Europe, 316; and East Germany, 338; and Europe, 337; and German unification, 340; and Latin America, 175; and Madrid Peace Conference, 130; and Malta Summit, 317, 340; and military, 324, 330, 334; and nuclear testing, 360; and Panama, 180; and United Nations, 262
Gore, Albert, 38, 375
Grassley, Charles, 211
Gray, Robert, 476
Great Britain: and Arab-Israeli conflict, 117; and Bosnia, 279; and Conventional Forces in Europe Treaty, 331; and Cuba, 251; and Falklands, 471; and Germany, 316, 341; and Iraq, 508; and Kurds, 509, 515; and Persian Gulf War, 544; and Yugoslavia, 294
Greene, Harold, 204, 205
Gregg, Don, 81, 82–83
Grenada, 471
G-7 Economic Summit, 24, 25–26, 32
Guatemala, 228
Gulf of Tonkin Resolution, 207, 211
Gunter, Michael M., 507–16, 521, 522, 524, 525, 546–47
Gures, Dogan, 512
Gutman, Roy W., 291–94, 298, 299, 303, 305–6
Guzelaydin, Hussein, 510

Haas, Richard, 117, 140, 151–55, 157, 160, 164, 169–70
Haiti, 224, 228, 229, 230, 232, 261, 263
Halabja, 510

Haley, Edward P., 91–106, 153, 169, 544–45
Haley, Robert W., 528–34, 540, 542
Halliburton, 423
Hamdoon, Nizar, 103
Hamilton, Lee, 96, 99, 100, 106, 110 n.36, 208, 210
Hamilton-Gephardt resolution, 208, 210, 211
Harahan, Joseph P., 335–46, 359
Harkin, Tom, 206
Harris, Joseph, 370
Hart, Peter, 476
Hashemites, 509
Hashimoto, Ryutaro, 64
Hassan, king of Morocco, 483
Hatch, Orin, 209
Hatfield, Mark, 199, 211
Havel, Vaclav, 343
Hawke, Robert, 70
Haynes, Ulric, 290, 298, 302, 309
Heimbach, Daniel R., 441–54, 502–3
Helms, Jesse, 179, 253, 307, 377, 467
Helms-Burton Act, 187, 191, 225, 253
Helsinki Final Act, 342, 345
Hill and Knowlton, 476
Hills, Carla: appointment of, 46, 47; background of, 46; and cabinet nomination, 373–74, 376; and Canada, 221; and European Community, 21; and free trade, 47; and GATT (Uruguay Round), 20, 51–52, 53; and Korea, 78–80; and retaliation, 47, 48; and Super 301, 66; and trade, 63–65, 73, 85, 87
Hoar, Joseph, 265
Hodel, Donald, 371, 372
Hollings, Ernest, 381, 385
Hong Kong, 75, 82
Hosokawa, Morihiro, 54–55
Howard Air Force Base, 178
Hughes, G. Philip, 226–30, 240
Hughes, Philip, 232
Humphrey, Hubert, 372
Hungary, 280, 316, 335, 338, 356
Hurd, Douglas, 146, 341
Hussein, king of Jordan, 125, 140, 491, 493, 502
Hussein, Saddam, 85–86; and aggression, 447, 449, 450, 453; and Arab Cooperation Council, 108 n.22; and Arab-Israeli conflict, 123,

494, 495, 500; and Bush, 85–86, 93, 96, 108 n.23, 143, 145–46, 198, 199, 202, 203, 205, 206, 207, 260, 443, 468, 469, 473; and Bush just war doctrine, 443, 446, 447; and character, 145, 146; and chemical weapons, 497–98, 543; and deceit, 93–94, 104, 490, 493, 502; and economy, 92; and Egypt, 164; goals of, 490; and Hitler, 477, 487–88; and human rights, 94; and Iran-Iraq War, 99; and Israel, 125, 491; and justification, 448; and Kelly, 98; and Kurds, 512; and Kuwait, 468, 487; and leadership, 138; and motivation, 92–93; and Noriega, 176; and nuclear weapons, 477; and Persian Gulf War, 125; pre-war policy towards, 91–106, 153, 170; and rhetoric, 143; and Schultz, 103; and strategy, 497–98; survival of, 468, 469; and terrorism, 498; and weapons, 104–5, 144. *See also* Iraq

Husseini, Faisal, 130
Hutchings, Robert L., 337, 338
Hu Yaobang, 83
Hyde, Henry, 179

Iacocca, Lee, 12
Ibrahim, Izat, 510
Immigration and Naturalization Service v. Chadha, 214 n.6
India, 9, 19, 48
Indyk, Martin, 117
Intermediate-range Nuclear Forces (INF) Treaty, 333, 336–37
International Atomic Energy Agency (IAEA), 332
International Monetary Fund, 33, 284
Intifada, 120, 124, 132, 134
Iran, 94, 100, 101, 105–6, 153, 501; and Kurds, 507, 513, 514, 515, 516
Iran-Contra, 101, 379
Iran-Iraq War, 94, 95, 99, 101–2, 103, 167, 333
Iraq, 91; and Arab-Israeli conflict, 123, 124; and balance of power, 501, 503, 513, 524; and Central Intelligence Agency, 496, 497–99; and chemical weapons, 331, 510, 511; and economy, 102, 143, 507; and Egypt, 164; importance of, 153; and Iran, 501; and Israel, 123, 124, 162, 164, 498; and Kurds, 507–16, 546–47; and Kuwait, 196, 468; and military, 499, 501; misunderstanding of, 92–106, 167; and nuclear weapons, 477; and oil, 140; post-war policy towards, 154; pre-war policy towards, 91–106, 153, 170; and Reagan, 473; sanctions against, 143, 144, 147, 154–55, 198, 202, 204, 209, 210, 450–51, 468, 469, 473, 474, 476, 488, 498; and Soviet Union, 100; and United Nations, 262. *See also* Hussein, Saddam; Iran-Iraq War

Islamic Conference, 490, 491
Israel, 113–36, 151–52; and defense policy, 168; and Hussein, 491; and Iraq, 123, 124, 162, 164, 498; and Madrid Peace Conference, 501; and media, 494–95; and Persian Gulf War, 161–62, 493, 494–95, 498, 500–501; and United States, 170–71

Israeli-Egyptian Treaty, 113

Jackson-Vanik Amendment, 185, 191 n.3
Janow, Merit, 50, 55
Japan: agreement with, 50–51; and agriculture, 54–55, 62 n.76; and Asia, 71; and Congress, 48; and economy, 24–25, 33, 48, 64; and foreign aid, 71; and GATT (Uruguay Round), 52, 53, 54–55, 62 n.76; and Keiretsu, 22, 24, 64, 75; and Mosbacher, 47–48; and nuclear weapons, 328; and public opinion, 47; and Super 301, 67; and trade, 9, 10–12, 19, 22, 24–25, 26, 28, 31, 33, 36, 44, 46, 49–51, 54, 55, 57, 64, 67, 75–76, 81, 232; and World Trade Organization, 31
Jarvis, Robert, 105–6
Jeffords, James, 208–9
Jeremiah, David, 139
Jerusalem, 123, 162–63. *See also* East Jerusalem
Jews: American, 116, 127, 128, 156, 157, 158–59, 160, 170, 224; Soviet, 114, 121, 123, 125, 126, 152, 158. *See also* American Israel Public

Affairs Committee; Israel
Johnson, James Turner, 442, 447, 456 n.16, 457 nn.24, 45
Johnson, Lyndon B.: and cabinet nominations, 375; and decisions, 261, 271 n.6; and Israel, 162, 163; and military, 142, 147, 153, 394; and Tower, 378; and war, 472
Johnston, J. Bennett, 208–9
Jones, Charles O., 385
Jones, David, 202–3
Jordan, 125, 128, 130, 491, 493, 495, 501–2
Jordan-Israeli Peace Treaty, 164
Juster, Kenneth I., 295–301, 302–3, 307–8

Kagan, Robert, 280
Kaiser, Karl, 339
Kanter, Arnold, 349–54, 356, 357
Kantor, Mickey, 79
Karadjic, Radovan, 281, 282
Kassebaum, Nancy, 384, 385
Kazakhstan, 326
Keiretsu, 22, 24, 64, 75. *See also* Japan
Kelly, John, 96–98, 105, 106, 109 n.25
Kelly, Thomas, 474
Kemp, Jack, 158
Kennan, Sy, 119
Kennedy, Edward, 199, 202
Kennedy, John F., 243, 244, 372, 394, 409, 472
Kerrey, Robert, 199, 202
Khamisiyah, 537, 538, 540, 541
Kilberg, Bobbie Greene, 156–60, 170
Kimmitt, Robert, 181
King, James D., 369–86, 420, 431
Kissinger, Henry, 129, 393, 402, 428
Klein, George, 159
Kleindienst, Richard, 374
Klurfeld, James M., 355–58, 359, 428–30
Kohl, Helmut, 340, 342, 343
Korea, 78–80, 86, 399
Korean War, 154, 262
Kosovo, 280, 284
Krauthammer, Charles, 397–98
Kristol, William, 280
Kurds, 262, 499, 507–16, 521, 524, 525, 546–47
Kuwait, 98, 140, 142, 161, 196, 443, 446–47, 448, 468, 477, 487, 488

Laboa, Sebastian, 181
Lake, Anthony, 398
Lantos, Tom, 94, 97, 98, 99
LaRocque, Jules N., 185–91, 223, 240
Latin America, 32, 63, 175, 185–86, 187, 188, 189, 190, 191, 224, 225, 226–30, 234–35, 237–40, 250. *See also specific countries*
League of Nations, 400, 508
Lebanon, 134
Lee, Burton J., III, 535–36
Lee Teng-hui, 81
Levin, Carl, 202, 380
Levy, David, 122, 128
Lewis, Anthony, 279
Lewis, Sam, 162
Libya, 121, 153, 176
Li Lanquing, 74, 75
Lilley, James, 74, 80, 81–86
Lilley, Peter, 251
Limited Test Ban Treaty, 333
Longrigg, Stephen H., 508
Lubrani, Uri, 116
Lugar, Richard, 200, 201
Lynch, John E., 410–11

Mack, Connie, 248
Mackenzie, G. Calvin, 372
Madigan, Edward, 46, 54
Madrid Peace Conference, 113, 126, 127, 128, 129–34, 164–66, 171, 495, 501
Mahathir bin Mohamad, 70
Major, John, 117, 515
Malaysia, 70
Malta Summit, 317, 340
Market Strategies, 476
Markovic, Ante, 299
Marshall, Ray, 371, 377
Marshall Plan, 303–4, 305
Massey, Joe, 85
Mavroules, Nicholas, 414
McClure, Frederick, 385
McCormack, Richard T., 20, 22–26, 27, 31, 33, 36, 38
McCurdy, David, 467
McGinnis, John O., 27–29, 30, 36
McGovern, George, 409
McMillan, Robert, 240
McNamara, Robert, 364, 372
McSherry, Ray, 21
Medellin cartel, 181–82

Index

Media: and Big Three automakers, 56; and Bosnia, 307; and Israel, 494–95; and Japan, 63, 64; and Panama, 179, 181, 240; and Persian Gulf War, 264, 307–8, 444, 452, 475, 477, 478–79, 480, 494–95; and Somalia, 264, 307; and Soviet Union, 315; and Tower, 383; and trade, 6. *See also* Public opinion
Meese, Edwin, 374, 376, 384, 387 n.21
Meguid, Ismat Abdul, 119
Menier, Jose Antonio Rodriguez, 247
Metzenbaum, Howard, 93
Metzger, Leigh Ann, 444, 458
Mexico, 221, 227, 228, 231–32
Meyers, Jan, 99
Meyerson, Christopher C., 43–57, 63–64, 66, 87
Miami Summit of the Americas, 227, 232, 235
Michel-Solarz resolution, 208, 209, 211
Middle East, 91–106, 113–36, 146; and balance of power, 501, 503, 513; El Reedy on, 164–66; and Europe, 299; Haas on, 151–55; and Kurds, 514; and Persian Gulf War, 291, 499; Peters on, 161–63; and U.S. forces, 395. *See also* Arab-Israeli conflict; Arab states; *specific countries*
Miller, Aaron, 117
Milosevic, Slobodan, 281, 287, 293, 298–99, 305
MIRV, 365–66
Missile Defense Act, 323
Missile Technology Control Regime (MTCR), 353
Mitchell, George, 198, 201, 206, 208, 221
Mitchell-Nunn proposal, 208, 211
Mitterrand, François, 117, 343
Miyazawa, Kiichi, 11, 51
Modai, Yitzhak, 126
Mogadishu, 263, 266, 268
Mohamed, Ali Mahdi, 263
Montenegro, 278
Mosbacher, Robert, 46, 47–48, 49, 76, 220, 221, 229, 231–33
Most favored nation status, 38, 65, 84
Movsesian, Mark L., 34, 35
Moynihan, Daniel P., 285
Mubarak, Hosni: and Arab-Israeli conflict, 117, 119–20, 121, 124, 164, 165; and Bush, 159; and Iraqi invasion, 491; and Persian Gulf War, 140, 197, 483
Mulroney, Brian, 73, 221–22, 291
Murphy, Richard, 101, 102, 169
Muslims, 277, 278, 280, 282, 300, 305
Mutual Balanced Force Reductions (MBFR), 330, 352

National Council of Churches, 470
National Jewish Coalition, 158
National Religious Broadcasters, 445
National Security Council, 95, 142, 226, 265, 349, 470, 513
National Security Review 3, 319
NATO: and arms control, 424; and Conventional Forces in Europe, 330; and Conventional Forces in Europe Treaty, 352; and Eastern/Central Europe, 337; and Eastern Europe, 330; enlargement of, 355–56, 359; and Germany, 316–17, 340, 341, 342; and international system, 403; and nuclear weapons, 329; and peacekeeping, 330; and Somalia, 265, 270; and Warsaw Pact, 317; and Yugoslavia, 279, 281, 293
Netanyahu, Benjamin, 168
Newman, Robert A., 537–38, 541–42
Ney, Edward N., 220–22, 228
Nicaragua, 176, 186–87, 189, 191, 226, 227, 234, 261, 317
Nimeiry, Jaafar, 116
Nisayeh, Muhammed Hasi, 165
Nixon, Richard M., 74; and cabinet nominations, 372, 374, 375, 387 n.13; and defense policy, 393, 401, 402; and military force structure, 394; and war, 472; and War Powers Resolution, 194
Nofal, Mamdouh, 133–34
Noriega, Manuel Antonio, 175–79, 180, 181–82, 195, 238, 239, 240, 466–67
North American Free Trade Agreement (NAFTA), 5, 8–10, 12, 19, 28–29, 32, 63, 220–21, 228, 231
North Atlantic Cooperation Council, 336
Northern Telecom, 75

North Korea, 86, 333
Novak, Robert, 383
Nuclear Suppliers Group, 332, 353
Nunn, Sam: and Persian Gulf War, 143, 201, 202, 208, 209–10, 211, 218 n.61, 449, 450, 498; and Tower, 381, 382, 390 n.71

Oakar, Mary Rose, 414
Obey, David, 210
Office of Public Liaison, 156, 157–58, 159
Office of U.S. Trade Representative, 46, 48, 55
Omnibus Trade and Competitiveness Act, 9, 20, 45, 48, 49
Open Skies Treaty, 331, 336
Operation Blue Spoon, 180
Operation Greyhound, 246
Operation Just Cause, 180, 181, 195, 260, 270
Operation Opera, 116
Operation Provide Comfort, 262, 264, 516, 521
Operation Provide Hope, 262, 318
Operation Restore Hope, 259, 265, 266, 267, 269
Operation Staunch, 102
Organization of African Unity, 270
Organization of American States (OAS), 177, 181, 182, 228, 230, 244, 261, 263
Organization of American States Democracy Initiative, 228
Ortega, Daniel, 234
Orthodox Church, 281
Oslo Agreement, 161, 162, 164, 495
Overseas Private Investment Corporation (OPIC), 72
Ozal, Turgut, 512, 514, 515
Ozceri, Tugay, 511

Pach, Chester, 375
Pakistan, 101
Palestine Liberation Organization (PLO), 113, 117, 119, 120, 121, 122, 123, 128, 129, 130, 132, 494, 495. *See also* Arab-Israeli conflict; Arafat, Yasir
Palestinians, 114, 117, 120, 121, 122, 126, 128, 130, 131–32, 134, 151, 168, 291

Panama, 175–82, 194–96, 213, 228, 238–40, 260, 263, 270, 302, 471
Panama Canal, 176, 181, 195
Panamanian Defense Forces, 177, 178, 179, 180, 195
Panamanian National Assembly, 195
Papaioannou, George, 304, 307
Patten, Chris, 82
Peace of Paris, 335
Pearl Harbor attack, 213
Pearson, Charles, 47
Pell, Claiborne, 199
Pentagon. *See* Department of Defense
Peres, Shimon, 115, 119, 120, 121, 122, 134, 162, 168
Perez, Carlos Andres, 232–33
Perot, Ross, 4, 22, 38, 57, 481
Persian Gulf, 395
Persian Gulf War: and Arab-Israeli conflict, 114, 115, 116, 123, 124–25, 133, 161, 494, 495, 500, 501–2; and Arab states, 487–89, 490–92, 493–94; and biological weapons, 522, 529; and budget, 421–22; and Bush's leadership, 137–48, 483–86; and casualties, 524–25; and Central Intelligence Agency, 496–99; and chemical weapons, 522, 528, 531, 532, 537, 538, 540, 543; and collective security, 400–401; cost of, 198; and deployment, 434–35; disagreements on, xviii; and El Reedy, 490–91; end of, 167–68, 433, 498–99, 501, 503, 512–14; Haas on, 153–54; and illness, 521–23, 525–26, 528–34, 535–36, 537–38, 539–40, 541–45; and Israel, 161–62, 493, 494–95, 498, 500–501; and Kurds, 510; and Madrid Peace Conference, 495; and media, 307–8, 475; and Perez, 233; and public opinion, 228, 444, 446, 468, 469–70, 471–72, 474–75, 476–77, 478–80; reasons for, 152–53, 477, 484, 513, 524; and Russia, 317; typicality of, 429; and United Nations, 167, 262; and United States, 152–53; and War Powers Resolution, 196–213, 238–39
Peru, 228
Peters, Joan, 161–63
Pfau, Richard, 375, 376

Philippines, 260
Phillips, Kevin, 472
Phillips, William G., 380
Pickering, Thomas, 86, 116
Pilgrimage of Peace to the Middle East, 447, 451
Poland, 335, 338, 356
Politics: and Bush, 484; and human rights, 39; and military, 408, 416, 423, 429; and Persian Gulf War, 471, 472, 475–76, 484, 513; and trade, 22–24, 39. *See also* Democratic party; Election, of 1988; Election, of 1992; Republican party
Pol Pot, 86
Pomper, George, 385
Poos, Jacques, 299
Popular Democratic Front for the Liberation of Palestine (PDFLP), 133
Porter, Roger, 43
Post-Ministerial Conference, 69
Powell, Colin: as advisor, 261, 297; and Base Force Concept, 395, 397; and Bosnia, 292; and defense policy, 395, 397, 403; and Panama, 176, 178, 179, 180, 181; and Persian Gulf War, 139, 143, 144, 147, 475, 485, 497, 524; and Somalia, 265, 267, 269, 270, 294
President/presidency: and advisors, 271 n.5; and Congress, 369; and Cuba, 189; and economy, 6, 46; and foreign policy, 193–94; and industry advisory groups, 63–64; and jobs, 22, 37–38; and Middle East policy, 151; power of, 141; and protectionism, 15, 34; and rhetoric, 5, 6, 34–35; and trade, 4–5, 6, 7, 12, 14–15, 27–28, 34–35, 37; and War Powers Resolution, 203, 204–5, 238; and World Trade Organization, 36
President's Conference of Major National Jewish Organizations, 116, 158
Proxmire, William, 374
Pryce, William T., 228, 234–36, 239
Public opinion: and Bosnia, 292; and Cheney, 485–86; and Cuba, 224; and drugs, 466; and economy, 46, 50, 55–56; and election of 1988, 466; and foreign assistance, 305; and Japan, 47, 55–56; and jobs, 12, 37–38, 39; and New World Order, 481; and Noriega, 467; and Panama, 179, 181, 182; and Persian Gulf War, 228, 444, 446, 468, 469–70, 471–72, 474–75, 476–77, 478–80, 481 n.11, 485–86, 488, 489; and Somalia, 259, 269; and Tower, 383; and trade, 4, 14, 37–38, 46, 55–56; and United States, 465; and Yugoslavia, 279, 287. *See also* Media
Punta del Este Declaration, 52

Qaddafi, Muammar, 176, 178
Quandt, William, 478
Quayle, Dan, 124, 139

Rabin, Yitzhak, 115, 119, 120, 121, 122, 134, 151, 160, 168, 493
Radway, Laurence Ingram, 465–81, 483
Ramlawi, Nabil, 119
Rauner, Robert E., 413
Ravenal, Earl C., 391–404, 421, 427, 428, 431–32, 434
Reagan, Ronald: and arms control, 334, 348; and Bush, 6, 12, 45, 54, 119, 121, 138, 186, 238, 261, 270, 323, 334, 409, 471; and cabinet, 101, 111 n.50, 371–72, 374, 377, 387 nn.13, 21, 388 n.37; and Canada, 220, 228; and Caribbean, 228–29; and character, 138; and Congress, 45, 193; and Cuba, 189, 244–45; and decision-making, 261, 270; and economy, 25; and federalism, 276; and foreign *vs.* domestic policy, 101; and free trade, 5; and GATT (Uruguay Round), 51, 52; and Grenada, 471; and Hussein, 93; and Iran, 101; and Iran-Contra, 101; and Iraq, 101–4, 153, 473; and Israel, 116, 119, 121; and Japan, 49, 50, 54; and Jewish community, 158; and Latin America, 186, 226, 260–61; and managed trade, 57; and military, 323, 362, 408, 409, 410; and military budget, 319, 361; and military force structure, 394;

and Nicaragua, 189; and Noriega, 176, 238; and protectionism, 5; and Soviet Union breakup, 277; and Tower, 379, 383–84; and trade, 5, 6, 45, 47, 49, 50, 228; and war, 470, 472
Reilly, Bill, 221
Republican National Convention, 12–13, 44
Republican party: and Bush, 260, 443, 472, 475; and cabinet nominations, 372; and defense policy, 428; and federalism, 276; and government, 29; and Israel, 127; and Persian Gulf War, 201, 208, 210, 211, 443, 475; and protectionism, 34; and Tower, 378; and trade, 5, 7, 13–14, 29, 37; and United Nations, 280
Rice Council for Market Development, 49
Rice Millers' Association, 49, 50
Richardson, Elmo, 375
Riddlesperger, James W., Jr., 369–86
Ridge, Tom, 14
Rollins, Ed, 472
Roman Catholicism, 277, 281
Romania, 121, 316, 335, 338
Rooney, Andy, 479
Roosevelt, Franklin D., 261, 270
Rosenthal, Abe, 477
Ross, Dennis, 117
Rostow, Eugene, 356
Russia, 282; and arms control, 318, 324–25, 353, 355, 359–60; and chemical weapons, 331; and Communism, 314, 336; and Conventional Forces in Europe Treaty, 331; and economy, 32–33, 284; and International Monetary Fund, 33; and military preparedness, 319, 321–22, 324, 326; and NATO, 355–56; and nuclear materials, 357–58; and nuclear testing, 333; and Open Skies Treaty, 331; and Persian Gulf War, 317; and Strategic Arms Reduction Treaty, 324–25; and Strategic Arms Reduction Treaty II, 325, 353; and United States, 317; and World Bank, 33. *See also* Soviet Union

Russian Federation, 262
Rwanda, 269

Sabah, Saud Nasir Al-, 487–89, 500
Sabato, Larry, 382–83
Sadat, Anwar, 113, 161
Safire, William, 279
Sahnoun, Mohamed, 263, 270
Salinas, Carlos, 227, 228, 232
Sandinistas, 176, 186, 187, 227, 234, 238. *See also* Nicaragua
Santiago Declaration, 182, 228
Sarajevo, 294
Sarbanes, Paul, 200, 204
Sargent, John G., 373
Sasser, Jim, 407
Saudi Arabia: and Madrid Peace Conference, 166; and Persian Gulf War, 142, 144, 161, 196–97, 201, 204, 468, 474, 475, 483, 497; and U.S. security, 101
Schindler, Alexander, 127
Schlesinger, James, 202
Schultz, George M., 101, 102–3, 109 n.25, 117, 238, 470
Schultz, Kathryn M., 359–63, 364, 365–66
Schwartzkopf, Norman, 143, 144, 475, 477, 513, 524
Scowcroft, Brent: as advisor, 261, 297; and China, 84, 85; and Congress, 145; and defense policy, 425; and Eastern Europe, 338; and Israel, 117; and Jewish community, 160, 170; and Panama, 179, 180, 181; and Persian Gulf War, 91, 139, 142, 143, 145, 473–74; and Somalia, 265, 270; and Soviet Union, 303–4
SCUD missiles, 494, 495, 497, 501
Section 301, 48, 49
Segev, Samuel, 113–36, 157, 164, 168, 170–71, 493–95, 498, 500, 501–2
Senate, 361, 369, 370–86. *See also* Congress
Serbia: and Baker, 293; and Croatia, 278–79; and Dayton process, 300; and economy, 284; and Germany, 278; greater, 305; and nationalism, 281; and New World Order, 263; and Tito, 280; and Vukovar, 307;

Index 565

and Yugoslavia, 277
Shafi, Haidar Abdul, 130, 131–32
Shamir, Yitzhak: and American Jewish community, 170; and Arab-Israeli conflict, 115, 117–18, 120, 121, 122, 123, 124, 125, 126–27, 128, 129, 130, 131, 133, 134; and Bush, 126–27, 128, 129, 130, 133, 134, 157, 159–60, 165, 168, 170, 493; and Hussein of Jordan, 502; and Persian Gulf War, 161, 501–2, 502
Shenon, Philip, 539–40, 545
Shevardnadze, Edward, 191 n.3, 340, 341, 351
Shifter, Dick, 85
Shiites, 499, 507, 508, 511, 525
Shoval, Zalman, 125, 126
Silberman, Murray, 167–68
Simes, Dimitri K., 279–80
Simpson, Alan, 93
Six Day War, 162
Slovakia, 284–85
Slovenia, 278, 279, 284, 286, 288 n.8, 293, 305, 336
Smith, Curt, 445
Snyder, Joseph, 252
Solarz, Stephen, 208, 211
Somalia, 259–60, 263–71, 290, 291, 293–94, 295–96, 299, 302, 307
Sorensen, Theodore, 319
South Africa, 252–53
Southeast Asia, 69–70
South Korea, 86
Southwest Asia, 395
Soviet Union: and Arab-Israeli conflict, 117, 121, 165; and arms control, 348, 350–51, 356–57, 362–63; and Baltic states, 341, 342; breakup of, 32, 260, 277, 296, 314–16, 323, 335–36, 345, 350, 391, 424, 425; and captive nations, 277; and Carter Doctrine, 101; and chemical weapons, 331; and Cold War's end, 314; and Communism, 314, 315, 324; and Conventional Forces in Europe Treaty, 342; and Cuba, 185, 187, 188, 189, 223, 227, 244, 245, 247, 250; and Eastern/Central Europe, 337, 338; and Eastern Europe, 316, 353; and East Germany, 335, 339; economic assistance to, 190; and economy, 187, 188, 189, 284, 315; and ethnic groups, 315, 316; and European security, 341; and federalism, 275–76, 282; and German unification, 339, 342, 343; and Germany, 316; and glasnost, 314, 315; and Iraq, 100; and Korea, 399; and Latin America, 175; and Madrid Peace Conference, 132; and media, 315; and Middle East, 101; and military, 319, 325, 339, 340, 342, 343, 350–51; and Nicaragua, 187; and nuclear weapons, 336; and Panama, 180; and perestroika, 188, 315; and Persian Gulf War, 196; and Strategic Arms Reduction Treaty, 351; and trade, 63; and United Nations, 262; and United States, 296, 342, 360, 393; and Yugoslavia, 275, 293. *See also* Commonwealth of Independent States; Russia; Russian Federation
START. *See* Strategic Arms Reduction Treaty
State Department: and Cuba, 248, 251; and ethnic cleansing, 292; and Latin America, 227; and Panama, 176, 177; and Persian Gulf War, 144, 148, 470; and Somalia, 267
Stein, Jacob, 116, 127, 159
Strategic Arms Limitation Treaty (SALT), 348
Strategic Arms Reduction Treaty, 260, 324–25, 329, 333, 348, 351–52, 360
Strategic Arms Reduction Treaty II, 325, 326–27, 336, 353, 365, 426, 427
Strategic Defense Initiative, 323
Strauss, Lewis, 375–76, 384
Structural Impediments Initiative (SII), 24, 25, 33, 51, 64, 66, 67, 75
Suez War, 494
Sullivan, Louis, 377
Sunnis, 507
Sununu, John, 134, 139, 156–57, 160, 385, 442, 444, 458
Super 301, 19, 24, 28, 35, 48, 49, 66–67
Supreme Court, 214 n.6

Sweden, 124
Syria, 114–15, 121, 134, 164, 165–66, 499, 513

Taiwan, 75, 81, 82, 83
Takesita, Noboru, 25
Talabani, Jalal, 509–10, 511, 513, 516
Talbert, Melvin, 447
Tannanbaum, Duane, 193–214
Technology Competitiveness Act, 411
Teeter, Robert, 466
Thatcher, Margaret, 82, 142, 146, 197, 343, 471, 496
Third World, 25, 71–72, 327, 328, 333, 334
Thomas, Clarence, 390 n.70
Thornburgh, Dick, 10
Thurman, Maxwell, 178
Thurmond, Strom, 209, 218 n.59
Tibi, Ahmed, 119
Timmerman, Kenneth, 100, 101, 102
Tito, Marshal, 276, 284, 294, 298
Tokyo Declaration, 10, 76
Tower, John, 369, 376–86, 388 n.43, 389 n.69, 390 n.71, 420, 421, 431
Towery, Ken, 379
Trade Act (1974), 63, 191 n.3
Trade Act (1988), 19
Trade Promotion Coordinating Committee, 49
Treasury Department, 48
Treaty of Sevres, 507–8
Treaty of Union, 339
Treaty on Non-Proliferation of Nuclear Weapons, 332
Truman, Harry, 472
Tudjman, Franco, 281, 287
Turkey, 23, 101, 507, 508, 509, 511–12, 513, 514–15
Turner, Stansfield, 105
TV Marti, 247
Two Plus Four Meetings, 341

Ukraine, 326, 331, 336
Ullman, John E., 275–88, 291, 297–98, 299, 303–4, 305, 307, 309, 420, 423, 431, 432, 437
UNITAF, 267
United Methodist Church, 447
United Nations: and Arab-Israeli conflict, 118, 120, 152; and Bosnia, 300; and Bush, 142, 158, 165, 214, 262–63, 271 n.1, 297, 392, 397, 448, 484; and collective security, 321, 397, 400; and Cuba, 250, 252; and intervention, 287; and Iraq, 262; and Jews, 158; and just war doctrine, 442, 487; and Kurds, 515, 516; and Persian Gulf War, 167, 196, 202, 205, 206, 207, 208, 212, 214, 262, 267, 448, 468, 477, 484, 487, 499, 503, 513; Resolution 242, 118, 129, 131; Resolution 338, 131; Resolution 660, 487; Resolution 678, 207, 208, 488; Resolution 687, 489; Resolution 688, 516; and Rwanda, 269; and Somalia, 263–64, 265, 266, 267, 268, 269, 270, 295, 296; and United States, 267, 269, 270, 280, 399, 400
United Nations Commission on Human Rights, 250
United Nations Protection Force (UNPROFOR), 280
United States: and Arab-Israeli conflict, 133; and arms control, 323–34, 348, 356–57, 359–60; and Asia, 71, 73; and bipolarity, 402; and Bosnia, 299, 306; and business, 94; and captive nations, 276–77; and Castro, 246; and chemical weapons, 331–32; and China, 74, 436–37; and Cold War, 22, 249, 276, 424–25; and collective security, 397, 398–99; and Conference on Security and Cooperation in Europe, 343, 344; and Cuba, 185, 188–89, 191, 223, 243–45, 248–49, 364; and defense conversion, 409–17, 423–24, 429; and defense policy, 424–25, 431–32; and democracy, 280; and drugs, 176, 179; and Eastern Europe, 316; and economy, 6, 283, 285–86, 411, 413, 415, 480; and Egypt, 165; and energy, 413, 431; and ethnic blocs, 277, 279, 283; and ethnic cleansing, 292; and European security, 341–42, 424; and exports, 53–54; and federalism, 276, 283, 285–86, 288; and foreign aid, 71; and German unification, 339, 340; and Good Neighbor Policy, 187; and infrastructure, 413, 431; and

interest groups, 27, 28, 55; and international system, 403; and intervention, 279–80; and Iran, 94; and Iran-Iraq War, 94; and Iraq, 94, 96, 102, 170; and Israel, 162, 170–71; and Japan, 50–51; and jobs, 8–9, 22, 23, 27; and just war doctrine, 442; and Korea, 399; and Kurds, 509, 510, 512, 515; and Latin America, 187, 189–90; and lobbyists, 27; and Madrid Peace Conference, 132, 151; and manufacture, 4; and Mexico, 227, 228; and military, 6, 71, 189, 340, 342, 404; and military bases, 415–17; and military budget, 361–62, 432, 435–36; and military conversion, 415; and military deployment, 434–35; and military doctrine, 403; and military force structure, 394, 401, 432, 434; and military industry, 409–17; and military intervention, 309; and military preparedness, 318–34, 321–22; and military (Southern Command), 177, 178, 179; and multilateralism, 48; and multipolarity, 392–93, 402; and nationalism, 27; and NATO, 355–56; and New World Order, 404; and nuclear testing, 333; and nuclear weapons, 324–30, 332–33; and oil, 401; and Open Skies Treaty, 331; and Organization of American States, 263; and Persian Gulf War, 152–53, 267, 320, 335; and post-Cold War relations, 152–53; and public opinion, 465; and recognition, 277; and Russia, 317; and Somalia, 264, 267, 269, 270, 299; and Soviet Union, 190, 296, 323, 342, 360, 399; and Strategic Arms Reduction Treaty, 324–25; and Strategic Arms Reduction Treaty II, 325; and terrorism, 403; and trade, 4, 8–9, 22, 23, 27, 30, 37; and transparency, 23, 24; and unilateralism, 399; and United Nations, 267, 269, 270, 280, 399, 400; and weapons of mass destruction, 320, 332; and weapons suppliers, 362; and Yugoslavia, 275, 277, 279, 280, 286, 298–301. *See also specific agencies and leaders*

United States-Asia Environmental Partnership, 73
United States-Canada Environmental Bill, 221
United States-Canada Free Trade Agreement, 228, 231
United States Commodity Credit Corporation, 102
Uno, Sosuke, 51
UNOSOM II, 268, 269, 270
USS *Stark*, 99
Uthman, Mahmud, 512

Vance, Cyrus, 357
Vatican, 181
Venezuela, 224
Veterans Administration, 525–27, 537, 538
Vienna Document, 345
Vietnam, 317
Vietnam War, 194, 197, 200, 202, 207, 210, 280, 281, 287

Walsh, Thomas, 373, 384
War Powers Resolution, 193–214, 214 n.6, 238–39, 499; defined, 194
Warren, Charles B., 372, 373, 376, 384, 387 n.15
Warsaw Pact, 317, 330, 334, 339, 343, 352, 424, 434
Washington Institute for Near Eastern Policy, 117
Washington Summit, 342
Watanabe, Kozo, 76
Watt, James, 371, 377
Webster, William H., 176, 178, 237–40, 495
Weidenbaum, Murray: *Small Wars, Big Defense*, 410
Weinberger, Caspar, 116, 238, 408, 470
Weiss, Ted, 414
Weizman, Ezer, 119
West Bank, 114, 118, 119, 120, 121, 123, 125, 133, 164
Wethington, Olin L., 30–33, 35
Weyrich, Paul, 380–81, 382
Wilson, Charles E., 372, 386 n.10
Wilson, Woodrow, 270, 277, 282, 507, 525

Wirthlin Group, 476
Wisner, Frank, 264
Woerner, Frederick, 178
Wolfowitz, Paul, 264, 303, 307
World Bank, 33
World Federation of Public Health Associations, 251
World Trade Organization, 21, 23, 31, 35, 36
World War I, 400
World War II, 210, 213, 316, 443
Wormuth, Francis, 218 n.55
Wright, Jim, 389 n.69

Yeltsin, Boris, 315, 325, 327, 328, 334, 360
Yetiv, Steve, 137–48, 154
Yeutter, Clayton, 46–47, 49, 50, 53, 54

Yom Kippur War, 129
Yugoslavia: breakup of, 275–76, 316, 336; and Dayton process, 300; and economy, 281, 283–84; and ethnic cleansing, 294, 300; and Europe, 299–300; and federalism, 275, 281, 291, 299; makeup of, 277–78; and New World Order, 263; and Slovenia, 305; and Tito, 276, 284, 294, 298; and United States, 297–301; and Wilson, 525. *See also specific states*

Zacks, Gordon, 159
Zevari, Hoshyar, 511
Zhao Ziyang, 83
Zimmerman, Warren, 304

About the Editors and Contributors

SAUD NASIR AL-SABAH served as Kuwait's Ambassador to the United States from 1982–1992. Following the Gulf War, he returned to Kuwait and was Minister of Information (1992–1998) and Minister of Oil (1998–2001).

JAY R. AVELLA is a professor and former Academic Vice President at Capella University in Minneapolis, Minnesota. He served in the U.S. Navy, retiring in 1995 at the rank of captain. Just prior to retirement, he was attached to the staff of the secretary of defense and served as a member of the Crisis Management Group for the Persian Gulf War.

SUSUMU AWANOHARA served as Washington, DC, Bureau Chief for the *Far Eastern Economic Review* from 1989 to 1994, capping a 20-year career with the journal that included assignments in Hong Kong, Indonesia, and Singapore. Following his Washington posting, he was a visiting scholar at the Woodrow Wilson Center and is currently an adviser to Nikko Research.

DAVID G. BLANCHARD is a former senior administrator at Hofstra University. He is a graduate of the U.S. Military Academy at West Point, and he is a retired Colonel (O6) from the U.S. Army Reserves.

MEENA BOSE is Associate Professor of Political Science at the United States Military Academy. She taught at Hofstra University from 1996–2000. She is the author of *Shaping and Signaling Presidential Policy: The National Security Decision Making of Eisenhower and Kennedy* (Texas A&M University Press, 1998).

DOUGLAS G. BRINKLEY is Director of the Eisenhower Center for American Studies and Associate Professor of History at the University of New Orleans. He is the author of numerous books and journal articles, including *FDR and the*

Creation of the United Nations (1997), *The Majic Bus: An American Odyssey* (1993), and *Dean Acheson: The Cold War Years, 1953–1971* (1992).

DOUGLAS A. BROOK is Dean of the School of Business and Public Policy at the Naval Postgraduate School at Monterey, CA. He served as Assistant Secretary of the Army (Financial Management) from 1990–1993 and was detailed by President Bush to serve as Acting Director of the U.S. Office of Personnel Management from 1992–1993.

STEPHEN F. BURGESS is Assistant Professor of International Security at the U.S. Air War College. He has been a faculty member at the University of Zambia, Vanderbilt University and Hofstra University. He is the author of *Smallholders and Political Voice in Zimbabwe* (University Press of America, 1997), as well as several journal articles, book chapters and monographs.

RICHARD B. CHENEY is the vice president of the United States. He has served under four U.S. presidents and as Wyoming's sole representative in the U.S. House of Representatives. As Secretary of Defense from 1989 to 1993, he directed Operation Just Cause in Panama and Operation Desert Storm in the Middle East.

PETER B. COLLIS is a practicing physician, university professor, and national adviser on health policy. In 1990 he became Deputy Assistant Secretary of Defense for Medical Readiness, and was responsible for the medical policy of all U.S. forces deployed to Desert Shield and Desert Storm.

DELIA B. CONTI is Associate Professor of Communications at Penn State McKeesport. She is the author of *Free Trade, Fair Trade and Interdependence: The Rhetoric of Presidential Economic Leadership* (1998), as well as several articles on presidential trade rhetoric.

EDWARD J. DERWINSKI is President of Derwinski and Associates. From 1989 to 1992, he was Secretary of the Department of Veterans Affairs; previously, he had served as Administrator of the Veterans Administration, held positions in the State Department, and represented the Fourth District of Illinois in the U.S. House of Representatives from 1959 to 1983.

MICHAEL D'INNOCENZO holds the Harry H. Wachtel Distinguished Teaching Professorship for the Study of Nonviolent Social Change at Hofstra University. A professor of history, he has been a candidate for U.S. Congress and a political columnist for weekly newspapers.

CAROLYN EISENBERG is Associate Professor of History at Hofstra University. She is the author of *Drawing the Line: The American Decision to Divide Germany, 1944–49* (1996). She has published numerous articles on U.S. foreign and nuclear policy.

About the Editors and Contributors

ABDEL RAOUF EL REEDY served as Ambassador of Egypt to the United States from 1984 to 1992. From 1980 to 1983, he was Permanent Representative of Egypt to the United Nations as well as Leader of the Egyptian Delegation to several international organizations and conferences, including GATT and the UN Conference on Disarmament.

DONALD BURNHAM ENSENAT is currently chief of protocol for the State Department. He served in the Bush Administration on the Board of Directors of the Overseas Private Investment Corporation (OPIC) and as U.S. Ambassador to Brunei.

MARK FALCOFF is resident scholar at the American Enterprise Institute. He has taught at the Universities of Illinois, Oregon, and California (Los Angeles), as well as at the U.S. Foreign Service Institute. His most recent books are *A Culture of its Own: Taking Latin America Seriously* (1998) and *The Cuban Revolution and the United States, 1958–1960: A History in Documents* (2001).

STEPHEN P. FARRAR is Director of International Business for Guardian Industries Corp., a leading worldwide manufacturer and fabricator of flat glass products used in automotive and construction industries. Before joining Guardian, he served as Chief of Staff to U.S. Trade Representative Carla Hills and worked in White House under presidents Reagan and Bush.

BERNARD J. FIRESTONE is Professor of Political Science and Dean of the College of Liberal Arts and Sciences at Hofstra University. He is the author of *The Quest for Nuclear Stability* (1982) and editor of *Lyndon Baines Johnson and the Uses of Power* (1988) and *Gerald R. Ford and the Politics of Post–Watergate America* (1993).

HENRIETTA HOLSMAN FORE currently serves as the 37th director of the U.S. Mint. She has served as chairman and CEO of the Holsman Companies, a management and investment company with manufacturing, real estate, and international businesses. In the George Bush administration, she was Assistant Administrator for Private Enterprise (1990–1991) and Assistant Administrator for Asia (1991–1993).

BARBARA HACKMAN FRANKLIN served as the 29th Secretary of Commerce and was the highest ranking woman in the George Bush administration. Currently she is President and CEO of Barbara Franklin Enterprises, an international trade consulting and investment firm headquartered in Washington, DC.

MARTIN E. GOLDSTEIN is Professor of Government and Politics at Widener University. In 1991–1992, he was a William C. Foster Fellow in the Arms Control and Disarmament Agency. Serving in the Bureau of Non-proliferation Policy, he helped devise and implement U.S. policy concerned with preventing the spread of nuclear weapons.

DONALD P. GREGG is Chairman of the Korea Society in New York. He served as Ambassador to the Republic of Korea from 1989 to 1993. As a career CIA officer for more than 30 years, he served in Japan, Burma, Vietnam, and Korea. He was Director of Asian affairs on the National Security Council staff and later became National Security Adviser to Vice-President Bush.

MICHAEL M. GUNTER is Professor of Political Science at Tennessee Technological University. He has written or edited seven books on the Kurds, including *The Kurdish Predicament in Iraq* (1999).

ROY W. GUTMAN is diplomatic correspondent for *Newsweek*. From 1990 to 1994, he reported from Europe for the Long Island newspaper *Newsday* on such events as the unification of Germany and the violent disintegration of Yugoslavia. A collection of his award-winning articles on Bosnia, *A Witness to Genocide*, was published in 1993.

RICHARD N. HAASS is Director of Policy Planning in the U.S. Department of State. From 1989 to 1993, he was Special Assistant to President George Bush and Senior Director for Near East and South Asian Affairs on the National Security Council. He is the author of numerous books, including *The Reluctant Sheriff: The United States after the Cold War* (1997) and *Intervention: The Use of American Military Force in the Post-Cold War World* (second edition, 1999).

P. EDWARD HALEY holds the W. M. Keck Foundation Chair of International Strategic Studies at Claremont McKenna College. He is a Senior Research Associate at the Keck Center for International and Strategic Studies, of which he was the founding director. He previously served as a staff member in the U.S. Senate and House of Representatives. He is the author of numerous books and other writings on American foreign policy.

ROBERT W. HALEY is Professor of Internal Medicine and Director of the Division of Epidemiology in the Internal Medicine Department at the University of Texas Southwestern Medical Center in Dallas. He spent 10 years (1973-1983) at the U.S. Centers for Disease Control and Prevention, serving in the Epidemic Intelligence Service and other positions.

JOSEPH P. HARAHAN is Public Historian with the On-Site Inspection Agency, U.S. Department of Defense. He has served as an arms control inspector and team leader on special treaty documentary projects. His recent books include *On-Site Inspections under the CFE Treaty* (1996), and *On-Site Inspections under the INF Treaty* (1993).

PAUL F. HARPER is Professor Emeritus at Hofstra University, where he chaired the Political Science Department from 1975 to 1996. He has written about labor unions in the People's Republic of China. He served as Director of Hofstra's John F. Kennedy Presidential Conference in 1985 and co-edited *John F. Kennedy: The Promise Revisited* (1988).

ULRIC HAYNES, JR. is a consultant to Hofstra University and the university's former Executive Dean for University Relations. A former United States Ambassador to Algeria, he has had a wide ranging career covering diplomacy, public service, education, and the private sector.

DANIEL R. HEIMBACH is Professor of Christian Ethics at Southeastern Baptist Theological Seminary in Wake Forest, North Carolina. During the George Bush administration, he served on White House staff as Deputy Executive Secretary of the Domestic Policy Council and as Associate Director for Domestic Policy. He also served as Deputy Assistant Secretary of the Navy for Manpower.

CARLA A. HILLS is Chairman and Chief Executive Officer of Hills & Company, International Consultants, which advises companies on global trade and investment issues, particularly in the emerging markets. Ambassador Hills served in the George Bush administration (1989–1993) as U.S. Trade Representative.

G. PHILIP HUGHES served in the George Bush Administration as Executive Secretary of the National Security Council from 1989 to 1990 and as Ambassador to Barbados and the Eastern Caribbean from 1990 to 1993. From 1981 to 1985, he served as Deputy Assistant for National Security Affairs to Vice President Bush. He is currently Senior Director at the White House Writers Group (WHWG) in Washington, DC.

KENNETH I. JUSTER is the Undersecretary of Commerce for Industry and Security in the Administration of President George W. Bush. Prior to his current government service, he was a senior partner in the Washington, DC, law firm of Arnold & Porter. During the Administration of President George Bush, Mr. Juster served as Counselor (Acting) of the U.S. Department of State from 1992 to 1993, and as Deputy and Senior Adviser to Deputy Secretary of State Lawrence S. Eagleburger from 1989 to 1992.

ARNOLD KANTER is Senior Associate with the Forum for International Policy and a principal in the Scowcroft Group, an international business consulting firm. He served in the Bush administration as Special Assistant to the President for Defense Policy and Arms Control from 1989 to 1991 and as Undersecretary of State for Political Affairs from 1991 to 1993.

BOBBIE GREENE KILBERG is an attorney who served in the Bush administration as Deputy Assistant to the President and Director of the Office of

Intergovernmental Affairs from 1992 to 1993. She also served as Deputy Assistant to the President for Public Liaison (1989–1992) and Public Liaison Officer (1988–1989).

JAMES D. KING is Professor and Head of the Department of Political Science at the University of Wyoming. He is the author or co-author of numerous publications, including *The Equality State: Government and Politics in Wyoming* (2000).

JAMES M. KLURFELD is Editor of the Editorial Pages of *Newsday*, where he has worked since 1968. He has served as Washington Bureau Chief and Albany Bureau Chief and as a reporter in the Suffolk office. He has received a number of rewards for his writing.

JULES N. LAROCQUE has taught in the Department of Economics at Lawrence University in Appleton, Wisconsin, since 1963. His current research focuses on economic nationalism in advanced industrial, developing, and transitional economies.

BURTON J. LEE III served as Physician to the President and Director of the White House Medical Unit from 1989 to 1993. He is a specialist in internal medicine and spent his career running a large clinical practice in New York City, doing clinical research and teaching postgraduate physicians.

JAMES R. LILLEY is a Senior Fellow at the American Enterprise Institute. He served as Assistant Secretary of Defense for International Security Affairs from 1991 to 1993, U.S. Ambassador to the People's Republic of China from 1989 to 1991, and U.S. Ambassador to the Republic of Korea from 1986 to 1989. He is coeditor of several books, including *China's Military Faces the Future* (1999) and *Beyond MFN: Trade with China and American Interests* (1994).

RICHARD T. McCORMACK served as Undersecretary of State for Economic Affairs from 1989 to 1991, and was the chief Personal Representative of President Bush at the 1989 and 1990 G-7 Economic Summits.

JOHN O. McGINNIS is Professor at Northwestern University School of Law. He was a Deputy Assistant Attorney General in the Office of Legal Counsel in the administrations of Presidents Reagan and Bush.

MICHAEL J. McISAAC is pursuing a Master's in Business Administration at the Frank G. Zarb School of Business at Hofstra University. He graduated summa cum laude from Hofstra University in 1998 with a bachelor's degree in political science.

ROBERT McMILLAN is a practicing attorney on Long Island and partner in the law firm of McMillan, Rather, Bennett & Rigano. He was appointed by

President Bush and confirmed by the U. S. Senate as a member of the Board of Directors of the Panama Canal Commission in 1989, serving through 1994. Since 1999 he has chaired the U.S.–Panama Business Council.

CHRISTOPHER C. MEYERSON is a member of the District of Columbia bar who has worked on international trade issues at the U.S. Department of Commerce and at Venable, Baetjer, Howard & Civiletti. Mr. Meyerson received a JD and an MPhil from Columbia University, and was awarded the 2000 Junior Scholar Award by the International Political Economy Section of the International Studies Association.

ROBERT MOSBACHER is chairman of Mosbacher Energy Company and Mosbacher Power Group. He was Secretary of Commerce in the Bush administration from 1989 to 1992.

MARK L. MOVSESIAN is Professor of Law at Hofstra University. He has served as an Attorney-Adviser in the Office of Legal Counsel at the Department of Justice, and as a Law Clerk to Associate Justice David H. Souter of the Supreme Court of the United States. His scholarly interests include contracts and international trade.

ROBERT A. NEWMAN recently retired as an investigator with the House Committee on Government Reform and Oversight, where he specialized in veterans issues with a focus on Persian Gulf War veterans' illnesses. He served in the U.S. Air Force. In the Bush administration, he served as Director of External Affairs for the National Oceanic & Atmospheric Administration (NOAA).

EDWARD N. NEY is Chairman of Marsteller Advertising and Chairman of the Board of Advisers of Burson-Marsteller. He served as U.S. Ambassador to Canada from 1989 to 1992 and played a key role in efforts to expand the U.S.–Canada Free Trade Agreement to include Mexico.

ROSANNA PEROTTI is Associate Professor of Political Science at Hofstra University and general editor of the Bush proceedings project. She has published articles and presented conference papers on national immigration policymaking. She teaches courses in American Politics, Public Opinion, and the Media and Politics.

JOAN PETERS is author of the award-winning national best seller *From Time Immemorial: The Origins of the Arab–Jewish Conflict over Palestine* (1985). A historian and investigative reporter, she has appeared on more than 200 television and radio programs and contributed to *Harper's*, *The New Republic*, *The New Leader*, and *Commentary*.

WILLIAM T. PRYCE is Vice President for Washington Operations of the Council of the Americas, where he has served since 1997. Formerly a career

Foreign Service officer, he served as a Special Assistant to the President for National Security Affairs, covering Latin America from 1989 to 1992.

LAURENCE INGRAM RADWAY is Professor Emeritus in the Government Department at Dartmouth College. He has served as Chairman of the New Hampshire Democratic Party, deputy leader of the New Hampshire House of Representatives, and captain in the U.S. Army. He is the author of *Soldiers and Scholars: Military Education and National Policy* (1957) and *Foreign Policy and National Defense: The Liberal Democracy in World Affairs* (1969).

EARL C. RAVENAL is Distinguished Research Professor of International Affairs at the Georgetown University School of Foreign Service. He has been a Senior Fellow of the Cato Institute, a Fellow of the Woodrow Wilson International Center for Scholars and the Washington Center of Foreign Policy Research, and a Faculty Member of the Salzburg Seminar in American Studies. He is author or coauthor of 11 books on foreign military policy.

JAMES W. RIDDLESPERGER, JR. is Professor of Political Science at Texas Christian University. He has published numerous articles in professional journals and is coeditor of *Presidential Leadership and Civil Rights Policy* (1995).

KATHRYN R. SCHULTZ, currently a Foreign Affairs Specialist in the Department of State, was a Senior Research Analyst at the Center for Defense Information in Washington, DC, at the time of the conference.

SAMUEL SEGEV is a former editorial writer and political analyst for the Israeli newspaper *Maariv*. He has also served as New York Correspondent for the French weekly *L'Express* and as Correspondent for the Israeli daily *Davar*.

PHILIP SHENON is the Defense Department Correspondent of the *New York Times*, based in Washington. He served as a foreign correspondent in the Middle East and was actively involved in coverage of the Gulf War, reporting from Iraq, Saudi Arabia and Kuwait. In 1997, he was awarded the Sigma Delta Chi award from the Society of Professional Journalists for his coverage of Gulf War illnesses.

MURRAY SILBERMAN is Adjunct Professor at the Austrian Diplomatic Academy in Vienna, where he has worked since 1982. He also is a consultant to the United Nations and to nongovernmental organizations. His publications include *Crisis in the Persian Gulf* (1980) and *Slavery in the Arab World* (1989), as well as numerous articles on the Middle East, Africa, and Europe.

DUANE TANANBAUM is Associate Professor of History and Chair of the History Department at Lehman College, the City University of New York. His research focuses on the relationship between Congress and the president in foreign affairs. He is the author of *The Bricker Amendment Controversy: A Test of Eisenhower's Political Leadership*, and numerous articles on the War Powers Resolution.

JOHN E. ULLMANN is Professor Emeritus of Management and Quantitative Methods in the School of Business at Hofstra University and an industrial engineer. Much of his recent work has dealt with the changes in Central and Eastern Europe, and he has written and lectured extensively on these topics here and in Europe. He is the author of 30 books and monographs and over 100 articles in his fields.

WILLIAM H. WEBSTER became Director of Central Intelligence (DCI) in 1987 and continued into the Bush administration until 1991, when he retired from government service and joined the law firm of Milbank, Tweed, Hadley & McCloy. A former U.S. circuit judge, he became Director of the Federal Bureau of Investigation in 1978 and held this position until his appointment as DCI.

DERRICK BRADFORD WETHERELL is a senior writer at the Center for Public Integrity and has contributed to two books, *The Buying of the President 2000* (2000) and *The Cheating of America* (2002), both published by Harper Collins. He received his B.A. in print journalism and political science from Hofstra University and his M.A. in international public affairs journalism from The American University.

OLIN L. WETHINGTON is a partner in the Washington, DC, law firm of Steptoe & Johnson. He served as Assistant Secretary for International Affairs in the U.S. Department of the Treasury from 1991 to 1993. From 1990 to 1991, he worked in the White House as Special Assistant to the President and Executive Secretary to the Economic Policy Council.

STEVE A. YETIV is an Associate Professor of Political Science at Old Dominion University. He is an award-winning author of the book, *The Persian Gulf Crisis* (1997), has published widely on international and Middle East affairs and is regularly interviewed by the national media.